Recognizing
Race and Ethnicity

This best-selling textbook explains the current state of research in the sociology of race/ethnicity, emphasizing white privilege, the social construction of race, and the newest theoretical perspectives for understanding race and ethnicity. It is designed to engage students with an emphasis on topics that are meaningful to their lives, including sports, popular culture, interracial relationships, and biracial/multiracial identities and families.

The new third edition comes at a pivotal time in the politics of race and identity. Fitzgerald includes vital new discussion on white ethnicities and the politics of Trump and populism. Prominent attention is given to immigration and the discourse surrounding it, police and minority populations, and the criminal justice system. Using the latest available data, the author examines the present and future of generational change. New case studies include athletes and racial justice activism, removal of Confederate monuments, updates on Black Lives Matter, and Native American activism at Standing Rock and against the Bayou Bridge pipeline.

Kathleen J. Fitzgerald is a Teaching Assistant Professor at the University of North Carolina, Chapel Hill. Her teaching and research focus on social inequalities, specifically race, racism, and privilege; gender and sexualities; and food justice. She is author of *Beyond White Ethnicity: Developing a Sociological Understanding of Native American Identity Reclamation*, coauthor of *Sociology of Sexualities*, second edition, and has published in *The Sociological Quarterly*, *Humanity and Society*, and *Sociological Focus*.

THIRD EDITION

Recognizing Race and Ethnicity

Power, Privilege, and Inequality

Kathleen J. Fitzgerald

Routledge
Taylor & Francis Group

NEW YORK AND LONDON

Third edition published 2020
by Routledge
52 Vanderbilt Avenue, New York, NY 10017

and by Routledge
2 Park Square, Milton Park, Abingdon, Oxon, OX14 4RN

Routledge is an imprint of the Taylor & Francis Group, an informa business

First edition published 2017 by Westview Press
Second edition published 2018 by Routledge

Trademark notice: Product or corporate names may be trademarks or registered trademarks, and are used only for identification and explanation without intent to infringe.

Library of Congress Cataloging-in-Publication Data
Names: Fitzgerald, Kathleen J., 1965– author.
Title: Recognizing race and ethnicity / Kathleen J. Fitzgerald.
Description: Third edition. | New York, NY : Routledge, 2020.
Identifiers: LCCN 2019059182 | ISBN 9780367182236 (hbk) | ISBN 9780367182243 (pbk) | ISBN 9780429202353 (ebk)
Subjects: LCSH: United States–Race relations. | United States–Ethnic relations. | Whites–Race identity. | Minorities–United States–Social conditions. | Race awareness–United States. | Power (Social sciences)–United States. | Equality–United States.
Classification: LCC E184.A1 F5755 2020 | DDC 305.800973–dc23
LC record available at https://lccn.loc.gov/2019059182

ISBN: 978-0-367-18223-6 (hbk)
ISBN: 978-0-367-18224-3 (pbk)
ISBN: 978-0-429-20235-3 (ebk)

Typeset in Myriad Pro
by Wearset Ltd, Boldon, Tyne and Wear

Brief Table of Contents

Part 4: Contemporary Issues in Race/Ethnicity

Expanded Table of Contents

Part 3: Institutional Inequalities

Part 4: Contemporary Issues in Race/Ethnicity

Preface

WHEN I WROTE the first edition of this book, political pundits were still talking about the prospect of the United States being a postracial society, since the first non-white man, President Barack Obama, had been reelected as president of the United States. As I wrap up the writing of this third edition, in August of 2019, no one mentions the word "postracial" in the same sentence as the "United States" anymore. Clearly, race, racism, and privilege remain defining features of our culture. This past week there were three mass shootings (in Dayton, OH, El Paso, TX, and Gilroy, CA), two of which occurred in a twenty-four hour period. All three shooters were white men and two of the three held white nationalist, anti-immigrant views. Most of the victims were people of color, yet officials in two of the cases were hesitant to describe race as a motive for the crime. In the El Paso shooting, with the death toll reaching twenty-two, authorities are describing the incident as an act of domestic terrorism and are considering charging the suspect with federal hate crimes. While it feels like an exceptionally dark moment for our country, as a race scholar, I know this is, unfortunately, not our darkest moment. The third edition of *Recognizing Race and Ethnicity: Power, Privilege, and Inequality* looks squarely at this moment as well as at the United States' violent racial/ethnic history.

NEW TO THE THIRD EDITION

Results of the 2017 GenForward Survey "**The 'Woke' Generation? Millennials on Race**" frame the discussions in this text, from Millennials' opinions on Black Lives Matter to Confederate monuments, to the extent of racial progress today, whether or not Donald Trump is a racist, and whether racism is one of the most important problems facing our nation. This survey is the first of its kind, a bimonthly survey of a nationally representative sample of 1,750 young adults' (between the ages of eighteen and thirty-four in 2017) attitudes on and experiences with race. The

Millennial generation is the most racially diverse and the largest in the country, so they provide a good barometer for the future of race relations. While traditional-aged college students, the primary audience for this book, are Generation Z rather than Millennials, their lives are not so different despite being in the shadow of the Millennial generation.

This edition contains a new chapter on **Housing**, which expands the previous edition's discussion of the role of housing in contributing to the racial wealth gap. This new chapter critically investigates residential segregation in detail, including the role of federal policies and laws, real estate industry practices in intentionally segregating communities, and social dynamics that unintentionally perpetuate residential segregation. The consequences of housing segregation, including environmental racism, are explored as well.

This text has always focused on the manifestations of racism and privilege in arenas important to students, such as the sports world and Hollywood films, so this new edition expands its discussion of **racial justice activism** in sports, from a focus on Colin Kaepernick, Eric Reid, Chris Long, and Malcolm Jenkin's protests against police brutality beginning in the 2016 National Football League (NFL) season, to professional soccer player Megan Rapinoe and WNBA player Maya Moore's protests in support of racial justice. A focus on racial justice activism permeates this text, and that continues with an expanded look at the Black Lives Matter movement and coverage of Native American activism at Standing Rock against the Dakota Access Pipeline.

This text is one of the first on the market to focus heavily on **white privilege** and we continue that in this new edition. The chapter on white privilege has been expanded to include discussions of white ethnics, white fragility, and the mani-festation of white supremacy in violence. The role of whiteness in politics is also necessarily a key topic in this new edition, as the Trump presidency makes clear.

In addition to fully updated statistics, this new edition contains the latest scholar-ship in the sociology of race/ethnicity and in-depth discussion of topical issues including police shootings of racial minorities, battles over Confederate monuments, cyber racism, the 1619 Project on slavery and the founding of this nation, and the school-to-prison pipeline, among others.

Kathleen J. Fitzgerald
University of North Carolina
August 2019

Preface to the Second Edition

WHEN THE FIRST African American president, Barack Obama, was elected in 2008, many political pundits erroneously declared the United States to be "postracial." As President Obama is finishing his second and final presidential term, race remains a central cleavage in American society, and the racial divide may be starker than ever. Perhaps the most glaring evidence of this are police shootings of unarmed black men. When I completed the first edition of *Recognizing Race and Ethnicity* in the summer of 2013, George Zimmerman had just been acquitted in the shooting death of unarmed African American teenager Trayvon Martin. Martin's killing and Zimmerman's acquittal inspired the emergence of an online campaign, #BlackLivesMatter, which became a traditional campaign the next summer after the killing of 17-year-old African American Michael Brown by white police officer Darren Wilson in Ferguson, Missouri. Months of protests followed that shooting. The three years since have witnessed dozens more killings of unarmed African American men by police, over a hundred in 2015 alone, many caught on cell phone video and widely shared on social media. The most recent, as of this writing, are Alton Sterling in Baton Rouge, Louisiana, and Philando Castile in Minnesota. This new edition necessarily focuses attention not only on the extrajudicial shootings of black men by police officers but also on the mobilization and activism of the Black Lives Matter movement, which seeks to draw sustained attention to these killings and hold police accountable for their actions.

In addition to the widely covered shootings and protests, the Republican presidential nominee for 2016, Donald Trump, is using race/ethnicity explicitly for political leverage, specifically using the age-old tactic of xenophobia to successfully generate votes. He referred to Mexican immigrants as "rapists" and "criminals," made anti-Semitic and antiblack comments, and campaigned on building a giant wall along the US–Mexico border, deporting the estimated eleven million undocumented immigrants already in the country, and banning the immigration of Muslims. Ku Klux Klan member David Duke thanked Trump for creating a climate that was welcoming to views like his when he announced his intention to run for a Louisiana Senate seat in July 2016. This new edition thus covers the racialized political rhetoric that exploded in the summer of 2015 and continues unabated.

The second edition of *Recognizing Race and Ethnicity* also significantly expands the global race/ethnicity discussions. In addition to the "Global Perspectives" boxes found in each chapter, this text explores France's official policy of color-blindness; global white supremacy, specifically with an exploration of eugenics policies in Brazil; decolonization movements in the 1960s; police violence in Brazil; a global focus on the war on drugs; Dutch slave history; the globalization of hate groups; and the current racialization of immigrants and the expansion of anti-immigrant sentiment, particularly pertaining to Syrian immigration to the US.

Expanded attention to intersectionality is also a key feature of this new edition, including a look at new research on black women's mobilization against sexual violence, which was the foundation of civil rights movement mobilizing throughout the South; new research on interracial same-sex intimacies; an expanded discussion of gender and incarceration; and a discussion of the violent victimization of lesbian, gay, bisexual, transgender, and queer (LGBTQ) people, with LGBTQ people of color disproportionately targeted. Additionally, the text has been thoroughly updated with the most current statistics, the latest sociological research on race/ethnicity, and an expanded discussion of C. Wright Mills' sociological imagination and the usefulness of this perspective for studying race/ethnicity.

The second edition of *Recognizing Race and Ethnicity* maintains its seminal focus on white privilege, critically examining how whites historically and currently benefit from the existing racial order, and the social construction of race/ethnicity. The new edition retains the expanded theoretical discussion that includes an exploration of critical race theory, the white racial frame, color-blind racism, the diversity ideology, and intersectionality, moving beyond the more traditional functionalist, conflict, and symbolic interactionist perspectives on race/ethnicity. Race is presented through a sociohistorical lens to facilitate students' understanding of the social construction of race. This text shifts the discussion of social policies from a narrow focus on a few social policies that are perceived as race related, such as affirmative action, to an understanding of the historical racialization of the US welfare state overall. Topics of interest to students, including biracial/multiracial identities, multiracial families, and the intersections of race and sports and race and popular culture, continue to make this text particularly relevant to their lives and provide opportunities for thought-provoking class discussions. Finally, each chapter contains boxed inserts that focus on racial justice activists and organizations, helping students to understand the ongoing mobilization and activism to end racial inequality.

Kathleen J. Fitzgerald
July 28, 2016

Acknowledgments

WHILE ONLY MY name graces the cover of the text, there are so many more people who deserve a "shout out" at the completion of this work. First, I would like to thank my new department at the University of North Carolina. I am deeply honored to be working with such an amazing group of sociologists. It is a mere bonus that they are also some of the finest people I have ever met. The students at UNC live up to their outstanding reputation every day. I am lucky to have so many students excited about, interested in, and engaged with the subject of race. To those of you speaking up in class, asking good questions, sending me emails about current events that our class has made you rethink or simply see in a new way—thank you. There could not be a more important moment for us to take these issues seriously. To some who sent me info on topics that *needed* to be in the new edition (Miranda Veal), you were right. Thank you! To the graduate students I have worked with at UNC—thank you for your thoughtful comments and interest. Thanks to Ken Cai Kowalski, especially, for always suggesting new research on the various topics covered. In the second edition of this text, I acknowledged the amazing work being done by scholars in the sociology of race/ethnicity. That remains true. Writing a new edition allows one to scan the field of new research—and there is so much good work being done. Thanks to those of you I know personally and to those whose work I have engaged with, but whom I have not had the chance to meet.

A big thank you to my new team at Routledge—especially my editor, Dean Birkenkamp. When mergers happen in the publishing industry, sometimes books fall through the cracks. I am so happy that did not happen. Not only that, I was placed with an editor who truly knows not only the publishing industry, but the sociology of race/ethnicity, and the importance of a book like this. Thanks, Dean! I am delighted with the way things have worked out. To the rest of the team at Routledge, who I have yet to meet, thank you.

There are always others, outside of our professional worlds who make us think and help make us who we are. While there are too many of those folks to name here,

I do want to mention a few. My eternal thanks go to Sally Ann Schultz—for teaching me the importance of social and racial justice when I was a clueless high-schooler. Thanks to Bridget Schultz Joseph for always telling me in high school, "You would love sociology!" You were right. Thanks to Gael Thompson for keeping me grounded. And, forever, my thanks and my love go to my dear husband, fellow sociologist, and favorite person, Tony Ladd. For all the support you offer, above and beyond your keen sociological insights (which are priceless), thanks for keeping the home fires burning and food on the table, so I could get the book done!

REVIEWERS

We would like to thank the following peer reviewers for their time and comments toward making this a better book:

First Edition
   Hazel Arthur, Lipscomb University
   Keith Mann, Cardinal Stritch University
   Vivian L. Carter, Tuskegee University
   David G. Embrick, Loyola University Chicago
   G. Reginald Daniel, University of California, Santa Barbara

Second Edition
   Taylor Cedric, Central Michigan University
   Karyn McKinney, Penn State Altoona
   Kyle Anne Nelson, University of Northern Colorado
   Bobby Potters, University of Indianapolis

PART ONE

Thinking About Race

Taking Account of Race, Racism, and Privilege

CHAPTER LEARNING OUTCOMES

By the end of this chapter, you should be able to:

- Differentiate between race and ethnicity
- Define sociology and the sociological imagination
- Distinguish between different forms of racism
- Understand what is meant by the social construction of race
- Describe demographic shifts in American society along racial/ethnic lines
- Explain how race functions at the level of identities, ideologies, and institutions
- Discuss the Millennial generation's attitudes on race

As I write this introduction to the third edition of *Recognizing Race and Ethnicity*, Sacramento County District Attorney Anne Marie Schubert announced that the two police officers who fatally shot African American Stephon Clark almost one year prior, on March 18, 2018, would not face charges in the shooting. Clark was unarmed and shot to death in his grandmother's backyard as he was being pursued as a vandalism suspect. Police mistook the cell phone Clark was holding for a gun and fired twenty shots at him. A feeling of déjà vu came over me, as I realize the first sentence of the second edition of this text begins with a similar story—the announcement that Caesar Goodson Jr., the sole Baltimore police officer charged with murder in the death of 25-year-old African American Freddie Gray during an encounter with police on April 12, 2015, had been found not guilty.

After a string of similar incidents in which unarmed African Americans—such as Trayvon Martin, Oscar Grant, Michael Brown, Tamir Rice, Eric Garner,

Alton Sterling, Philandro Castile, Rekia Boyd, Tanisha Anderson, and so many others—were killed by police or self-proclaimed neighborhood watchmen, it seems hard not to see this as part of a larger pattern. In the face of so many incidences, we must ask, "Is the violence against black bodies a result of isolated incidences which can be reduced to the poor decisions of those involved? Or is there a larger problem at hand—one that indicates that 'all lives' do not, in fact, matter?" (Weissinger, Mack, and Watson 2017:1). Police shootings of unarmed African Americans have inspired protests, activism, and the emergence of a new social movement, Black Lives Matter.

While it is still rare for a police officer to be charged and convicted of an on-duty shooting, there are two recent examples where police officers were held accountable for their actions. Chicago police officer Jason Van Dyke, who shot and killed unarmed 17-year-old Laquan McDonald, was found guilty of second-degree murder and received a sentence of six years and nine months, far shorter than the eighteen years prosecutors were seeking. Michael Slager, the North Charleston, South Carolina, police officer who shot and killed unarmed African American Walter Scott, was sentenced to twenty years in prison for his actions in late 2017. In this case, Judge David C. Norton described the shooting as "reckless, wanton and inappropriate" (Blinder 2017).

W. E. B. Du Bois begins his seminal work, *The Souls of Black Folk*, with the prophetic statement: "The problem of the Twentieth Century is the problem of the color-line" (1989:1). His comment remains true today, but we would instead say the problem of the twenty-first century remains a problem associated with the **racial order**, the collection of beliefs, suppositions, rules, and practices that shape the way groups are arranged in a society; generally, it is a hierarchical categorization of people along the lines of certain physical characteristics, such as skin color, hair texture, and facial features (Hochschild, Weaver, and Burch 2012). The United States has not resolved the "race problem," as it has historically been referred to by social scientists, and part of the reason is that white people have never considered it to be their problem to solve. The term *race problem* implies a problem of racial minorities. Du Bois expresses this implication in his first chapter: "Between me and the other world there is ever an unasked question ... How does it feel to be a problem?" (1989:3). Race relations in a society, whether problematic or not, involve all racial groups, including the dominant racial group.

The election of President Barack Obama led to immediate claims in the media that the United States was a **postracial** society, a society that had moved beyond race, because Obama could not have won the presidency without a significant number of white votes. However, as sociologists point out, Obama may have won the presidential elections in 2008 and 2012, but most whites did not vote for him (Wingfield and Feagin 2010). While Obama won significant majorities of racial minority votes, from 62 percent of the Asian American vote and 66 percent of the Latino vote to 95 percent of the black vote, he won only 43 percent of the white vote in 2008 (Wingfield and Feagin 2010). The kind of opposition he faced while governing was virulent and unlike anything past presidents have experienced. For instance, he is the only president to have his birthright questioned. Perhaps even more disturbing, the US Secret Service reported approximately thirty death threats against Obama daily, which is four times the number made against the previous president (Feagin 2012).

The election of Donald Trump stifled any discussion of the United States as postracial, as he began his political career by promoting the idea that President Obama was not born in the United States and thus was not a legitimate president, and he made racism a central aspect of his campaign and presidency (see Chapter 13). A few examples include his campaign kick-off when he referred to Mexican immigrants coming to the US as rapists and as bringing crime and drugs, which he followed with, "some, I assume, are good people" (Silva 2018). He later criticized federal judge Gonzalo Curiel, who is of Mexican descent and was born in Indiana, claiming he could not possibly be impartial in his decision making because he was Mexican. Perhaps most surprising was when he not only refused to condemn the white nationalists' deadly violence at the Unite the Right rally in Charlottesville, VA, in 2017 but also claimed that there were good people on both sides. The white supremacist who murdered forty-nine people gathered for worship at a mosque in Christchurch, New Zealand, in March of 2019 cited President Trump as an inspiration in his manifesto, describing him as a symbol of "renewed white identity and common purpose." While Donald Trump has claimed that he is the "least racist person that you have ever met," his own comments and the avowed support he receives from white supremacists challenge that account (O'Connor and Marans 2016). Ta-Nehisi Coates counters Trump's claim, stating, "In Trump, white supremacists see one of their own … To Trump, whiteness is neither notional nor symbolic but is the very core of his power" (2017:4).

While much has changed over the last century in terms of race, race remains a central organizing principle of our society, a key arena of inequality, and the subject of ongoing conflict and debate. Race also influences our identities, how we see ourselves. Ongoing evidence of the continuing significance of race manifests in both significant and obscure ways, as the following exemplify:

- White nationalists held a "Unite the Right" rally in Charlottesville, VA, in August of 2017 and were met by antiracist counter protesters. Violence erupted and one counter protester, Heather Heyer, was killed in the conflict.

- On July 17, 2019, a noose was found on Stanford University's campus near a residence hall where a group of largely minority high-school students were staying for a summer program (Griffith 2019).
- The State of New York recently convicted a white supremacist of terrorism; this is the first time in the state's 231-year history that a white supremacist was convicted on terrorism charges (Kalmbacher 2019).
- For the first time in American history, the November 2018 elections saw two Native American women elected to the House of Representatives. Sharice Davids, a member of the Ho-Chunk nation, will represent Kansas and Deb Haaland, a Laguna Pueblo, will represent New Mexico.
- Numerous incidences of white women calling the police on black people for nonexistent offenses have drawn national media attention during 2018–2019. These include an incident at a corner store in Brooklyn where 53-year-old Teresa Klein called the police on a black child and accused him of sexual assault when his backpack brushed up against her as he walked past (Phillips 2018). Another involved a black man who was detained by a white police officer at gunpoint as he picked up trash in front of the building where he lived and worked in Boulder, CO (Stevens and Mervosh 2019).
- Rachel Dolezal ignited a nationwide debate in 2015 about racial identity when it was discovered that she, a woman born to two white parents, identified as black and had been passing as black for most of her adult life.
- According to the Institute for Women's Policy Research, women earn 81.1 cents for every dollar a man earns; but for black women, that pay gap is even greater. Black women earn 66.8 cents for every dollar white men earn, even when they have the same education, skills, and experience (Rankin 2016).
- After a sixty-two-year court battle over school integration, on May 18, 2016, the middle schools and high schools of Cleveland, Mississippi, were ordered by a judge to desegregate.
- Democratic Virginia Governor Ralph Northam faced demands for his resignation when a racist medical school yearbook photo emerged. As he admitted to wearing blackface during that time period, the Attorney General of the state, Mark R. Herring, also acknowledged wearing blackface at a party as an undergraduate. As of this writing, neither official has resigned over the scandal (Martin and Blinder 2019).
- LGBTQ people of color face disproportionate rates of violent victimization (Mogul, Ritchie, and Whitlock 2011). The year 2015 was the most violent year on record for transgender people: twenty-two transgender people were murdered, and nineteen of those were people of color (Fitzgerald 2017; Meyer 2015).

THE SIGNIFICANCE OF RACE

Despite the undeniable racial progress that has been made during the twentieth century, ongoing racism exists and even harkens back to the racism of earlier eras. As the opening vignette describes, being a young person of color in the United States can be lethal. Oscar Grant, Michael Brown, Eric Garner, Tamir Rice, Alton Sterling, Philandro Castile, Stephon Clark, and Jamar Clark are just a few of the black men who have been killed at the hands of police in the last few years. In fact, some have referred to the police shootings of unarmed black men as a "blatant disregard for black and brown bodies" and an example of "modern day lynching" (Embrick 2015:836–837). After the acquittal of George Zimmerman in the shooting death of Trayvon Martin, three African American women, Alicia Garza, Patrisse Cullors, and Opal Tometi, began an online campaign known as #BlackLivesMatter (#BLM). This has since grown into an international social movement, moving the hashtag from social media to the streets with, according to Garza, thirty-three chapters in the US and some abroad. Their initial goal was to draw attention to the injustices African Americans face, particularly at the hands of police. Ultimately, their objectives include celebrating blackness in a nation that denigrates it (see Chapter 6).

While Black Lives Matter activism has helped focus necessary attention on police killings of unarmed black men, the killings of African American women, LGBTQ

IMAGE 1.1: Unite the Right Rally. In August of 2017, white nationalists held a Unite the Right rally in Charlottesville, VA. An antiracist counter protester, Heather Heyer, was killed by one of the white nationalists at the rally.

people of color, Native Americans, and Latinos have generated less media attention. Rekia Boyd, Sandra Bland, Gynnya McMillen, and Ty Underwood are just some of the African American or LGBTQ women of color recently killed, most while in police custody. The #SayHerName movement has emerged as a gender-inclusive racial justice movement to rectify this oversight.

In addition to these examples of "modern day lynching," which reflect the racism of earlier eras, racist symbolism of previous eras also remains, providing evidence of the existence of ongoing racism. Nooses, for instance—visual reminders of an era when whites lynched African Americans, as well as Mexican Americans, Native Americans, Jewish Americans, and many other racial minorities, for real or imagined offenses—are still hung today to intimidate people of color. In 2019, nineteen black UPS workers in Ohio filed suit against their employer for the repeated racist discrimination they faced that their employer refused to address, including the hanging of nooses at an African American employee's workstation and repeated uses of the 'n' word (Simon and Sidner 2019b). In 2018, eight African American employees of a General Motors plant in Toledo, OH, filed a lawsuit against GM for the daily racism they faced on the job, including the hanging of a noose and a declaration that the bathrooms were for "whites only" (Simon and Sidner 2019). Lynching imagery was pervasive on the internet during President Obama's 2008 and 2012 election campaigns as well as during his presidency (Feagin 2012). In 2007, a noose was hung on the office door of an African American professor who taught courses on race and diversity at Columbia University. That same year on the same campus, a Jewish professor found a swastika on her office door. Both are professors of psychology and education and are involved in teaching multicultural education.

What is the message being sent by this kind of racial imagery? President Obama and the professors targeted in these examples violate what Feagin, Vera, and Imani (1996) refer to as **racialized space**, space generally regarded as reserved for one race and not another. Columbia University was being defined by some students as a **white space**, not only a racialized space where nonwhites are perceived as intruders and unwelcome but also an institutional space where white privilege is reproduced (Moore 2008). Additionally, research on the experiences of Latino college students finds they often refer to institutions of higher education as a "white space," thus, as an environment where they feel less than welcome (Barajas and Ronnkvist 2007).

Are these isolated incidents? According to the Southern Poverty Law Center, a nonprofit group that tracks hate crimes and hate-group activity, the prevalence of nooses and other symbols of hate, such as swastikas, is not unusual (see Chapter 13). Often such incidents are explained as a practical joke, which raises the question, what exactly is funny about a noose? A noose is the ultimate symbol of terror directed primarily, but not exclusively, toward African Americans. This symbol is hard to joke about.

Lynching is generally regarded as a southern type of mob justice perpetrated by whites against blacks. Indeed, the great majority of lynchings fit this profile and thus became the focus of a major antilynching movement during the first half of the twentieth century (see Chapter 4). However, many other racial/ethnic minorities were also targeted for this type of violence. Part of the perceived "taming of the West" involved the lynching of thousands of Chinese, Native Americans, and Latinos, particularly Mexicans, by Anglo-Americans (Gonzales-Day 2006; Romero 2019). In Atlanta in 1915, Leo Frank, a Jewish factory manager from Brooklyn, was lynched for the murder of a young female factory worker, despite the fact that the evidence overwhelmingly pointed at someone else as the perpetrator of this crime. After Frank's conviction, a mob broke into the jail and dragged him off to be lynched, rather than allowing his life sentence to stand. He was described as someone worthy of paying with his life for this horrendous crime, "not just some black factory sweeper, but a rich Jew from Brooklyn" (Guggenheim 1995).

Lynching is a public act—often occurring at night, yet nevertheless drawing large crowds of supporters. Photographers in the early part of the twentieth century routinely captured such moments, and often these photographs were made into postcards for popular consumption (Gonzales-Day 2006). Sociologically speaking, the use of public execution is meant to send a message to all members of the community. Lynchings are acts of terror, not just actions meant to punish one particular individual; terrorism is designed to instill fear in more people than the individual or individuals targeted. Thus, anyone currently teaching courses that challenge white supremacy could well interpret the hanging of a noose or a swastika on a professor's door as being directed at them as well. The presence of souvenirs and postcards complicates the picture; beyond terrorizing minority communities, the lynching becomes a morbid celebration of dominant-group privilege.

Not long after the hanging of a noose at Columbia University, an African American man was elected president for the first time in US history. The success of Barack Obama's presidential campaign clearly indicates racial progress. And yet, Obama's presidency has been followed up by President Trump, a man who won by overtly deploying racism in his campaign and his governing. Such contradictions are actually part of a long history of societal contradictions surrounding the issue of race and are quite common; these may even become obvious to us if we take the time to reflect on some of the lessons we have been taught about race. According to white author and professor Helen Fox, "Everything I learned about race while growing up has been profoundly contradictory. Strong, unspoken messages about how to be racist shamefully contradict the ways I have been taught to be a good person" (2001:15). Students often note that they were taught to love everyone because "we are all children of God" while being simultaneously warned against interracial dating. Clearly, there is a fundamental, though often unrecognized, contradiction embedded in such messages.

REFLECT AND CONNECT

Can you identify any contradictory messages surrounding race that you have been exposed to through the media, at home, in school, or in church?

Defining Concepts in the Sociology of Race and Ethnicity

This book approaches the study of race/ethnicity through a sociological lens. **Sociology** refers to the academic discipline that studies group life: society, social interactions, and human social behavior. Sociologists who study race and ethnicity focus on such things as historical and current conflict between racial/ethnic groups, the emergence of racial/ethnic identities, racial/ethnic inequality and privilege, and cultural beliefs about race/ethnicity, otherwise referred to as racial ideologies.

Sociologist C. Wright Mills (2000) introduced the concept of the **sociological imagination** to help us understand the ways history, society, and biography intersect; in other words, the sociological imagination is a perspective that encourages us to understand our lives as historically and culturally situated. This perspective can be used to more thoroughly understand your current situation as a college student. For instance, if you are an African American male student, the sociological imagination allows you to understand that you getting accepted into an institution of higher education is a product of more than just your own hard work (although that certainly played a role). It encourages you to see where you are today (your biography) as a product of a particular historical time and place. If you had been born in the southern United States in 1929, for instance, your odds of getting a college degree were much lower. Fewer Americans attended college overall, and it was even more difficult for African Americans, as most colleges and universities in the South were racially segregated.

Such a perspective keeps us from being overly individualistic in our thinking, which makes it an especially useful perspective for understanding race/ethnicity, which operates simultaneously at the historical, institutional, and individual levels. We live our lives as racial beings, as members of one or more racial groups that have a history that informs the present, and we constantly interact with institutions that have their own racial histories and present, which informs our experiences with those institutions. This textbook will focus on all of these angles: the US racial/ethnic history, racialized institutions, and racial identities.

Many students are uncomfortable with the discipline of sociology. It is tempting to counter every statement in sociological research about whites, blacks, or Latinos with, "Well, this is not true for all members of this group." But sociologists take that as a given. Sociologists study groups and patterns of behavior rather than individuals. By definition, sociologists acknowledge that there are always outliers, those who do not fit the pattern. However, the emphasis in sociology is on the *patterns* rather than on those exceptions to the rule. This is important for understanding the sociology of race/ethnicity because there will always be exceptions to the research presented, but the presence of such exceptions does not negate the research results. In American society, where individualism reigns supreme, this is often difficult to accept, but this text will be making claims about groups of people based upon scientific research, and the research is not going to apply to every member of a particular group.

While the sociology of race/ethnicity is interested in the racial hierarchy and the positioning of all racial groups in that hierarchy, much of the empirical research is focused on blacks and whites. This is not intended to ignore the experiences of Latinos, Asian Americans, American Indians, or any other racial group in America, but instead is meant to recognize that the black–white binary is the foundation of the racial hierarchy in the United States and remains so today. Thus, if we want to understand how couples in an interracial relationship negotiate race, we can opt to study black–white couples because they are the most stigmatized and historically it is their relationships that have been the "most forcibly prohibited" (Steinbugler 2012). Such research limitations can sometimes mistakenly portray racial politics as black–white and contribute to the invisibility of other racial minority groups.

We live in a culture where the meaning of race appears to be clear, yet scientists challenge our commonsense understandings about race. **Race** specifically refers to a group of people who share some socially defined physical characteristics, for instance, skin color, hair texture, or facial features. That definition more than likely reinforces our commonsense understanding of race. Most of us believe we can walk into a room and identify the number of different racial groups present based upon physical appearances. But is that really true? Many people are racially ambiguous in appearance, for any number of reasons, including the fact that they may be multiracial.

A term that is distinct from race yet often erroneously used interchangeably with it is **ethnicity**. *Ethnicity* refers to a group of people who share a culture, nationality, ancestry, and/or language; physical appearance is not associated with ethnicity. Both race and ethnicity are socially defined and carry significant meaning in our culture; they are not simply neutral and descriptive categories. A challenge social scientists offer is to understand race and ethnicity as social constructions rather than biological realities, despite the fact that the definition of race refers to physical appearance. The details concerning this very important distinction will be introduced later in this chapter.

While social scientists distinguish between the two categories of race and ethnicity, these are not mutually exclusive. In other words, people can identify according to their race and their ethnicity. For instance, a Nigerian American immigrant, an African American whose ancestors have been in the United States for hundreds of years, and a black Puerto Rican all have very different ethnicities, yet they are still classified as "black" in our culture. This text uses the term **racial/ethnic** to acknowledge that race and ethnicity overlap. In addition to using the term *racial/ethnic*, the term **people of color** will be used to collectively refer to racial/ethnic minority groups that have been the object of racism and discrimination in the United States, rather than using the term *nonwhite*. To use the term *nonwhite* reinforces white as the norm against which all other groups are defined, which is a perspective this text argues against.

Sociologists often use the terms **minority group** or **subordinate group** to express patterned inequality along group lines. From a sociological perspective, a minority group does not refer to a statistical minority (a group smaller in size). Instead, sociologists are referring to a group that is cumulatively disadvantaged in proportion to their population size. For instance, Native Americans are a minority group because they are disproportionately impoverished. Women are a minority group according to the sociological understanding of the term; however, while they qualify as a sociological minority, women are a statistical majority as they represent 51 percent of the US population. The opposite of this is also true: if there are disadvantaged groups, there are advantaged groups that sociologists refer to as **majority groups** or **dominant groups**. Again, we are not referring to statistics but instead to a group's disproportionate share of society's power and resources. In terms of race, whites are the dominant, majority group in the United States.

This text primarily emphasizes one status hierarchy: race. However, multiple status hierarchies are significant: there is a gender hierarchy, in which men are the dominant group and women are the minority group. Another status hierarchy of significance relates to sexuality: heterosexuals are the dominant group, while lesbians, gay men, and bisexuals comprise what we refer to as sexual minorities. Status hierarchies intersect with one another, resulting in unique experiences with discrimination and privilege: we may be members of a dominant group in one hierarchy and members of subordinate groups in others.

Sexualizing Racial/Ethnic Minorities

One of the primary areas where we can see the intersection of status hierarchies is the sexualizing of racial/ethnic minorities. As sociologist Joane Nagel states, "Sex matters in ethnic relations, and ... sexual matters insinuate themselves into all things racial, ethnic, and national" (2003:1).

> ## WITNESS
>
> "Sex is the sometimes silent message contained in racial slurs, ethnic stereotypes, national imaginings, and international relations … Ethnic and racial boundaries are also sexual boundaries" (Nagel 2003:2, 3).

Racial/ethnic minority group members in the United States must negotiate their sexual identities through a maze of demeaning and sometimes contradictory sexual stereotypes that work to portray them as deviant, "other," and potentially threatening to the dominant group. African American men are portrayed as hypersexual, while black women struggle with often contradictory controlling images that are sexual in nature: mammies, matriarchs, welfare recipients, and the Jezebel (Collins 1990) (see Chapter 11). The image of black men as hypersexual, animalistic, sexually immoral, and threatening is deeply rooted in American culture. After slavery ended, American literature and folklore were flooded with images of sexually promiscuous black men as threats to white women (Staples 2006).

Latino males are stereotyped as hypersexual, aggressive, and "macho." Another stereotype is that of the "Latin lover," who is seen as sexually sophisticated and thus a threat to white women. Latina portrayals follow a virgin/whore dichotomy: either she is a passive, submissive virgin or she is a sexually aggressive whore (Asencio and Acosta 2010).

Asian American sexuality is socially constructed to maintain white male dominance (Chou 2012). Asian American women are stereotyped as exotic and eager to please men sexually, specifically white men, while also passive and subordinate. Instead of being stereotyped as hypersexual as African American and Latino men are today, Asian American males are portrayed as weak and effeminate; they are emasculated, hyposexual, or even asexual (Chou 2012).

Sexual stereotypes of Native Americans are in many ways similar. For many decades, whites viewed Native Americans as savages and Native women as promiscuous and sexually available to white men. This later morphed into an image of Native women as "dirty little squaws" who slept with married white men, thus threatening white women and their families (D'Emilio and Freedman 2012). The bottom line is that sexual ideologies define racial and ethnic "others" as "oversexed, undersexed, perverted, or dangerous" (Nagel 2003:9).

Racism: Past and Present

Despite some racial progress, our society remains divided along racial lines and racial inequality persists. However, one can look at the previously discussed noose incidents as a sign of that progress: while they are disturbing, racist acts whose intent is to terrorize minorities, they are only symbolic. Three or more generations ago, instead of nooses we would more than likely have seen the "strange fruit" that 1940s-era African American jazz singer Billie Holiday sang of—lynched bodies hanging from trees.

However, in the face of such a history, we must not underestimate the power of symbols. We live in a symbolic world, which means that we develop a shared understanding of our world through a variety of symbols; meanings are culturally conveyed and understood through symbols. Yet we do not all have equal power in defining symbols as meaningful. Part of the symbolism of a noose is recognition that, in the United States, white supremacy exists.

The act of hanging nooses, the cultural meaning of this symbol, and any denials of the significance of such symbolism all amount to **racism**. *Racism* refers to any actions, attitudes, beliefs, or behaviors, whether intentional or unintentional, that threaten, harm, or disadvantage members of one racial/ethnic group, or the group itself, compared to another. Thus, racism can take many forms. It can manifest as **prejudice**, a belief that is not based upon evidence but instead upon preconceived notions and stereotypes that are not subject to change even in the face of contrary evidence. Prejudice relegates racism to the realm of ideas and attitudes rather than actions.

The type of racism that most people envision when they hear the word *racism* is actually **individual discrimination**, which refers to discriminatory actions taken by individuals against members of a subordinate group. Not hiring people because they are Latino is an example of individual discrimination. The minority applicants are not given a chance to even compete for the job, their candidacy dismissed due to the racial/ethnic group to which they belong. This type of racism has declined since the civil rights era simply because it is illegal and thus many employers discriminate less, or less overtly, out of fear of legal retribution.

The most prominent type of racism today is also the hardest to see: **institutional racism**. It is hard to see because it is found not in individual actions but in everyday business practices and policies that disadvantage minorities and offer advantages to dominant-group members; it is often written off as "just the way things are." For instance, schools disproportionately rely on personal property taxes for the majority of their funding, something we will explore in great detail in Chapter 7. This type of system disadvantages schools that serve predominantly poor communities (the residents have less personal property and what they do have is valued less, thus fewer tax dollars are collected). As we will discover in the coming chapters, race and class overlap significantly; this type of funding system, while possibly not intentionally racist, manifests as racism because schools that have predominantly minority populations also tend to be the most impoverished and, thus, tend to get the least funding.

Racism has changed over the generations, yet it remains a significant facet of our society; "Malcolm X used to say that racism was like a Cadillac: they make a new model every year. There is always racism, but it is not the same racism" (Lipsitz 2001:120). Today's racism is certainly different from the racism of the post–Civil War and post-Reconstruction era of segregation known as Jim Crow; however, that does not negate the fact that racism is alive and well and is something people of color experience in their daily lives and to which white Americans are often oblivious. Race and racism are constantly changing, responding to changing social contexts, societal demands, social movements, and varying political climates, to name a few significant influences.

The Continuing Significance of Race

One of the primary arguments in this text is that all of us are required to take account of race, to recognize the various ways race functions in our lives. As a white woman, I have to constantly reflect on the ways my race and gender (as well as social class, age, and sexuality) influence my experiences; I have to interrogate the ways my racial privilege, for instance, operates (see Chapter 2). Many of you are taking this course because it is a requirement. That is no accident. In our rapidly changing world, employers need a workforce that is familiar with and comfortable with all kinds of diversity, including, but not limited to, racial/ethnic diversity (see Box 1.1 Race in the Workplace: Diversity Training in Higher Education). Too often we Americans have fooled ourselves into thinking we understand one another when we clearly do not. During slavery, for instance, southern slaveholders were astonished at the demands of abolitionists, insisting that they treated "their" slaves well and that it was a mutually beneficial system. Later, during the civil rights movement, many southern whites again misunderstood race relations in their own communities, repeatedly claiming that "their Negroes" were happy and that only outside agitators, primarily those who were communist influenced, were the ones fighting for civil rights. During the early to mid-1970s, as busing became the solution to segregated schools in the North, intense rioting and violent opposition occurred in many cities throughout the North, most notoriously Boston. However, individuals in northern states did not consider themselves racially prejudiced, certainly not in the way southerners were stigmatized as racist. Their reactions to busing revealed a very different picture, however.

More-current examples of the continuing significance of race include the race-baiting Republican president Donald Trump has engaged in, specifically his claims that Mexicans are rapists and that we should build a wall to keep them out, and his campaign promise that if he became president of the United States he would deport all Muslims (see Chapter 13). The implementation of strict voter ID laws, which are

BOX 1.1

Race in the Workplace:
Diversity Training in Higher Education

Diversity and *multiculturalism* are often words associated with educational settings—schools of education explore curricular and pedagogical approaches to teaching students from diverse backgrounds and how best to educate all students about the multi-ethnic and multiracial US history. Many institutions of higher education have also signaled their commitment to diversity by hiring Chief Diversity Officers. Multicultural education challenges traditional historical narratives that focus narrowly on a white, male, and middle- to upper-class history.

However, diversity education reaches well beyond schools and has become an influence in the workplace as well. One reason for implementing diversity training is that the American workforce is changing demographically. Today there are more women and people of color in the paid labor force and entering professions; occupations are less segregated along racial and gender lines than they once were. Thus, there is more interaction among whites and people of color as well as among women and men in occupational settings. Additionally, employers are increasingly recognizing the need for hiring, training, retaining, and promoting minority workers. Diversity in all ranks of employment means that different people bring different skills, management styles, knowledge, and approaches to problem-solving, among other things, which, if tapped, work to the advantage of employers. Beyond

such benefits, due to affirmative action policies and the various civil rights acts, employers are no longer free to overlook qualified minority candidates for employment or promotion without the threat of legal action.

Institutions of higher education are workplaces as well. On most campuses, the student body has become more racially/ethnically diverse, yet faculty diversity has been found to lag behind. One study found that even the hiring of Chief Diversity Officers has not influenced faculty demographics (Hansen 2018). While many in higher education are committed to diversity, it turns out that most college campuses are white spaces and too often embrace diversity as a brand rather than showing a real commitment to campus change (Berrey 2015). In fact, diversity agendas are generally "accompanied by the (unspoken) expectation that such minority representation should not threaten the status of white people and other dominant groups" (Berrey 2015:7).

The fall of 2015 witnessed minority student protests on numerous college campuses, including the University of Missouri, where they led to the ouster of two top-level administrators. Minority students are demanding their institutions hire more minority faculty, make a commitment to increasing racial diversity in admissions, and offer a more racially inclusive curriculum—demands that remain remarkably similar to those made in the 1960s (see Chapter 6).

What does a true institutional commitment to diversity on a college campus look like? It "permeates every aspect of the campus and is widely collaborative. It does not rest mostly on chief diversity officers, administrators in multicultural affairs and ethnic cultural centers, and faculty and staff of color. Instead, trustees, presidents, provosts, deans, department chairs, and others all across campus play meaningful roles in advancing it" ("Forum: What Does a Genuine ..." 2016).

found in thirty-three states and require people to show a government-issued photo ID in order to vote, is also a good example of the continuing significance of race. Conservatives claim that such laws are necessary in order to protect against voter fraud. Liberals are critical of such laws for a number of reasons. First, there is no evidence of massive voter fraud that needs to be addressed. Second, such ID requirements would not stop voter fraud. Finally, liberals see this as a Republican tactic to suppress voter turnout among key constituencies, primarily African Americans and other racial minorities, students, and poor people, all of whom tend to vote Democratic. Former senator Jim DeMint claimed that where strict voter ID laws had been enacted, "elections begin to change towards more conservative candidates" (Graham 2016).

To take account of race is to bring it out into the open—to recognize how membership in particular racial/ethnic groups advantages some while hindering others. It exposes how race remains a significant social divide in our culture and, further, how it is embedded in our identities, ideologies, and institutions. Supreme Court justice Harry Blackmun used similar language in his opinion in the affirmative action case *Regents of the University of California v. Bakke* (1978):

> A race-conscious remedy is necessary to achieve a fully integrated society, one in which the color of a person's skin will not determine the opportunities available to him or her. ... In order to get beyond racism, we must first take account of race. There is no other way. ... In order to treat persons equally, we must treat them differently.

In this opinion, Blackmun emphasizes that we must recognize race to get beyond it, that color-consciousness is preferable to color-blindness. Many Americans, particularly white Americans, would rather avoid recognizing the issue of race. Not being victimized by racism can lead many whites to believe that racism is fading away and that any emphasis on race only revives it. Even many progressive white people believe that acknowledging race is a form of racism and that denying race is equivalent to not discriminating against or holding stereotypical views about racial minorities. This **color-blind ideology** dominates US culture; it's the idea that we don't see race, that racism is a thing of the past, and that if racial inequality still exists, it must be due to other factors, such as culture or personal ineptitude. Claiming we live in a color-blind society isn't polite; it is problematic because it fails to challenge white privilege or acknowledge ongoing racism (Bonilla-Silva 2006; Haney Lopez 2006; Omi and Winant 1994). Instead, **color-consciousness**, recognizing race and difference rather than pretending we don't, allows us to celebrate difference without implying difference is equivalent to inferiority.

REFLECT AND CONNECT

Do you claim to be color-blind? If so, what social pressures exist to encourage color-blindness? Does being color-conscious make you uncomfortable? If so, why?

Cyber Racism

The world has changed dramatically in the last three decades, particularly in terms of digital technologies, the internet, and the emergence of social media. Today's generation of college students have not known a time when such technologies did not exist. In this new era, anyone with an internet connection can find white supremacists and their messages online, and white supremacist ideologies are easily spread across the globe. White supremacists were some of the earliest adopters of digital media technologies, creating, publishing, and maintaining some of the earliest web pages on the internet (Daniels 2009).

Due to this, scholars have coined the term **cyber racism**. Cyber racism refers to the widespread use of digital technologies and the internet by white supremacist movements throughout North America and Europe, spreading white supremacist ideologies across national boundaries (Back 2002; Daniels 2009). In addition to white supremacist websites, these groups also use cloaked websites, which are sites with a hidden agenda and whose authorship is concealed, and can be understood as a form of propaganda, a strategic disinformation campaign (Daniels 2009). Such sites allow regular people, casually surfing the internet, to encounter white supremacist ideas. An example of a cloaked website is Martin Luther King: A True Historical Examination, which is designed for a young audience and appears initially to be a tribute to him, yet contains misleading information designed to delegitimize him (Daniels 2009).

Other research has found negative biases against women of color embedded in search engine results and algorithms. Scholar Safiya Umoja Noble (2018) encourages readers to run a google search for "black girls" and compare the results to a search for "white girls." Search algorithms privilege whiteness and discriminate against people of color. Most of us mistakenly assume algorithms are objective or unbiased, yet, since they are designed by humans, they reflect the biases of their creators. And since the tech industry is overwhelmingly composed of white men, racial and gender biases are prevalent (Noble 2018).

RESISTING RACE

Discussing loaded topics, such as those related to racial issues, can make some people uncomfortable or even defensive and resistant. If any part of the previous section made you uncomfortable, remain engaged and learn from your sense of discomfort rather than avoid it. White college professor Helen Fox explains, "I learned from being forced to confront my blind spots, my resistance, the points at which my emotions take over from reason" (Fox 2009:12). You may be uncomfortable with discussions of race-related issues because our society generally does not encourage open, honest, and substantive discussions about race. Thus, some discomfort with an open discussion of race is to be expected. However, it is only through such discomfort that we truly grow.

> ### WITNESS
>
> An African American undergraduate student noted, "I firmly believe that you cannot change your perceptions of people who come from unfamiliar cultures while having safe and superficial chit-chat. It is only when you get uncomfortable and passionate that the true work towards reform can begin" (Fox 2001:51).

The way we view the world is influenced by our particular social statuses, such as race, class, sex, gender, and sexuality. We can only understand others by first understanding ourselves and how our social statuses influence our experiences in and understanding of the world. This text encourages readers to embrace an idea known as the **standpoint perspective**, which argues that knowledge is perspectival; meaning, people's understanding of the world stems from their own social location, as women, or as people of color, or as a person with a disability, or as heterosexual, or some combination of these (Harstock 1987; Smith 1987).

One of the goals of this text is to stimulate honest rather than superficial conversations about race. In 1997, President Bill Clinton appointed a new commission to study the problem of race in the United States and to conduct a national dialogue on race. Clinton declared his initiative, entitled "One America in the 21st Century," in a commencement address at the University of California at San Diego: "Over the coming year I want to lead the American people in a great and unprecedented conversation about race" (Franklin 2009:xi). Clinton began this process with town hall meetings across the country, while opposition to the commission mounted. Much of the media coverage of Clintons initiative declared the racial dialogue initiative to be racially biased rather than progressive.

WITNESS

African American W. Ralph Eubanks grew up in Mississippi during the tumultuous 1960s. Exemplifying the standpoint perspective, he describes in his memoir, *Ever Is a Long Time* (2003), the dramatically different reactions of the local black and white communities to the assassination of President John F. Kennedy in 1963. At his all-black school, Eubanks' teacher relayed the news to the students through tears; later the black community gathered quietly at a neighbor's home. Their mourning was interrupted by shouts spilling from a passing white school bus filled with children cheering, "They got him! Yay! They finally got him!" (Eubanks 2003:61).

Clinton was not the first president to direct attention to the issue of racial inequality or to face a backlash because of it. President Truman formed a Committee on Civil Rights in 1946. President Johnson appointed a White House Conference on Civil Rights in 1966, and in 1967 he created the National Advisory Commission on Civil Disorders, more commonly known as the Kerner Commission, to address urban rioting. Perhaps ironically, the nation's first black president barely addressed race, with the exception of one eloquent campaign speech about race given on March 18, 2008. President Obama worked to balance embracing black America with a belief in policies that benefited everyone rather than those that targeted specific groups. When criticized by some prominent black Americans, such as Cornel West, for not addressing racism explicitly, he responded with, "I'm not the president of black America, I'm the president of the United States of America" (Kantor 2012).

Examining Our Own Belief Systems Surrounding Race

Conversations about race, which were the goal of the Clinton initiative, first require that we engage in a process of **self-reflexivity**, examining our conscious and unconscious beliefs about race. To be self-reflexive means to engage in an ongoing conversation with ourselves concerning what we are learning and to reflect on how it mirrors our experiences or challenges our long-held assumptions. Throughout this text, you will be asked to understand and question your preconceived notions about race, racism, privilege, and racial inequality.

Self-reflexivity allows us to recognize that we are all oppressors, not only in our society but globally as well. A poor white man, for instance, has race and gender privilege but faces inequality along class lines. It is no healthier to be an oppressor than to be oppressed, although it is fair to say that the experience of being oppressed is the more damaging of the two. There are multiple status hierarchies, for instance, based on social class, gender, sexuality, age, and ability/disability. The only truly privileged person may be a wealthy, white, heterosexual man with no disabilities who claims citizenship in a wealthy country. And even then, should that privileged person live long enough, age becomes the great equalizer for two reasons: aging is an increasingly disabling process, and we live in a youth-oriented culture that does not value the elderly. Thus, even those who appear to have privilege on every status hierarchy can eventually face subordination when it comes to age.

Speaking "Race" Honestly

So, how do we have honest dialogues about race in a society that has taught us to avoid them, without putting people off? First, we must have the necessary tools to speak intelligently about race: to debate one another, to challenge false statements, and to critically interrogate media content. This text is designed to provide students with a foundation for this—you are being provided with a language for talking about race (which is why terminology is important), statistics for visualizing the extent of racial discrimination and privilege, and a sociohistorical framework for understanding race/ethnicity in the US and the world.

Second, the primary thing that is necessary for being able to talk about race is to break from our cultural norm of color-blindness. In her TED Talk, African American finance executive Mellody Hobson (2014) encourages us to abandon our commitment to color-blindness and instead to be color-brave (see Recommended Multimedia at the end of the chapter). She argues we need to speak openly about race—and that it makes good business sense to do so. The first step to fixing any problem, she argues, is to not hide from it, but instead to bring awareness to the issue. We need to be less anxious and more bold in our conversations about race. She continues, "We have to be willing to have pro-active conversations about race with honesty, understanding, and courage … because it is the smart thing to do" (Hobson 2014).

Third, honest discussions about race emerge in classrooms in which students and faculty listen to one another respectfully. Antiracist activist and author Paul Kivel (2008) argues that the first thing we must do if we are to do antiracist work is to trust the stories told by people of color concerning their experiences with racism and discrimination rather than disregard them. Many whites, for example, tend to assume people of color are exaggerating the racism they claim to have experienced or that they are placing too much emphasis on history. Some white people have faced racial discrimination that deserves to be heard and acknowledged as well. However, since non-Hispanic whites significantly outnumber all other racial/ethnic groups and hold the power in US society, white people do not encounter the ongoing, systemic racism that is too often experienced by people of color. White people may experience individual acts of discrimination or be prejudiced against by some people of color, but it is not systemic as the racism directed at people of color is, both historically and currently. As students, it is partially your responsibility to help establish norms of respect in your classroom so that you can have productive conversations about a topic that many of us have been taught is taboo.

To be self-reflexive about race forces us to acknowledge not only societal racism but the racism inevitably within us. The use of strong language ("inevitably") is intentional. We live in a racist society; so we cannot be nonracist without actively working toward that goal. Anyone can be racist—meaning any person can hold prejudicial views regarding racial/ethnic others, and/or discriminate against racial/ethnic others. White people in no way corner the market on racial prejudice and discrimination. However, white people's racism gets reinforced by society through the media, the attitudes of family members, political rhetoric, and educational institutions. This implies that racism can be understood as *prejudice plus power*. It may be that much harder for white people to see their racism because it is constantly being culturally reinforced, so it is the norm. **Cultural norms** are unquestioned practices or beliefs and thus are taken for granted. Racism manifests itself not only in attitudes but in cultural belief systems, individual actions, and institutional practices. Because people of color do not collectively hold enough positions of power, they tend not to have as much influence in creating cultural belief systems, known as racial ideologies, or institutional practices.

Because racism tends to be normalized in our color-blind society, organizations and individuals have emerged to actively fight racism (see Box 1.2 Racial Justice Activism: Eracism). This text focuses on **racial justice activism**, sometimes referred to as *antiracist activism*, which concerns groups and individuals who are actively working to eradicate racism. Each chapter will contain a special feature, "Racial Justice Activism," by a racial justice activist or about an antiracist organization, so that you can see the work being done to counter the dominant pattern of racism within our society.

Racial Justice Activism:
Eracism

"Eracism" is the slogan of a nonprofit, volunteer-run organization known as ERACE, which formed in New Orleans in the summer of 1993 and now includes a chapter in Atlanta. It grew out of a series in a local newspaper, the *Times-Picayune*, entitled "Together Apart: The Myth of Race." ERACE's objectives are to facilitate conversations between people of all races, to create an atmosphere in which people feel free to explore their perceptions, assumptions, and biases about race in a nonjudgmental setting, and to ultimately help put an end to racism. The idea is that honest discussion can help eliminate stereotypes and misconceptions.

ERACE sponsors monthly group discussions that are designed to foster an open, critical exchange of ideas. In addition to its monthly discussions, ERACE sponsors social gatherings and children's play groups, and its members speak to schools, businesses, and the media. Additionally, their website also includes documents to help people learn to address racism in the home, in schools, the workplace, and in everyday interactions.

In 2010, the organization launched Eracism in Schools to connect two New Orleans schools, one with a predominantly black student population and the other with a predominantly white student population, for dialogues. For more information on ERACE, check out its website: www.eracismnew orleans.org/.

UNDERSTANDING RACE AS A SOCIAL CONSTRUCTION

Have you ever questioned this concept called race? Most white people have not, because they view the world from a position of **race privilege**, the unearned advantages associated with being a member of a society's dominant race. Having race privilege allows people to rarely even think about race, much less question its validity. White (race) privilege and the ways it manifests itself will be explored in much more detail in Chapter 2. However, it is not only white people who fail to question the notion of race. For people of color, their experiences with racial prejudice and discrimination emphasize the significance of race, and such experiences cause them not to question the concept of race, either. If you experience racial discrimination, race feels very real.

People who question the validity of race tend to be those who live in the racial margins—biracial and multiracial individuals, for instance. Racial categories in our society are treated as absolute, as either/or, and as biologically real. Yet biracial individuals live in a world of both/and—they are members of more than one racial group, so discrete racial categories don't apply to them. For example, monoracial people can fill out their demographic information on standardized tests or census forms without question, while biracial and multiracial people find themselves in a predicament. They are forced to think of themselves as *either* black, white, Hispanic, or Native American, when they may be all or some combination of the above categories. Their very existence challenges our societal racial categorization system. Thus, their standpoint on the world and their lived experience allow them to see what for many of us is difficult not only to see but to understand: that race is not real in a biological sense.

Race is a **socially and politically constructed** phenomenon. In other words, race is not biologically or genetically determined; racial categories, groups of people differentiated by their physical characteristics, are given particular meanings by particular societies in particular eras. It is political in that groups of people are socially constructed as different in order to exploit some groups and advantage others. Evidence for the social construction of race includes the presence of biracial and multiracial people, described above, who live in the racial margins and whose existence challenges the racial categorization system (where people have historically been said to be one race or another, not more than one).

Second, there is also more genetic variation within a so-called racial group than between groups. Think about this last statement for a moment and challenge how

IMAGE 1.2: Despite the fact that Kian looks black and Remee looks white, these two girls are twins, born just a minute apart. The images exemplify the idea that race is a social construction.

SOURCE: Barcroft Media.

you have been taught to think about race and the world. We all encounter very light-skinned African Americans who are identified and classified as black (in personal interactions or on official documents, for instance) and individuals with very dark skin who are similarly identified and classified as white. We see these physical variations every day; however, we tend not to let them challenge our assumptions about race. The idea of the social construction of race forces us to recognize that if such glaring contradictions exist, we must challenge our racial categorization system.

A third piece of evidence that race is a social construction is that racial categories change across time and place (see Box 1.3 Global Perspectives: The Social Construction

BOX 1.3

Global Perspectives:
The Social Construction of Race in Latin America

To say that race is a social construction is to recognize that definitions of race change across time and place. In Latin America, for instance, race is understood differently than in the United States. A common theme of Latin American race relations is the notion of *mestizaje*, cultural and racial mixing that involves a progression toward whiteness. This is a concept generally applied to indigenous peoples, however, rather than to Latin Americans of African descent. In Peru, for instance, questions of race tend to refer to Indians rather than Afro-Peruvians (Golash-Boza 2012). For indigenous people in Peru, their racial status is determined by their educational attainment, social class, and certain cultural markers; thus, they hold the possibility of changing their racial status by changing these markers. However, for black Peruvians, their racial status strictly refers to skin color; thus, changing their racial status is not possible (Golash-Boza 2012).

In Brazil, race is defined differently than in the United States and is closer to that of Peru. Brazilians have never defined race in biological terms and instead embrace a form of colorism, whereby lighter-skinned citizens hold a higher social status. This is not defined as racism because these are not distinctions made upon biological-group membership. Mulattoes hold a special status in Brazil that is unheard of in the United States, one that is neither "black nor white" (Degler 1971). Historically, in the United States, the "one-drop rule" has applied, by which anyone with any African ancestry was considered to be black.

What is important about this is that throughout Latin America there is considerable racial mixing and understandings of race are different than those of the United States. However, the presence of extensive race mixing does not challenge white supremacy in these countries or the racial hierarchy, where racial minorities are disadvantaged compared to those designated as whites or those who are lighter skinned (Bonilla-Silva 2010).

of Race in Latin America). If race were biologically real, this would not be true. The racial category "white" has always been in flux. Groups that were once considered non-white include Americans of Irish, Greek, Italian, Armenian, and Jewish descent. Their physical appearance never changed, but their social status did, which offers more evidence that race is a socially constructed category. Prior to "becoming white," members of these groups were discriminated against, assumed to be of inferior intelligence, and faced some of the same obstacles that black Americans have faced. For example, when Irish Americans were viewed as nonwhite, they were not considered qualified for certain jobs and their housing choices were limited (Ignatiev 1995). Over time, all of these groups came to be considered white, and with that changing racial/ethnic status came advantages that they could use every day (the social construction of whiteness is discussed in detail in Chapter 2).

For more evidence of race changing across time, consider a seemingly objective document: the census. Census data have been collected every ten years by the federal government since the first census of 1790, which was overseen by Thomas Jefferson. The census is supposed to provide us with a demographic snapshot of the United States: data on educational level, age, race, gender, socioeconomic status, and much more illustrate the US population at a particular time (see Image 1.2). The census is assumed to contain objective and unbiased information. Social scientists use census data regularly in scientific research, thus affirming the validity of the document and the data collected.

REFLECT AND CONNECT

Speculate as to why such differentiations and subgroupings of blacks were considered necessary during the decades leading up to and immediately after the Civil War, yet have been considered unnecessary since 1890. Can you explain why such racial categorizations of African Americans were politically advantageous in some eras but not others?

However, racial categories on the census are always changing, which confirms the social construction of race as a reflection of sociohistorical eras (see Recommended Multimedia at the end of this chapter). For instance, the first census documented "whites" and "nonwhites," with instructions to not count Native Americans at all. Prior to and following the Civil War, the census had multiple categories for blacks. For instance, in 1840, 1850, and 1860, census takers were provided with a racial category called mulatto, a person of mixed African and white ancestry, although this category was not explicitly defined at the time. In the 1870 and 1880 censuses, the category "mulatto" was defined and differentiated into two subgroups, **quadroons** (children of a white person and a mulatto) and **octoroons** (children of a white person and a quadroon, thus, someone having one black great-grandparent), as well as a category referring to "people having any perceptible trace of African blood." By 1890, census takers were asked to record the exact proportion of African blood, based upon physical appearance and the opinion of the census taker (the census did not begin using racial self-definitions until 1960).

Over the years, such groups as Japanese Americans have been classified on the census as "nonwhite," "Orientals," "other," and currently "Asian or Asian Pacific Islander." A relatively new ethnic category on the census is that of "Hispanic." Many Latinos do not see themselves as "Hispanic," as it is not a term they have used to define themselves. It is instead a term originated by the United States federal government. The term *Latino* references the Latin American origins of such people and thus tends to be more commonly used. On the 2000 census, the race question was split in two; the first question asking about the respondent's Hispanic ethnicity and the follow-up question asking about the respondent's race, which does not include a "Hispanic" option (see Image 1.3). Currently, "Hispanic" is not classified as a race on the US census despite the fact that whites are referred to as "non-Hispanic whites." However, the US Census Bureau considered adding "Hispanic" as a racial category on the 2020 census in order to more accurately reflect how people self-identify their racial and ethnic origin. In fact, the Census Bureau recommended merging the race and ethnicity questions into one, as it was prior to 2000 (Bayoumi 2019). As previous eras exposed great interest in African Americans, as emphasized by their census categorizations in the eras surrounding the Civil War, political interest in Hispanics has existed since the 1970s.

➡ NOTE: Please answer BOTH Question 5 about Hispanic origin and Question 6 about race. For this census, Hispanic origins are not races.

5. Is this person of Hispanic, Latino, or Spanish origin?

☐ No, not of Hispanic, Latino, or Spanish origin
☐ Yes, Mexican, Mexican Am., Chicano
☐ Yes, Puerto Rican
☐ Yes, Cuban
☐ Yes, another Hispanic, Latino, or Spanish origin — *Print origin, for example, Argentinean, Colombian, Dominican, Nicaraguan, Salvadoran, Spaniard, and so on.* ☑

6. What is this person's race? *Mark ☒ one or more boxes.*

☐ White
☐ Black, African Am., or Negro
☐ American Indian or Alaska Native — *Print name of enrolled or principal tribe.* ☑

☐ Asian Indian ☐ Japanese ☐ Native Hawaiian
☐ Chinese ☐ Korean ☐ Guamanian or Chamorro
☐ Filipino ☐ Vietnamese ☐ Samoan
☐ Other Asian — *Print race, for example, Hmong, Laotian, Thai, Pakistani, Cambodian, and so on.* ☑   ☐ Other Pacific Islander — *Print race, for example, Fijian, Tongan, and so on.* ☑

☐ Some other race — *Print race.* ☑

IMAGE 1.3: The social construction of race is exemplified by the changing racial categories on the census. This image is of the racial category question on the 2010 census. Currently, "Hispanic" is not a racial category, according to the US census; however, the Census Bureau is considering adding it as a racial category on the 2020 census.

SOURCE: US Census Bureau, 2010 census questionnaire.

Another change the Census Bureau considered making for the 2020 census was adding more racial categories, including a new category, "Middle Eastern or North African (Mena)." This category would include people from Turkey, Iran, and Israel, who currently are counted as white by the census, but who are racialized as non-white in daily interactions, which means they experience prejudice, discrimination, and racial profiling based on their skin color and presumed race. Arabs and Middle Easterners are "neither fully white nor recognized as people of color" (Zopf 2018). The Trump administration rejected the suggested changes to the 2020 census (Bayoumi 2019).

Why keep track of the racial demographics of society at all? Aren't we all just human beings? The American Civil Liberties Union urged the race category be removed from the census in 1960, but once various civil rights acts were passed, census data on race became useful for gauging compliance with laws barring various forms of discrimination. Thus, we come back to Justice Blackmun's point—to get beyond racism, we must first take account of race.

Finally, from a biological science standpoint, it is not hard to recognize that racial categories are social constructions. Quite simply, their argument is that if two animals (and humans are animals) can breed, they are of the same species. Any further breakdown in the species "human being," then, is socially generated rather than biologically determined. Additionally, after mapping the human genome, geneticists have not identified a gene that is found strictly in one racial group and not in another. Thus, there is no genetic marker for race.

But despite the lack of biological validity, race is a significant aspect of American society because we attach particularly salient meanings to specific physical characteristics and these meanings result in some very real consequences. Dislodging the notion that race is real in a biological sense is often difficult, particularly if this is your first encounter with this idea (after all, our genes determine what we look like, right?). Next time you walk into a room, see whether you can identify how many racial groups are present. While this may make you uncomfortable, as some people are racially ambiguous and you might hate to be wrong, most people assume that this task is possible. However, scientists know otherwise. Despite the lack of biological validity, race and ethnicity are important socially, which is why a critical investigation of race, racism, and race privilege is so important. It may be difficult to dislodge our misconceptions surrounding the biological validity of race, but it is important to recognize that there is power in the notion of race as a social construction. Anything that is constructed can be *deconstructed*. In other words, there is nothing inevitable about race, racism, and racial inequality. We could have a society without these problematic divisions, a society without a racial hierarchy.

Of course, the United States is not the only nation to struggle with the issue of racial categorization. France has implemented an antiracism model that has official color-blindness at its core. The basis of this model is a 1978 law that prohibits the collection of racial/ethnic data, on the census or any other official document, such as those explaining educational demographics. It is also illegal for public or private institutions to collect racial/ethnic data. Similarly, most French people disavow racial/ethnic categorization, viewing these as divisive (Bleich 2003).

DEMOGRAPHIC SHIFTS IN THE UNITED STATES

Courses on race and ethnicity are required in many colleges and universities because the face of America is changing demographically. Figure 1.1, based upon Pew Research Center data, shows the demographic breakdown of racial/ethnic groups in the United States in 2017 and predictions for 2050.

REFLECT AND CONNECT

Take a minute to look over the demographic data in Figure 1.1. A Pew Center report says "non-Hispanic whites" will lose majority status by 2050. Based upon your understanding of race as a social construction, can you identify potential flaws in this prediction/interpretation of the data?

As the previous discussion makes clear, we cannot be sure that in thirty-something years these will be the census racial categories. Census racial categories have changed over time and it is reasonable to assume this will continue. If so, what changes do you predict in terms of future census racial categories?

A second flaw in the statement is the assertion that "non-Hispanic whites" will "lose majority status." Sociologically speaking, to say that "non-Hispanic whites" will lose majority status speaks only to numerical status and says nothing about power and societal dominance. There is no evidence that whites will lose power, resources, and status and certainly no evidence that whites will become a minority group. Additionally, it is problematic because interpreting the data to mean whites will become a minority group only makes sense if we lump all racial minority groups together, in which case it would appear that whites will be 47 percent of the population in 2050 and nonwhites will be 53 percent. However, we disaggregate the data along racial-group lines. When viewed that way, non-Hispanic whites (at 47 percent) as a group are still considerably larger than the next largest group, Hispanics (at 29 percent). Interpreting changing racial demographics to mean that whites will lose majority status can be viewed not only as inaccurate but as incendiary in the current climate. It is the kind of statement that strikes fear in whites, increases antagonism toward immigrants, fuels racial tensions, and creates a climate of hostility overall.

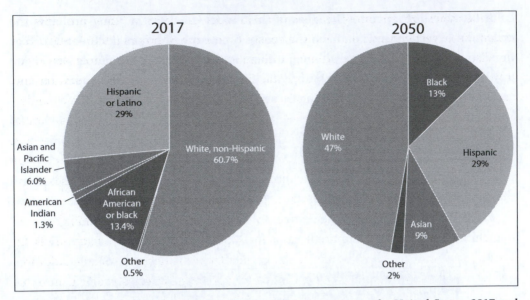

FIGURE 1.1: Demographic breakdown of racial/ethnic groups in the United States, 2017 and 2050 (predicted). Please note: does not include people of more than one race.

SOURCES: Passel and Cohn 2008. Retrieved June 21, 2016; US Census Bureau 2017.

At the same time, these are significant demographic changes confronting American society; essentially, the face of America is changing dramatically. In two short generations, American society will look very different. Thus, such changes require that we learn to understand one another, particularly cultural differences across racial/ethnic lines. Future teachers, a population that is still disproportionately white, middle class, and female, will be facing classrooms with much more racial/ethnic diversity than those they grew up in. The hope underlying courses in racial/ethnic diversity or a multiculturalism requirement is that today's college students will come to embrace, not just tolerate, racial/ethnic differences.

Millennials on Race: The 'Woke' Generation?

This new edition of *Recognizing Race and Ethnicity* is framed by an exciting new survey entitled "The 'Woke' Generation? Millennials Attitudes on Race in the US" (Cohen et al. 2017). It is a first-of-its-kind, nationally representative survey of over 1,750 young adults, who were between the ages of 18 and 34 in 2017 and is designed to gauge what young people think about race today. The **Millennial generation**, sometimes referred to as Generation Y, refers to the generation of people born between the years 1981–1996. If you are a traditional-age college student reading this book, you are likely not a Millennial; instead you are a member of the Post-Millennial generation, those born in 1997 or later. You may have older siblings or cousins or friends who are Millennials, so their experiences are not too dramatically different from yours.

Millennials are an interesting generation demographically. They are now the country's largest generation, having surpassed the Baby Boomers (1946–1964). They are also the most racially and ethnically diverse generation in the country (see Figure 1.2). There is also a perception that Millennials are a more liberal generation and, indeed, more than 80 percent of voters under the age of 30 voted for Bernie Sanders in the 2016 Democratic primary. They are also overwhelmingly liberal on a handful of social issues, including gay rights, immigration, and marijuana. And yet, we have to be careful treating this generation, or any generation, as a monolithic group. On gun rights and abortion, for instance, they mirror the wide range of attitudes found in the rest of the country (Thompson 2016). Millennial attitudes on racial issues, as we will explore throughout this text, are diverse as well (Cohen et al. 2017).

This survey finds, for instance, that Millennials of all racial backgrounds list racism as one of the most important problems facing American society. Additionally, a majority of Millennials surveyed feel that African Americans and Latinos are the groups that experience the most discrimination in our society. Millennial respondents were asked whether they felt the projected demographic changes described above would strengthen the country, weaken it, or not make much of a difference (see Figure 1.3). The diversity of the responses are telling: almost half of white respondents (49 percent) felt that this change would not make much of a difference, while people of color were more likely to say that these changes strengthened the country (46 percent of African Americans, 61 percent of Asian Americans, and 59 percent of Latinos) (Cohen et al. 2017).

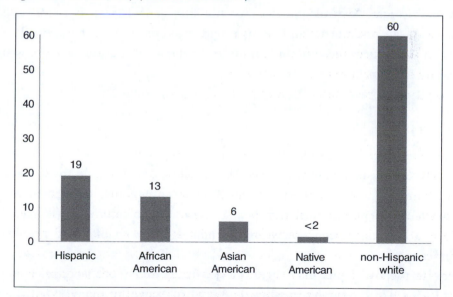

FIGURE 1.2: As of 2018, Millennials surpassed Baby Boomers (1946-1964) as the largest generation. They also are the most racially diverse generation in American history.

SOURCE: Cohen et al. 2017.

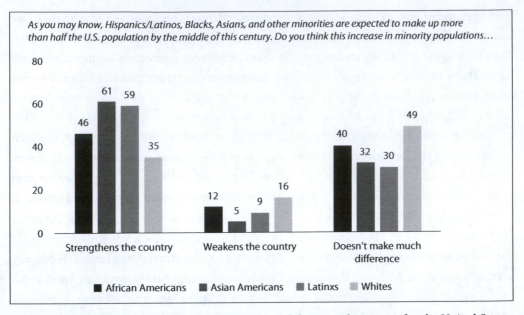

As you may know, Hispanics/Latinos, Blacks, Asians, and other minorities are expected to make up more than half the U.S. population by the middle of this century. Do you think this increase in minority populations...

FIGURE 1.3: When asked what the changing racial demographics mean for the United States, Millennials showed some significant differences along racial lines, with almost half of white Millennials saying it would not matter, and even fewer African Americans (46 percent) stating that it would matter, while majorities of Latino and Asian American respondents felt it would strengthen the country. Notably, whites had the highest percentage of respondents who viewed these changes as weakening the country, at 16 percent (Cohen et al. 2017).

Other questions explore Millennials' opinions on the Black Lives Matter movement, Confederate symbols, whether or not President Trump is racist, and the extent of racial resentment and racial progress among their generation. We will return to these survey results throughout the book as we address these important topics and more.

A Note on Terminology

Racial terminology, specifically what terms are acceptable for describing a group of people, has changed over time. Many white students, particularly those who have not had much interaction with people of color, often feel hesitant to interact with students of color because they "don't know what to call them" (Fox 2009:27). There is a fear that using the wrong terminology can be offensive and lead to misunderstanding.

Prior to the civil rights movement, most African Americans were referred to as "Negroes" and the term *black* was considered offensive by many (Martin 1991). During the Black Power movement of the late 1960s, people were encouraged to substitute the term *black* for *Negro*. Twenty years later, at a 1988 news conference, African American leader Jesse Jackson announced that "African American" was the preferred term for blacks. It was considered a more acceptable term than *black* because it referenced a land base and a cultural heritage (Martin 1991).

While this shift in terminology has been relatively successful, some blacks are hesitant to embrace it as an identity. As one undergraduate of African descent explains:

> My mother calls herself Black—capital B—my aunt won't hear of anything but African American, and I prefer to be called an American of African Descent, which stresses the American-ness of my experience. We are an extremely diverse community that values our individualism and our independent thinking.
>
> (Fox 2009:30)

Another black undergraduate explains, "I am not an African American, I'm black. I refuse to be called American until the day that this country treats me with the same value and respect as everyone else" (Fox 2009:30). Ultimately, neither *black* nor *African American* is considered to be an offensive term, although individuals differ as to whether or not they personally feel comfortable with them. Both the terms *Negro* and *colored* are considered outdated and inappropriate terms for describing black people.

The term *Latino* is often preferred by Latinos to the term *Hispanic*. *Hispanic* is a term describing people of Spanish (and sometimes Portuguese) descent in the United States. It was a term created by the federal government in the early 1970s and is an umbrella term that includes over twenty different nationalities (Fox 2009). Because of its origins, it is not a term that many Latinos use to describe themselves. Some feel that the term needs to be retired. Others find the umbrella nature of both *Hispanic* and *Latino* problematic, preferring to see themselves as Mexican American or Puerto Rican, for instance. The term *Latino* is now used interchangeably with *Hispanic*, although *Latino* is the preferred term in this text.

The term *Chicano* was created by Mexican American activists during the Brown Power movement of the 1960s and 1970s (see Chapter 6). "During the 60s, young Mexican Americans started to use 'Chicano/Chicana' as an affirmation of pride and identity and to say, 'We're not Mexicans or Americans. We're a combination—a special population with our own history and culture'" (Martinez 1997, quoted in Fox 2009:33). Thus, all Chicanos are Mexican Americans, but not all Mexican Americans embrace the term *Chicano*.

The terms *Native American*, *Native people*, *Indian*, *American Indian*, *indigenous people*, and *First Nations* are used interchangeably by Indians and non-Indians without offense; however, much like with the previous discussion, individuals have preferences for specific terms. One of the leaders of the American Indian Movement (see Chapter 6), Russell Means, commented:

You notice that I use the term *American Indian* rather than *Native American* or *Native indigenous people* or *Amerindian* when referring to my people. There has been some controversy about such terms. ... Primarily it seems that American Indian is being rejected as European in origin—which is true. But all of the above terms are European in origin [italics in the original].

(Nagel 1996:xi)

This text will use Native American, American Indian, Indian, and Native people interchangeably.

There has been less contestation surrounding terms used to describe Asian Americans. The term *Asian American* is an umbrella term that refers to a wide range of Asian ethnic groups in the United States. While the term *Asian American* is not considered offensive, it is more accurate to describe people as members of their particular ethnic group: Korean American, Japanese American, Chinese American, and so on. Using the term *Oriental* to describe Asian Americans is inappropriate due to the outdated and offensive nature of the term, similar to the use of the words *Negro* or *colored* to describe African Americans.

There are even fewer debates over what to call white people, with one notable exception, *Caucasian*, which is a term introduced in the late eighteenth century to refer to people of European origin (broadly defined) with white skin, referring to people from the Caucasus Mountains region, from Russia to northern Africa. Although it is not a term the US Census Bureau ever used to describe white people but is instead a racial classification employed by anthropologists, it quickly became synonymous with *white*. However, the term is losing its meaning, as most white people do not use it to describe themselves.

REFLECT AND CONNECT

Were any of the terms we just discussed new to you? If so, why do you think that is? Would you consider yourself someone who has avoided interracial interactions because you were unsure "what to call them"?

RACIAL IDENTITIES, RACIAL IDEOLOGIES, AND INSTITUTIONAL RACISM

There are three interlocking aspects of race: identities, ideologies, and institutions. Racism and privilege are manifested in all three, so we must understand all three in order to fully grasp the intricacies of race in our society. Race is an arena of power and, as French theorist Michel Foucault emphasizes, power can be exercised as control through scientific knowledge. Chapter 3 focuses on the changing science of race and the many ways this has acted as a system of control. This text takes a different approach than standard sociological texts that emphasize only social scientific research on racial inequality. This kind of approach fails to account for how science itself informs identities, ideologies, and institutions and actually helps maintain the racial hierarchy.

Racial Identities

What do we mean by "racial identity"? Our identity is how we see ourselves. We establish our **racial identity**, our sense of who we are racially and how we view ourselves, through interaction with others. In addition to interactions with others, the way race is discussed and presented in society contributes to the creation of individual and collective racial identities. The potential racial/ethnic identities one has to choose from change across time, similar to the changing census categories. A current example of such change is the increasing salience of biracial and multiracial identities. There is nothing new about people with multiple racial ancestries. What is new is that people are identifying as biracial or multiracial. Historically in the United States, the one-drop rule reigned, which meant that individuals with more than one

IMAGE 1.4: The emergence of people who identify as biracial or multiracial is relatively new, despite the fact that there is nothing new about biracial/multiracial people. Racial identity options expand or contract in different historical eras.

racial heritage, one of which was black, identified themselves or were identified by others as black (in other words, to have "one drop" of black blood made one black, a policy that has not been applied to any other racial/ethnic minority group). The so-called biracial baby boom of the post-1960s era has resulted in many of the children of black–white interracial unions, those that have been defined as the most taboo in our culture, claiming a biracial identity rather than a black identity, as previous generations had (Korgen 1998).

Native American identity reclamation is another example of the significance of race as an identity and emphasizes the idea that identities are always in flux. In this case, many individuals who formerly viewed themselves as white are now reconnecting with their Native heritage and identify as Native American, specifically their tribal identity (Fitzgerald 2007; Nagel 1996). Thus, people who have assimilated, are perceived as white, and benefit from white privilege are instead claiming a nonwhite racial identity.

A final argument for why racial identity is important pertains to the idea of racial identity development. Psychologists have long studied identity development, particularly in adolescents; however, racial identity development has too often been overlooked. All people go through stages of development as they begin to define themselves in relation to others. Racial identity development is a part of this process, yet often not a conscious part of it. Researchers argue that racial identity development differs for white people and people of color (Helms 1990; Cross, Parham, and Helms 1991; Tatum 1992, 1994). For instance, whites in the first stage of racial identity development base their notions of people of color on media stereotypes because they tend not to have had much contact with people of color. For students of color, stage one involves internalizing many of the stereotypes about their own racial group and other people of color. For some, this can be the result of being raised in a primarily white environment. Thus, Tatum (1992) argues, they tend to distance themselves from the more oppressed members of their own group. Social psychologists use the term **internalized racism** to describe individuals who believe what the dominant group says about them; in other words, they internalize negative messages about their racial group.

WITNESS

"The greatest weapon in the hands of the oppressor is the mind of the oppressed." South African liberationist and martyr Steven Biko, *I Write What I Like* (1978)

Racial Ideologies

Racial ideologies, or cultural belief systems surrounding race, are also significant and have changed over time, generally to meet the needs of the dominant group in a particular era or in response to changing social conditions. Societies establish racial hierarchies to benefit some groups while disadvantaging others, and ideologies serve to justify such arrangements. The current reigning racial ideology in the United States is that of color-blindness, or the **color-blind ideology**. Color-blindness is the idea that race no longer matters, particularly since the civil rights movement, and that if there is evidence of ongoing inequality along racial lines, it must be based on some nonracial factor, such as culture. This is a significant racial ideology because it allows white people, even those who consider themselves liberal and/or progressive, to deny the significance of race in our current society (Bonilla-Silva 2006; Omi and Winant 1994).

This is a justifying ideology because it allows us to think that the social activism of the 1960s resolved racial inequalities and thus we are a society that is beyond race. Color-blindness suggests that race no longer matters, which in turn implies that policies designed to address racial inequality, such as affirmative action, are no longer needed. And yet, such policies are designed to address not only current racial (and gender) inequality but also the ongoing effects of historical inequalities; as long as inequality remains, a need for social policies to address them remains. In previous eras, ideologies based on white supremacy predominated to justify slavery long after slavery had been introduced. Such ideologies served to deflect questions about the morality of slavery because they allowed white people to believe in the complete inferiority and inhumanity of blacks. White supremacist ideologies allowed Anglo-Americans to justify taking land away from Native peoples and engage in genocidal policies against them, due to the perceived inferiority of the Native peoples, who were viewed as "uncivilized heathens."

Millennials on Race

Racial ideologies change over time and while scholars still describe the reigning ideology of the current era as color-blindness, Millennials' attitudes on race may indicate that is shifting. For instance, Millennials of all racial backgrounds cite racism as one of the top three concerns facing our country (see Table 1.1). Additionally, when asked if racism remains a major problem in our society, a majority of all Millennials agree it is (see Figure 1.4). While there is great variation in the attitudes of whites and people of color on these questions, it might be evidence of the declining power of color-blindness among young people.

	African American	Asian American	Latinx	White
Most cited problem	Racism (52%)	Health Care (45%)	Immigration (39%)	Health Care (39%)
Second most cited problem	Health Care (30%)	Racism (32%)	Racism (33%)	Environment and Climate Change (27%)
Third most cited problem	Police Brutality (25%)	Education (25%)	Health Care (29%)	Racism/ Terrorism and Homeland Security (26%)
N =	503	258	505	510

TABLE 1.1: Millennials' Perceptions of the Three Most Important Problems, by Racial Group. While racism is a top concern among Millennials of all racial backgrounds, there is considerable variation between groups. It is only among African Americans that a majority of respondents cite racism as a top concern (Cohen et al. 2017).

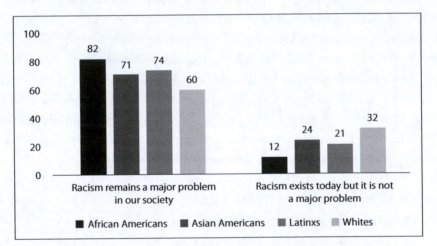

FIGURE 1.4: Perceptions of racism as a major problem in the United States, according to Millennials. Large majorities of African Americans (82 percent), Asian Americans (71 percent), and Latinos (74 percent), and a solid majority of white, non-Hispanic Americans (60 percent) believe racism remains a major problem in the United States today (Cohen et al. 2017).

Institutional Racism

Finally, institutional racism is found in the ways societal institutions, such as those in the educational, economic, political, media, and legal spheres, are "raced." Institutional racism is the most pervasive form of racism today and also the most subtle because it is found in everyday business practices, laws, and norms that create or maintain racial inequality, whether intentional or not. Institutional racism is often considered to be the most difficult kind of racial discrimination to see because it tends not to be an action taken by a particular person that others can point to and recognize as racism. It is much more subtle than that, despite the fact that the racial manifestations are very real. Because this is the most prominent type of racism in the United States, it may explain why white people and people of color have such divergent views on the extent of racism that still exists in our society. As you can see by scanning the table of contents for this book, the second half of the book explores institutional racism and privilege in great detail.

Racial identities, ideologies, and institutions are intricately interconnected. For instance, when the ideology of white superiority reigned and the one-drop rule was established, biracial individuals saw themselves as black. They did not consider their white heritage as informing their identity in any way, nor were they encouraged to do so. Claiming a biracial or a multiracial identity is a post-1960s phenomenon. Additionally, ideologies inform institutional practices such as public-policy making, and vice versa. For instance, the emergence of a biracial or multiracial identity came as interracial relationships increased in the post-1960s era, after the last laws forbidding interracial marriage were overturned by the Supreme Court in 1967.

Another example of the interconnections between identities, ideologies, and institutions occurred during the 1990s with the battle for a multiracial category on the census, a clear institutional reflection of this growing movement of people who claim a multiracial identity. The Census Bureau did not opt for a specific biracial or multiracial category, but it did allow individuals for the first time to check more than one racial category (see Chapter 12).

CHAPTER SUMMARY

This chapter introduced key concepts necessary for understanding the history and current status of race in American society, particularly the idea that race is a social construction rather than a biological reality. We began by distinguishing between race and ethnicity while acknowledging that they are interrelated concepts, then explored the various types of racism, from prejudice to institutional racism to colorism. While there has been racial progress since the Jim Crow era, when whites terrorized minorities through lynching and other forms of violence, we do not live in a postracial society.

Studying race, racism, and race privilege is essential in our rapidly changing world. Most businesses recognize the changing face of America and expect future employees to be able to adapt to a diverse workforce. For that to occur, it is necessary that Americans of all racial/ethnic backgrounds understand one another and understand how race operates at the level of individual identities, as well as through ideologies and institutions. This text encourages us to take account of race in society by providing an essential history of racial/ethnic relations in the United States and explaining the significance of that history to current society. Additionally, the emphasis on self-reflexivity, the call to look within ourselves to understand how racial ideologies inform our attitudes and beliefs concerning racial "others" as well as how such ideologies inform our identities, allows us to personally take account of race. While color-blindness remains the dominant racial ideology in the United States, it is more helpful to recognize race, racism, and privilege—in other words, to embrace color-consciousness.

KEY TERMS AND CONCEPTS

Color-blind ideology, color-blindness	Quadroon
Color-consciousness	Race
Colorism	Race privilege
Cultural norms	Racial identity
Cyber racism	Racial ideologies
Ethnicity	Racial justice activism
Individual discrimination	Racial order
Institutional racism	Racial/ethnic
Internalized racism	Racialized space
Majority group (dominant group)	Racism
Millennial generation	Self-reflexivity
Minority group (subordinate group)	Social construction
Octoroon	Sociological imagination
People of color	Sociology
Postracial	Standpoint perspective
Prejudice	White space

PERSONAL REFLECTIONS

1. Describe the life experiences that have informed your racial attitudes and beliefs and reflect on your level of interaction with members of other racial/ethnic groups. What in your life has facilitated or hindered you in interacting with members of different racial/ethnic groups?

2. Look around your campus (cafeteria, classes, and dormitories). Is there evidence of racial segregation? Why do you think self-segregation occurs? Is it harmful? What does it tell us about our society, if anything? Should we work to eradicate self-segregation? Why or why not?

CRITICAL THINKING QUESTIONS

1. Speculate on what changes you think will occur in census racial categories over the next fifty years, keeping in mind that census categories always reflect the prevailing notions of race and result from an intensely political process.

2. Explain how the racism of the dominant group can be understood as prejudice plus power and how the color-blind ideology is an example of dominant-group power.

ESSENTIAL READING

Coates, Ta-Nehisi. 2017. *We Were Eight Years in Power: An American Tragedy.* New York: One World Publishing.

Davis, F. James. 1991. *Who Is Black? One Nation's Definition.* University Park: Pennsylvania State University Press.

Du Bois, W. E. B. 1989 [1903]. *The Souls of Black Folk.* New York: Penguin Books.

Fox, Helen. 2009. *When Race Breaks Out: Conversations about Race and Racism in College Classrooms,* revised ed. New York, Washington, DC: Peter Lang Publishers.

Kendi, Ibram X. 2016. *Stamped from the Beginning: The Definitive History of Racist Ideas in America.* New York: Bold Type Books.

Nagel, Joane. 2003. *Race, Ethnicity, and Sexuality: Intimate Intersections, Forbidden Frontiers.* New York and Oxford: Oxford University Press.

Noble, Safiya Umoja. 2018. *Algorithms of Oppression: How Search Engines Reinforce Racism.* New York: New York University Press.

Omi, Michael and Howard Winant. 1994. *Racial Formation in the United States: From the 1960s to the 1990s,* 2nd ed. New York, London: Routledge.

RECOMMENDED FILMS

The Talk: Race in America (2017). Directed by Sam Pollard. This documentary explores the necessity of conversations between parents of color and their children, especially their sons, about how to behave if they are stopped by police. Parents, children, academics, police officers, and community activists are interviewed in this engaging and timely documentary.

A Girl Like Me (2007). Directed by Kiri Davis. This film explores the ways racial stereotypes affect the self-image of young African American women and children. Through interviews with young African American women, the film explores racialized beauty standards surrounding skin color, body type, and hair texture, as perpetuated in the media.

Race: The Power of an Illusion, Vols. 1–3 (2003). Produced by Larry Adelman. One of the best documentaries on race, this film explores the idea of race as a social construction and questions the idea that race is biological by exploring the science of race, historically and currently, how the idea of race was legitimized, and the ways race manifests itself in our daily lives.

What's Race Got to Do with It? (2006). Written, directed, and produced by Jean Chang. This film is a sequel to *Skin Deep* (1995), a look at race relations on college campuses. This new film explores the experiences of a diverse group of college students as they engage in a sixteen-week intergroup dialogue program. They challenge one another on issues such as minority underrepresentation, multiculturalism, individual responsibility, and affirmative action, and their experiences exemplify the attitudinal changes that can occur over a period of sustained dialogue.

RECOMMENDED MULTIMEDIA

Check out the "Millennial Attitudes on Race in the US" survey results in their entirety online at https://genforwardsurvey.com/assets/uploads/2017/10/Gen Forward-Oct-2017-Final-Report.pdf

Write a paper, three to four pages, reflecting on the survey results and the following questions: To what extent are the "Millennials Attitudes on Race in the US" survey results surprising to you? Or do you find the results consistent with the attitude of young people today? Explain your answer. What kinds of racial attitudes do you think Post-Millennials (those born in 1997 or later) will have? Why? Ask your parents and a couple other people their age some of the same questions from the survey. Reflect on how their answers are similar to or different from the attitudes of Millennials on race.

Explore the Census Bureau's online graphic showing US population statistics by race between the years 1790 and 2010. Make an argument that this is evidence that race is a social construction. What about the changing US racial categories surprised you the most? What are the most consistent patterns, and why do you think this is so? www.census.gov/population/race/data/MREAD_1790_2010.html

Listen to *A More Perfect Union*, the speech on race given by Barack Obama during his 2008 campaign for the Democratic presidential nomination. As you listen, think about the following questions: What points do you agree with? What do you disagree with? Does the speech make you think about race in a new way? Why or why not? Reflect on this speech and President Obama's eight years in office. To what extent did President Obama affect race relations in the United States during his two terms? Give evidence to support your position. www.youtube.com/watch?v=p We7wTVbLUU

Color Blind or Color Brave? A TED Talk by Mellody Hobson. www.google.com/ search?ei=g7lwWvvEBpLIjwOR0Ia4BQ&q=mellody+hobson+ted+talk&oq=Melody +Hobson&gs_l=psy-ab.1.1.0i10k1l10.43914.59493.0.60856.23.19.1.0.0.0.172.1707. 1j14.16.0...0...1.1.64.psy-ab..7.16.1802.6..0j35i39k1j0i131k1j0i131i67k1j0i67k1j0i20i 264k1j0i20i263k1j33i160k1.191.N_uXSp939U4

What do you think of Mellody Hobson's suggestion that we become "color-brave" rather than color-blind? What would this look like in your life?

White Privilege: The Other Side of Racism

CHAPTER LEARNING OUTCOMES

By the end of this chapter, you should be able to:

- Describe the social construction of whiteness and the process of "becoming" white
- Explain the concept of white privilege
- Evaluate the ways social class, social mobility, and whiteness are interconnected, historically and currently
- Describe the lingering embrace of ethnicity among white ethnics
- Demonstrate the ways cultural belief systems support white privilege and the ways white privilege is institutionalized
- Explore potential and existing challenges to white privilege

Part of white privilege involves the treatment of white people as individuals, without their actions being attributed to their membership in a racial group or reflecting on other members of a racial group. An example of white privilege involves media treatment of terrorists or mass murderers. When a white Norwegian man, Anders Behring Breivik, murdered seventy-seven people on July 22, 2011, the media immediately declared him a "lone wolf." The lone-wolf appellation implies that this heinous act was committed by a deranged or evil individual and was not the result of the radical ideologies of some larger group he may be connected to. While we may never fully understand why Breivik committed this horrendous act, the important point for our discussion is that all white people were not implicated in his actions. And yet, this is part of a larger pattern. On March 15, 2019, Brenton Harrison Tarrant, a 28-year-old white supremacist, murdered forty-nine people worshiping at two different mosques in Christchurch, New Zealand. White supremacist Dylann Roof entered the Emanuel African Methodist Episcopal Church in Charleston, South Carolina, on June 17, 2015, and after sitting for almost an hour with a small group of African American bible study participants, he pulled out a gun and began executing them, killing nine and injuring one. In 2014, a white supremacist, Frazier Glen Miller, Jr., shot and killed three people at a Jewish Community Center in Overland Park, KS. In 2012, a white supremacist, Michael Page, shot ten people, fatally wounding six of them, at a Sikh temple in Oak Creek, WI.

Terrorist acts committed by Muslims result in the extension of collective guilt to the entire Muslim community (Chen 2011). Muslim community leaders are forced to denounce such radical actions and to defend their community and their religion. Similarly, African Americans experience a collective shaming when a mass murderer is found to be black, such as the case of the DC sniper in October 2002. When the news reported the arrest of the sniper and it turned out he was a black man, all black people were shamed by his individual actions (Harris-Perry 2011). His actions were at least partially interpreted as if they were connected to his blackness.

The examples above are easily understood as white supremacist actions, but it might be harder to see how they are also examples of white privilege. Research by Mingus and Zopf (2010) finds that the race of a mass shooter influences the media framing and the public's response to the event. In this way, they argue, mass shootings are racial projects that reinforce white privilege. White people have the privilege of being treated as individuals whose actions are not a reflection of their whiteness. Most mass murderers, for instance, have been white. Yet white Americans do not feel a collective guilt or shaming when the racial identity of a white serial killer is discovered. Even in the case of lynching, which we will explore in greater detail in Chapter 5 and which is, at its core, a race-related phenomenon, there is no evidence that whites felt a sense of collective guilt when a person of color was lynched by a white mob. In the late 1990s, there were a number of disturbing mass shootings at US high schools, and the FBI insisted there was no profile for the perpetrators. Frustrated by this denial, antiracist activist Tim Wise writes, "White boy after white boy after white boy, with very few exceptions to that rule … decide to use their classmates for target practice, and yet there is no profile?" (Wise 2001).

In this chapter, the focus is on whiteness: the social construction of whiteness, white ethnicity, white privilege, white supremacy, and white fragility. Race privilege is the idea that if some racial/ethnic groups experience disadvantages, there is a group that is advantaged by this very same system. Studying whiteness forces us to acknowledge that all of us have a place in the relations of race. As obvious as this may seem, this is a concept many people are unfamiliar with, and it is also a relatively new focus in the social sciences. Prior to the late twentieth century, sociologists were guilty of either ignoring race or focusing on racial/ethnic "others" in their analysis of the "race problem." Scientists avoided analyzing and interrogating the role of whites in American race relations, as did the average white American. For people of color, the advantages whites receive due to their racial-group membership are more than obvious. As mentioned in Chapter 1, such differences in perspective are at least partially the result of people's standpoint: where one exists in the social structure influences how one views the world. Examples of whiteness as a social construction and white privilege follow:

- Hollywood celebrities, CEOs of private and public companies, real estate moguls, and other wealthy, powerful, white people were charged in March of 2019 with fraud and bribery in connection with college admissions scandals, while a federal court hears yet another challenge to affirmative action in college admissions, showing some cognitive dissonance concerning questions of fairness surrounding college admissions.
- A student showed up to his school, Nicolet High School in Wisconsin, in early June 2016 with a Confederate flag, declaring it White Privilege Day. The school suspended the student for his actions (Sater 2016).
- White privilege plays out in the restaurant industry: front-of-the-house, tipped employees are overwhelmingly white while back-of-the-house, hourly wage employees are overwhelmingly black or Latino.
- White privilege provides its recipients with protection from suspicion; thus, whites are unlikely to face the kind of situation Trayvon Martin faced in February 2012 when a neighborhood watchman decided he looked suspicious and eventually shot the unarmed 17-year-old to death.
- European soccer is seen by some fans as the privileged domain of whites, as black players are taunted with racist chants from fans, causing at least one of the black players and his teammates on AC Milan to walk off the field during a match ("AC Milan Players ..." 2013).

THE SOCIAL CONSTRUCTION OF WHITENESS

We introduced the idea of the social construction of race in the previous chapter; to say race is socially constructed is to recognize that racial groups are socially designated categories rather than biological ones; thus, racial categories change across time and place. Whiteness is also a social construction, although recognizing this requires that we first acknowledge that "white" is a race rather than simply the norm. Thus, to say that whiteness is socially constructed is to emphasize that the groups which have been defined as white have changed across time and place (see Box 2.1 Global Perspectives: Constructing Whiteness in Brazil).

Being designated as white is not about skin color or one's genetic makeup as we have been socialized to understand it; instead, it is a social and political process. Many racial/ethnic groups that are considered white today have not always been defined as white. Americans of Irish, Italian, Greek, Armenian, and Jewish descent have, instead, become white over time. "Becoming white" is a process whereby a formerly racially subordinate group is granted access to whiteness and white privilege, with all the benefits this entails. **White privilege** refers to the rights, benefits, and advantages enjoyed by white persons, or the immunity granted to whites that is not granted to people of color; white privilege exempts white people from certain liabilities others are burdened with.

Racial Categorization and Power

The privileges associated with being designated white may make it seem like the option of becoming white is in the best interest of racial/ethnic minority groups. However, while racial categorization is fluid and does change over time, racial/ethnic minority groups do not have complete agency in determining whether they become white. During some eras in US history, Mexican Americans legally demanded they be recognized as white, while at other times they have actively worked to maintain their Mexican heritage (Foley 2008; Rodriguez 2005). This has resulted in Latinos' having a somewhat ambiguous racial status even to this day. Another reason for a group's ambiguous racial status is the power given to official documentation, such as who has been defined as white in legal decisions (Haney Lopez 1996). The US census, for instance, uses such racial and ethnic categories as "non-Hispanic white" and "Hispanic," which are intended to emphasize the ethnic status of Latinos but are also about race. Thus, there are **structural constraints**—restrictions placed on one's options by either lack of access to resources or one's social location, such as government racial categorizations and legal decisions—to defining a group's racial/ethnic status. This is important to keep in mind as the Census Bureau considers including "Hispanic" as a race in 2020 (see Chapter 1).

However, there is also **agency**, the extent to which a group of people have the ability to define their own status. People are not simply pawns existing within larger social structures. Individuals and groups act within these structures and, through such actions, can change them.

Since the 1960s, many Mexican Americans have embraced pluralism rather than assimilation. **Pluralism** is when a group embraces and adapts to the mainstream

BOX 2.1

Global Perspectives:
Constructing Whiteness in Brazil

Racial categories change across time and place. Someone who is defined as white in Brazil may not be defined as white in the United States, whereas someone who is classified as an African American here may be classified as white in Brazil. Much like the United States, Brazil has a multiracial history, with people of indigenous, African, and European ancestry making up its population. Brazil has had a much more pronounced history of interracial relationships, however, which has resulted in an amalgamation of races to a greater extent than in the United States. Due to such amalgamation, Brazil used to be referred to as a racial democracy, a notion that is today considered to be a misrepresentation of Brazilian race relations.

While Brazil never established a system of racial segregation like that in the United States, other strategies were used to privilege whiteness. During the period of massive immigration into Brazil, from 1882 to 1934, the Brazilian government openly expressed a preference for white migrants (Pinho 2009). During other periods in Brazilian history, "whitening" was promoted through encouraging miscegenation: Brazilians were encouraged to marry white to better the race (Telles 2009). During the 1930s, there was an emphasis on "behavioral whitening," which involved rejecting cultural practices associated with African or indigenous cultures and instilling new habits of education, health, hygiene, and diet

that were considered to be closer to white (Pinho 2009).

While Brazilians are less likely to use the term *race* and instead refer to color, due to the discrimination associated with blackness, many Brazilians seek to avoid that designation (Telles 2009). On the 2000 census, 54 percent of Brazilians declared themselves to be *branco* (white) (Bailey 2008). However, racial census categories are rarely used in everyday speech. Instead, Brazilians tend to use terms referring to skin color, of which there are over one hundred, albeit only about six of those terms are used with any consistency: *branco* (white), *moreno* (brown, although not the census term for brown), *pardo* (the census term for brown), *moreno claro* (light brown), *preto* (the census term for black), and *negro* (a common term for black not found on the census) (Telles 2004). To be defined as white in Brazil is about more than skin color. It involves concerns with gradations of skin colors and hair types, as well as social class affiliation (Pinho 2009). While in the United States, gradations of color within racial groups are noted (for instance, the light skin preference found within Latino and African American communities), in Brazil, color differences within the entire population are significant. Being white in Brazil, as in the United States, imparts economic advantages, social prestige, and political power to its recipients.

IMAGE 2.1: Native American students at the Carlisle Indian School, a government-run boarding school. The primary objective of Native American boarding schools was the forced assimilation of Native American children, as this photo exemplifies by the children's appearance, specifically, their short haircuts and mainstream (white) clothing.

SOURCE: Courtesy of the Barry Goldwater Historic Photographs, Arizona Historical Foundation Collection, Arizona State University Libraries.

society without giving up their native culture. For instance, Mexican Americans' choosing to keep their language alive by speaking Spanish in their homes while also learning English so as to participate in the dominant culture is an example of pluralism. **Assimilation**, long the preferred model for race relations among the dominant group in American society, is the push toward acceptance of the dominant, Anglo culture at the expense of one's native culture (see Chapter 5). Groups are expected to become American by dropping any connection to their native culture, such as language, customs, or even a particular spelling of their name.

Historically, immigrants were encouraged to assimilate into "American" society. What this really meant was that they were expected to assimilate to the white norm, known as Anglo-conformity. Thus, "American culture" was synonymous with "white culture." Previous generations of immigrants were pressured to become American by dropping their accents or native language and cultural practices associated with their native country. Today, the assimilationist thrust remains, as the English-only movement emphasizes. This is a movement that attempts to make English the national language, to get states to pass laws eliminating bilingual education in schools, and to make government materials, such as signs in Social Security offices or Medicaid brochures, for instance, available only in English.

There are both push and pull factors at work when it comes to whitening: the dominant group may embrace the assimilation of the subordinate group for political reasons, and the subordinate group may seek assimilation, and thus embrace whitening, for access to the privileges it accords. This is accomplished by embracing, or at least acquiescing to, the racial hierarchy. As mentioned previously, racial/ethnic groups do have agency, yet they are not always operating under conditions that allow them to exercise their agency. While some groups challenge the assimilationist push, as did many Chicanos (a term Mexican activists embraced during the 1960s), most succumb. They succumb because access to white privilege makes life easier, such as by offering children advantages that every parent hopes for. White privilege is a difficult offer to resist—acceptance versus exclusion, benefits versus obstacles.

Becoming White

Many groups of people that are today unquestionably seen as white have not always been so. Irish, Greek, Jewish, and Italian Americans have all experienced a "whitening process" in different historical eras, when their group shifted from being perceived as nonwhite to being seen as white. The process of becoming white varied for each group, but each group became white in response to larger social and cultural changes. There are three specific eras in the history of whiteness in the United States (Jacobson 1998). The first began with the passing of the first naturalization law in 1790, which declared "free white persons" to be eligible for citizenship. The second era (from the 1840s to 1924) emerged as significant numbers of "less desirable" European immigrants, such as the Irish, challenged this notion of citizenship and required a redefinition of whiteness and, ultimately, the implementation of a white racial hierarchy. Whiteness was redefined again in 1920 at least partially in response to the rural-to-urban migration of African Americans, which solidified the previously fractured white racial grouping. Groups such as the Irish and Jews, who had held a "probationary" white status in previous generations, were eventually "granted the scientific stamp of authenticity as the unitary Caucasian race" (Jacobson 1998:8).

Irish Americans

Historian Noel Ignatiev (1995) explored how an oppressed group in their home country, the Catholic Irish, became part of the oppressing racial group in the United States. The whitening process for Irish Americans involved the denigration of blacks. This transformation was even more shocking because Irish Americans were not considered white during the early periods of Irish immigration. In fact, early Irish immigrants lived in the black community, worked with black people, and even intermarried with blacks.

The Irish becoming white, thus increasing their status in the racial hierarchy, has essentially been attributed to a larger political agenda. In this case, the Democratic Party sought the support of the Irish during the antebellum and immediate post-bellum eras and was able to attract them primarily due to the party's pro-immigrant position at the time. This was a very successful strategy, as Irish voters became the most solid voting bloc in the country by 1844, throwing their support overwhelmingly behind the Democratic Party (Ignatiev 1995).

Although the Democratic Party is recognized today as the party that passed civil rights legislation and generally is supported by the black community, at the time, racial politics looked very different. By the end of the Civil War, southern whites ruled the Democratic Party, and President Lincoln, a Republican, was held responsible for the emancipation of slaves. African American men who could vote during Reconstruction and in the North during Jim Crow tended to support the Republican Party. Most southern whites, on the other hand, overwhelmingly supported the Democratic Party, including their explicitly racist ideologies. Thus, in the mid-nineteenth century, Irish Americans were assimilated into American society through a politics of race: their acceptance as whites hinged on their acceptance and perpetuation of a racist system, particularly antiblack sentiment (Ignatiev 1995).

Irish Americans intentionally distanced themselves from blacks and even supported Jim Crow and other racist policies that were designed to oppress blacks. An essential truth emerged: in the United States, to be considered white, a person must not be associated with blackness and subordination. Black and white are relational concepts, meaning they only have meaning in relation to each other. We learn to understand who we are partially through an understanding of who we are not. For many groups that are now considered white, distancing themselves from blacks involved accepting the American racial hierarchy and participating in the racism directed at people of color.

Mexican Americans

Racial categorization is not a straightforward process. Some racial/ethnic groups maintain a more fluid racial status. As mentioned previously, Hispanics represent this kind of ambiguity. The term *Hispanic* refers to US residents whose ancestry is Latin American or Spanish, including Mexican Americans, Cuban Americans, Central Americans, and so on. The term *Hispanic* was first used by the US government in the 1970s and first appeared on the US census as an ethnic category in 1980. Thus, all Mexican Americans are considered to be Hispanic, but not all Hispanics are Mexican Americans.

The racial status of Mexican Americans has shifted throughout the nineteenth and twentieth centuries. Mexicans in the newly conquered Southwest at the close of the Mexican–American War in 1848, for instance, were accorded an intermediate racial status: they were not considered to be completely uncivilized, as the indigenous Indians of the region were, due to their European (Spanish) ancestry (Almaguer 1994). They were treated as an ethnic group, similar to white European ethnic immigrants. However, by the 1890s, as whites began to outnumber Mexicans throughout the Southwest, Mexicans became racialized subjects (Rodriguez 2005).

Mexican Americans have been legally defined as white, despite the fact that their social, political, and economic status has been equivalent to that of people of color (Foley 2008). According to the 2010 US census, "Hispanic" is an ethnic group, not a racial group. This was not always how the census categorized Mexicans, however. In 1930, the Census Bureau created a separate racial category for Mexicans that, for the first time, declared Mexican Americans to be nonwhite. This designation did not end the ambiguity surrounding the racial categorization of Mexicans. Census takers at the time were instructed to designate people's racial status as "Mexican" if they were born in Mexico or if they were "definitely not white," with no real instruction for differentiating how anyone would know which Mexican was "definitely not white." Consequently, due to such ambiguity, the Census Bureau discontinued this designation in subsequent censuses. In 1980, the bureau created two new ethnic categories of whites: "Hispanic" and "non-Hispanic" (Foley 2008). This resulted in many Latinos' choosing "other" for their race, which motivated the Census Bureau to add a question concerning ethnic-group membership after the question concerning racial-group membership, to try to determine who is Hispanic. This has not proven to be an effective solution, however, so the Census Bureau is considering adding "Hispanic" as a racial category on the 2020 census.

While such official maneuverings provided structural constraints on the racial/ethnic identification choices of Latinos, Latinos also exercised their agency. Many Mexican Americans during the 1930s through 1950s, for instance, demanded to be recognized as white as a way to avoid Jim Crow segregation. Much like the whitening process for Irish Americans, for Mexican Americans, distancing themselves from blacks became the objective, rather than challenging the racial hierarchy through an embrace of a nonwhite racial status. Mexican Americans, particularly those in the middle class, often supported the racial segregation of schools and the notion of white supremacy. Today, while some Latinos enjoy a status as white ethnics, many others, primarily Mexicans and recent Latino immigrants, remain excluded from the privileges of whiteness. Often this exclusion has been linked to their social class or skin color, as "a dark-skinned non-English-speaking Mexican immigrant doing lawn and garden work does not share the same class and ethnoracial status as acculturated, educated Hispanics. ... Hispanicized Mexican Americans themselves often construct a 'racial' gulf between themselves and 'illegal aliens' and 'wetbacks'" (Foley 2008:62–63).

New research finds that many Mexican Americans identify racially as "white" on the census because they conflate "whiteness" with being an American. In fact, this practice of identifying as white on the census is a subversive act that they engage in "not because they are accepted as white or even because they see themselves as white. Rather, by reframing the borders of whiteness to include them, Mexican Americans resist racial 'othering,' in an effort to be accepted as fully American" (Dowling 2014:7). Additionally, other variables influence whether or not Mexican Americans racially identify as white. For instance, over 80 percent of Latinos in Texas border towns identify as racially white, regardless of their skin color or social class (Dowling 2014).

REFLECT AND CONNECT

Do you belong to a racial/ethnic group that has experienced a changing racial status, such as those discussed here, and become white? If so, were you aware of this? If not, why do you think you were unaware of this? Reflect on the significance of this for your life today.

Social Class, Mobility, and "Whitening"

The process of becoming white has often been directly linked to **collective social mobility**, a group's changing class status over time in the United States. For instance, whitening often occurs simultaneously with a group's entrance into the American middle class, making becoming white and becoming middle class interconnected phenomena (Brodkin 2008). Whiteness has also been closely connected to the formation of the American working class (Roediger 1991). Finally, class has been used to divide whites, as in the case of the derogatory notion of "white trash."

Because race is socially constructed, it is always changing, always open to challenge, which means there is always potential for destabilization. Yet, despite this potential, the societal racial hierarchy endures. One of the reasons is that some groups have been provided with membership into the dominant group and have obtained access to white privilege. Thus, the hierarchy remains, with whites at the top and people of color at the bottom. For instance, when Irish immigrants were relatively limited in number, their association with the black community and marginalization from the white community were tolerated and even encouraged by many whites. But as their numbers grew and they became a potentially powerful political force, their assimilation into the white mainstream was encouraged and embraced.

Jewish Americans

The process through which Jewish Americans became white involved their simultaneous entrance into the middle class. Today, much like the situation for Irish Americans, most US citizens see Jewish Americans as white ethnics. However, Jewish Americans have not always been considered white in the United States. Prior to World War II, there was considerable anti-Semitism in the United States, which manifested in immigration restrictions for Jews and limits on Jewish admission to elite universities, among other forms of discrimination (Karabel 2005; Tichenor 2002). Their whitening process involved access to the GI Bill, which was overwhelmingly denied to black soldiers in the post–World War II era (see Chapter 8). Access to this basic government program enabled Jewish Americans, along with thousands of white Americans, to obtain college educations and enter middle-class professions. In this example, class and race are intertwined, as entering the middle class was part of the whitening process for this previously nonwhite group. It is unclear whether becoming white paved the way to their middle-class status or whether their middle-class status contributed to their whitening (Brodkin 2008).

Psychological Wage

One of the most significant ways white privilege has manifested itself has been in the economic sphere, so it is not surprising that there is also a significant link between the emergence of the American working class and whiteness. In 1935, African American sociologist W. E. B. Du Bois argued that white workers, despite their extremely low wages, received an intangible benefit, which he called a **psychological wage**, because they were white. What he meant was that, while all workers were exploited, a racially divided labor force meant that white workers received a psychological boost from simply not being black. This psychological wage was manifested in public deference; titles of courtesy, such as "Mr." or "Mrs."; and inclusion at public functions, parks, and countless places that excluded blacks. Later, labor unions continued the practice of offering white workers access to good jobs by excluding black workers from many unionized occupations.

Historian David Roediger (1991) argues that the formation of the US working class is intimately linked to the development of a sense of whiteness because the United States is the only nation where the working class emerged within a slaveholding republic. Thus, the working class defined itself in opposition to slavery, with race attached to each concept; whiteness was connected to the working class while blackness was linked to slavery. As Roediger argues, "In a society in which Blackness and servility were so thoroughly intertwined—North and South—assertions of white freedom could not be raceless" (1991:49). Part of the whitening process for Irish Americans involved avoiding the stigma of blackness, and one way they did this was through their access to what was known as "white man's work," which simply referred to employment that excluded African Americans (Ignatiev 1995). They were unwilling to work in the same occupations as free blacks in the North, thus solidifying their whiteness by insisting on racially differentiated employment.

Whiteness and Class

Race is a fluid category, rather than fixed; the boundaries of whiteness are continually in flux. Inequality exists even within the white racial/ethnic group. We can see this through an exploration of the ways whiteness is related to social class in the notion of "poor white trash" or "white trash." This clearly derogatory notion emerged in the mid-1800s and was created by higher-status whites not just to describe poor whites but to imply their moral inferiority (Wray 2006). The term *cracker*, emerging in the late 1700s, has similar origins. While today *cracker* is a term often used as a generalized racial slur against whites by people of color, it originated as a term higher-status whites used to describe poor whites who were viewed as dangerous, lawless, shiftless, lazy, and people who often associated with other stigmatized groups (Wray 2006). This intersection of class and race is evidence of the power of higher-status whites to define who is included in the category of "white." Such derogatory terms are used to describe poor whites not just to emphasize their poverty but to make their racial status questionable as well.

Race Matters

While sociologists speak of race as socially constructed rather than biologically based, it is not meant to imply that race is insignificant and can thus be disregarded. Race still matters. We live in a society that attaches meaning to race, and individuals attach meaning to their own race. It informs who we are, is an aspect of our identity if for no other reason than it has been externally ascribed to us our entire lives. We learn to see ourselves as white, black, Asian American, Native American, or Latino through our interactions with others. Thus, the fact that people racially identify does not negate the idea of the social construction of race. Instead it emphasizes the power of socially defined ideals.

White Ethnicity

The discussion above introduces you to the idea that some groups have experienced a racialization process and have become white over time. The idea that these groups had at some point in the past been understood as nonwhite is likely surprising to you since they are unquestionably white today. While the race (whiteness) of these groups is hardly questioned today, it is common to think of Irish, Italian, Greek, and Jewish Americans as **white ethnics**. This is a term that refers to white Americans who are not Anglo-Saxon Protestants and instead descend from Ireland, Southern and Eastern Europe and, of course, are not Protestant. Much sociological research explores white ethnicity, from early research predicting their inevitable assimilation, to the "ethnic revival" of the 1970s, and the political implications of ethnicity. Importantly, this body of research overlooks race and prioritizes ethnicity among whites, while mostly ignoring the ethnic diversity among groups seen as racial minorities (African Americans, Native Americans, Latinos, and Asian Americans).

Sociologists of the Chicago School focused considerable attention on the experiences of white ethnic immigrants, treating the city of Chicago and its myriad immigrant communities as their natural laboratory (see Chapter 3) (Park and Miller 1921; Thomas and Znaniecki 1918–1920). This focus is unsurprising as at the time 30 percent of the inhabitants of the city of Chicago were foreign born (Erdmans 1995). It was understood that initially immigrants would seek communities of other immigrants in which to live and work. Referred to as **ethnic enclaves**, these are communities where immigrants of particular racial/ethnic groups live in close proximity to one another and where there are ethnic groceries, restaurants, and other businesses catering to their particular culture.

Ethnic enclaves can provide a buffer from the hostilities of mainstream society and provide employment and residential opportunities for newcomers. This buffer was necessary, as these Greek, Polish, Italian, and other white ethnic immigrants coming to the United States in the late nineteenth and early twentieth centuries experienced considerable prejudice and discrimination. Italian immigrants were referred to as "wops, dagos, and guineas," and referred to as the "Chinese of Europe" and "just as bad as the Negroes" (Dinnerstein and Reimers 1982). Greek immigrants were forced out of several communities and Polish immigrants were decried as stupid and animal like (Dinnerstein and Reimers 1982). Anti-Catholic bias and anti-Semitism were still very prominent in the United States during this time period as well, which resulted in hostility directed at many of these immigrant groups (Lieberson 1980).

After this initial transition phase, immigrants were expected to assimilate into the dominant culture by dropping their ties to the "old world" and becoming American. During the first half of the twentieth century, white immigrants appeared to embrace assimilation (see Chapter 5). English-speaking white immigrants might work to minimize their accents while those who did not speak English learned it; other immigrants might change the spelling of their last name to appear more American; for others, giving their children American sounding first names exemplified their commitment to assimilation. A casual glance at white immigrant America in the early twentieth century would have you agreeing with sociologists that assimilation was the desired and inevitable path for immigrants.

Ethnic Revival of the 1970s

Dropping their ties to the "old world" completely, however, did not happen. Historian Marcus Hansen (1996 [1938]) proposes the "third generation thesis," to explain this lingering ethnicity among white ethnics. His argument was that the immigrant was very much invested in assimilating and dropping ties to their home culture. But by the third generation, the grandchild of the immigrant, there was a desire to reconnect with one's heritage. Hansen explains it this way: "What the son wishes to forget the grandson wishes to remember" (1996 [1938]:206).

The sociological focus on white ethnics continued into the 1970s, culminating in what some have called an **ethnic revival**. During this era, sociological research revealed that, instead of leaving their ethnic heritage behind as assimilationist theories had predicted, white ethnics were embracing and celebrating it through festivals, foods, and other cultural expressions. These findings demonstrate that, to a certain extent, white ethnics continue to embrace aspects of their ethnic heritage as opposed to completely melting into the dominant American culture. Herbert Gans (1979) refers to these expressions as **symbolic ethnicity**, individualistic expressions of ethnicity that celebrate Americans' ethnic heritage through leisure-time activities, such as St. Patrick's Day celebrations for Irish Americans and St. Joseph's Day for Italian Americans. He argues that these claims to an ethnic heritage are merely symbolic because they do not challenge the individuals' middle-class, mainstream American status.

Around this same time, sociologists began to focus on the political implications of ethnicity—ethnic identities, they argued, were also political interest groups (Glazer and Moynihan 1970). According to this perspective, ethnic-group members maintained their ethnicity through politics, acting in ways that supported the collective interest of their particular group. Latinos are a case in point. They are the largest and one of the fastest-growing racial/ethnic minority groups in the United States. They tend to be concentrated in key states with crucial electoral votes and are assumed to share interests with one another that would likely cause them to vote as a bloc. For all of these reasons, since the 1980s, the Democratic and Republican Parties have actively sought the Latino vote (see Chapter 13).

WHITE PRIVILEGE

While the privileges associated with whiteness are not new, the academic exploration and understanding of white privilege is relatively new. Sociologists who study race have shifted the analysis from a focus solely on people of color to one that includes whites and their role in race relations. This necessary shift focuses on what Paula Rothenberg (2008) refers to as "the other side of racism," white privilege.

In the United States, individuals identified and defined as white make up the group with the unearned advantages known as white privilege. This shift to an analysis and an understanding of white privilege requires that we recognize "white" as not only a race but also a social construction.

Whiteness refers to the multiple ways white people benefit from institutional arrangements that appear to have nothing to do with race (Bush 2011). George Lipsitz (2006) refers to this as a "possessive investment" in whiteness, where whiteness has a cash value in the housing market, educational sphere, and employment opportunities. He uses the term *possessive* intentionally in order "to stress the relationship between whiteness and asset accumulation in our society" and to emphasize that whites become possessed by whiteness unless they work to "develop antiracist identities [and] disinvest and divest themselves of their investments in white supremacy" (2006:viii).

Racial hierarchies, status hierarchies based upon physical appearance and the assumption of membership in particular categories based upon these physical features, exist in the United States and throughout the world, albeit with much variation. Hierarchies imply that a group exists at the top while others exist somewhere in the middle and still others on the bottom rungs of the hierarchy. The group at the top is the group that benefits from the racial hierarchy in the form of race privilege. Sociologist Herbert Blumer (1958) argues that race is essentially about group position. The dominant racial group feels a sense of superiority over subordinate racial groups and perceives subordinate-group members as different, alien, and "other." Importantly, the dominant racial group has a sense of entitlement toward societal goods and resources and perceives their privilege as threatened by the subordinate group.

The seminal work on white privilege is the self-reflexive essay by Peggy McIntosh (2008), "White Privilege: Unpacking the Invisible Knapsack." McIntosh defines *white privilege* as

> an invisible package of unearned assets which I can count on cashing in each day, but about which I was 'meant' to remain oblivious. White privilege is like an invisible weightless knapsack of special provisions, maps, passports, codebooks, visas, clothes, tools, and blank checks.
>
> (2008:123)

There are several aspects to this definition that warrant attention: that white privilege is invisible, that it is unearned, and that white people are socialized to count on this while simultaneously not recognizing it as privilege.

As the above definition by Peggy McIntosh exemplifies, the idea that white privilege is invisible has been fundamental to our understanding of the concept (Doering 2016; Fitzgerald 2014). We should challenge this assumption, however. First, white privilege is only invisible to white people. People of color have no trouble seeing the various ways race privilege plays out in day-to-day life. Second, using the term *invisible* is misleading "because it does not refer to an optical phenomenon but to low levels of racial self-awareness" (Doering 2016:106). Instead of describing white privilege as "invisible," we should describe it as "unacknowledged," because knowingly "not knowing" is different from invisibility (Fitzgerald 2014). Finally, there are certain contexts that disrupt white privilege and increase racial self-awareness for whites. Racial self-awareness can emerge from **racial challenges**, interactions that make whites account for their whiteness. A racial challenge can refer to a charge of racism, or it can be something more moderate, such as pointing out that on an otherwise multiracial campus, a campus organization is all white, or that a syllabus for a class includes only white writers (Doering 2016).

It is not in the interest of whites to draw attention to the privileges they receive (DiTomaso 2013). Part of this involves denying the racism that people of color experience or denying knowledge of the extent of racial inequality in the world. Other scholars have explored this, referring to it as a "convenience of ignorance" (Myrdal 1944) or an "epistemology of ignorance" (Mills 1997), which involves "*a process of knowing designed to produce not knowing* surrounding white privilege, culpability, and structural white supremacy" (Mueller 2017:220).

Race affects every aspect of our lives: it informs how all of us view the world, our daily experiences, and whether or not opportunities are available to us. While the importance of race has long been recognized for racial/ethnic minorities, until recently even social scientists have overlooked the significance of race in the daily lives of whites. Part of this problem emerges from a lack of recognition that "white" is a race, rather than merely the norm, the human standard against which all other groups are measured (a perspective that is itself part of white privilege). Some have called for the development of a **new white consciousness**, "an awareness of our whiteness and its role in race problems" (Terry 1970:17). Social scientists have finally heeded this call, and white people are now being asked to recognize how race and privilege operate in their world.

White Privilege as Taboo

The discussion of white privilege will undoubtedly make many students uncomfortable. In 2013, a high school in Wisconsin came under fire for teaching white privilege in an "American diversity" class. Some parents complained that the subject matter was akin to indoctrination and meant to divide the students and provoke white guilt ("'White Privilege' Lesson ..." 2013).

This is the unacknowledged side of racism—the advantages offered to the dominant group by an unjust system. Why has it taken so long for social scientists to focus on something as seemingly obvious as the "other side of racism"? A racial bias embedded not only in the discipline of sociology but in our culture is part of the explanation. Additionally, whiteness has been normalized in both our culture and in science, and privilege is meant to remain unacknowledged. Those benefiting from such societal arrangements, even if these are people who actively oppose racism, have difficulty acknowledging the advantages they reap from these arrangements.

In Chapter 1, we discussed the need for examining our own belief systems surrounding race and for learning to speak honestly about it. In this chapter, the objective is not just to introduce you to the concept of white privilege, but to get you to recognize it and to be able to address it. Speaking about privilege is difficult, particularly for those who benefit from it. The first obstacle has to do with a deeply ingrained sense of **white fragility**. White fragility refers to the ways white people become highly fragile in conversations about race, and where the smallest amount of racial stress becomes intolerable, triggers discomfort and anxiety, and can result in argumentation, withdrawal, anger, and silence (DiAngelo 2018). White fragility is an exercise in power and control, a form of bullying, because it "keeps people of color in line and 'in their place'" and is designed to "protect, maintain, and reproduce white supremacy" (DiAngelo 2018:112, 113).

Interrogating white privilege is not meant to alienate white people or exclude people of color from conversations concerning race. Instead, it is meant to bring everyone to the table to discuss race, racism, racial inequality, and race privilege. Professor Helen Fox provides a strong argument for why it is so essential to engage white people in discussions of race and privilege:

> I am convinced that learning how to reach resistant white students is central to our teaching about race. These are the future power brokers of America, the ones who by virtue of their class, their contacts, and their perceived "race" will have a disproportionate share of political and economic clout.
>
> (2001:83)

For people of color, conversations surrounding race are not new; such conversations have likely been quite common for them. People of color experience explicit **racial socialization**, meaning they are taught in their families, in schools, and through the media that their race matters. White people, on the other hand, may have difficulties with the topic of race and privilege for the simple fact that such conversations have likely been uncommon in their lives.

White people experience racial socialization as well, but it is usually more subtle. White racial socialization comes in the form of an unspoken entitlement. Whites are socialized to protect their privilege, partially through denial of such privilege.

White privilege allows whites the privilege of not having to think about race—not having to think about how race might affect them that day.

Research on the racial socialization of white children from wealthy families finds that children's racial context matters: when compared to children raised by parents who take a color-blind approach, children raised by parents who take a color-conscious approach—they choose a racially diverse school for their children, talk about issues of race and privilege, and embrace diversity—are more likely to "possess the rhetorical tools and agency necessary to challenge" the racial status quo and racism (Hagerman 2014:2612). Despite some differences, there are also similarities in the ways both conservative and liberal whites address race in their parenting. For instance, talking about race is an option for them, in a way that is not true for parents of color. For parents of color, talking about race is a requirement, not an option. White parents in this study also wanted their children to remain racially innocent for as long as possible, which is only possible because of white privilege; their children do not experience racism personally. Even white liberal parents who adhere to an ideology of fairness find themselves "faced with a conflict between their *abstract values* of fairness and their own personal *interests* of securing for their child the best education possible" (Hagerman 2018:73).

Despite this recognition and embrace of white privilege, whiteness is understood by whites as a culture void, as lacking culture, as an unmarked category, in direct opposition to the view that minorities have rich and distinct cultures (Frankenberg 1993). People of color are seen to have a recognizable culture (evidenced, for instance, in Black Entertainment Television, Latin music, Asian food, and so on) that whites are perceived to lack. For example, Frankenberg (1993) found that white women in interracial relationships often viewed themselves as having no culture and often cited envy of racial/ethnic minorities because of their obvious culture and accompanying identity.

REFLECT AND CONNECT

Take a moment and think about your childhood, specifically reflecting on when you discovered your race. When did you discover you were white, African American, Latino, or whatever? Try to identify an example of when you were racially socialized. For people of color, this is generally not a difficult task. For whites, this might be more difficult.

There are some problems with viewing white culture as actually cultureless. The first is that it reinforces whiteness as the cultural norm. Whites are everywhere in cultural representations—advertising, film, television, books, museums, public history monuments—yet the claim is made that this is just culture, not white culture.

Additionally, by claiming to be cultureless, whites can ignore white history. The political, economic, and social advantages whites have accumulated historically are easier to overlook when claiming there is no such thing as white culture (Frankenberg 1993).

WITNESS

"And here I am, just another alienated middle-class white girl with no culture to inform my daily life, no people to call my own." Interviewee quoted in Frankenberg (1993).

Seeing Privilege

White privilege—"an elusive and fugitive subject," as Peggy McIntosh described it in 1998—has gone unexamined primarily because it is the societal **norm**. For sociologists, social norms are a significant aspect of culture and refer to the shared expectations about behavior in a society, whether implicit or explicit. There are several reasons why white privilege is hard for white people to see. The first problem is that white privilege is intentionally unacknowledged. Privilege is maintained through ignoring whiteness. Part of privilege is the assumption that your experience is normal; it does not feel like a privileged existence.

While inequality is easy to see, privilege is more obscure. White people can easily see how racism "makes people of color angry, tired, and upset, but they have little insight into the ways that not having to worry about racism affects their own lives" (Parker and Chambers 2007:17). For people of color, white privilege is not a difficult concept to grasp—it is clear from their standpoint that racial disadvantage has a flip side that amounts to advantages for the dominant group. Despite this, for white people, seeing race is difficult and is the "natural consequence of being in the driver's seat" (Dalton 2008:17).

It is difficult for most white people to discuss ways they benefit from white privilege, and many get offended when asked to think about some advantage they have accrued due to being white. Many students can recognize whether they attended a well-funded public school that adequately prepared them for college. Recognition of privilege does not negate hard work, but it is an acknowledgment that not everyone has the same educational opportunities, particularly individuals who attended poor schools predominantly populated with racial/ethnic minority students.

White privilege is problematic for many white people because it can feel insulting. Americans are taught that we live in a **meritocracy**, where individuals get what they work for and rewards are based upon effort and talent. This ideology helps us understand poverty along individualized "blame the victim" lines rather than as a social problem. In other words, if people are poor, it is presumed to be due to some inadequacy on their part. The opposite of the "blame the victim" ideology is also true. When people succeed in American society their success is often attributed to hard work, motivation, intelligence, or other individualized characteristics that are meant to set the person apart from less-successful individuals. The idea of white privilege challenges this. It forces us to recognize that some people, due to their membership in particular racial/ethnic groups, are systematically disadvantaged and face more obstacles in their lives while members of other racial/ethnic groups are systematically advantaged, with more open doors and more opportunities available to them. It may take their individual talents, motivation, and intelligence to take advantage of the open door, but it must be acknowledged that not everyone had the door opened for them in the first place. This is often how privilege manifests itself.

White privilege is uncomfortable for many white students to grasp because the word *privilege* does not appear to describe their life. Poor and working-class white people are often offended by such a notion because they do not see themselves as beneficiaries of the system in any way. They work hard and have very little, relatively speaking. Indeed, many white people are members of the **working poor**, people who work full time and still fall below the poverty line in the United States. How can they be considered privileged? To be able to understand this, we have to recognize the complexities involved in the multiple status hierarchies that exist in American society. One can lack class privilege but still have race privilege, for instance.

The idea of white privilege is that all people identified and treated as white benefit from that status, even if they face disadvantages in other arenas, such as social class. To truly understand how race operates in the United States, it is essential that we recognize this. White privilege offers poor whites something: the satisfaction that at least they do not exist on the bottom rungs of the societal hierarchy—that, despite their poverty, they are at least not black. Additionally, despite any other disadvantages a white person may have, when they walk into a job interview, or restaurant, or any situation, the primary characteristic noted is that they are white, which is their passport for entry, as Peggy McIntosh (2008) describes. Race and gender are what sociologists call **master statuses** in our society, statuses that are so significant they overshadow all others and influence our lives more than our other statuses.

The combination of the presumed invisibility of white privilege and the fact that all white people are implicated in the racial hierarchy through their privilege also makes it a disturbing concept for many white people. Interrogating white privilege is a particularly difficult task because it is both structural and personal. It forces those of us who are white to ask questions that concern not only structural advantage (such as, how are schools structured in ways that benefit white people?) but individual privilege as well (in what ways was my educational attainment at least partially a result of racial privilege?). Again, while it is uncomfortable to acknowledge being unfairly advantaged, this is exactly what white privilege is.

Additionally, it is important to recognize in what arenas we may be advantaged (oppressors) and in what arenas we may be disadvantaged (oppressed). As a white person, I have race privilege (see Box 2.2 Race in the Workplace: White Teachers Making Meaning of Whiteness). As a woman, I have disadvantages within a **patriarchy**, a male-dominated society. On a global scale, I have certain advantages, from my odds of survival to the educational and economic opportunities I have had access to, to having been born in a wealthy, First World country rather than in an impoverished nation.

White Privilege Versus White Racism

Discussing white privilege makes many whites feel uncomfortable because it implicates them in a racist social structure. Thus, doesn't that make them racist? Is there a difference between white privilege and **white racism**? Feagin, Vera, and Batur (1995:7) define white racism as "the socially organized set of attitudes, ideas, and practices that deny African Americans and other people of color the dignity, opportunities, freedoms and rewards that this nation offers white Americans." That is clearly a broad definition of white racism—it certainly goes above and beyond the idea that many whites take comfort in, which is that a racist is someone who is actively involved in a white supremacist organization, participates in hate crimes, or believes in the innate inferiority of people of color. However, it is not that clear cut. As the definition implies, as long as people of color are denied opportunities, it is white racism, and what goes unspoken is that the flip side of this racism is that those become opportunities for white people. In other words, these are two sides of the same coin—without white racism, there is no white privilege. To work actively against racism, whites also have to work against privilege. For instance, if a white employee of a restaurant recognizes racialized patterns, such as people of color working in the kitchen and white staff working the dining room, they can point these out to management and challenge them to justify these staffing decisions. Additionally, there are those who argue that simply living in American society makes one racist—it is the norm in our society, found in the subtle messages we all receive every day. Thus, neutrality is not equated with being nonracist. The only way to be nonracist in American society is to actively work against racism, such as by joining a racial justice organization. Many racial justice organizations are affiliated with religious institutions, for instance, or can be found on university campuses. They can also easily be found online by searching for "antiracist activism" or "racial justice activism." Beyond actually joining a racial justice organization, one can simply work to be an ally to people of color in the struggle to end racism. Being an ally involves speaking up when you see racial injustice occurring, assuming racism is everywhere, every day, and understanding the history of whiteness and racism (Kivel 2011).

BOX 2.2

Race in the Workplace:
White Teachers Making Meaning of Whiteness

Today's teaching force is still overwhelmingly white, middle class, and female. Their classrooms, however, are much more racially diverse than the classrooms they encountered growing up. For many white teachers, this has required they not only understand diversity but come to terms with themselves as *white*. Debby Irving, teacher and author of *Waking Up White and Finding Myself in the Story of Race* (2014), describes her process of unlearning color-blindness, learning to see herself as raced (white), and exploring how she learned so many distorted ideas about race and racism. She explains, "In order to convey racism's ability to shape beliefs, values, behaviors, and ideas, ... I share personal and often humiliating stories, as well as thoughts I spent decades not admitting, not even to myself" (2014:xii). Similarly, Alice McIntyre, teacher and author of *Making Meaning of Whiteness: Exploring Racial Identity with White Teachers* (1997), explains that entering the teaching profession offered her "numerous occasions to 'see' my whiteness and to experience the ways in which race and racism shaped my life, my teaching, my politics, and my understanding of privilege and oppression, especially as they relate to the educational system in the United States" (1997:2). Upon returning to graduate school after twelve years of classroom teaching, she became interested in how white student teachers embraced the cultural understandings of children and how those understandings reinforced white privilege. One of the primary questions motivating her research was what impact does one's white racial identity have on one's notion of what it means to be a teacher?

McIntyre believes that for white teachers to be more effective in the classroom, they must interrogate their own racial socialization, specifically how they are socialized into a position of privilege and a sense of entitlement. She argues that white teachers have an obligation to reflect on their race and its influence on their teaching. "White student teachers need to be intentional about being self-reformers ... *purposefully thinking through their racial identities as salient aspects of their identities*" (italics in original, 1997:5). This cannot be achieved without linking identities to the larger social structure and institutions.

Her goal is to help white student teachers "develop teaching strategies and research methodologies aimed at disrupting and eliminating the oppressive nature of whiteness in education" (1997:7). She is aware of the difficulties surrounding such a task. As she explains, "There is no comfort zone for white people when it comes to discussing white racism" (1997:43).

White Privilege Versus White Supremacy

While the term *white privilege* causes discomfort in many white people, *white supremacy* can be an even more shocking term, because when we hear the phrase we often think of white supremacist and white power organizations such as the Ku Klux Klan (KKK) (see Chapter 13). However, the term **white supremacy** is broader than that; it refers to the systemic ways the racial order operates to the benefit of whites and discriminates against people of color (Bonilla-Silva 2006; Feagin 2006; Smith 2005; Strmic-Pawl 2015; Takaki 1993; Yancey 2008). White privilege is just one manifestation of white supremacy (Strmic-Pawl 2015). Too often, a focus on white privilege allows us to individualize racism and miss the fact that it is structural (Leonardo 2004; Strmic-Pawl 2015; Yancey 2008).

Sociologist Hephzibah Strmic-Pawl uses a white supremacy flower to represent this (see Image 2.2). As the image depicts, in order to understand white supremacy, we must begin with the roots, which "represent the foundation of the United States with events such as Native American genocide, plantation slavery, and the writing of the Constitution" (Strmic-Pawl 2015:193). Out of the roots, a stem grows. The stem

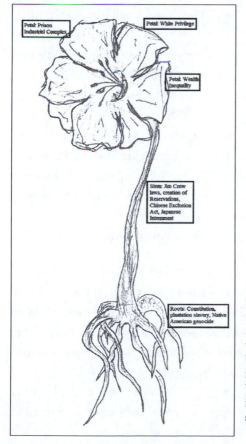

IMAGE 2.2: The white supremacy flower model illustrates the roots of racism and white supremacy in Native American genocide and slavery: the stem represents most of US history, including Jim Crow, the Chinese Exclusion Act, and more; and the bloom represents the contemporary United States, including white privilege. Introduced by Hephzibah V. Strmic-Pawl (2015). (Copyright© 2015 by American Sociological Association. Reprinted by Permission of SAGE Publications, Inc.).

represents much of US history, including the Jim Crow era, the Indian Wars, the Chinese Exclusion Act, and the internment of Japanese Americans during World War II. Each petal on the bloom represents manifestations of racism and white supremacy in the contemporary United States, including mass incarceration, residential segregation, and white privilege. Importantly, "the loss of one petal does make the flower weaker, but it does not kill the plant" (Strmic-Pawl 2015:194).

IDEOLOGIES, IDENTITIES, AND INSTITUTIONS

In the previous chapter, we explored the ways race operates in the form of racial ideologies, racial identities, and institutional racism. We expand on that discussion here to show the ways race privilege informs racial ideologies and racial identities, as well as fosters institutional privileges.

Racial Ideologies of Color-Blindness

Ideologies are not just powerful; they operate in the service of power by providing a frame for interpreting the world (Bonilla-Silva 2010; Thompson 1984). It is through cultural belief systems that so many nonwhite groups embrace the racial hierarchy, embrace racism, as a way to obtain white privilege. The current reigning racial ideology is that of color-blindness.

Color-blindness supports white privilege because it encourages a mentality that allows us to say we don't see race, that essentially we are color-blind. Paradoxically, this ideology persists within a society literally obsessed with race. The elections of President Barack Obama are a good example. In 2007, discussions of race surrounded Super Bowl XLI because never before had an African American head coach led a team to the Super Bowl—and both teams, the Chicago Bears and the Indianapolis Colts, had black head coaches (see Chapter 12). People of mixed-race ancestry continually report being asked, "What are you?" which is evidence of the ongoing significance of race rather than a commitment to color-blindness.

Clearly, Americans see color, we see race, and we attach significance to it. The power of the color-blind ideology is threefold:

1. **We ignore racism.** We have a racist society without acknowledging any actual racists (Bonilla-Silva 2006). Racism is alive and well, yet individuals cling to color-blindness, thus avoiding personal responsibility for it. Sociologist Eduardo Bonilla-Silva argues that the color-blind ideology "barricades whites from the United States' racial reality" (2010:47).
2. **We ignore white privilege.** Haney Lopez (2006) refers to this as "colorblind white dominance." By claiming color-blindness, white people can ignore the ways white privilege benefits them and can ignore ongoing racism.

3. **We perceive whiteness as the norm.** Color-blindness fuels perceptions of whiteness as the norm and as synonymous with racial neutrality.

A glaring example of the normativeness of whiteness was found in media coverage of Hurricane Katrina in 2005. For days, media coverage showed thousands of displaced and desperate people, overwhelmingly black, seeking shelter from the rising flood waters, yet race was never mentioned. When it finally was mentioned, many white people were angered by what they saw as the media "racializing" what they perceived as a race-neutral tragedy. Clinging to color-blind ideologies, they insisted that those left behind to face the devastation were simply people, not black people. The fact that they were black was somehow deemed irrelevant or mere coincidence. Yet this tragedy was clearly "raced" and "classed" as well. It was not simply a coincidence that it was predominantly poor black people who were left behind to drown as the levees broke and the city of New Orleans experienced devastating flooding.

New Orleans is an overwhelmingly black city and a very poor city. When the mayor announced a mandatory evacuation due to the impending hurricane, transportation should have been provided because so many poor black New Orleanians did not own an automobile. In addition, as a matter of public policy, when considering a mandatory evacuation, one has to consider not just transportation but

IMAGE 2.3: A home damaged by the flooding of New Orleans due to the levee breaches after Hurricane Katrina in 2005. These homes are in New Orleans's Ninth Ward, an overwhelmingly poor and African American community that suffered some of the worst flooding. (Photo by Harold Baquet. The Historic New Orleans Collection, Gift of Harold F. Baquet and Cheron Brylski, acc. no. 2016.0172.).

where people are going to go. Poor people are not able to simply get a hotel room in another city to wait out the storm, as a middle-class person could.

Racial ideologies change over time as culture changes. What is essential is that we recognize how the racial ideologies manifest themselves in different eras, that we gauge the influence of such ideologies, and, perhaps most important, that we recognize how the dominant group benefits from such ideologies.

White Racial Identity

Social scientists have only recently begun studying white racial identity development (Helms 1990; McDermott and Samson 2005). Much effort has been put into the study of white ethnic identity development (Alba 1990; Rubin 1994; Stein and Hill 1977; Waters 1990), black racial identity development (Burlew and Smith 1991; Helms 1990; Resnicow and Ross-Gaddy 1997), and shifting racial identities (Fitzgerald 2007; Korgen 1998; Rockquemore and Brunsma 2002), while white racial identities went unexamined. When sociologists have focused on white racial identity development, it has generally been in conjunction with white supremacist movements, but, of course, all whites have a racial identity, not just those belonging to such organizations (Dees and Corcoran 1996; Gallaher 2003). Some research finds that white racial identity development is surprisingly similar for white supremacists and white racial justice activists (Hughey 2010, 2012).

For the most part, people of color have been forced to think about race not just in the abstract but as something fundamental to who they are, how they are perceived, and, thus, how they see themselves. Whites, however, develop a white racial identity without much conscious thought or discussion. As James Baldwin has said, being white means never having to think about it. Janet Helms (1990) identifies stages of white racial identity development, beginning with whites who have had no contact with other races, moving to those who learn about race and privilege, and then to those who see inequalities as the fault of the other races. For white people progressing through these first three of six stages of racial identity development, the question becomes how do they get to see themselves as white in a raced world rather than as neutral, nonraced, or the norm?

In the first stage of white racial identity development, whites have had little contact with people of color and thus have developed a sense of superiority over them based upon social stereotypes and media representations. Whites in stage one have difficulty seeing white privilege and may even resist the idea. Some of these folks are outright racists while others are not blatant racists but may perceive people of color in stereotypical ways, for instance, as lazy or dangerous. There is nothing inevitable about identity development—most whites are in stage one and many never move beyond the first stage (Helms 1990).

For those whites who progress in their identity development, according to Helms (1990), stage two is characterized by fear and guilt that stems from seeing themselves, perhaps for the first time, as holding racial prejudices and as benefiting from structural racism, historically and currently. As they learn more about race in American society, it challenges what they thought they knew about the world. They are seeing racism and privilege for the first time. Often, whites respond to this guilt and fear through retrenchment, which is the third stage.

In the retrenchment stage, whites deal with their guilt by blaming the victim, declaring that racial inequality is the fault of minorities. Not all white people move backward at this stage. Instead, some progress through the next stages, eventually developing a healthy white racial identity that is not based on guilt or a sense of superiority.

Many whites struggle with seeing themselves as white. As mentioned previously, whiteness is viewed by many whites as bland, cultureless; thus, white people are more likely to lack an overt racial identity. In fact, this lack of a sense of white identity is due to the fact that whiteness is generally seen as the norm. By bemoaning their lack of a racial identity, whites help maintain the separate status of racial/ethnic minorities, who are perceived as different, as "other," in American society. What is in operation is white privilege: the privilege to *not* think about race, the privilege to *not* recognize the dominant culture as white culture and instead see it as racially neutral, and the privilege to overlook the fact that whiteness, rather than being absent, is ever present as the unnamed norm.

Identities are more than personal. They are products of particular sociohistorical eras. Thus, white identities, like all racial identities, are social, historical, and political constructions. The fact that white as a racial identity is rarely visible is evidence of the operation of white privilege in our lives today. Identities are political, and they are a response to changing social and political contexts. Native American activism during the 1970s resulted in more individuals' officially identifying as Native American (Nagel 1996). The racial identity of white Americans often goes unacknowledged, with the exception of historical eras that challenge the taken-for-grantedness of whiteness and white privilege. For instance, during the civil rights movement, many white Americans began to explicitly claim their whiteness if for no other reason than they viewed the privileges associated with their whiteness as being threatened. The racial socialization of whites, their sense of entitlement, was being challenged every day. As black civil rights activists demanded equal rights, whites counterattacked with rhetoric concerning the perceived loss of their own rights (Sokol 2006). Today, in a less racially charged atmosphere, most whites are unlikely to see themselves in racial terms. However, white people working toward racial justice do view white as a race and their life experiences as racialized (see Box 2.3 Racial Justice Activism: Tim Wise on White Identity and Becoming a Racial Justice Activist).

BOX 2.3

Racial Justice Activism:
Tim Wise on White Identity and Becoming a Racial Justice Activist

Tim Wise has been working as an anti-racist activist since he was 21 years old. He details his path to antiracist work in his book *White Like Me: Reflections on Race from a Privileged Son* (2005). During his college years at Tulane University in New Orleans, he immersed himself in activist work, primarily working as an anti-apartheid activist and a Central American peace activist.

Wise explains that he was not aware that, even as he worked to eradicate racism across the globe, he was doing absolutely nothing about racism in his own community and thus was reinforcing his own white privilege despite his activism. This contradiction was pointed out to him by an African American woman and New Orleans native during a question-and-answer period concerning the university's decision to divest in South Africa. She pointedly asked him, in his four years of living in New Orleans, "What one thing have you done to address apartheid in this city, since, after all, you benefit from that apartheid?" (2005:114). After his inability to adequately respond to that question and much self-reflection, he realized, "I had been blind to the way in which my own privilege and the privilege of whites generally had obscured our understanding of such issues as accountability, the need to link up struggles (like the connection between racism in New Orleans and that in South Africa), and the need to always have leadership of color in any antiracist struggle,

however much that requires whites to step back, keep our mouths shut and just listen for a while" (2005:117).

After graduating from college, Wise took that lesson seriously and began his career as an antiracist activist, working as a youth coordinator for the Louisiana Coalition Against Racism and Nazism, which opposed the political candidacy of neo-Nazi Senate candidate David Duke. He moved up the ranks of the organization and eventually became one of the most visible faces associated with the anti-Duke effort (2005:11). Wise now earns a living lecturing and writing about white privilege and antiracist activism.

Wise acknowledges that there is significant resistance to whites' engaging in antiracist activist work because they lack antiracist role models to whom they can look for guidance, they fear alienating family and friends with their views, and "because resistance is difficult ... many whites who care deeply about issues of racism and inequality will find ourselves paralyzed either by uncertainty, fear or both" (2005:62). He emphasizes that despite these obstacles to resistance, "experiences taught me that to be white in this country doesn't have to be a story of accepting unjust social systems. There is not only one way to be in this skin. There are choices we can make, paths we can travel, and when we travel them, we will not be alone" (2005:63).

While engaging in this kind of work has resulted in some death threats, hate mail, and being followed by skinheads on at least one occasion, Wise argues that "I put up with whatever cost I have to put up with, because the cost of not doing the work is greater. ... People of color have to do this work as a matter of everyday survival. And so long as they have to, who am I to act as if I have a choice in the matter? Especially when my future and that of my children in large part depends on the eradication of racism? There is no choice" (2005:6).

Institutional Privilege

Just as sociologists have identified racial discrimination within all of our major social institutions, white privilege can be found in these arenas as well: banks/lending institutions, educational systems, media, criminal justice systems, and government, to name just a few. This is the most difficult arena in which to make race privilege visible. Institutional racism was introduced in the first chapter and refers to everyday business practices and policies that result in disadvantage for some racial groups, intentionally or not. **Institutional privilege** is even more difficult to identify because privilege is designed to be unacknowledged, and in its institutionalized form it becomes even more obscured. In addition to the advantages individuals accumulate through white privilege, institutional privilege also takes the form of customs, norms, traditions, laws, and public policies that benefit whites (Williams 2003). Throughout this text, various societal institutions will be explored, exposing not only the racial inequality embedded in them but also the ways white privilege is built into the specific business practices and policies within each institution. In exploring institutional privilege, it is useful to ask what group benefits from a particular arrangement, policy, or practice?

Another way to understand the cumulative advantage that institutional privilege amounts to is to use the idea of **locked-in advantage**, which was introduced by economists. In economics, locked-in advantages are the competitive advantages that early technology leaders have by being the first on the market. Daria Roithmayr (2014) uses this idea to explain continuing racial inequality. For instance, during the Jim Crow era whites were advantaged by racial exclusion policies held by homeowners' associations, unions, schools, and banks, all of which contributed to white advantage and racial minority disadvantage (and which will be explored in greater detail throughout this book).

To help understand what is meant by institutional privilege, we explore several policies and practices that have allowed whites to accumulate wealth and prevented people of color from doing the same. These include the policies and practices of banking and lending institutions as well as government policies and practices.

Racial minorities have been systematically excluded from wealth creation with very real, concrete consequences. Slavery is the most obvious example. In addition to the cruelty and inhumanity of this institution, it was also a system that deterred wealth accumulation by the great majority of blacks and supported the massive accumulation of wealth by some whites. For over 240 years, blacks labored in America without being compensated. Clearly that placed them in a disadvantaged position in terms of wealth accumulation. While only a small portion of the population owned slaves, it is estimated that about fifteen million white Americans today have slave-owning ancestors (Millman 2008). Of our first eighteen presidents, thirteen owned slaves. Two recent presidents, father and son George H. W. and George W. Bush, are descendants of slave owners, contributing, of course, to their great wealth and political power to this day.

Upon emancipation, reparations for former slaves were promised, most in the form of land. The promised "forty acres and a mule," however, never materialized. During the Reconstruction era, the federal government established the Freedmen's Bureau to provide food, education, medical care, and, in some cases, land to newly freed slaves as well as to needy whites (see Chapter 5). Although this agency only lasted one year and was unable to meet the needs of the great majority of newly freed slaves, it is significant that more whites benefited from this government agency than blacks.

Native American Land Loss

The exploitation of Native Americans often involved the taking of land; an estimated two billion acres of land was transferred to the United States government from American Indian tribes through treaties in exchange for tribal sovereignty (Newton 1999). European Americans confiscated land that Native peoples populated, forced their removal, and sometimes engaged in acts of genocide so as to acquire land. This theme of Native land loss at the hands of whites is hardly news; most of us learned of this in grade school. However, we need to reflect more on its significance. Native land loss is always presented as a collective problem, which it was, as tribes lost their lands and livelihoods as they were repeatedly relocated to less-valuable lands. What we tend not to realize is that this is a significant loss at the individual level as well. Land is equivalent to wealth in the white mainstream culture (Native peoples, however, generally did not believe people could own the land and instead saw themselves as stewards of the land). Who benefited when all those Native people were forced off of the land on which they lived? White people took the land as their own, thus acquiring wealth. Native land loss at the hands of whites goes beyond giant land swindles involving treaties between the federal government and tribal governments. Throughout the country there were smaller, everyday, localized swindles. Additionally, many states established laws that did not allow Native people to own land, thus limiting their ability to accumulate wealth and simultaneously contributing to the ability of white people to accumulate wealth.

An egregious example of the distance some whites went to swindle Native people out of their wealth involved the murder of at least twenty-four Osage Indians in Oklahoma during the 1920s (some estimates suggest that over one hundred were murdered). The Osage had been relocated to land in Oklahoma that was presumed to be useless—rocky, sterile, and unfit for cultivation. However, oil was found under the land and, subsequently, the Osage tribal members became some of the wealthiest people in the world. In order to get their hands on the mineral rights associated with this oil wealth, some white men married Osage women and began killing them. While most of the murders went unsolved, three men were convicted and sent to prison (Grann 2017).

White Advantage: Wealth Accumulation

These historical examples of the exploitation of racial minorities in terms of wealth accumulation have a flip side: white advantage. Whites historically and currently benefit from the exclusion of other racial/ethnic groups. For instance, laws supported the rights of white Americans to own homes and businesses while banks and lending institutions provided them with the necessary capital to do so. This was not a given for people of color. Until the 1960s, laws explicitly excluded people of color from obtaining business loans in many places. White people were subsidized in acquiring their own homes and thus establishing equity, which eventually became wealth that was passed on to the next generation (Oliver and Shapiro 1995). This is significant if for no other reason than wealth accumulates. Federal Reserve studies confirm that even today, minorities get fewer home loans, even when their economic situations are comparable to those of whites. "The poorest white applicant, according to this [Federal Reserve] report, was more likely to get a mortgage loan approved than a black in the highest income bracket" (Oliver and Shapiro 1995:20). The consequences of this are profound because, for most Americans, home ownership represents their primary and often only source of wealth (see Chapter 9). Research finds that over the past thirty years, white household wealth has grown 84 percent, which is 1.2 times the growth rate of Latino household wealth and 3 times the rate of black household wealth (Asante-Muhammed et al. 2016).

Ideologies of white supremacy fuel white identities and a sense of entitlement, and, thus, the creation of institutions that deny access to anyone but whites has been deemed acceptable. Ideologies of color-blindness in our current era fuel a "raceless" identity in whites that allows them to deny ongoing racism while still enjoying race privilege.

REFLECT AND CONNECT

Think about how much white privilege you may have. If you are white, did your ancestors own slaves? Ask your parents the following questions: Did your parents or grandparents have access to home and/or business loans? Did they own their own homes or land? Did your parents or grandparents own a business? Did your parents or grandparents attend college? Have you received or do you expect to receive an inheritance? Are your parents paying for your college education, thus making significant student loans unnecessary? If you can answer yes to any of these, you have more than likely benefited from white privilege in a very material, concrete way.

CHALLENGING WHITE PRIVILEGE

What can or should be done about white privilege? Is it necessary to challenge white privilege? Is it possible? It is easier to condemn racism than to challenge one's own privilege. Understanding white privilege is essential yet incomplete, because, as McIntosh notes, "describing white privilege makes one newly accountable" (2008:109). In other words, if we see privilege, do we not have an obligation to work to eradicate it? While white privilege allows whites to ignore their race and avoid confronting the advantages associated with it, many white Americans actively challenge white privilege as part of their commitment to racial justice and as a way to challenge their own sense of entitlement (e.g., Warren 2010; Wise 2005). White civil rights activists have rejected their own race privilege through their activism on behalf of full civil rights for people of color, for instance (e.g., Murray 2004; Zellner and Curry 2008).

Racial justice activists argue that white privilege is the proverbial "elephant in the room" that white people agree to ignore (Parker and Chambers 2007). White theologians have called for an end to the silence surrounding white privilege within religious institutions (Cassidy and Mikulich 2007). Stories of racial justice activism are featured in "Racial Justice Activism" boxes in each chapter. Now, we are going to explore why challenging white privilege is not only necessary but also actually in the interests of white people; although, as one of my former students pointed out, it bears emphasizing that we should reject white privilege because it is the right thing to do, not because it is in our interest as white people.

For many white people, being introduced to the concept of white privilege invokes intense feelings of guilt. They often respond by saying they should not be made to feel guilty for being white, as it was hardly their choice. Or they feel that by focusing on privilege, it takes away from their achievements or the achievements of their parents. This is not the intent. White guilt is a normal reaction to learning about historical and current atrocities inflicted upon racial minorities by whites. When it comes to race, our country has an ugly history that cannot be ignored. Guilt is uncomfortable psychologically, so people tend to work to alleviate the feeling. Thus, such guilt has the potential to motivate change, to get white people to understand how they are racist, how they contribute to racial oppression, and what they can do to end it. It is important to recognize white privilege. It is necessary for a complete understanding of the role race plays in all of our lives, both at the individual and societal levels. Additionally, opposing the racial inequities associated with whiteness is not the same thing as opposing white people (Williams 2003).

It is important to critically investigate white privilege because while privilege offers advantages, whites are also losers under this system of structural inequality. There are many unrecognized ways whites lose under this system: for example, it is expensive, financially and morally, to ignore white privilege in the workplace because it remains an uncomfortable environment for people of color and, thus, their retention is less likely. The only way white people can remain part of this racial hierarchy is to compartmentalize—separate their heads from their hearts. There are long-term consequences of such compartmentalization, primarily in terms of failing to recognize our common humanity (Kendall 2006). Helms' stages of racial identity development are helpful in understanding our common humanity. Through this model, we can see that racial identity is not fixed. We can change; we can progress in terms of understanding ourselves along racial lines as well as understanding the operation of our societal racial hierarchy.

Tim Wise (2008) argues that white people pay a tremendous price for maintaining white privilege and that it is actually in the interest of whites to dismantle the racial hierarchy. Wise offers the following bit of advice to whites interested in working for racial justice:

IMAGE 2.4: Antiracist activist, author, and speaker Tim Wise.

The first thing a white person must do to effectively fight racism is to learn to listen, and more than that, to believe what people of color say about their lives. … One of the biggest problems with white America is its collective unwillingness to believe that racism is still a real problem for nonwhite peoples, despite their repeated protestations that it is.

(2005:67)

> ## WITNESS
>
> "I think it's the price of the soul. You're internally diminished when you dominate other people or when you're trying to convince yourself you're not dominating others" (Warren 2010:88).

One of the reasons offered by whites fighting for racial justice is the moral one: that this is an unjust system and, thus, it should be dismantled. Ignoring both inequality and privilege dehumanizes all of us. Racial justice activists find that when they engage in this work it is personally fulfilling. They believe that working for racial justice will produce a better society for all. For racial justice activists, having healthier communities, more empowered citizens, and a more humane culture that focuses on compassion and community will provide a better society for all (Warren 2010).

> ## WITNESS
>
> One of the racial justice activists interviewed by Warren (2010) explains why she believes this work is part of her civil and political responsibility: "We have got to do something about that for the good of democracy. It's just not healthy for a democracy to have that kind of racism at its core" (Warren 2010:85).

Another reason it is in the interest of whites to dismantle white privilege is economic. It is costly to maintain inequality. Whiteness privileges some whites more than others. It is estimated that an affluent 20 percent of whites reap most of the benefits of whiteness (Hobgood 2007). Having a labor force that is divided along racial lines (see Chapter 9) deflates all workers' wages. The prison industrial complex (see Chapter 10) disproportionately incarcerates racial minority males. The mass incarceration of minority males becomes self-perpetuating in that they become the face of crime, leaving white criminals privileged in that they are not immediately suspect. However, whites are disadvantaged by the mass incarceration of minorities simply because more and more tax dollars go toward incarcerating citizens rather than toward supporting schools, for instance.

Recent research finds that, in addition to the reasons cited above for why whites might consider challenging white privilege, a commitment to whiteness can be deadly (Metzl 2019). Through interviews with lower- and middle-class white republicans in Missouri, Tennessee, and Kansas, Metzl finds their support of a politics fueled by racial resentment is resulting in higher death rates for whites. He argues that their support of the Republican agenda—including a hostility to gun control, taxes, and government programs such as the Affordable Car Act—is resulting in dramatically declining life expectancy for those very same people. Non-Hispanic, white men, for instance, make up the overwhelming number of gun suicides in this country; specifically, between 2009 and 2015, they accounted for "nearly 80 percent of all gun suicides in the United States, despite representing less than 35 percent of the total population" (Metzl 2019:47). Ultimately, politicians sell white working- and middle-class voters on the idea that they should be voting for policies that defend of a "white way of life," that are, instead, lethal.

WITNESS

"As these policy agendas spread from Southern and midwestern legislatures into the halls of Congress and the White House, ever-more white Americans are then, literally, *dying of whiteness*. This is because white America's investment in maintaining an imagined place atop a racial hierarchy—that is, an investment in a sense of whiteness—ironically harms the aggregate well-being of US whites as a demographic group, thereby making whiteness itself a negative health indicator" (Metzl 2019:9).

Millennials on Race

The "The 'Woke' Generation? Millennial Attitudes on Race in the US" survey measured **racial resentment** among the respondents. Beliefs associated with racial resentment emphasize the idea that blacks no longer face discrimination and that any difficulties African Americans face emerge from their poor work ethic. Racial resentment, then, fuels beliefs that racial minority groups are undeserving of government benefits, as they refuse to live up to American values of individualism, independence, and hard work (Kinder and Sanders 1996).

To measure racial resentment, survey respondents were asked if they agree or disagree with the following statement: "Irish, Italian, Jewish and many other minorities overcame prejudice and worked their way up. Blacks should do the same without any special favors." As Figure 2.1 shows, the majority of whites (59 percent) and Latinx (51 percent) respondents agreed with the statement, thus expressing some

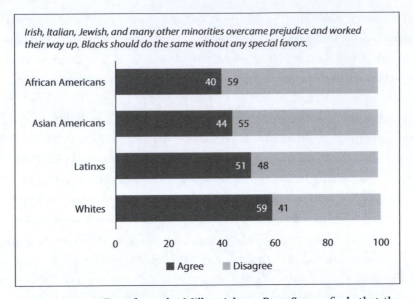

Irish, Italian, Jewish, and many other minorities overcame prejudice and worked their way up. Blacks should do the same without any special favors.

FIGURE 2.1: Data from the Millennials on Race Survey finds that the majority of whites (59 percent) and Latinos (51 percent) showed some racial resentment by agreeing with the statement, "Irish, Italian, Jewish, and many other minorities overcame prejudice and worked their way up. Blacks should do the same without any special favors," while the majority of African Americans (59 percent) and Asian Americans (55 percent) disagreed with the statement, showing less racial resentment (Cohen et al. 2017).

racial resentment, while majorities of African American (59 percent) and Asian American (55 percent) Millennials disagreed with the statement, illustrating less racial resentment.

A second question designed to gauge racial resentment asked respondents whether they agreed or disagreed with the following statement: "Generations of slavery and discrimination have created conditions that make it difficult for Blacks to work their way out of the lower class." Figure 2.2 summarizes those results, with African Americans (79 percent), Asian Americans (78 percent), and Latinxs (59 percent) expressing agreement, and sometimes overwhelming agreement, with the statement, while white Millennials were evenly split on the question (49 percent agree and 49 percent disagree).

CHAPTER SUMMARY

This chapter focuses on the social construction of whiteness, including how some groups have become white over time. For many groups, such as Jewish Americans, becoming white is intimately connected to social class and social mobility. The desire to assimilate into whiteness is a result of benefits associated with white

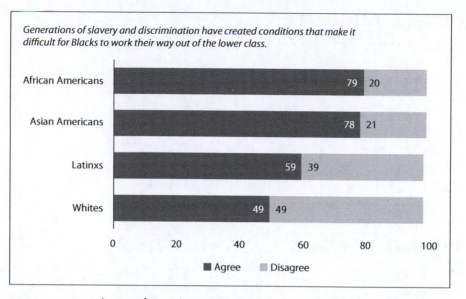

FIGURE 2.2: A second question measuring racial resentment among Millennials asked, "Generations of slavery and discrimination have created conditions that make it difficult for Blacks to work their way out of the lower class," found respondents of color overwhelmingly agreed with the statement, while white Millennials were evenly split between agreement and disagreement (Cohen et al. 2017).

privilege. White privilege can be thought of as the other side of racism. White privilege tends to be unacknowledged by its recipients. Part of the benefits associated with our racial hierarchy involves establishing cultural belief systems that contribute to the invisibility of privilege. White racial identities emerge out of the intersection of these cultural belief systems and institutionalized privilege. Ultimately, many whites working for racial justice argue that white privilege actually hurts whites as well as people of color. They maintain that it is necessary to dismantle the racial hierarchy by ending both racism and white privilege so as to create a more compassionate society.

As we work to bring white people into discussions of race, we must be careful not to render racial/ethnic "others" invisible. To address this, the goal should be to work at understanding the racial hierarchy—what groups are designated as dominant, what groups are subordinate, and how this system inequitably distributes power, privilege, and oppression. Understanding the totality of the system is essential to adequately take account of race, racism, and privilege.

KEY TERMS AND CONCEPTS

Agency

Assimilation

Collective social mobility

Ethnic enclave

Ethnic renewal

Ethnic revival

Institutional privilege

Locked-in advantage

Master status

Meritocracy

New white consciousness

Norm

Patriarchy

Pluralism

Psychological wage

Racial challenges

Racial hierarchies

Racial resentment

Racial socialization

Structural constraints

Symbolic ethnicity

White ethnics

White fragility

White privilege

Whiteness

White racism

White supremacy

Working poor

PERSONAL REFLECTIONS

1. If you are white, describe at least five ways you have benefited from white privilege. Discuss whether it was difficult to think of five examples and, if so, speculate on why that was. Discuss whether you had considered yourself privileged in any way, but specifically along racial lines, before. In other words, was white privilege visible to you? If so, why do you think that was so? If not, explore why that was not the case. Discuss the effects your white privilege has on other people.

   If you are a nonwhite student, reverse the questions. For instance, list five ways you have been discriminated against due to your race. Were these examples difficult to come up with? Speculate on why or why not. Additionally, speculate on a few ways you think your life might have been different had you been born white in American society.

2. If possible, describe white privilege to two white people you know—friends, coworkers, or family members. What is the general reaction to this notion? Why do you think this is so? Is it possible for you to not see white privilege after reading this chapter? If so, why do you think that is? If not, why not? Describe white privilege to two people of color that you know—friends, coworkers, or family members. Describe the general reaction to this notion. Tie this in to the idea of standpoint perspective described in Chapter 1.

3. Define and reflect on the concept of white fragility. Give an example of white fragility in your life—if you are white, focus on a time when you exhibited symptoms of white fragility. What is it about the conversation or situation that

unsettled you and resulted in your experiencing white fragility? If you are non-white, give an example of white fragility that you witnessed in someone else. What triggered the reaction? How was the situation resolved?

CRITICAL THINKING QUESTIONS

1. Thinking about Tim Wise's story (Racial Justice Activism), to what extent do you think this kind of transformation (his development of a white racial identity and eventually becoming an antiracist activist) is likely for most whites? What do you base your speculation on? Explain how white racism and white privilege are two sides of the same coin (in other words, without one, the other does not exist).

   Provide examples that go beyond those provided in the text to show how white racism and white privilege are interconnected.

2. Think about some arena in which you hold privilege (race, gender, sexual orientation, disability, nationality). Identify five ways you see privilege operating in your life.

ESSENTIAL READING

DiAngelo, Robin. 2018. *White Fragility: Why It's So Hard for White People to Talk about Racism.* Boston, MA: Beacon Press.

Hagerman, Margaret A. 2018. *White Kids: Growing Up with Privilege in a Racially Divided America.* New York: New York University Press.

Ignatiev, Noel. 1995. *How the Irish Became White.* New York: Routledge.

Irving, Debby. 2014. *Waking Up White.* Cambridge, MA: Elephant Room Press.

Leonard, David J. 2017. *Playing While White: Privilege and Power On and Off the Field.* Seattle, WA: University of Washington Press.

Lipsitz, George. 2006. *The Possessive Investment in Whiteness: How White People Profit from Identity Politics*, revised and expanded ed. Philadelphia, PA: Temple University Press.

McIntosh, Peggy. 1988. *White Privilege and Male Privilege: A Personal Account of Coming to See Correspondences through Work in Women's Studies.* Working Paper 189. Center for Research on Women, Wellesley College, Wellesley, MA.

Metzl, Jonathan M. 2019. *Dying of Whiteness: How the Politics of Racial Resentment is Killing America's Heartland.* New York: Basic Books.

Rothenberg, Paula S., ed. 2016. *White Privilege: Essential Readings on the Other Side of Racism*, 5th ed. New York: Worth Publishers.

Warren, Mark R. 2010. *Fire in the Heart: How White Activists Embrace Racial Justice.* Oxford, New York: Oxford University Press.

Waters, Mary. 1990. *Ethnic Options: Choosing Identities in America*. Berkeley, CA: University of California Press.

Wise, Tim. 2005. *White Like Me: Reflections on Race from a Privileged Son*. Brooklyn, NY: Soft Skull Press.

RECOMMENDED FILMS

Mirrors of Privilege: Making Whiteness Visible (2006). Produced by Shakti Butler. This film features stories of antiracist activists and how and why they choose to fight not only racism but also white privilege. These stories of racial justice activism emphasize the stages of white racial identity development.

The Great White Hoax: Donald Trump and the Politics of Race and Class in America (2017). Featuring Tim Wise, Executive Producer Sut Jhally, Director Jeremy Earp. This documentary explores how politicians of both parties tap into white anxiety and white grievances while scapegoating people of color, using a divide-and-conquer strategy on the working class. The film shows how Trump's race-baiting in his 2016 campaign has a long history in American politics.

White People (2015). Directed by Jose Antonio Vargas. MTV asks what does it mean to be young and white in America today? The film follows journalist Jose Antonio Vargas as he travels across America, asking white people the hard questions: about affirmative action, color-blindness, privilege, and many more.

Tim Wise on White Privilege: Racism, White Denial, and the Costs of Inequality (2008). Produced and edited by Sut Jhally. This video is an engaging lecture by one of the most prominent antiracist activists today, Tim Wise. Emphasis is placed not only on the damage white privilege does to people of color but also on its costs to white people and, thus, why it is in all of our interests to challenge white privilege.

RECOMMENDED MULTIMEDIA

Check out the White Privilege Conference (WPC) website, particularly the WPC University, which offers online courses (some for credit) exploring issues of diversity, white privilege, and social justice. www.whiteprivilegeconference.com/university.html.

Check out the website for the National Collegiate Dialogue on Race. If you find this interesting, ask your professor to sign your class up for the dialogue so that you can participate in it. www.usaonrace.com/category/department/national-collegiate-dialogue.

CHAPTER 3

Science and the Sociology of Race

CHAPTER LEARNING OUTCOMES

By the end of this chapter, you should be able to:

- Understand the key characteristics and dynamics of science, and how they contributed to the eugenics movement and modern-day racism
- Critique the current uses of race in genomic science
- Demonstrate an understanding of the sociological approach to race and ethnicity
- Explain the latest developments in sociological theorizing about race

---

Pharmacogenomics is a branch of pharmacology that operates on the assumption that there are differences in the ways we respond to drugs based on our race. Such assumptions raise questions about the role race plays in the sciences, as well as about the validity of studies that use race as their basis.

Racial disparities in rates of hypertension in the United States are often cited as evidence of a need for specific drugs for African Americans. In 2005, the Food and Drug Administration (FDA) approved a new drug, BiDil, that it claimed could effectively treat congestive heart failure in African Americans (Hochschild, Weaver, and Burch 2012; Kahn 2013). BiDil was the first drug approved by the FDA to be marketed to patients of a specific race. This was hailed as progress toward a new era of "personalized medicine," in which pharmaceuticals can be designed to work with someone's specific genetic makeup. Others embraced BiDil because it was designed to treat an otherwise underserved population of patients.

However, there are critics of pharmacogenomics. Some believe that racial disparities in rates of heart disease and hypertension have been exploited by large companies so as to market drugs to particular populations. Others worry about the implications of race-based medicines: that their existence biologizes race in dangerous ways, fueling racial prejudice in new ways. Some warn that this is a new era of **racialized medicine** in which race is treated as a genetic fact for medical purposes (Kahn 2013).

In the case of BiDil, the research sample used to determine its effectiveness was limited to individuals aged 45 to 64, an age range that accounts for only 6 percent of heart failure mortality. For those over the age of 65, the statistical differences in rates of heart disease between African Americans and whites disappear. Moreover, the study data used to approve BiDil did not describe patients of other racial groups, leading many to question its racialized marketing, and so also its integrity.

According to anthropologist Audrey Smedley and psychologist Brian Smedley, race is more than a socially constructed way of categorizing people; it is a knowledge system, a worldview, "a way of knowing, of perceiving, and of interpreting the world, and of rationalizing its contents" (Smedley and Smedley 2012:13). Whereas the previous two chapters introduced the idea of race as a social construction, this chapter will explore the role science has played in establishing and rationalizing that social construction.

First, we examine how scientific understandings of race/ethnicity have changed over time. Then, we look at how sociologists have studied race and ethnicity, and how their perceptions have evolved from the study of racial inequality to an interest in race privilege. This chapter concludes with a look at the most recent theoretical perspectives on race, racial formation theory, the white racial frame, and critical race theory (CRT), among others.

Consider how the science of race remains a potent force and also how sociologists have reified race through seeking evidence of its reality, despite the understanding of race as a social construction:

- Every modern era has supported a "science of race" that emphasizes race as biological, because "science is the most effective tool for giving claims about human differences the stamp of legitimacy" (Roberts 2011:27).
- African American scholar W. E. B. Du Bois established the first scientific school of sociology in the United States and challenged prevailing scientific racism of the time, despite the fact he was marginalized by the white, mainstream discipline of sociology until the late twentieth century (Morris 2015).
- The sociological study of race has historically focused on race relations—which is argued to embrace the pacification of subordinate groups—rather than

focusing on racism, which provides a conceptual framework for working toward racial justice for oppressed groups (Steinberg 2007).

- Nearly four million people have pursued genetic ancestry testing (sometimes referred to as genetic genealogy) since 2002 (Roth and Ivemark 2018).

- Race and genetic ancestry testing has continued to make headlines. Massachusetts Senator Elizabeth Warren has been criticized for claiming her Native American ancestry on law school faculty records from the 1980s. In the face of critiques that she wasn't really Native American, and being ridiculed by President Trump who referred to her as "Pocahontas" and dared her to take a DNA test to prove her ancestry, she took the test and released the results which confirmed her Native American ancestry. This led to criticism from Native Americans, who claim tribal membership is much more complicated than a simple DNA test.

- One of the most discussed topics on the white nationalist organization Stormfront's website concerns white pride and the results of genetic ancestry tests. When results confirm multiracial ancestry for white nationalists, fellow white nationalists offer potential explanations, including that the results cannot be trusted, or conspiracy theories that the testing companies are Jewish owned, among others (Murphy 2019).

SCIENTIFIC RACISM

Science is a systematic attempt to produce knowledge about the world. Using science, we are able to generate new understandings of human behavior ranging in application from the cellular level to the level of human social interactions. Scientists have long aimed to make generalizations based on the data they gather with the goal of establishing predictable patterns and attaining some degree of control over our world. But what we consider to be scientific knowledge is constantly changing, and, often, new knowledge overturns previously held truths.

Scientific findings carry more validity than opinions that are based on casual observations. This is because science practices a commitment to specific methods, agreed-upon ways of observing and analyzing the world. Science also distinguishes itself from opinion by making claims of objectivity, which means that scientists' personal biases do not influence their research. However, eliminating bias from scientific observation and study is easier said than done. The social context in which knowledge is produced and the particular era out of which scientific research emerges influence scientists' findings.

Despite scientists' claims to the contrary, scientific interest in race has never been objective. In fact, for generations scientists repeatedly sought to prove the innate inferiority of blacks and the superiority of whites. In different historical periods, scientific claims of inferiority were extended to American Indians, Mexicans, and the Chinese. Collectively, these claims fall into the category of **scientific racism**, which refers to using science to prove the innate racial inferiority of some groups and the superiority of others.

Scientific racism emerged in response to questions concerning the morality of slavery and gained traction as the global abolitionist movement grew in the mid-1800s. For generations to follow, attempts were made to prove that the enslavement of black people was not a moral wrong because blacks were not fully human. Scientific racism, like other forms of racism, served the purpose of justifying the social order.

Scientific Interest in Race

The social, historical, and political contexts within which scientists live and work influence their perceptions of the world, and these perceptions inform both the research questions they ask and their interpretation of data. For example, in the cultural climate of the mid to late 1800s, responses to abolitionist challenges to the institution of slavery and then the attempts at reestablishing black subordination after emancipation called for a new area of scientific research—one that sought evidence of white superiority and black inferiority.

An early example of scientific racism was the study of **phrenology**, a now defunct branch of science that compared the skull sizes of various racial groups and used those data to try to determine group intelligence, social and cultural characteristics, and the presumed innate group differences between the races. Other scientists measured facial angles in an attempt to prove that blacks were closer to the primitive in their physical characteristics and therefore inferior. In support of such practices, scientific journals published countless articles seeking to show fundamental racial differences, all ultimately supporting the social order of the time.

The skull sizes of Native American peoples were also compared to those of whites, to similar political ends. In the 1830s, American phrenologist Dr. Charles Caldwell was one of the first to make this argument with regard to Native Americans. According to Caldwell, Native Americans' inferiority meant they were bound for extinction (Horsman 1975) and for this reason efforts to "civilize" them were a waste of time and money. Ideas like these influenced the work of many other scientists during that period.

In his academic article "Race Traits of the American Negro" (1896) Frederick L. Hoffman compared mortality rates, in particular infant mortality rates, in white and black communities to establish his "extinction thesis." In studying black communities, Hoffman attributed high infant mortality—the number of babies that die before the first year of life—and high death rates to the physical inferiority of the black population. Much like Caldwell, he argued that any public or social investment in a dying race would be a waste of funds. While Hoffman's data were accurate—blacks did have higher infant mortality rates and death rates than whites—his interpretation of the data was faulty. Hoffman failed to take into account the socioeconomic factors faced by black Americans during that period, including poverty, malnutrition, poor sanitation, and lack of health-care, all of which contribute to high infant mortality rates. African American scholars W. E. B. Du Bois and Kelly Miller disputed these and similar findings, arguing they were based on flawed science, yet Hoffman's thesis fit with the prevailing racial ideologies of the era and, thus, gained traction (Morris 2015).

Other scientists of this period argued that Mexicans and Chinese immigrants were likewise racially inferior to whites. Although couched in the objectivity of science, all of these arguments reflected the politics of the time. For example, the idea of *Manifest Destiny* convinced many white Americans that it was their divine right to claim and occupy all the land from the Atlantic to the Pacific Oceans. By claiming that the American Indians, Chinese immigrants, and Mexicans living throughout the American West were inferior, white landowners were able to justify a seemingly insatiable demand for land and westward expansion.

In the late 1860s, Chinese immigrant labor was used to build the western half of the Transcontinental Railroad (Irish immigrants built the eastern half). The use and abuse of immigrant labor, during this and other periods in American history, were facilitated by ideologies that argued for the innate inferiority of the exploited group. The exploitation of the Chinese meant, for instance, that they were forced to work through harsh winters in the Sierra Nevada Mountains, where many crews were lost, some buried alive under snowdrifts. As growing numbers of white Americans moved west to California, they felt threatened by the presence of Chinese immigrants in so many industries, including agriculture. In 1882, the Chinese Exclusion Act made it illegal for Chinese laborers to enter the country and denied citizenship to those who were already here (Takaki 1989) (see Chapter 5, 13).

Eugenics Movement

The proliferation of scientific racism ultimately led to the eugenics movement. Englishman Sir Francis Galton coined the term **eugenics**, arguing that the healthiest and ablest should be encouraged to have more children for the betterment of society. His views were considered a positive form of eugenics because his intention was to encourage the healthiest citizens to reproduce more. A decidedly negative interpretation of eugenics emerged during the chaos of the post–Civil War era and gained currency in the United States. During this period, the focus shifted from encouraging healthy individuals to bear children to sterilization, inhibiting pregnancy in those deemed the least fit for procreation. It was understood that upper-class whites were "a superior stock of humans who deserved to be propagated through breeding across generations" (Morris 2015:18).

During the early half of the twentieth century, white birth rates dropped while those of immigrants and African Americans either increased or remained the same. This became a source of great concern for many white Americans. White women were encouraged to have more children out of a sense of "republican motherhood" (a phrase of the era referring to women's contribution to the nation, the growth of the "republic"). From these attitudes emerged the demand to reduce immigration and to force sterilization on those deemed "unfit," all in the name of a better society.

Additionally, at this time, **antimiscegenation laws**, laws prohibiting interracial marriage, emerged in many states because of fears that intermarriage would lead to the deterioration of the white race. The science of the day supported the argument that it was in the best interest of society to sterilize the "feebleminded," a catchall phrase often used against racial/ethnic minority group members. Many white American social scientists and even some founders of the discipline of sociology were drawn to the eugenics movement. Evidence of this support includes the fact that the lead article in the first American sociological journal was Galton's "Eugenics: Its Definition, Scope, and Aims," and one of the earliest well-known sociology textbooks reprinted Galton's article in its entirety (Morris 2015).

By the 1940s, eugenics was considered a discredited science, but practices associated with eugenics, such as involuntary sterilizations, continued until the 1970s in the United States. It is estimated that more than seventy thousand persons, women and men, were involuntarily sterilized in the United States (Roberts 1997). Perhaps most significantly, sterilization abuse against women of color skyrocketed in the 1960s and 1970s at the hands of government-paid physicians. In New York, Boston, and throughout the South, for instance, teaching hospitals routinely performed unnecessary hysterectomies on black and Puerto Rican women for practice. Many women of color were coerced into signing consent forms for tubal ligations while they were in labor. It is estimated that more than one-third of women of childbearing age in Puerto Rico, a United States territory, were involuntarily sterilized between 1950 and 1958, with the consent of the Puerto Rican government. Native American women on reservations were also subject to sterilization abuse. By the 1970s, an estimated 25 percent were infertile as a result of these systematic efforts (Roberts 1997). While policies vary by state, many still encourage the sterilization of poor women as a form of birth control by paying for these services through Medicaid but not providing equal access to other forms of birth control (Roberts 1997).

While the overwhelming majority of scientists today concur that race is a social construction, there are still some who attempt to attribute biological explanations to social inequalities. In *The Bell Curve* (1994), scholars Richard Herrnstein and

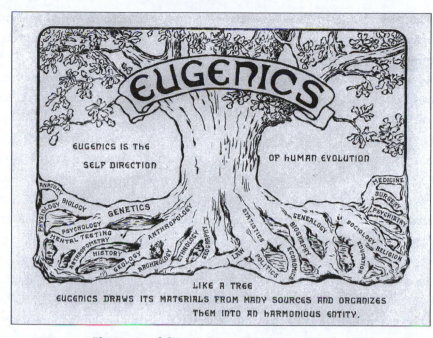

IMAGE 3.1: The image of the eugenics tree was meant to show that the then-new science of eugenics combined insights from other scientific fields (noted in the roots of the image) into a science of human evolution that was more advanced than the scientific disciplines from which it emerged. (Logo used by the Second International Congress on Eugenics in 1921 at the American Museum of Natural History, courtesy of The Harvard Medical Library.)

Charles Murray argued that intelligence explains inequalities along class and racial lines. Previous research had found that intelligence had only a modest effect on social class (Jencks et al. 1972). This book was widely publicized and generated considerable media attention (Fischer et al. 1996). While social science research rarely makes the best-seller list, this work did, raising the question, why was *The Bell Curve*—an eight-hundred-page tome of quantitative analyses—an exception? It is impossible to answer this question conclusively; however, it is likely that many people in the United States are still drawn to biological explanations of social inequalities, however fragile or ill-conceived the science; its arguments still resonate with many people. Books such as *Inequality by Design* (Fischer et al. 1996) and numerous scientific articles by sociologists (e.g., Duster 1995; Nisbett 1995) success-fully refuted Herrnstein and Murray's arguments; however, they failed to similarly capture a mass audience.

Race and the Human Genome Project

By 2003, scientists had mapped the **human genome**, the genetic sequence of the human species, a significant scientific accomplishment. The Human Genome Project

(HGP) represents an important advancement in genetic research and biotechnology. Its potential uses include finding cures for existing diseases, addressing life-threatening genetic disorders, and preventing future illness through gene therapies (manipulation of genes that cause disease). Another direction for the field of bio-technology is to uncover genetic explanations for crime, intelligence, and mental illness, among other things (Duster 2003).

According to researchers on the HGP, despite the wide range of physical appearances present in the human species, we are genetically 99.99 percent similar to one another. Thus, HGP research has been used to support the argument that race is a social construction and is not expressed genetically or biologically. However, recent developments in genetics research have begun to emphasize the minute genetic differences (0.01 percent) among us.

Many scientists fear that interest in the 0.01 percent of human genetic difference is leading to a new era of scientific racism (Brewer 2006; Duster 2003, 2005). HGP research is being used in fields as diverse as pharmacogenomics, as illustrated in this chapter's opening vignette, and genealogical research, which claims to be able to use genetic technology to trace ancestral lineage. Genetic ancestry research runs the risk of rebiologizing race, reinforcing the false notion that race is not a social construction but, instead, a genetic trait. HGP research also encourages genetic explanations for very complex phenomena such as crime and mental illness. For all of these reasons, many social scientists are questioning whose interests are being served by this new direction in genetic research.

Genetic Ancestry Testing and Race

Tracing genetic ancestry has become big business. As of 2016, seventy-four companies have emerged to sell genetic ancestry testing to consumers and more than four million people have done these tests (Roth and Ivemark 2018). Companies such as 23andMe, African Ancestry, Decode Genetics, Ancestry.com, Family Tree DNA,

IMAGE 3.2: Dozens of companies now exist that use DNA to trace ancestry. African Ancestry appeals specifically to customers of African descent, helping individuals trace their lineage to a specific location in Africa and to specific African ethnic or tribal groups. (African Ancestry, Inc. Reprinted with permission.)

and many others claim to be able to uncover their client's "genetic ancestry" using a DNA sample. The business of genetic ancestry testing has been popularized by the PBS series *African American Lives* and *Finding Your Roots*, both hosted by Henry Louis Gates, Jr., which focus on the use of DNA in family genealogy. The popularity of both shows has led to millions of people turning to what is perceived as an objective scientific approach to genealogy: genetic ancestry testing (Duster 2011). Much research exists criticizing genetic ancestry testing and specifically its ability to make claims about a subject's racial/ethnic ancestry (e.g., Duster 2011; Greely 2008; Nelson 2008; Shriver and Kittles 2008; Tallbear 2008). Despite these limitations, companies that do genetic ancestry testing often sell their results as more accurate than they really are. As Greely (2008) argues, these companies are not necessarily dishonest; they just are not completely honest about the limitations of the science and therefore likely mislead consumers.

Several types of tests are used to trace genetic ancestry. The first tests either an individual's mitochondrial DNA (mtDNA), part of our DNA that is passed down from our mother's side, or a Y chromosome, which can obviously only be done on males; both mtDNA and the Y chromosome remain relatively unchanged from one generation to the next (unlike the rest of our DNA). Although mtDNA and Y chromosome tests can certainly provide links to our genetic past, drawing conclusions about race based upon them is problematic. Investigating the genetic ancestry of individuals cannot help us to understand racial identity in the present day. Race is a socially created category distinguished by certain physical features, such as skin color, hair texture, and facial features. However, these parts of our DNA have no influence on our appearance. Another problem is that these tests analyze one of literally thousands of our ancestral lines; thus, what they can tell us about our ancestry is quite limited.

Another type of genetic ancestry test emerged from forensic research in the mid-1990s. At that time, forensic researchers claimed they had developed a test that could distinguish between "Caucasian" and "Afro-Caribbean" in nearly 85 percent of cases (Carter 2007). This test compares a sample of DNA—specifically, single nucleotide polymorphisms—with DNA samples from West Europeans, West Africans, East Asians, and indigenous Americans to see if they match ancestry information markers (AIMs) from those populations. The results of these DNA searches have been interpreted as a measure of racial makeup (results claim that someone is 48 percent African, for instance). However, assessing the probability that someone belongs to a particular continental group is not the same as discovering one's racial ancestry and, by extension, one's current racial makeup.

Another factor that these tests attempt to account for is human migration patterns, which have occurred over millennia. Over time, certain genetic mutations appear as evolutionary responses to the environment, such as melanin concentrations in people adapting to sunny climates or the presence of sickle cell gene as an antimalarial mutation (Williams 2005). This is referred to as **genome geography**, in which portions of a genetic sequence are associated with specific geographic locations (Fujimura and Rajagopalan 2011). To shift discussions of population geography to race is to make a giant leap; geography and race do not always correspond, as anyone who has ever traveled knows, and ancestry and race are not the same thing. In fact, it would be more accurate to conclude that we are all African because all humans originate from East Africa (Williams 2005).

While all of these tests have the appearance of scientific objectivity, their findings can be ambiguous and are often inaccurate. People who know of their African ancestry, for instance, have found these tests to reveal no African genetic ancestry. Approximately half of participants who expect to find Native American roots instead find no supporting genetic evidence (Broyard 2007). While some scientists might argue that errors in traditional genealogical research are to blame for these discrepancies, the high margin of error also points to the limitations of genetic genealogy, making it "feel more like a parlor game" than hard science (Broyard 2007:473).

Genetic ancestry testing is being marketed directly to certain racial/ethnic minority group members, particularly African Americans, Jews, and Native Americans. Some have found DNA ancestry testing to be much more common among African Americans, primarily due to the limitations placed upon them in pursuing traditional genealogical research due to the slave trade and the erasure of much of African culture in America (Duster 2011; Greely 2008; Nelson 2008). For instance, the company African Ancestry claims to help people find out where in Africa their ancestors came from.

Other companies, such as Gene Tree and Family Tree DNA, claim to offer genetic ancestry testing specifically for so-called Native American DNA markers (Tallbear 2008). Many people who believe they have Native American ancestry are unable to provide adequate evidence of this to gain tribal membership (Fitzgerald 2007). Thus, however flawed the science, genetic ancestry testing holds some appeal to people who have no other way to prove their Native American ancestry (Tallbear 2008). Massachusetts Senator Elizabeth Warren caused quite a stir when she claimed to be Native American. As a white woman unconnected to a specific tribe and Native American culture, some encouraged her to take a DNA test to "prove" her Native American ancestry. However, even companies offering these tests replied that such test results should be treated with caution, as "genetic testing cannot provide complete information about one's ancestors … and scientists currently have limited information about the genetic signatures of Native Americans" (Begley 2016). This is because many Native American tribes have resisted being involved in data collection for DNA databases for a number of reasons, including fear of exploitation, but also because the results challenge their tribal origin stories (Bliss 2012).

The idea that simply taking a DNA test would prove one is Native American is not something that sits well with all Native American tribes as tribal membership is complex, varies considerably among the 562 federally recognized tribes, and it is more than biological and cannot be reduced to a genetic test. Tribal membership is about culture, ancestry, relations, and the land. However, some tribes have embraced using genetic ancestry testing for determining tribal membership. The Meskwaki tribe, for instance, has a profitable casino, and once they started sharing profits with tribal members in 1994, they were flooded with tribal membership applications. They decided to require results from a sixteen-factor DNA paternity test to determine membership (Kaplan 2005).

Many Jewish people have also embraced this technology because genetic testing can provide clues about a person's origins and ancestral migrations, and some AIMs indicating migration patterns have been discovered. One company offers to test for Jewish ancestry, specifically offering the Cohanim chromosome test (Greely 2008). Jewish ancestry has been the most consistently identifiable in terms of allele frequencies because Jews, both through choice and coercion, have experienced relatively isolated reproduction and have been more endogamous than most human groups and, thus, tend to share more genetic similarities. One of the most consistent Jewish DNA markers has been the Cohanim chromosome. However, some scientists challenge the accuracy of this interpretation because even with the consistencies in allele frequencies that scientists find among Jews, as Lewontin (2012) points out, none of the genetic elements found are characteristic of all or even a large majority of Jews.

Another body of research has emerged from sociologists interested in genetic ancestry testing—this research questions the impact such tests may have on a consumer's racial/ethnic identity (Fitzgerald 2014b; Roth and Ivemark 2018). Research finds that consumers do not merely accept the results of genetic ancestry tests as given and they do not privilege these accounts because they have a scientific "halo of legitimacy" (Duster 2003; Roth and Ivemark 2018). Instead, consumers choose which aspects of the results to embrace and which to disregard, based on their own identity preferences and whether or not others are likely to accept their identity claims, something Roth and Ivemark (2018) refer to as **genetic options theory**.

Sociologist Alondra Nelson (2016) studied African Americans who engaged in genetic ancestry testing and found that they were using the test results in surprising ways. Broadly speaking, she found that instead of focusing exclusively on one's personal ancestry, many African Americans used the tests as a tool for healing and racial reconciliation, "to restore lineages, families, and knowledge of the past and to make political claims in the present" and to repair "the social ruptures produced by transatlantic slavery" (2016:6, 9).

REFLECT AND CONNECT

Has anyone in your family ever done genetic ancestry testing? If so, what motivated them to do it? What were the results? How does the information you learned in this chapter challenge what you thought you knew about your racial ancestry, if at all?

THE SOCIOLOGY OF RACE

By the early 1930s, scientific racism was fading in popularity, particularly among social scientists. Anthropologists Franz Boas, Ruth Benedict, and Ashley Montagu critiqued the notion of racial purity and racism. African American scholars such as W. E. B. Du Bois were the first to argue that race was a social construction, while white sociologists of the Chicago School, such as Robert Ezra Park, popularized that idea (Morris 2015). Chicago School social scientists challenged biological notions of race and thus defied the dominant scientific paradigm on race, while they simultaneously reified problematic notions of black cultural inferiority (Steinberg 2007). Once the horrors of the Nazi regime were uncovered in the post–World War II era, the nail appeared to be securely in scientific racism's coffin.

WITNESS

"Du Bois's sociological arguments stressing that races were socially constructed and blacks were not biologically inferior flew in the face of white racial beliefs. … White social scientists concurred with the general white consensus that blacks were created inferior and incapable of functioning as social equals of whites" (Morris 2015:3).

When sociologists discuss research into the educational attainment of Native Americans, or the socioeconomic status of Asian Americans, or wealth disparities between whites and blacks, for instance, we are not making claims about all Native American, Asian American, white, or black people. Sociologists focus on patterns rather than rarities, but there will always be deviations from the norm. For example, you will likely think of contrasting examples for almost any statistic presented in this text; however, keep in mind that exceptions to the norm do not negate overall patterns. For example, in Chapter 8 we explore how economic inequality is racialized; in other words, wealth and poverty are patterned along racial lines. This does not mean that all people of color are poor or all white people are wealthy. It does mean that wealth is disproportionately held in the hands of whites and poverty disproportionately affects racial/ethnic minorities.

Sociologists represent a diverse group of academics, all of whom are interested in the role of social structure and how it influences individuals. The discipline as a whole has been traditionally composed of three theoretical perspectives, each with very different assumptions and explanations for aspects of the social world. The first perspective is referred to as the **functionalist perspective** and emphasizes social order over conflict: the value of consensus, harmony, and stability for a society, and the interdependence of social systems. Thus, from a functionalist perspective, diversity along racial/ethnic lines is potentially problematic because it often results in social conflict, which they believe societies should try to reduce. The functionalist perspective on race/ethnic relations will be discussed in more detail in Chapter 5.

The second theoretical perspective is conflict theory. The **conflict perspective** emerges out of Marxist thought and emphasizes conflict between dominant and subordinate groups over scarce and valued resources in a society. A conflict analysis of race relations is understood in terms of the competition between the dominant, privileged racial group—whites—and the less-privileged, subordinate racial groups, such as African Americans, Native Americans, Latinos, and Asian Americans. From a conflict theorist's perspective, societal conflict is not always a bad thing because it can lead to necessary social change. The civil rights movement, for instance, caused great social upheaval, yet in the long run it benefited racial/ethnic minority groups and society as a whole through the passage of legislation that expanded civil and political rights to include African Americans (see Chapter 6).

Sociologist Robert Ezra Park and the Chicago School took a functionalist approach to the study of race and ethnicity, specifically focusing on "race relations." The nomenclature of *race relations* became the dominant language within the discipline for discussing racial issues for decades, from the 1920s through the 1960s. Sociologist Stephen Steinberg (2007), who adheres to the conflict perspective, argues that such language is problematic because it obscures the reality of race in the United States, a reality better captured by the conflict theory language of *racial oppression*. The language of *race relations* implies an innate hostility between groups due to their differences, whereas *racial oppression* implies that racism is embedded in the structure of society (Steinberg 2007). Because *race relations* was the dominant paradigm at the time, mainstream sociologists failed to anticipate the civil rights revolutions of the post–World War II era (Hughes 1963).

The third theoretical perspective, **symbolic interactionism**, argues that we can understand society and social structures through a focus on small-scale human interactions, the use of symbols in interaction, and the meanings we assign to symbols. According to symbolic interactionists, social structures are reproduced and maintained through interactions. For instance, during the era of Jim Crow, the post–Civil War and post-Reconstruction era of legal segregation and subordination of blacks throughout the South, whites routinely referred to black men of all ages as "boy." This interactional pattern was far from meaningless. It reinforced and reproduced a social order that emphasized the inferiority of all blacks to all whites. Even age did not grant black men and women authority. If a 16-year-old white girl referred to an 83-year-old black man as "boy," she was, consciously or not, emphasizing his status as subordinate to her. Some of the most significant research emerging out of the symbolic interactionist tradition focuses on racial/ethnic identity formation and the emergence of biracial and multiracial identities in the post–civil rights era (see Chapter 12).

Exploring Social Inequality

As an academic discipline, sociology emerged partially as a response to the dramatic social changes brought about by the Industrial Revolution. Karl Marx, one of the founders of the discipline, observed how industrial capitalism resulted in new forms of social inequality and exploitation. Marx focused on class inequalities that resulted from small groups of people controlling the productive resources of a society while other, much larger, groups had only their labor to offer, placing them at a distinct disadvantage.

Max Weber, another founder of the discipline, expanded the sociological analysis of class inequalities by focusing more broadly on **status inequalities**—differences in prestige and honor—which are not necessarily related to one's economic status. Research on inequalities along the lines of race, ethnicity, gender, sexuality, and age emerge out of Weber's notion of status inequalities.

Despite these foundations for study, during the second half of the nineteenth century and the first half of the twentieth century, white American sociologists were overwhelmingly silent on the subject of race. At a time when Jim Crow segregation was the law of the land throughout the South, when African Americans could not vote and were denied access to even their most basic civil rights, sociologists were relatively silent on the subject of race. Around the same time, the Chinese Exclusion Act was passed by Congress; eugenics influenced scientific research; white supremacist groups, such as the Ku Klux Klan, wielded local power and terrorized blacks to keep them "in their place"; and incidents of lynching were at an all-time high. Why were mainstream sociologists silent on these important issues?

W. E. B. Du Bois and E. Franklin Frazier

Sociologists of color were the first to question what some have referred to as an academic conspiracy of silence on the subject of race. Most sociologists during the late 1800s and early 1900s were white males and so were not interested in issues of race and gender inequality. At the forefront of the effort to open the eyes of white America to issues of oppression were African American sociologists W. E. B. Du Bois (1868–1963) and E. Franklin Frazier (1894–1962). Although both were marginalized from the mainstream of sociology because of their race, Du Bois and Frazier managed to make important contributions to the field of sociology and, more specifically, the study of race.

Du Bois earned a PhD from Harvard, wrote over twenty books and thousands of essays and articles over the course of his life, and helped to establish the discipline of sociology in the United States when it was still in its infancy; yet he was virtually ignored by the discipline (see Box 3.1 Racial Justice Activism: The Activism of

BOX 3.1

Racial Justice Activism:
The Activism of W. E. B. Du Bois

In addition to contributing to the academic field of sociology, Du Bois was also an activist for racial justice. In 1905, he co-founded the Niagara Movement, the first civil rights organization in the United States to call for an end to racial segregation, disenfranchisement, and oppression. In 1909, this organization became the National Association for the Advancement of Colored People (NAACP), which is still considered the nation's most prominent civil rights organization.

Du Bois was an activist in the anti-lynching movement in the United States and an outspoken critic of eugenics, and he was engaged in the Pan-African Movement, which sought to unite the global African community through efforts against colonialism. Du Bois viewed racism as essentially a problem of ignorance. Because he believed that education alone could not eliminate racism, his objective was to "educate and agitate."

Using his scholarship, Du Bois exposed the oppressive conditions under which black Americans lived in the hope that white Americans would recognize the wrongs of racism. His scholarship did not have the effect on white America that he had hoped, and in 1903 he published *The Souls of Black Folk*, an emotional appeal to white Americans to recognize their shared humanity with black Americans through the Christian metaphor of the "soul" (Gibson 1989).

His much later work *Black Reconstruction, 1860–1880* (1935) documented the significant and historically overlooked roles of blacks during the Civil War and Reconstruction. Documenting this history was crucial, as the white South, despite losing the war, quickly emerged as victorious in establishing the dominant narrative surrounding the Civil War and Reconstruction: that it was a war of northern aggression, that southerners were fighting for states' rights rather than to maintain slavery, and that Reconstruction was a failure of black leadership, marred by corruption.

Du Bois died in 1963, just prior to the passage of one of the most important victories associated with the civil rights movement, the 1964 Civil Rights Act, for which his lifetime of work laid the foundation.

IMAGE 3.3: Sociologist W. E. B. Du Bois, author of over twenty books and thousands of essays and articles dealing with race and racism during the Jim Crow era. Du Bois was virtually ignored by the discipline of sociology during his lifetime.

IMAGE 3.4: Sociologist E. Franklin Frazier. (Reprinted with permission of the American Sociological Association, www.asanet.org).

W. E. B. Du Bois). He did not gain the credit he deserved during his lifetime, and his work remained marginalized from the sociological **canon**, the body of knowledge considered fundamental to an academic discipline, until recently. His work *The Philadelphia Negro* (1899) provided the first empirical study on black life and racial dynamics in the United States that was not marred by the racial stereotypes of the era. Morris (2015) argues that Du Bois is actually the founding father of American sociology, yet because he built a sociological school that challenged popular ideas, such as scientific racism, and instead emphasized that social conditions contribute to racial inequality, his work went unrecognized by white, mainstream sociology. While Du Bois is currently receiving long overdue recognition for his contributions to the discipline, during his lifetime, he was not considered to be a significant figure in the discipline simply due to racism. Du Bois was black and he studied black America—a subject the majority of sociologists did not consider worthwhile at the time.

Frazier (1947) was one of the first to argue that the scientific practice of white American sociologists was based on the assumption that blacks were an inferior race. In 1927, he published an article equating racial prejudice with insanity. The article so disturbed white readers that he was forced to resign from his position at Atlanta University. From there he went to Chicago, where he earned his PhD in sociology at the University of Chicago.

Unlike Du Bois, Frazier garnered attention in the field of sociology during his lifetime. Frazier's most significant sociological works include *The Negro Family in the United States* (1939) and *Black Bourgeoisie* (1957). Frazier was an African American sociologist studying black life. His success relative to Du Bois's more than likely stems from the fact he was younger than Du Bois and entered the discipline several decades after him. Another reason for the greater marginalization experienced by Du Bois could pertain to his activism (see Box 3.1 Racial Justice Activism: The Activism of W. E. B. Du Bois): activism challenges scientific claims of objectivity and is frowned upon in the scientific community. Despite the controversy that his work inspired among white sociologists, Frazier became the first African American to preside over a national academic organization as president of the American Sociological Society.

Both Du Bois and Frazier were the subjects of multiple investigations by the FBI for being communists. These accusations were never substantiated in Frazier's case. Du Bois, on the other hand, openly admitted to being a socialist and, at the age of 93, joined the Communist Party (Keen 1999).

WITNESS

In FBI documents, the following arguments were used to justify the investigation of any connection Du Bois might have had to communism: "He constantly writes of racial discrimination and how his race is oppressed, especially in the south. ... Further, he believes there should be social equality between all people, regardless of color" (https://vault. fbi.gov/E.%20B.%20(William)%20Dubois).

Ethnicity Paradigm

Relative to sociological research on ethnicity, sociological research on race throughout the first half of the twentieth century was rare. Some of the most significant research in the sociology of ethnicity includes, but is not limited to, the experiences of white ethnic immigrants, the lingering presence of ethnicity for white ethnics, ethnic conflict, ethnic stratification, ethnic identity, and the political implications of ethnicity (see Chapter 2). Generally speaking, when attention has been paid to the experiences of racial minorities, they have been awkwardly packaged within this ethnicity paradigm.

Race and ethnicity are distinct if overlapping concepts, and theories of ethnicity do not translate well to the experiences of racial minorities. For example, most white ethnics in the United States have not had the experiences of slavery, colonization, or attempted genocide, as have many racial minorities. Some sociologists have acknowledged a push within the discipline to substitute the term *ethnicity* for *race*, as the latter carries with it the negative associations of racism (Sollors 1996). But the word *ethnicity* has not become a substitute for the word *race*, either in the discipline of sociology or in popular culture.

The Chicago School

Sociologists associated with the Chicago School, between 1915 and 1935, used the city of Chicago as their "lab" and produced studies of white European ethnic immigrants that remain influential to the study of ethnicity. W. I. Thomas and Florian Znaniecki researched Polish immigrants for their study *The Polish Peasant in Europe and America* (1918–1920). This work has been described as the most descriptive account of immigrant society and the effects of immigration and industrialization on immigrant families and communities ever documented.

While the Chicago School focused on white ethnics and extended their assimilationist paradigm to racial minorities, its sociologists were ahead of many scientists of the era who focused on the biological basis of race. According to Robert Ezra Park and his colleagues, race was not biological but instead socially created. Park promoted what was known as the **ethnicity paradigm**, which viewed race as part of ethnicity—but as a less important factor in people's lives than ethnicity—and equated ethnicity with culture. According to Park, the determinants of ethnicity involved race, religion, nationality, and language. This perspective shifted understandings of race from a biological to a social phenomenon, and so was considered progressive for its time.

Park's ethnicity paradigm is linked closely to the assimilationist paradigm: the idea that ethnic minorities should eventually give up their ties to their home countries and become part of the dominant, Anglo-American culture of the United States. From a functionalist perspective, the assimilation of immigrants is desirable because it decreases differences between groups and so also decreases the potential for group conflict. Members of the Chicago School argued that it was necessary for immigrants to retain ties to their old country initially because "a premature severing of his [sic] ties to the past left the immigrant in a demoralized condition" (Persons 1987:53–54). After this necessary transitional phase, immigrants were expected to assimilate into the dominant culture. From here emerges the ideology of the **melting pot**, the idea that diverse streams of immigrants come to America and eventually merge into another distinct group, that of the "American."

Park proposed four stages of assimilation: contact, conflict, accommodation, and assimilation. Contact occurs when diverse ethnic groups meet and live together, as they do in communities across the country. In these communities, groups compete (conflict) with one another for such things as jobs and housing. The accommodation stage describes the period during which immigrants are expected to change and adapt to the dominant American culture. Park acknowledged that the accommodation stage could result in a subordinate status for immigrants, an outcome also known as **ethnic stratification**. However, Park believed that ethnic groups would eventually reach the final stage and assimilate, or merge, with the dominant, Anglo-American culture.

E. Franklin Frazier, one of Park's doctoral students at the University of Chicago, believed the paradigm to be flawed in terms of its application to the experiences of racial minorities. He pointed out that the model of ethnic assimilation did not adequately reflect the diverse range of experiences of racial minorities in the United States. For example, blacks at that time were still not assimilated into the dominant, Anglo-American culture. The same argument holds true today for other groups defined as racial minorities, such as Native Americans, Asian Americans, and Latinos. One of the weaknesses of the ethnicity paradigm was Park's attempts to apply it to racial and ethnic minorities. When racial minority groups failed to assimilate, Park viewed it as a cultural deficiency on their part, rather than as a reflection of the different experiences and opportunities to assimilate among racial and ethnic minority groups. Frazier believed that it was not possible to treat all contact between dominant and subordinate groups as the same, as the assimilationist paradigm does. While he promoted the assimilation of blacks into the dominant culture, he felt their path was ultimately more difficult due to exclusion by white society. Frazier's critique emphasizes the limitations on a subordinate group's ability to assimilate in the face of opposition by the dominant group.

Beyond Frazier's critique that vastly different experiences separated white ethnics from racial minorities in the United States, many questioned the assumption that all immigrants and racial minorities should be expected to assimilate into the dominant culture. Some criticized assimilation as mere Anglo-conformity. **Anglo-conformity** means that instead of becoming a melting pot, in which all groups come together and forge a new identity, all groups coming to the United States are expected to drop their cultural identities in favor of an Anglo-American culture. Others criticized this assimilationist paradigm for ignoring the possibility of **cultural pluralism**, the idea that numerous ethnicities are capable of coexisting without threatening the dominant culture.

First introduced by Horace Kallen, cultural pluralism was initially perceived as radically anti-assimilationist (Whitfield 1997). Although Kallen's idea of cultural pluralism challenged assimilationism, it too failed to address the diverse experiences of racial minorities. For example, as slaves, African Americans were once forcibly stripped of their cultures. Native Americans experienced a similar attempted cultural genocide at the hands of white Americans. Neither group was in a position to voluntarily maintain many of their native cultures and traditions. Cultural pluralism tended to favor relatively privileged people, people in a position to choose which cultures they embrace, a decision that sometimes means challenging the dominant group. Social scientists continue to debate the relative values of cultural pluralism and assimilation. In the United States, the assimilationist perspective took hold as the prominent ideology and remains influential to this day.

REFLECT AND CONNECT

If you have ancestors who immigrated to the United States or you are an immigrant yourself, can you identify any pressures to assimilate that the immigrant generation faced or faces? To what extent have you or your family members embraced cultural pluralism, if at all? Provide evidence.

Power, Conflict, and Stratification Theories

Assimilationist theories emerged out of the functionalist perspective on race relations. However, another theoretical perspective factors into the traditional sociological discussion of race: conflict theory. Conflict theorists have offered a number of explanations for racial/ethnic inequality, specifically Marxist theory, the split labor market theory, and theory of internal colonialism.

Marxist theorists generally view the world as stratified along class lines. When Marxists look at racial inequality, they see it as an extension of capitalist exploitation. They view capitalists as benefiting from racial inequality as well as class inequality. African American Marxist sociologist Oliver Cromwell Cox (1948) argues that slavery was first and foremost a capitalistic enterprise. Ideologies of black inferiority were introduced after slavery was instituted, thus serving to justify this form of capitalist exploitation. He emphasizes that racial exploitation and racial prejudice emerged in conjunction with the rise of capitalism; thus, in his view, racial inequality is an extension of class inequality. According to Marxist theory, workers are most powerful when they are united. Therefore, many Marxists perceive racism as a means of dividing the working class along racial lines to the advantage of business owners and corporations who seek to exploit them.

Another influential conflict perspective on racial inequality is the **split labor market theory** (Bonacich 1972, 1975, 1976), which emphasizes the ways both race and class contribute to inequality. Whereas Marxists focus on the division between workers and owners, split labor market theorists believe workers can be divided into two classes: higher-paid workers and lower-paid workers. These groups are often divided along racial/ethnic lines as well. Members of certain racial/ethnic groups find themselves confined to certain jobs and exempt from other generally higher-paying jobs, thus splitting the labor market. Split labor market theorists disagree with Marxists on the issue of who benefits from this type of market. Whereas Marxists emphasize how racial inequality in the labor market benefits capitalists, split labor market theorists argue that in many cases capitalists are not the beneficiaries of this system. Instead, this system is maintained by the higher-paid labor group, which works to maintain its privileges in the labor market. Under this model, higher-paid, white workers enforce discriminatory practices in the labor market so as to maintain their privilege.

Internal colonialism theory (Blauner 1969, 1972) argues that colonialism, which is the process through which one country dominates another by stripping it of its human and economic resources, can actually take place within one country. In other words, dominant racial groups establish a system of oppression and exploitation of subordinate racial groups within their own nation in ways that benefit them. According to this perspective, African Americans, Native Americans, and Mexican Americans were subordinated by white Americans for economic gain—African Americans were used for free labor during slavery, Native Americans were exploited for their land, and Mexican Americans were exploited for both their land and their labor (Farley 2005).

The exploitation of African Americans, Native Americans, and Mexican Americans differs from that of white ethnic immigrants, such as Irish Americans, Jewish Americans, and German Americans. Sociologist Robert Blauner (1969, 1972) distinguishes between **immigrant minorities**, also known as voluntary minorities, members of subordinate groups who willingly choose to immigrate to a country, and **colonized minorities**, also known as involuntary minorities, members of groups that are forced to participate in another society. In the United States, African Americans, Native Americans, and Mexican Americans, historically at least, fell into the category of involuntary, or colonized, minorities. Involuntary minorities face assaults on their cultural traditions, struggle with limited housing options (including being segregated and forced into ghettos), and are the targets of racist stereotypes and ideologies. Their situation differs from that of, for example, Irish and German immigrants, who as voluntary minorities faced a lesser degree of discrimination, oppression, and marginalization.

Although Blauner did not directly consider Asian Americans, they tend to fall somewhere between immigrant minorities and colonized minorities because not all Asian Americans found themselves in the United States voluntarily (Farley 2005). Many Chinese, for instance, came to the United States as indentured laborers. The early immigration of Filipinos occurred while their country was a US colony, which would make their situation similar to that of Native Americans. In the 1970s, Vietnamese immigrants came here as refugees of the Vietnam War (Farley 2005).

REFLECT AND CONNECT

Are you descended from people who are or were considered to be immigrant minorities or colonized minorities, or both? If you know enough about your family's history in the United States, describe the extent to which their experiences fit Blauner's theory of internal colonialism. If you are an immigrant, do any of your experiences fit with Blauner's theory of internal colonialism?

CURRENT RESEARCH INTO THE SOCIOLOGY OF RACE

In the field of sociology, race relations is largely understood as a conflict between whites, the dominant racial group, and people of color, the various subordinate racial groups. Therefore, much of the current sociological research exploring race, racism, and race privilege is in the conflict tradition, in addition to the contributions sociologists have made to our understanding of how racism works. Racism does not merely consist of discriminatory actions or interactions between individuals. In fact, most often racism is systemic and institutionalized. Current studies of race avoid focusing exclusively on conflict between groups and instead often seek to understand the emergence of new racial identities, particularly biracial and multiracial identities, the process by which race is institutionalized, and how racial ideologies emerge from these institutions, justifying racism as the status quo. The latest research on race privilege was presented in the previous chapter.

Symbolic Interactionism on Racial/Ethnic Identity

Symbolic interactionists who study race are concerned primarily with issues of racial/ethnic identity. Ethnic identity research emerged in the early 1900s in the Chicago School. Even more current researchers focused on white ethnics and excluded racial/ethnic minorities (e.g., Alba 1990; Waters 1990). More recently, however, symbolic interactionists have begun studying biracial and multiracial identities, as well as racial identity development (Korgen 1998; Rockquemore and Brunsma 2002). While there is nothing new about the existence of biracial/multiracial *people*, the embrace of biracial/multiracial *identities* is a relatively recent development. Because symbolic interactionists hold strong to the sociological tenet that context matters, many have become increasingly interested in the emergence of new racial/ethnic identities in the post–civil rights era.

Racial Formation Perspective

The racial formation perspective argues that we live in a postcolonial, post–civil rights, color-blind era whose circumstances challenge earlier class-based theories and the ethnicity paradigm. In the current era, racial classification persists, despite claims of color-blindness and official commitments to racial equality and multiculturalism. In their book *Racial Formation in the United States: From the 1960s to the 1990s*, sociologists Michael Omi and Howard Winant (1994) shift the discussion away from the ethnicity paradigm and its assimilationist focus to what they call **racial formations**, the ways racial categories are created, inhabited, transformed, and destroyed over time. In doing so, they attempt to link the "macro" with the "micro" by examining the ways race plays out structurally and in our everyday lived experiences. It is through racial formations that race becomes "common sense," a way of making sense of our world.

A current example of racial formation involves the changing understanding of race and place surrounding the immigration of Latinos into the southern United States, particularly into small towns and rural areas. The understanding of race in the southern United States has historically been a simple black–white binary, despite increasing racial diversity throughout the rest of the country. However, the dramatic increase in Latino immigration into southern communities has resulted in new questions about race, place, and belonging, and asks how Latino immigration challenges the traditional southern black–white racial stratification system (Massey 2008; Smith and Furuseth 2006; Winders 2005).

Racialized Social Systems Theory

Sociologist Eduardo Bonilla-Silva (1997) introduced the **racialized social systems** perspective as a way to move sociology away from a focus on prejudice, social psychology, and the notion that racism amounted to a set of ideas, and toward a more structural understanding of racism. The racialized social system perspective refers to the ways all aspects of a society, from the economy to politics and ideologies, are structured by the placement of individuals in racial categories. These categories are not simply different: they are hierarchical, and thus they inform social relations between the groups. The race in the superordinate position is granted higher esteem in society; thus, its members are awarded privileges in the economic and political systems, among other benefits.

White Racial Frame

Sociologist Joe Feagin (2010) has introduced one of the latest sociological perspectives on race/ethnicity, referred to as the **white racial frame** (see Box 3.2 Race in the Workplace: Sociologist Joe R. Feagin's Research on Race, Racism, and Privilege). He describes the white racial frame as a worldview that includes racial beliefs, racially loaded terms, racialized images, verbal connotations, and racialized emotions and interpretations, as well as discriminatory actions that help justify ongoing racism. Frames help us make sense of our world by structuring our thinking and influencing what we see, or fail to see, in our daily lives. Feagin argues that a new perspective for

---

BOX 3.2

Race in the Workplace:
Sociologist Joe R. Feagin's Research on Race, Racism, and Privilege

Although race was not a topic most white sociologists considered worthy of examination during the early decades of the discipline, there has been a dramatic shift in attention to race issues since the civil rights movement. Sociologist Joe R. Feagin is one of the most prolific race scholars today, authoring or coauthoring over sixty books and hundreds of articles.

Feagin's current research sheds light on the systemic nature of US racism, the ways racism manifests in the political sphere, and he offers us a new theoretical perspective for understanding the persistence of racism in the US: the white racial frame. His current work also explores the racialization of Latinos, the racism faced by Asian Americans, white racism, how children learn racism, and the many costs of racism to us all.

While the bulk of his work has challenged the discipline of sociology to address race, racism, and privilege as valid sociological topics, his coauthored book *Liberation Sociology* (with Hernan Vera in 2008) challenges the discipline in terms of its commitment to scientific objectivity. The authors argue that the goal of sociology should be to help eliminate oppression and create a more egalitarian society. They define the objective of **liberation sociology** as "not just to research the world but to change it in the direction of democracy and social justice" (2008:1). They argue that the sociological canon is replete with examples of liberation sociology, despite the fact that the modern-day discipline has distanced itself from this tradition.

understanding racism and racial inequality is needed to address the systemic nature of racism in the United States. Feagin (2012) defines **systemic racism** as the deeply rooted, institutionalized racial oppression of people of color by whites. Whiteness is deeply entrenched in US society, and indeed across the globe, and it is resistant to change because the white racial frame operates, historically and currently, through all major social institutions to justify and rationalize white privilege and power. He argues that it is essential to understand US racism as more than mere prejudices and stereotypes.

Feagin (2013) also argues that both collective memory and collective forgetting are essential for the reproduction of the white racial frame. We understand our racialized present through our knowledge of our racialized past; our collective memory legitimates the racial present. Collective forgetting, what we as a culture ignore or suppress about our past, is also essential to the perpetuation of the white racial frame. Contested meanings surrounding the Confederate flag in the southern United States can best be understood through this lens. For many African Americans, the "stars and bars" is a symbol of a brutal era, slavery, and the war to maintain it. While ultimately successful, black students at the University of Mississippi had to fight for decades to have the Confederate flag removed from official campus events (see Chapter 11).

Many white southerners maintain that the Confederate flag is a symbol of their southern heritage, not a symbol of slavery or racism, and thus should be a source of pride. Approximately half of white southerners today descend from Confederate soldiers. The contributions of their family members to the Civil War, a war in which 25 percent of southern men of military age died, are a significant part of their family lore (Horwitz 1998).

Southern whites and blacks hold significantly different collective memories of the past and the present, and this is reflected in their interpretations of the Confederate flag. These are not equally valued collective memories, however, because whites hold more power in American society. The collective memories of major historical events, such as the Civil War, that are most likely to be reflected in history textbooks, films, and public monuments are memories that are more likely to emerge from white racial understandings of the world (Feagin 2010).

REFLECT AND CONNECT

In what way is the US legal system an expression of systemic racism? Specifically consider the potential dilemmas surrounding the fact that we still live under a Constitution that disproportionately reflects the influence of slaveholders, for instance (Feagin 2012).

Critical Race Theory

The most significant interdisciplinary development in racial theorizing is known as **critical race theory** (CRT) (see Box 3.3 Global Perspectives: Global Critical Race Feminism). CRT argues that ideologies of assimilation and color-blindness actually help perpetuate white dominance rather than eliminate it. The group of theorists who created CRT, Derrick Bell, Allen Freeman, and Richard Delgado, began with the assumption that American society was anything but race neutral; in fact, they argued that racism was an ordinary aspect of our society. This theory emerges out of critical legal studies and has had considerable impact on the fields of education and policy studies. CRT takes on particular significance when applied to the legal arena, where laws are assumed to be fair, universal, and not biased toward or against any particular group. CRT challenges the presumed racial neutrality of law and argues that there is very little incentive to eradicate racism, as so many people benefit from race privilege and the racial hierarchy (Delgado and Stefancic 2001).

CRT embraces an activist agenda rather than a commitment to objectivity, which means that it is more than a theoretical perspective, it is also a method. Central to CRT is the concept of narrative and storytelling as a method of knowledge production and an emphasis on counterstories. **Counterstories** are told by people of color (or members of nondominant groups) to reflect their view of the world from their particular social location. Counterstories challenge the dominant narratives relayed through history textbooks, Sunday sermons, mass media, and legal decisions and are designed to help dominant-group members understand the world from the standpoint of subordinate groups (Delgado and Stefancic 2001). Thus, narratives by members of nondominant groups are powerful tools for both subordinate groups and the dominant group. Some argue that the dominant group uses stories to justify and perpetuate their privilege; thus, stories are powerful tools for challenging privilege as well.

Native American author Vine Deloria Jr. offers an example of a counterstory that addresses the ongoing anthropological study of Native peoples: "The massive volume of useless knowledge produced by anthropologists attempting to capture real Indians in a network of theories has contributed substantially to the invisibility of Indian people today" (1988:81). In other words, white America sees Native Americans as (often white) anthropologists have portrayed them, rather than as Native Americans see themselves. Deloria's critique may seem a bit harsh, as anthropologists, like all scientists, also offer useful knowledge. The significance of his counterstory, however, is the perspective it gives—that of a Native activist and author who believes that anthropologists have helped to silence indigenous peoples in favor of the academic voice of anthropology.

CRT is also interested in understanding the narratives of the dominant group, at least insofar as these narratives can contribute to a greater understanding of racial inequality. For example, these narratives are often used to persuade juries to accept the perspective of a member of a dominant group, as happens in cases charging police brutality. In the shooting of Tamir Rice as he played with a toy gun in a park in Cleveland, Ohio, police aggression was justified by the argument that the 12-year-old victim was seen as a threat, thereby justifying police aggression (so the dominant narrative goes); and in the case of Trayvon Martin, the unarmed 17-year-old African American who was shot to death by a volunteer neighborhood watchman on February 26, 2012. The police did not arrest the shooter until public outcry forced the district attorney to issue an arrest warrant. CRT theorists would argue that by understanding these narratives as such, we are less likely to accept them as truth.

Another significant contribution of CRT is **intersectionality**, which focuses on the interactions between different systems of oppression (Crenshaw 1989). All individuals hold positions in multiple status hierarchies (such as gender, race, class, sexuality, nationality, and age). These categories of difference are also complex and sometimes contradictory axes of identity. We can experience oppression due to our membership in certain status categories (being female in a patriarchy, for instance) while simultaneously being privileged by another status hierarchy (being white in a racist country, for instance).

Intersectionality does not portray social inequalities and status hierarchies as separate and discrete phenomena. Rather, it is relational in that race, gender, sexuality, and other dimensions of status hierarchies "are always considered *in relation to one another*, not simply parallel but always intertwined" (Grzanka 2014:xv; italics in the original). Intersectionality recognizes that the systemic and structural inequalities stemming from these status hierarchies—racism, sexism, homophobia, and so on—are oppressions that do not operate independently of one another; instead, they intersect and influence one another, often creating new and distinct forms of oppression (Dill et al. 2001). Intersectionality can best be envisioned in the following way: "If we imagine racism and sexism metaphorically in space, they'd look more like a double helix than two lanes on a highway" (Grzanka 2014). Currently there is an epidemic of violence directed at gay and transgender people of color; 2015 was the most violent year on record, with twenty-two transwomen of color murdered. By June 1, 2016, thirteen transgender women had been murdered that year, eleven of whom were black or Latina. When gay or transgender people of color experience violence, it is about more than homophobia; it is about racialized homophobia (and for lesbians and transwomen, it is gendered as well) (Fitzgerald 2017). The significance of intersectionality is explored throughout this book, but Chapter 8 provides one example in its exploration of population policies and reproductive rights. All women have not been treated equally when it comes to the state and reproductive rights. The regulation of the reproductive lives of women of color has been a key aspect of racial oppression throughout American history (Davis 1983; Roberts 1997).

Initially, CRT was ignored by academics. When it was acknowledged, it was deemed too radical. Despite this challenge, the critical race movement is thriving. Critical legal studies is now taught in law schools across the country, with its approach expanding to critical race feminism, global critical race feminism, critical white studies, Latino critical thought, Asian critical thought, and queer critical theorizing (see Box 3.3 Global Perspectives: Global Critical Race Feminism).

CRT has been used to study Asian American experiences in educational institutions and in education discourse, for instance. The Asian American experience is unique in that they are perceived to be the **model minority**, a minority group that has succeeded in American society, specifically evidenced by their success in educational institutions. However, Asian CRT theorists argue that the model minority image is harmful to Asian Americans because it problematically homogenizes the experiences of over twenty-five different Asian ethnic groups, each with its own culture, history, and immigration experience (Buenavista, Jayakumar, and Misa-Escalante 2009). Educators also often fail to acknowledge the needs of many Asian American students because they are presumed to be academically successful, which is problematic for those who are struggling.

Diversity Ideology

Diversity ideology emerges out of CRT and color-blind racism (Berrey 2011; Embrick 2011). **Diversity ideology** refers to the institutional co-optation of notions of diversity that originally emerged out of the civil rights movement. While these notions of diversity are intended to advocate for racial and gender equality, instead they result in the maintenance of highly inequitable environments. According to this perspective, there is a diversity discourse and an apparent celebration of diversity in corporations, schools, and universities while these institutions simultaneously maintain racial and gender hierarchies (Berrey 2011; Embrick 2011; Moore and Bell 2011; Randolph 2013).

In his research with upper-level managers in Fortune 1000 companies, sociologist David Embrick (2011) finds that while diversity is a common theme in the business world and is often well publicized on corporate websites, managers tend to embrace such a broad understanding of diversity that they actually exclude gender and race in their definitions of diversity. Additionally, while most managers claimed to be enthusiastic about their company's diversity initiatives, when pressed, they were unable to adequately explain those policies and practices. Berrey's (2015) research on diversity programs and policies finds that while diversity discourse and programs are quite popular and may even appear progressive, they often get co-opted by reformist groups.

Research on higher education finds that in the 1980s university administrators began adopting a **racial orthodoxy**—a set of beliefs, narratives, and practices within

BOX 3.3

Global Perspectives:
Global Critical Race Feminism

Critical race theory emerged out of critical legal studies and has given birth to many other branches of thought, perhaps most significantly that of critical race feminism and global critical race feminism (GCRF). Whereas critical legal studies challenged the presumed racial neutrality of the law, critical race feminism makes a similar challenge along gender and racial lines. The legal system makes no mention of gender because neutrality is assumed. However, within this discourse of neutrality one finds a privileging of men, men's bodies, and men's experiences. For instance, the legal understanding of self-defense is based upon the assumption of similar body size and strength between perpetrator and victim, which is generally not the case in a male assault on a female victim. Women who kill their abusive spouses, for instance, often commit the act when the spouse is asleep. However, if they claim that they acted in self-defense, their pleas are rarely effective in court because they did not kill their spouses in the heat of a violent confrontation, in the moment when their lives were being threatened, which is what the standard of self-defense is based on.

GCRF examines the legal treatment of women of color across the globe. For instance, theorists within this tradition have challenged international law for its failure to address problems, such as domestic violence, that take place in the private sphere of the family and the home, which is where the majority of the world's women can be found (Wing 2000). One of the challenges is fighting for women's international rights while retaining a respect for cultural contexts within which women live. 50 Million Missing is an organization that is fighting female genocide in India, for instance, while still respecting Indian culture. Another organization, Global Campaign to Stop Killing and Stoning Women! (SKSW Campaign), works to eliminate all forms of culturally justified violence against women, particularly their killing and maiming for presumed violation of sexual norms, with the claim that "[Muslim] culture is not violent."

Global critical race feminists also work for the rights of women of color in the global workplace. Women of color are the most exploited in the global marketplace, and any efforts to change this must be global in origin (Wing 2000). What are the best approaches to support working women of color, whether in the First World or the Third World? In this era of globalization, international law exists, at least in part, to protect human rights. However, this protection is more difficult to implement than it sounds. All humans do not have equal experiences; thus, laws benefiting some may disadvantage others. International laws must avoid marginalizing women and particularly women of color, which is the challenge global critical race feminists aim to present (Wing 2000).

an organization, supported by discourse, that make up commonly recognized under-standings of race (Berrey 2011)—that included "diversity." In this context, diversity included many cultural identities, not just racial identities, and was described as a benefit to all, not just to minority groups.

While paying attention to cultural diversity can be understood as progress, sociol-ogists find this problematic because it shifts our focus away from racial/ethnic minority issues in higher education:

> Rather than emphasizing the imperative of social justice, diversity discourse and many diversity programs stress the instrumental benefits of racial identity and of interpersonal interaction along racial and other lines. ... Diversity discourse and initiatives often incorporate, represent, and even cater to white students.
>
> (Berrey 2011:577)

For instance, a structural issue faced by racial/ethnic minority students is that they are underrepresented in higher education, but the racial orthodoxy does nothing to address that. Instead, there is a focus on teaching the disproportionately white student body about cultural diversity. Diversity programs in higher education focus on preparing white students for a diverse world, and they are much less successful at making their campuses diverse.

Ultimately, while embracing a discourse of diversity, schools and corporations are actually found to reproduce existing status hierarchies that a commitment to diver-sity is intended to dislodge. It takes more than merely having a diverse workforce or student body to achieve racial justice.

WITNESS

Sociologist Antonia Randolph explores the ways the diversity ideology plays out in schools. She finds that "teachers granted immigrant minor-ities such as Asians and Latinos advantages (*ethnic credits*) that Blacks did not receive [while] Black students and schools suffer *racial penal-ties* including stigma and its consequences, for being the wrong kind of different" (2013:2, italics in the original).

Research finds that while Americans are open to and optimistic about diversity, seeing it as a strength for our country, there is considerable tension surrounding the issue, specifically because diversity talk is generally deeply informed by race (Hart-mann 2015)—so much so that "all of the debates, contradictions, and confusions that mark and define American thinking about race ... get projected onto all the differences associated with multiculturalism. This is where race comes to be about so much more than race" (Hartmann 2015:633). Even more problematic is the fact that diversity discourse emerges out of a white cultural perspective, where privilege and inequalities are masked and there is an expectation of assimilation (Bell and Hartmann 2007).

Racialized Organizations

Much of our lives are spent within large organizations; for instance, as a student, you are part of an organization that provides students with an education; most of you will someday be employed by a large, bureaucratic organization. Sociologist Victor Ray (2019) has introduced the theory of racialized organizations to shift analysis away from the understanding of organizations as race-neutral bureaucratic structures and instead makes visible how race and racism are reproduced through various organizational mechanisms. The idea that organizations are race neutral simply obscures the fact that they operate in white interests. One organizational mechanism is how, through rules and regulations, racialized organizations limit employee agency, including the range of acceptable emotional responses (Ray 2019). The NFL can be understood as a racialized organization through its response to Colin Kaepernick's protest against police brutality: as he took a knee during the pre-game national anthem throughout the 2016 season, he experienced a swift and severe backlash from the NFL. After being released from the San Francisco 49ers, he was never again signed to an NFL team, despite starting in two NFC championship games and one Super Bowl and being only 29 years old. He sued the NFL, arguing they pressured teams to not sign him in the following two seasons due to his protests. In February of 2019, the NFL settled a collusion lawsuit with Colin Kaepernick and Eric Reid, who also faced discrimination in the NFL for taking a knee during the pre-game national anthem in protest against police brutality (see Chapter 12).

CHAPTER SUMMARY

Scientific knowledge is always evolving, and while all scientists maintain a commitment to objectivity, scientific knowledge often reflects the social and political context in which it is created. This is perhaps best exemplified by looking at the history of the science of race, much of which, from current-day perspectives, appears to have justified racial minority exploitation and oppression. The science of eugenics, for instance, is plainly racist by today's standards. However, it was at one time understood to be unbiased and objective science. Despite the progress made in identifying racist scientific practices, modern-day versions of scientific racism remain, for example, in certain interpretations and applications of the human genome.

Table 3.1: Summary of Sociological

Traditional Theoretical Approaches

Functionalist Perspective—emphasizes social order over conflict, the value of consensus, harmony, and stability for a society, and the interdependence of social systems. Diversity along racial/ethnic lines is potentially problematic because it often results in social conflict, which they believe societies should try to reduce.

Conflict Perspective—emphasizes conflict between dominant and subordinate groups over scarce and valued resources in a society. Race/ethnic relations is understood in terms of the competition between the dominant, privileged racial group, whites, and the less privileged, subordinate racial groups, such as African Americans, Native Americans, Latinos, and Asian Americans. Societal conflict is not always a bad thing since it can lead to necessary social change.

Ethnicity Paradim—research includes, but is not limited to, the experiences of white ethnic immigrants, the lingering presence of ethnicity for white ethnics, ethnic conflict, ethnic stratification, ethnic identity, and the political implications of ethnicity. The experiences of racial minorities have been awkwardly packaged within the ethnicity paradigm rather than understood as unique.

Marxist Perspective—argues that racial exploitation and racial prejudice intersect with capitalism; thus, racial inequality is an extension of class inequality. According to Marxist theory, workers are most powerful when they are united. Therefore, many Marxists perceive racism as a means of dividing the working class to the advantage of business owners and corporations who seek to exploit them.

Chicago School—shifts understandings of race from a biological to a social phenomenon, and so was considered progressive for its time. Chicago School sociologists viewed race as part of ethnicity—but as a less important factor in people's lives than ethnicity—and equated ethnicity with culture.

Split Labor Market Theory—split labor market theorists argue that workers can be divided into two classes: higher-paid workers and lower-paid workers, often divided along racial/ethnic lines. Members of certain racial/ethnic groups find themselves confined to certain jobs and exempt from other, generally higher paying, jobs, thus *splitting* the labor market. Higher-paid, white workers enforce discriminatory practices in the labor market in order to maintain their privilege.

Assimilationist Paradigm—emphasizes the idea that ethnic minorities should give up their ties to their home countries and become part of the dominant, white, culture of the United States. The assimilation of immigrants is desirable because it decreases differences between groups and so also decreases the potential for group conflict.

Internal Colonialism—argues that colonialism, the process through which one country dominates another by stripping them of their human and economic resources, can actually take place within one country when dominant racial groups establish a system of oppression and exploitation of subordinate racial groups within their own nation in ways that benefit them.

Current Theoretical Approaches

Symbolic Interactionism—places emphasis on small-scale human interactions, emphasizing that social structures are maintained through interactions, thus reproducing a social order that emphasizes the inferiority of all blacks to all whites.

Racial Formation Theory— emphasizes the ways racial categories are created, inhabited, transformed, and destroyed over time. Racial formation theory examines the ways race plays out structurally and in our everyday, lived experience.

Racialized Social Systems Theory— perspective refers to the ways all aspects of a society, from the economy, politics, to ideologies, are structured by the placement of individuals in racial categories that are not simply different, they are hierarchical, and thus they inform social relations between the groups.

——— Related Paradigms

• • • Similar theories within a broad approach

White Racial Frame—a white racial frame is a worldview that emphasizes the systemic nature of racism and includes racial beliefs, racially loaded terms, racialized images, verbal connotations, racialized emotions and interpretations, as well as discriminatory actions that help justify ongoing racism and supports the deeply entrenched whiteness that operates in our society, both historically and currently.

Critical Race Theory (CRT)—argues that racism is central to US society rather than aberrational and specifically challenges the rhetoric of racial neutrality and color-blindness found within policies and law. CRT is more than a theory, it is a methodology in that CRTs embrace an activist agenda rather than objective science.

Diversity Ideology—emphasizes the pervasiveness of diversity discourse and a superficial celebration of diversity in organizations, particularly corporations and schools, which simultaneously maintain racial and gender hierarchies.

Sociology emerged in the mid to late 1800s and initially focused exclusively on class inequality as brought about by industrial capitalism. Early American sociology, dominated by white scholars, largely ignored race and racism, focusing attention on ethnicity and the inevitability of assimilation. W. E. B. Du Bois and other African American scholars have focused on race and racism, but their work was marginalized from the mainstream discipline of sociology. Conflict theorists contribute to our understanding of racial inequality by portraying it as linked to capitalist exploitation. By the second half of the twentieth century, research on race, racism, and race privilege had become important arenas of sociological investigation. New eras result in the need for new explanations; thus, sociologists have contributed two new theoretical paradigms for understanding the persistence of race as a concept and a category: racial formation theory and the white racial frame. The emergence of CRT, an interdisciplinary project, has resulted in challenges to the presumed racial neutrality of law and policy. Although scientific developments over the last fifty years have resulted in a more complete understanding of race, it is inevitable that scientific knowledge will continue to be challenged and some of it overturned as new knowledge is presented.

KEY TERMS AND CONCEPTS

Anglo-conformity

Antimiscegenation laws

Canon

Colonized minority

Conflict theory

Counterstories

Critical race theory

Cultural pluralism

Diversity ideology

Ethnic stratification

Ethnicity paradigm

Eugenics

Functionalist perspective

Genetic options theory

Genome geography

Human genome

Immigrant minorities

Internal colonialism theory

Intersectionality

Liberation sociology

Marxist theory

Melting pot

Model minority

Phrenology

Racial formations

Racial orthodoxy

Racialized medicine

Racialized social systems

Scientific racism

Split labor market theory

Status inequalities

Symbolic interactionism

Systemic racism

White racial frame

PERSONAL REFLECTIONS

1. Based upon your educational experiences to date, what are the key characteristics of science? In what ways has the science of race failed to live up to these characteristics? Can you think of any scientific assertions being made today that you think we will look back on as critically as we look back on the early science of race or eugenics?
2. Provide evidence of the "ethnic revival" or "symbolic ethnicity" in your family or community. Were these hard to identify? If so, why do you think that is? If not, why?

CRITICAL THINKING QUESTIONS

1. What do critical race theorists mean when they refer to counterstories? Identify a counterstory you are familiar with (whether historical, in popular culture, or in scientific research). How does emphasizing counterstories affect how we all view the world?
2. Would you argue that immigrants are pressured to assimilate into the dominant, Anglo-American culture, or would you argue that the United States today embraces cultural pluralism more than it does assimilation? Provide evidence to support your answer. Make an argument for white assimilation as the preferred approach to immigration. Make the counterargument: that pluralism should be the preferred approach.

ESSENTIAL READING

Delgado, Richard and Jean Stefancic. 2001. *Critical Race Theory: An Introduction.* New York: New York University Press.

Feagin, Joe R. 2010. *The White Racial Frame: Centuries of Racial Framing and Counter-Framing.* New York and London: Routledge.

Morris, Aldon D. 2015. *The Scholar Denied: W. E. B. Du Bois and the Birth of Modern Sociology.* Oakland: University of California Press.

Nelson, Alondra. 2016. *The Social Life of DNA: Race, Reparations, and Reconciliation after the Genome.* Boston, MA: Beacon Press.

Omi, Michael and Howard Winant. 1994. *Racial Formation in the United States: From the 1960s to the 1990s*, 2nd ed. New York and London: Routledge.

Zuckerman, Phil, ed. 2004. *The Social Theory of W. E. B. Du Bois.* Thousand Oaks, London: Pine Forge Press.

RECOMMENDED FILMS

No Más Bebés (2015). Produced and directed by Renee Tajima-Pena. This documentary follows the story of Mexican American women who were coercively sterilized at Los Angeles County+USC Medical Center in the 1960s and 1970s.

Race: The Power of an Illusion (2003). Produced by Larry Edelman. In exploring the social construction of race, this film also provides a detailed history of scientific racism.

RECOMMENDED MULTIMEDIA

Race: Are We So Different? A project of the American Anthropological Association, this is a website and a traveling exhibit. If you do not get the opportunity to see it live, check it out online! Pay particular attention to their discussion of the science of race. www.understandingrace.org/home.html. Write a short paper, two to three pages, summarizing the key insights you gained from exploring this website.

PART TWO

A Sociological History of US Race Relations

Emergence of the US Racial Hierarchy

CHAPTER LEARNING OUTCOMES

By the end of this chapter, you should be able to:

- Describe the emergence of racial/ethnic inequality
- Apply the various power/conflict theories toward understanding the emergence of racial stratification in the United States
- Understand the unique historical exploitation of African Americans, Native Americans, and Mexican Americans
- Critically examine the intersection of race, gender, and sexuality
- Examine minority group resistance to racial inequality

While most of us know that the United States was built upon the appropriation of Native American lands, we are rarely confronted with the extraordinary levels of violence associated with these actions, often at the hands of government officials. When Columbus reached the Bahama Islands, the Arawaks, the indigenous peoples of the islands, welcomed him with food and water. Columbus responded by enslaving the Arawaks. By 1550, they were nearly eradicated; over three million had died from war and enslavement (Zinn 2003). Geographically speaking, Columbus did not arrive in what would become the United States; he did, however, instigate the colonization of the Americas and certainly set the tone for how future colonizers would interact with the indigenous people of the Americas.

While the "Indian Wars" refers to conflict between the US government and Native American tribes after the Revolutionary War, most of the images of these wars are those involving the Plains Indians of the late 1800s, such as the Battle of Little Big Horn in 1876; many conflicts pre-date this and were fought in the eastern United States. King Philip's War (1675) in New England is considered to be the most violent Indian war of all, with casualties greater than in any other American war when considered in proportion to the population (Loewen 2007). Florida became part of the United States after General Andrew Jackson engaged in raids on the Seminoles in 1818, burning villages and seizing Spanish forts in reaction to Spain's harboring of runaway slaves (Carrier 2004). These raids are known as the First Seminole War. In 1835, President Jackson ordered the Seminoles to leave Florida, and when they refused, he sent in troops. This Second Seminole War lasted over seven years and cost over fifteen hundred US lives and over $40 million (Carrier 2004). Despite their resistance, ultimately over four thousand Seminoles were forced out of Florida.

History textbooks could not possibly describe every Indian war because they were so numerous, but "precisely because there were so many, to minimize Indian wars misrepresents our history" (Loewen 2007:118). To minimize the violence involved in the appropriation of this country also misrepresents history.

The United States is a country with a long history of racial and ethnic conflict. European Americans "discovered" a populated continent and proceeded to lay claim to it, thus initiating hundreds of years of conflict with the various native tribes already inhabiting the country. This was followed by the exploitation of blacks through 240 years of slavery and another hundred years of Jim Crow racism in the form of segregation and terror, and the subordination and exploitation of Mexicans throughout the southwestern United States, beginning with the Treaty of Guadalupe Hidalgo in 1848. Examples of early racial/ethnic contact and conflict follow:

- According to historian Howard Zinn, "Columbus and his successors were not coming into an empty wilderness, but into a world which in some places was as densely populated as Europe itself, where the culture was complex, where human relations were more egalitarian than in Europe" (2003:21).
- "By 1800, 10 to 15 million blacks had been transported as slaves to the Americas, representing perhaps one-third of those originally seized in Africa. It is roughly estimated that Africa lost 50 million human beings to death and slavery in those centuries we call the beginnings of modern Western civilization" (Zinn 2003:29).
- The US Constitution, our declaration of democracy, makes no mention of Native Americans, declares slaves to be counted as three-fifths of a person, and ignores women completely.
- "History" is presented as if only European Americans contributed to it; even history textbooks "obliterate the interracial, multicultural nature of frontier life" (Loewen 2007:107).

- In encouraging the Mexican–American War, the media displayed considerable support for American aggression and helped justify it, as the following quotation from an article in the *Illinois State Register* exemplifies: "Shall this garden of beauty be suffered to lie dormant in its wild and useless luxuriance? … Myriads of [sic] enterprising Americans would flock to its rich and inviting prairies; the hum of Anglo-American industry would be heard in its valleys; cities would rise upon its plains and sea-coast, and the resources and wealth of the nation be increased in an incalculable degree" (Zinn 2003:154).

However, mere contact between different racial/ethnic groups does not necessarily imply that one group will become dominant and the others subordinate. Sociologists focus on why racial/ethnic inequality emerges when two or more racial/ethnic groups come into contact with one another. This chapter provides a sociological analysis of the early exploitation of Native Americans, African Americans, and Mexican Americans by European Americans as well as the dominant sociological explanations for such racial/ethnic conflict. Social scientists argue that to understand race, racism, and race relations today, it is important to take history into account in order to comprehend why these patterns of racial inequality first arose and the ways they influence modern-day race relations.

From a sociological perspective, it takes more than mere prejudice to explain the institution of slavery, the unequal treatment of Native Americans, and discrimination against Mexican Americans. While negative attitudes toward another group are part of the perpetuation of racial inequality, they alone are not enough to result in an institution of such magnitude and cruelty as slavery, for instance.

Sociologists rely more on structural explanations, particularly power-conflict theories, to understand racial/ethnic inequality. In this chapter, we will use the power-conflict perspective on racial/ethnic inequality to understand the ways racial exploitation manifested itself in, for instance, the form of slavery, the confiscation of Native American land, and the land and labor exploitation of Mexican Americans from early European contact in the 1500s through the late 1800s. We will conclude this chapter with an analysis of the various ways racial minority groups actively resisted their oppression during that era.

THE EMERGENCE OF RACE

To understand the history of racial/ethnic relations we have to first suspend our historically specific understandings of race; in other words, we must consider that how we understand race has not always been part of people's worldview. For instance, the world has not always been "raced"; societies have not always been organized along the lines of physical features, such as skin color, with economic, political, social, and psychological rewards awarded or denied along such lines. Race emerged in a particular historical era in conjunction with a specific set of social circumstances, such as colonialism, the transatlantic slave trade, and the emergence of the plantation system (Allen 1994; Berkhofer 1978; Jordan 1968).

Africans were not oppressed, exploited, and enslaved because they were *black.* The emergence of the transatlantic slave trade actually helped create "race," the idea of dividing humanity into hierarchical categories based upon physical appearances. It is through the slave trade that Europeans began viewing themselves collectively as "white" and Africans as "black." The continent of Africa is and has always been home to people with a wide range of skin colors; thus, collectively defining them as "black" has been a social construction.

Prior to this racialized view of the world, the significant division between groups of people was religious. During the colonial era, European Christians felt considerable prejudice toward the non-Christians they encountered in Africa, Asia, and the Americas, viewing them as uncivilized, inferior heathens. New World slavery began in the late 1500s, and Europeans at that time justified their exploitation of Africans and Indians along religious rather than racial lines (Ennals 2007; Noel 1972; Zinn 2009).

Cultural beliefs of superiority and inferiority along racial lines emerged almost one hundred years into the slave trade, roughly between 1667 and 1682, as a way to justify the exploitation of Africans (Bennett 1961). The myth of race emerged not only to justify exploitation but also to persuade both whites and blacks of white superiority and black inferiority. Racism is a circular process: it is used to justify exploitation and, in turn, helps perpetuate beliefs of racial inferiority in both dominant and subordinate-group members, which, in turn, act as rationalizations for the inequality.

SOCIOLOGICAL PERSPECTIVES ON RACIAL/ETHNIC INEQUALITY

European Americans came to the New World for a multitude of reasons, from the pursuit of wealth to the search for religious freedom. These desires inevitably placed them in conflict with the original inhabitants of the continent for land and resources. Research finds numerous examples of racial and ethnic prejudices, conflicts, and inequalities emerging whenever different racial and ethnic groups come into contact and compete for resources (Olzak and Nagel 1986; Takaki 1979).

From a sociological perspective, much racial and ethnic conflict can be explained through the conflict perspective (see Chapter 3). The *conflict perspective* refers to a collection of theories that emphasize competition for scarce resources, unequal power relations between groups, and the opportunity for economic exploitation of one or more groups by another. We will explore the necessary conditions for inequality to emerge and then focus on the various conflict theories that can help us understand the origins of racial/ethnic inequality: Marxist theories, the theory of internal colonialism, and the split labor market theory. While these three theories were introduced in Chapter 3, they will be explored in further depth here and used specifically to explore the origins of racial/ethnic inequality in the United States.

Conditions Necessary for Inequality to Emerge

Before we explore theories of racial and ethnic inequality, we have to look at why racial and ethnic contact resulted in racial and ethnic inequality in the United States. The origin of racial and ethnic **stratification**, or group inequality, is explained through the identification of three conditions necessary for inequality to emerge (Noel 1968, 1972). First, there must be widespread **ethnocentrism**, where one group believes its culture is superior to the cultures of other groups. Second, there must be some kind of opportunity for exploitation. A group that holds economic, geographic, or technological advantage over another is in a position to exploit that other group. And third, there needs to be a relationship of unequal power in which one group is able to dominate and force the other group into a subordinate position. In other words, it takes more than contact between different groups and the emergence of prejudice for inequality to emerge. There is a huge difference between disliking or even fearing another group of people and the mass enslavement of that group (Zinn 2009).

Viewing the origins of racial/ethnic stratification in this way is useful for explaining how Europeans and later European Americans were able to subordinate Africans, indigenous people, and Mexican Americans. First, Africans and indigenous peoples, as non-Christian, were perceived by Europeans as heathens, uncivilized, and thus not just different but inferior to them. Second, Europeans were motivated to subordinate these people because of the economic benefits associated with exploiting them for their land and/or labor. And finally, the fact that they had more-sophisticated weapons ensured Europeans were able to dominate these groups and directly benefit from their subordination, thus establishing a situation of racial/ethnic inequality between European American whites and Native Americans, African Americans, and Mexican Americans.

Marxist Theories

Marxist theories take as their starting point Karl Marx's assertion that capitalism is an economic system that is inherently inhumane because huge profits are generated through the exploitation of human beings. While Marx focused exclusively on class inequality instead of racial/ethnic inequality, some social scientists extend his argument to racial minorities by pointing out that not all humans—or workers, as Marx viewed them—are exploited equally. Racial/ethnic minority group members, for instance, tend to face greater exploitation under capitalism than do white workers, and women laborers are more exploited than men.

Sociologist Oliver Cromwell Cox (1948) explains that the emergence of racism was intrinsically connected to the emergence of capitalism, particularly when viewed from a global perspective. Capitalism as an economic system emerged in conjunction with **colonialism**, the European contact with and exploitation and domination of the native peoples of Africa, Asia, and the Americas. Europeans began to take advantage of these people for their land, labor, and resources and then created racial ideologies, cultural beliefs about racial inferiority and superiority, to justify such treatment. Cultural belief systems, as described in Chapter 1, can be quite powerful in shaping group members' perceptions.

Applying this perspective to American racism, particularly race relations in the South, Cox argues that white capitalists created and perpetuated racial prejudices because it benefited them: they could exploit black workers and keep white workers from realizing their potential solidarity with the black working class. Such a "divide and conquer" strategy benefits capitalists in that a divided workforce holds less leverage against capitalists in the labor market. This idea challenges the notion that it is primarily poor and working-class whites who are more likely to be racist, a misperception that is often still held by many. Cox used rather strong language to make this point, explaining that it is "sheer nonsense to think that the poor whites are the perpetrators of the social system in the South" (1948:577).

While it is hard to deny the connection between capitalism and colonialism, a critique of Marxist explanations for racial/ethnic inequality is that they overemphasize the benefits white capitalists earn from the establishment and perpetuation of a racist hierarchy, while overlooking the benefits all whites earn under such a system —what is today referred to as *white privilege.* In other words, even poor whites benefit from this racial hierarchy. Under slavery, for instance, only a small percentage of whites owned slaves and thus benefited directly from slavery; poor whites lived in desperately impoverished conditions but benefited psychologically from the realization that at least they were not slaves.

Another problem with Marxist analyses of racial/ethnic inequality is that capitalists may exploit racial and ethnic tensions, but many argue that capitalists do not consciously set out to create those tensions. In other words, a divided labor force can be taken advantage of, but how it became divided is an entirely different question. There is some evidence that, at least in some situations, capitalists have done exactly that: set out to create racial divisions in the labor force that work to their advantage (Bloom 1987). However, in most situations, such maneuvering by capitalists cannot be substantiated.

Split Labor Market Theory

Other social scientists, while acknowledging that racial/ethnic conflict is linked to capitalism, challenge the idea that only wealthy whites create and benefit from racial tensions in the labor force. The split labor market theory emphasizes how white workers fuel antagonisms between racial groups in the labor force that ultimately benefit them as white workers (Bonacich 1972, 1975, 1976; Brown and Boswell 1995; Wilson 1978). This theory focuses on three competing groups in the labor force: capitalists (owners), higher-paid labor (white workers), and cheaper labor (racial/ethnic minority workers). Strict Marxists focus instead on two competing groups: workers and capitalists.

From a Marxist perspective, capitalists' goal of attaining the most profit possible rests on their ability to pay workers the lowest wages possible. From a split labor market perspective, white workers create and maintain a split labor market in which they control the higher-paid jobs, while workers of color are marginalized to less desirable jobs and are unable to compete with white workers for the good jobs. One of the ways white workers have been able to secure their dominance in the workforce and decrease the power of racial/ethnic minority workers has been through unions. Prior to World War II, unions had a long history of racial segregation that was maintained through violence and coercion and that served the interests of white workers by keeping competition in the job market to a minimum. Thus, from the split labor market perspective, racial discrimination in the labor force benefits white workers, disadvantages minority workers, and is not in the interest of capitalists, either, because their goal would be to pay all workers the cheapest possible wage so as to maximize profits. Being a significant majority of the labor force, white workers are arguably able to exert this kind of influence in the labor market.

WITNESS

"Shortly after the turn of the [twentieth] century, there were 2 million members of labor unions … 80 percent of them in the American Federation of Labor. The AFL was an exclusive union—almost all male, almost all white, almost all skilled workers. Racism was practical for the AFL … it won better conditions for some workers, and left most workers out" (Zinn 2003:329).

While some evidence supports the split labor market perspective, its explanatory power is limited. Ultimately, a divided labor force disadvantages all workers: capitalists can use minority workers as strikebreakers, thus decreasing a union's bargaining power and the advantage white workers are able to wield. Indeed, using racial/ethnic minority workers as strikebreakers was a main union-busting strategy during the labor unrest of the early twentieth century (Bonacich 1976; Wilson 1978).

Internal Colonialism

The initial racial/ethnic conflicts in this country between European Americans and Native Americans, African Americans, and Mexican Americans remain significant for understanding racial/ethnic conflict and inequality today. All three of these groups fall into Blauner's category of colonized minorities. Blauner (1969, 1972) emphasizes that despite the experiences of prejudice and discrimination faced by many European white ethnic immigrant groups, colonized minorities have faced dramatically different historical circumstances, more severe discrimination, and societal barriers to advancement, all of which set them apart from immigrant minorities. The exploitation colonized minorities faced also tended to be ongoing and intergenerational, whereas white ethnics faced intense discrimination for shorter durations, sometimes even for less than a generation. The intent of this distinction is not to downplay the discrimination white ethnic immigrants faced, as it was very real and debilitating; instead, it is to emphasize how the experiences of immigrant minorities differed from those of colonized minorities and that these differences have influenced the status of such groups today.

Because colonized minorities enter a country involuntarily, members of these groups are coerced into participating in an entirely different culture, while their traditional culture is treated as inferior. Colonized minorities find themselves in a society where their traditional cultural practices, customs, and rituals, from religion to language to family structures, are destroyed, and where even engaging in traditional cultural practices can be severely punished (Indian boarding schools are a primary example). Additionally, the experience of colonized minorities often involves enslavement or severe labor market marginalization. Such discrimination limits group members' **social mobility**: their opportunities for economic advancement and their chances of moving into a higher social class. The initial subordinate position of colonized minorities in a society also contributes to increased prejudice and discrimination from the dominant group and thus becomes self-perpetuating. The dominant group begins to view the subordinate status of racial minorities as a natural outgrowth of their inferiority (Blauner 1972).

Race and the State

While the theories we have just discussed explore the link between capitalism and racial/ethnic inequality, the role of government cannot be denied, particularly when analyzing the origins of racial/ethnic inequality in the United States. Sociologists Oliver and Shapiro (1995) use the term **racialization of state policy** to describe how government policies have impaired the ability of blacks to accumulate wealth and facilitated white wealth accumulation, with slavery being the most blatant example. However, the idea can also be applied to any racial/ethnic minority group. The displacements of Native Americans and Mexicans from their native lands for the purpose of westward, particularly white, expansion are also examples of the role of government in supporting white wealth accumulation in the United States.

Similarly, sociologists Omi and Winant (1994) emphasize the role of the United States government in shaping race. One example is found in the US Constitution, our declaration of democracy, which makes no mention of Native Americans, declares slaves to be three-fifths of a person, and ignores women completely. They go on to argue that for most of US history, including the colonial era, the United States has operated as a **racial dictatorship**, since most racial minorities were marginalized from the political process. Such language is alarming because we tend not to think of American society as a dictatorship, of course, as our democratic principles seem contrary to the idea of a form of government in which a small group of people hold absolute power. But their point is that one racial group, whites, has operated as a dictatorship right here in our own democracy through the ongoing disenfranchisement of people of color. Omi and Winant optimistically conclude that, while we are moving toward a **racial democracy**, where all racial groups share in our democracy and thus hold at least a minimum of political power, the state played a major role in the creation and maintenance of a racial hierarchy throughout most of the United States' history.

Institutions, Ideologies, and Identities

As Marxist theorists help us understand, with the emergence of capitalism came an immediate need for abundant land and cheap labor. Out of these needs, the institution of slavery emerged. Ideologies of racial inferiority emerged long after this institution was in place. In other words, slavery existed prior to the emergence of cultural beliefs of black inferiority. These cultural ideologies emerged as a way to justify this cruel institution and were all the more powerful because they were perceived as the natural order of things (Parenti 1994). Cultural ideologies are fueled through **stereotypes**: exaggerated and/or simplified portrayals of an entire group of people based upon misinformation or mischaracterizations. As cultural ideologies take hold, they inform how individuals see themselves. For the first time in history, individuals of this era began establishing racial identities, understanding themselves at least partially in terms of racial-group membership. Through the early slave trade, Europeans began defining themselves as white and Africans as black, identities that up until that point had been mostly unheard of. In addition to racialized identities came perceptions of inferiority and superiority. Those defined as white began to see themselves as innately superior to people of color across the globe. Racism itself can be thought of as an ideology, "a set of interrelated values which functions to justify a particular existence or desired social order" (Noel 1972:155).

EUROPEAN CONTACT WITH NATIVE AMERICANS

The European arrival in the New World in 1492 was the beginning of five centuries of devastation for the original inhabitants of this continent. There is considerable debate over the number of people that were here upon European arrival. The North American indigenous population prior to European contact is estimated to be between seven and eighteen million, made up of an estimated six hundred different tribes (Snipp 1989; Stiffarm and Lane 1992; Thornton 1987). Initial low population estimates were politically motivated: they helped portray the European conquest of North America as legitimate because it was depicted as a relatively uninhabited continent. Tens of thousands of Native Americans and even entire tribes were decimated by European diseases, such as smallpox, cholera, bubonic plague, scarlet fever, whooping cough, and pneumonia, to which indigenous people had no immunity. Within the first decade of the Spanish arrival in what is today Florida there was a smallpox pandemic (1520–1524) that is estimated to have reduced the native population by 75 percent (Stiffarm and Lane 1992; Thornton 1987). This is often viewed as a "natural disaster," yet the introduction of disease at least at some times and in some places by European colonizers was intentional and thus could be viewed as an early form of biological warfare (Stearn and Stearn 1945; Thornton 1987).

It is beyond the scope of this book to provide a sufficient description of the various Native American tribes encountered by Europeans. The many tribes varied dramatically in terms of culture, language, family structures, modes of economic production, and customs. Some Native American tribes built great cities and established flourishing agricultural systems, while other tribes were nomadic. Native Americans are responsible for the initial cultivation of over 60 percent of the foods eaten around the world today, including corn, potatoes, peanuts, and many grains (Weatherford 1991). European founders were so enamored of the governance structure of the Iroquois Confederacy, which included tribes from the northeastern United States and parts of Canada, that they modeled the US Constitution and federal government after it (Robbins 1992). Despite such accomplishments, Europeans still felt a collective sense of superiority over Native Americans.

The European invasion of North America was comprehensive, as various European colonizers came from many directions: the Spanish came up through the South, particularly through Florida and Mexico; the French came down the

Mississippi River from northeastern Canada; the British colonized the region along the Atlantic coast; the Dutch colonized what is now New York; and last—and often overlooked—the Russians explored the Pacific Northwest and California (Loewen 1999; Nies 1996). Each of the European colonizers brought distinctive ideas about how best to interact with the particular tribes they encountered: some colonizers were more hostile than others, but all viewed the natives as a hindrance to their quest for fur, gold, land, and/or souls.

Colonists considered themselves superior and viewed Native tribes as primitive; however, the colonists were reliant on Native people for survival, so they initially established good relations with them. The survival of early colonists was due directly to aid Indians provided, primarily in the form of food, during the first harsh winters. Trade with the Indians provided not only much-needed resources but also generated wealth, particularly for French colonists interested in the fur trade. Despite such alliances, as the needs of European American settlers changed as they sought wealth instead of mere survival, their opinions of Native people changed accordingly. As European colonists arrived in the New World in increasing numbers and sought permanent settlements, which required further encroachment on Native lands, their beliefs about Indians shifted from that of the "friendly Native" to that of the "hostile savage," the idea that Native Americans were dangerous, bloodthirsty, and uncivilized (Nash 1974).

WITNESS

Artist Benjamin West's 1771 painting *Penn's Treaty with the Indians* captured this sense of whites as civilized and Indians as primitive. According to James Loewen, "West followed the usual convention of depicting fully clothed Europeans—even with hats, scarves, and coats—presenting trade goods to nearly naked Americans. In reality, of course, no two groups of people have ever been dressed so differently at one spot on the earth's surface on the same day. The artist didn't really try to portray reality. He meant to show 'primitive' (American Indian) and 'civilized' (European)" (2007:94).

Between the end of the American Revolution in 1783 and the end of the Civil War in 1865, Native American tribes ceded hundreds of millions of acres of land to the United States federal government in what were publicly espoused to be freely negotiated transactions (Fitzgerald 2007). In reality, Native Americans were coerced into acquiescing to the sale of lands through a variety of ways, including the use of the military, government treaties, and discriminatory laws. Land west of the Appalachians was in demand by white settlers by the 1800s.

IMAGE 4.1: Population of an Indian village moving, drawn by Theodore R. Davis. (Courtesy of the Library of Congress, LC-USZ62-102450).

By Andrew Jackson's presidency, 1829–1837, the demand for land by whites was so intense that his administration boldly announced a policy of Indian removal in the 1830s. The Indian Removal Act of 1830, an example of the racialization of state policy, began the forced removal, under the direction of the US military, of tens of thousands of Native Americans to land west of the Mississippi, a region that was dubbed at the time "Indian country." Over twenty thousand Choctaw were forcibly removed from their homeland in southern Mississippi and Alabama between 1831 and 1833. In total, over forty-five thousand Indians were removed from their land and relocated west of the Mississippi during Jackson's presidency alone. In response to the numerous US attempts at forced relocation, some tribes turned around and marched hundreds of miles back to their homelands in protest.

The Cherokee fought the state of Georgia on state-level relocation demands prior to the federal Indian Removal Act in US courts, eventually reaching the Supreme Court. The Cherokee relied on their "foreign nation" status as the basis of their claim that the state of Georgia did not have authority to settle land disputes involving the Cherokee. While the Supreme Court decision actually favored the Cherokee, ruling that Native Americans were domestic independent nations and, thus, could not negotiate with states, President Jackson blatantly ignored the ruling and relocated them anyway with use of the US military.

The Trail of Tears is perhaps the most well-known enactment of Native American removal policy. Between fifteen thousand and twenty thousand Cherokee were forced to march over one thousand miles through the winter from their homeland of over a thousand years in the Appalachian mountain region of Georgia and the Carolinas to territory west of the Mississippi. Over four thousand died during the march from hunger, exhaustion, and disease.

Still, the most gratuitous massacre of Native Americans is believed to have occurred during the early to mid-1800s as white settlers moved into California and Nevada and encountered the indigenous people there (Johansen 2005). The white settlers received support from the federal government during the 1850s when it financially supported volunteer "Indian fighters," who were reimbursed for the bullets they used to kill Indians in this region. It is estimated that during the 1850s, the government paid over a million dollars for the slaughter of Indians by white citizens in this region of the country (Johansen 2005).

For the native people of this continent, contact with Europeans and European Americans was devastating. Between the 1500s and the mid-1800s, Native Americans experienced a **genocide**, the deliberate and systematic attempt to eradicate a group of people, at the hands of whites through the introduction of disease, war, forced relocation, and cultural denigration. The three conditions for racial inequality to emerge came into play. There was evidence of ethnocentrism, whites stood to gain from swindling Native people out of their land, and there was unequal firepower, which allowed whites to act on their desire for land. Racial/ethnic conflict between whites and Native Americans was also facilitated by government actions. The needs of the dominant group were reflected in the implementation of government policies that supported racial inequality, and these became self-perpetuating as government policies and practices fueled racial prejudices that justified ongoing racial inequalities.

REFLECT AND CONNECT

To what extent has this summary of early Native–white relations mirrored what you were taught in your K–12 education? To what extent does it differ? Speculate on why.

SLAVERY IN THE UNITED STATES

From our current perspective, the 400 years of the global slave trade, 240 of which involved the United States, appear to be a moral conundrum. How could such an inhumane institution exist simultaneously with the development of a nation that prided itself on its democratic principles? Why was slavery established in the burgeoning colonies? Why were West Africans taken from their homes and transported to the United States for lifetime, intergenerational enslavement? The answers to these questions, indeed, the information covered in this chapter, may surprise you. While we all learned something about slavery in our K–12 education, research by the Southern Poverty Law center finds there is widespread illiteracy about slavery among students. Most US history textbooks in use in schools today receive a failing grade for their coverage of slavery. Teachers are too often unwilling to teach the ugly truth about this period in our history, sometimes out of fear of frightening young students and sometimes due to their own historical ignorance (Stewart 2019). For generations, this history was intentionally misrepresented by "white southerners and their sympathizers [who] adopted an ideology called 'the lost cause,' an outlook that softened the brutality of enslavement and justified its immorality" (Stewart 2019).

Sociological theories on racial/ethnic inequality point to the development of capitalism in conjunction with colonialism as directly linked to slavery and as the facilitator of much racial/ethnic conflict and inequality. As sociologist Matthew Desmond (2019) explains:

> Like today's titans of industry, planters understood that their profits climbed when they extracted maximum effort out of each worker. So they paid close attention to inputs and outputs … The cotton plantation was America's first big business … and behind every cold calculation, every rational fine-tuning of the system, violence lurked.

Because huge profits could be made from the enslavement of blacks, government policies and practices supported the exploitation, and ideological justifications emerged to rationalize such an inhumane system.

WITNESS

"Our founding ideals of liberty and equality were false when they were written. Black Americans fought to make them true. Without this struggle, America would have no democracy at all" (Hannah-Jones 2019).

Why Africans?

Africans were not the first choice for enslavement, as indentured servitude involving white European servants already existed. But whites were difficult to successfully enslave because they could more easily blend into the population if they escaped. They were also Christian; thus, lifetime servitude was harder to justify for the dominant group. There were also attempts at enslaving Native Americans. The Spanish had enslaved southwestern Native Americans since the 1500s, until Mexico won its independence from Spain in 1821 and began eradicating slavery. Indian slavery in most parts of the South was eventually abandoned because slaves often got sick and died, or they could more easily escape and rejoin their tribes, often knowing the terrain better than the whites (Bennett 1961). Indian slaves were often used as export trade—thousands of Native Americans were sent to the West Indies, where it was assumed they could never escape, in exchange for black slaves (Loewen 2007). Thus, the attempted enslavement of these groups in most cases proved futile.

The exception to this was in the Appalachian Mountain south region, where the enslavement of Indians did not end with the importation of African slaves. Indians represented one-quarter of the total slave population in South Carolina in the early 1700s (Dunaway 2003). Despite this exception, slavery eventually became associated with blackness while whiteness became associated with wage labor (Roediger 1991).

Africans, in time, became the preferred choice for North American slavery, beginning with the arrival of the first African slaves in Virginia in 1619, because they were viewed as relatively inexpensive, costing the same price for a lifetime of service (with offspring) as an indentured servant did for a limited number of years. Africans were presumed better suited to the climate and the type of agricultural work needed in the South, even though this was untrue for many, since many enslaved Africans came from nomadic tribal cultures and, thus, were not suited for agriculture. It was also considered acceptable to enslave Africans because they were not Christians and thus were perceived as not fully human. They were also viewed as less likely to successfully run away, due to their distinctive physical features' increasing their

IMAGE 4.2: Photo of a newspaper advertisement from the 1780s for the sale of slaves at Ashley Ferry outside of Charleston, South Carolina.

visibility (Bennett 1961). Over the course of the trans-Atlantic slave trade, over 15 million Africans were forcibly taken from their homes and enslaved in the "New World."

Today we think of slavery as associated only with the southern United States; however, slavery initially existed throughout the American colonies. By 1804, all northern states had abolished slavery. Despite abolishing slavery, however, northerners made millions of dollars off slavery, in shipbuilding, banking, and distilleries, to name a few industries, throughout its duration in the United States.

The slave trade lasted over four hundred years, during which an estimated fifteen million Africans were forcibly taken from their homes and communities in West Africa and brought to the Americas, required to march long distances, sometimes as far as five hundred miles, from the interior of their country to the coast, where they were incarcerated for up to a year before boarding a slave ship (Burton 2008). An estimated 1.8 million died en route to the New World. Slavery was not only devastating for the enslaved but also for the families they left behind. The various tribes and countries of West Africa faced the ongoing loss of their most precious resource, people, for hundreds of years (Burton 2008; Rediker 2007). Europeans traded goods for Africans, then shipped Africans to the Americas, then sold the slaves in exchange for goods they took back to Europe. The middle of these three events, the passage on the slave ships, is known as the Middle Passage.

The slave ship was its own horror. Human beings were branded and chained, packed as tightly as possible, sometimes in spaces no higher than eighteen inches, in unbearable conditions, for six to ten weeks. By all historical evidence, the trip across the Atlantic was an intolerable journey for the captives. Epidemics of disease swept the ships. Included in the degradation was the rape of female captives by the crew, partially for their enjoyment and partially for economic value in the form of slave breeding. It is estimated that 15 percent of Africans died within their first year in captivity in the New World, from everything from diseases to physical abuse (Bennett 1961; Zinn 2003).

Much of the creation of the idea of race began on slave ships. The crews of slave ships defined themselves in opposition to their African cargo. Never before had people defined themselves as white or black, but during the Middle Passage, the crew became "white" and the cargo became "black" (Rediker 2007). It was through the slave trade of the fifteenth and sixteenth centuries that Europeans began racializing the world in the way we know it today (Stewart 1992).

New World Slavery

Cruel and inhumane as it may have been, there was nothing new about slavery itself, although slavery took a unique form in the New World. Slavery was found in ancient societies, but in the ancient world, conquered peoples were enslaved as part of the spoils of war, or they were enslaved because of poverty or because they were convicted of a crime. Slavery in the United States bore very little resemblance to the slavery of the ancient world (Bennett 1961; Ennals 2007; Genovese and Fox-Genovese 2008; Handlin 1972). In other times and places, slaves could escape their status at some point, through valiant wartime service or through purchasing their own freedom, as it was not a lifetime condition of servitude. Another major difference was that New World slavery involved forced relocation and **cultural genocide**, which refers to efforts to destroy the culture of a group of people. Slaves were taken from West Africa and stripped of their names, cultures, languages, and families, in addition to the loss of their freedom and their humanity (Ennals 2007).

The first Africans who came to colonial America landed in Virginia in 1619; they were in some form of servitude, yet in this period slavery did not yet exist as we know it. The first blacks entering colonial America were in a type of servitude in a society where a large part of the population was at least to some degree unfree; thus, their lack of freedom was not particularly unusual. Thousands of European indentured servants, for instance, were in servitude at this time working off the price of their passage to the New World. However, this changes in slightly more than half a century, as blacks found themselves in a position of lifelong, intergenerational servitude that was defined legally and had been an unknown condition prior to the 1660s (Handlin 1972).

Thus, the enslavement of blacks was a gradual development in the American colonies. Slavery became associated with blacks and wage labor became associated with whites, although there was some debate about which was a lower status (see Box 4.1 Race in the Workplace: White Slavery).

In 1807 Congress abolished the international slave trade, making it a felony to import slaves. Since slavery remained in place in the United States until the end of the Civil War in 1865, when Congress ratified the Thirteenth Amendment, a brutal domestic slave trade emerged. Over a million African Americans were forcibly relocated from the upper South, a tobacco-growing region, to the lower South, a cotton-and-sugar-producing region. Some scholars refer to this as the Slave Trail of Tears; almost a million slaves marched at gunpoint over a thousand miles, many all the way from Virginia to Louisiana. The roots of chain gangs emerged here (see Chapter 10), as the male slaves were handcuffed together for the entire march (Ball 2015).

Prior to the 1820s, southerners often apologized for their reliance on slave labor; however, afterward, particularly in response to the rise of abolitionism (see Box 4.2 Racial Justice Activism: The Abolitionist Movement), southern views of slavery shifted from seeing it as "a necessary evil to a positive good" (Burton 2008:66). Many white southerners literally convinced themselves that they were doing God's work by enslaving Africans (Burton 2008). Part of the ideology that surrounded slavery

BOX 4.1

Race in the Workplace:
White Slavery

Many southerners argued that slavery was a more humane system than wage labor and that southern slaves fared better than most laborers (Genovese and Fox-Genovese 2008). The emphasis on the security, comfort, and humanity of slavery was an idea held by slaveholders and not slaves themselves. Indeed in the North, early industrial laborers were widely exploited in the name of profit. They worked thirteen- to fourteen-hour days, often seven days a week, for minimal pay in dangerous environments. These laborers referred to their situation as "wage slavery" or sometimes "white slavery." White workers began defining themselves in relation to slaves, and the use of the phrase *white slavery*

was specifically intended to argue that *white* workers should not be enslaved at all, rather than as a critique of the institution of slavery (Roediger 1991). Early industrial workers received wages for their labor, the rights of citizenship, and the right to relocate, all of which black slaves were denied. Stereotypes of slaves as lazy and shiftless, despite the fact that they worked from sunup to sundown most days, also helped differentiate them from waged workers. Stereotypes of African Americans as lazy continued into the Jim Crow era. Such stereotypes reemerged with the attacks on the welfare state that began in the 1980s and culminated in welfare reform in 1992 (see Chapter 8).

involved the idea that it was the "masters who made most of the sacrifices, sparing no paternalistic effort and expense to care for the Blacks and uplift them from their African barbarism" (Parenti 1994:122). Some leading white historians of slavery used to perpetuate a paternalistic perspective, emphasizing the notion that Africans were childlike, irresponsible, and primitive, and thus whites had a moral obligation to take care of them. This argument extended, therefore, to the belief that slavery was necessary and actually good for blacks. Ulrich Phillips (1918) was an early historian of slavery who perpetuated this myth, a myth that went unchallenged by historians throughout the first half of the twentieth century (Burton 2008). Later, historians such as Herbert Aptheker, in his work *American Negro Slave Revolts* (1974 [1943]), and Kenneth Stampp, in *The Peculiar Institution* (1956), challenged Phillips by highlighting instances of slave rebellion.

Scholarly analyses of slave narratives have found that, while all slaves were denied constitutional rights that all whites could count on, there were sometimes distinctions among slaves in terms of privileges. These privileges took the form of limited material resources or social advantages, such as wearing cast-off clothing of the master and mistress of the house, or being allowed to hold dances periodically in the

BOX 4.2

Racial Justice Activism:
The Abolitionist Movement

There was opposition to slavery from its very beginning. Many Americans, both white and black, northerners and southerners, were deeply divided over the institution and believed it was morally wrong. Many organized into an abolitionist movement that aimed to pressure both state governments and the federal government to abolish slavery (Maltz 2007). The abolitionist movement involved interracial organizations as well as international supporters. Abolitionism in the United States is often described as a crusade in the tradition of evangelical Protestant religious movements. Quakers made up a major portion of the abolitionist movement, particularly in the early years, and were influential in getting Pennsylvania to be the first state to abolish slavery in 1789 (Emery, Gold, and Braselmann 2008).

As in most social movements, different organizations making up the abolitionist movement used different strategies to reach their goal of eradicating slavery. Prior to 1830, many white abolitionists thought slavery should be abolished and former slaves should be sent back to Africa (Emery, Gold, and Braselmann 2008). This was a solution that most black abolitionists did not support. Some abolitionists thought freedom should come gradually, while other abolitionists called for the immediate abolition of slavery. Despite differences between abolitionists, the common theme uniting them was the idea that "to hold another human being in bondage was morally wrong" (Burton 2008:154).

One of the most well-known white abolitionists was William Lloyd Garrison (1805–1879), who used the press to mobilize opposition to slavery. He was editor of *The Liberator*, and his editorials were often blamed for inciting slave rebellions. He formed the New England Anti-Slavery Society in 1832 and was part of the founding of the American Anti-Slavery Society a year later. He was jailed and his life was threatened for his unpopular opinions. Frederick Douglass (1818–1895) was born into slavery, escaped, and became perhaps the best-known abolitionist, author, and speaker of his day. Garrison and Douglass worked together for a while, until philosophical differences divided them. Douglass viewed many white abolitionists, however well intentioned, as paternalistic and racially biased in their own way.

While Lincoln is ultimately given credit for the abolition of slavery, credit should more accurately be given to abolitionists and the long-struggling abolitionist movement (Mitchell 2007). Many abolitionists, both black and white, were so dedicated to their cause that they ended up serving extensive prison sentences in state penitentiaries for various crimes associated with their activism, such as helping slaves gain their freedom. Their crimes were often considered more heinous than murder.

slave quarters, that were often seen by whites as an outgrowth of an indulgent master (Andrews 2019). While such privileges may have created status distinctions among slaves, they also drew the ire of white slave patrollers. These were groups of armed, mounted whites who rode at night among the slave plantations "seeking out runaway slaves, unsanctioned gatherings, weapons, and contraband, and generally, any sign of potential revolt" (Fountain 2018). Slaves with such privileges drew "resentment among the poorly fed and shabbily clothed white patrollers" who sought to "flog some of 'those pampered [slaves] … who were spoiled' and needed to be taught a lesson" (Andrews 2019:3).

African Americans clearly fit what Blauner (1972) refers to as a colonized minority within the United States: they were brought to this country involuntarily; their participation in a culture that was not their own was mandatory; they experienced the denigration of their original cultures; and finally, they were forced to engage in free labor for over 240 years. Thus, as a colonized minority, blacks were oppressed and kept economically subordinate for hundreds of years, influencing their socioeconomic status today, as wealth, and the lack of it, is cumulative.

REFLECT AND CONNECT

Despite the eventual elimination of slavery, how might this history influence African Americans today? What specific aspect of this history do you think has been most enduring?

THE UNIQUE EXPLOITATION OF MEXICAN AMERICANS BY WHITES

At some level, the story of Mexican American and white contact in the United States is more complicated than that of the previous groups described. That is because the Southwest region was initially populated by various Native American tribes, then colonized by Spain in the 1500s, turned over to Mexico in the aftermath of the Mexican War of Independence in 1821, and finally became part of the United States at the close of the Mexican–American War of 1846–1848 with the Treaty of Guadalupe Hidalgo. Thus, the history of Mexican Americans is a complex story of shifting nationalities as well as changing racial designations reflecting differing historical eras.

Who are Mexican Americans? These are either people who populated portions of Arizona, California, New Mexico, Nevada, Utah, Wyoming, and Colorado upon annexation by the United States in 1848, or individuals who have immigrated to the United States from present-day Mexico. **Annexation** is when one group, in this case the United States government, takes over a territory formerly under the control of another group, in this case the Mexican government, through military action or through a cooperative agreement. Mexican Americans, then, are people who have Indian, Spanish, and Mexican heritage. There is an African heritage as well, as the Spanish colonizers initially brought African slaves to Mexico. Some Mexicans immigrated to the United States voluntarily and some are descendants of people who were involuntarily incorporated into the United States territory. Mexican Americans are the result of a **racialization process**, the process by which a group is assigned a racial identity and a place in a societal racial hierarchy, a ranking system where some racial groups are privileged while others experience oppression and discrimination (Omi and Winant 1994).

Spain's colonization of Mexico, which included the southwestern United States, began in the 1500s and was accomplished through religion and the establishment of missions. New Mexico, Arizona, Texas, and California were all regions where the Catholic Church, as the arm of the Spanish Crown, attempted to establish missions, convert the Indians, and have them become taxpaying citizens of the Crown (Samora and Simon 1993). Missionaries were unsuccessful in Arizona, as Native tribes in the region violently resisted the presence of the Spanish. While alleging to save souls, the Spanish missionaries were notorious for their brutal treatment of the Indians. In fact, some have argued that these missions were merely a form of slavery under a different name (Johansen 2005).

Mexico gained independence from Spain in 1821. United States citizens began heading west and settling on Mexican lands in significant numbers in the 1820s. Interestingly, many of these white settlers chose to become Mexican citizens, converting to Catholicism and even adopting Spanish names in their efforts to assimilate into what was then Mexican culture (Samora and Simon 1993). At this time, both the incoming white settlers and the original Mexicans were farmers and ranchers and there was no racial/ethnic stratification (Meier and Rivera 1972). This situation was about to change, however. As more and more white settlers moved into Mexico, the United States government began to show great interest in acquiring this land. During this time, the belief in Manifest Destiny reigned, which was the idea that the United States had a preordained right to all the land between the Pacific Ocean and the Atlantic Ocean and even an obligation to occupy this territory.

Controversies arose in Texas and California initially, and after 1845, when the United States approved statehood for Texas, President James Polk "began to entertain the idea of acquiring all the land to the west of Texas—unwarranted aggression in Mexico's eyes" (Samora and Simon 1993:93). On the night of his inauguration, Polk confided to his secretary of the navy his desire to acquire California. In a direct challenge to Mexico, he ordered troops to the Rio Grande (Zinn 2003).

These events led to the Mexican–American War (1846–1848), concluding with the Treaty of Guadalupe Hidalgo, which turned over half of Mexico's territory to the United States. This treaty established the right of residents of that territory to preserve their Mexican culture, including their language, their land, and their Mexican citizenship if they so desired.

Despite these explicit designations in the treaty, the climate changed dramatically as whites flooded into the region at the close of the war. Individual whites sought land that belonged to Mexicans, and the federal government failed to support the treaty by setting aside Mexican-owned land for public domain. By the mid-1800s, Mexican Americans throughout the Southwest had lost political and economic power, been driven off their lands, had their rights denied, and been relegated to performing menial labor. Mexicans were now perceived by whites as unskilled and incapable of performing important jobs, stereotypes that linger today.

The new settlers, unlike those who came in the 1820s, came as conquerors with the aim of displacing Mexicans, which they did (Samora and Simon 1993). As Menchaca explains, "racial status hierarchies are often structured upon the ability of one racial group to deny those who are racially different access to owning land. This process leads to the low social prestige and impoverishment of the marginalized" (2001:1). Like Native Americans, Mexican Americans were initially exploited by whites for access to their land. As mentioned in Chapter 1, land is equivalent to wealth, and such a massive transfer of land from one group to another is a major transfer of wealth. Mexican Americans were then forced into low-wage labor on land that had previously belonged to them. Mexican Americans were the only group of those discussed in this chapter who were exploited for both their land and their labor, whereas Native Americans were exploited almost exclusively for their land and African Americans for their physical and reproductive labor (Farley 2005).

Initial contact between whites and Mexican Americans needs to be understood in terms of dominant- and subordinate-group relations. Mexicans were not initially voluntary immigrants to the United States, nor was their culture respected. They were stripped of their land and ideologies of inferiority emerged to justify their subordination, all contributing to and complicating their current status.

REFLECT AND CONNECT

Explain how an understanding of Mexican American history challenges current anti-immigrant rhetoric and sentiment.

GENDER, SEXUALITY, AND RACE

In addition to discrimination, upon contact with Europeans and European Americans between the 1500s and late 1800s, each of the racial/ethnic minority groups discussed in this chapter was subjected to notions of gender and sexuality that often challenged their cultural norms.

Gender refers to the societal norms and expectations associated with the behavior of men and women. Gender, like race, is a social construction in that definitions of appropriate behavior for males and females have changed across time and place. The specific forms of racism women of color face are referred to as **gendered racism** (Essed 1991). It refers to the ways that gender is also raced: the expectations about appropriate behavior for males and females vary along racial lines, and minority women face discrimination because they are both women and racial minorities. **Sexuality** refers to how people express themselves as sexual beings. Like gender and race, sexuality is also a social construction in that we live in societies that define appropriate sexual behaviors and sanction inappropriate ones. Just as there is gendered racism, one can understand sexuality along racial/ethnic lines as well (Nagel 2003).

How racial/ethnic minority women were treated and understood by whites is a burgeoning area of scholarship as most historical analyses have been **androcentric**, meaning they have been focused on men and men's experiences at the exclusion of women's experiences. African American, Native American, and Mexican American women were uniquely exploited based upon both their race and their sex. Definitions of appropriate sexuality were intertwined with notions of gender and race as well, causing conflict between whites and many Native American tribes. Essentially, "gender and sex were at the heart of both how Europeans perceived Indians and Africans as different" (Spear 2007:582).

To a certain extent, enslaved males and females had similar experiences in that slave marriages were not recognized; slaves were often sold away from family members, whether husband and wife or parent and child; the slave master was considered to be the head of the household; and all were exploited for their physical labor. Slave women, though, suffered in additional ways. While generations of historians remained silent on the sexual exploitation of slave women, there is now irrefutable evidence that it was commonplace for slave owners to take sexual advantage of slave women.

Gender and race intersect in our understandings of the experiences of male and female slave owners as well. Journalistic and historical accounts of slavery proclaimed that southern white women were unaware of the horrors of slavery, as slave masters handled the buying, selling, and violent reprimanding of slaves. Some argued that southern white women of the antebellum era lived restricted lives within a patriarchal and paternalistic culture, making their lives more closely resemble those of enslaved women rather than their white husbands (Glymph 2008). Such a perspective relied on the cultural understandings of white women as fragile, passive, sensitive, and emotional, and white men as dominant, unemotional, aggressive, and logical. Viewing slavery through this kind of gendered lens, it is easy to see men, masters, overseers, and slave drivers as perpetrating violence against slaves and to overlook women's role in the violent maintenance of slavery. More recent scholarship by Thavolia Glymph (2008) and Stephanie E. Jones-Rogers (2019), which relies on historical documents as well as slave narratives collected through the Federal Writer's Project (see Recommended Multimedia at the end of this chapter) challenges these understandings and instead finds that there were plenty of married, slave-owning women who actively participated in the brutality of slavery; they were active in the buying and selling of slaves, took part in the violent disciplining of slaves, and personally profited from slavery. In reality, white women held power in the private sphere; violence inside the plantation house was rampant and it was perpetrated by white women (Glymph 2008).

WITNESS

"Violence permeated the plantation household, where the control and management of slaves required white women's active participation and authorized the exercise of brute or sadistic force. Mistresses became expert in the use of psychological and physical violence … Hellish punishment did not require large transgressions" (Glymph 2008:33).

Slave Breeding

Slave owners took advantage of slave women as a way to increase their wealth by literally breeding more slaves, thus forcing slave women to participate in the perpetuation of the institution of slavery itself by bearing children who were the property of their master (Roberts 1997). Some male slaves were cruelly exploited by being used as breeders as well.

Slave breeding was justified through ideologies that compared slave women to animals: since they were breeders rather than mothers, their children could be sold away from them just as a calf was sold from a cow. Slave owners considered slave breeding to be part of their rights of ownership and a good business practice because it increased their wealth through little effort of their own. Additionally, and somewhat paradoxically, slave owners took advantage of slave women's maternal instincts, threatening the sale of their children to encourage their submissiveness (Davis 1983).

The law did not protect slave women from the crime of rape, and many slave owners consciously used rape as a weapon of terror against them. Additionally, a child born to a slave woman legally belonged to the slave master, not the mother, regardless of the identity of the father. This was encoded in law in many states as early as 1662, when the first statute in Virginia declared that children born of slave women and fathered by white men were themselves slaves. In 1809, two years after the international slave trade was abolished, a South Carolina court ruled that female slaves had no legal claims on their children (Roberts 1997). Once the slave trade was abolished, the only way a slave owner could increase his wealth was through slave breeding or participation in the illegal slave trade.

WITNESS

Slave men who were exceptionally strong were rented as studs, "used like animals to sire chattel for their masters. … Some slave owners practiced a cruel form of negative breeding. An ex-slave reported that 'runty niggers' were castrated 'so dat dey can't have no little runty chillums'" (Roberts 1997:28).

Native American Women and the European View of Women

Native American women today claim that their bodies bear the scars of colonization and that gender violence is linked to colonialism (Smith 2009). Native women were depicted by Europeans as sexually deviant, dirty, and thus deserving of rape and sexual assault. In the southwestern United States, Native women were sexually exploited by their colonizers, even without the economic incentive white southern slave owners had. Children born of such interracial unions were stigmatized by their tribes and forced into servitude at Spanish missions (Menchaca 2001).

The sexual exploitation of slave women, Mexican women, and indigenous women is fundamentally related to the European American belief that women of color were not really women and thus were not deserving of the same protections as white women. While slave women were abused as breeders, Native American women were targeted for destruction because of their capacity to give birth and ensure at least the physical survival of their tribes; thus, they were targeted with sterilization campaigns (see Chapters 5 and 8).

Europeans brought their established ideas about women's roles in society, particularly that women were weak, passive, and subservient to men and required male protection, to the New World. When they encountered women living in tribal cultures, they were confronted with women serving in sometimes powerful ways. As Europeans attempted to change tribal societies, to help them progress and become civilized, these transformations included altering gender roles:

Believing their own system of gender was natural, indeed God-given, many Europeans emphasized the ways in which Africans and Indians organized labor and power differently and judged them as inferior if not unnatural for doing so; the Europeans judged sexual mores and practices in similar terms.

(Spear 2007:582–583)

In many Native tribes, women held power, and European colonizers sought to impose patriarchal gender relations as a way to weaken and eventually destroy Native cultures, all in the name of progress (Jaimes and Halsey 1992). Many Native American tribes did not function with the same family norms as European societies; for instance, they did not establish monogamous, patriarchal, nuclear families. As the first missionaries encountered Natives and worked to convert them to Christianity, the missionaries viewed Native family structures as inherently flawed and inferior. Prior to the removal of the Cherokee in the early 1800s, the Cherokee had attempted to assimilate into white society as a way to avoid this fate. As part of their assimilationist efforts, Cherokee men wrote a Cherokee constitution that was modeled after the United States Constitution (Tucker 1969, quoted in Jaimes and Halsey 1992). In this document they disenfranchised women, relegating them to chattel, contrary to women's previously held positions of authority in the tribe.

Women played central roles in many Native tribes, and their contributions were seen as having great value. Some tribes were matrilineal and the feminine was celebrated instead of denigrated; it was "a worldview in which men balance women rather than the European conception of a hierarchical universe in which men rank above women" (Perdue 1997:78). This led to some misunderstanding as Europeans interpreted cultural patterns through their own cultural lens, rarely attempting to understand Native women or gender or sexuality from the perspective of Native people. For instance, European Americans who encountered the presence of "women's houses" or "menstrual huts" interpreted these as evidence of a Native belief that menstruating women were unclean and were to be avoided, a view shared by Western men of the era. Instead, "women's houses" were evidence of the belief in women's power and spirituality, in that menstruating women were separated from the rest of the tribe because they were perceived as too powerful during this time (Perdue 1997).

Sexuality, as a social construction, also differed for many Native American tribes and was a source of conflict between them and the European colonizers. In addition to differences in family forms discussed here, evidence shows that some tribes had three or four genders rather than merely the two found throughout the Western world: women, men, two-spirit/womanly men, and, less frequently, two-spirit/manly women (Lang 1997). Since the earliest European contact there were reports of Native American males who took up the culturally defined roles of women, or did women's crafts, or wore women's clothing, and sometimes established sexual relationships with other men. While on the surface these may appear to refer to distinctions of sexuality, these categories were not always defined sexually but instead were gender distinctions, referring to individuals who combined masculine and feminine characteristics, and thus challenged the Western understanding of gender as binary (one is either male/masculine or female/feminine) (Lang 1997). Upon encountering societies that celebrated more than two genders, Europeans immediately stigmatized them and deemed them inferior and uncivilized. Gender variance within Native American tribes had mostly disappeared by the 1930s, as a result of Euro-American repression and forced assimilation (Nanda 2020).

Indians were strongly encouraged to adopt patriarchal family structures, monogamous marriage, and a gendered division of labor, so as to progress (Newman 1999). These significant differences in social organization, gender roles, family structures, and sexuality fueled ideologies of Native American inferiority among the colonizers due to their ethnocentrism, their belief that European cultures were superior. When such ideologies of inferiority exist, it becomes easy to dehumanize, exploit, or even destroy other cultures, which is exactly what happened in contact between Europeans and Indians, Mexican Americans, and African Americans.

RESISTANCE

The fact that whites were able to successfully oppress and exploit African Americans, Native Americans, and Mexican Americans erroneously presents these racial/ethnic groups as passive. The reality is very different. In the face of such brutality, racial/ethnic minorities have actively and creatively, individually and collectively, resisted their oppression at every step. James C. Scott (1992) argues that subordinate-group resistance takes the form of a **hidden transcript**, the actions and interactions that occur outside the gaze of members of the dominant group that challenge the **public transcript**, which is the actions and interactions that subordinate groups engage in while in the presence of the dominant group that make them appear to accept their subordination.

Understanding resistance to oppression requires understanding the tension between social structure and individual agency. Social structure refers to patterns of behavior and relationships between groups in a society, the way norms and social institutions become embedded, and the ways these can begin to shape the behavior of individual actors within a social system. It can be thought of as the web of relationships in which we exist and that informs our behaviors (Merton 1938). For instance, during the slave era, blacks and whites were born into the existing system or social structure, which limited or facilitated their options and choices in life. The flip side of this notion is what we call agency. While sociologists tend to focus on social structures, we also recognize individual agency, a person's capacity to act within any social structure. Focusing on agency allows us to avoid inaccurately portraying people as passive pawns of the social system. Both structure and agency are important for understanding individuals and societies. To paraphrase Karl Marx on this issue: people make history, although they do not always do so under conditions of their own choosing. Resistance to racial/ethnic oppression is evidence of minority group agency in the face of the serious structural constraints of racial oppression (see Box 4.3 Global Perspectives: The Haitian Revolution).

BOX 4.3

Global Perspectives:
The Haitian Revolution

Haiti stands alone as a nation that emerged out of a successful slave rebellion. Between the years 1791 and 1804, Toussaint L'Ouverture led Haitian slaves in a military rebellion that at varying times took on the French, Spanish, and British colonial powers, eventually winning their independence (Ennals 2007). At the time of the revolution, Saint-Domingue, as it was known, was an immensely wealthy French colony that produced, through slave labor, three-quarters of the world's sugar and a quarter of the world's coffee (Knutson 2004).

The Haitian Revolution struck fear in slave owners throughout the hemisphere. At the time of the revolution, slavery was ensconced in the United States, Brazil, and the Caribbean. All of the major European colonial powers had an interest in maintaining slavery in the Americas. Through this successful revolution, the fragility of the system had been exposed. Within one month of the uprising, slaves in Jamaica, Cuba, Brazil, and Virginia were aware of it, discussing it, and singing songs about it and slave owners were complaining of a new "insolence" among their slaves. This revolution provided the exemplar for black slaves across the globe (Geggus 2001). It showed whites and blacks that black slaves could organize, successfully rebel, and establish their own government (Ennals 2007).

In a world where white supremacy reigned, L'Ouverture mounted a serious challenge to the prevailing racist ideology with this victory. As Haiti's military leader and first governor, he established a constitution that prohibited land ownership by whites and offered citizenship to anyone of African or Indian descent (Geggus 2001). The global effect of the Haitian Revolution cannot be underestimated.

Africans who found themselves on slave ships bound for the New World engaged in hunger strikes, committed suicide, or united to overthrow the ship's crew. The high death rates noted previously on the passage sometimes were the result of failed insurrections or successful suicides (Burton 2008). The story of the *Amistad*, a slave ship whose crew was successfully overthrown by the Africans on board, is perhaps the most famous example of such insurrections.

Once in the United States and sold into slavery, blacks continued to resist their subordination. Slaves would attack overseers, sabotage equipment, feign illness or injury, engage in work slowdowns, and in rare instances, engage in large-scale slave rebellions. The most common form of resistance was running away. Historian Herbert Aptheker (1974) insisted that the image of slaves as docile was erroneous and found slaves engaged in daily acts of defiance, including evidence of approximately

Harriet Tubman (1823–1913)
nurse, spy and scout

IMAGE 4.3: Harriet Tubman, known as "Moses" for her work freeing slaves through the Underground Railroad, was born into slavery and escaped. It is estimated that she helped over three hundred slaves escape to freedom.

250 slave plots and uprisings. Harriet Tubman, known as "Moses," was a runaway slave herself and made nineteen trips into the South to help three hundred slaves escape to their freedom through what became known as the Underground Railroad (Burton 2008).

Slave rebellions were the ultimate form of resistance and the most feared by whites. Nat Turner's rebellion in 1831 and the discovery of Denmark Vesey's conspiracy to engage in rebellion in 1822 are two of the most significant examples of the threat of slave insurrection in the United States; the overthrow of colonial rule in Haiti by slaves is an example of a successful slave rebellion. The largest slave revolt in US history occurred in 1811 in Louisiana. After killing a plantation owner's son, dozens of armed slaves marched from plantation to plantation toward New Orleans, burning several in the process. The militia suppressed this revolt quickly and dozens of participants were executed.

Learning to read was also a form of agency and an act of resistance for slaves as antiliteracy laws were designed to dehumanize and control the enslaved population. Literacy was a sign of potential social mobility, and as most southern whites at the time were illiterate, maintaining black illiteracy was essential in order to maintain ideologies of white superiority (Burton 2008).

Another form of documented resistance to slavery involves slaves suing their masters in court for their freedom. Many of the masters being sued were well known —for instance, Henry Clay, a sitting Secretary of State, was sued by his slave,

Charlotte Dupuy, for her freedom. Known as freedom suits, over five hundred of such court cases have been compiled and digitized for the decade between 1820 and 1830 alone (Dunker 2019; see Recommended Multimedia at the end of the chapter).

Women resisted the sexual advances of their masters and many female slaves did what they could to not bear children as a way to resist their role in the reproduction of slavery. Slave owners speculated that slave women deliberately terminated their pregnancies, and there is even evidence of the ultimate form of resistance engaged in by female slaves, the use of infanticide, "killing their newborns to keep them from living as chattel" (Roberts 1997:48).

Evidence of Native and Mexican American resistance to oppression also exists. When enslaved, Native people had a reputation for getting sick and dying as opposed to remaining in their oppressed condition (Bennett 1961). The Native American tribes the Spanish colonizers met in Arizona so ferociously resisted the Spanish that they abandoned attempts to establish missions in that region. Native resistance was also manifest in more recognizable ways as centuries of military conflicts between colonists or the United States government and various Indian tribes, from the Pequot War of 1637 to the closing of the frontier after the massacre at Wounded Knee in 1890. In response to the federal government's forced relocations, some tribes turned around and marched thousands of miles back to their homelands to protest their initial relocation.

Resistance is evidence of minority group agency and will be highlighted throughout the book as a reminder that the social order is always a process of ongoing negotiation. While whites have been the dominant racial group since their arrival on this continent, their dominance is always contested, always challenged by subordinate racial/ethnic groups. Resistance to the racial hierarchy also comes from members of the dominant group who view the system as inequitable. Agency, sociologists remind us, can occur at both the individual and the collective levels.

REFLECT AND CONNECT

Why is it important to emphasize subordinate-group agency in the face of oppression?

CHAPTER SUMMARY

United States history seen through a racial/ethnic lens is unavoidably a story of conflict and violence. Race is a creation of a particular historical era and is a result of particular social conditions. Sociologists working within the power-conflict perspective emphasize that the origins of racial/ethnic inequality are linked to the emergence of colonialism and capitalism; one group dominates and exploits another so as to benefit from that exploitation. Racist beliefs emerge to justify this exploitation and to reinforce the status quo. Racial/ethnic inequality and exploitation manifest in many ways in this country, from the usurpation of Native American lands to the enslavement of African Americans, the appropriation of land and labor from Mexican Americans throughout the Southwest, and the gendered racism racial/ethnic minority women have faced.

In addition to the opportunity for exploitation, sociologists also focus on the role of government, the racialization of state policy, in establishing and maintaining racial/ethnic inequality in the United States. Finally, sociologists focus on more than social structures for understanding racial and ethnic inequality. We also emphasize the role of agency, the active resistance to oppression that racial and ethnic minority groups engage in.

Understanding the history of racial/ethnic inequality in the United States facilitates our understanding of current racial/ethnic inequalities. It allows us to understand the cumulative effects of oppression as well as the cumulative effects of privilege. History is also essential for understanding the social construction of race; it permits us to see how racial categories are created and change across time. In this chapter, we explored how the concept of race emerged in conjunction with colonialism and the slave trade. It expanded as whites encountered Mexicans and Native American tribes of the interior of the United States in their interminable desire for land.

KEY TERMS AND CONCEPTS

Androcentric

Annexation

Colonialism

Cultural genocide

Ethnocentrism

Gender

Gendered racism

Genocide

Hidden transcript

Public transcript

Racial democracy

Racial dictatorship

Racialization of state policy

Racialization process

Sexuality

Social mobility

Social structure

Stereotypes

Stratification

PERSONAL REFLECTIONS

1. How much did you know about the racial/ethnic history of this country prior to reading this chapter? How much do you know about your family history as it may pertain to the racial history presented in this chapter? In other words, do

you know whether your ancestors were involved in the slave trade or governmental oppression of Native Americans, were forcibly removed from their homelands by the federal government, or were enslaved? Ask your family members about your family history. How do you feel about your family history? Put yourself in the shoes of someone from a different racial/ethnic group than your own. How would it feel to view history from their perspective compared to yours?

2. Had you previously considered the gendered nature of early racial/ethnic conflict and inequality? If not, why do you think that is? Using this chapter's historical lesson on the intersection of gender and race as a guide, speculate on the ways racial/ethnic inequality is gendered today.

CRITICAL THINKING QUESTIONS

1. Why is it important to understand slavery from the perspective of those enslaved as well as the perspective of the dominant group (see *Unchained Memories* under Recommended Films)? Why have these voices only been discovered recently? What does this tell us about history and how we understand the past?

2. Based upon the information relayed in this chapter, how are the US government, capitalism, and racism linked and how have they historically reinforced each other?

ESSENTIAL READING

Bennett, Lerone. 1961. *Before the Mayflower: A History of the Negro in America, 1619–1964.* New York: Penguin Books.

Dunbar-Ortiz, Roxanne. 2014. *An Indigenous Peoples' History of the United States.* Boston, MA: Beacon Press.

Jones-Rogers, Stephanie E. 2019. *They Were Her Property: White Women as Slave Owners in the American South.* New Haven, CT: Yale University Press.

Loewen, James. 2007. *Lies My Teacher Told Me: Everything Your American History Textbook Got Wrong,* revised ed. New York: Simon and Schuster.

Zinn, Howard. 2003. *A People's History of the United States: 1492–Present.* New York: Harper Perennial Modern Classics.

RECOMMENDED FILMS

The Abolitionists (2013). Written, produced, and directed by Rob Rapley. Weaving together dramatic performances with documentary evidence, this film looks at the lives of passionate antislavery activists such as Frederick Douglass, William Lloyd Garrison, Angelina Grimké, Harriet Beecher Stowe, and John Brown, the movement they founded, and the intense opposition they faced.

The Canary Effect: Kill the Indian, Save the Man (2006). Directed by Robin Davey and Yellow Thunder Woman. This documentary explores the history of European–Native contact and the disastrous effects the United States' policies and practices have had on indigenous people, with particular attention paid to the horrific abuses Native people faced at the hands of whites and the genocidal strategies of the US government.

Slavery and the Making of America (2004). Written, produced, and directed by Dante J. James (Episode 1), Gail Pellett (Episode 2), Chana Gazit (Episode 3), and Leslie D. Farrell (Episode 4). This four-part PBS series explores American slavery, from its earliest days through the Civil War, and includes a detailed account of Reconstruction. Particular importance is placed upon the latest scholarship on the economic importance of slavery to the making of America as well as on the brutality of daily life as a slave.

Traces of the Trade: A Story from the Deep North (2008). Produced and directed by Katrina Browne. This poignant film explores one white woman's discovery that her family's status and privilege was based upon an ugly secret: that they were the largest slave-trading dynasty in American history. This film is unique not only in its portrayal of the role slavery played in the entire American economy but in the fact that it is the story of how one northern family and their entire community benefited from the slave trade. Producer/director Katrina Browne invites family members on her exploratory trip to Ghana, discusses the impact of slavery on African societies, and details the effect this information has on each of them. A major theme is racial reconciliation.

Unchained Memories: Readings from the Slave Narratives (2003). Directed by Ed Bell and Thomas Lennon. This film brings to life the Federal Writers' Project slave narratives from the 1930s (see Recommended Multimedia), read by well-known actors.

RECOMMENDED MULTIMEDIA

1619 Project—The *New York Times Magazine* and the Pulitzer Center. The idea behind the 1619 Project is to reframe American history and mark the date of the arrival of the first Africans as the real founding of this nation and to make explicit how slavery is the foundation on which the United States was built. This website contains the original essays from the *New York Times Magazine*, a reading guide, and lesson plans. https://pulitzercenter.org/lesson-plan-grouping/1619-project-curriculum.

Slave narratives from the Federal Writers' Project of 1936–1938, Library of Congress. This site contains more than 2,300 first-person accounts of slavery and over five hundred photos of former slaves and is considered to be the most complete portrait of what life in slavery was like. http://memory.loc.gov/ammem/snhtml.

The University of Nebraska—Lincoln's Center for Digital Research in the Humanities has compiled and digitized court documents from more than five hundred freedom suits. These are available through their online database "O Say Can You See: Early Washington, DC, Law and Family." http://earlywashingtondc.org/.

A Guide to the Mexican–American War—Virtual Programs and Services, Library of Congress. This digital collection of materials associated with the Mexican–American War includes maps, manuscripts, photos, government documents, and even sheet music. www.loc.gov/rr/program/bib/mexicanwar.

Race Relations in the Nineteenth and Twentieth Centuries

CHAPTER LEARNING OUTCOMES

By the end of this chapter, you should be able to:

- Understand the assimilationist perspective and why it is the preferred model for race/ethnic relations among functionalists
- Evaluate the strengths and limitations of Park's race relations cycle for understanding intergroup contact
- Describe the changing racial ideologies associated with the shift from slavery to Jim Crow
- Critically examine the power-threat hypothesis for understanding lynching and race riots
- Explain the obstacles to assimilation African Americans and Chinese Americans historically faced and the efforts taken at forcing the assimilation of Native Americans

In the post–Civil War era, many white southerners were interested in reestablishing white supremacy in the aftermath of slavery. One of the primary tools for doing so was the prison system. States throughout the South began passing vagabond laws designed to allow the incarceration of people for minor crimes, and these laws generally targeted black people. Once arrested, criminals were forced to labor throughout the South; they picked cotton, cleared swamps, built railroads, and paved roads. The convict-leasing system in Florida was so horrific that the state became known as the American Siberia (Carrier 2004). Most prisoners were arrested for minor offenses. Mississippi passed the *Pig Law* in 1876, which redefined the theft of a farm animal or any property valued at ten dollars or more as punishable by up to five years (Oshinsky 1996).

Many convicts died due to the abuse of convict labor, as "records of this era tell a story of endless brutality and neglect" (Oshinsky 1996:45). Prisoners ate and slept on the ground, without blankets or mattresses, and many died of shackle poisoning (caused by the constant rubbing of chains and leg irons on bare flesh) or such diseases as pneumonia or tuberculosis. Convict leasing was referred to as "worse than slavery."

By the end of the 1880s, at least ten thousand black men were again working as slaves, only this time their enslavement was due to accusations of or convictions for criminal behavior (Blackmon 2008).

Racial hierarchies are not static; instead, they are constantly responding to changing social and historical conditions, as well as to challenges from subordinate groups. With the termination of slavery in the United States, an entire social order was eliminated, leaving whites, as the dominant racial group, desperately trying to maintain their power and privilege. In addition to the human, economic, and emotional toll of the Civil War and the emancipation of four million former slaves, many other cultural changes influenced the racial order and made the late nineteenth and early twentieth centuries an unstable and brutally oppressive period for racial/ethnic minorities in the United States.

Certain social conditions, primarily rapid urbanization and industrialization, contributed to societal instability at this time. It was a time of dramatic economic inequality, as industry leaders reaped huge profits while workers faced extreme exploitation, with few rights or benefits. The United States was also experiencing unprecedented immigration from Southern and Eastern Europe. With the completion of the Transcontinental Railroad and the "opening of the West," even forcibly relocating Native Americans to points farther west proved insufficient to satisfy the European American desire for land. All of these changes produced a society in flux, where the social order could not be taken for granted and where clashes between racial/ethnic groups intensified. One of the manifestations of this instability was the establishment of Jim Crow, the era of segregation, terror, and extreme subjugation of African Americans throughout the southern United States, a period referred to as "worse than slavery" (Oshinsky 1996). Examples of the ways racism manifested itself in this era include the following:

- Even Las Vegas, Nevada, was rigidly segregated during the first half of the twentieth century, which was problematic because shows relied on a lot of black talent. When black actor Sammy Davis Jr. swam in a whites-only pool at a hotel, the manager drained the pool. African American actress Lena Horne was an exception to the whites-only rule at the Flamingo Hotel: she was allowed to stay, as long as she avoided the casinos, restaurants, and other public spaces. Additionally, when she checked out, her towels and bedsheets were burned (Cook 2012).

- In the 1870s, the US government sought to destroy the Cheyenne, Lakota, and other tribes of the Great Plains by exterminating sixty million buffalo, their primary form of subsistence (Stiffarm and Lane 1992).
- "Jews were increasingly seen as a racial group ... in the mid to late nineteenth century—particularly as the demographics of immigration tilted away from German and other West European Jews, and toward the Yiddish-speaking Jews of Eastern Europe" (Jacobson 1998:172).
- "By 1900, the South's judicial system had been wholly reconfigured to make one of its primary purposes the coercion of African Americans to comply with the social customs and labor demands of whites" (Blackmon 2008:7).
- "The first transcontinental railroad was built with blood, sweat, politics and thievery. ... The construction was done by three thousand Irish and ten thousand Chinese, over a period of four years, working for one or two dollars a day" (Zinn 2003:254).

SOCIOLOGICAL PERSPECTIVES ON INTERGROUP RELATIONS

In the previous chapter, power-conflict perspectives on racial/ethnic inequality were introduced. While those theories are helpful for understanding racial/ethnic conflict and inequality, the dominant perspective in the sociology of race/ethnic relations has been the functionalist perspective. The functionalist tradition emphasizes the importance of social order and stability, societal consensus, and equilibrium. Order and stability are preferred over conflict so that society functions smoothly. Functionalists argue that inequality between groups can result in conflict, and well-functioning societies must find ways to reduce racial/ethnic stratification or inequality with the ultimate goal of eradicating racial/ethnic conflict.

From a functionalist perspective, the primary solution to the problem of racial and ethnic inequality is assimilation, which literally means "the act of making similar." Minority groups go through a process of adapting to the culture of the dominant group. If groups become more similar, there will be less racial/ethnic conflict and more societal stability. Assimilation has been viewed not only by sociologists but also by society as the desired outcome for minority groups in a society. The expectation that immigrants to the United States speak English is an example of the continuing pressure to assimilate.

Sociologist Robert E. Park provides one of the earliest and most influential assimilationist perspectives in sociology, the **race relations cycle**. Park's cycle was composed of four stages: contact, competition, accommodation, and assimilation

(Park 1950). He argues that as groups come into contact with one another through migration, they initially compete for valuable resources. This competition results in conflict, which leads to accommodation, where the immigrant group is compelled to adjust to the dominant group's norms as a way to reduce the conflict. Accommodation paves the way for assimilation, which is the desired goal from this perspective. Once the group assimilates, it becomes so similar to the dominant group that there are no longer differences that can result in discord.

According to Park, this is a pattern that repeats itself across the globe and is progressive and irreversible, although the length of time it takes groups to go through this cycle can vary. While this model helps explain white ethnic assimilation patterns, such as the Irish American experience in the United States, it fails to adequately address the lack of assimilation of racial minority groups, such as African Americans. Park tries to address this by acknowledging that "racial barriers may slacken the tempo of the movement; may perhaps halt it altogether for a time; but cannot change its direction" (1950:150). In other words, it will simply take longer for racial minorities to assimilate than it does for white ethnics. Assimilation is inevitable and desirable, according to the functionalist perspective on racial/ethnic stratification, even if it will be a slower process for groups defined as racial minorities.

Milton Gordon (1964) expands on Park's race relations cycle by identifying several subprocesses of assimilation. Park's position only emphasized what Gordon calls **cultural assimilation**, whereby the minority group absorbs the culture of the dominant group, its norms, values, and behavioral expectations. However, complete assimilation also requires **structural assimilation**, the merging of dominant and subordinate groups in interpersonal relationships. Structural assimilation involves integration in intimate relationships, such as families, friendship networks, social circles, and marriages. Until this happens, assimilation is not complete. According to Gordon, African Americans, for example, can be seen as culturally assimilated; however, there is still a divide in terms of structural relationships: most families, friendship networks, and marriages are intraracial (see Chapter 12).

Gordan (1964) further analyzes three ways assimilation can occur: the melting pot, Anglo-conformity, and cultural pluralism. Most Americans are taught to think of US society as a melting pot, which refers to the idea that people from all over the world come to this country and blend together to create a new identity, that of the "American." In this view, subordinate groups are not alone in being asked to change; the dominant group also changes. No one comes here already an "American." All groups that immigrate to the United States must drop some of their cultural characteristics and adopt those associated with American culture if they wish to be "American." This is an assimilationist ideology because it encourages downplaying racial/ethnic/cultural differences among groups over time and merging into a new group identity.

While the idea of American society as a melting pot is a deeply ingrained belief, it is more accurate to view the United States society as one of assimilation through **Anglo-conformity**. Anglo-conformity differs from the notion of a melting pot in that it's not both groups that are expected to change. In this view, subordinate groups are expected to conform to a white, Protestant, English-speaking society. Anglo-conformity became the norm simply due to the fact that white, Protestant, English-speakers were the ones who held the most power when the country was founded. By definition, then, racial minorities, groups whose physical distinctions at least partially set them apart from the dominant group, can never fully and completely assimilate. Anglo-conformity can help explain why assimilation is easier for white ethnic immigrants, like Irish Americans or German Americans, and is even easier for those who already speak English.

A third assimilationist ideology, cultural pluralism, states that it is not necessary for immigrants to give up all aspects of their culture to assimilate into the dominant American society. Instead, they can be fully functioning members of mainstream society while retaining their ethnic heritage. For instance, US citizens may speak Spanish in their home, but, from the perspective of cultural pluralism, a certain amount of cultural assimilation is anticipated; for example, they are expected to speak English in schools and in the workplace. While Anglo-conformity has been the dominant thrust in American society, pluralism has always existed as a competing belief system, challenging ideologies of both the melting pot and Anglo-conformity.

The assimilationist perspective became the dominant perspective within the sociology of race/ethnicity. Assimilation was viewed as the unquestioned goal of immigrant groups and was particularly good at explaining the experiences of white European ethnics in American society. Despite its usefulness for understanding the experiences of white ethnic immigrants, there are some well-documented weaknesses with the assimilationist perspective. For instance, this perspective has not been very useful for understanding the experiences of racial minorities. Additionally, the assimilationist perspective fails to acknowledge that minority groups may not wish to assimilate; people may wish to maintain their original cultures. Finally, this perspective is also accused of being one-way assimilation: the dominant group is not forced to change; instead subordinate groups alone bear the burden of change (Farley 2005).

Despite these weaknesses, the assimilationist perspective had considerable influence in American society, and, in the case of the American Indian during the late nineteenth and early twentieth centuries, government policies mandated minority-group assimilation. For instance, a full-blown *Americanization movement* emerged between 1909 and the early 1920s that involved explicit attempts at assimilating immigrants, primarily those who differed culturally or religiously from Anglo-Americans. Public schools were instructed to teach immigrants more than English; they were expected to teach civics, middle-class values, and discipline to ensure loyalty and cultural conformity (Daniels 1998).

REFLECT AND CONNECT

In what ways do you see schools helping with immigrant assimilation? In addition to schools, what other institutions help assimilate immigrants? Give an example.

FROM RECONSTRUCTION TO JIM CROW

The explanatory power of the assimilationist perspective has not been very effective for understanding the experiences of African Americans. Even after emancipation, race relations in the United States, particularly those between blacks and whites, can still best be understood through a conflict perspective.

President Abraham Lincoln issued the *Emancipation Proclamation* in 1863, freeing all the slaves held within the Confederacy and imposing a federal occupation of southern states that had seceded from the union; thus, the federal government militarily occupied and politically ruled some southern states for a period after the Civil War. When the Confederate Army surrendered in 1865, officially ending the Civil War, there was no consensus as to what should be done with the newly freed slaves, although former slave and abolitionist Frederick Douglass suggested that whites should "do nothing. ... Your *doing* with [Blacks] is their greatest misfortune" (Bennett 1961:186).

Lincoln had to be convinced that the situation in the South required federal action to prevent the passage of legislation that was designed to maintain black subordination despite emancipation. Pennsylvanian congressman Thaddeus Stevens pushed for giving blacks the most basic political right: the right to vote. Massachusetts senator Charles Sumner was concerned about the plight of the former slaves and proposed the federal government break up plantations to provide the freed slave with "forty acres of land and treat him like a human being" (Bennett 1961:187). It was understood that some basic economic security would be a necessary foundation for newly freed slaves to establish themselves and start their new lives. In the immediate postwar period, prior to 1870, it is estimated that nearly one-quarter of the four million newly freed slaves died or suffered from illness. Many ended up in refugee camps near union army bases where they were exposed to infectious disease and hunger; "so bad were the health problems suffered by newly freed slaves, and so high the death rates, that some observers of the time even wondered if they would all die out" (Harris 2012).

Instead of addressing the survival needs of the newly freed slaves, with the end of the Civil War, white political leaders of southern states began enacting legislation to meet what they saw as their greatest needs: to maintain a cheap labor supply in the South and to reestablish white supremacy. This was established through Black Codes, laws restricting black freedom of movement, travel, and access to better jobs. These codes included complex and changing rules concerning appropriate racial etiquette, as well as vagrancy laws that forced blacks to work or be incarcerated. Black Codes differed from state to state and were often absurd, specifically forbidding blacks to engage in any work other than farming, for instance, or declaring it a crime for black people to quit their job, or even denoting insulting gestures as violations of the law in some southern states. As the opening vignette describes, vagrancy laws targeted blacks for minor crimes and, once incarcerated for the crime, they were rented to individuals and businesses as convict labor in mines, factories, and cotton fields. By 1890, the South had eighteen thousand prisoners, 90 percent of whom were black, engaged in convict labor, a form of exploitation (see Chapter 10) (Blackmon 2008).

These laws also resulted in the emergence of sharecropping, an agricultural system in which farmers worked land owned by others in return, theoretically, for a share of the profits from the crops. Newly freed slaves, who were usually uneducated, lacked employment options, and had limited opportunities for travel, often found sharecropping to be their only means of employment. Sharecropping allowed southern landowners to get their needed labor very cheaply, while former slaves found themselves victims of rampant fraud that indebted them further and led to a new form of servitude.

Reconstruction Era

Whereas slavery can be viewed as an example of a racial dictatorship, the ten years known as the Reconstruction era, during which the actions of the federal government supported the full civil and political rights of blacks, can be viewed as the beginning of a racial democracy. Three significant pieces of legislation, passed after the Civil War ended, transformed southern race relations dramatically for a short period of time: the Thirteenth Amendment (1865) permanently abolished slavery throughout the United States; the Fourteenth Amendment (1868) made former slaves citizens of the United States with full citizenship rights; and, finally, the Fifteenth Amendment (1870) gave black men the right to vote by prohibiting the denial of that right on the basis of race or color. These amendments were deemed necessary because there was fear that the Emancipation Proclamation would be interpreted as a temporary war measure. The era of Reconstruction, pushed by "Radical Republicans" in Congress, had begun.

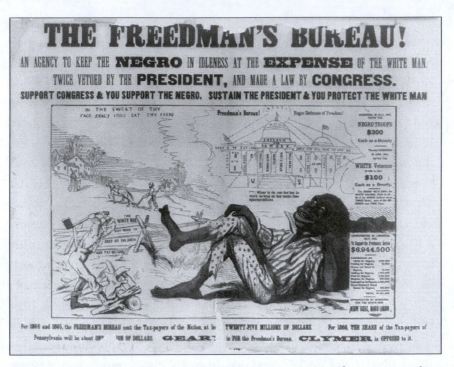

IMAGE 5.1: This cartoon from 1866 is one in a series of posters attacking Radical Republicans on the issue of black suffrage.

The heart of Reconstruction involved the *Reconstruction Acts of 1867*, which provided for the protection of the rights of newly freed blacks through federal military intervention in southern states, and passage of the Civil Rights Act of 1866. This act was designed to protect the rights of newly freed blacks by, much like its 1960s successor, prohibiting discrimination on the basis of race, creed, or color in theaters, hotels, and all public accommodation, and by nullifying the Black Codes, those state-by-state legal efforts implemented to maintain black subordination. President Andrew Johnson had vetoed the Civil Rights Act; however, Congress overturned the veto by a two-thirds majority vote.

As part of the federal reconstruction efforts, the Freedmen's Bureau was established in 1865. Officially entitled the Bureau of Refugees, Freedmen, and Abandoned Lands, it provided basic necessities, such as food, medical care, education, and sometimes land, to newly freed blacks and poor whites in Reconstruction states. While the intentions behind this federal agency were to help the newly freed slaves to prosper, its success was limited due to lack of funding and intense local opposition. The Freedmen's Bureau was unable to adequately address many of the needs of former slaves and displaced refugees of the Civil War; however, it was successful at helping establish schools throughout the South (see Chapter 7).

Such actions by the federal government represented a formal challenge to the existing racial hierarchy. The idea of who was an American was being challenged.

IMAGE 5.2: During the Reconstruction era, many African Americans held political offices throughout the former Confederacy: secretary of state in Florida, state supreme court justice in South Carolina, and lieutenant governors of Mississippi, Louisiana, and South Carolina, just to name a few. This image is of the first African American senator and representatives of the 41st and 42nd Congress. Pictured: Senator Hiram Revels and Representatives Benjamin S. Turner, Josiah T. Walls, Joseph H. Rainey, Robert Brown Elliott, Robert C. De Large, and Jefferson F. Long.

Through the extension of full citizenship rights, including the right to vote, plus government protection in the form of the military occupation of the South, and the establishment of the Freedmen's Bureau, the government was proclaiming, for the first time, that the United States was more than a white person's country.

During the Reconstruction era, former slaves embraced their new freedom and citizenship by enthusiastically seeking education, employment, and political participation. There was a dramatic rise in black literacy during this period. Many black colleges, such as Fisk, Howard, Morehouse, Spelman, and the Hampton Institute, were established during the Reconstruction era, at least partially with federal funds through the Freedmen's Bureau (Bennett 1961; Davis 1983; Du Bois 1989). The first public school systems for white and black children in the South were established during this era as well (see Chapter 7).

Blacks gained political offices throughout the former Confederacy: secretary of state in Florida, the state supreme court justice in South Carolina, and lieutenant governors of Mississippi, Louisiana, and South Carolina (Bennett 1961). While the vast majority of black Americans during the post–Civil War era remained mired in desperate poverty, some became extremely wealthy. It was an era of hope and promise, but unfortunately it was short lived.

Legal Disenfranchisement and the Emergence of Jim Crow

Reconstruction ended by 1877 as the final federal troops were removed from southern states. By 1883 the Supreme Court had overturned the Civil Rights Act of 1875, which protected the right to serve on juries, as well as access to public transportation and the right of all Americans to accommodations such as restaurants, regardless of race. Overturning the Civil Rights Act shifted federal judicial support away from the protection of blacks and toward the reestablishment of white supremacy in the South. The Supreme Court ruled repeatedly against civil rights for blacks during this era, culminating in the 1896 decision *Plessy v. Ferguson*, which declared segregation constitutionally protected, as long as "separate but equal" facilities were provided. In this decision, the majority of the court found that the Thirteenth and Fourteenth Amendments provided blacks with political equality but not social equality, which they felt could not and should not be legislated.

The impact of *Plessy v. Ferguson* was profound and the decision led to the legalization of racial segregation in all aspects of southern life. Many of us have seen grainy black and white images of "White Only" and "Colored" signs above water fountains from this era; however, segregation was far more extensive than this. Legal racial segregation involved educational institutions, public transportation, hospitals, cemeteries, elevators, hotels, public parks, public pools, beaches, restaurants, restrooms, physician waiting rooms, theaters, taverns, prisons, churches, and generally any public place. African Americans could not try on clothes or shoes in a store, go to the state fair except on designated "colored days," or call a white person by his or her first name (Carrier 2004). Florida made it illegal to store black children's schoolbooks in the same place where white children's schoolbooks were stored. In Alabama, blacks and whites were prohibited from playing checkers together. New Orleans created separate red-light districts for black and white prostitutes. Additionally, all southern states prohibited interracial marriage.

This system of extreme segregation became known as Jim Crow. The term *Jim Crow* comes from an early minstrel song and character, "Jump Jim Crow," popularized by T. D. "Daddy" Rice. Rice is considered to be the father of American minstrelsy, which was a form of entertainment in the mid to late 1800s in which white actors wore blackface and ridiculed black slaves and ex-slaves for the benefit of white audiences (see Chapter 11). The Jim Crow caricature was based upon a white person's interpretation of the real-life awkward walk of a disabled African American stable hand in Louisville, Kentucky (Oakley 1997). It is unclear how the term came to be used to describe the system of segregation in the post-Reconstruction South, but once used the term took on a life of its own.

There were two primary goals associated with Jim Crow in the South: to reestablish black subordination and to disenfranchise black male voters. Post-Reconstruction Black Codes that denied black males their constitutional right to vote were first passed in Mississippi in 1890 (no women of any race could legally vote at this time). Such legislation denied anyone from voting if his grandfather had not voted, legislation known as the grandfather clause. Poll taxes were enacted, as were highly subjective reading comprehension tests, all designed to turn away black voters at the polls, without explicitly stating in the law that they were denying blacks their constitutional right to vote. Such methods also had the effect of excluding many poor whites from political participation as well. In Louisiana, black voting fell by 90 percent due to such measures, while white voting fell by 60 percent (Bloom 1987). Many southern states also excluded blacks from serving on juries and working in law enforcement.

The enthusiasm of ex-slaves for such basic civil rights was threatening to southern whites, particularly elite white plantation owners. For these landowners, maintaining the class structure was integral to maintaining the racial hierarchy. Upper-class southern white rhetoric espousing the fear of "Negro domination" emerged as a way to generate widespread white support for the disenfranchisement of blacks (Bloom 1987). As the threat of blacks gaining political office was very real, many southern whites took a multipronged approach to maintaining their political power through legal maneuvering as well as terror.

Racial Subordination Through Terror

Often, violent tactics were used to support black political disenfranchisement, as blacks who attempted to resist often became the victims of lynching. Maintaining white supremacy became an overt goal of whites in the post–Civil War and post-Reconstruction South. Newly organized white supremacist organizations would terrorize blacks who dared to embrace their newly gained citizenship rights. Nathan Bedford Forrest, a former Confederate cavalry general, organized and led the first Ku Klux Klan meeting in April 1867 with the explicit goal of reducing black political participation. There were dozens of race riots, during which hundreds of newly freed blacks were massacred. Klan murders of blacks took place in broad daylight without fear of prosecution because it was commonly accepted that a black person "had no rights that a white person had to respect," as stated in the 1857 *Dred Scott v. Sanford* Supreme Court decision, which declared slaves and their descendants, whether free or slave, could never be citizens of the United States and thus were not granted constitutional protections.

White use of terror and intimidation not only doomed Reconstruction but also ensured the reestablishment of a racial hierarchy resembling that which had existed in the antebellum era. The institution of oppression changed with the elimination of slavery; however, racial ideologies of black inferiority were still dominant and new ideologies of black inferiority emerged. For instance, the fear of a violent, criminal black male was not a necessary belief system during slavery but became a fundamental part of Jim Crow as a way to justify their segregation and disenfranchisement. Thus, whites established new forms of institutional discrimination in the form of Jim Crow, legal segregation, discrimination, disenfranchisement, and terror. Under slavery, particularly in the face of growing calls for abolition, ideologies of black inferiority were created and perpetuated. Emancipation and black progress during the Reconstruction era called such ideologies into question, however, and evidence of black competence was threatening to whites. African Americans who were successful in business, were professionals, owned their own land, or were in businesses that competed with local white businesses, or threatened beliefs of black inferiority invited hostile retaliation from whites.

Blacks who did not "know their place," those who dared to challenge their subordination, were at risk of being lynched. **Lynching** is a form of vigilante justice, a murder carried out in public, administered by mobs, and involving torture such as burning, castration, shooting, or dismemberment. According to sociologist Herbert Blumer (1958), feelings of hostility and competition emerge between different racial/ ethnic groups because people have a sense of their **group position**, the position their group occupies, and should occupy, relative to out-groups in the social order. Thus, whites felt threatened by evidence of black success because black people, in their view, were supposed to be subordinate.

It is estimated that over 3,000 people were victims of lynch mobs between 1892 and 1940 and more than 2,600 of them were African American (Brown 2000). This violence was directed at black women as well as black men, with at least 130 black women lynched during roughly the same time period (Feimster 2018). Estimates from Ida B. Wells, a noted antilynching activist (see Box 5.1 Racial Justice Activism: Ida B. Wells and the Antilynching Movement), are that over ten thousand black people died at the hands of whites between the 1880s and the 1940s (Feagin, Vera, and Batur 1995). While there is considerable variation between these estimates, since lynchings often went unreported and no federal agency kept track of these crimes, Wells did her best to keep track of lynchings; thus, her estimate is considered valid. These estimates are evidence of the impunity with which the widespread use of terror was directed against blacks.

One of the more accepted sociological explanations for lynching was proposed by Hubert M. Blalock (1967). His theory, referred to as the **power-threat hypothesis**, argues that lynching increased when competition over economic resources increased or when there was increasing competition for political power. Later research by Susan Olzak (1990) found that both political and economic competition helps explain many forms of racial violence, from lynching to race riots. Other researchers found the power-threat hypothesis to be useful for understanding lynching in the Deep South, specifically *before* the implementation of Jim Crow legislation (Corzine, Creech, and Corzine 1983). Thus, in the absence of formal laws restricting black options, these extralegal methods were implemented in order to keep blacks subordinate and second-class citizens. However, lynching continued as a practice long after Jim Crow laws were established. Lynching in the American South was often the result of "a growing belief among whites ... that Negroes are getting out of hand—in wealth, in racial independence, in attitudes of self-assertion especially as workers or in reliance upon the law" (Cox 1945:577). Lynching was used by whites whenever they believed blacks threatened their privileged access to political or economic resources (Tolnay and Beck 1995).

While lynching occurred throughout the United States, it became the terror tactic of choice in the South in the post-Reconstruction era. By the 1880s it had become an elaborately staged event, sometimes drawing as many as fifteen thousand spectators (Pinar 2001). Lynchings became ritualized affairs in a carnival atmosphere, and these elaborate and vicious occasions were meant not only to punish the accused but also, perhaps more importantly, to send a warning to all blacks to stay "in their place."

IMAGE 5.3: Flag flown from an upper-story window of the NAACP headquarters in New York City, 1936.

Photographs of lynching were sold as postcards, and audio recordings of the victim's anguish were exhibited around the country (Goldsby 2006). Mobs could witness and celebrate the murders in person and later audiences thousands of miles away could revel in the spectacle as well.

Lynchings and the carnivalesque climate surrounding them exemplified social theorist Émile Durkheim's (1964) understanding of social control. Lynching is a form of public execution intended to do more than punish an offender: it reinforces the social norms of the community and is an opportunity for **social solidarity**, the creation of a sense of community among whites, of belonging to a group. Lynchings were rituals that reinforced white supremacy and solidarity, which is why they often involved mobs, were public spectacles, and inspired the collection of morbid souvenirs, such as postcards and body parts of the victim, that memorialized the event.

Research on 3,767 completed lynchings in 11 southern states between 1877 and 1950 finds that torture and desecration of the bodies of lynching victims was not common—as only 7.7 percent of lynching victims were tortured prior to their death and in 8.2 percent of cases victim's bodies were desecrated (Beck and Tolnay 2019). Both torture and desecration were more common if the victim was accused of a gender-related crime like rape or sexual assault. Such extreme actions were also more common in the presence of large mobs and after 1910, perhaps paradoxically, a time period when the number of lynching victims was declining. One possible explanation for this temporal pattern is that, during the post–World War I era, the "social and economic foundations of southern society were showing signs of crumbling" and the stability of the white racial order was threatened (Beck and Tolnay 2019:334).

While most lynchings occurred in the South, research by sociologist Charles Seguin (2018) finds that both northern and southern newspapers justified these crimes by referring to lynching victims as "brutes," "fiends," and "ravishers." Northern newspapers slowly became more critical of lynching around the 1890s, as the practice became known by Europeans. The antilynching activism of Ida B. Wells included a speaking tour in England that drew European attention to these crimes. Additionally, the British press ran the first international news story on American lynching in their coverage of the lynching of eleven Italian immigrants in New Orleans in 1891. In this coverage, *The Manchester Guardian* referred to this as a "massacre" and questioned whether, in the face of such barbaric practices, the United States was even civilized. It is at this point that northern newspapers began to change their coverage of lynching; southern newspapers continued to justify lynching.

In addition to lynchings, communities throughout the country experienced what were called **race riots**: mob attacks by dominant-group members on black communities, with violence against racial minorities and property (see Table 5.1). The

City	Year	Estimated Number of Blacks Killed
Colfax, LA	1873	150
Wilmington, NC	1898	19
Atlanta, GA	1906	25–40
Springfield, IL	1908	7
East St. Louis, IL	1917	39
Chicago, IL	1919	28+*
Tulsa, OK	1921	50–300
Rosewood, FL	1923	8

T A B L E 5 . 1 : Major Race Riots Between the Civil War and the Great Depression

S O U R C E : www.pewresearch.org/fact-tank/2017/10/25/many-minority-students-go-to-schools-where-at-least-half-of-their-peers-are-their-race-or-ethnicity/

N O T E : * The "official" death toll in the Chicago race riot of 1919 is disputed, but general consensus is that "dozens" of people died and hundreds were injured (Oakley 1997).

term *race riot* came into existence in the 1890s and refers to a form of mob violence centered on race. Race riots left tens of thousands of black people homeless and thousands injured or dead. Sociologists understand riots and lynching as examples of **collective violence**, a process by which a group of people respond to deviance or perceived deviance, an extralegal form of social control (Black 1976, 1984; Senechal de la Roche 2001). Lynchings and race riots are considered collective acts because these actions solidify bonds between individuals holding similar views. In other words, blacks felt a collective sympathy for the victims of lynching, and whites felt little concern for the black offenders of their white supremacist rules but were concerned with maintaining white supremacy and solidarity.

Federal antilynching legislation was proposed by Missouri representative Leonidas C. Dyer in 1918 in response to the horrors of the East St. Louis race riot of 1917. If the Dyer bill had passed, it would have made lynching a federal crime, distinct from murder, which was under the purview of the state. Thus, a lynching charge could be prosecuted in the federal courts and removed from the control of the local southern judicial systems, which tended toward maintaining white supremacy and offering leniency toward perpetrators of lynchings. Due to intense southern opposition, federal antilynching legislation never passed despite bills being repeatedly brought before Congress.

Gender, Sexuality, and Lynching

White southerners justified the barbaric practice of lynching through several myths, most commonly that white men needed to protect the purity of "white womanhood." Despite the fact that less than one-third of lynching victims were even *accused* of raping white women, southern whites were easily convinced that lynching was a necessary form of punishment for a new social problem, the rape of white women by black men (Brown 2000; Grant 1975). Interestingly, the myth of the black male rapist did not exist before 1830, which leads to speculation that black economic prosperity, or even the potential of it, was the real motive.

At the same time, black women were systematically raped as part of the post-Reconstruction terror tactics used by white supremacists. According to Ida B. Wells, "white men perpetrated sexual violence against black women, while black men were brutalized by white mobs for having consensual sex with white women" (Feimster 2018). Race riots often included sexual attacks on black women. Few white Americans publicly expressed outrage over the rape and sexual exploitation of black women by white men, which began in slavery and continued into the Jim Crow era (Brown 2000).

A lynching often took on a sexualized nature. In the carnival-like atmosphere that lynching had developed, sometimes members of the mob dressed in women's clothing, presumably representing the victimized white woman (Brown 2000). Lynching victims were often stripped naked and castrated (Pinar 2001). For a young black male coming of age at the turn of the century, fear of being lynched was more than likely all-consuming, and for black females fear of rape at the hands of white men had to be equally consuming. The dynamics and intersection of race, gender, and sexuality play themselves out in gruesome ways in the practice of lynching, the threat of or experience of rape, and in race riots during the late nineteenth and early twentieth centuries.

African American Resistance to Jim Crow

African Americans, faced with the retrenchment of their recently won rights as well as mob violence and terror, actively opposed their renewed subordination under Jim Crow. An active antilynching movement emerged, educational institutions flourished, the National Association for the Advancement of Colored People (NAACP) was formed to fight for civil rights, and black workers mobilized into unions. Such activism proved to be dangerous for participants as well as sympathizers. Many whites viewed such activism on the part of blacks as a sign of their "uppity-ness," as them challenging their second-class status, resulting in a violent backlash from whites hostile to such change. Despite such risks, racial hierarchies and the beliefs and behaviors that support them were constantly being negotiated and challenged.

An **antilynching movement** was active from 1883 (after the Supreme Court overturned the Civil Rights Act of 1875) to 1940, when lynchings diminished and the NAACP shifted its focus from fighting for antilynching legislation (which Congress never passed) to challenging school segregation in courts (see Chapter 7)

(Brown 2000). Gender and sexuality may lie at the heart of the *practice* of lynching, but gender was also an important dynamic in the *anti*lynching movement. Ida B. Wells was an integral part of the antilynching movement, as were many black activist organizations, such as the NAACP (see Box 5.1 Racial Justice Activism: Ida B. Wells and the Antilynching Movement).

While originating in the black community, the antilynching movement ultimately became an arena of activism for both white and black women. Aside from fighting for the right to vote, most women's activism of the late 1800s and early 1900s was in the name of morality, virtue, and social improvement. The endorsements of women's organizations were sought after, because they were perceived as moral guides, and lynching became one of the moral causes that activist women of all races signed on to. After 1920, women voters were also sought out by the NAACP in the fight to pass antilynching legislation. As new voters, they were perceived as a

---

BOX 5.1

Racial Justice Activism:
Ida B. Wells and the Antilynching Movement

One of the first people to systematically study lynching in order to campaign against it was Ida B. Wells (1862–1931), an African American journalist and antilynching activist. Wells lived in the Jim Crow South and worked as an activist fighting for women's rights as well as civil rights. She used her journalistic skills as well as her public speaking skills to expose this crime not just to northerners but also to the international community. She was particularly interested in presenting the problem sociologically, so she quantified the problem at a time when no official statistics were kept on lynching. Until the work of Wells, the deaths of blacks at the hands of whites were not included as part of official crime statistics. In 1895 she published this information in *The Red Record*, a detailed account of lynching in the United States.

Wells was the first person to publicly decry the myth of black male rape of white women. In a controversial Memphis newspaper article, Wells argued that many of the alleged rapes of white women by black men were not rapes and that sometimes white women chose voluntarily to be with black men. Because such relationships were prohibited in the South, she argued, a white woman was forced to cry rape to protect herself. Wells' own life was threatened due to her public pronouncement, and she had to permanently flee her home in Memphis, Tennessee.

Wells was one of the founders of the NAACP, and partially due to this influence the antilynching campaign was a major focus of this early civil rights organization. Wells spent her entire life active in the fight to expose and end mob violence against African Americans.

IDA B. WELLS.

IMAGE 5.4: Ida B. Wells, journalist and anti-lynching activist.

powerful voting bloc, and many of them responded by lobbying their representatives to pass antilynching legislation (Brown 2003). By 1930, for instance, the largest organization of white women opposing lynching, the Association of Southern Women for the Prevention of Lynching, emerged, led by Jessie Daniel Ames (Brown 2000). It is possible that the antilynching movement consisted of so many women activists simply because women were not viewed as threatening to the power structure in the same way that black men were. No woman could vote prior to 1920, for instance. This may have provided white and black women with the freedom to mobilize against lynching.

One of the goals of the antilynching movement was to get a federal antilynching bill passed, which was never accomplished, but the movement did succeed in exposing this horrific practice and contributed to the decrease in lynching (Brown 2000).

In addition to the antilynching movement, African American resistance included the formation of an interracial civil rights organization, the NAACP, in 1909 as a response to lynching, race riots, and the lack of basic civil rights for African Americans. Key founders of this organization were white activists Mary White Ovington, William English Walling, and Oswald Garrison Villard and African American activists W. E. B. Du Bois, Walter White, Ida B. Wells, and Mary Church Terrell.

The primary strategy of the NAACP was to secure civil rights for African Americans through the courts by making sure the laws already in existence were enforced (Emery, Gold, and Braselmann 2008; Greenberg 1994). The NAACP challenged segregated graduate and professional schools. For instance, in 1938, Lloyd Gaines brought a case to the Supreme Court against the University of Missouri for being denied admission to its law school simply because he was black. The strategy of the NAACP was to force the courts to enforce the *Plessy* ruling or to desegregate. Since the state of Missouri did not offer a "separate but equal" law school for black students, the university was in violation of the Supreme Court ruling of 1879. This behind-the-scenes work paved the way for the more overt civil rights activism of the 1950s and 1960s. One of the most memorable NAACP cases that inspired the civil rights movement was *Brown v. Board of Education* (1954), which declared segregated schools to be unconstitutional and emerged directly out of this NAACP litigation campaign (see Chapter 7).

WITNESS

Mary White Ovington described her perspective on the origins of the NAACP and on the fund-raising necessary to sustain the organization: "We were primarily a group of white people who felt that while the Negro would aid the committee's work, the whites, who were largely responsible for the conditions and who controlled the bulk of the nation's wealth, ought to finance the movement" (Sullivan 2009:13–14).

African Americans also resisted Jim Crow laws through black labor organizing. Racially segregated unions had been formed in almost all industrial arenas as capitalists exploited workers for profit in every way possible: forcing them to work in dangerous conditions, paying them very little money, and requiring them to work painfully long hours. Most of the major unions, such as the Brotherhood of Locomotive Engineers and the Order of Railway Conductors, excluded blacks from membership. While some union leaders viewed interracial unions as beneficial because laborers would be united and more threatening to capitalists, white members remained hostile to the inclusion of blacks (Harris 1977). By 1869, the Knights of Labor had made significant efforts to organize black workers. This organization, which was a federation of unions, later became the American Federation of Labor (AFL). Southern white hostility toward black workers resulted in AFL president Samuel Gompers' refusal to force unions to include black workers, despite his personal belief that racially integrating unions could only increase their overall power and success. At the same time that the AFL officially excluded blacks, the United Mine Workers of America, founded in 1890, actively organized all miners regardless of race (Harris 1977).

Conflict theorists explain this through a split labor market theory (see Chapter 4). White laborers demand rights from employers and unions and discriminate against people of color, so that the good jobs are reserved for white workers. White workers, then, act as an interest group that defends, at least in the short term, a two-tiered job market: good jobs, those that are unionized and have high pay and benefits, become reserved for white workers, and low-paying, nonunionized jobs remain for people of color. This strategy can backfire when minorities are brought in as strikebreakers in union disputes.

Despite the potential benefits of belonging to the unions and the potential power of racially integrated unions, black workers did not always view alignment with white workers as their best option. Being used as strikebreakers provided them entry into occupations they were otherwise excluded from, even as their role in strike-breaking fueled white worker animosity. Because of this, some leaders of the black community discouraged black laborers from organizing, and sometimes the black press advocated against organizing as well.

One of the most respected jobs for African Americans in the late 1800s was that of sleeping car porter. Many porters feared they would lose their jobs if they joined a union. Despite such a deterrent, A. Philip Randolph organized the Brotherhood of Sleeping Car Porters in 1925 (see Box 5.2 Race in the Workplace: Sleeping Car Porters: Racial Subordination and Opportunity). This organization became the most powerful black union and worked for labor rights for all black workers, above and beyond sleeping car porters, as well as for basic civil rights for African Americans. Randolph and the Brotherhood repeatedly called for the end of racial discrimination within all unions in the AFL (Adams 1992).

The late nineteenth and early twentieth centuries provided African Americans with a glimpse of liberty during the Reconstruction era, but ongoing racism resulted in the reinstitution of the racial hierarchy, which was brutally enforced for almost another hundred years. In the face of—and in response to—this brutal period, the foundation of the modern civil rights movement was established. The political mobilization involved in the organization of the antilynching movement brought evidence of the brutality of this period to the world. The NAACP and other black political organizations legally challenged racial segregation, and labor organizing resulted in improved economic conditions for some black workers during the Jim Crow era. Perhaps even more important, this period showed the ability of the black community to organize to fight racism.

Sociologists emphasize the importance of assimilation to achieve racial harmony. However, in the nineteenth and twentieth centuries in the United States, whites prevented African Americans from fully assimilating into the dominant culture and, instead, promoted racial/ethnic conflict. As we are about to explore, the assimilation of some racial/ethnic groups was constrained by the dominant group, while the assimilation of others was facilitated.

Blacks in the Urban North

Many blacks responded to their disenfranchisement and the exploitation of Jim Crow by migrating north. Ultimately, 1.6 million blacks migrated out of the rural South and to the urban North, Midwest, and West between 1910 and 1930, a period known as the *Great Migration*, with a second migration of 5 million southern blacks north and west between 1940 and 1970. After immigration restrictions were passed in the early 1920s, black job opportunities in the North increased dramatically and acted as a "pull" factor, encouraging black migration from the rural South to the urban North. While the North may have felt like the "Promised Land" to migrating blacks, they encountered racism there, too, which resulted in conflicts over jobs, schools, and housing.

REFLECT AND CONNECT

Identify three reasons African Americans would desire to leave the South during the Jim Crow era. To this day, most African Americans still live in the South. Can you identify two reasons why many blacks might have stayed in the South during the Jim Crow era, rather than participating in the rural-to-urban migration?

Passing

It was during the Jim Crow era that a different type of resistance to the racial hierarchy emerged: **passing**. *Passing* refers to a member of one racial group becoming accepted as and understood by others to be a member of another racial group; it generally refers to African Americans passing as white to avoid discrimination. Many African Americans who could pass for white, those who had light skin and European features, did choose to pass. Research finds that between 1890 and 1940, approximately 19 percent of black males passed for white at some point in their lives, with around 10 percent of them "reverse passing" back to black at some point (Nix and Qian 2015).

In order to successfully and completely pass, people had to cut ties with their families. Many moved to different areas of the country during the mass migration of African Americans out of the South and to the urban North or to California, which made cutting the ties easier. Otherwise, it would have aroused suspicion if they lived in the black community or were seen associating with blacks; their white status would be threatened. We know of stories of people who, in doing their family genealogy, find that at a certain point in history, their family split; some passed as white and some remained in the black community (Broyard 2007).

Passing was an incredible trade-off, a loss, an exile (Hobbs 2014). People did it in order to have better life chances and economic opportunities. But they paid a significant price in terms of loss of family and community ties. Historian Allyson Hobbs (2014) emphasizes that racial passing was often a collaborative endeavor—family members, friends, and neighbors would pretend not to know their white-looking family member or friend if they passed them on the street so as not to blow their cover, since in the absence of proof of a specific black ancestor, simply being known as black in the community was accepted by the courts as evidence of black ancestry. There was often significant pain and loss not just for those left behind but also for the individual who chose to pass as white.

While we can understand racial passing as a type of resistance to the racial hierarchy, since it clearly challenges the rigidity and essential nature of racial categories, it can also be seen as an acquiescence to it. People who passed often faced harsh criticism from the black community—first, because their appearance allowed them to escape the brutality of Jim Crow (and for some in earlier eras, even slavery), and second, because passing as white challenged the sense of racial pride many African Americans were trying to cultivate during this period. As Hobbs states, "to pass as white was to make an anxious decision to turn one's back on a black racial identity and to claim to belong to a group to which one was not legally assigned. It was risky business" (2014:5).

Some scholars have identified examples of "reverse racial passing," where a person who is legally defined as white successfully passes as nonwhite; they are "white people who either envision themselves or are envisioned by others as becoming black," (Dreisinger 2008:2; Harper 1998). Reverse-passing narratives can be found throughout popular culture (Dreisinger 2008). Rachel Dolezal is someone who fits that description today.

REFLECT AND CONNECT

Do you know of any other examples of passing, of individuals shifting their identity from one group to another in order to obtain the privileges associated with being a member of the dominant group, historically or currently?

NATIVISM AND THE ERA OF EXCLUSION

The immediate post–Civil War period witnessed gains made by African Americans, only to have these reversed as Jim Crow set in. The late 1800s also witnessed progress and backlash for other racial/ethnic groups. The mid to late 1800s was one of the most significant eras of immigration in United States history. Defining who qualified as an "American" became a major focus of the era, and African Americans

BOX 5.2

Race in the Workplace:
Sleeping Car Porters: Racial Subordination and Opportunity

The late nineteenth century witnessed a revolution in rail traffic—the transportation of not just goods but also people over long distances. George Pullman sought to make traveling by rail a luxurious experience rather than a long, miserable ride through his Pullman sleeping cars and the assistance of porters. Pullman intentionally sought African American men for this occupation and, initially, these were all newly freed men. By World War I, Pullman was the largest employer of African Americans and the word *porter* had become synonymous with *black*. The occupation of porter and Pullman as an employer illustrate considerable tensions for black male laborers in the post-Reconstruction era.

Pullman was one of the largest employers of blacks and did actively seek out former slaves for his employ, yet many in the black community remained critical of this "opportunity." Pullman chose black males for this work not only because they could be paid less but also because it allowed white passengers to feel elegant as they were waited on by black servants. This practice was resented by many in the black community because it too closely resembled the master–servant relationship of slavery. Porters were expected to meet all the needs of travelers, from handling their baggage and preparing their bedding to shining their shoes and performing other personal services.

Pullman defended his exclusive hiring of black males for this position by citing his concern for the job opportunities of former slaves. Despite such concern, he was unwilling to hire blacks for other jobs at Pullman, and his company town in Pullman, Illinois, had no black residents.

Even if in the role of servant, the black porters were sharing in the luxurious atmosphere of a Pullman sleeping car, which differentiated Pullman porters' experiences from those of the average black American. Pullman porters held the respect of the black community and were even considered part of the black bourgeoisie. They traveled the country at a time when most blacks were still confined to sharecropping in the rural South. Their constant movement allowed them to carry messages of importance to black communities across the country, from information concerning northern migration to civil rights activism. While economically exploited by Pullman, porters were still relatively economically independent compared to other African Americans of the era. The status of the Pullman porter only increased with the successful organizing of the Brotherhood of Sleeping Car Porters. As the generations passed, porters were often well educated, owned their own homes, and were leaders in their communities (Adams 1992; Brazeal 1946; Harris 1977).

and Native Americans were not yet included in that identity. Initially, tens of thousands of immigrants, mostly European Catholics, Eastern European Jews, Asians, and Middle Easterners, also found themselves defined out of the elusive category of "American." A spread of **nativism**, a surge in anti-immigrant beliefs and policies, occurred. Nativists saw themselves as the true Americans because they were native born and expressed anti-Catholic hostilities and **xenophobia**, the fear and contempt of strangers. Thus, while this historical era was one of terror and oppression for recently emancipated African Americans, it was also an extremely repressive era for many immigrant groups. Nativism resulted in the first immigration restrictions in the United States, such as the Chinese Exclusion Act.

Global White Supremacy

White racial supremacy is a global phenomenon linked to global capitalism; thus, one can see similar immigration legislation throughout the world. For instance, similar immigration restrictions were enacted in Australia during the same period and were, tellingly, referred to as the "white Australia policies" (see Box 5.3 Global Perspectives: White Australia Policies). **Global white supremacy** can be defined as a "historically based and institutionally perpetrated system of exploitation and oppression of continents, nations, and peoples classified as 'non-white'" by those classified as white (Blay 2011). This definition presupposes the existence of white nations. White nations had to be created, and government policies and programs, such as those in the United States described above and those in Australia, were avenues for the historical creation of white nations.

White nations were also created through race science, as a growing number of scientists devoted themselves to creating racial hierarchies by categorizing the people of the globe, and through the ways such science influenced policy (see Chapter 3). Race science influenced how emerging nation-states dealt with immigrants and different populations already within their borders (Loveman 2014). Eugenics influenced Brazilian racial history as well. Brazilian scholars adhered to the neo-Lamarckian strand of eugenics, which operated on the assumption that genetic deficiencies could be overcome in a single generation (Telles 2004). In Brazil, this translated into an emphasis on "whitening." It was believed that black inferiority could be overcome through miscegenation: "race mixture would eliminate the black population, resulting in a white or mostly white Brazilian population" (Telles 2004:28).

Irish Immigration: From "Paddies" to Patriots

Irish immigration to the United States changed dramatically during the early 1800s. Prior to 1820, most Irish immigrants were Scottish-Irish Protestants. After 1820,

IMAGE 5.5: : "The Usual Irish Way of Doing Things." This 1871 cartoon by Thomas Nast reflects both dominant-group fears of the influx of Irish immigrants during the mid-1800s and Anglo stereotypes of the Irish as animal-like, violent, and drunk. (Thomas Nast, "The Usual Irish Way of Doing Things," wood engraving, *Harper's Weekly*, September 2, 1871).

political oppression in Ireland resulted in increasing Irish Catholic immigration to the United States. Their emigration out of Ireland accelerated during the mid to late 1840s as a result of the Irish potato famine and the resulting poverty and starvation. Over one million impoverished Irish Catholics fled the famine and arrived in the United States between 1845 and 1849. They faced a hostile reception in their new country. The desperate poverty of most Irish immigrants frightened native-born citizens. In the constantly evolving racial hierarchy, the Irish were viewed as having a status well below that of whites but just above that of African Americans. Their Catholicism was also perceived as threatening and led to their further marginalization.

The Irish were not initially perceived as white in the United States (see Chapter 2). While African Americans faced the Jim Crow caricature in the South, the Irish faced the Jim Dandy stereotype in the North—that of a drunken, belligerent, and foolish Irish person (Ignatiev 1995). Cartoons in influential periodicals during the 1870s and 1880s depicted Irish Americans as ignorant and apelike, closely resembling dehumanizing stereotypes of black men popular during the same era (Curtis 1997). Part of the challenge of assimilating for the Irish meant becoming white, and becoming white meant distancing themselves from people of color. Thus, the Irish had to learn to discriminate along racial lines, something unfamiliar to them in their native land, as part of their acceptance into American society.

No other European ethnic group faced the degree of discrimination that the Catholic Irish faced in the United States. It was not uncommon for help wanted ads to discourage Irish men and women from applying by stating, "No Irish need apply," even for menial jobs (Dolan 2008). Prior to emancipation, there was a split labor market, where the lowest-paying jobs were all that were open to Irish immigrants and Irish Americans and good jobs were reserved for whites. Employers recognized the desperation of famine immigrants and used it to suppress wages even more. In the South, work considered too dangerous for slaves was considered ideal for Irish laborers. Slaves at the time were property and thus were viewed as valuable; Irish workers, however, were disposable. The Irish contributed to the building of much of the most dangerous infrastructure of many US cities, as well as the eastern leg of the Transcontinental Railroad and the Erie Canal. The Irish experience in the United States, particularly for the famine immigrants, was that of miserable subsistence and discrimination.

WITNESS

Historian Kerby Miller notes, "Irish immigrants were disproportionately concentrated in the lowest-paid, least-skilled, and most dangerous and insecure employment; with few exceptions, they also displayed the highest rates of transience, residential density and segregation, inadequate housing and sanitation, commitments to prisons and charity institutions, and excess mortality" (1985:315).

In addition to the employment discrimination they faced, which contributed to their poverty, intense anti-Catholic prejudice worked against the Irish immigrants, particularly during the first half of the nineteenth century. Anti-Catholic sentiment took political form in the emergence of the Know-Nothing political party in 1849 (Dolan 2008). One of their primary goals was to keep Catholics and immigrants from being allowed to hold political office. The Know-Nothings were fervently anti-immigrant, believed that America should be a Protestant country, and feared that Catholics were hostile to US values and would be more loyal to the pope than to the United States.

Despite this, between the late 1800s and the early 1900s, the status of Irish Americans changed from that of a despised nonwhite minority to that of a white ethnic group, a term used to describe white immigrants who are not European Protestants (see Chapter 2). This path to whiteness was paved primarily through increasing Irish American access to political power. In the post–Civil War period, there was a rise of machine politics and many Irish became involved in local and state governments. Irish immigrants to America quickly learned that whiteness entitled them to political rights and employment opportunities (Roediger 1991). The Democratic Party of the mid-1800s recognized the advantage of appealing to immigrant voters through a rejection of nativism and the Know-Nothings. While the Democratic Party rejected the anti-immigrant rhetoric of the period, it embraced racial ideologies of black inferiority and white supremacy. For the Irish, "the Democratic Party eased their assimilation as whites, and more than any other institution, it taught them the meaning of whiteness" (Ignatiev 1995:76).

Irish Americans worked to distinguish themselves from blacks and emphasized their whiteness. They did this through their political affiliations as well as through violence; the Irish had a "terrible record of mobbing free Blacks on and off the job—so much so that Blacks called the brickbats often hurled at them 'Irish confetti'" (Roediger 1991:136). Irish Catholic immigrants, a people oppressed in their native land, potentially could have bonded with black Americans over their shared oppression; instead they struggled against blacks, viewing antiblack sentiment as the more certain path to assimilation and access to the benefits whiteness offered.

Irish assimilation was a result of the intersection of race and politics, and is evidence of both "push" and "pull" factors involved in the "whitening" process: as the number of Irish immigrants dramatically increased through the mid to late 1800s, they became politically valuable to the dominant group, specifically to the Democratic Party, providing the pull from the dominant group toward whiteness and Irish assimilation. Becoming white was also viewed as beneficial and thus was desired by the Irish as a way to benefit from white privilege, providing the push toward assimilation. During the second half of the nineteenth century, Irish immigrants went from being a despised minority, derisively referred to as "Paddies," to being viewed as white and part of the American melting pot.

Sinophobia: Chinese Exclusion

While Irish Americans' status was improving over the course of the nineteenth century as they assimilated into the white mainstream society, Chinese immigrants found their path to assimilation blocked. The 1850s to 1880s were a major period of Chinese immigration to the United States, primarily centered in California. Fear and hatred of the Chinese and Chinese culture, called **sinophobia**, emerged and resulted in violence against Chinese immigrants, restrictive legislation not faced by other immigrant groups, and damaging stereotypical portrayals in the media.

Chinese migrants were disproportionately male, many initially entering as **sojourners**, people who immigrate for a period of time for work but have no intention of remaining in the new country. Others had more typical immigrant desires and intended to remain in the United States. While their motive for coming to the United States was work, most were relegated to only low-wage and dangerous jobs, such as building railroads or mining.

Many engaged in agricultural work that was vital to the economy of California. As the United States industrialized, Chinese laborers became a valuable part of the factory labor force in the West. Additionally, many worked in domestic service and laundries. Many Chinese immigrants engaged in labor that whites were unwilling to do. During the mid-1800s, California was experiencing a labor shortage and relied on Chinese immigrants to meet labor needs. Despite this, the Chinese faced intense hostility. Chinese immigrants faced both government antagonism in the form of legal and social policies and hostility and violence from dominant-group members.

Some government-sanctioned discrimination was regional. For instance, in California in 1854, the state legislature passed a law imposing taxes solely on Chinese gold miners (Chan 1991). The Chinese were entering California in significant numbers during the height of the gold rush, and white miners sought to limit Chinese competition in the gold mines through additional tax burdens and sometimes violence.

Chinese workers made up over 90 percent of the labor force of the Central Pacific Railroad and were responsible for the completion of the western half of the Transcontinental Railroad, working through the winter, plowing through the granite of the Sierra Nevada mountain range (Cassel 2002). While the Chinese were often doing the work whites did not want, they faced hostility from white workers, who claimed that their willingness to work for such low wages ultimately hurt all workers. Despite their contributions to American society, discrimination against the Chinese was rampant. Anti-Chinese riots are part of the historical record throughout the West, including in cities such as Rock Springs, Wyoming, in 1885; Seattle, Tacoma, and Portland in 1886; and Denver in 1880. Additionally, there were over thirty riots in California cities, which included the burning of Chinatowns and the expulsion of Chinese citizens (Tichenor 2002). Even in areas of the country where there were few Chinese, one finds evidence of intense racial prejudice against them. Milwaukee, Wisconsin, was the site of an anti-Chinese riot during the spring of 1889. This particular riot was inspired by fear of interracial relationships involving Chinese men and white women.

White fears of Chinese immigrants fueled racial ideologies that the Chinese were culturally and biologically inferior to whites. Chinese immigrants were accused of carrying diseases, particularly leprosy and venereal diseases. These beliefs led to the first piece of legislation that prohibited Chinese women from immigrating to the

IMAGE 5.6: Image of an anti-Chinese riot in Denver, Colorado, on October 31, 1880, showing Chinese residents being beaten and property destroyed.

United States. Most Chinese immigrants were men and the Chinese women that did come were often prostitutes. The Page Law of 1875 was passed with the overt purpose of abetting prostitution by disallowing entry of Chinese women into the United States. Indirectly, but perhaps not unintentionally, the law kept male Chinese laborers from staying in the United States for long periods of time and establishing families, since antimiscegenation laws already made it illegal for Chinese men to marry non-Chinese women (Cassel 2002).

The discrimination culminated in the Chinese Exclusion Act of 1882, the first law in US history to restrict immigration, which is unique in its prohibition of immigration on the basis of race/ethnicity. It banned Chinese immigration for ten years under penalty of imprisonment or deportation and made Chinese immigrants already in the United States ineligible for citizenship, with exemptions for diplomats, teachers, tourists, merchants, and scholars (Cassel 2002). This law captured white views of the era: the Chinese were viewed as incapable of being assimilated into the larger American society. In a period of American history in which there was a dramatic influx of literally millions of immigrants, primarily from Ireland, Italy, and Eastern Europe, it is significant that the Chinese immigrants were the first to face restrictions.

Rather than being a historical anomaly, the Chinese Exclusion Act was repeatedly extended through federal legislation in 1888, 1892, 1894, 1902, and 1904. Chinese Americans did not passively accept this discrimination, however. They resisted in several key ways: through labor strikes and lawsuits and in print journalism (Wong 1998). The Chinese were victims of racial discrimination but hardly passive victims of it, and they were "angered by the discriminatory laws enacted to humiliate and exclude them" (Chan 1991:20). The formation of Chinatowns was also a response to their marginalization from mainstream American society. The creation of such ethnic enclaves, communities where immigrants of particular racial/ethnic groups live in close proximity and where there are ethnic restaurants, groceries, and other businesses, provides immigrants a supportive buffer from the hostilities of the mainstream as well as employment opportunities otherwise unavailable to them (see Chapter 2). Ethnic enclaves are adaptive responses by minority groups to racial oppression and discrimination and blocked paths to assimilation.

Xenophobia and hostility toward Asians continued into the twentieth century and resulted in the passage of more immigration restrictions. In 1924, Congress passed the Immigration Act, which included the National Origins Act and the Asian Exclusion Act (see Chapter 13). These laws excluded Asian immigration and sought to severely restrict immigration from Southern and Eastern Europe by restricting immigration from any other country to 2 percent of the population from that nation that was already here (thus having the effect of favoring the largest immigrant groups already here, which were Northern European groups).

WITNESS

"The racial character of Jewishness in the New World ebbed and flowed over time" (Jacobson 1998:171).

Anti-Semitism in the United States

Jewish immigrants also faced hostility and anti-immigrant sentiment during the late nineteenth and early twentieth centuries, due to both religious and cultural differences from white, mainstream American society. The Jewish American community was experiencing a transformation during this era—from a small community of mostly German Jews in 1880 to a much larger and more diverse population of Jews primarily from Eastern Europe, Poland, and the Soviet Union in the decades that followed. While previous Jewish immigrants to colonial America faced political repression through restrictions on voting and holding political office, they were not perceived as threatening to the dominant culture and, thus, were generally tolerated by the dominant group.

Most Jewish immigrants who arrived after 1880 were escaping persecution in their native lands in the form of *pogroms*, which were violent attacks against Jews, Jewish businesses, and synagogues, and Jews' systematic murder at the hands of government officials. One-third of all Russian and Eastern European Jews had emigrated by 1914, most to the United States (Takaki 1993). With the dramatic influx of Eastern European Jewish immigrants in this era of US nativism and anti-immigrant sentiment, anti-Semitism in the United States increased dramatically.

Most of the new Jewish immigrants, while as impoverished as other immigrants of the era, were skilled workers and settled in urban areas in the northeastern United States. They also tended to be relatively well educated, with literacy rates at 80 percent for men and 63 percent for women (Takaki 1993). The majority of Jews put their skills to work in the burgeoning garment industry. While the work was considered skilled, the garment industry exploited the desperate immigrants through exceedingly long workdays and crowded, dangerous work environments. Jewish immigrants of this period entered the United States with more industrial experience than most other immigrant groups of the period, who were mostly peasants or farm laborers. This placed Jews at a slight advantage (Steinberg 1981).

Despite some skills and educational credentials that distinguished them from many other immigrants of the era, Jewish immigrants were perceived negatively and in racial terms as genetically distinct and inferior. By the 1920s, a very prominent white American, Henry Ford, was regularly publishing his anti-Semitic views in his newspaper, the *Dearborn Independent*, declaring Jews "un-American," among other critiques. Jews were victims of discrimination in neighborhoods, clubs, resorts, and private boarding schools (Steinberg 1981). As Jews gained some socioeconomic success and began moving out of the Lower East Side of New York City, a Jewish ethnic enclave, they encountered rental restrictions in the form of signs exclaiming, "No Jews, and no Dogs." Essentially, Jewish success fueled anti-Semitism and their assimilation was not universally welcomed (Takaki 1993).

Jewish immigrants faced discrimination in housing, employment, and in higher education. Because education is considered part of the very foundation of Jewish culture, the new immigrants worked hard to help their children attend college, which they did in significant numbers. Not surprisingly, the Protestant elite reacted with alarm at the increased numbers of college-educated Jews and soon established restrictions that limited their access to higher education. Some elite institutions, Harvard University among them, began complaining of a "Jewish problem," and "fear that colleges 'might soon be overrun by Jews' was publicly expressed at a 1918 meeting of the Association of New England Deans" (Brodkin 2008:45). Admissions quotas were soon common, particularly in professional schools of law and medicine, thus restricting Jewish access to some of the most prestigious occupations in American society. Anti-Semitic feelings among non-Jewish students became common on college campuses.

As they entered colleges, they encountered resistance. As they entered professional fields, they found opportunities blocked. Sometimes classified job ads explicitly stated "Christians only" to deter Jewish applicants. Often hospitals and law firms turned down Jewish interns, and colleges and universities often refused to hire Jewish faculty (Takaki 1993).

As second-generation Jewish Americans sought to leave their urban enclaves for suburban America, they encountered housing options blocked through **restrictive covenants**, agreements made by homeowners, and backed by law, not to sell their homes to members of particular racial/ethnic minority groups. Despite these obstacles, Jews eventually assimilated and "became white" (Brodkin 2008). For Jews, their successful assimilation seemed to fuel anti-Semitism in American society, at least prior to World War II, contrary to functionalist beliefs that assimilation should result in less racial/ethnic antagonism (see Chapter 2).

Western Expansion and the "Indian Problem"

As whites worked to reestablish white supremacy in the post-Reconstruction South, anti-Chinese sentiment in the West resulted in the nation's first immigration restriction laws, and European immigration was changing the demographics of northern cities, the Indian Wars raged on, only they now were primarily found in the Great Plains. European settlers exploited Native Americans almost from their earliest contact. Hostilities against Native Americans intensified dramatically during the mid to late nineteenth century, resulting in the institutionalization of racist policies and practices against them. Whites saw only two options concerning Native Americans: extermination or assimilation. The push toward one or both of these ends took increasing priority during the second half of the nineteenth century. The West had opened for white settlement, and transportation improvements made it easier for people to head west after the Transcontinental Railroad was completed in May 1869.

The policies of the federal government toward Native Americans at this time involved various efforts at forced assimilation, including numerous relocations to government-run reservations, military conflicts, the breaking up of communal lands, and the boarding school movement. These are all examples of institutional racism: government policies, fueled by racist ideologies asserting the inferiority of Native American tribal cultures, were enacted to encourage Native people to drop their cultural ways and assimilate into the Anglo-American culture.

There was a significant shift during the mid-1800s in the relationship between Indians and the federal government. In 1834, the federal government formed the Bureau of Indian Affairs (BIA) as a division of the War Department, reflecting the ongoing conflict between Indian tribes and white European Americans. By 1849,

IMAGE 5.7: Native Americans relocated to reservations by the US government. Pictured are four Lakota women, three with children on cradleboards, and a Lakota man on horseback on or near the Pine Ridge Reservation in 1891.

the BIA was shifted to the Department of the Interior, reflecting a more paternalistic stance in which Native Americans would eventually become wards of the US government (Collier 1972). As wards of the government, Indians were relocated to reservations, most of which were created between 1850 and 1880.

Forced relocations were one of the ways the US government tried to address the "Indian problem." These were essentially military actions in which tribes were escorted off of their homeland at gunpoint by the US military. These relocations not only moved Indians westward and, presumably, out of the way of whites but also took tribes off their land and out of their familiar environments, and disrupted their cultural systems, so that assimilating them would be easier.

Decades after the Trail of Tears (see Chapter 4), in 1864, the US military forced over ten thousand Navaho on a three-hundred-mile march from their homeland in eastern Arizona to Fort Sumner in New Mexico as part of government efforts to assimilate them, to re-create the Navaho in the "white man's image." Hundreds of tribal members perished during the relocation, which is referred to by Navaho as the "Long Walk." In another example, the Nez Perce tribe was forcibly relocated from the northwestern United States to a reservation in eastern Kansas and then again relocated to Oklahoma. Predictably, many of the tribal members died during this relocation, and many of those who survived the long march died of diseases once they settled onto reservations (Johansen 2005).

WITNESS

According to the United States secretary of the interior, "on these reservations they can be taught, as fast as possible, the arts of agriculture, and such pursuits as are incident to civilization … to build churches and organize Sabbath schools, whereby these savages may be taught a better way of life than they have heretofore pursued" (quoted in Berkhofer 1978:169).

In the post–Civil War era, United States Indian policy shifted from a focus on armed resistance to the assimilation of the Indian, and the US government found reservations to be the most efficient path for Native American assimilation. Indians who did not obey the federal government and go to reservations were considered to be at war with the United States and, thus, subject to military retaliation. Reservation Indians were denied freedom of travel, self-governance, and the right to practice their culture, including their religion. Despite the government's stated goal of teaching Indians as "fast as possible the art of agriculture" (Berkhofer 1978:169), reservations were located on the most uninhabitable land, which was unfit for farming. Reservations were guarded by the US military and tribal leadership was usurped by Indian agents working for the federal government. Indians had to rely on the federal government for all of their needs, from health-care to food rations to education, and the federal government often failed to provide adequately the basic necessities of life. The stage was set for cultural genocide as well as severe poverty.

The United States government had spent most of the second half of the nineteenth century focused on removing Native people from their land and relocating them to reservations. In 1887 Congress passed the Dawes Allotment Act, which called for the breakup of communally held lands for the purpose of providing individual Indian families with plots of land to farm. Indian tribalism ran counter to the American ideology of individualism, which was part of the reason individual land ownership was so strongly encouraged (Berkhofer 1978). It was another attempt to get Native people to drop their "Indian ways" and assimilate, specifically by engaging in white forms of landed agriculture, which differed dramatically from tribal patterns of food production and consumption. While this piece of legislation was intended by its white political proponents to be progressive, the ethnocentrism behind it is hard to overlook as it was based upon the belief that individual land ownership and the nuclear family were superior to the communal lifestyle of tribes.

It was further doomed by the fact that the land provided for Native families to farm tended to be the least suitable for farming and many severely impoverished Native people could not afford the supplies to begin farming.

This legislation inadvertently resulted in tribal land being given to whites because the legislation declared that once the tribal land was divided up and given to individual Indians, any surplus could be sold to whites. Prior to this legislation in 1887, tribal lands had been declared to be under tribal ownership for perpetuity; however, under the Dawes Act, after twenty-five years, individual allotments could be sold to anyone. In the face of the dire poverty that so many Native Americans endured, many took advantage of this opportunity and sold their land to non-Natives. More than sixty million acres of land were lost to Indian tribes and turned over to white settlers through this piece of "progressive" legislation (Bonvillain 2001).

During the 1890s, a new resistance movement, referred to as the Ghost Dance, was spreading among Sioux Indians on the Dakota reservation that inspired them and correspondingly frightened white government agents. This movement was threatening to whites because it began with the vision of a Paiute Indian named Wovoka who announced that the earth would be covered with new soil and all the white men buried, thus allowing Indians to regain their land and reassert their cultures. This hopeful message drew Indians from across the nation to the Dakota reservation. At intertribal gatherings, Indians danced the Ghost Dance until they collapsed, celebrating Wovoka's vision. The commitment and passion Indians showed for this new movement, as well as the message behind it, caused US government agents to panic.

In response, the military decided to arrest Chief Sitting Bull but instead killed him in the attempt. Over 350 Sioux headed to the Pine Ridge Reservation upon hearing of Sitting Bull's death. While they were camping at Wounded Knee Creek in December 1890, the US Army surrounded them. A gun fired and a massacre ensued. Over three hundred Sioux were gunned down, many of whom were unarmed men, women, and children. This massacre is now considered to mark the end of the Indian Wars and Native American autonomy.

One of the most significant attempts to assimilate Native people into the white mainstream society was the boarding school movement, which officially began in 1869. By 1909, there were hundreds of boarding schools, both on and off reservations. One of the primary goals of boarding schools was to "kill the Indian and save the man" by forcibly separating children from their parents, instilling white cultural values, Christian beliefs, and patriarchal values in Indian children (Smith 2005). The boarding schools had a profoundly devastating effect on Native American cultures as eventually more than one hundred thousand children were forced (parents who resisted were imprisoned) to attend these schools, where they spent years at a time away from their families. On the one hand, boarding schools could be perceived as progressive because their position indicated that Indians could be reformed and could be educated to become productive members of society. Ultimately, however, racism and ethnocentrism were embedded in the curriculum as girls were essentially taught domestic skills and boys were taught vocational skills, ostensibly preparing them only for low-status, low-paying jobs (Johansen 2005) (see Chapter 7).

Further attempts at assimilation came about through federal legislation. For instance, in 1924 the US government passed the Indian Citizenship Act, which granted citizenship to all Indians. Previously, Indians could become citizens through marrying a male citizen, through military service, or through accepting plots of land through the Dawes Act. The Indian Citizenship Act was not the result of Indian demands. This move by the federal government was simply another incentive for Indians to assimilate into the white mainstream and drop their Native cultures.

A particularly disturbing example of discrimination against Native Americans by whites during the early twentieth century involves the murders of at least twenty-four Osage Indians (Grann 2017). Members of the Osage tribe in Oklahoma during this time were some of the richest people in the world simply because oil had been discovered on their land. The US government turned their paternalistic lens on the Osage, deciding that they were incapable of handling their own money and would require guardians, who were prominent white citizens of Osage County. While many of these guardians used their position to swindle money away from the Osage, gaining the mineral rights to the land was the only way for whites to completely control the wealth, but this was much more difficult, as the rights could only be inherited. Thus, many men sought to marry into the tribe, and then when the tribal member died, or was killed, the white person had the mineral rights to the land and the wealth-creating oil. Headright inheritance, as it was called, was found by the FBI to be the cause of many of the deaths. At least three white men were found guilty and imprisoned for several of the murders. Most of the murders, however, went unsolved (Grann 2017).

The post–Civil War era was a period of decreasing warfare with Indians and increasing attention to their assimilation into the dominant culture. Appealing to racist ideologies of the inferiority of Native American tribal cultures, the federal government engaged in various actions to ensure the cultural genocide of Native Americans: forced relocations to government-run reservations, detribalization through land allotment policies, prohibition of cultural rituals and practices, boarding schools, and the granting of US citizenship to Indians. While some minority groups, such as the Irish, wished to assimilate into the dominant white American culture, Native Americans had assimilation imposed on them. They resisted the imposition of white culture at every step.

Native American Resistance

Native Americans actively resisted US government policies and practices that were established to ensure their subordination. Sociologically speaking, minority group agency is evidence of the ongoing challenge to dominant-group ideologies and institutions. Whites with political power defined Indians as inferior, uncivilized, and dangerous, and these beliefs became the dominant beliefs of the era and were used to justify the relocation of Indians and the usurpation of their lands. However, Native Americans actively resisted not only their oppression but the racist ideologies being espoused as well. In addition to the Ghost Dance movement, resistance took the form of tribes' returning to their homelands after being relocated, armed resistance against the military, and violence against settlers.

A group of almost three hundred Cheyenne Indians walked a thousand miles back to their homeland from their assigned reservation in Oklahoma. Chief Joseph of the Nez Perce tribe of what is today the northwestern United States strongly opposed the attempts to relocate his tribe. In 1879 he approached President Rutherford B. Hayes to appeal the relocation of his people, but it was not until 1885 that the remaining Nez Perce tribal members were relocated back to the Northwest, although not to their original reservation.

Native Americans also won military battles against whites during this era, if not the overall war. In 1876 the Battle at Little Bighorn, also known as "Custer's Last Stand," provides an example. The Seventh Calvary of the United States Army under George Armstrong Custer was defeated by Lakota and Cheyenne Indians who were led by Sitting Bull. Thousands of Cheyenne and Lakota Indians had left their reservation in protest of US government policies, and the US Army was attempting to forcibly relocate them back to the reservation the federal government had assigned for them.

The Santee, a Minnesota Sioux tribe, revolted against the American government that had interned them on reservations and failed to provide the promised food supplies. They began by attacking farms and killing immigrants and engaged in three days of raiding farms and killing whites, eventually killing more than seven hundred settlers and one hundred soldiers before the army took control (Johansen 2005). Under the authority of President Lincoln, the largest mass hanging in US history took place as thirty-eight Santee were found guilty of taking part in the massacre and were hung at Fort Mankato.

Native American resistance is not only evidence of subordinate-group agency, it also exposes the weakness of the assimilationist perspective on race/ethnic relations. Native Americans did not want to give up their cultures—they did not seek to become part of white society—thus, the idea that assimilation was inevitable, a core sociological belief throughout the first half of the twentieth century, was not fully supported by the evidence.

BOX 5.3

Global Perspectives:
White Australia Policies

Australia has a somewhat parallel history to the United States in that it was a country with an Aboriginal population that was ruthlessly subordinated and displaced to make room for European settlers. In 1901, Australia passed the Immigration Restriction Act, which quickly became known as the "white Australia policy" and resulted in the expulsion of thousands of Pacific Islanders who had been brought in to work the sugarcane fields during the late 1800s, and which sought to prevent other people of color from settling in Australia (Lake and Reynolds 2008). Its goal was to establish a white continent as Australia aligned itself with Great Britain and the United States. This policy of immigration restriction amounted to racial segregation on a global scale. Australian political leaders looked to the United States for direction and, in turn, were viewed by many Americans as enacting progressive reforms (Lake and Reynolds 2008).

The white Australia policy, interestingly, did not mention race, yet the idea behind the policy was that whites were superior. The legislation was enforced through literacy tests: immigration was limited to those who could pass a literacy test in any European language. Due to Australia's proximity to Asia, "invasion narratives" emerged whereby Australia's homogeneous, white future was perceived as threatened by invading hordes of Asians (Ang 2003).

The white Australia policy was more than an immigration restriction: it was an explicit attempt to align the Commonwealth of Australia with the white nations of the world rather than with its closest neighbors. There "was no reason to believe that a White Australia could not be maintained. This was the zenith of the British Empire and of the belief that the British, as a self-proclaimed race, were born to rule. Australians saw themselves as part of this" (Jones 2003:112). White Australia policies were not seriously challenged until after World War II—except by the Japanese, who were offended that they were included within the category of "Eastern" people, along with Pacific Islanders and Indians (Jones 2003; Rivett 1992).

CHAPTER SUMMARY

Racial and ethnic relations were explosive during the late nineteenth and early twentieth centuries. The country was experiencing rapid social changes combined with unprecedented immigration. The question of "who is an American?" loomed large, and how "American" was defined influenced the assimilation processes for different racial/ethnic groups.

The defining racial institution of US society, slavery, had been eliminated. Racial hierarchies were constantly being negotiated and challenged by subordinate groups. Resistance to slavery was evidenced throughout its tenure by white and black abolitionists as well as by slaves themselves. After slavery was abolished many whites worked to maintain the status quo. Thus, Jim Crow was established in the South as a new form of institutional racism intended to replace slavery, with racial ideologies of black inferiority and white superiority becoming more pronounced.

Many immigrant groups coming to the United States during this era, such as the Irish, Jews, and the Chinese, found themselves defined as subordinate. They were denied access to good jobs, ridiculed in the media, and mired in poverty, and they often did not have access to higher education. The Chinese eventually faced unprecedented immigration restrictions. Some immigrant groups eventually were able to assimilate into the dominant white culture, while others encountered ongoing obstacles to their assimilation.

The United States government played a key role in facilitating assimilation for some groups, forcing it on others, and blocking it for still others. In the late nineteenth and early twentieth centuries, Native Americans faced numerous attempts at forced assimilation, from being rounded up on reservations to the boarding school movement. While some groups, such as the Irish, embraced assimilation into the dominant, mainstream white culture, others, particularly Native Americans, actively resisted this.

KEY TERMS AND CONCEPTS

Anglo-conformity

Antilynching movement

Collective violence

Cultural assimilation

Global white supremacy

Group position

Lynching

Nativism

Passing

Power-threat hypothesis

Race relations cycle

Race riots

Restrictive covenants

Sinophobia

Social solidarity

Sojourners

Structural assimilation

Xenophobia

PERSONAL REFLECTIONS

1. To what extent did you understand the significance of race to US history prior to reading this chapter? Reflect on where your historical perspective comes from (in other words, try to understand why it is what it is). What aspect of US racial history did you find the most shocking and why?
2. Do you have ancestors belonging to any of the groups discussed in this chapter (whites, Native Americans, Chinese Americans, Irish Americans, Jewish Americans, or African Americans)? If so, how does this information make you feel?

CRITICAL THINKING QUESTIONS

1. To what extent has the United States favored the assimilation of racial/ethnic minorities? Provide examples of when assimilation has not been an option for particular racial/ethnic groups. What are some factors that influence the ability of a group to assimilate into the dominant culture? What are some factors that inhibit a group's chances of assimilating into the dominant culture?
2. Provide evidence that this period in history, the late nineteenth and early twentieth centuries, was a racial dictatorship. Conversely, provide evidence that this period could be described as the beginning of a racial democracy.

ESSENTIAL READING

Blackmon, Douglas A. 2008. *Slavery by Another Name: The Re-Enslavement of Black Americans from the Civil War to World War II.* New York: Anchor Books.

Curtis, Lewis Perry. 1997. *Apes and Angels: The Irishman in Victorian Caricature,* revised ed. Washington, DC: Smithsonian Institution Press.

Daniels, Roger. 1998. *Not Like Us: Immigrants and Minorities in America, 1890–1924.* Chicago, IL: Ivan R. Dee Publishers.

Downs, Jim. 2015. *Sick from Freedom: African American Illness and Suffering during the Civil War and Reconstruction,* reprint ed. Oxford, New York: Oxford University Press.

Feimster, Crystal N. 2011. *Southern Horrors: Women and the Politics of Rape and Lynching.* Boston, MA: Harvard University Press.

Grann, David. 2017. *Killers of the Flower Moon: The Osage Murders and the Birth of the FBI.* New York: Doubleday.

Wilkerson, Isabel. 2010. *The Warmth of Other Suns: The Epic Story of America's Great Migration.* New York: Random House.

RECOMMENDED FILMS

Reconstruction: America After the Civil War (2019). Produced by Henry Louis Gates, Jr. and Dyllan McGee. This PBS documentary offers comprehensive coverage of one of the most overlooked and misunderstood eras in American history.

The Iron Road (1990). Produced by Neil Goodwin. This documentary, broadcast on PBS's *American Experience*, explores the building of the first transcontinental railroad. Over twenty thousand men, most of whom were Chinese and Irish immigrants, labored to build the railroad, while working through dangerous conditions.

The Rise and Fall of Jim Crow, Vols. 1–4 (2002). Produced by Bill Jersey and William R. Grant. This film series provides excellent documentary coverage of the post–Civil War and pre–civil rights era, examining both African American oppression and civil rights organizing. Topics include the formation of the Reconstruction, the Ku Klux Klan, lynching, race riots, W. E. B. Du Bois, Booker T. Washington, Walter White, the formation of the NAACP, and labor organizing. It exposes the complexities of this often-overlooked period in American racial history.

We Shall Remain, Vols. 1–5 (2009). Produced by Mark Samuels and Sharon Grimberg. In this groundbreaking PBS documentary film series, part of *American Experience*, Native American scholars, activists, and laypeople relay their history and heritage. The film series explores Native American resilience in the face of cultural genocide, from early contact with Europeans through the activism of the 1970s. It addresses the specific conflicts and issues faced by Native tribes throughout the United States.

RECOMMENDED MULTIMEDIA

Visit the website Without Sanctuary for photographs and postcards of lynching in America: http://withoutsanctuary.org.

Lynching in the United States, 1883–1941, interactive map, from Penn State's Institute for CyberScience (David Rigby, Alison Appling, and Charles Seguin). This map identifies lynching victims by name, race, location, date of the murder, and cause of death. It serves to highlight that such mob violence occurred across the country and many racial/ethnic groups were targeted, although Southern blacks were by far the most likely victims of lynch mobs. www.charlieseguin.com/dot_map.html.

For more information on the Freedmen's Bureau and the Jim Crow era, check out this PBS website: www.pbs.org/wnet/jimcrow/stories_events_freed.html.

Race Relations in Flux: From Civil Rights to Black Lives Matter

CHAPTER LEARNING OUTCOMES

By the end of this chapter, you should be able to:

- Differentiate between social movements and collective behavior
- Describe the social and cultural conditions that contributed to the minority activism of the post–World War II era
- Define nonviolent direct action and provide examples of these strategies that were used by racial/ethnic minority activists and organizations in this era
- Identify and describe the key social movement organizations associated with the civil rights movement, the Red Power movement, Chicano activism, and Asian American activism
- Differentiate between political activism and cultural activism
- Explore the intersection of identities and activism
- Describe the emergence of the Black Lives Matter and #SayHerName movements and Dakota Access Pipeline protests at Standing Rock, and the similarities and differences of each movement to their 1960s counterparts

Inspired by the militancy of the late 1960s, specifically the Black Power, Red Power, and Chicano rights movements, Asian Americans began mobilizing for change. Explicitly rejecting Asian stereotypes of passivity, in 1968, Asian American students at the University of California, Berkeley, formed the Asian American Political Alliance (AAPA). The AAPA developed close ties with the Black Panther Party and used some of its tactics and strategies as a model. It demanded an end to the Vietnam War, more faculty and students of color in the University of California system, and an end to police brutality. The group also worked with Asian Legal Services to help those who resisted the Vietnam War draft (Ogbar 2001). Some Asian American activism focused on demands for reparations for the internment of Japanese Americans during World War II.

The AAPA also struggled to develop a "yellow consciousness," a pride in being Asian American, independent of white America. Until this point, most Asian Americans identified with their specific ethnic group, such as Japanese or Vietnamese or Chinese, and did not think of themselves as "Asian American." Part of the development of this new racial consciousness involved the development of a pan-Asian identity rather than specific ethnic identities associated with Japanese Americans, Vietnamese Americans, or Chinese Americans, and so forth. The AAPA was the first group to refer to itself as "Asian American," and the term became a unifying force among various Asian ethnic groups.

SOURCE: "Asian American Political Alliance 1968." 2008. Asian American Movement 1968, January 15. http://aam1968.blogspot.com/2008/01/asian-american-politcal-alliance-1968.html.

The post–World War II era witnessed an explosion of resistance in the form of activism on the part of African Americans, Native Americans, Chicanos, and Asian Americans as the civil rights movement helped inspire other racial minority groups to demand full equality. The 1950s through 1970s marked an era of dramatic social changes in the United States, particularly for racial/ethnic minorities, who mobilized, protested their subordination, and demanded their full civil and political rights. Minority activists challenged demeaning stereotypes in the media and misrepresentation in educational institutions and sometimes reclaimed racial/ethnic identities that had previously been shed in often futile attempts at assimilating into the dominant white society.

We begin this chapter with an exploration of the sociological framework for understanding social movements, followed by an analysis of the social and historical conditions that provided the impetus for the civil rights movement, the Red Power movement, Chicano activism, and Asian American mobilization. Finally, we will conclude with an examination of the strategies and tactics used by movement activists to generate attention to minority oppression, their demands for change, the success of their activism, and the response to their demands. While white resistance to civil rights activism is well documented, this chapter also highlights the involvement and contributions of white Americans to the movement for black equality. Examples of such activism include:

- Civil rights activist Diane Nash explains, "I've been amazed and upset with the way the media and history have portrayed the [civil rights] Movement as though it was Martin Luther King's movement. It was not. It was truly a people's movement. Martin was not the leader of the Movement, he was the spokesman. … It's so important to portray it as a people's movement" (Ingram 1990:221).

- Jo Ann Robinson was an English professor at Alabama State University when she organized the Montgomery bus boycott. Despite the fact that she was employed at a historically black college, her activism cost her her job (Carrier 2004).

- In 1965, Cesar Chavez helped organize a national grape boycott to protest the poor working conditions migrant farmworkers faced. By the 1970s, the boycott "had become a national concern. For the first time in American history, consumers understood the plight of farmworkers, and 17 million of them stopped buying grapes" (Ingram 1990:105).

- Despite traditional gender roles defining women as passive, women of color were actively involved in all minority protest movements of the post-WWII era. White women were also politically active; some were fighting alongside people of color for civil rights for all and others were fighting to maintain the status quo and actively resisted the demands of the civil rights movement.

- The Black Lives Matter movement began online in 2013 after the acquittal of George Zimmerman in the shooting death of unarmed Florida teenager Trayvon Martin and became a full-blown social movement in the wake of the shooting death of Michael Brown by police officer Darren Wilson in Ferguson, Missouri.

- In early 2016, Native Americans began protesting the construction of an oil and gas pipeline designed to run from North Dakota to Illinois, under the Missouri and Mississippi Rivers, near the Standing Rock Indian Reservation. Native Americans viewed the pipeline as a threat to their clean water and an assault on ancient burial grounds. The activism, known as the Dakota Access Pipeline Protests and #NoDAPL, generated international attention, and has been described as transformative in its merging of "the climate movement with indigenous communities" (Solnit 2016).

SOCIOLOGICAL PERSPECTIVES ON SOCIAL MOVEMENTS

Sociologists define a **social movement** as organized activism intended to be engaged in over a long period of time, with the objective of changing society in some way through collective action. The minority protest movements of this era involved all the key characteristics of a social movement: they were organized, involved activism over a sustained period of time, engaged the mobilization of a large number of supporters, and used all of the major forms of mass communication available. Additionally, the racial/ethnic movements of this era can be understood as **grassroots movements**, meaning they were inspired and organized by the masses, by everyday people who were simply tired of racism and discrimination. Prominent leaders such as Martin Luther King Jr. emerged out of the civil rights movement, but such well-known movement leaders are not credited with starting the social movement.

There are many types of social movements. The minority protest movements in this chapter can all be described as **reform movements**, meaning their goals were to make changes within the existing system (instead of attempting to overthrow the system, as revolutionary movements would), and **left-wing social movements** because they are "attempting to increase freedom and equality for submerged groups" (Wood and Jackson 1982:9). But a social movement should not be confused with **collective behavior**, which refers to unorganized, spontaneous, and often short-lived actions of a large group of people, such as riots, fashion, or fads.

Why did these movements occur when they did? There was nothing new about racial oppression in the United States; therefore, these social movements were not merely a response to racial oppression. Sociologically, to understand the emergence of social movements, one must understand the social and historical contexts out of which they emerge. The next section examines the conditions that facilitated the emergence of minority protest movements in the post–World War II era.

Social and Cultural Context

Human beings act within social, cultural, and historical contexts. Thus, analyzing social action requires attention to these contexts. The post–World War II era was a period of economic growth and increasing urbanization, which contributed to minority group activism. The official beginning of the civil rights movement is generally defined as 1954 with the Supreme Court decision *Brown v. Board of Education*. However, much had occurred prior to that that facilitated the emergence of the civil rights movement. President Harry S. Truman, for instance, had already taken a strong stand on civil rights, particularly through Executive Order 9981, which integrated the US armed forces in 1948. In an entirely different arena, Major League Baseball had racially integrated in 1947, providing hope for individual African Americans and momentum for the budding movements (see Chapter 12).

Sociologists who study social movements point out that for subordinate groups to challenge their status through protest, it takes more than **relative deprivation**, the perception of a subordinate group that its situation is worse than that of the dominant group in terms of economics, power, and privilege (Gurr 1970). This is true for the minority protest movements of the post–World War II era: the civil rights and Black Power movements; Native American activism, also known as the

Red Power movement; Chicano activism; and Asian American activism, sometimes called the Yellow Power movement. For clarification, **Chicano** is a term and an identity that refers specifically to Mexican Americans, particularly those who are politically active, while *Latino* refers more broadly to all Spanish-speaking and Portuguese-speaking people from Latin America.

Thousands of African Americans, Latinos, and Native Americans fought in World War II, most in racially segregated units. After fighting racism in Europe, these groups hoped that they could return to the United States and be treated as something other than second-class citizens. Yet this was not the case. Instead, they found themselves still facing discrimination, oppression, and second-class citizenship.

Additionally, at this time, the US system of segregation and racial inequality was coming under increasing scrutiny throughout the world. Former European colonies began declaring their independence from colonial rule; for example, India successfully overturned British rule in 1949 after a massive nonviolent civil disobedience campaign led by Mahatma Gandhi. The overthrow of European colonial powers throughout Africa followed. The bulk of Africa had been claimed by European governments by 1905 (Liberia and Ethiopia were the only two nations that were not colonized), and colonial powers had viewed it as their obligation to "civilize" Africa, while stripping them of their wealth and natural resources. The post–World War II era led Africans to take India's lead and challenge their subordination to colonial powers; the year 1960 is called the "Year of Africa" because that year seventeen African territories gained their independence from European colonial rule. Psychiatrist and philosopher Frantz Fanon viewed violent resistance to colonialism as cathartic because colonialism denied colonized peoples their humanity and imposed a subjugated colonial identity on them. This activism on the part of subordinate groups across the globe influenced the post–World War II climate and put international pressure on the United States to dismantle its system of racial segregation.

The post–World War II era of US economic growth was also influential in that it had a two-pronged effect: first, it resulted in increasing expectations for many impoverished minorities, and, second, it created a certain amount of economic security for the working and middle classes, which allowed them the freedom to participate in a social movement. Finally, increasing urbanization of racial minorities throughout the first half of the century resulted in their concentration in urban areas, which helped facilitate communication and **mobilization**, the crucial recruitment of movement participants. Living in urban areas allowed minorities to more easily share their grievances and feed off of their strength in numbers, something less possible when they had been scattered throughout rural southern areas.

Sociologist Doug McAdam (1988) proposes an additional factor that helped facilitate the civil rights movement: the fact that this was the era of the baby boomers. College students during the 1960s were "uniquely optimistic about the future ... and enamored of [their] 'history-making' presence in the world" (McAdam 1988:14). Black Americans possibly held even more optimism regarding the future, due to several Supreme Court victories and the integration of Major League Baseball and the armed forces. Change and progress appeared possible (McAdam 1988). Sociologists refer to this optimism as a **sense of efficacy**, the belief that people can change their situation, and a **sense of feasibility**, the sense of possibility, the potential of actors to carry out the action successfully (Turner and Killian 1987).

Ideologies, Institutions, and Identities

Participation in social movements contributes to the emergence of new ideologies and new identities (Gamson 1992). Social movement participants bring identities to the movement and their identities are changed through their participation in the social movement as one's "identity becomes consistent when it is built in a common ideological orientation that renders it meaningful" (Johnston, Larana, and Gusfield 1994:14). The activism of the Red Power movement, for instance, led people with Indian ancestry to proudly reembrace their American Indian ethnic identity (Nagel 1996). It provided Indians with a positive image of Indianness that inspired them to reconnect with their culture and their Indian identity.

Prior to 1968, "Asian American" did not exist as an identity or a racial category (Okamoto 2014). It was the development of an Asian American identity, referred to as a pan-Asian identity, that precipitated the activism of the Asian American movement of the 1970s (Espiritu 2009). Also referred to as **panethnicity**, or the broadening of ethnic-group boundaries to forge a new group identity, a **pan-Asian identity** emerged, referring to the development of a shared consciousness among individuals of Asian background to identify as Asian American as recognition of their shared experiences with racism in American culture. As the opening vignette explored, one of the major challenges facing organizing the Asian American social movement was getting Asian Americans to see themselves as Asian Americans, above and beyond their ethnic identification. Prior to the development of a pan-Asian identity, Asian Americans did not form alliances with one another or understand themselves as having a shared history, and instead lived in separate ethnic communities (Okamoto 2014).

WITNESS

Sam, a Korean American attorney, discusses his sense of Asian American unity: "I ended up marrying a Korean woman, but it could have been another Asian. … In college, my Asian, no my Asian American identity became very important to me. … The slogan then was Asian unity, yellow power and all that" (Kibria 1997).

Sociologists emphasize how social movements create both **collective identities**, the re-creation or resurgence of a racial/ethnic group's culture, traditions, or history (Fitzgerald 2007; Nagel 1996), and **individual identities**, a new sense among participants of being defined at least partially along racial/ethnic lines (Hunt and Benford 1994; Gamson 1992; Nagel 1996). Identities are a significant mobilizing force and are formed within social movements. This is a burgeoning area of research for social movement theorists, as "new social movements" are often referred to as identity-based movements, because identity is central to why people mobilize (Johnston, Larana, and Gusfield 1994; Melucci 1980).

THE CIVIL RIGHTS MOVEMENT

The civil rights movement, considered an identity-based social movement because participants mobilized around their black racial identities, sought to extend full citizenship rights to African Americans. These rights had been guaranteed in the Thirteenth (1865), Fourteenth (1868), and Fifteenth (1870) Amendments, which had passed in the years following the Civil War, yet they remained unenforced. The civil rights movement began during the early 1900s, as discussed in Chapter 5, and witnessed its first success in 1948 with the efforts of President Truman, and continued through the late 1960s (see Figure 6.1). Civil rights activists confronted Jim Crow segregation, fought for the right to vote, and pursued educational and economic equality, and the right to be free from terror. An often-overlooked aspect of civil rights activism involved mobilization and protests against the sexual violence directed at African American women perpetrated by white men throughout the Jim Crow era. Black women had begun testifying to family, friends, and the NAACP of their experiences of sexual violence in the 1940s, and through this activism, black women reclaimed their bodies and demanded respect. This also marked some of the earliest activism on the part of African American women (McGuire 2010).

Social Movement Organizations

Social movements are made up of a variety of organizations that are working to meet the needs of the movement. The civil rights movement was no exception. Sociologists who study social movements emphasize the significance of social movement organizations (**SMOs**), which are formal organizations that share the goals of the larger social movement and help organize strategies, resources, and mobilization efforts (McCarthy and Zald 1977).

One of the most important organizations to the movement was the NAACP, which actually began in 1909 and set the foundation for the modern civil rights

1947	President Harry S. Truman's Committee on Civil Rights publishes *To Secure These Freedoms*, encouraging federal action to end lynching, racial segregation, and voting restrictions for blacks
1947	Major League Baseball integrates when Jackie Robinson joins the Brooklyn Dodgers
1948	President Harry S. Truman issues Executive Order 9981, which integrates the American armed forces
1954	Supreme Court decision *Brown v. Topeka Board of Education* declares public school desegregation illegal
1955	Emmett Till is murdered in Money, MS
1955	Montgomery bus boycott begins after Rosa Parks is arrested for refusing to give up her seat to a white man
1956	Supreme Court orders University of Alabama to admit black applicant Autherine Lucy
1957	Arkansas governor Faubus orders the Arkansas National Guard to block black students from Little Rock Central High School; President Dwight Eisenhower sends in federal troops to enforce *Brown* decision
1957	Southern Christian Leadership Conference (SCLC) is formed in New Orleans
1960	First student sit-ins at Woolworth's lunch counters in Greensboro, NC, and Nashville, TN
1960	Student Nonviolent Coordinating Committee (SNCC) is formed
1961	Freedom Rides, organized by Congress of Racial Equality (CORE) and SNCC, begin
1961	Voter registration drives in the South begin
1962	James Meredith becomes the first black person to attend classes at the University of Mississippi
1963	SCLC launches protests of school desegregation in Birmingham, AL
1963	March on Washington for Jobs and Freedom; Martin Luther King Jr. gives his "I Have a Dream" speech at the March on Washington
1963	Civil rights activist Medgar Evers is shot to death in Jackson, MS
1963	Black church in Birmingham is bombed by the KKK killing four little girls
1963	President John F. Kennedy is assassinated in Dallas, TX
1964	Freedom Summer begins in Mississippi; Freedom Schools formed
1964	Civil rights workers James Chaney, Mickey Schwerner, and Andrew Goodman are murdered
1964	*Civil Rights Act* is signed by President Lyndon Johnson
1965	Malcolm X is assassinated in New York
1965	Selma to Montgomery March—Alabama state troopers attack civil rights protesters on Edmund Pettus Bridge
1965	*Voting Rights Act* is passed
1966	Black Panther party is formed in Oakland, CA
1968	Martin Luther King Jr. is assassinated in Memphis, TN
1968	Presidential candidate Robert F. Kennedy is assassinated in Los Angeles

FIGURE 6.1: Timeline of key events of the African American Civil Rights Movement.

SOURCES: Blumberg 1984; Honey 2007.

movement. The NAACP Legal Defense Fund, for instance, challenged racial inequality in the courts and brought forward many cases that were crucial to the civil rights movement. Another is the Congress of Racial Equality (CORE), which also pre-dated the civil rights movement, having organized in 1942 in Chicago. CORE embraced the use of nonviolence to challenge segregation.

Two organizations emerged out of successful civil rights movement activism specifically to fight for civil rights for African Americans: the Southern Christian Leadership Council (SCLC) and the Student Nonviolent Coordinating Committee (SNCC, pronounced "snick"). The SCLC emerged in 1957 out of the success of the Montgomery bus boycott, and Martin Luther King Jr. was the organization's first president.

BOX 6.1

Racial Justice Activism:
Bob Zellner

Bob Zellner, a white southerner, the son and grandson of KKK members, was one of the first white members of the SNCC, the interracial student activist civil rights organization. Zellner's racial justice activism began innocently enough through a sociology class assignment on race relations during his senior year in 1960. Instead of heading to the library, Zellner and several colleagues chose to do primary research, much to the dismay of their sociology professor. They were interested in meeting with Martin Luther King Jr. and the Montgomery Improvement Association, organizers of the Montgomery bus boycott, as well as black students at a local black college. Although such actions seem innocent enough from our current vantage point, these were radical actions that placed these students on the radar of local law enforcement agencies.

Many white civil rights activists participated in the movement despite lack of support for their work from their parents and their communities. Many families of black student activists feared physical or economic reprisals against them or their families (Zellner and Curry 2008). Over his years of activism, Zellner was beaten, arrested, jailed, and nearly killed, yet his commitment to racial justice activism never wavered.

In his memoir, Zellner describes some of the threats whites sympathetic to civil rights faced: "A white person who got involved or took any action would be punished—you could suffer an economic boycott by the White Citizens Council, your house might be shot into, the traditional cross might be burned in your lawn, you could receive threatening telephone calls. Then your choices were to stay and fight, or to flee" (Zellner and Curry 2008:255). Executive producer Spike Less is bringing Zellner's life story to the big screen in the upcoming film *Son of the South*.

The success of the sit-in movement inspired the formation of another SMO, a formal organization of college students intending to fight racism, SNCC. SNCC was organized nonhierarchically, which meant it was group centered rather than leader centered and was an interracial organization (see Box 6.1 Racial Justice Activism: Bob Zellner). SNCC organizers were committed to building grassroots leadership, which meant they were interested in training leaders from the bottom up rather than looking to black elites for leadership (Emery, Gold, and Braselmann 2008). They embraced democratic decision-making within their organization, welcomed white allies, and engaged in more **civil disobedience**, the practice of refusing to obey discriminatory laws, and nonviolent activism than the more traditional civil rights organization, SCLC.

They brought their demands for racial equality to the Deep South, one of the most dangerous places in the country for such activism. New leaders of the civil rights movement emerged, such as Diane Nash, John Lewis, Bob Moses, and Stokely Carmichael. Their first organized actions involved registering voters throughout Mississippi. They organized workshops in nonviolence throughout the Deep South. Such actions were not taken lightly by the white power structure and SNCC members faced violence and arrest, seriously undermining their ability to register blacks to vote (Goldberg 1996).

As a civil rights organization, SNCC best represents the eventual disillusionment of the civil rights movement. While in hindsight it is easy to see the successes of the civil rights movement, during the years of activism, in the face of violent opposition to black demands for basic equality and the failure of the federal government to offer blacks basic protections, SNCC became increasingly militant in their message. Although initially committed to interracialism, by 1967 SNCC had shifted its emphasis from integration to building black community organizations, and eventually it expelled all white members of the organization.

Social Movement Strategies and Tactics

All social movements use a variety of strategies and tactics to attain their goals. While some of the strategies of the civil rights movement, such as nonviolent civil disobedience, present us with the most iconic and enduring images of the movement, most of these strategies were borrowed from Gandhi or from the labor movement of previous eras. This section explores some of the key strategies and tactics used during the 1950s and 1960s by civil rights movement activists.

Montgomery Bus Boycott

Jim Crow segregation emerged in the South after the Civil War as a way to physically signify black subordination in an era when that could no longer be taken for granted. In 1955, black citizens of Montgomery, Alabama, successfully challenged racial segregation in transportation through a massive boycott of city buses that lasted for 381 days. The boycott was ignited by the actions of Rosa Parks, an African American seamstress and member of her local NAACP, who refused to give her seat to a white man, as was the custom and law in Alabama and throughout the South. Parks was not the first African American to be arrested for challenging segregation laws in Montgomery or elsewhere in the South, nor would she be the last. However, her arrest was the catalyst for the Montgomery bus boycott, a significant moment in civil rights movement history.

The bus boycott was incredibly hard on Montgomery's black residents as most were reliant on public transportation. In addition to giving up the convenience of bus transportation, walking many miles to and from their jobs, they faced violent retaliation for their well-publicized activism. Despite this, there was almost 100 percent participation in the boycott by the black community. Black riders accounted for 75 percent of the bus company's business; thus, the boycott presented the bus company with serious financial hardship.

A young minister new to Montgomery, Martin Luther King Jr., was recruited to coordinate the bus boycott. King may have become the most visible face of the movement, but it was a grassroots movement. In other words, the civil rights movement found King; King didn't found the movement.

In response to the bus boycott, Alabama whites formed White Citizens' Councils, groups of middle-class whites organized specifically to fight desegregation. Black activists faced political and economic opposition, as well as violence at the hands of some local white supremacists, for their activism. Many local blacks, including Rosa Parks, were fired from their jobs for their participation in the boycott. The homes of local activist E. D. Nixon and Martin Luther King Jr. were bombed due to their activism. While white opposition was considerable, some whites supported the Montgomery bus boycott by contributing financial support; some did so anonymously to avoid retaliation while others exhibited more overt support, such as marching with blacks or providing rides to those participating in the boycott. Sympathetic whites also faced economic and political retaliation from other white people for their actions.

By 1956, the court case challenging Montgomery's desegregation laws had reached the Supreme Court, which ruled that the city's segregation laws were unconstitutional. The success of the Montgomery bus boycott inspired the formation of the SCLC in 1957, and Martin Luther King Jr. was elected the first president. This organization united black ministers across the South, who met to discuss plans for future activism. The SCLC was committed to **nonviolent direct action** (see Box 6.2 Global Perspectives: Gandhi, Nonviolent Protest, and the End of British Rule in India): engaging in confrontational tactics, such as strikes, sit-ins, and demonstrations, while remaining nonviolent, generally in the face of violence (Fitzgerald and Rodgers 2000).

WITNESS

Diane Nash, a civil rights activist, emphasizes that the civil rights movement has been misrepresented as "Martin [Luther King Jr.]'s movement. It was not. It was truly a people's movement. … People are surprised when I tell them that the Freedom Rides, the sit-ins at lunch counters, the Montgomery bus boycott, the March on Washington, the Selma Campaign—those major elements of the Movement—were not things which Martin thought up and suggested we do" (Ingram 1990:221–222).

School Desegregation

Most historians mark the 1954 Supreme Court decision in *Brown v. Board of Education* as the beginning of the civil rights movement. *Brown v. Board of Education* declared segregated schools unconstitutional, overriding the previous Supreme Court decision *Plessy v. Ferguson* (1896), and opening the door for desegregation in all aspects of life.

The first real test of the *Brown* decision was in Little Rock, Arkansas. The local chapter of the NAACP decided to enforce the decision through the integration of Little Rock's Central High School. This strategy was chosen because Little Rock, a moderate southern city, was considered to be a more enlightened community regarding race issues. For instance, its local police force was already integrated and the law school at the University of Arkansas had voluntarily admitted blacks since 1948; thus, it was believed that the implementation of the *Brown* decision would stand more chance of success there than in the Deep South. The resistance the NAACP encountered, however, was astounding. The desegregation plan was limited to nine stellar black students, all from middle-class families, who were seeking the best high school education in their city, which was being provided at all-white Central High.

Arkansas governor Orval Faubus ordered the Arkansas National Guard to surround the high school and not allow the black students to enter on the first day, sincerely fearing for the safety of the black students. A judge ordered that integration should proceed, and so on the second day of classes, the group of students who became known as the Little Rock Nine attempted to enter Central High School. Eight of the nine came together, but the ninth girl, fifteen-year-old Elizabeth Eckford, had not gotten the message that the nine should come to school together and tried entering the school on her own. She faced a hostile mob and shouts of "Lynch her! Lynch her!" (Williams 1987). The Arkansas National Guard refused her entrance into the school. As she headed back to the bus stop, she was spat on and cursed by the angry mob.

This case exemplifies the conflicts over states' rights that characterized much of the civil rights movement: the dilemmas posed when federal and state laws conflict.

President Eisenhower was eventually forced to send in federal troops to enforce the judicial order and protect the black students. The federal troops confronted a mob the following day and made clear their intentions of enforcing the law. Each of the nine black students had a bodyguard assigned to him or her for the entire school year so that all could get to their classes safely. The next year, Governor Faubus closed the schools to avoid integration, depriving all children whose families could not afford private schools the right to an education. The Supreme Court stepped in and declared the closing of the public schools to be unconstitutional. By 1959, the public schools were reopened and racially integrated (Williams 1987).

BOX 6.2

Global Perspectives:
Gandhi, Nonviolent Protest, and the End of British Rule in India

The commitment of civil rights activists to nonviolent direct action and civil disobedience was modeled on Gandhi's successful campaign to end British colonial rule in India. Mohandas Gandhi, an Indian citizen and a British-educated lawyer, initially became politically active during his years in South Africa. His experiences with racism there led him to begin a massive twenty-year campaign protesting the race laws that held both blacks and Indians in subjugation.

Upon his return to India, he brought his strategy of *satyagraha*, a type of nonviolent resistance combined with activism. In his first nationwide *satyagraha* in 1920, he urged Indians to boycott all British goods and institutions, including schools, and to refuse to pay taxes, and he agitated for the rights of disadvantaged groups in India. One of his most famous actions was the Salt March in 1930. He encouraged thousands to march with him to the sea, a distance of over 248 miles, to protest the British tax on salt. He and the other protesters illegally made salt from the seawater. Thousands were imprisoned, which did little to subdue the movement, as by 1931 over twenty-four thousand resisters were in jail, and over sixty thousand were jailed throughout the campaign (Herman 2008).

It took over fifteen years, but Gandhi's campaigns brought about what has been described as a "seismic shift in Indian politics" (Herman 2008:343). These actions eventually resulted in the Government of India Act 1935, which was the beginning of the end of British rule in India. After another fifteen years of civil disobedience, British rule officially ended in 1950. Gandhi's commitment to nonviolent civil disobedience has been used across the globe by subordinate groups demanding equality, including racial minorities in post–World War II United States.

The Sit-in Movement

Another social movement strategy that civil rights activists relied on was the sit-in. In 1960, four well-dressed African American college students in Greensboro, North Carolina, challenged southern norms by sitting down at a lunch counter and requesting service. The response to their request was a curt, "We don't serve colored here." The actions of the four students ignited similar protests across the South. The sit-ins, and the white reaction to them, were headline news across the country.

Students from Fisk University and Vanderbilt University in Nashville engaged in similar nonviolent direct action, forcing the desegregation of lunch counters in their communities. As a social movement strategy, *nonviolent* means they accepted beatings without hitting back and *direct action* refers to people engaged in disruptive protests: strikes, sit-ins, boycotts, mass meetings, and demonstrations (Fitzgerald and Rodgers 2000). Nashville, like Little Rock, was considered a moderate southern city and thus possibly more receptive to demands for civil rights than cities in the Deep South. However, the student demonstrations were challenged by groups of white Nashville young people who attacked the protesters. None of the black protesters fought back. When the Nashville police arrived, they arrested eighty-one black protesters for disorderly conduct.

White southerners who were opposed to black demands for civil rights suggested that the college students were outside agitators, communists, or northern Democrats—the protesters could not have been local because "their Negroes" were

IMAGE 6.1: Whites protesting integration.

happy. However, local black communities showed their support for the sit-ins by boycotting downtown merchants. The sit-ins not only hurt the reputation of Nashville and the South but hurt the city financially as well. Many northern white students showed their support for the sit-ins by picketing branches of the same department stores in their locales. In a mere two weeks, there were sit-ins in eleven cities. By the end of 1960, sit-ins had occurred in every southern state except Mississippi, and "a citizen army of 70,000 crossed the color line in 150 cities to desegregate many public venues," including swimming pools, churches, beaches, libraries, theaters, parks, and museums (Dierenfield 2008:58).

A mere few weeks later, Nashville became the first major southern city to desegregate its lunch counters; however, "it would take four more years of sit-ins, marches, beatings, and arrests before blacks in Nashville could desegregate hotels, movie theaters, and fast-food restaurants" (Dierenfield 2008:58). Facing very real dangers, black college students, throughout 1960, politely demanded equality and eventually won many of their battles. This kind of activism was copied elsewhere as "pray-ins" were held to protest racially segregated religious congregations and "wade-ins" were held to protest white-only beaches and swimming areas.

Freedom Rides

The CORE, a civil rights organization that formed in the early 1940s, decided to protest segregation in transportation through the Freedom Rides in 1961. The strategy of the Freedom Rides was to have interracial groups riding buses throughout the South, defying segregation laws along the way. The white activists would sit in the back of the bus while the black activists would sit in the front. At every stop, they violated the norms of segregated waiting rooms by doing the same thing: black activists entered "white-only" areas while the white activists entered the "colored only" sections. They were well aware that these actions would ignite violent reactions from southern racists and that the federal government would have to step in and force compliance with the 1955 Supreme Court decision that had declared segregation in interstate transit to be illegal. The Freedom Riders encountered enraged mobs of whites at many stops. In Alabama, CORE riders were beaten with bats, their bus was fire-bombed, and one participant was nearly lynched. At some locations, police stood by while whites attacked the riders, exposing the lack of basic protections for civil rights activists, a clear example of the power structure's operating to maintain white supremacy.

Freedom Summer

Members of SNCC declared an ambitious goal for the summer of 1964: to bring the civil rights movement to Mississippi through a program it called Freedom Summer. At the time, Mississippi was considered to be a "closed society" and one of the most dangerous places civil rights activists could find themselves. It also had the most impoverished and the least-educated population, as well as the most stringent enforcement of black voter disenfranchisement. Mississippi was also home to the majority of African Americans in the United States (Dierenfield 2008).

Freedom Summer trained young people, black and white, to register voters throughout Mississippi and to establish Freedom Schools to educate black citizens of all ages. SNCC intentionally sought the collaboration of not just white students but northern white students of privilege. After a decade of civil rights activism and three particularly hard years of voter registration efforts, one valuable lesson had been learned: the murder of black civil rights workers did not raise alarm. SNCC

IMAGE 6.2: African American resistance to racism had blossomed into a full-blown civil rights movement by the early 1960s. This image shows hundreds of thousands of people gathered at the National Mall in Washington, DC, for the March on Washington for Jobs and Freedom in 1963. It was here that Martin Luther King Jr. delivered his historic "I Have a Dream" speech.

members were sure that if the sons and daughters of America's wealthy white families were injured while fighting for democracy, the federal government and law enforcement would have to take notice (McAdam 1988).

Although Freedom Summer lasted only three months, over one thousand white northern college students were trained and headed south to Mississippi to work on one of forty-four local projects conducted by SNCC. While in Ohio at a workshop in nonviolent direct action, they received word that three civil rights workers had gone missing in Mississippi. African American James Chaney and two white northerners, Michael Schwerner and Andrew Goodman, were in Mississippi and had gone to investigate the burning of a black church. They were taken to jail for speeding, released later that night, and never seen again. President Lyndon Johnson sent federal agents to help search for the missing men.

The bodies of the three civil rights workers were found buried in an earthen dam in early August 1964. The three men had been shot to death; the black man, James Chaney, had additionally endured a brutal beating. Twenty-one white Mississippians and Klan members, including a local deputy sheriff, were taken into custody a few months later. Charges were dropped in the state court and it looked like these men were going to get away with murder; however, in 1966, seven of them were federally charged and convicted of violating the civil rights of the young men, rather than for their murders (Williams 1987). Eventually, Edgar Ray Killen was found guilty of manslaughter in the case in 2005 and was sentenced to sixty years in prison.

The murders of these young men did not deter the Freedom Summer volunteers. They came in droves, with the hope of turning Mississippi inside out (Dierenfield 2008). White Mississippians felt they were being invaded by the North—again. They dug in their heels to maintain segregation. The violence continued as "racists beat eighty civil rights workers, shot at thirty-five of them, and killed four. Seventy black homes, businesses, and churches were bombed or burned. The police excused the white Mississippians who perpetrated the crimes and arrested a thousand activists" (Dierenfield 2008:109). Despite this, there was progress. Over three thousand black children attended Freedom Schools, and the voter registration drive led seventeen thousand black Mississippians to register as Democrats.

REFLECT AND CONNECT

To what extent do the cultural images of the civil rights movement reflect organized strategizing? To what extent do they appear to be spontaneous protest, or episodes of collective behavior, rather than organized activism? Why might this matter?

Women and the Civil Rights Movement

Many women were fundamental to the civil rights movement, including Fannie Lou Hamer, Diane Nash, Ella Baker, Frances Beal, Daisy Bates, Dottie Zellner, and Victoria Gray, among others. While male civil rights activists saw racial inequality clearly, gender inequality, especially within their own organizations, was much harder for them to acknowledge. Even an organization such as SNCC was male dominated. Two white female members of SNCC, Mary King and Casey Hayden, wrote a position paper in 1964 outlining women's secondary status in the organization: women were unlikely to be project directors, they were generally asked to take minutes at organization meetings and to sweep the floor after meetings, and they were less likely to speak to the press as the face of the organization. In response to the paper, an African American male member of SNCC, Stokely Carmichael, joked that "the position of women in SNCC is prone," and while the comment was understood to be a joke, "his jest came to symbolize the collection of slights suffered by women in SNCC" (Brownmiller 1999).

IMAGE 6.3: African American Fisk University college student and civil rights activist Diane Nash (right).

Belinda Robnett (2004) argues that after 1966, SNCC became more macho in style under the leadership of Stokely Carmichael, and this change left little room for women. This was a shift away from their original organizational style, which had previously involved a commitment to **participatory democracy**, an organizational ideology that discourages centralization of leadership and is nonhierarchical. Organizations committed to participatory democracy tend to empower women more, even if they are not committed to feminist ideologies (Robnett 2004). Perhaps in response to that macho leadership style, Frances Beal founded the Black Women's Liberation Committee within SNCC in 1968. In an early exploration of the ways intersectional status hierarchies intertwine and cocreate structural hierarchies, Beal called attention to the unique position of black women in an era of liberation movements:

> The new world that we are struggling to create must destroy oppression of any type. … This will mean changing the traditional routines that we have established. … If we are going to liberate ourselves as a people, it must be recognized that black women have very specific problems [distinct from those of white women or black men] that have to be spoken to.
>
> (Beal 1969)

Despite the sexism within the civil rights movement, women who participated in it found their work to be liberating and empowering. Many women activists who had been involved in the movement later became involved in the women's movement. Some scholars see women's participation in SNCC as contributing to shifts in cultural gender norms that should be understood as a successful political outcome of the activism and as leading directly to the 1970s women's liberation movement (Robnett 1997).

WITNESS

"Since the advent of black power, the black male has exerted a more prominent leadership role in our struggle for justice in this country. He sees the system for what it really is for the most part. But where he rejects its values and mores on many issues, when it comes to women, he seems to take his guidelines from the pages of the Ladies Home Journal" (Beal 1969).

Black Power

By the mid-1960s, there were some significant shifts in civil rights activism. In the face of violent opposition to demands for civil rights, failures at all levels of government to protect activists or even to enforce existing laws, and persistent racial inequality, disillusionment among activists grew and a new militancy emerged that became known as the Black Power movement. The message and more defiant approach of Black Power was more threatening to white America than the mainstream civil rights movement's focus on civil disobedience. Instead of advocating nonviolence, Black Power advocates, such as the Black Panthers and Black Muslims, argued that blacks should use violence as self-defense when confronted with violent whites.

In 1966, the Black Panther Party was formed in Oakland, California, by Huey Newton and Bobby Seale to address the needs of urban blacks. One of their primary issues was the policing of black urban communities, specifically the fact that black urban residents faced rampant police brutality. Their activism also involved establishing much-needed social programs in low-income black communities, such as community schools and breakfast programs. But it was their revolutionary language, such as their emphasis on black self-defense, and their militant posturing, including the carrying of weapons, that not only frightened whites but also drew the attention of the FBI. At the time, FBI director J. Edgar Hoover declared the Black Panthers to

---

BOX 6.3

Race in the Workplace:
Community Action Programs: Race, Place, and Activism

As part of President Lyndon B. Johnson's War on Poverty, the Economic Opportunity Act was signed into law in 1964. This legislation promoted the establishment of Community Action Programs that encouraged the hiring of low-income community members as paid community workers; these were "neighborhood-based community action programs (CAPs), designed, directed, and staffed by low-income residents" (Naples 1998:39).

CAPs provided low-income people of color, many of whom were women, with paid work in their own communities— work that would address the needs of their particular communities. The goal was to empower low-income people to become self-sufficient. Under these

programs, federal funds were directed to urban Latino and African American communities and to Native American tribes so that they could direct and administer their own social programs, rather than having federally dictated, one-size-fits-all programs. CAP workers "described their commitment to community work as part of a larger struggle for social justice and economic security for people of color and low-income residents of all racial-ethnic backgrounds" (Naples 1998:63). Many individuals who worked in CAPs had been active in movements for racial justice. It was their experience in community organizing that made them such good candidates for becoming paid community workers.

be the greatest threat facing the country (Dierenfield 2008). The Panthers faced tremendous opposition from the US government and political repression by authorities through violence, arrests, infiltration of organizations associated with the Black Power movement, and investigations of movement participants. These actions discredited the organization and severely curtailed the ability of such radical groups as the Black Panthers to operate effectively.

Legislative Victories

In the face of such political, legal, and extralegal violence, it is perhaps surprising that some of the demands of the civil rights movement were actually met. Segregation was dismantled throughout the South. President Kennedy sent a civil rights bill to Congress, where it faced an uphill battle. When Kennedy was assassinated in 1963, Lyndon Johnson, his successor—a white southerner—surprised many when he wholeheartedly embraced the bill. President Johnson used his political skills to get the Civil Rights Act through Congress and signed it on July 2, 1964. While believing this was the morally correct thing to do, he also understood it was political suicide, telling an aide at the time, "I think we delivered the South to the Republican Party for your lifetime and mine" (Dierenfield 2008:94). This legislation prohibited discrimination in public accommodations, made job discrimination illegal, and allowed the federal government to withhold funds from any program that was found discriminating. The Voting Rights Act of 1965 followed, overturning almost a century of Black Codes that kept African Americans from exercising their constitutional right to vote. Significant resistance to these laws was rampant. Many cities closed public parks and pools rather than integrate them. There was violent opposition to school desegregation in major cities in the North throughout the 1970s.

Finally, President Johnson established his War on Poverty, whose programs would help black Americans disproportionately because they were disproportionately impoverished. One of the most successful programs to come out of this was federal funding for Community Action Programs through the Economic Opportunity Act (see Box 6.3 Race in the Workplace: Community Action Programs: Race, Place, and Activism).

White Reaction to the Civil Rights Movement

Many whites were actively involved in the struggle for full civil rights for African Americans. Many other whites violently resisted those demands. It is far too simplistic, not to mention inaccurate, to portray all white northerners as holding progressive racial views and all white southerners as having dissenting views on integration. Much current historical scholarship struggles with teasing out the complexity of white reactions to the civil rights years. For instance, almost all white southerners were aware of civil rights movement protests. While most white southerners opposed the demands of the civil rights movement, sometimes proximity to activism shifted white opinion in favor of civil rights protests (Andrews, Beyerlein, and Tucker Farnum 2016). While the shift from nonviolent direct action to Black Power struck fear in many whites, even the initial nonviolent demands of the movement were perceived as threatening the southern way of life.

The civil rights movement was often a source of confusion to many southern whites. Whites clung to the myth that blacks in their community were content and that race relations were good in their communities (Sokol 2006; Tyson 2004). This perspective stems less from a refusal to see the problem than from the lack of much overt conflict over segregation and racism prior to the 1950s. Civil rights activism was repeatedly portrayed as the influence of outside agitators. It is no surprise that the civil rights movement was interpreted differently by whites than by blacks, as blacks made what they saw as demands for long overdue equality while whites expressed confusion at what appeared to be a sudden case of discontentment. White blindness to the oppression of black Americans was a matter of convenience and also an expression of white privilege.

WITNESS

As the civil rights movement exploded across the South, whites "longed for the days of perceived peace and perfection—of unquestioned white supremacy and habitual black deference" (Sokol 2006:66).

For many whites, any freedoms blacks gained were perceived to come at the expense of their freedoms. Many whites felt that their rights were violated when desegregation laws decided who their children would sit next to in their classrooms or who they would have to sit next to in a restaurant. Civil rights changed everyday interactions in the South. Whites were now expected to refer to blacks with the same formality that had previously been reserved for whites (using "Mr." or "Mrs."). Blacks no longer displayed deference to whites. The bottom line was that many southern whites felt their lives were literally turned upside down over civil rights, and they struggled with the dramatic social changes they faced (Sokol 2006).

While the face of white resistance to the civil rights movement has been male, recent scholarship finds that white women played important roles in resisting the demands of the civil rights movement and working to maintain Jim Crow (McRae 2018). Their activism focused primarily on politics, popular culture, and social welfare and educational institutions. White women's activism is "at the center of the history of white supremacist politics in the South and the nation" (McRae 2018). For these women, being a good white woman meant enforcing racial segregation and pressuring community members to maintain the status quo. They policed the racial identities and relationships of their neighbors, demanded schools censor textbooks and movies that challenged segregation, and influenced electoral politics through canvassing, voter registration, and volunteering at the polls. Their work was not restricted to the South, either. Anti-busing activists in Boston in the early 1970s were a national extension of this work.

There were, of course, white southerners who sympathized with the civil rights movement but were not activists. Vocalizing such views was incredibly risky, though, as sympathetic whites faced the violent repercussions of the Ku Klux Klan. The Klan often directed its violence at white businesses that complied with the Civil Rights Act. Even in the face of this, thousands of whites marched in support of civil rights in various protests in cities across America and joined the two to three hundred thousand protesters at the March on Washington in 1963 (Anderson 1999).

REFLECT AND CONNECT

Reflecting on some of the white reactions to the civil rights movement discussed here, are there any social justice movements today that you are not associated with (such as gay rights, animal rights, or some form of local activism on your campus or in your community) that you find yourself dismissing without much understanding? Or do you find yourself supporting such movements, as a sympathizer or as an active participant, despite some risks associated with such support?

The Demise of the Civil Rights Movement

Many civil rights scholars mark the year 1968 as the official end of the civil rights movement. That year was marred by tragedy: the assassination of Martin Luther King Jr., urban rioting, student antiwar protests on over one hundred campuses nationwide, the assassination of Robert F. Kennedy, and the escalation of the Vietnam War. By 1968, King's focus had shifted from demands for civil rights for blacks to fighting poverty and to anti–Vietnam War activism; he was planning a Poor People's March on Washington when he was assassinated. His wife, Coretta Scott King, and other movement leaders continued with the march despite his death.

It was at the Poor People's March on Washington on May 12, 1968, that some contact and cooperation occurred between civil rights, Chicano, Asian American, and Native American activists. Antiwar activism was a mobilizing force for both King, in his final years, and Asian American activists. Despite lack of much direct contact between these four movements (blacks, Chicanos, Native Americans, and

Asian Americans) and the decreasing visibility of the civil rights movement, it provided the foundation for the other minority protest movements, in that they borrowed from the civil rights movement organizational forms, tactics, rhetoric, grievances, and targets, as well as inspiration (Nagel 1996; Rollins 1986). Other similarities between the four movements extend to the prominent role of college students in the activism and the repressive response of the federal government to their mobilization. In the following sections, we will explore the activism of Native Americans, Chicanos, and Asian Americans.

NATIVE AMERICAN ACTIVISM

The Indian Wars were long over, and more than half a century had passed since Indians had been removed to and isolated on reservations. It was presumed that Indians had acquiesced to the federal government. However, 1961 through 1978 witnessed a resurgence of organized Indian activism, referred to as the Red Power movement. While inspired by the same post–World War II social and cultural conditions that spawned the civil rights movement, the Red Power movement also had some catalysts specifically related to the Indian experience. We will discuss these catalysts, the Native American movement organizations that emerged, the types of activism they engaged in, and the demise of the Red Power movement.

The Red Power movement began among rural and reservation Indians, including Clyde Warrior, Karen Richard, and Melvin Thom, who took pride in their traditional cultures (Shreve 2011). Red Power ideas soon resonated with urban Indians. Large numbers of Indians were living in urban areas due to the implementation of the federal government's *termination policy* in 1950, a policy that sought an alternative approach to assimilating Indians. Under this paternalistic approach, the federal government identified certain tribes they felt were ready to survive on their own and cut off government support of the tribe, encouraging them to leave their reservations for major American cities. This policy resulted in over thirty-five thousand Indians' moving from reservations to urban areas between the years 1952 and 1960. They were concentrated in Denver, Los Angeles, Phoenix, Salt Lake City, San Francisco, and Minneapolis (Smith and Warrior 1996).

Urban Indians faced all the challenges other urban minorities faced, such as poverty, police brutality, and unemployment, but they also had unique challenges that stemmed from being disconnected from their tribal cultures and feeling alienated from the white, mainstream culture. Supratribal Indian organizations, those representing Indians of various tribes, emerged to address the needs of Native Americans, specifically the American Indian Movement (AIM), which was founded in Minneapolis in 1968, and the National Congress of American Indians, founded by Indian veterans of World War II.

IMAGE 6.4: Tipi with a sign reading "American Indian Movement" on the grounds of the Washington Monument in Washington, DC, during an American Indian–organized protest known as the Longest Walk.

Red Power activism began as a Native youth movement, specifically with the founding of the National Indian Youth Council in 1961. While the role of youths in the Red Power movement was not different from other social movements of the era, Native youth were unique in that they were not rebelling against their elders. Instead, they were interested in upholding tribal traditions (Shreve 2011).

Indian activists engaged in numerous high-profile events to draw attention to their ongoing discrimination and oppression; almost all involved the occupation of national monuments, landmarks, or government offices. These locations are significant because they are part of the **collective memory** of a nation, "that set of beliefs about the past which the nation's citizens hold in common and publicly recognize as legitimate representations of their history" (Rhea 1997:2). At a basic level, Native people challenged what we call American history by questioning whose history is being told: does what we call American history represent all groups fairly or does it have a Eurocentric bias?

Sociologists refer to this as part of a larger **race pride movement**, the reassertions of racial identity and cultures that have occurred since the mid-1960s (Rhea 1997). Universities were also targeted by Indian activists as they fought for the creation of Native American studies programs as well as the hiring of Native American faculty to teach in such programs. While there were many similarities between the civil rights movement and the Red Power movement, we see Indians protesting for more than basic civil and political rights. Red Power activists engaged in **cultural activism**: efforts to be able to freely live their Native cultures by participating in traditional ceremonies, fighting for more racially inclusive education, and learning and preserving native languages. In essence, *cultural activism* refers to all the efforts racial/ethnic minority groups engage in to sustain their cultures, cultures that whites have actively attempted to destroy (Fitzgerald 2007).

Red Power Strategies

Like the civil rights movement and all social movements, the Red Power movement used a variety of strategies and tactics to attain its goals. Instead of sit-ins, Native Americans in the Northwest organized "fish-ins" to protest their inability to fish waters their respective tribes had been fishing for hundreds of years. While federal treaties with the Puyallup, Nisqually, and Muckleshoot tribes had guaranteed them the right to fish in their usual places, game wardens in Washington State began arresting them for fishing out of season. The National Indian Youth Council used the media to generate attention to their cause (Shreve 2011). They also used the occupation of federal monuments and government offices as a strategy. These were specific to Native protest—as they exemplified their long-standing conflicts with the federal government.

Indian Occupations

A group of young Indians, most of them college students, calling themselves the Indians of All Tribes decided to take over Alcatraz Island, an abandoned federal prison off the coast of San Francisco. Upon arriving, they were immediately met by the coast guard and they proceeded to read their Alcatraz Proclamation and lay claim to the property. The basis of their land claim was an 1868 Sioux treaty that granted Indians the right to unused federal property.

WITNESS

Native American activists began their Alcatraz Proclamation with this statement: "We, the Native Americans, reclaim the land known as Alcatraz Island in the name of all American Indians by right of discovery. We wish to be fair and honorable in our dealings with the Caucasian inhabitants of this land, and hereby offer the following treaty: We will purchase said Alcatraz Island for twenty-four dollars (24) in glass beads and red cloth, a precedent set by the white man's purchase of a similar island about 300 years ago" (quoted in Smith and Warrior 1996:29).

Their goal was to attain the title to the land and establish the Center for Native American Studies, the American Indian Spiritual Center, the Center of Ecology, the Indian Training School, and the American Indian Museum (Smith and Warrior 1996). These goals reflect what the activists perceived as the major threat facing Native Americans in the face of government termination policies: the loss of Indian tribal cultures. While none of these goals materialized at this time and at this location, the occupation of Alcatraz drew international attention to the plight of Native Americans. This attention captivated Indians across the country and inspired more activism. Native American studies programs have since been implemented across the country, as part of a wider ethnic studies movement, all pushed by minority activism of this era.

In 1972, the Trail of Broken Treaties, a caravan of hundreds of Indians from across the country, headed to the Bureau of Indian Affairs (BIA) building in Washington, DC. Indians occupied the BIA offices for over a week, just prior to the November 1972 presidential election, and presented the federal government with a twenty-point program for improving the lives of American Indians. While the occupation was short lived, it received national news coverage. Much like the occupation of Alcatraz, the Trail of Broken Treaties also succeeded in drawing mainstream America's attention to the ongoing plight of Native American people.

Wounded Knee 1973

Indian activism shifted toward more violent confrontations with the conflict at Wounded Knee in 1973. Eighty years after the historic massacre at Wounded Knee (see Chapter 5), AIM and many Indians of the Oglala Pine Ridge Reservation in South Dakota seized the town of Wounded Knee and announced its independence from the United States. This activism was not nonviolent. Instead, the participants were armed and ready to fight any unauthorized person who entered the reservation. The FBI was called in and joined with armed BIA agents and local police against the armed protesters, creating a volatile situation. This standoff lasted for more than two months, with intermittent exchanges of gunfire that resulted in the deaths of two Indians and an injury to an FBI agent that paralyzed him. This major event, while marred by tragedy, was significant for Indians. It is credited with creating a new sense of Indian pride in tribal Indians and "spiritually reclaiming Wounded Knee as a source of fighting pride rather than submissive shame. ... Indians challenged America culturally for generations by refusing to disappear, but the takeover of this historic site was their first direct assault on collective memory" (Rhea 1997:14–15).

Cultural Activism

There were many other instances of activism both on and off reservations. For example, Native American activists in the Northwest, modeling their protests after the success of the civil rights movement sit-ins, organized fish-ins, occupying national parks and historic sites, such as the one formerly known as the Custer Battlefield National Monument (see Chapter 11). Native American activists successfully demanded a more balanced portrayal of the Battle at Little Bighorn, rather than one that showed Custer and his men as victims of an Indian massacre. After a ten-year battle with the National Park Service, they succeeded in getting the name of the site changed to the Little Bighorn Battlefield National Monument, changing the presentation of the war itself at the memorial, adding Indian perspectives on white westward expansion, and even getting Native Americans hired as staff at the site (Rhea 1997).

While these changes may seem less important than, for example, the right to vote, part of a dominant group's power is the power to define history and cultural representation. Thus, the success Indians have had in this arena as well as in the implementation of Native American studies programs is evidence of a shift in power relations (Fitzgerald 2007; Rhea 1997). These successes have led to other successes, such as President Carter's signing the American Indian Religious Freedom Act in 1978 and the passage of the Native American Graves Protection and Repatriation Act in 1990, which provided Indian tribes with the power to take back from American museums tribal items, particularly those considered to be sacred (Rhea 1997).

WITNESS

"For America's ethnic minorities it was a time to cast off negative stereotypes, to reinvent ethnic and racial social meanings and self-definitions, and to embrace ethnic pride. For American Indians it was the beginning of a period of tribal insurgence and of the emergence of supratribal identification and activism" (Nagel 1996:122).

Indian Women's Activism

Women played significant roles in the Red Power movements, as they did in other racial justice movements of the era. The occupation of Wounded Knee was the brainchild of female elders, for instance (Jaimes and Halsey 1992; Langston 2003). Native American Anna Mae Aquash gave her life for the movement when she was killed at Wounded Knee in 1974 (Crow Dog and Erdoes 1990). During the 1969 occupation of Alcatraz Island, the first nationally recognized Native activism of the era, Native women, such as Wilma Mankiller, LaNada Boyer/Means, Madonna

Gilbert/Thunderhawk, Grace Thorpe, and Stella Leach, contributed significantly to the occupation. Because this activism involved the occupation of an abandoned prison on the island by over one hundred people for an extended period of time, being sustainable was essential. It was the work of women in the community kitchens, schools, and health center that made this occupation possible (Langston 2003).

One of the significant contributions made by Native women activists involved cultural preservation. Most other racial/ethnic minority groups of the era were fighting for integration; however, Native Americans had a history of forced assimilation into the dominant, mainstream American culture, and, thus, the Red Power movement was focused on cultural integrity (Langston 2003). LaNada Boyer/Means wrote a $300,000 grant proposal to support turning Alcatraz Island into an Indian cultural education center, for instance. Women such as Janet McCloud and Ramona Bennett took leading roles in the fish-in movement of the Northwest.

WITNESS

Ramona Bennett, a leader of the fish-in movement, explains the importance of fishing to tribal culture: "At this time, our people were fighting to preserve their last treaty right—the right to fish. We lost our land base. There was no game in the area. … We're dependent not just economically but culturally on the right to fish. Fishing is part of our art forms and religion and diet and the entire culture is based around it. And so when we talk about [Euroamerica's] ripping off the right to fish, we're talking about cultural genocide" (Institute for Natural Progress 1992:213).

Elder women have been at the forefront of resistance against the forced relocation of the Navaho (or Dine, as they refer to themselves) from Big Mountain, Arizona. In 1974 Congress passed the Navajo and Hopi Settlement Act, which required over ten thousand Native people to relocate off this land after coal, oil, and uranium deposits were discovered there (Jaimes and Halsey 1992). Despite the legislation, hundreds of families resist by remaining on the land to this day.

When the male leadership of the Red Power movement found themselves targeted by state and federal law enforcement and the movement faced its demise, a group of Native women who were part of the American Indian Movement responded by founding Women of All Red Nations (WARN) in 1974. Native women and WARN continue to be at the forefront of Native activism, including protesting the continued use of Native American mascots in sports (see Chapter 12), the sterilization abuse of Native women throughout the 1970s (see Chapter 8), Indian exposure to environmental racism (see Chapter 9), treaty rights and tribal sovereignty issues, and Native women's health issues, among others.

Demise of the Red Power Movement

Despite the successes of the Red Power movement, federal repression efforts directed at Native organizations, particularly AIM, resulted in the destruction of AIM
and the eventual demise of the Red Power movement, similar to the federal suppression of the Black Panther Party. Federal authorities engaged in a campaign of infiltration, often using paid informants, surveillance, and the eventual indictments of
members of both the Black Panther Party and the Red Power movement. Leaders of
AIM were declared to be a threat to the United States, they were repeatedly arrested
and charged, and the organization as a whole was targeted for investigations and
arrests, actions that undermined the organization.

MEXICAN AMERICAN AND CHICANO ACTIVISM

Chicano activism involved mobilization of both rural and urban Mexican Americans. *Chicano* is a term many Mexican American activists embraced during this era
(see Chapter 2), and the Chicano movement involved an attempt to unify Mexican
Americans on the basis of a nonwhite and working-class identity and culture
(Muñoz 2007). Mexican American activism began in the grape fields in California
under the leadership of civil rights activist Cesar Chavez, extended to the urban
organizing of the Crusade for Justice and the Brown Berets, and became a nationwide movement for Chicano and Latino pride. The Chicano movement involved
economic, political, and cultural activism, and young people played an integral role
in the activism of the era.

The Chicano movement began in 1968 when over ten thousand East Los Angeles
high school students walked out of their classes. The student strike lasted for over a
week and "disrupted the largest school district in the nation and captured front-page
headlines and national attention" (Muñoz 2007:1). The students were protesting
racism in their schools: the presence of explicitly racist teachers, the lack of teachers
of Mexican descent, racist school policies, and an absence of classes on Mexican
American culture and history.

Brown Power Strategies and Tactics

Chicano activism was inspired by other activism of the era, primarily the civil rights
movement. Some of the issues addressed by the Chicano rights movement are
similar to those addressed by African Americans and Native Americans, but some
are reactions to the unique exploitation of Chicanos.

Organizing Farmworkers

The Chicano rights movement began by uniting Filipino and Chicano farmworkers in the 1962 National Farm Workers Association, which became the United Farm Workers in 1966. Cesar Chavez was a student of Gandhi, nonviolence, and the civil rights movement. While his activism focused on earning farmworkers the same protections as other workers had under the National Labor Relations Act of 1935, such as the right to organize, he also viewed this as more than a labor struggle. Chavez engaged in voter registration drives in the Mexican American community (Ingram 1990). He believed in education and personally taught reading and writing skills to many Mexican Americans failed by the public school system. The farmworkers' activism focused on their low wages, poor working conditions, and dangerous work environments, particularly through their efforts at limiting the use of pesticides. The United Farm Workers played a significant role in getting one of the most harmful pesticides, DDT, banned in the United States in 1972.

They initiated a nationwide grape boycott against the largest grape growers. By 1970, national attention to the boycott had resulted in the participation of an estimated seventeen million people (Ingram 1990). This forced agribusinesses—large-scale farming operations that engage in the production, processing, and distribution of agricultural products and supplies—to deal with farmworkers and their issues. Eventually the farmworkers' activism resulted in a ban on the carcinogenic chemical pesticide DDT, and they won their right to unionize and the right to better working conditions, although these have not yet all been fully implemented. Despite the DDT ban, the pesticide fight continues, as more and more pesticides are created and being used on crops in the fields, and inadvertently on farmworkers themselves.

Urban Organizing: The Crusade for Justice and the Brown Berets

By 1966, urban Chicanos were organizing in Denver under the name Crusade for Justice and the leadership of Rodolfo "Corky" Gonzales. Chicanos, like Native Americans and African Americans, had become increasingly urbanized since the 1950s and thus were dealing with urban problems of poverty, unemployment, poor housing, police harassment and brutality, and underfunded education systems.

Gonzales initially organized the Crusade for Justice to fight police brutality against Chicanos by the Denver Police Department. Like so many racial minority activists of this time, Gonzales was declared by the FBI to be a potentially violent radical and thus warranted surveillance (Vigil 1999).

A group referring to itself as the Brown Berets was formed in 1967 primarily by college students and, like the Black Panther Party and AIM, embraced militant self-defense and community organizing against police brutality. Educational equality was also a major focus, prompting the Brown Berets to organize high school walkouts throughout the country in 1968, protesting the lack of quality education for Chicano youth. By 1970, they were protesting the Vietnam War as well.

Urban organizations such as the Crusade for Justice and the Brown Berets tended to be composed of younger participants and were more radical in their demands than Chavez and the farmworkers. They operated from a platform of cultural nationalism rather than one of assimilation, emphasizing that Chicanos were racially oppressed in the United States and experienced racial, economic, and cultural exploitation; they cited as the origins of their oppression the Mexican–American War and the Treaty of Guadalupe Hidalgo (Armbruster-Sandoval 2004). Gonzales believed that for Chicanos to reclaim their culture, they needed to take control of school boards and other community-based institutions. They demanded Chicano studies programs, bilingual education programs, and pride in and the preservation of Chicano culture. Chicanos in Texas and Colorado formed a political party called La Raza Unida Party and won control of the school board and city council in several cities in Texas, and their candidate even got 6 percent of the vote for Texas governor in the 1972 election (Moore and Pachon 1976).

The activism of the Chicano movement resulted in increased political participation and ethnic pride for Chicanos as well as the implementation of bilingual education programs in schools throughout the country. Meanwhile, the more radical organizations were infiltrated by the FBI and faced police surveillance and harassment, leading to their demise. The largest Latino civil rights advocacy organization in the United States, the National Council of La Raza, emerged in 1968, modeled after the NAACP, and remains active today. This is a Latino civil rights organization, rather than a specifically Chicano group, because it is working to end discrimination against all Latinos.

Women and Chicano Activism

While women were integral to the Chicano movement, the patriarchal nature of Mexican American and American cultures meant they were not seen as movement leaders, despite whatever leadership capabilities they had (Muñoz 2007). Latinas played major roles in the Chicano activism of the 1960s and 1970s. Dolores Huerta, along with Cesar Chavez, helped organize and eventually lead the United Farm Workers union. About half of the striking farmworkers were women. Some of the Latinas who were on strike traveled the country, appealing to women, to support the grape boycott. The long history of Latinas as community builders and social activists challenges the stereotype that they are socially conservative, apolitical, and domestic (Rose 1995). Thus, while men were the visible leaders of the Chicano movement, women were responsible for much of the everyday work of organizing and the behind-the-scenes work that is so fundamental to a movement (Muñoz 2007).

ASIAN AMERICAN ACTIVISM

The post–World War II social and cultural conditions that inspired the civil rights movement played a role in Asian American activism, as did specific conditions of oppression faced exclusively by Asian Americans. Some of those specific conditions included a new awareness of inequalities perpetrated against Asian Americans, such as the Chinese Exclusion Act of 1882; the National Origins Act of 1924, which excluded Japanese immigration; the internment of over 110,000 Japanese Americans during World War II; and the anti-Asian sentiment behind American wars: Japan in World War II, the Korean War, and Vietnam.

IMAGE 6.5: Asian American activism in the 1960s and 1970s. (Courtesy of Alysa Sugiyama).

It was primarily Asian American college students who founded the Asian American movement. This movement tends to be the least well known of the post–World War II minority protest movements because it did not have national visibility and had comparatively fewer participants. Additionally, the invisibility can be at least partially attributed to the idea that race relations in the United States are black and white, overlooking other racial/ethnic groups. One of the first pan-Asian organizations was the Asian American Political Alliance (AAPA), which was formed at the University of California, Berkeley. This organization rejected assimilation as a solution to racial inequality (Okamoto 2014).

The Asian American movement emerged during the late 1960s and early 1970s as the Vietnam War escalated and triggered a growing antiwar movement in response. Many Asian American college students were involved in the antiwar movement and believed that the war was racist, something mainstream antiwar activists were less likely to emphasize. The US military used the racist term *gook* to describe the South Vietnamese enemy as a way to dehumanize them, and this image was often extended to Asian Americans as well. Asian American activists became disillusioned with the white-dominated antiwar movement and started their own organizations, which resulted in the Asian American movement.

WITNESS

"When the Asian American movement was still mainly on campuses, the Vietnam War was a very major factor. It brought Asian Americans into political activity—making us conscious about policies about the use of certain types of armaments and munitions on Vietnam, leveling the country into a parking lot, and analyzing what was happening to Asians in Asia" (Dong 2014).

The Asian American movement helped create and was in turn fueled by the emergence of a pan-Asian identity. Certain conditions in the 1960s converged to help create this new sense of ethnic consciousness: due to immigration restrictions, by this time, US-born Asian Americans outnumbered Asian immigrants. Thus, they shared a common language and could communicate their shared oppressions. Additionally, US citizens tended to treat Asian Americans similarly, unable or unwilling to distinguish among the various ethnicities. These things converged to create an Asian American identity that proved valuable for mobilizing and demanding full political, civil, and cultural rights (Espiritu 2009).

The Asian American movement also made demands on American educational systems: activists insisted on the establishment of Asian American studies programs in universities and expressed concern over the underenrollment of Asian

Americans compared to European Americans in colleges and universities. Over ten thousand students participated in protests demanding the establishment of ethnic studies programs and the hiring of faculty of color at San Francisco State College and UC Berkeley over the course of several months (Okamoto 2014). They fought for bilingual and bicultural education, including incorporation of ethnic studies into the K–12 curriculum. At Princeton University, Asian American students held sit-ins in the president's office, and a hunger strike was held at Northwestern University to demand the establishment of Asian American studies programs on its campuses. Finally, the movement fought for full civil rights for Asian Americans, justice for victims of anti-Asian violence, and changes in immigration laws (Wei 2004).

One of the most significant victories concerned redress for Japanese Americans interned during World War II. The Asian American movement fought a *Campaign for Redress* for an official apology and reparations for the Japanese internment during World War II and won that battle when President Ronald Reagan signed the Civil Liberties Act in 1988, which authorized $1.25 billion in reparation payments to approximately seventy thousand Japanese American survivors of the camps (see Chapter 13) (Rhea 1997; Wei 2004).

REFLECT AND CONNECT

Why have the later social movements, such as the Red Power, Chicano, and Asian American movements, tended to focus more on cultural activism than the civil rights movement did?

ACTIVISM IN THE LATE TWENTIETH AND EARLY TWENTY-FIRST CENTURIES

Most accounts of the civil rights movement mark its demise in 1968, with the murder of Martin Luther King Jr. And though that marker accurately reflects the end of major mobilization and activism, the fight for civil rights has continued and certain organizations, such as the NAACP, have remained active during the fifty years since, an era historians refer to as the "long civil rights movement." Whereas the minority protest movements discussed in this chapter did fade in terms of both visibility and activism by the mid-1970s, one racial/ethnic minority group, Arab Americans, actually witnessed increasing mobilization against racism and discrimination in the 1980s and 1990s. Beyond Arab American activism, the late twentieth century was an era of white backlash against racial/ethnic minority activism. Currently, there is a resurgence of racial minority activism in the form of the DREAMers, Black Lives Matter, and #SayHerName movements.

Arab American Activism

While racism and discrimination against all racial/ethnic groups continue, despite the successes of the minority protest movements of the post–World War II era, Arab Americans are the only racial/ethnic group who experienced increasing racism and discrimination in the last few decades; thus, their activism emerged later than that of the other racial/ethnic groups discussed in this chapter (Tehranian 2009). The racialization of Arab Americans began under President Nixon in the 1970s when he initiated a series of "special measures" targeting Americans of Middle Eastern descent: limitations on Arab immigration and increased FBI surveillance of Arab Americans, among others (Tehranian 2009). This racialization was further facilitated by several international events: the Iranian hostage crisis in 1979, the first Gulf War in the early 1990s, and, ultimately, 9/11.

In response to this racialization and "othering," the American-Arab Anti-Discrimination Committee was founded in 1980 to defend the rights of people of Arab descent. It provides organized opposition to discrimination faced by Arab Americans, including legal support for those who have faced discrimination, similar to the role the NAACP plays for African Americans. Arab American activism is generally centered around three issues: the Palestinian–Israeli conflict, the wars in Iraq, and violations of civil liberties since 9/11 (David 2007).

WITNESS

Iranian American law professor John Tehranian reflects on generational shifts in perceptions of Arab Americans: "My dad, who grew up in Eisenhower's America, often reminisces at how enthralled people used to be with his ethnic background. From the snowy mountains of New Hampshire, where my dad attended college at Dartmouth, to the plains of Wyoming, where he visited his college roommates during Christmas holidays, being Persian in the 1950s was perceived as exotic and exciting. … No one associated the Middle East with fundamentalism and terrorism back then. … In the post-9/11 world, the negative associations with and hostility toward Americans of Middle Eastern descent have only gotten worse" (2009:120–1).

White Backlash

By the late 1970s, white tolerance for racial/ethnic mobilizing and, particularly, civil disobedience began to dissipate. Such actions were viewed by many whites as lacking respect for law and order, as simply chaotic lawbreaking. Many whites viewed the passage of the Civil Rights Act, the Voting Rights Act, and affirmative action as marking the end of racism. This has resulted in increasing racial resentment among whites, manifesting in decreasing support for social policies perceived as disproportionately benefiting minorities (see Chapter 2). Some of this decreasing tolerance has had severe negative consequences for minorities—for instance, in the formation of the prison industrial complex (see Chapter 10) and the mass incarceration of black and Latino men. Another detrimental consequence has been the emergence of the color-blind ideology (see Chapter 1). Color-blindness amounts to "racism without racists," an ideology that manages to subordinate racial minorities through covert means instead of the overt racism of the Jim Crow era (Bonilla-Silva 2010). Ongoing racial inequalities are now defined as the consequence of something other than race, for instance.

The Long Civil Rights Movement: Black Lives Matter and #SayHerName

The Black Lives Matter (BLM) movement began as an online campaign in 2013 after the acquittal of George Zimmerman in the shooting death of Trayvon Martin and became a movement after the shooting death of Michael Brown in Ferguson, Missouri, by white police officer Darren Wilson. Founded by Alicia Garza, Patrisse Cullors, and Opal Tometi, its first in-person protest was called a "Black Lives Matter Freedom Ride," acknowledging the historical lineage of black activism in this country. The words "black lives matter" reflect a sentiment "as old as the desire to be free from slavery ... a civic desire for equality and a human desire for respect ..." (Lebron 2017:viii). The group draws its inspiration from the civil rights movement, LGBT (lesbian, gay, bisexual, and transgender) movement, Black Power movement, and the Occupy movement. Like the civil rights movement, the BLM movement fights for the dignity and humanity of black Americans. Its primary activism has been against the violence blacks have faced at the hands of police officers and vigilantes. There are currently thirty-three BLM chapters in the US, Canada, and Ghana. Since August 2014, they have organized more than one thousand demonstrations.

WITNESS

"Thus, it was the death and failure of our justice system to account for the unnecessary death of a black American that prompted three women to offer these three basic and urgent words to the American people: black lives matter" (Lebron 2017:xi).

There are many similarities between the post–World War II minority protest movements and the Black Lives Matter movement. They are motivated by similar problems, primarily racism and police brutality. Both are challenging the US to uphold its laws and are part of a long tradition of activism. They embrace similar tactics: nonviolent direct-action protests. For instance, in December 2015, Black Lives Matter protesters in Minneapolis blocked a freeway and shut down a terminal at the Minneapolis–Saint Paul International Airport in protest of the police shooting of Jamar Clark. Protesters staged a "die-in" at the October 2015 Twin Cities Marathon to protest the police shooting death of Native American Philip Quinn. In 2016, protesters began confronting presidential candidates at public forums on their silence around issues such as police brutality and the prison industrial complex. During the civil rights movement, whites spoke of *their* civil rights being violated; similarly, whites critique the Black Lives Matter movement with the claim that "all lives matter." Another similarity is their use of media. Today, the BLM movement relies on social media; the civil rights movement relied on a relatively new medium, television. As mentioned previously, media can play a crucial role in social movement mobilization. The movement mirrors SNCC's nonhierarchical organizational style.

One of the primary differences between the civil rights movement and the BLM movement is that the BLM movement is also committed to intersectionality, specifically fighting for the rights of Black queer and transgender folks and opposing the violence they face, which is rarely covered by the mainstream media; the civil rights movement, in contrast, was focused on racial inequality and discrimination.

IMAGE 6.6: New Orleans, LA. A July 8, 2016 protest of the police killing of unarmed black men, specifically Alton Sterling and Philando Castile. Note the protest is at Lee Circle, under a statue of Confederate general Robert E. Lee, before that was removed (see Chapter 11). (Photo: Kathleen J. Fitzgerald).

While the Black Lives Matter movement has successfully brought attention to police shootings of men of color, black women, especially queer and transgender women of color, are also disproportionately affected by police violence, yet their stories are not making headlines. The police killings of Alexia Christian, Natasha McKenna, Rekia Boyd, and many more remained invisible. This was a catalyst in 2015 for the #SayHerName campaign, a gender-inclusive racial justice campaign.

WITNESS

"That blacks have consistently found themselves at the business end of whites' chains, ropes, fists, guns, and nooses is America's shame—our standards of equal liberty and protection under the law to which we, as a nation, claim to be committed, tend to falter and collapse when blacks depend on those standards and commitments" (Lebron 2017:2).

The "Woke" Generation? Millennial Attitudes on Race in the US

The media has framed the nonviolent protests engaged in by Black Lives Matter activists as riots and the group has been referred to as racist and anti-law enforcement. Such framing seeks to delegitimize the movement and to decrease support for it (Banks 2018). The GenForward survey "The 'Woke' Generation? Millennial Attitudes on Race in the US" asked respondents about the two most visible protest movements today—the Black Lives Matter movement and the growing visibility of white nationalist groups (see Chapter 13 for a discussion of white nationalist groups). As can be seen in Figures 6.2 and 6.3, Millennials' opinions on this topic vary by race, but overall Millennials are more supportive of Black Lives Matter than they are of the alt-right. When asked about the validity of the Black Lives Matter movement, 56 percent of African Americans, 43 percent of Asian Americans, 27 percent of Latinos, and 19 percent of whites responded that "they have a lot of good ideas and should be a major part of the political discussion." The other options were "I just don't know enough" and "They are nothing but racists and are totally invalid." Only 5 percent of African Americans, 11 percent of Asian Americans 10 percent of Latinos, and 23 percent of whites felt that Black Lives Matter activists were racist and totally invalid (Cohen et al. 2017) (see Figure 6.2).

However, whites are more evenly split when asked about the extent of similarities between the Black Lives Matter movement and white nationalist groups, with 51 percent of whites agreeing that the groups are similar, while less than one-third of African Americans see the groups as similar. For Latinos, 40 percent see white nationalist and Black Lives Matter movements as similar, along with 34 percent of Asians (see Figure 6.3).

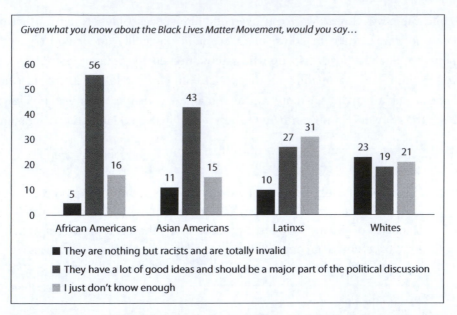

FIGURE 6.2: Millennial attitudes toward Black Lives Matter, by racial group (Cohen et al. 2017).

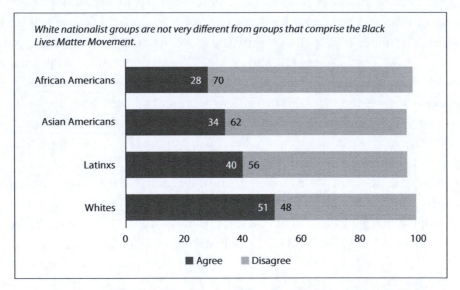

FIGURE 6.3: Millennial attitudes toward the alt-right, by racial group (Cohen et al. 2017).

WITNESS

"What happened at Standing Rock was the most recent iteration of an Indian War that never ends" (Estes 2019:10).

Current Native American Activism—Standing Rock and #NoDAPL

Some of the most visible activism by Native Americans in the current era involved a protest camp north of Standing Rock Indian Reservation, from April 2016 to February 2017. Native people and supporters from across the country were there to block construction of the Dakota Access Pipeline (DAPL) by Energy Transfer Partners, because the oil pipeline threatened the reservation's water supply. The pipeline was designed to run under both the Missouri and the Mississippi Rivers and cross four states, threatening the water supply for more than just the Standing Rock Indian Reservation. The Standing Rock Sioux tribe had filed a lawsuit against the Army Corps of Engineers who had approved the construction of the pipeline without engaging in the appropriate assessment as to whether or not the tribe would face disproportionate risk due to the proximity of the pipeline to their water and the risk of oils spills (Estes 2019).

These protests were a historic gathering, uniting all seven nations of Dakota-, Nakota-, and Lakota-speaking peoples, which had not happened in more than one hundred years (Estes 2019). They called themselves the Water Protectors, and at its peak the camp was so large that it was North Dakota's tenth largest city, with a population of ten thousand to fifteen thousand people. These have been the largest protests by Native people since the 1970s.

The Water Protectors faced violence at the hands of local police, military, and a private security contractor known as TigerSwan, which was hired to infiltrate the camps. Television images of police deploying water hoses against nonviolent protesters during freezing North Dakota winter nights were broadcast across the world. On September 9, 2016, the Department of Justice called for a stop to construction on the pipeline and for the tribe to have meaningful input on such infrastructure projects. Later, the US District Court denied the tribe's request to halt the construction. The tribes have appealed the court decision. Despite the protests, construction continued and the pipeline became operational in June of 2017. After only six months in operation, there have been five spills, highlighting the "unavoidable reality—pipelines leak" (Brown 2018).

CHAPTER SUMMARY

The minority protest movements of the post–World War II era ushered in dramatic changes in American society. Ordinary people organized social movements, engaged in activism, and demanded full equality for racial/ethnic minorities in the United States. There were particular social and cultural conditions, such as industrialization, urbanization, and international changes after World War II, that helped facilitate this unparalleled period of activism. For many whites, things were moving too quickly, and, thus, these changes were perceived as threatening. For racial/ethnic minorities, such changes were long overdue. While not all social movement organizations of this period shared the same ideologies or approached their causes with the same tactics and strategies, they all shared the goal of racial/ethnic equality in the United States. Some sought this through assimilation into the dominant mainstream American society. Others sought it through a cultural pluralist approach, embracing their particular racial and ethnic cultures.

African Americans were the first to begin organizing for their full civil and political rights. Using nonviolent direct action, they engaged in boycotts, sit-ins, voter registration drives, Freedom Rides, and desegregation campaigns. Native Americans, Asian Americans, and Chicanos all followed with activist movements that were both distinct from one another and overlapping. Native Americans and Chicanos both organized against urban problems facing other urban minority populations as well, such as police brutality, poor schools, and unemployment. They each took unique approaches to address these problems, reflecting their particular social and historical circumstances. Although many civil rights movement activists later found themselves drawn to the antiwar movement, Asian American activism was an outgrowth of the limitations of the antiwar movement.

Institutionalized racism and reigning beliefs of the racial inferiority of African Americans, Native Americans, Latinos, and Asian Americans were overtly challenged, and new, more positive racial identities emerged for people of color. The minority protest movements of the post–World War II era permanently altered race relations in American society, yet they have failed to eliminate racism, as the racialization and targeting of Arab Americans and the ongoing police brutality that inspired the Black Lives Matter movement continue. Current racial/minority activism remains, primarily in the form of Black Lives Matter, #SayHerName, and the Dakota Access Pipeline protests at Standing Rock Indian reservation. In all of these modern movements, one can see the influence of post-WWII movements and activism.

KEY TERMS AND CONCEPTS

Chicano

Civil disobedience

Collective behavior

Collective identities

Collective memory

Cultural activism

Grassroots movement

Individual identities

Left-wing social movement

Mobilization

Nonviolent direct action

Pan-Asian identity

Panethnicity

Participatory democracy

Race pride movement

Reform movement

Relative deprivation

Sense of efficacy

Sense of feasibility

Social movement

Social movement organizations (SMOs)

PERSONAL REFLECTIONS

1. Think about what you knew about slavery, Jim Crow, and the civil rights movement prior to reading the previous three chapters. Explain how what you knew was a result of your particular "social location" (who you are, where you are from, your race, class, gender, and so on).

2. Ask your parents and grandparents what they were doing during these decades of activism. What do they remember of the movements described in this chapter? Were they activists or sympathetic to the causes? How did they perceive these activists? Would you have engaged in activism in this era? What kinds of things might have facilitated your activism? What may have hindered it?

CRITICAL THINKING QUESTIONS

1. Explain why the four minority protest movements discussed in this chapter had such similar strategies, tactics, successes, and failures. Give an example of a current social movement that has borrowed a strategy or tactic from the minority protest movements of the post–World War II era.

2. Why did these protest movements choose to use nonviolent direct action to challenge the white power structure in the beginning of the movement? Explain why most of the movements (with the exception of the Asian American movement) shifted away from nonviolent direct action toward more militant positions.

3. Describe similarities and differences between Black Lives Matter and Standing Rock protests and activism with racial/ethnic activism and protests of the 1950s to 1970s.

ESSENTIAL READING

Branch, Taylor. 1989. *Parting the Waters: America in the King Years, 1954–63*, reprint ed. New York: Simon and Schuster.

Estes, Nick. 2019. *Our History is Our Future: Standing Rock Versus the Dakota Access Pipeline and the Long Tradition of Indigenous Resistance.* New York: Verso.

Lebron, Christopher J. 2017. *The Making of Black Lives Matter: A Brief History of an Idea.* New York: Oxford University Press.

Louie, Steven G. and Glenn Omatsu, eds. 2006. *Asian Americans: The Movement and the Moment.* Los Angeles, CA: UCLA Asian American Studies Center Press.

McAdam, Doug. 1988. *Freedom Summer.* New York: Oxford University Press.

McGuire, Danielle L. 2010. *At the Dark End of the Street: Black Women, Rape, and Resistance—A New History of the Civil Rights Movement from Rosa Parks to the Rise of Black Power.* New York: Vintage Books.

McRae, Elizabeth Gillespie. 2018. *Mothers of Massive Resistance: White Women and the Politics of White Supremacy.* New York: Oxford University Press.

Muñoz, Carlos, Jr. 2007. *Youth, Identity, Power: The Chicano Movement,* revised and expanded ed. New York: Verso Press.

Rhea, Joseph Tilda. 1997. *Race Pride and the American Identity.* Cambridge, MA: Harvard University Press.

Robnett, Belinda. 1997. *How Long? How Long? African-American Women in the Struggle for Civil Rights.* New York, Oxford: Oxford University Press.

Smith, Paul Chaat and Robert Allan Warrior. 1996. *Like a Hurricane: The Indian Movement from Alcatraz to Wounded Knee.* New York: The New Press.

Tyson, Timothy B. 2004. *Blood Done Sign My Name.* New York: Three Rivers Press.

Zellner, Bob and Constance Curry. 2008. *The Wrong Side of Murder Creek: A White Southerner in the Freedom Movement.* Montgomery, AL: New South Books.

RECOMMENDED FILMS

Chicano! History of the Mexican American Civil Rights Movement (1996). Produced by PBS-NLCC Educational Media. This four-part documentary provides an overview of the growing unrest in Mexican American communities, their consciousness raising, and ultimate activism, from Cesar Chavez to La Raza Unida, between 1965 and 1975.

Eyes on the Prize Volumes 1–8 (1987). Produced by Blackslide. Broadcast on PBS's *American Experience*, this series is an exemplary, award-winning documentary of the civil rights movement, exploring every major event between 1954 and 1968, from the Montgomery bus boycott to the Black Power movement. The series explores both southern and northern whites' and blacks' reactions to integration, including interviews with many activists, both famous and unknown.

RECOMMENDED MULTIMEDIA

The Civil Rights Movement, Lesson Plan Library, Discovery Education. This website is useful for future teachers but also can be good for college students. www.discovery education.com/teachers/free-lesson-plans/the-civil-rights-movement.cfm.

Teaching a People's History, Zinn Education Project. This website is loaded with material on social justice and racial/ethnic minority group history. In particular, check out the section on Asian American oppression and activism. http://zinned project.org/teaching-materials/#filter_themes_top.

PART THREE

Institutional Inequalities

Education

CHAPTER LEARNING OUTCOMES

By the end of this chapter, you should be able to:

- **Evaluate the identities students develop in educational institutions in relation to cultural ideologies surrounding race and intelligence**
- **Critically evaluate whiteness in education**
- **Demonstrate the historical inequities racial/ethnic minorities faced in public educational institutions and the cumulative nature of such inequities**
- **Describe white resistance to school integration in the post–** *Brown v. Board of Education* **era**
- **Demonstrate an understanding of the concept of the achievement gap, noting its strengths and weaknesses**

Schools in the Jim Crow South were racially segregated, a practice declared constitutional by the Supreme Court decision *Plessy v. Ferguson* (1896), which made "separate but equal" the law of the land. Black and white schools were indeed separate; however, they were nowhere near equal. African American Robert Pershing Foster attended Monroe Colored High School in the 1930s in Monroe, Louisiana. While it was officially named the "Colored High School," it actually was the only school for black students in Monroe and housed over 1,100 black students from kindergarten through eleventh grade, with one teacher for each grade. The school acquired their textbooks by driving to the white high school every few years to pick up the books the white school was throwing away. Although a new white high school was built in 1931, complete with laboratories for chemistry and physics classes, a two-thousand-seat auditorium, and an expanded library, the school for black children operated with used books, secondhand supplies, and underpaid teachers.

No matter how smart Pershing was, he would never be able to attend the new school. The unfairness was glaring to Pershing, who vowed to work harder than ever to disprove his assumed inferiority. He eventually went to medical school and became a physician (Wilkerson 2010).

Today, Luther Burbank Middle School in San Francisco serves predominantly low-income students of color and can be described in eerily similar terms to Monroe Colored High School in the 1930s, despite being separated by eighty years. In many classes, there aren't enough textbooks for students; the social studies textbook is so dated that it doesn't even reflect the breakup of the former Soviet Union, which occurred in 1991. The classrooms do not have computers and the school library employs no librarian. Art classes have been deleted from the curriculum due to budgetary constraints. The heating system does not work well, requiring students to wear coats, gloves, and hats in the classrooms during winter. As of 2001, seventeen of the thirty-five teachers at Luther Burbank were in their first year of teaching, and many lacked credentials. This information on the inadequate state of affairs in which Luther Burbank was attempting to function was introduced by plaintiffs in a 2001 school-funding lawsuit, *Williams v. State of California* (Darling-Hammond 2007).

Education can provide tools to overcome adversity, as well as contribute to the development of critical-thinking skills. For you or some of your classmates, especially those whose ancestors were historically denied access to formal education, going to college can be about liberation. A college education represents an opportunity for a better life.

Your decision to go to college is a personal one, based on your individual circumstances. But that decision is made within a larger social and historical context, which is often given very little thought. Sociologists look for structural explanations, rather than individual explanations, for why certain people tend to have the same goal you do—to get a postsecondary degree—and why other people may not. Personal decisions are constrained or facilitated by structural circumstances, and it is these structural circumstances that draw the attention of sociologists.

A sociologist might look at a graph like that in Figure 7.1 to analyze educational attainment rates by race. While all racial groups saw an increase in the number of bachelor's degrees attained between 1988 and 2015, there is still considerable racial variation. From a sociological perspective, the significance of this is that educational attainment appears to be related to race rather than being a random phenomenon. According to the US Census Bureau, the percentage of Asian Americans with a bachelor's degree in 2015 was 54 percent, up from 38 percent in 1995 and higher than the overall percentage of Americans with a bachelor's degree in 2015

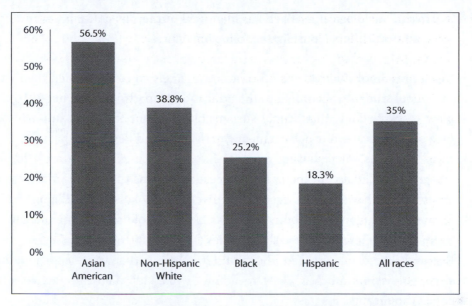

FIGURE 7.1: Percentage of people 25 years and over with a Bachelor's degree or higher, by race and Hispanic origin, 2018.

SOURCE: US Census Bureau. 2019.

(33 percent). While 36 percent of non-Hispanic whites held a bachelor's degree or higher in 2015, only 22 percent of African Americans and 15 percent of Hispanics did. The fact that educational attainment is racialized rather than random is a major focus of this chapter.

Another educational statistic that falls along racial lines pertains to high school dropout rates. While over 70 percent of high school graduates today pursue higher education, dropout rates for most racial/ethnic minorities are alarmingly high compared to dropout rates for whites and Asian Americans. This has persisted for at least forty years. Overall dropout rates declined between 1972 and 2016, from 15 percent to 6.1 percent, but dropout rates are still much higher for many minority youth, particularly Native Americans and Hispanics.

REFLECT AND CONNECT

What do you think accounts for these statistics? Why do some people pursue higher education while others do not? What factors influence whether or not someone completes high school or drops out? Why does race correlate with educational attainment in these ways?

Although personal efforts certainly influence school success, structural factors, such as social class, gender, race, nationality, and sexuality, correlate with educational success as well. Sociological research has identified numerous patterns pertaining to race, class, and education. Consider the following data:

- Black preschool students are 3.6 times more likely to be suspended than white preschool students, according to the Education Department (Turner 2016).
- New research finds that school suspensions account for approximately one-fifth of the black–white achievement gap (Morris and Perry 2016).
- Even in places where busing worked, like Louisville, KY, there are efforts to resegregate schools: "In the past two decades, dozens of affluent, mostly white communities have tried to secede from diverse school districts" (Eligon 2019).
- Whites with high verbal abilities are less likely to hold racially prejudicial attitudes than whites with low verbal abilities (Wodtke 2016).
- Research by sociologist Ted Thornhill (2018) finds that white college admissions counselors are less likely to admit "woke," or politically active, black college applicants.
- In a study of 2,500 college students, students of color reported high levels of negative diversity interactions—those defined as hostile, hurtful, or tense interactions with those who are racially different from themselves. Specifically, 43 percent of African Americans, 37 percent of Hispanics, and 40 percent of Asian American students reported high levels of negative interactions (Tate 2017).
- Teachers are more likely to hold negative views or low expectations of lower-class and racial minority children than of white, middle-class children (Baron, Tom, and Cooper 1985; Ferguson 1998; Leacock 1969).
- In February 2016, a group of mostly African American high school students from Dallas were visiting Texas A&M university when they were approached by a white woman wearing earrings containing a Confederate flag image. She pointed at the earrings as she and several other white females taunted the high school students and called them racial slurs (Moore and Bell 2017).
- On all indicators of academic success at the high school level, such as enrollment in honors or advanced-placement classes, black males are underrepresented. By contrast, they are overrepresented on all indicators of academic failure, such as dropout rates, being held back, or being disciplined (Noguera 2008).
- Research finds schools to be alienating places for Puerto Rican youth, who tend to fare worse on educational outcomes than African Americans, whites, and other Latinos (Nieto 2000).
- Despite the 1954 Supreme Court decision, *Brown v. Board of Education*, which declared segregation unconstitutional, increasing numbers of black students, including half of black students in Chicago and one-third of black students in New York City, attend apartheid schools, those that are more than 99 percent black (Lieb 2017).

These facts paint a troubling picture about educational disparities along racial lines. This chapter will explore those disparities in detail, beginning with sociological perspectives on race and education, including some of the ways whiteness in education manifests itself. Then we explore the ways student identities are racialized and how such educational identities are linked to race and the history of minority education in the United States. Particular attention will be paid to the ramifications of *Brown v. Board of Education*, the case that declared segregated schools unconstitutional, and the subsequent shift to de facto segregation that has occurred since that decision. This chapter will close with an exploration of current issues, including bilingual education programs, funding disparities, the achievement gap, tracking, the No Child Left Behind Act (NCLB), and some key current racial issues in higher education, including attacks on affirmative action.

SOCIOLOGICAL PERSPECTIVES ON RACE AND EDUCATION

There are many ways to assess a problem from a sociological perspective, and educational inequality is no exception. This section will examine race and education from several perspectives, including social reproduction theory, critical race theory, and the concept of whiteness.

Social Reproduction Theory

Sociologist Pierre Bourdieu observed the relationship between cumulative disadvantage and economic inequities. He argued that access to economic capital—money—increases people's opportunities because it allows access to social and cultural capital as well. **Social capital** refers to people's social networks: if they know others in positions of power, then they can more easily use those relationships to advance in life. Those who attend Harvard, for instance, have more than a Harvard degree opening doors for them. They also have connections to other Harvard graduates across the country, which is a significant form of social capital. **Cultural capital** refers to things such as social skills, linguistic styles, habits, and tastes that take the form of credentials, connections, and knowledge (Bourdieu 1977; Bourdieu and Passeron 1977). For example, the perceived quality of your accent, the clothing you choose to wear, the foods you enjoy—these send daily signals to others about your cultural worth, and the higher that worth is estimated, the easier it is for you to advance in society.

Bourdieu worked within the sociological tradition called **social reproduction theory**, the study of the myriad ways that societies reproduce their status hierarchies, particularly class hierarchies. If applied to education, this perspective counters the idea that education can be a path to liberation for oppressed groups. Instead, students who have more social and cultural capital are more successful in school than their peers with less social and cultural capital.

It is more difficult for black parents to meet the institutional standards of schools than it is for white parents due to racial differences in cultural capital (Lareau and Horvat 1999; Yosso 2005). Educators strongly emphasize the role of parents in a child's educational success; however, after a long history of racial discrimination in education, it is often difficult for minority parents to trust teachers. Teachers tend to assume that all parents trust them, regardless of their race. White parents, who do not have the same racially charged history as minority parents, have an easier time trusting their children's teachers and schools. Therefore, white parents are more easily able to meet schools' expectations than minority parents. In addition to trust, white parents are more likely to have a sense that they are entitled to interact with teachers as equals. They are more often able to attend school events during the day, and they may have larger vocabularies, all of which amounts to cultural capital that facilitates their interaction with teachers and school administrators (Lareau and Horvat 1999). Racial/ethnic minority parents, impoverished parents, and non–English speakers typically lack the sense of entitlement to interact with teachers; in turn, teachers interpret the limited interaction with minority parents as reflecting their lack of interest in their children's education. This is one way the social and cultural capital of families can affect a student's educational experiences.

Some research finds that even in well-resourced suburban schools, white families' participation and advocacy is welcomed while black families are discouraged from similar participation and advocacy. In other words, schools play a significant role in shaping parents' engagement (Lewis-McCoy 2014). Thus, it is more than the social and cultural capital of families, but the expectations of school personnel that affect the influence parents can have on their child's educational experience.

Another way social capital varies along racial/ethnic lines involves parental information networks. These are important for gaining access to better educational experiences and opportunities, such as access to high-performing schools or reputable teachers. In this era of alternative and charter schools, strategic information is required that is not equally available to all groups. Racial/ethnic minority parents are more likely to lack the social capital necessary to navigate school district policies, which then puts their children at a disadvantage (Lewis 2003).

While the language of "school choice" associated with alternative and charter schools is appealing to some parents, research by sociologist Mary Pattillo (2015) finds that for poor and working-class African American parents, the experience is less than empowering. If they want to choose a school other than their assigned neighborhood school, they must do a significant amount of research into a wide variety of types of schools available. Then, if they find a quality school they wish to send their child to, there are numerous barriers to access. For instance, schools make their admissions decisions based on a myriad of factors, most of which are not under the control of parents. Additionally, transportation is a significant barrier because many low-income urban families do not own a vehicle. The cost of public transportation can be prohibitive, and safety can be a concern. Another barrier can be time constraints. Often parents' work schedules interfere with their ability to get their child to a school that is not in their neighborhood. Thus, despite the language of choice, "schools outside of the neighborhood were a hard sell. ... The preference for nearby schools ... did not stem from a limited worldview or a reluctance to make sacrifices for their children's learning" (Pattillo 2015:55).

Critical Race Theory and Community Cultural Wealth

Some sociologists challenge Bourdieu's notion of cultural capital because it highlights only the cultural competencies of whites and establishes those competencies as the cultural norm. It overlooks potential cultural capital of people of color and instead views them as operating from a deficit. Critical race theorists have suggested an alternative to the standard definition of cultural capital, **community cultural wealth**, which seeks to broaden what qualifies as cultural capital to include the unique assets that communities of color are able to provide to their members: specifically, different sets of skills that tend not to be recognized or valued by dominant institutions (Yosso 2005). The notion of community cultural wealth exposes how the apparently race-neutral concept of cultural capital reflects white culture and disregards skills and knowledge more likely to be found in communities of color. These theorists, instead of using a deficit model that views children of color and their families as lacking in skills in their interaction with schools and teachers, emphasize that communities of color have knowledge and skills that they draw on and share in order to succeed in the world, and thus bring their own, often unrecognized, cultural competencies to the table. Community cultural wealth factors in skills, such as bilingualism or other communication skills, into the notion of cultural capital. By the community cultural wealth model, a student does not enter school with a deficit but simply a different set of skills.

Whiteness in Education

Whiteness studies is another lens through which sociologists explore inequities in the educational system. As defined in Chapter 2, *whiteness* refers to how the rules, ideologies, values, norms, and institutions of our society are all constructed by white people, yet are made to appear normal and race neutral. Whiteness studies questions these assumptions and attempts to recognize how defining everything according to white standards affects our interpretation of ourselves and our neighbors. This section explores some of the ways that whiteness affects educational institutions, specifically the ways that school campuses are understood as racialized spaces and how white teachers are socialized to overlook their whiteness and the ways it influences their classroom (see Box 7.1 Race in the Workplace: Investigating Whiteness in Teacher Education).

From a sociological perspective, most schools are racialized spaces, more specifically, white spaces, places where cultural biases influence perceptions of the space as belonging to whites and where people of color feel unwelcome (Feagin, Vera, and Imani 1996; Moore 2008). In the United States, most neighborhoods, schools, playgrounds, and even nightclubs are racialized spaces. When baseball fans at an Atlanta

---

BOX 7.1

Race in the Workplace:
Investigating Whiteness in Teacher Education

The United States teaching force is disproportionately white, middle class, and female, while the K–12 student population is becoming increasingly diverse (Fuller 1992). Due to such demographic changes facing schools, there is considerable research on multicultural education and understanding how white teachers negotiate racial differences when they enter the classroom (Deering and Stanutz 1995; Fry and McKinney 1997; Irving 2014; Jordan 1995; Lawrence 1997; McIntyre 1997; Rosenberg 2004; Tatum 1994). Educators argue that white teachers are most effective when they reflect on and come to understand their own white privilege rather than take a color-blind approach in their classroom. Teachers all too often enter their classrooms without having had "the opportunity to explore their own beliefs about student differences and the role these play in teaching and learning" (Weist 1998:358). Color-blindness is so ingrained in them that pre-service teachers often have difficulty simply acknowledging another's race (Rosenberg 2004).

Several white teachers have written of their experiences negotiating race and white privilege in the classroom (Davis 2005; Fox 2001; Howard 2006; Irving 2014; McIntyre 1997, 1997b; Paley 2000; Pearce 2005; Rosenberg 2004). Some authors document their struggles in the classroom, whereas others enter the conversation from the perspective that racial justice demands white involvement (Sleeter 1994). In direct contrast to the message sent by the dominant ideology of color-blindness, these authors argue that it is imperative that white teachers explore their own racial location and work to understand their own roles as racial beings and how this influences their classroom teaching (McIntyre 1997b). Learning to view oneself as white, as a racial being, rather than simply as the norm is a challenge to white privilege and can help dismantle racism within educational institutions (McIntyre 1997b; Sleeter 1994). As Debby Irving states, "If I, a middle-aged white woman raised in the suburbs, can wake up to my whiteness, any white person can" (2014:xii).

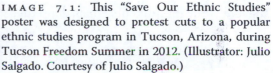

IMAGE 7.1: This "Save Our Ethnic Studies" poster was designed to protest cuts to a popular ethnic studies program in Tucson, Arizona, during Tucson Freedom Summer in 2012. (Illustrator: Julio Salgado. Courtesy of Julio Salgado.)

Braves baseball game engage in the ritual arm motion known as the "tomahawk chop" in support of their team, they are, perhaps unintentionally, marking that space as a white space, because by engaging in such action they are creating a hostile place for Native Americans who take offense at the tomahawk chop and similar uses of Native American imagery for sports mascots (see Chapter 12).

Most Americans live in racially segregated worlds, and an individual's experience in that world accounts for how they react to the racial diversity on a college campus or in any other new social environment. For many college students, stepping onto campus means stepping into the most racially diverse environment they have ever been in. For others, that same college campus is an overwhelmingly white space, spaces where people of color feel unwelcome and like intruders. Swastikas and nooses hanging on minority professor's doors, for example (see Chapter 1), are evidence of college campuses as white spaces. Another example of the assumption that college campuses, other than those specifically designated as historically black colleges and universities or Hispanic-serving institutions, are white spaces was introduced earlier in the chapter—the white women who verbally harassed the black high school students who were visiting Texas A&M university. The harassment is an example of the women policing those boundaries by explicitly letting the black students know they are not welcome at Texas A&M (Moore and Bell 2017). Another example involves Simkins Hall, a dormitory at the University of Texas, which sparked a controversy in 2010 when people were reminded of the fact that the building was named for William

Simkins, a Ku Klux Klan leader and University of Texas law professor from 1899 to 1929. The hall was built and named in 1954, a time of fervent anti-integration sentiment among many whites, and only four years after the first African American students were admitted. While the University of Texas Board of Regents voted to strip the Simkins name from the building in 2010, there were some who defended the name, despite the fact that its presence made some students feel unwelcome. Dave Player, an editor for the student newspaper, was quoted as saying, "Honoring an individual by putting his or her name on a facility does not mean the University is condoning every aspect of that individual's character" (Vertuno 2010). Other examples include Confederate monuments on college campuses, such as Silent Sam, a controversial monument on the campus of the University of North Carolina. After decades of protest over the presence of the statue, in August of 2018 some student activists toppled the monument, forcing the administration to act (Moody 2018). To this day, the fate of the monument remains unsettled.

WITNESS

Twenty-year-old African American University of Texas student Brittany McCoy expressed shock over learning of the dorm's namesake, saying, "Texas is a school that stresses diversity. I know I wouldn't want to stay in that dorm, and wouldn't want my people staying there" (Vertuno 2010).

Another example of schools as racialized spaces involves the Texas State Board of Education and decisions it made concerning the K–12 history curriculum in Texas in 2010. The board's majority voted to downplay Cesar Chavez's role in history in favor of stressing the contributions of Ronald Reagan and the conservative movement of the 1980s, despite minority board members' attempts to seek the inclusion of more blacks and Latinos in the history curriculum. Furthermore, this new Texas statewide curriculum gave the civil rights movement less emphasis. Arizona also passed legislation that emphasized its white history in schools instead of a more diverse curriculum, such as that offered by a popular Mexican American studies program in the Tucson Unified School District. Arizona state lawmakers approved a bill that restricted any ethnic studies courses out of fear that they could stir up resentment.

WITNESS

Resentment among whom? Journalist Jeff Biggers asks, "Is teaching Arizona children that Arizona native and Chicano leader Cesar Chavez led nonviolent marches on behalf of farmworkers stirring up resentment?" (Biggers 2010).

Identity Development in Schools

From the time young children enter preschool or kindergarten, they spend the bulk of their waking hours in school environments, where they interact with peers and adults and encounter many social experiences for the first time. They observe and respond to teachers' expectations and attitudes. These formative experiences profoundly influence students' attitudes about education and contribute to their identity development. As discussed in earlier chapters, sociologists view identity as something that is constructed through a negotiation between how we see ourselves and how others perceive us. Schools have long been places where children engage in such identity construction and negotiation. As institutions, schools are informed by the dominant group's ideologies, which, in turn, help inform student identity development. Those identities can contribute to or inhibit school success for the rest of a student's life.

The Pew Research Center's *Race in America 2019* report asked respondents a number of questions designed to gauge whether or not they experience discrimination along racial lines. One of these questions asked whether or not, in their interactions with others, "people acted like they thought they weren't smart." In response to this question, 26 percent of non-Hispanic whites, 36 percent of Asian Americans, 48 percent of Latinos or Hispanics, and 60 percent of African Americans responded that this discrimination had happened to them due to their race or ethnicity (Horowitz, Brown, and Cox 2019). This data is important to consider when we think about how students perceive their academic abilities and develop identities that can facilitate or inhibit their success in school.

Students' attitudes about education and social mobility influence the identities they construct in school, and the identities they assume contribute to their success or failure in school. For example, sociologist Nilda Flores-Gonzalez (2002) spent a year studying Puerto Rican students at an urban high school and found that the students developed different identities in relation to school. Some students develop **school identities**, which means they learn student role expectations early, perform the role well, and develop meaningful relationships with peers and teachers. The development of a school identity contributes to students' perceptions of themselves as "stayers," students who do not view dropping out of high school as an option. Other students developed **street identities**; their lack of success in elementary school and subsequent feelings of humiliation, and lack of meaningful relationships with peers and teachers, lead to their disengagement from school in the elementary years. The development of a street identity can contribute to the likelihood of the student's eventually dropping out of high school (Flores-Gonzalez 2002).

A similar study on identities fostered in the educational system found that some African American students develop **oppositional identities**, a collective sense of identity formed in opposition to that of white Americans. This research found that children at a very young age began to perceive succeeding in school as "acting white." Good grades, taking school seriously, and positive attitudes about school were therefore stigmatized as an affront to the African American identity (Fordham and Ogbu 1986). Other research has challenged this notion that African American students discount school success as "acting white" (Diamond, Lewis, and Gordon 2007; Tyson 2002; Tyson, Darity, and Castellino 2005). In fact, such research found that both white and black high-achieving students experience negative peer pressure over their academic success and low-achieving black students experience positive peer pressure, such as encouragement to improve their academic performance. Karolyn Tyson's (2011) research finds that the "acting white" phenomenon is found in racially integrated schools but not in predominantly black schools and that it emerges out of the institutional practice of **racialized tracking**, where higher-level classes (gifted, honors, advanced placement) are overwhelmingly populated with white students while lower-level classes are disproportionately composed of minority students.

Stigma is an equally powerful force for children who learn that anything less than academic excellence will be stigmatized by their peers and the adults around them. Sociologists define **stigma** as an attribute that is deeply discrediting and challenges one's identity (Goffman 1963). Many Asian American students feel great pressure to excel academically, to live up to their stereotype as the **model minority**, the idea that Asian Americans academically excel and achieve a higher degree of socioeconomic success than other racial/ethnic groups. There is an assumption that Asian American academic success is the result of hard work and Asian cultural norms that emphasize educational success. This stereotype is problematic because Asian Americans are a large and diverse group with considerable variation in academic performance among individual Asians and among Asian ethnic groups. While the model minority identity is imposed on Asian Americans, they negotiate their school identities within the context of such assumptions about their abilities and their work ethic. Some researchers have found that Asian American parents teach their children in covert and overt ways that educational success is a way to combat their experiences with racism and oppression (Sue and Okazaki 1990). While the origins of the high expectations parents and peers hold for Asian American students' academic success are a matter of debate, certainly these expectations influence Asian American student identity development.

The research examined in this section provides snapshots of how racial/ethnic groups negotiate identity in the school environment differently. To understand how these attitudes and identities prevail along such racialized lines, it helps to take account of the history of education in the United States. The assumption of racial-minority intellectual inferiority was overt and widespread throughout US history. In the current era, racism may be less overt, but it still exists, and its historical impacts are still palpable.

A HISTORY OF RACE AND PUBLIC EDUCATION IN THE UNITED STATES

The first public schools, called common schools, emerged in the 1840s at a time of significant political, economic, and social upheaval in the United States. While education was not mandatory at this point, these early schools were funded by local taxes and free to all white children, regardless of religion. There were few educational opportunities for children of color at this time, not even for free African Americans in the North. Neither of the earliest proponents of the common schools, Horace Mann or John Dewey, spoke out against racial/ethnic minority children's exclusion from educational institutions (Weinberg 1977).

There were several reasons for local governments to encourage education. First, it was believed that a democracy required at least a relatively educated populace and that a basic level of literacy was necessary to vote and participate in a democracy. Second, as the nation shifted from an agricultural economy to an industrial one, there was a greater need for a more literate workforce. Third, schools were viewed as institutions capable of Americanizing the ever-increasing flow of new immigrants to the country. Public schools taught immigrants civics, middle-class values, the English language, loyalty, and cultural conformity (Daniels 1998). Fourth, as the United States became increasingly urbanized, many social problems such as crime, disease, and poverty were exacerbated; some public policy experts viewed these as best addressed through education.

When the Civil War ended in 1865, the federal government became involved in public education. As a requirement to gain readmission to the union after the Civil War, Congress required former Confederate states to establish free public schools for both black and white children (McGuinn 2006). Soon all states had established educational systems and made school mandatory for all children until the age of sixteen. Schools of this era were racially segregated.

The United States committed to universal education earlier than many European countries, which were still limiting education to elite white males at this time. However, the public education that was extended to minorities was not equal to that extended to white children. African Americans, Mexican Americans, Asian Americans, Native Americans, and other racial/ethnic minority groups were historically denied access to education. When public education was extended to minorities, they were not as invested in as white children were; thus, they received a substandard education by design. Each racial/ethnic group resisted their exclusion from educational institutions. When local and state governments failed to meet their needs, they sought access to this basic privilege in creative ways, which this chapter will describe in detail.

Two Landmark Cases: *Plessy v. Ferguson* and *Brown v. Board of Education*

One of the most powerful and effective ways that minority groups sought access to equal education in the United States was through formal litigation. Two cases in particular dramatically influenced educational institutions and set precedents for scores of cases to come, a few of which will be discussed in this chapter.

In 1892, Homer Plessy boarded a train in New Orleans, Louisiana, and took a seat in a car designated for whites only as an explicit challenge to the company's segregation policies. Plessy, who was so light-skinned that he could pass for white but was still considered black according to Louisiana law, was asked to move to the train car for black passengers. When he refused to move, he was arrested and thrown in jail. Plessy sued the state of Louisiana, claiming that in enforcing the Louisiana Separate Car Act, the East Louisiana Railroad was violating his right to equal treatment as granted by the Fourteenth Amendment. After a series of losses and appeals by Plessy, the case made it to the Supreme Court in 1896. The court declared that states could continue to enforce racial segregation as long as the facilities provided for each race were equal. Under the ruling, which declared that facilities must be "separate but equal," black students could be relegated to their own schools, but the schools ostensibly had to have the same quality of classrooms, desks, books, and teachers as the neighboring white schools. Practically speaking, minorities were still treated as inferior because this ruling legalized segregation and made no real commitment to maintaining equal facilities. However, it was an important case because it set the precedent for numerous challenges to racially segregated schools.

Perhaps the most famous of the challenges that stood on the shoulders of *Plessy v. Ferguson* was the landmark Supreme Court decision *Brown v. Board of Education of Topeka* (1954), which officially, unanimously, and powerfully declared segregated schools illegal. The case was a compilation of four desegregation cases—one from South Carolina; the Topeka, Kansas, case; a case from Delaware; and one from Virginia—that were initially brought by groups of African American parents. This was part of a decades-old strategy by the NAACP Legal Defense Fund, engineered by legal scholar Charles Hamilton Houston, to challenge racial discrimination in the courts by making states adhere to the language of the *Plessy* decision. In other words, states had to either integrate schools or provide equal facilities for whites and blacks.

One of the earliest challenges to *Plessy* brought by the NAACP was *Missouri ex rel. Gaines v. Canada* (1938), in which Lloyd Gaines, an African American college graduate, was denied admission to the University of Missouri School of Law because he was African American. NAACP attorneys argued that, according to *Plessy*, the state of Missouri was obligated to either admit Gaines to the University of Missouri or provide an equivalent law school for African Americans in Missouri. The Supreme Court decided in favor of Gaines, stating that if a state provides educational opportunities to whites, such as a law school, it must also provide such opportunities for their black residents. This case is a significant precursor to the *Brown* decision, yet it differs significantly from that decision in that, in this case, the Supreme Court upheld the "separate but equal" condition of *Plessy*, while in *Brown*, it was overturned.

In the *Brown* case, the NAACP Legal Defense Fund used evidence to show that while educational institutions were separate, they were not equal. Houston contributed a video documentary of unequal schooling that provided persuasive evidence that states were violating the Supreme Court standard of "separate but equal." Additionally, social scientific research, specifically Kenneth and Mamie Clark's research on children's self-perceptions related to race through their well-known doll experiments, was used to support the argument that separate was inherently unequal. In this research, conducted during the 1930s, they found that African American children in segregated schools had lower self-perceptions than did African American children who attended integrated schools. In their research, they presented the children with two dolls, identical except for the doll's skin color and hair. The children were then asked questions, such as which one was the nice doll and which one they would like to play with. Their findings showed a clear preference for the white dolls, arguably providing evidence of internalized racism, which is a

1896	*Plessy v. Ferguson*—Declared "separate but equal" the law of the land.
1927	*Gong Lum v. Rice*—Allowed states to define Chinese students as nonwhite.
1931	*Alvarez v. Lemongrove*—California court declared that Mexican American children could not be segregated because they were white.
1936	*University of Maryland v. Murray*—Court orders state's white law school to admit black students because they violate "separate but equal" standard by not having a law school for blacks.
1938	*Missouri ex rel. Gaines v. Canada*—Similarly to the previous case, the court ordered the University of Missouri Law School to admit black students since the state failed to provide a separate black law school for Missouri residents.
1945	*Mendez v. Westminster*—A federal appeals court strikes down segregated schooling for Mexican American and white children.
1950	*Sweatt v. Painter*—Supreme Court rejects the plan by the state of Texas to create a separate law school for black students rather than admit a black student to the all-white University of Texas Law School. The court ruled that learning in law school "cannot be effective in isolation from the individuals and institutions with which the law interacts."
1954	*Brown v. Board of Education*—Unanimously overturned *Plessy*, declared separate schools to be inherently unequal.
1955	*Brown II*—Court orders school desegregation to proceed "with all deliberate speed."

FIGURE 7.2: Timeline of significant school desegregation court cases leading up to *Brown v. Board of Education*.

self-hatred that emerges when members of subordinate groups believe the negative stereotypes perpetuated about them by the dominant group (see Chapter 1). These research results were presented as evidence that segregation harms black children; thus, there could be no such thing as "separate but equal."

Presented with such evidence, the Supreme Court acknowledged what lower courts, and the *Plessy v. Ferguson* ruling, had not acknowledged, that "separate educational facilities are inherently unequal." The case declared "separate but equal" schools unconstitutional and marked a dramatic change in US education policy in terms of race.

WITNESS

In his final opinion on the case of *Brown v. Topeka Board of Education* (1954), Chief Justice Earl Warren declared that "to separate [students] from others of a similar age and qualification solely because of their race generates a feeling of inferiority as to their status in the community that may affect their hearts and minds in a way unlikely to ever be undone."

African Americans

African American educational inequality has a long history. Slaves were denied education; compulsory ignorance was an essential part of the enslavement of people (Weinberg 1977). It was illegal to teach a slave to read or write, although some slaves, including Frederick Douglass, learned clandestinely to read and write despite the prohibitions. Upon emancipation, former slaves enthusiastically sought education and went to great lengths to gain access to education for their children, including pooling their already meager resources to build schools and pay teachers themselves (Hahn 2003). They also sought access to the federal funds available to establish the first public school systems for white and black children in the South. The Freedmen's Bureau, a federal program that was set up to help former slaves, also helped establish these schools. During the thirty-year period following the Civil War, dozens of black colleges were established, many of which remain in existence today. In 1854, there was only one predominantly black college, but by the middle of the following century, there were more than one hundred (Franklin and Moss 2000). The size of the elementary and secondary school teaching force swelled quickly, with over 9,500 teachers in schools for former slaves by 1869. White and black women, from the South and the North, enlisted to teach in these schools.

This burst of success was short lived. By 1869, the Freedmen's Bureau's facilitation of the education of former slaves had all but ceased. By the mid-1870s, Reconstruction was losing political support in Washington, and the withdrawal of northern troops

IMAGES 7.2 AND 7.3: Images of a white school (top) and a black school (bottom), both in Virginia. Images such as these were used in the *Brown v. Board of Education* Supreme Court case, proving that segregated schools were unequal and thus violated the precedent established by *Plessy v. Ferguson* (1896).

from the South in 1877 signaled the end of federal oversight of the southern states. Administration of the fragile new black schools fell to local governments, many of which were run by people who viewed the education of former slaves as dangerous. Efforts were made in the southern states to reestablish the racial hierarchy and to ensure black subordination, even though laws stipulated that schools for black and white children must be provided. The Ku Klux Klan, for instance, burned schools and harassed teachers so as to terrorize them into quitting (Weinberg 1977).

Perhaps even more damaging to African American education were the covert ways in which whites in power sought to maintain black subordination. Many communities began what would become a long tradition of disparate school funding: money allotted to black schools dropped to one-third of what was spent on white schools. As a result, the education that a black student received was inferior to that which was afforded a white student in the same county. Many counties throughout the South did not have high schools for black students, even though the law required children to attend school until the age of sixteen (Kharem 2006). In 1899, the Supreme Court offered its tacit approval of such practice in *Cumming v. Board of Education of Richmond County*, in which, in a unanimous decision, the court refused to grant any relief to blacks whose high school had been closed by county officials while two white high schools remained open. In addition to racially disparate funding, the amount of instruction varied by race as well. The school year for black students was considerably shorter than it was for white students. This practice was justified by the expectation that black children had to work in the fields when the cotton needed to be picked, inspiring some to refer to black education in the Jim Crow era as a "sharecropper education" (Payne 2008).

Many African Americans migrated north in the hope of providing their children with educational opportunities that did not exist in the South (Walters 2001). In many major cities of the post–Civil War North, a Jim Crow system of segregation did not officially exist; however, black children who attempted to attend schools that were predominantly white were often harassed to the point of being prevented from attending school (Kharem 2006). In some northern states, public schools simply served whites only, even when African Americans paid taxes that helped finance the schools they were prevented from attending (Weinberg 1997). African American access to colleges and universities was also severely limited at this time, and northern universities completely excluded blacks from enrolling prior to 1940. Only thirty blacks graduated from predominantly white colleges and universities between 1826 and 1890 (Feagin, Vera, and Imani 1996).

Different political forces and ideologies continued to influence education for African Americans into the twentieth century. Scientific racism, discussed in Chapter 3, fueled the perception of the natural inferiority of African Americans. As a result, it was believed by many that education for blacks should prepare them for a

IMAGE 7.4: Japanese American fourth graders pledging allegiance at Raphael Weill School in San Francisco in 1942, weeks before they and their families were taken by the War Relocation Authority to internment camps.

subservient role in society (Cole 2006). Even within the African American community itself, opinions differed about what roles education should prepare black students for. Some prominent black leaders, such as Booker T. Washington, encouraged a policy of **accommodationism**, which posited that blacks could gain more autonomy by cooperating with whites rather than demanding full civil rights. This message appealed to whites because it appeared to emphasize that African Americans needed to "learn their place," that of subordinate, second-class citizens, not only in society but specifically in the new economic order, industrial capitalism.

Asian Americans

As African Americans fought for their freedom from bondage, Chinese Americans were still relative newcomers to the United States. Between the years 1849 and 1854, approximately forty-five thousand migrants left China for the United States. Like most immigrants, they were hoping for better lives than they had in their home country. They faced discrimination and found their employment options limited to dirty, dangerous work, such as mining and agriculture. Like African Americans in the North, Chinese Americans in the West were denied access to public education, despite paying taxes that supported local schools, because the public schools admitted white children only. Even if a Chinese American child was fortunate enough to get some formal education, the child was likely to be denied education beyond the fifth grade because there were virtually no high schools for nonwhite students (Weinberg 1997).

Chinese American parents fought early and hard so their children could benefit from the same education afforded to white children. In 1857, Chinese American community leaders formally requested that the San Francisco school board allow their children to attend the public schools. This request was denied and the board addressed the issue by saying that Chinese American children could attend the segregated school with African American students (Weinberg 1997). Chinese American parents in the San Francisco area sued the school board when their children were denied access to the local white school. The court decided that the school board could not force the Chinese American students to go to the local black school but instead had to create a separate "Oriental school," in the terminology of the day, for Chinese children in 1885.

Amid broad anti-Asian sentiment, the San Francisco school board instituted a policy that relegated Japanese and Korean children to so-called Oriental schools in 1906. Having been allowed in the public schools with white children up until then, Japanese families filed a lawsuit, claiming that such segregation violated international treaties between the United States and Japan. The plaintiffs appealed to the Japanese government, which played a more influential role in defending its emigrants' lives than did any other Asian country's government. The Japanese government concurred that such segregation was an insult to the Japanese people. Japan applied significant political pressure on the United States government, and the issue attracted international media attention. This political clout, which other marginalized groups in the United States did not have in their own fights for equal education, paid off for the Japanese families. Eventually, a deal was struck between Japan, President Theodore Roosevelt, and the San Francisco school board. It was agreed that Japanese children would be allowed back into mainstream schools, provided Japan ceased allowing its citizens to immigrate to the United States (Weinberg 1997).

Although the Japanese families' challenge of the San Francisco school board was successful, Chinese and Korean students remained segregated. Also, the victory did little to quell growing anti-Asian sentiment among white Americans, who feared that Asian immigrants were a threat to national security, labor, and the economy. The educational discrimination historically faced by Asian Americans stemmed from the same racial ideologies of white supremacy and minority inferiority that dominated the era.

Mexican Americans

The story of school segregation and desegregation as it relates to Latinos in the United States is largely a story of Mexican American children. Mexican Americans went from being citizens of one republic (Mexico) to being citizens of another (the United States) as a result of the US government's acquiring the land they lived on in 1848 at the close of the Mexican–American War. And from that time on, Mexican Americans formed the largest national-identity group among Latinos in the United States, followed by Puerto Ricans (residing primarily in the Northeast) and Cuban Americans (residing primarily in Florida). Like African Americans and Asian Americans, Latino children faced educational exclusion and discrimination. However, the fact that they spoke Spanish made it even easier to discriminate against them. Language barriers continue to be an issue in contemporary education (see the discussion of bilingual education, page 279), but early on they were used to justify segregating Mexican American children from white children in schools. Mexican American children were sent to Mexican schools, or, in smaller communities with only one school, they were segregated in Mexican classrooms in otherwise predominantly white schools (Donato 1997). Like black schools in the South, schools for Mexican American children were underfunded in comparison to the schools for white children, and the school year for Mexican American children was deliberately shorter so that they could work in the fields the rest of the year (Donato 1997). When they did have access to schools, the education they received was intended to prepare them for subordinate roles in society and socialize them for a life of cheap labor, educational goals that reflected the needs and ideologies of the white community, not the Mexican American community. Mexican Americans, like African Americans and Asian Americans, were often denied access to a high school education.

Mexican Americans challenged racial segregation in schools. The first successful desegregation case in the United States, *Alvarez v. Lemon Grove*, was brought by Mexican Americans in California in 1931. Lemon Grove was a small community outside of San Diego that, unlike the rest of Southern California at the time, did not have segregated schools. In January 1931, the day students returned from their winter break, the principal directed the Mexican American students to their "new" school: a two-room structure with secondhand equipment, supplies, and books. The parents of the Mexican American children immediately reacted, boycotting the school and suing the school district. In the court's decision, it was found that Mexican American children could not be segregated because they were white. Thus, the decision did not challenge racially segregated schools, just the definition of who should be relegated to nonwhite schools.

The League of United Latin American Citizens (LULAC) formed in 1929 to fight for the civil rights of people with Latin American ancestry, much as the NAACP was created to advocate for the civil rights of African Americans. One of LULAC's primary fights was against school segregation. It brought forward another key desegregation case, *Mendez v. Westminster School District of Orange County.* In the spring of 1945, a group of Mexican American parents, including Gonzalo Mendez, sued their local school district for requiring that Mexican American children attend segregated schools with only Mexican American students. Mexicans were considered "white" under the law, and the parents argued that they were being discriminated against based on their Mexican nationality, a clear violation of the Fourteenth Amendment, which grants equal protection under the law. When the judge ruled in the parents' favor, the Westminster school district appealed to the federal courts, maintaining that the Spanish-speaking students' language barriers made them unfit for white schools. Various multiracial organizations rallied support for the Mexican American families, and they again won in the appeal. The result of the case was monumental: the state of California became the first state in the country to end racial segregation in schools. This case is known as a significant forerunner to *Brown v. Board of Education*, the better-known Supreme Court decision that ended segregated schooling nationwide.

In *Keyes v. School District No. 1* (1973), parents of African American and Latino students sued the Denver school board for intentionally creating a segregated school system. This was the first Supreme Court case that did not concern a school system with a history of blatant segregation and was also noteworthy for being the first case brought by both African Americans and Latinos. The court ruled that desegregation was not just about having more than one race of students in the school (Latinos and African Americans, for instance) but that desegregation had to involve whites. The court also found, however, that the plaintiffs had to provide evidence that the school board intentionally created a segregated school system. Thus, if policies resulted in segregated schools even if they were not designed to, then no intent to segregate could be inferred.

Native Americans

In their pursuit of equal education, Native American children faced a different set of barriers than other minority groups. Mexican Americans, African Americans, and Asian Americans contended with racism, xenophobia, and benign neglect on the part of their local governments. However, the education of Native American children was part of deliberate and systematic efforts by the federal government to destroy Native American tribal cultures (Trafzer, Keller, and Sisquoc 2006).

In America's earliest days, Native Americans and white settlers coexisted, if not always peacefully. Tribes maintained the responsibility of educating their youths. White missionaries established schools for Indian students, teaching them Christianity and English literacy. As settlers fanned out across the country in the 1840s and 1850s, coexistence with Native Americans became inconvenient for the whites, and by the late 1800s most Native American tribes had been relocated by the United

States military from their homelands to reservations. Federal policy of the era, especially after the Civil War, supported the notion that Native Americans, once reformed and stripped of their unique cultural identities, could assimilate into the white world.

This marked the beginning of the **boarding school movement**, in which thousands of Indian children were taken from their parents and sent to boarding schools under the leadership of the Bureau of Indian Affairs. Native Americans were perceived by whites as uncivilized heathens, and federally controlled boarding schools were intended to civilize them, destroy tribal cultures and identities, and indoctrinate Native children with white cultural values and beliefs, including Christianity and the English language. Some parents agreed to send their children to the boarding schools, although the government made it difficult to refuse. Parents who declined to send their children risked having their food rations withheld and being intimidated by federal troops. Many Native American children were taken away from their families by the military and brought to boarding schools against their will. Australia established similar practices with their Aboriginal population (see Box 7.2 Global Perspectives: Aboriginal Education in Australia).

The first boarding school for Native Americans was the Carlisle Indian Industrial School of Pennsylvania, which opened under the leadership of former army officer Richard Henry Pratt in 1879. Indian students were brought there from reservations

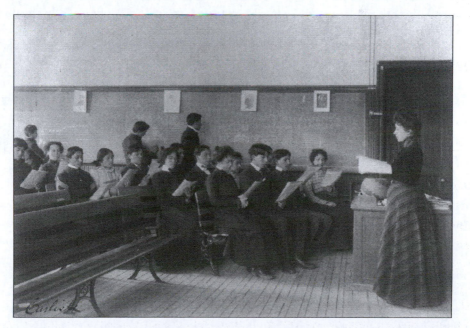

IMAGE 7.5: Image of the Carlisle Indian School, the first of over five hundred Native American boarding schools established to forcibly assimilate Native American children.

BOX 7.2

Global Perspectives:
Aboriginal Education in Australia

The educational history of racial minority groups in the United States has numerous parallels to the history of the education of Australian Aborigines, the original inhabitants of the Australian continent. For over 150 years, schools in Australia were used to protect white interests, whether that was through maintaining segregation or assisting with racial integration (Fletcher 1989).

At times, Aboriginal children were simply banned from attending white schools; at other times schools were viewed as important tools for assimilating Aborigines. Decades of racial segregation were justified by racial ideologies claiming Aborigines were incapable of learning, diseased, and unclean, and therefore a threat to white Australian children. In other eras, the assimilation of Aborigines into the mainstream, white culture was viewed as essential, and, thus, Aboriginal children were forcibly taken from their families and placed in boarding schools or with white foster families. Western Australian Aborigines describe the period of 1880 to 1940 as the "stolen generations" because so many children were taken from their families during this era. One crucial difference between the US approach to indigenous education and the Australian approach is that US authorities sought to remove Indian children for a period of three to five years, whereas the Australian government sought permanent removal of children from their parents and communities (Jacobs 2009).

The boarding schools established for Aboriginal children, like those established for Native Americans in the United States, were generally industrial schools that sought to prepare the boys for agricultural labor and girls for domestic labor, as well as to teach them English literacy and Christianity. The justifications for these policies were remarkably similar to those used in the United States. In both countries, for instance, policy makers justified their actions as humanitarian because they were taking children out of presumably backward environments and allowing them the opportunity to become white and civilized (Jacobs 2009).

Aborigines have not had much success within the Australian educational system, and only recently has this been attributed to the extreme racism that Aborigines confront in schools and in the rest of society. In the 1960s, a student organization by the name of Student Action for Aborigines, influenced by the civil rights activism in the United States, demanded an end to racial discrimination in all arenas. The requests were similar to the educational demands made by racial minority groups in the United States. The Aborigines requested accurate representation in curricula, an end to racial segregation in schools, and minority access to higher education. Additionally, there have been efforts to introduce Aboriginal studies into Australian schools so as to increase respect for Aboriginal culture and decrease the racism directed at them.

in the Northern Plains and Dakota territories. They were subjected to a structured and militaristic way of life that was meant to strip them of their Native American identities. They marched in formation between their dormitories and classes. Carlisle students received a traditional education for just half of the day and were required to spend the second half working, so as to keep school expenses down (Noriega 1992). Girls were taught to be housekeepers and maids while boys learned a trade or agricultural techniques.

Boarding schools spread across the country in the decades following the opening of the Carlisle School and most followed a similar model. Indian children were not allowed to wear their traditional clothing, their given names were replaced with Anglo-sounding names, their long hair was cut off, and they were not allowed to speak their native languages. Boarding school experiences were traumatic for Indian students. They were often separated from their parents for years at a time. The environment was abusive. When children cried, or spoke their Native language, or in any way resisted their acculturation, they were severely beaten.

As was the case for other minorities, the education that Indian children received was predominantly vocational because it was assumed that they would take on subordinate roles once they had assimilated into mainstream society. The children were trained for occupations that did not exist on reservations, which made going home problematic.

This was all part of the systematic **resocialization** of Indian children. Identified by sociologist Erving Goffman (1961), resocialization is the process by which people's environment is controlled in such a way as to get them to abandon their current identity and accept a new one. Resocialization begins with the dismantling of the subject's existing identity, which was why Indian children had their names and clothes confiscated and were prohibited from speaking their native languages. Resocialization tends to be even more successful in what Goffman called **total institutions**, environments in which every aspect of the inhabitants' lives is controlled. Prisons, the military, asylums, and Indian boarding schools are examples of total institutions.

Historically, the dominant racial group in the United States used schools to perpetuate cultural ideologies of racial inferiority and superiority. Education can be about liberation for oppressed people, as it was for newly freed slaves. However, it can also be a tool used against a group of people by a dominant group, as the federal government did against the Native Americans. Karl Marx observed in his **dominant ideology thesis** that the dominant group, which he called the ruling class, uses social institutions such as schools to promote ideas, values, and morals that support their dominance. Subordinate groups resist the ideologies of the dominant group. For example, consider the many lawsuits covered in this chapter, which were brought by diverse groups of subordinated people.

REFLECT AND CONNECT

Dominant groups go to great lengths to limit the education of minority groups. Is this evidence of the potential liberating power of education? Why or why not?

Native American children resisted boarding school life in numerous ways. Some ran away; although they were usually found and brought back, a few froze to death without shelter (Littlefield 2001). Despite being forbidden to do so, they spoke their languages quietly to other students as a form of resistance. Indian communities began to demand rights in the education of their children. In the 1920s, the federal government began to respond to these demands. Carlisle Indian School closed in 1918, and by midcentury most other Indian boarding schools were shuttered as well. Schools opened on reservations and attempted to preserve Native languages and traditions rather than destroy them.

School Desegregation After *Brown*

After generations of racially segregated schools, the Supreme Court declared school segregation to be unconstitutional. Even though the *Brown* decision technically mandated an end to segregation in 1954, minorities still had to fight to attend schools of their choice. School desegregation was a slow and often violent process, as white resistance to it took many forms. In one of the first tests of the *Brown* decision, an African American woman, Autherine Lucy, applied and was admitted to the University of Alabama in 1956. However, white students reacted so violently to the situation that the school expelled her, allegedly for her own safety. James Meredith attempted to become the first African American student to attend the University of Mississippi. He was rejected twice due to his race; in 1961, he filed a complaint with a district court. By a two-to-one margin, the judges decided in favor of Meredith, stating that, indeed, his first two rejections were based solely upon race and thus were discriminatory and in violation of federal law. Campus riots ensued, and Attorney General Robert F. Kennedy sent in federal marshals to protect Meredith on campus. Despite such controversy and conflict, Meredith eventually graduated from the University of Mississippi, at least partially as a result of the *Brown* decision.

While the *Brown* decision was unanimous and powerful in its declaration that schools had to be desegregated, the implementation of this decision—the actual, practical process of desegregating every school in the country—was another matter entirely. The *Brown* decision was followed by a second Supreme Court decision in 1955, referred to as *Brown II*, which came in response to the concerns of schools, who were claiming that immediate desegregation would incur untenable financial

IMAGE 7.6: Hostility to school integration did not just happen in the South. This image shows white adults jeering at black elementary school students as they integrate at a school in New York.

burdens. *Brown II* established the constitutionally unique provision that school integration was to proceed "with all deliberate speed." Although an edict to desegregate as soon as possible sounds like a victory for integration, the language of *Brown II* has been highly criticized for its lack of clarity. Interpretations of "all deliberate speed" varied widely, and it meant that schools remained officially segregated even into the 1990s in some parts of the country. Critics claim that the Supreme Court feared resistance and hostility from whites and went out of its way to avoid offending white segregationists in its *Brown II* decision (Minow 2004; Ogletree and Sarat 2006). The language of *Brown II* has been blamed for encouraging noncompliance with, and even outright resistance to, desegregation, and it is just one of the ways that people resisted the mandate to desegregate their schools. Such resistance began immediately after the ruling, and the repercussions of that resistance are still visible today.

The fact that it took federal troops to get James Meredith past angry mobs and safely to class is suggestive of the backlash felt in many communities as a reaction to the *Brown* decision. Some districts even closed schools entirely rather than desegregate. For instance, certain municipalities in Virginia viewed abandoning public education altogether as preferable to integrating. As their public schools remained closed or nearly empty, whites throughout the South established *segregation academies*, private schools that provided education for white students only. However, there were not enough segregation academies to meet the needs of all the white students being denied education through school closures. The closing of the public schools infuriated many white and black parents as well as the courts and were eventually declared unconstitutional. A more passive form of resistance on the part of whites was that of **tokenism**, admitting only three or four black students into white schools as a minimal form of compliance with the law. The Supreme Court refused to hear cases brought forth that challenged such tokenism, inadvertently bolstering white resistance to school integration with their support of tokenism (Wilkinson 1979). Alabama avoided integrating schools in 1955 by passing a "pupil placement law" that allowed "local school boards the authority to deny black students entry into white schools based on racially biased intelligence and psychological tests or because of the 'psychological effect' desegregation had on white students. No black child was deemed fit," (Hannah-Jones 2017). In 1956, they went even farther, closing some public schools rather than allowing integration.

Many white Americans avoided sending their children to integrated schools by moving their families away from areas where minorities lived and went to school. They moved to suburbs where their neighbors were mostly white and, therefore, the other schoolchildren were mostly white. This movement was not limited to a few families in a few cities. In fact, the exodus of so many whites from once-diverse urban areas became a noticeable phenomenon known as **white flight**. White flight is a solid example of white privilege in that it highlights white families with options unavailable to people of color (the option to "vote with their feet"). State governments have tended to establish school district boundaries and funding formulas that favor suburban schools, thus making them better than many of their urban counterparts (Walters 2001). Until the Fair Housing Act passed in 1968, and some enforcement was added through an amendment in 1988, racial minorities did not have complete freedom to choose their residential location. People of color were systematically excluded from suburbs for decades, and as a result suburban America remained overwhelmingly white (see Chapter 9).

Researchers have documented a phenomenon they refer to as **Latino flight**, the pattern of Latinos' enrolling their children in private schools to avoid sending them to school with black children. Latinos are one of the fastest-growing racial/ethnic groups in the country. By 2020, they are expected to make up 21.5 percent of the school-age population, a dramatic increase from 11.9 percent in 1990. The choices that Latinos make about the types of schools to attend and their locations will have a considerable impact on the potential future of school integration (Fairlie 2002).

Busing

Resistance to the *Brown* decision remained strong, but patience for those who opposed integration, and the era of "all deliberate speed," was over by the early 1970s. At that time, the courts began to order school districts to take more immediate action for ending school segregation. In 1971, in the landmark case of *Swann v. Charlotte-Mecklenburg Board of Education*, the Supreme Court ruled that a district could desegregate its schools by *busing* students from black schools to white schools to achieve a racial balance at each school. Busing was a proposed policy solution because, due to white flight, blacks and whites usually did not live in the same communities, and since American public schools have historically been neighborhood based, integration could only be achieved by sending some children to schools that were not in their neighborhoods. In some communities, this meant that both white and black children were bused out of their own neighborhoods to attend school across town. But more often than not, it meant busing urban minority children out of their neighborhoods and into predominantly white suburban schools. There was, again, violent resistance to this latest attempt at school integration in cities across the country: San Francisco, Louisville, Boston, St. Louis, and Pontiac, Michigan. White parents in Boston screamed racial epithets and threw stones at school buses full of black children. In Pontiac, Michigan, empty school buses were bombed (Hochschild and Scovronick 2003).

Although studies find that desegregation through busing has been successful in some cases, busing does not hold much promise as the perfect solution to the problem of school segregation. The great majority of children of color are left behind in underfunded, understaffed, ill-equipped urban schools while a handful of their peers are sent to better schools in the suburbs. Research suggests that even schools that are racially integrated are segregated internally, a problem that busing clearly cannot resolve (Caldas and Bankston 2005; Maran 2000; Tyson 2011). For instance, students are steered into different educational tracks along racial lines, and race correlates strongly with whether students are in remedial courses or honors courses, something known as racialized tracking (Tyson 2011).

From De Jure *Segregation to De Facto Segregation*

The *Brown* decision was less successful at its intended purpose, integrating schools, than it was at paving the way for integration in all other areas of life and at providing a catalyst for the civil rights movement. After showing some progress toward desegregation in the 1980s, schools today are more segregated than they have been since the late 1960s, with urban schools 95–99 percent nonwhite, and some never integrating (Kozol 1991). Today, most minority students attend schools with fewer whites than a typical minority student did in 1970 (Fiel 2013). In the South, this resegregation has proceeded quickly since courts have released many school districts from desegregation orders previously imposed on them (Hannah-Jones 2017). A judge in May 2016 ordered schools in Cleveland, Mississippi, to desegregate, ending a sixty-two-year battle over school integration. Latino, black, and white children experience rigid racial segregation in schools, with Latino children in the Los Angeles area even more racially segregated than black children in Mississippi (Carter, Flores, and

Reddick 2004; Lockette 2010; Portales 2004). As Figure 7.3 shows, in 2014, just over 80 percent of white students attended schools where at least half the students were also white, 44.1 percent of black students attended schools where at least half the students were also black, and almost 57 percent of Hispanic students attended schools where at least half the students were also Hispanic (Geiger 2017).

The *Brown* decision succeeded at making ***de jure* segregation** illegal, which refers to segregation protected and enforced by laws; however, it has not addressed what is called ***de facto* segregation**, segregation that exists in fact, even if it's not legally supported. The resegregation of American schools is partially a result of the decades of white resistance to school segregation, particularly white flight, which results in suburban schools' being predominantly white while urban schools are predominantly composed of students of color. Another reason for resegregation is that schools in the United States historically have been controlled at the local level and school desegregation has been virtually impossible to enforce in the absence of federal political and financial control over schools (Walters 2001).

Supreme Court decisions since the mid-1970s have also created obstacles to school integration (Chemerinsky 2005). The role of the federal courts in desegregation is

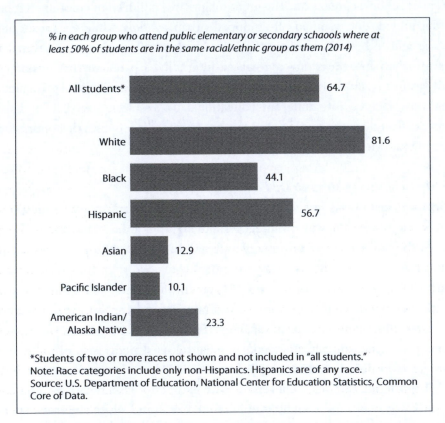

FIGURE 7.3: Racial composition of schools attended by the average student of each race, 2014.
SOURCE: Geiger 2017.

fundamental because they constitute the only branch of the federal government that has authority over schools nationwide. When the federal courts step in, however, the result is not always desegregated schools. The Supreme Court decision *Milliken v. Bradley* (1974), for instance, ruled that interdistrict desegregation efforts were not permissible. However, because urban areas and urban school districts tend to be predominantly minority while suburban areas and school districts are predominantly white, busing students from an urban school district to a suburban one would be the only viable way to achieve racial integration. The *Milliken* decision, however, did not allow desegregation programs to operate between school districts and has dramatically contributed to school resegregation (Clotfelter 2002). By the 1990s, several key Supreme Court decisions had ended previous desegregation orders, thus paving the way for the resegregation of America's schools.

Finally, the implementation of "school choice" has contributed to the resegregation of schools. School choice has been part of educational reform proposals since the 1980s. The idea is that parents should have options concerning their children's education, particularly if they are faced with failing schools. Sometimes school choice programs involve allowing children access to charter schools or to alternative public schools (other than their neighborhood school), or they can take the form of vouchers, where the public dollars that would have been spent on a child attending the local public school can be used toward a private school. As mentioned previously, school choice turns out to be a false choice for low-income and working-class black families, who face numerous barriers to obtaining the optimal educational opportunities for their children (Pattillo 2015).

School choice can result in the resegregation of schools because the application process for charter schools and vouchers is more complicated than enrollment in traditional public schools, thus favoring middle-class parents, who are more likely to have the cultural capital necessary to navigate the difficult enrollment processes and the privilege to transport their child long distances for school. One outcome of this is racial resegregation. According to one study, "White students were represented in alternative schools at 200 to 300 percent of their representation in the district as a whole" (Lewis 2003:88).

School choice also contributes to the racial segregation of schools because it can draw white students away from racially diverse public schools (Renzulli and Evans 2005). The language of school choice presumes that parents will make their choices based upon the academic reputation of a school; however, some research finds that nonacademic factors, particularly a school's racial composition, are also a major variable in their decision making (Billingham and Hunt 2016; Wells and Crain 1992). For white parents, the racial composition of the school is a significant influence on their selection of a school for their children; "The likelihood that white parents will choose a hypothetical school for their children drops significantly as the proportion of black students in the student body increases" (Billingham and Hunt 2016:112).

Resistance to Racial Discrimination in Schools

Minority groups continued to take responsibility for their education into the middle of the twentieth century, when it became part of the civil rights agenda. The effects of substandard education were felt by those who had grown up in underfunded, discriminatory school environments, and minority groups made efforts to overcome this. Adult education programs, known as citizenship schools, began in 1957 as a way to prepare African Americans for voter registration. Civil rights proponents also advocated **Afrocentric education**, an educational strategy that taught African American students about black history and culture. The Black Panther Party established schools throughout urban ghettos in the 1960s, providing black students with Afrocentric curricula, which were not offered in public schools. Much of the activism of the civil rights and other racial justice movements revolved around access to education, as the discussions of the Little Rock Nine and James Meredith in Chapter 6 exposed.

During this era, minority groups demanded full civil equality, including school curricula that reflected their group's experiences, from elementary through college. In 1969 the first four-year black studies program was implemented at San Francisco State University. By 1973, hundreds of black studies programs had been established at colleges and universities throughout the country. Ethnic studies, Asian American studies, Native American studies, and Chicano studies programs, among others, emerged as a response to minority group activism of the post–World War II era.

The Red Power movement of the late 1960s and 1970s focused on establishing tribal colleges and universities and influencing school curricula at all levels to more accurately reflect Native American history and cultures. Tribal colleges, most of which are community colleges, were created to serve local Indian reservations, celebrating Native cultures and traditions while also preparing Indian students to transfer to mainstream four-year colleges and universities.

Native peoples have insisted on maintaining schools on the reservations and offering a curriculum that represents Indian cultures and histories. Although the boarding schools for Native Americans were originally designed to "kill the Indian and save the man," they ultimately had a transformative effect. The boarding schools triggered the preservation of a pan-Indian identity beyond the tribal level, a sense of community among tribes, and the preservation of tribal languages (Cornell 1988; Trafzer, Keller, and Sisquoc 2006). Today, grassroots organizations, such as the Boarding School Project, attempt to address the lingering issues associated with traumas experienced in Indian boarding schools. Many argue that a lot of problems facing Native communities today can be linked to the terrible legacy of abuse experienced by so many Native Americans in boarding schools (Pember 2010).

Numerous resources are available to help instructors offer a more inclusive account of American history. For example, the Southern Poverty Law Center's Teaching Tolerance program (see Box 7.3 Racial Justice Activism: From Teaching

BOX 7.3

Racial Justice Activism:
From Teaching Tolerance to Educational Justice Movements

This chapter has exemplified racial inequality in education. Of course, organizations fighting for racial and social justice in schools have long existed. Here we introduce the efforts of the Teaching Tolerance program and the beginnings of a larger educational justice movement. The Southern Poverty Law Center started its Teaching Tolerance program in 1991 with the goal of reducing prejudice and improving intergroup relations among schoolchildren. They provide educational materials for teachers and schools that encourage tolerance, which they define as "respect, acceptance and appreciation of the rich diversity of our world's cultures, our forms of expression and ways of being human. Tolerance is harmony in difference" (Teaching Tolerance 2016). The organization offers teaching toolkits and classroom exercises for addressing both historical and current racial issues. Some examples of the types of teaching programs offered are "Viva la Causa," a lesson on the migrant farmworkers strike and national grape boycott organized by Cesar Chavez and Dolores Huerta; a rock musical entitled *White Noise* that offers a critical look at hate speech; a lesson that looks at Vietnamese American history; a lesson that teaches social justice through photographs; and other lessons on various aspects of the civil rights movement. Other lessons explore global women's activism, sexuality and gender expression, immigrant history, the backlash against President Obama, and more.

One of the center's most innovative campaigns is Mix It Up at Lunch Day, which is a national campaign to help K–12 teachers develop more-inclusive school communities by addressing the self-segregation that often occurs in school cafeterias. Their goal is to get students to identify, question, and cross the social boundaries that direct us to socially segregate in the absence of legal segregation. On Mix It Up at Lunch Day, students are asked to move out of their comfort zone for one lunch period and connect with someone new.

Sociologist Mark Warren (2018) has documented a burgeoning educational justice movement that includes numerous organizations fighting for gender justice in schools, supporting queer and trans youth in schools, dismantling the school-to-prison pipeline, fighting school closures, supporting teachers' unions, among others. He argues that "for African Americans and many Latinos, the struggle for education was not solely about economic well-being. It was bound up with the struggle for liberation, for political power and full citizenship, and for their very lives" (2018:xvii). The educational justice movement challenges racism in education by understanding that this is part of a larger system of white supremacy,

continues

continued

> which must be challenged. It is ultimately about creating schools that are more humane, democratic, and caring, and empowering communities (Warren 2018:173).
>
> For more information, visit the Teaching Tolerance website, www.tolerance.org and Warren, Mark R. 2018. *Lift Us Up, Don't Push Us Out.* Boston, MA: Beacon Press

Tolerance to Educational Justice Movements) offers summer institutes for teachers and literature on teaching the civil rights movement (Armstrong et al. 2002). More current models for educating students about the civil rights movement are critical of the content of many high school history textbooks, which are simplistic in portraying the civil rights movement as Martin Luther King Jr.'s alone rather than as a grassroots movement with a long history and many other influential actors (Aldridge 2002; Ingram 1990). The curriculum of the 1964 Mississippi Freedom School is available to teachers, along with up-to-date teaching materials, so that one of the main lessons of that summer of activism can be taught: that we can all be creators of history and active agents of social change (Emery, Gold, and Braselmann 2008).

Indigenous people also continue to challenge educational institutions and demand recognition of their **counterhistories**, historical accounts of nondominant groups. By demanding a more inclusive history, they challenge the racial hierarchy and contest dominant historical narratives that have long been presented as truth. This is an ongoing battle. Montana implemented a controversial initiative to mandate the teaching of American Indian history in K–12 classrooms through passage of the Indian Education for All Act in 1972, and actually began funding the initiative in 2005 (Melcher 2009). By linking Indian education to funds, the legislature incentivized the teaching of Indian histories and cultures in public school classrooms. The objective of this bill was to increase the visibility of Native Americans and decrease the dropout rates among American Indian students. In 2007, South Dakota modeled their Indian Education Act off of Montana's, and educators in Wisconsin are working to strengthen their Indian education, specifically with a focus on Wisconsin's indigenous history (Jawort 2012).

A final example of resistance to racial inequalities in educational institutions involves parents' finding ways to send their children to better schools, outside their districts. In the face of limited educational options, some parents attempt to subvert district rules and enroll their children in schools in better-funded districts by using another person's address, for instance. One woman, Kelly Williams-Bolar of Akron, Ohio, was arrested and convicted in 2011 of using her father's address to send her child to a better school outside of her district. The schools in her daughter's district were failing and her low income did not allow her the privilege of moving to a better school district. The school district suspected her and hired a private investigator, and, ultimately, she was charged with a felony and incarcerated (Easter 2011).

CONTEMPORARY ISSUES OF RACIAL INEQUALITY IN EDUCATION

The long history of racial inequality in education contributes to racial inequality in schools today. We explore the status of bilingual education programs, current funding inequities, and the effects of vastly different educational opportunities for children of color and white children. We then shift our attention to the achievement gap and racial discrepancies in test scores, critically evaluating the concept and its use and explore its links to the school-to-prison pipeline Additionally, this chapter looks at the effect of the No Child Left Behind education reform bill on racial minority children. Finally, we explore some current racial issues in higher education, including attacks on the use of affirmative action in college admissions.

Bilingual Education in the United States

Bilingual education, educational programs that cater to non-English-speaking students by providing instruction in both their native language and in English, have come under attack in the last thirty years. This is an especially pertinent discussion in the current era as record numbers of non-English-speaking children have fueled the greatest growth in public schools since the post–World War II baby boom. Approximately 5.1 million English-language learners were enrolled in public schools in 2005, which represents a 60 percent increase from 1995 (Thompson 2009).

Various languages other than English have been used in both private and public schools in the United States since the 1600s (San Miguel 2004). In fact, until after the turn of the twentieth century, the United States was surprisingly accepting of the preservation of certain languages through German-, Norwegian-, and Dutch-speaking public schools.

The tolerance of the use of foreign languages in public schools ended with World War I, as fear of the massive numbers of immigrants entering the country increased. As Chapter 5 describes, nativist beliefs reigned at the turn of the twentieth century, resulting in legislation that essentially required immigrants to Americanize. The Nationality Act (1906) required that whoever wanted to be naturalized had to speak fluent English, thus proving their loyalty to their new country (Baker 2006). Individual states followed by passing legislation that required English to be the only language of instruction in schools.

The bilingual education that a student gets today is the result of demands for bilingual education initiated by Cuban Americans in Dade County, Florida, during the

To think Indian is to save a plant that can save a people.

ALLYSON TWO BEARS, 30 years old
Environmental Science major
Sitting Bull College, ND

A gatherer of herbs who's learning about restoration handed from her to medication she has accomplished a chart.

HELP TRIBAL COLLEGE
STUDENTS PRESERVE
THEIR WAY OF THINKING.
1-800-776-FUND

AMERICAN
INDIAN
COLLEGE
FUND

thinkindian.org

IMAGE 7.7: This ad appeared in high-profile publications, including the *New York Times Magazine*, *Harper's*, *U.S. News and World Report*, *Fortune*, and *Marie Claire*. The campaign was intended to bring attention to American Indian College Fund scholarships, about six thousand of which are awarded to Native American college students each year.

civil rights era. This set the stage for the passage of legislation around the country designed to help non-native English-speakers whose success in school was hindered by language barriers. Initially, school districts were given the right to offer bilingual education programs in 1968. However, many districts were resistant to such instructional methods, so not enough of them were implemented. In response, a landmark case was brought in 1972 by the Puerto Rican Legal Defense and Education Fund against the largest board of education in the nation, in New York City. The plaintiffs claimed that eighty thousand language-minority children were being denied equal education. This case resulted in a consent decree that mandated bilingual education for all children who need it. This legislation requires that students who are not proficient in English receive help in the form of English as a Second Language classes, English tutoring, and some form of bilingual education. Access to bilingual education has become a major civil rights issue for Latinos nationwide (Nieto 2000).

Bilingual education programs vary among schools, and one of the standard approaches has been to segregate English-language learners into their own classrooms, away from native English-speakers—that is, non-English-speaking students attend a school within a school where they are provided with intensive English language support. Under No Child Left Behind guidelines, all students are subjected to standardized tests that are intended to hold schools accountable for student performance in specific subject areas. Attaining fluency in a new language is a long and difficult process; it takes an average learner two years to be able to hold conversations and five to seven years to write essays or understand a novel (Thompson 2009). Students who are new to the English language do not typically do well on the tests required by No Child Left Behind. Funding is allocated to schools with better performance on these tests, so schools with large numbers of English-language learners face a disadvantage in funding.

Current Funding Inequities

In 1991, writer and activist Jonathan Kozol shocked the nation with his book *Savage Inequalities*, which exposed the incomprehensible inequality among public schools in the United States and the fact that these inequities fell along racial and class lines. He found that in the United States, wherever poor children of color were concentrated, public schools were almost always very bad; they were underfunded and underperforming, rarely had teachers certified in the content area in which they were teaching, and had unacceptably high student-to-teacher ratios. Kozol studied over thirty public schools, one of which was in one of the poorest cities in America, East St. Louis, Illinois, and another in a wealthy suburban area of Great Neck, Long Island. Kozol revisited this topic in *Shame of the Nation: The Restoration of Apartheid Schooling in America* (2005), which found the patterns of racial inequality in education remained entrenched into the new century.

Due to inequitable funding, students of color are more likely to be in overcrowded classrooms, have a teacher who is not certified in his or her subject area, lack textbooks and other basic resources, and be offered limited curricular options.

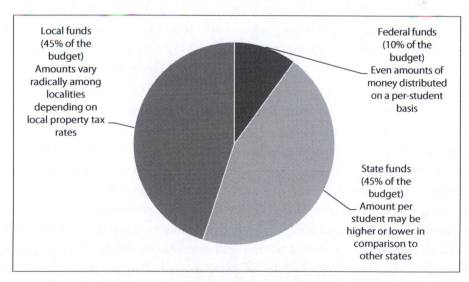

FIGURE 7.4: Typical federal, state, and local contributions to an American School.
SOURCE: Hacsi 2002.

Public schools receive funds from federal, state, and local municipalities (see Figure 7.4). Federal dollars are distributed as a certain amount per pupil and tend to be equitable from state to state and school to school. Federal contributions to education are minimal, amounting to only about 10 percent of a school's budget. The funds handed down to schools from the state tend to vary among schools more than federal funds do. For example, Vermont contributes about $15,175 per student, while Tennessee contributes $7,897. The student in Vermont gets approximately $7,278 more in resources—new computers and supplies, improved facilities, and better-paid teachers—than the student in Tennessee. Typically, about 45 percent of a school's budget comes from the state (Hacsi 2002). However, within states, school funding varies even more radically.

WITNESS

The list of problems articulated by an East St. Louis High principal to Kozol is startlingly similar to Robert Pershing Foster's story of black public schools in the 1930s in the chapter-opening vignette: "I need computers [to] bring the science laboratories up to date. Enlarge the library. Buy more books. The books I've got, a lot of them are second-hand. I got them from the Catholic high school when it closed. Most of all, we need a building renovation" (Kozol 1991:32).

The remaining 45 percent of a school's official budget comes from the most volatile of coffers: local funds, specifically, personal property taxes. In wealthy communities, residents are more likely to be homeowners and thus pay property taxes on their homes, as well as on luxury items such as expensive cars and boats. Wealthy communities with large, high-value properties collect more property taxes and have more money to direct toward their schools. Wealthy communities are also more able to contribute money to the school, which goes beyond a school's official budget. By comparison, in poor communities, residents are more likely to rent instead of own their own homes, thus they do not pay personal property taxes on homes. Residents in these communities do not have luxury items that generate significant property tax revenues for their local schools. As a result, the property taxes in poor communities are lower and the schools in those communities have much smaller budgets.

Wealthy communities resist altering school funding formulas because the current funding formula benefits their own children. Conflict theorists point out that schools reproduce the status quo as "inequalities in family wealth are a major cause of inequalities in schooling, and inequalities in schooling do much to reinforce inequalities of wealth among families in the next generation" (Hochschild and Scovronick 2003:23).

What was your high school like? What kinds of facilities and resources did you have access to? What types of extracurricular activities, college preparatory help, and support systems were available to you there? Do you think that the high schools that your college classmates attended offered the same kinds of programs and courses you were offered in high school? To what extent do you think race and class privilege played a role in your high school opportunities? Or were your high school experiences characterized by lack of opportunities?

Tracking

Racial/ethnic minority children are often in segregated classrooms, even if they are in integrated schools. Internal school segregation is an outgrowth of **tracking**, which refers to the sorting and placement of students into different educational programs, presumably based upon ability and prior academic achievement. Early research on tracking found that it contributed to a self-fulfilling prophecy, in that students in lower tracks believed they lacked intelligence and thus would withdraw their efforts in school, which essentially resulted in poor grades and a confirmation of their initial placement in the lower track (Howard 1995). Today's educational tracking is referred to by some sociologists as racialized tracking because higher-level courses, such as honors and advanced-placement courses, are disproportionately composed of white students while standard classes are disproportionately composed of racial minority students. A significant outgrowth of this pattern is that internal school segregation patterns contribute to the view that whiteness is linked with academic achievement (Tyson 2011). It is important to recognize that if minority students develop oppositional identities, as was discussed at the beginning of the chapter, and view school achievement negatively and as "acting white," this may be an extension of the organization of schools rather than an outgrowth of black culture (Tyson 2011).

The Achievement Gap

Measuring the cost of the inequality in American schools is a complicated and fraught process. African American and Latino students consistently score lower on standardized tests than white students, and Asian American students outperform all racial groups (Caldas and Bankston 2005). This discrepancy in standardized test scores along racial lines is called the **achievement gap**, and it is a major source of concern and controversy among educators and policy makers today. In this section, we are going to discuss the limitations of this measure and present more-responsible interpretations of this data.

Limitations of the Achievement Gap

Sociologists insist we go beyond the achievement gap and consider the data behind it when studying race and education. Using the results of standardized test scores alone is not enough to draw conclusions about academic achievement among races.

One of the problems with using these data, and with talking about race and education with statistics alone, is the risk of perpetuating the notion that race is real in a biological sense. As discussed in previous chapters, race is a social construction, not a biological reality. Despite this fact, part of the racial ideology in the United States includes the idea that racially distinct groups exist and therefore academic performance, among other things, can be measured along racial lines. School-children are categorized by race, however imperfect that measure is, and therefore we have data that distinguish academic performance along the lines of race. Because race has no genetic basis, the achievement gap cannot be due to some presumed genetic inferiority of certain racial groups or the genetic superiority of others; yet all too often, that is how the achievement gap is interpreted.

The black–white achievement gap is not due to the inferior intelligence of blacks but may instead reflect culturally biased tests and educational environments (Kharem 2006; Meier and Wood 2004; Orfield and Kornhaber 2001). Standardized test score data do not tell us that Asian Americans are innately smarter than whites, or that whites are innately smarter than Latinos and African Americans. What the data hint at are more complex issues, including economic, environmental, and social factors, some of which have been discussed in this chapter, that perpetuate de facto segregation and hinder the chances that minority students get to achieve high educational performance.

How does the constant discussion of a racial achievement gap influence teachers' perceptions of students of color? Do they expect less of students of color? Do they expect more of white students? Some theorists suggest that educators are so used to academic failure in minority youth, particularly boys, that it is no longer cause for alarm (Noguera 2008). Arguably, students read the negative attitudes of their teachers and this influences their own estimations of their potential. A large body of research finds that labeling students results in a **self-fulfilling prophecy**, a social-psychological term that refers to the process whereby people believe what is said about them and, in response, act in accordance with such views, which in turn results in a confirmation of the original assumption (e.g., Oakes 1985). The high schools that Jonathan Kozol observed in East St. Louis, for instance, offered an Advanced Home Economics course that provided students with preparation for employment at fast-food restaurants (Kozol 1991). This situation can easily become a self-fulfilling prophecy, with students in these courses likely to live up to such low expectations, assuming that the best future they can expect is a low-wage job in food service.

REFLECT AND CONNECT

Attempts to find scientific support for the intellectual inferiority of people of color have a long history (Jensen 1969). In the South, one of the strategies used to subvert *Brown* and combat desegregation was to publish standardized test scores of black children and compare them to those of white children, which fueled the perception that black children were inferior to white children and thus should not be in the same classroom (Ogbu 2003; Weinberg 1983). To what extent might the achievement gap reinforce racial ideologies of inferiority and superiority in the general population today?

Interpreting the Achievement Gap Responsibly

Despite a history of inequitable education in the United States, an examination of the last forty-plus years of standardized testing data reveals that between the 1970s and 1999, the racial achievement gap narrowed considerably (Caldas and Bankston 2005). This time period marked an era when the federal government was enforcing school integration and federal funding for schools was targeted toward low-income students. Federal education policy, specifically the Elementary and Secondary Education Act, which initially passed in 1965, directed federal funds to schools with disadvantaged students (McGuinn 2006). The late 1970s and 1980s witnessed many improvements in education: a decrease in the achievement gap, a decrease in racial segregation, and a narrowing funding gap between predominantly white and predominantly minority schools. Additionally, there was a dramatic increase in high school graduation rates for African Americans and Latinos since the 1970s, although their graduation rates overall were still lower than white graduation rates. More African Americans and Latinos were attending college than ever before, though their presence in higher education was still not proportional to that of whites. In fact, college attendance rates soared for both whites and blacks over that thirty-year period between the early 1970s and the late 1990s, with 65 percent of white adults and 51 percent of black adults having attended at least some college by 2001. Rates of college attendance increased for Latinos as well, to 32 percent by 2001 (Caldas and Bankston 2005). However, there is a gender disparity in these increasing college-attendance rates. It is primarily African American women and Latinas who account for this positive change. African American and Latino males are still severely underrepresented in higher education. As Table 7.1 shows, in 2013, 69 percent of

	1976–1977	1988–1989	1998–1999	2008–2009	2012–2013	2014–2015
White, non-Hispanic	88.0	84.4	75.6	71.5	69	67
Black/African American	6.4	5.8	8.5	9.8	11	11
Hispanic/Latino	2.0	3.1	5.8	8.1	11	12
Asian American/Pacific Islander	1.5	3.7	6.2	7.0	7	7
American Indian/Alaska Native	0.4	0.4	0.7	0.8	1	1
Nonresident alien	1.7	2.5	3.2	2.9	1	–

TABLE 7.1: Percent of Bachelor's Degrees Conferred by Race/Ethnicity, Selected Years, 1976–2015

SOURCE: National Center for Education Statistics 2014; Data for 2014–2015, National Center for Education Statistics 2014b.

bachelor's degrees were earned by whites, 11 percent by blacks, 11 percent by Latinos, and 7 percent by Asian Americans, showing continuing racial disparities in educational attainment.

During the 1990s, the federal commitment to school integration and to educational parity decreased; as a result, the rate of improving statistics stagnated and in some cases they even reversed. During the 1990s, there was actually a decline in black test scores in reading and science (Caldas and Bankston 2005). Statistics indicate that during eras of increasing investment in minority education, educational performance by minority students improves. And while rates of college attendance have mostly increased for all racial groups, there is still a racial gap in graduation rates. Thus, African Americans, Native Americans, and Latinos are underrepresented among college graduates, while whites and Asian Americans are overrepresented.

When sociologists investigate the achievement gap, they also note the increasingly low test scores of all students in the United States, regardless of race. The focus among educators has been on the fact that Latino and black students score below whites, but it is rarely noted that white students score below Asian American students and that no racial group scores at or above the level of proficient by the time they reach twelfth grade.

Another pattern that standardized test scores reveal is that girls outperform boys across the board, yet the achievement gap between genders is not discussed as often as the gap between the races. The pattern is typically interpreted as one of underperforming male students (Jones and Myhill 2004). This is a key difference between the interpretation of gender disparities and the interpretation of racial disparities in test scores. An underachieving boy is believed to have potential and his poor performance is perceived not as innate intellectual inferiority but as boredom (Jones and Myhill 2004). The data about underperforming students of color is extrapolated very differently, leading to the belief that race is a direct determinant of poor academic performance.

In fact, what standardized test score data appear to tell us is that the American educational system as a whole is in a crisis, not that racial minority children are inferior intellectually. Clearly, if so many students do not score at academic proficiency, there is something wrong; not enough students are learning what educators believe they should be learning. However, if the data on standardized test scores are to be believed, it is misleading to decide that the problem belongs to racial/ethnic minority children rather than educational institutions.

Arguably one of the causes of discrepancies in school performance along racial lines has to do with discrepancies in school funding. Historically there was intentional inequality; it was a standard practice that schools for racial minorities received less funds than white schools did. Critical race theorists argue that, to understand the achievement gap, unequal educational investments must be factored in (Ladson-Billings 2006). Since educational inequality has always existed in this country, it is unrealistic to expect anything other than differential performance. Instead of speaking of an achievement gap, critical race theorists argue that the achievement gap should instead be framed in terms of an **educational debt**; this language better captures the cumulative nature of racial disparities in education and the fact that these disparities are intergenerational (Ladson-Billings 2006).

Despite the fact that the achievement gap is a flawed measure, it is important to take the data seriously. The data tell us that public education, and by extension our society, offers too few opportunities for some. Perhaps the focus on standardized test scores leaves out a crucial piece of the puzzle (Hale 2004).

The School-to-Prison Pipeline

Scholars have become increasingly concerned about the criminalization of youth, which fuels a **school-to-prison pipeline**, where students are pushed out of schools and into the juvenile justice system by zero-tolerance disciplinary policies that mandate harsh punishment even for minor infractions. The effects of zero-tolerance policies snowball: once a child is suspended or expelled from school, they are less likely to complete high school. Those less likely to complete high school are more likely to be arrested and incarcerated (Cole 2019). Some scholars have found evidence of racial bias in disciplining of children: "When poor black or brown children act up, they are seen as 'troublemakers' and sent out into the hall or even suspended; when suburban white children do the same thing, they are called 'precocious,'" (Udoh 2018:105). Black and brown children are more likely to be funneled into the school-to-prison pipeline, contributing to the disproportionate rates of incarceration of black and brown people (see Chapter 10).

Additionally, scholars have recently identified a link between racial differences in school suspension rates and the achievement gap (Gregory, Skiba, and Noguera

IMAGE 7.8: A significant piece of the No Child Left Behind legislation requires high-stakes standardized testing of all students. Research finds that racial/ethnic minority students pay a "diversity penalty" due to the overreliance on high-stakes testing.

2010; Morris and Perry 2016). Approaches to school discipline began to change in the 1990s, becoming increasingly authoritarian and resembling "get tough on crime" rhetoric. Schools employed resource officers (uniformed police officers), security cameras, random searches, and zero-tolerance policies, all resulting in a dramatic increase in school suspensions. African American students are three times as likely as white students to be suspended from school (Gregory, Skiba, and Noguera 2010; Wallace et al. 2008). This pattern is referred to as a **discipline gap**, a disproportionate disciplinary response to behaviors engaged in by students of one race compared to others. Suspension does not appear to improve students' behavior or academic performance and has been shown to increase their anger and apathy (Contenbader and Markson 1998). Ultimately, "school suspensions account for approximately one-fifth of black–white differences in school performance" (Morris and Perry 2016:68).

Race and No Child Left Behind

In 2002, the Bush administration passed a major education reform bill known as No Child Left Behind (NCLB). The objectives of NCLB were to raise student achievement levels, close the achievement gap, improve student test scores, provide parents with more educational choices, and guarantee better-qualified teachers in every classroom. While these goals are certainly laudable, NCLB appears to be having a much more negative effect on schools that serve predominantly minority populations.

Under NCLB, schools that do not show improvements in academic achievement —that fail to make adequate yearly progress (AYP), in the language of the legislation —are penalized through the withholding of funds. Low-income students and students of color tend to be concentrated in schools that have larger class sizes, fewer qualified teachers, and fewer curricular options. Limited resources, such as books, computers, libraries, advanced-placement courses, and extracurricular activities, limit the effectiveness of these schools at meeting their students' needs.

The legislation requires that all students take part in high-stakes standardized testing; thus, schools with a higher percentage of English-language learners and those with more disabled learners are less likely to make AYP. This results in what some researchers refer to as the **diversity penalty**, in which schools serving the neediest students lose funds and are even less able to meet the needs of their students (Darling-Hammond 2007). This high-stakes testing results in increasing dropout and push-out rates for students of color, reducing their access to public education (Sunderman and Kim 2004). Some schools are boosting test scores by keeping certain students out of testing through questionable suspensions. Tens of thousands of students disappear from school during testing periods; the disappeared are overwhelmingly students of color (Dobbs 2003).

It was clear by 2010 that over 38 percent of schools were unlikely to meet AYP by the NCLB target date of 2013–2014. Thus, President Obama offered states waivers that would exempt them from many of NCLB's mandates in exchange for their embracing certain education reforms—specifically, setting standards that would prepare students for the workforce or higher education and establishing a teacher evaluation system that is linked to student performance on state standardized tests (Klein 2016).

NCLB is another example of whiteness in education despite its rhetoric of color-blindness (Leonardo 2007). NCLB standards are intended to be race neutral but clearly privilege predominantly white schools because these schools start out with advantages over predominantly minority schools. Under this legislation, public schools are evaluated through the standardized testing of schoolchildren as if they are being provided an equal education, despite what we know about current funding disparities, the achievement gap, and historical educational inequalities. When schools composed predominantly of students of color fail under presumably race-neutral criteria, the failure is interpreted as individual or cultural, not as a result of racial inequality: "NCLB gives whiteness the license to declare students of color failures under a presumed-to-be fair system" (Leonardo 2007:269).

Racial Issues in Higher Education

While most of this chapter has focused on K–12 educational institutions, there are a couple key issues currently facing higher education that we close the chapter with.

The first are the ongoing attacks on the use of affirmative action in higher education admissions and the second pertains to how racism proliferates on college campuses, despite their increasing diversity.

In late 2018, arguments in a lawsuit against Harvard University were heard in federal court. The case, brought by a conservative group known as Students for Fair Admissions that opposes race-based admissions policies, accuses Harvard of setting a quota on Asian American students admitted and says that Harvard holds Asian American students to a higher standard than applicants of other races (Hartocollis 2018). While most challenges to affirmative action have argued that whites are disadvantaged by affirmative action policies, this lawsuit argues that it is Asian American students who are being disadvantaged. Critics have accused Students for Fair Admissions of exploiting Asian American students in this politically motivated lawsuit.

Currently, university admissions committees are allowed to consider many factors, including race, in evaluating applicants for admission, and the Supreme Court has consistently recognized the value of diversity to the learning experiences of students. Historically, many whites have viewed affirmative action in college admissions as a form of "reverse racism." Millennials of all races show considerable opposition to that idea (see Figure 7.5).

A second issue pertains to freedom of speech on college campuses. In March 2019, President Trump signed an executive order tying college and university policies governing free speech to federal research funding. This move was a reaction against the presumption that college campuses inhibit free speech, particularly that of right-wing ideologies.

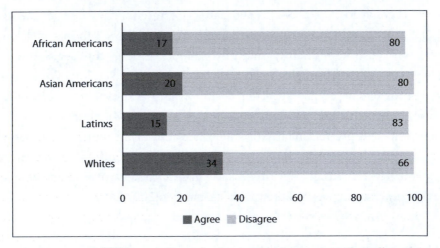

FIGURE 7.5: "White people are having trouble getting into the college they prefer because minorities are taking their spots." As the responses to this question show, Millennials of all races oppose the idea of affirmative action acting as a form of "reverse racism" in higher education admissions (Cohen et al. 2017).

Finally, for many of you reading this text, the college campus you are on is the most racially diverse community you have ever been part of. Most colleges and universities in the country have made some kind of commitment to diversity—from simply recognizing that there is a value to diversity, to increasing the diversity of the student body and the faculty, to requiring a diversity course as part of an institution's general education requirements. However, some research challenges the idea that simply putting people together in a diverse environment will reduce racial prejudice. Sociologist W. Carson Byrd (2017) studied college student interactions on twenty-eight selective colleges and universities, paying particular attention to whether these interactions influenced their racial beliefs. He finds that students live very race- and class-segregated lives on otherwise diverse campuses. This pattern extends beyond elite campuses. For instance, whites on college campuses are the most isolated and the least likely to interact across racial and ethnic lines; whites and Asian American/Pacific Islander students are the most likely to interact with each other on campuses; Latino students have the most integrated social networks; Asian and black students tend to be segregated (Bowman and Park 2014; Byrd 2017; Chang, Astin, and Kim 2004; Espenshade and Radford 2009; Saenz 2010; Stearns, Buchmann, and Bonneau 2000).

REFLECT AND CONNECT

To what extent does this describe your college experiences? Think about your interactions—at social events, organized campus activities, group work in classes, romantic life, with your professors. How many of these cross racial boundaries? How many of them are intraracial? Is this what you expected when you came to college? If your desire were to increase your interactions with people racially different from yourself, how would you go about that?

CHAPTER SUMMARY

While the United States led the world in public education, the historical record shows that not all children have been considered equally worthy of the investment. Racial ideologies of white superiority were a major influence on educational institutions, and children construct identities based at least partially on the messages they get in school about who they are and what they are capable of achieving. Schools are a perfect arena in which to observe how race operates in the current climate of color-blindness.

Historically, African American, Latino, and Asian American children all experienced racism in the form of benign neglect in public schools compared to the experiences of white students: shorter school years, disparate funding, limited opportunities to attend high school, and an exclusive focus on industrial education. Native American students experienced all of these things and more as the United States government sought to eradicate Native cultures through the establishment of boarding schools. Indian children were taken from their families and placed in boarding schools, where they were taught English, Christianity, and "white" ways. Such historical inequities contribute to ongoing educational disparities today.

The resegregation of American schools, tracking, and ongoing funding inequities hint at white resistance to school integration in American society. The achievement gap, while an imperfect measure, suggests ongoing inequities in American schools. Challenges to bilingual education programs and conflicts over ethnic studies programs and the social studies curriculum are all ongoing evidence of whiteness in educational institutions. Despite its race-neutral language, the federal education reform bill No Child Left Behind ends up disproportionately hurting children of color by penalizing "failing" schools, despite the fact that these schools have never had equal inputs. Despite these challenges, there is also evidence that significant progress has been made at including the voices and histories of people of color in curricula and on campuses and the challenges their presence poses to white supremacy.

KEY TERMS AND CONCEPTS

Accommodationism

Achievement gap

Afrocentric education

Bilingual education

Boarding school movement

Community cultural wealth

Counterhistories

Cultural capital

De facto segregation

De jure segregation

Discipline gap

Diversity penalty

Dominant ideology thesis

Education debt

Latino flight

Model minority

Oppositional identities

Racialized tracking

Resocialization

School identities

School-to-prison pipeline

Self-fulfilling prophecy

Social capital

Social reproduction theory

Stigma

Street identities

Tokenism

Total institutions

Tracking

White flight

PERSONAL REFLECTIONS

1. Use sociological theories and understanding to examine your personal educational experiences. Can you identify racial inequality and white privilege at work in your educational experiences? Describe how historical educational inequalities have benefited or disadvantaged you.

2. Exploring your personal educational experiences, what cultural capital, social capital, or community cultural wealth do you have access to and why? Explain the benefits this has provided for you.

CRITICAL THINKING QUESTIONS

1. Explain why schools have become more segregated over the past forty years, despite the Supreme Court ruling in *Brown v. Board of Education* (1954), which declared segregation illegal. What else is going on in American society that has facilitated the resegregation of American schools?

2. Compare and contrast the educational histories of racial/ethnic minority groups. Explain how historical inequalities contribute to current inequalities.

3. Critically consider the achievement gap. If we know race is a social construction, why are we so concerned with racial differences in standardized test scores? Why do we seem unconcerned that, collectively, American schoolchildren of all races perform below proficiency? Why does the gender achievement gap not garner the attention that the racial achievement gap has generated? Should it?

ESSENTIAL READING

Byrd, W. Carson. 2017. *Poison in the Ivy: Race Relations and the Reproduction of Inequality on Elite College Campuses.* New Brunswick, NJ: Rutgers University Press.

Feagin, Joe R., Hernan Vera, and Nikitah Imani. 1996. *The Agony of Education: Black Students at White Colleges and Universities.* New York and London: Routledge.

Flores-Gonzalez, Nilda. 2002. *School Kids/Street Kids: Identity Development in Latino Students.* New York: Teachers College Press.

Lee, Stacey J. 2009. *Unraveling the Model Minority Stereotype: Listening to Asian American Youth*, 2nd ed. New York: Teachers College Press.

Lewis, Amanda E. 2003. *Race in the Schoolyard: Negotiating the Color Line in Classrooms and Communities.* New Brunswick, NJ: Rutgers University Press.

Lewis-McCoy, R. L'Heureux. 2014. *Inequality in the Promised Land: Race, Resources, and Suburban Schooling.* Stanford, CA: Stanford University Press.

Trafzer, Clifford, Jean A. Keller, and Lorene Sisquoc. 2006. *Boarding School Blues: Revisiting American Indian Educational Experiences.* Lincoln: University of Nebraska Press.

Tyson, Karolyn. 2011. *Integration Interrupted: Tracking, Black Students, and Acting White After "Brown."* New York: Oxford University Press.

Warren, Mark R. 2018. *Lift Us Up, Don't Push Us Out: Voices from the Front Lines of the Educational Justice Movement.* Boston, MA: Beacon Press.

RECOMMENDED FILMS

Tell Them We Are Rising: The Story of Black Colleges and Universities (2018). Directed by Stanley Nelson and Marco Williams. Independent Lens/PBS documentary. This film explores the previously untold story of the rise, influence, and evolution of historically black colleges and universities.

The Kids We Lose (2019). Lisa Quijano Wolfinger, producer and director. This documentary film explores how school discipline techniques fuel the school-to-prison pipeline. The shift toward misguided, counterproductive, and punitive interventions in how children who face social emotional and behavioral challenges are handled is addressed.

A Class Apart: A Mexican American Civil Rights Story (2009). Directed by Carlos Sandoval and Peter Miller. This film explores the 1954 Texas legal case *Hernandez v. Texas*, which concerns the segregation of Mexican American schoolchildren and which eventually made it to the Supreme Court, where it was argued that Mexican Americans were a "class apart" and did not fit neatly into a legal structure that only addressed "blacks" and "whites."

The Angry Eye (2001). Directed by Jane Elliot. This film is an updated version of Jane Elliot's classic "blue-eyed/brown-eyed" exercise in discrimination. While the original exercise and film used grade-school-age children, this one focuses on white American college students as they experience discriminatory treatment usually reserved for students of color. The film highlights the experiences as well as the students' reactions and Elliot's observations.

Our Spirits Don't Speak English: Indian Boarding School (2008). Directed by Chip Richie. This film explores the true-life stories of Native American children taken from their homes and placed in boarding schools.

RECOMMENDED MULTIMEDIA

Learn more about the 1946 case *Mendez v. Westminster*, in which Mexican Americans won a class-action lawsuit to desegregate their schools in Orange County, California, at the following website: http://lpb.pbslearningmedia.org/resource/osi04.soc.ush.civil.mendez/mendez-v-westminster-desegregating-californias-schools/.

For more information on Native American education, see the website *American Indian/Indigenous Education* at www2.nau.edu/~jar/AIE/index.html. This website offers information on appropriate children's books, organizations, projects, and programs, as well as curriculum material on Native American education. Additionally, it provides links to Native American studies programs across the country as well as a link to Indian experiences at the Carlisle Indian School. The links page is particularly useful: http://jan.ucc.nau.edu/~jar/IndianLinks.html.

To learn more about Asian American history and education, check out the Center for Educational Telecommunications website at www.cetel.org/index.html. This website lists curricular resources for K–12 Asian American education and links to the Association for Asian American Studies and the UCLA Asian American Studies Center, one of the largest teaching, training, and research programs on Asian Americans in the United States.

Check out a discussion of the *Plessy v. Ferguson* and *Brown v. Board of Education* Supreme Court decisions in *Encyclopedia Britannica*: www.britannica.com/event/Brown-v-Board-of-Education-of-Topeka;www.britannica.com/event/Plessy-v-Ferguson.

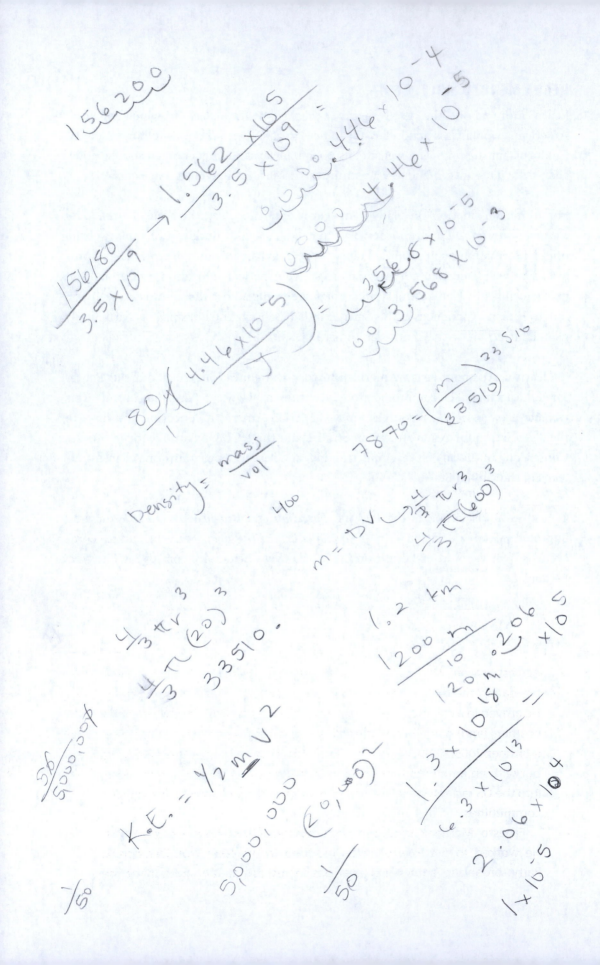

156200

$\dfrac{156/80}{3.5 \times 10^9} \rightarrow \dfrac{1.562 \times 10^5}{3.5 \times 10^9} =$

0.000446×10^{-4}

0.0000446×10^{-5}

$= 0.00003568 \times 10^{-5}$

$0.00003.568 \times 10^{-3}$

$\dfrac{80}{1} \left(\dfrac{4.46 \times 10^{-5}}{1} \right) =$

Density $= \dfrac{mass}{vol}$

400

$7870 = \left(\dfrac{m}{33510} \right) \underset{33510}{}$

$m = DV \quad \dfrac{4}{3} \pi r^3$

$\dfrac{4}{3} \pi (600)^3$

$\dfrac{4}{3} \pi r^3$

$\dfrac{4}{3} \pi (20)^3$

$\dfrac{4}{3} \quad 33510.$

$1.2 \; km$

$\dfrac{1200 \; m}{10}$

$120 \; m$ 0.206

$\times 10^5$

$\dfrac{56}{5000.000}$

$\dfrac{1.3 \times 10^{18}}{6.3 \times 10^{13}} =$

$K.E. = \frac{1}{2} m v^2$

$\dfrac{(20,000)^2}{5000,000}$

$\dfrac{1}{50}$

2.06×10^4

$\dfrac{1}{50}$

1×10^{-5}

Economic Inequality and the Role of the State

CHAPTER LEARNING OUTCOMES

By the end of this chapter, you should be able to:

- Understand the difference between income and wealth as well as the significance of both the racial wage gap and the racial wealth gap
- Describe various manifestations of racial economic inequality
- Understand the role of government policies and programs in the creation and perpetuation of racial wealth disparities
- Examine the racialized narratives surrounding the health-care and reproductive rights debates
- Understand the history and current status of affirmative action

---

Activist Ernesto Martinez migrated to New York from Puerto Rico in 1929, pre-dating the bulk of the Puerto Rican migration by almost two decades. He arrived in a city that, according to his daughter, "never wanted him or his brothers [and] offered them the lowest-paying jobs and the worst housing" (Martinez 2005:290). Puerto Ricans entered the United States as legal citizens but with an ambiguous racial status that did now allow them to fit neatly into the US racial system. Their racial status made them unwelcome in many communities.

Ernesto Martinez became a community activist in the early 1970s. He worked to get Puerto Ricans included in the New York Democratic Party, organized antipoverty agencies in his community, fought for the development of low-income public housing in Puerto Rican neighborhoods, and fought for integrated middle-income housing developments.

He spent forty years in New York City, a place that "never wanted him or his brothers," and for much of that time engaged in activism intended to claim his place in a city he loved. As a result of such activism, "Puerto Ricans made small, incremental gains that have slowly expanded opportunities to join the middle class" (Martinez 2005:303).

Puerto Ricans have a unique relationship with the United States. Since 1917, a specific form of US citizenship was extended to Puerto Ricans. They elect their own governor, are unable to vote in US presidential elections, and do not have a representative in Congress. They are subject to military service and must abide by US federal laws. During some eras Puerto Rican migration was discouraged by the US government, and in other eras it was encouraged. Whatever the era, Puerto Ricans were always considered second-class citizens on the mainland and faced considerable discrimination. The earliest migrants of the post–World War II era initially obtained manufacturing jobs that whites were leaving behind for professional opportunities. But such manufacturing opportunities were short lived. Because the bulk of the mainland Puerto Rican community arrived after the 1950s, when economic restructuring reduced the need for low-skilled laborers, the migrants encountered fewer opportunities for employment. Puerto Rican women found themselves pushed out of the garment industry by a more exploitable labor force, Haitian and Dominican immigrants.

The discrimination they faced resulted in their radicalization. Instead of pursuing assimilation into the white mainstream, Puerto Rican activists turned toward community pride and power. By the late 1960s, they turned to direct action to demand better wages and living conditions, protest their exclusion from public housing projects, and call for better educational facilities and bilingual education.

Puerto Ricans, like many other racial minority groups, faced discrimination that increased their likelihood of being impoverished and inhibited them from acquiring wealth. We tend to think of poverty or wealth rather narrowly, as how much people earn or are able to accumulate over the course of their lifetime. Individual effort and ability may play a role a person's economic position, but they are not the only factors that influence economic status. Nor are poverty and wealth random occurrences; instead, they are patterned along racial and gender lines. To make the case that racial inequality still exists in the United States, one need look no further than the economic sphere. From a sociological perspective, when economic indicators, such as income or wealth, are patterned along racial lines, they become group-level phenomena. In other words, people's racial-group membership influences their economic standing, in this case, privileging whites and putting people of color at a disadvantage. Consider some of the evidence of the link between race and economic status:

- The Institute for Women's Policy Research reports that despite the Lilly Ledbetter Fair Pay Act of 2009, the gender wage gap actually grew between 2015 and 2016, particularly for black women (Rankin 2016).
- As of 2016, the median net worth for African American families was $17,000, for Hispanic families it was $21,000, while the median net worth for white families was $171,000 (Oliver and Shapiro 2019).
- Approximately 35 percent of black households and 31 percent of Latino households had no assets in 2009, while only 15 percent of their white counterparts had similar net worth (Yen 2011).
- The Great Recession of 2008 resulted in a 30 percent drop in net worth across racial groups. However, for black and Hispanic families, their net worth dropped an additional 20 percent between 2010–2013 while white families' net worth was unchanged in these years (Dettling et al. 2017).
- While the overall unemployment rate declined to 5.1 percent in 2015, for African Americans, unemployment increased from 9.1 percent to 9.5 percent (Rankin 2015).
- The poverty rate for African Americans in 2017 was 20 percent; for Hispanics, 16 percent; for Asian Americans, 9 percent; for American Indian/Alaska Natives, 22 percent; while non-Hispanic whites had the lowest poverty rate at 8 percent ("Poverty Rate by Race/Ethnicity" 2017).
- In 2009, prior to the passage of the Affordable Care Act, 12 percent of non-Hispanic whites did not have health insurance through their jobs; for Asian Americans, it was 17.2 percent; for African Americans, 21 percent; and for Hispanics, 32.4 percent (DeNavas-Walt, Proctor, and Smith 2010).

Many factors account for such economic disparities, such as educational inequalities (see Chapter 7). However, this chapter will explore the persistence of institutional racism and privilege in the economic sphere, which contribute to one's residential options (see Chapter 9), access to health-care, educational opportunities, and overall life chances. This chapter will analyze historic and current economic inequalities as well as the role of government policies and practices in contributing to racial/ethnic economic disparity.

SOCIOLOGICAL PERSPECTIVES ON ECONOMIC INEQUALITIES

So as to understand racial inequality in the economic sphere, we begin with an overview of the US economic system, which is a capitalist system, meaning that businesses are for-profit entities, and, thus, business decisions are made with attention to the bottom line. However, capitalism has taken different forms over the years. In the late 1800s, the United States shifted from an agricultural economy, where most people were employed in some kind of agricultural labor, to an industrial economy, where the majority of jobs were in manufacturing. This shift dramatically affected every aspect of people's lives, from what kind of work they did to where they lived. Industrialization is accompanied by **urbanization**, whereby increasing numbers of people live in cities rather than in rural areas.

While US manufacturing led the world in the decades following World War II, not everyone benefited equally from this period of sustained economic growth. The post–World War II era of economic prosperity contributed to the emergence of a solid white middle class, as expanded production translated into increased wages (Cable and Mix 2003). Due to legal racial discrimination, racial minorities did not experience the same economic benefits. Eventually, because of the demands of the civil rights movement, black Americans were able to take advantage of these increasing economic opportunities as well.

By the early 1970s, however, the American economy had stagnated, just as racial minorities had begun to take advantage of these new economic opportunities. The 1970s witnessed a shift from an industrial, manufacturing economy to a service economy, in which the majority of new jobs were service jobs. Industrial jobs of the post–World War II era were good jobs, generally unionized and with high pay and benefits. However, the new service economy was two-tiered. High-end service-sector jobs were generally well rewarded and included such professions as teachers, computer technicians, lawyers, and medical professionals, all of which require higher education. Low-end service-sector jobs, however, tend to be low-wage, low-status work, such as being a hotel maid or in restaurant and retail service, occupations that lack benefits or prospects for career advancement and do not require higher education. Thus, the shift to a service economy punished workers without college degrees and has disproportionately negatively affected racial minority workers.

Defining Income and Wealth

To illustrate the racial disparities in income and wealth, we begin by distinguishing between the two concepts. **Income** refers to the amount of money a person earns in a given period of time for work, Social Security, or some other government transfer payment that person might receive. **Wealth** refers to a person's assets, which include savings, retirement accounts, and the equity in one's home, minus anything the person owes. Wealth can best be thought of as a "cushion," what people have to fall back on if they no longer have an income. Wealth can also be transmitted from one generation to the next, giving a person's children increased opportunities.

Sociologists have documented a significant **racial wage gap**, demonstrating that white workers earn more than nonwhite workers even when controlling for education, skills, and experience (see Figures 8.1, 8.2). In 1967, black men earned 65 percent of what white men earned for full-time, year-round work. By 2003, the racial wage gap had narrowed: black men were earning 78 percent of white male wages

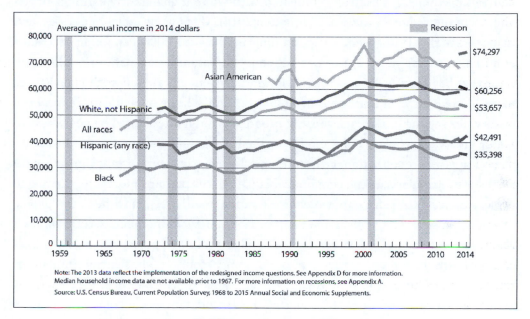

FIGURE 8.1: Real median household income by race and Hispanic origin, 1967–2014.

SOURCE: DeNavas-Walt and Proctor 2015.

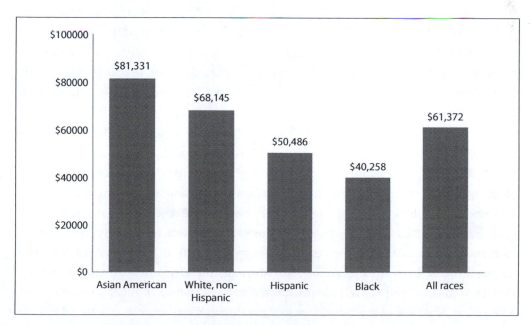

FIGURE 8.2: Median household income by race, 2017.

(Albelda, Drago, and Shulman 2004). After years of steady improvement, the racial wage gap has widened again since 2008 due to the economic crisis: in 2010 blacks earned 62 percent of white income and Latinos earned 68 percent of white income (Dillahunt et al. 2010). As of 2015, black workers earned 75 percent of what white workers earned, with the average hourly wages for black and Hispanic men at $15 and $14 per hour, respectively, compared with white men's hourly earnings of $21 and Asian men's hourly wage of $24 (Patten 2016). What gains racial minorities have made since the 1960s seem to be eroding in the post-2008 economic recession, emphasizing their more precarious economic situation. Such data exemplify progress that has been made since the civil rights movement, as well as the persistence of racial inequality. As illustrated in Figures 8.1 and 8.2, the overall pattern has been toward closing the racial wage gap, but progress is often interrupted by periodic economic crises, as people of color tend to be the hardest hit by economic downturns.

Sociologists argue that analyzing the racial wage gap is important but not sufficient for fully understanding economic inequality. It is perhaps more enlightening to explore the **racial wealth gap**, which is the gap in wealth between whites and people of color (Lui et al. 2006; Oliver and Shapiro 1995, 2019). Remember, wealth, which is also referred to as net worth, refers to a family's economic assets minus their debts and generally includes the equity in one's home, stocks, cash, pension funds, and retirement accounts. Far from steadily decreasing, the racial wealth gap actually increased between 1995 and 2001. During this period, families of color saw their net worth fall by 7 percent, while white families' net worth grew by 37 percent (Lui et al. 2006). While the black-to-white income ratio in 1984 was 77 percent, the wealth ratio was a mere 19 percent (Oliver and Shapiro 1995). In other words, for every dollar of wealth white families had in 1984, black families had only nineteen cents. Between 1983 and 2013, the wealth of the median black household declined by 75 percent and the median Latino household wealth declined by 50 percent, while wealth for the median white household increased 14 percent (Asante-Muhammad et al. 2017).

Since the current economic crisis began in 2008, the wealth gap between minorities has further expanded and is now at its widest level in twenty-five years (Yen 2011). The wealth of white households has grown 84 percent over the last thirty years, which is 1.2 times the rate for Latino households and 3 times the rate for black households. If black wealth accumulation continues at this slow rate, it will take black families 228 years to accumulate the same amount of wealth white families have today (Asante-Muhammed et al. 2016). Increases in income have little effect on the wealth gap. Even African Americans who earn high incomes are unable to accumulate wealth at the same pace as middle-income white families can. For most Americans, the bulk of their wealth is in their home; however, home ownership rates vary considerably by race (see Chapter 9).

The racial wealth gap holds true for Latinos and whites as well. For example, there is considerable variation in home ownership within the Latino community, with Cuban American home ownership rates of 52.2 percent, Mexican American rates of 45.9 percent, and Puerto Rican rates of 37.2 percent (Lui et al. 2006). Still, home ownership for non-Hispanic whites at 71.9 percent in 2015 remains much higher than for all Hispanic groups. The median net worth for Latinos was $11,458 in 2001, while for whites it was $120,989. This dramatic difference can be explained primarily by the disparity of home ownership rates (Lui et al. 2006). By 2016 median wealth per white household was $171,000, while Hispanic median wealth was $17,100 per household (see Figure 8.3).

The economic picture for Asian Americans tends to be bifurcated, with some doing very well economically and many others experiencing desperate poverty. Asian American poverty rates are higher than those for whites, contributing to wealth disparities between the two groups, although exact data on wealth disparities are harder to come by for Asian Americans and Native Americans due to their small population size, as are data on Asian American home ownership rates. The 2008 economic crisis has negatively impacted Asian Americans' median household wealth as well, as it dropped from $168,992 in 2005 to $78,066 in 2009, primarily as a result of the housing downturn (Yen 2011).

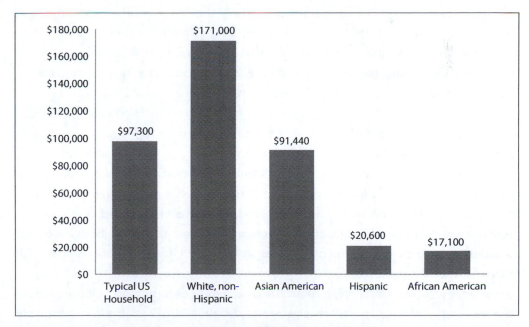

FIGURE 8.3: Median Wealth Per US Household by Race, 2016.

SOURCES: Kochhar and Cilluffo 2017; For Asian American wealth, Chen 2018.

NOTE: * Asian American statistics are from 2013.

Wealth must be understood as cumulative: it is passed down from one generation to the next. Thus, historical barriers to land ownership for some racial minorities have resulted in current wealth discrepancies between them and whites who were able to accumulate wealth through access to land. Legislation in the nineteenth century made citizenship illegal for Chinese and Japanese immigrants. As noncitizens, Asian immigrants were barred from owning land by the 1913 Alien Land Law, which restricted noncitizens from owning land in California (Lui et al. 2006). Other states adopted similar laws, and these laws resulted in considerable loss of land for Japanese and Chinese living in the United States in the early 1900s.

Faced with discriminatory laws and housing segregation, many Chinese, Japanese, and Filipinos turned toward self-employment and their own communities by forming ethnic enclaves. Ethnic enclaves are communities that are generally located in undesirable areas of a city and that provide economic opportunities and residential options for immigrants who otherwise struggle to find jobs and housing (see Chapter 5). They are an adaptive response to racism and discrimination felt by certain immigrant groups. Many Chinese, for instance, congregate in ethnic enclaves, known popularly as Chinatowns, where they often open small retail businesses, such as laundries or restaurants.

Lack of access to land ownership has significantly inhibited Native Americans from accumulating wealth since:

> The wealth of Native Americans, including the land, natural resources, and income generated from such resources, is 'held in trust' for them, meaning that the federal government controls when and how the land is leased, how much money the oil and gas and other resources sell for, and how the money earned is distributed.
>
> (Lui et al. 2006:30)

In essence, the federal government owns Indian assets and decides what to do with them. Specific government policies have played a significant role in Native American land loss as well. The 1862 Homestead Act transferred much of the Great Plains from Indian tribes to white homesteaders. Today, Native Americans face disproportionate poverty rates and high unemployment, and have the worst housing of any racial/ethnic group, all of which are a result of and help perpetuate their lack of wealth (Lui et al. 2006).

The rest of this chapter will explore racial differences in employment opportunities, poverty, and state policies that constrain the abilities of racial/ethnic minorities to accumulate wealth while facilitating white wealth accumulation. We then introduce potential solutions to the racial wealth gap proposed by scholars and, in some cases, being advocated by elected officials.

Scholars argue that, "Blacks cannot close the racial wealth gap by changing their individual behavior—i.e. by assuming more 'personal responsibility' … For the gap to be closed, America must undergo a vast social transformation produced by the adoption of bold national policies, policies that will forge a way forward by addressing, finally, the long-standing consequences of slavery, the Jim Crow years that followed, and ongoing racism and discrimination that exist in our society today" (Darity et al. 2018).

Unemployment

In addition to the racial wage and wealth gaps, the likelihood of being employed varies by race. Unemployment rates for white men and women are much lower than unemployment rates for blacks, Latinos, and Native Americans. As illustrated in Table 8.1, African Americans are twice as likely to be unemployed as non-Hispanic whites; even African American men who have a college education face double the unemployment rate of their white college-educated counterparts (Dillahunt et al. 2010).

When unemployment rates are reported in a social science textbook or on the nightly news, what exactly do these numbers mean? **Unemployment rates** specifically refers to data collected from unemployment offices around the country on people who are actively searching for work and are unable to find it. The limitations of this statistic are twofold: one, it does not include what are referred to as **discouraged workers**, those who would like to be employed but have given up the search and/or no longer report to their local unemployment offices; two, it does not include people who are **underemployed**, those who are working part-time or in temporary jobs, and are no longer part of the official unemployment statistics. However, they are not working in a job that provides sufficient income and economic security for them. Sociologist William Julius Wilson (2010) prefers using data on **joblessness**

Race/Ethnicity	1970	1980	1990	2000	2010	2015	2018
White	4.5	6.3	4.8	3.5	8.7	4.5	3.5
Black	8.2	14.3	10.1	7.6	16.0	8.5	7.6
Hispanic	N/A	10.1	8.2	5.7	12.5	6.5	4.9
Asian American	N/A	N/A	N/A	3.6	7.5	3.7	3.5

TABLE 8.1: Unemployment Rates by Race, Selected Years, 1970–2018.

SOURCES: Bureau of Labor Statistics 2011, 2016; For 2018 stats, Bureau of Labor Statistics 2018.

NOTE: Unemployment rates for whites are consistently lower than unemployment rates for racial/ethnic minorities.

instead of relying on official unemployment rates because it refers not only to those actively looking for work but also to those who have been marginalized from the labor force and are no longer actively looking for work. Looking at joblessness instead of official unemployment rates paints a much starker picture for urban minority males. In 2008, the official unemployment rate for men aged 25 through 54 was 4.1 percent; the jobless rate for this same group was 13.1 percent (Wilson 2010). Unemployment rates vary by race, as Table 8.1 shows.

During the 1970s, the United States went through an economic restructuring referred to as **deindustrialization**, in which manufacturing jobs moved from northern and midwestern cities to the nonunionized South or to Third World locations, to take advantage of cheaper labor. The burden of this economic transition has not been carried equally. African Americans and Latinos were disproportionately affected. For example, research shows that 60 to 70 percent of laid-off workers in 1973 through 1974 were African American, even when they amounted to only 10 to 12 percent of the workforce (Leondar-Wright 2008).

The economic downturn that began in 2008 had a much more detrimental effect on communities of color than it had on white communities, as has been the case historically. Describing this economic crisis as the Great Recession may be accurate in describing its effects on white America. For Americans of color, it is more accurately referred to as a depression, as in December 2009 black unemployment stood at 16.2 percent and for Latinos it was 12.9 percent, while for white America, the unemployment rate was 9 percent (Dillahunt et al. 2010). Minorities suffer more economically in a recession because they are often the first to be laid off, simply because they are more likely to have been the last hired; thus, seniority does not protect them.

What are the effects of job loss, beyond loss of income? Workers who lose their jobs do not quickly and easily find new jobs; instead, they generally experience long stretches of unemployment, which in turn become barriers to reentering the job market (Gibbons and Katz 1991). Displaced workers who do find work rarely find comparable work, suffering on average a 17 percent reduction in earnings (Farber 2005; Ruhm 1991). Income loss obviously inhibits asset building. Finally, job loss contributes to deteriorating mental and physical health and is even linked to increased mortality. Research by Desmond and Gershenson (2016) finds a connection between housing insecurity and job loss.

Racial discrimination in the job market is about more than large-scale economic shifts, however. There is also evidence that employers show preferences for white employees and that African Americans, more than any other racial/ethnic group, face negative employer perceptions about their work ethic and qualifications. Additionally, employers prefer black females over black males (Wilson 1996). Employer hiring can be described as a form of **statistical discrimination** in that individual applicants are disregarded based upon employer assumptions about inner-city black workers in general (Wilson 1996). Other research finds that even when black and white working-class men attend the same vocational high school, black men lack access to job networks that white men take for granted (Royster 2003). Employment opportunities are about more than supply and demand: "job matching is a social process in which actors are linked to jobs, often through personal relations that socially regulate employment information" (McDonald et al. 2016).

Job applicants with African American names, such as Lakisha or Jamal, get fewer callbacks for each résumé they send out, regardless of the skills these applicants bring to the table. Specifically, applicants with white names get a callback for every ten résumés they send out, whereas applicants with African American names need to send about fifteen résumés before getting a callback (Bertrand and Mullainathan 2004).

Racial Realism

Despite research showing clear evidence of racial discrimination in the job market, the belief persists, especially among whites, that racial minority workers actually face advantages in the job market due to their race (affirmative action will be explored later in this chapter). To what extent is this true? Some research finds a racial management strategy called **racial realism** at work in certain industries. There are two aspects to racial realism: racial abilities and racial signaling. An example of **racial abilities** can be found in the low-skilled sector. After Hurricane Katrina and the failure of the levees flooded 80 percent of the city of New Orleans in August 2005, there was considerable controversy over who was employed to rebuild the city. In 2000, New Orleans's Latino community was small—just 3 percent. Yet 50 percent of the reconstruction workforce after Katrina was Latino. Why? Because of employer perceptions of Latino and black workers: Latino workers were viewed more positively, as capable of working very hard for very little money, and black workers were perceived negatively, as lazy and inept. The second aspect of racial realism is **racial signaling**, which is when a business owner hires a minority group member because they believe their customer base will approve and reward them with their loyalty (Skrentny 2014). An example would be when an urban police department seeks to make sure their police force mirrors the racial demographics of the community they patrol.

Despite the fact that racial realism appears to benefit minorities, it actually benefits whites because it limits the mobility of minority workers by imposing a "glass ceiling" related to perceptions of what they are capable of (Skrentny 2014). For instance, a black salesperson is seen as valuable when it comes to reaching an African American customer base, but that same salesperson is not viewed as capable of succeeding in a white-populated market or of managing an interracial sales team, something white salespeople do not have to worry about. The ability of a black news anchor to appeal to white audiences is questioned in ways a white news anchor's appeal is not. This is referred to as the **African American mobility trap**, where black employees are hired to market to minorities and then find themselves stuck in racialized jobs (Skrentny 2014).

White Advantages in the Job Market

Some argue that we need to shift our attention away from the ways racial discrimination is manifest in the job market and toward the ways racial inequality is an outgrowth of favoritism whites show to one another through opportunity hoarding and the use of social capital, despite the fact that white people fail to see these things as advantaging them in any way in the job market (DiTomaso 2013). We introduced the idea of social capital in the previous chapter—it refers to people's social networks. Social networks are invaluable when searching for a job because most jobs are not listed in classified advertisements and personal contacts are the most effective ways to secure employment (Lipsitz 2006). Someone in your social network may tell you of a job opening that has not yet been made public, for instance, or a member of your social network can exercise their influence by providing a positive reference for you, or someone in your social network may actually be doing the hiring for a job. What we rarely talk about, however, is that social capital also involves social solidarity, "because it determines who is likely to help whom" (DiTomaso 2013).

Opportunity hoarding refers to the ways in which one social group restricts access to scarce resources, like job opportunities (Tilly 1998). In Chapter 2 we discussed how white privilege is designed to be unrecognized. Importantly, while excluding people from certain jobs is illegal, practices of inclusion or favoritism are not (DiTomaso 2013). In her interviews with whites about their job opportunities, Nancy DiTomaso (2013) found that they rarely described themselves as getting a job because they were the best person for the job. Instead, most jobs were obtained through the help of family and friends, an example of opportunity hoarding. This is the way white privilege works in the job market: "although the group-based nature of whites' advantages is invisible to them and hidden from their view, whites have to know how to access and use advantages, and they have to teach those skills to their children" (DiTomaso 2013:12).

Race, Poverty, and the Underclass

We have discussed three economic indicators: the racial wage gap, the racial wealth gap, and racial differences in unemployment rates. Poor people are often struggling on all three economic indicators, and race and poverty are interrelated. While most poor Americans are white, racial minorities are disproportionately impoverished in the United States. This section explores racial disparities in poverty rates, the sociological explanations for ongoing poverty, and how well these explanations account for the racial disparities.

REFLECT AND CONNECT

When you think of a typical poor person in the United States, what image comes to mind? A person of color, an elderly person, or a white child? We just learned that racial minorities are disproportionately impoverished. What variables contribute to their likelihood of being poor? How are poverty and employment related, if at all?

Poverty and Race

Racial minorities in the United States are much more likely to be poor than non-Hispanic whites. The poverty threshold, commonly referred to as the **poverty line**, is a designated income threshold, based upon household size. If a household falls below the federal poverty threshold, it is considered to be living in poverty. US poverty thresholds are low, as Table 8.2 shows.

The poverty line is an estimation of the cost of a minimal food budget for different family sizes; this estimated cost is then multiplied by three, under the assumption that a family spends one-third of its budget on food. However, this calculation is problematic today because food costs in the United States are relatively low and housing costs are extremely high, resulting in skewed data.

The US poverty rate in 2014 was 14.8 percent, just under the highest it had been in over 50 years, which was 15 percent in 2011, showing the lingering and significant effects of the economic recession. While the recession was hard on all Americans, it was particularly devastating for Americans of color. Poverty rates for American Indians/Alaska Natives were the highest at 27 percent. Hispanic poverty rates increased slightly, from 23.4 percent in 2011 to 23.6 percent in 2014, as did poverty rates for African Americans, which increased from 25.8 percent in 2011 to

Household Size	Federal Poverty Threshold
1 person	$12,490
2 people	$16,910
3 people	$21,220
4 people	$25,750

T A B L E 8.2: Federal Poverty Threshold by Household Size, 2019
S O U R C E: Paying for Senior Care 2019.

26.2 percent in 2014; while rates for Asian Americans were 12.0 percent in 2014, ranging from 11 to 18 percent depending on the Asian subgroup being considered. The poverty rate for whites not only is lowest, at only 10.1 percent in 2014, but declined from 11.1 percent in 2011. Blacks and Hispanics were still more than twice as likely to be impoverished as whites. If data on poverty rates include the island of Puerto Rico, Latino poverty rates are closer to 33 percent (De La Rosa 2000). Child poverty rates in the United States are even more startling, with one-third or more black and Latino children living in poverty. By 2017, poverty rates were lower, but still racialized, with white rates the lowest at 10.1 percent and African Americans with the highest rates of poverty at 21.2 percent (see Table 8.3).

Asian American families have higher poverty rates than do white families, whether they are foreign born or born in the United States (Takei 2008). The economic status of Asian Americans is bimodal: some do very well while others are extremely disadvantaged. There is considerable variation in poverty among Asian Americans: Koreans, Hmong, Vietnamese, Laotian, and Cambodians have substantially higher poverty rates than whites, while Chinese Americans, Indian Americans, Taiwanese Americans, and Japanese Americans have significantly lower poverty rates than whites (Takei 2008). In 2011, the poverty rate for Asian Americans was nearly 14 percent, which was higher than the poverty rate for whites, but still lower than that of other racial/ethnic groups. When broken down by subgroups, some of the poverty rates among Asian Americans are quite alarming and some of the highest in the country. For instance, in 2015, poverty rates among Americans of Hmong descent were 37.6 percent; among Cambodian Americans, 29.5 percent; and among Laotians, 18.5 percent (Chen 2018).

Explaining Poverty

How can we understand poverty sociologically? Sociologists look to structural explanations for social inequality rather than individualist explanations. If poverty were

Race	Percent
Native American/Alaska Native	19.2
Hispanic	18.3
African American	21.2
Asian American	10.0
White, non-Hispanic	8.7
Overall	12.3

TABLE 8.3: US Poverty Rates by Race, 2017

SOURCES: Duffin 2019b; For Native American poverty rates, www.census.gov/newsroom/facts-for-features/2017/aian-month.html.

random and not patterned along racial lines, individual explanations for poverty, such as lack of ability, motivation, or work ethic, would be sufficient. But because poverty is patterned, structural explanations are necessary for understanding it. The common explanations for poverty are unemployment, the pervasiveness of female-headed single-parent households, low educational attainment, and welfare dependency.

It is not surprising to hear that there is a link between unemployment and poverty. Racial minorities have much higher unemployment rates than do non-Hispanic whites. Thus, it stands to reason that people of color are more likely to be impoverished. This explanation for poverty is most appropriate for understanding urban poverty, particularly in the northeastern and midwestern cities that have been hit hardest by deindustrialization. Deindustrialization hit African Americans and Latinos the hardest because of their greater likelihood of living in cities, a pattern known as urbanization (Morales and Bonilla 1993). Manufacturing jobs relocated from central cities to distant suburbs. During the late twentieth century, as inner cities lost almost a million manufacturing jobs, the suburbs gained millions of manufacturing jobs. Sociologist William Julius Wilson (1987) calls this phenomenon the **spatial mismatch hypothesis**, in which blue-collar manufacturing jobs, which require less education, move far away from the population of people limited to these skills. The job growth that has occurred in inner-city areas has mostly been in occupations requiring higher education. For example, urban areas have become homes to the financial industry.

In the absence of urban manufacturing jobs, low-wage service-sector jobs have emerged to meet the needs of these new highly paid industries, opening up opportunities for work in restaurants, the hospitality industry, and other service businesses. This new demand for low-wage service work is often met by Latinos and new immigrants and contributes to their ongoing impoverishment (Moore and Pinder-hughes 1993). Restaurant workers, for instance, face some of the lowest wages and the poorest working conditions of any industry (Jayaraman 2013) (see Box 8.1 Race in the Workplace: The Workplace Project Benefits Latinos). Thus, unemployment is not a useful explanation for poverty rates among Latinos, because they tend to be impoverished despite being employed. Latinos, particularly Mexican Americans, are fast becoming entrenched as the working poor in the United States (C. Goldberg 1997). The working poor are households with at least one family member in the labor force that still fall below the poverty line. So, while unemployment may be a clear path to poverty, employment does not necessarily provide a path out of poverty. Someone working full time, year round at a job that pays minimum wage, which is all an employer legally has to pay an employee, will still fall below the poverty line. This is why we have seen a movement demanding a fifteen-dollars-per-hour minimum wage and witnessed fast-food workers strike to demand a living wage in cities across the country.

BOX 8.1

Race in the Workplace:
The Workplace Project Benefits Latinos

In 1992, an organization known as the Workplace Project emerged. Its goal was to organize the estimated quarter million Latino immigrants living on Long Island to fight for better working and living conditions. Between 1980 and 1990, the Latino population of Long Island increased by 80 percent; most were employed in the service industry: restaurants, landscaping, and domestic labor. Jennifer Gordon, the founder of the Workplace Project, decided that unionization was not a viable solution because unions had avoided organizing immigrant workers. Also, service-industry personnel change jobs frequently and work multiple jobs at a time, so it was unlikely that a union could meet all of their needs. Gordon decided to build a community-based organization.

One of the ways immigrant workers are routinely exploited is through non-payment of wages, a problem day-laborers are likely to face. The Workplace Project has successfully sued for back wages for over 250 workers, and pushed for and won the strongest wage-enforcement legislation in the country, called the New York Unpaid Wages Prohibition Act. The Workplace Project works to end the exploitation of Latino immigrant workers in Long Island (Sen 2003).

Other researchers argue that poverty is linked to female-headed single-parent households. Indeed, it is true that female-headed households are disproportionately impoverished, a pattern referred to as the **feminization of poverty**. Women earn less than men on average, and a single-parent household is likely to bring in less money overall, so the fact that African Americans and Puerto Ricans have disproportionately high rates of female-headed single-parent households is a likely explanation for their higher poverty rates. However, other data challenge the idea that female-headed households are a good explanation for household poverty. Mexican Americans have the highest levels of marital stability among Latinos and divorce rates that are below the national average, whereas Cuban Americans have higher-than-average divorce rates. These statistics on family structure do not explain Latino poverty very well, as Cuban Americans have lower poverty rates than the national average and Mexican Americans have higher rates. Poor Latino children are more likely to live in two-parent families (Brown et al. 2003).

While blaming single mothers for their poverty is a popular argument, in the face of such conflicting data, is family structure crucial for understanding high poverty rates? Some researchers argue no. Most single mothers were poor before they became single parents (Brown et al. 2003; Luker 1997). Having a child while unmarried may help keep a woman in poverty due to her additional expenses and time demands, but there is no evidence to support the notion that if an already impoverished woman does not have a child, she will be anything other than poor.

Low educational attainment is also an argument used to explain the higher poverty rates among racial/ethnic minorities. As Chapter 7 explores, whites attend better-funded schools and are more likely to graduate from high school and attend college than Latinos, African Americans, and Native Americans. How well does this explain the differential poverty rates? Not well when analyzing changes in poverty rates over the last fifty years. While high school graduation rates for African Americans, Latinos, and Native Americans are below those of whites and Asian Americans, they have risen dramatically over the past forty years, as have minority college-attendance rates. Yet, in that same period, we have witnessed declining wages for all workers, unemployment rates that are at least double those faced by white Americans, and increasing poverty for people of color since the 1980s. From the 1940s to the early 1970s, minority poverty rates declined rather significantly. Deindustrialization in the 1970s and the Reagan administration's economic policies in the 1980s resulted in increasing economic inequality and an eroding middle class, and were particularly hard on racial minority workers (Brown et al. 2003). The 1980s was an era of rising educational attainment for racial minorities and simultaneously a period of rising poverty. In the face of such evidence, poverty can be explained by paying more attention to changes in the economy, particularly those changes encouraged by government policies.

A final explanation offered for poverty is that it is a result of welfare dependency. One has to be poor to qualify for welfare, but welfare benefits are so low that in no state do they pull recipients out of poverty. Social scientists argue that current government policies and programs are insufficient to address poverty (Brown et al. 2003). This has not always been the case. During the 1970s, welfare did help reduce poverty rates by providing enough income to pull recipients above the poverty line, but the cuts and political attacks on welfare that began during the Reagan era have resulted in less-generous benefits, thus making welfare an inadequate solution to the problem of poverty.

The social policies in place are inadequate to address poverty because almost all policies address the nonworking poor even though a large percentage of people falling below the poverty line are working. Thus, they do not qualify for welfare benefits (currently known as Temporary Aid for Needy Families). The only US policy that attempts to help the working poor is the Earned Income Tax Credit, which is a refundable federal income tax credit that only low-to-moderate-income working individuals and families qualify for. Many poor people, especially the working poor, do not benefit from the few support programs for poor people in the United States.

The Underclass

Sociologists began using the term **underclass** to refer to the new face of poverty that emerged in response to deindustrialization. Members of the underclass are not just poor; they are chronically poor and living in areas of concentrated poverty (Wilson 1987). Many people become poor for a short period in their lives (usually less than two years), but the persistence of poverty facing urban minorities is the primary characteristic that sets the underclass apart (Bane and Ellwood 1986; Wilson 1987). Members of the underclass are generally able bodied, young, and black. The detachment of these young people from the labor force becomes self-perpetuating as their chronic unemployment leads to a lack of work experience. Such circumstances hinder access to potential future job opportunities, ultimately reinforcing their economic marginalization.

The underclass emerged in the late 1970s and early 1980s in northeastern and midwestern urban metropolitan areas due to the dramatic economic restructuring (referred to as deindustrialization) that was going on at the time. The existence of an underclass is also a result of the migration of middle-class and working-class blacks away from urban areas after the victories of the civil rights movement. What were once class-integrated communities became concentrations of impoverished people in black communities. Entire communities are now poor, with most of their residents isolated from mainstream institutions and behaviors, such as going to work every day (Wilson 1996).

The Black Middle Class

Despite the obstacles African Americans and other minorities have faced at educational institutions and in the economic sphere, many have managed to achieve economic success. One of the greatest accomplishments of the civil rights movement is the presence of a burgeoning black middle class in the United States. A black middle class first emerged during Reconstruction. They soon became targets for racial violence and literally disappeared due to the southern white backlash following Reconstruction (Bowser 2007). A second black middle class emerged after 1900, during the violence and terror of the Jim Crow era, despite the fact that signs of black financial success could trigger Klan violence. The black middle class that emerged during this era earned their status in occupations of service to their own communities—primarily, preaching and teaching (Bowser 2007). Such occupations were not threatening to whites because most whites had no interest in serving the black community in these ways. After World War II, a third wave of the black middle class took hold as a result of black access to manufacturing jobs. Unfortunately, these kinds of opportunities did not last long for black America. The current black middle class is primarily a result of the gains of the civil rights movement: affirmative action legislation, school desegregation, and the Civil Rights Act (Bowser 2007). The black middle class has always found itself in a more economically precarious position than has the white middle class, and today's black middle class is no exception, particularly in the face of attacks on affirmative action and a poor economy.

For some, the burgeoning of the black middle class since the civil rights movement is evidence of the demise of racial inequality. Instead, it needs to be understood as progress. African Americans, and all racial minority groups, are still disproportionately impoverished. Even when one compares the black middle class to the white middle class, we do not see true equality. Members of the black middle class experience residential segregation similar to that faced by poor black people, which restricts not only their opportunities for housing but also their employment and educational opportunities. They are also more economically precarious than the white middle class for two reasons: they tend to be concentrated in lower-middle-class occupations, such as sales and clerical jobs, and they tend to have less wealth (Pattillo-McCoy 1999). Even in educational institutions, black middle-class children do not perform as well as white and Asian children on standardized tests and have lower levels of academic achievement. Finally, the black middle class is still vulnerable to racial discrimination in all of its manifestations (Bowser 2007). For instance, poverty and low wages are more pervasive for uneducated black workers than for uneducated white workers. In addition, the unemployment rate for blacks is substantially higher than it is for white workers, regardless of age, education, occupation, or industry (Brown et al. 2003). Black middle-class neighborhoods struggle with issues that white middle-class neighborhoods have more of a buffer from: proximity to poverty, higher crime rates, poorer schools, and fewer amenities (Pattillo-McCoy 1999).

RACE AND SOCIAL POLICY

Social policies refer to government policies and programs designed to help citizens meet their needs: policies and programs that are intended to provide for some basic level of security for people. Whose needs are more likely to get met and why? Think about who is more likely to be protected from natural and unnatural disasters. We would like to believe that government support is applied equally to those who need it, but minorities in general, and poor communities of color in particular, are at greater risk (Brown 2013; Henricks 2015; Silverman 2016). They are more likely to be underserved in the event of an emergency, as images of New Orleans after Hurricane Katrina and Puerto Rico after Hurricane Maria reminded us (Bullard and Wright 2009). Even in the recovery and rebuilding of New Orleans after Katrina, researchers find evidence of racialization, specifically in the Road Home program, the largest housing recovery program in US history (Gotham 2014). Other research finds that during the Great Recession and its associated housing market crash, which began in 2008, median household income declined 28 percent between 2005 and 2009, with racial wealth disparities doubling and sometimes tripling during that same time period (Henricks 2015; Kochhar, Fry, and Taylor 2011).

Race is intimately connected to social policies. For instance, as deindustrialization and suburbanization changed the racial demographics of cities, support for urban programs decreased significantly (Wilson 1996). In addition, support for social programs, such as welfare, are influenced by race—more specifically, by racial group loyalty. In short, if members of one's own racial group are perceived as benefiting from a particular social program, one is more likely to support the program (Luttmer 2001). Research finds that whites are the least supportive of policies, such as affirmative action, that African Americans strongly support. Latinos and Asian Americans offer more moderate support of affirmative action policies, which is somewhat surprising because they are beneficiaries of such programs (Lopez and Pantoja 2004). Sociologists use the term **racial apathy** to describe the ways racial prejudice manifests itself among whites in the post–civil rights era (Forman 2004). *Racial apathy* refers to a lack of feeling or an indifference toward racial/ethnic inequality and an unwillingness to acknowledge or address racial/ethnic inequality. Racial apathy is on the rise and has important political consequences because whites object to programs designed to address these inequalities (Forman and Lewis 2006). Sociologists also explore a similar idea, that of racial resentment, introduced in Chapter 2, to capture the attitude held by many whites that people of color are undeserving of government benefits.

Politicians who support certain social programs go out of their way to promote them as race neutral. The reverse is also true; race is often used as a way to generate opposition to policies and programs. In fact, one of the ways white privilege operates is by negatively stigmatizing some programs, such as welfare, or by associating them with racial/ethnic minorities. At the same time, social programs that disproportionately benefit whites are perceived as race neutral. An example of the ways race influences our perceptions of social policies is the stigma associated with affirmative action. While the policy has benefited white women more than any other group, the perception exists that it is a policy designed to provide racial minorities special advantages in the labor force and college admissions, which has resulted in hostility toward the policy. The GI Bill, a package of programs disproportionately benefiting white servicepeople in the post–World War II era, has not been stigmatized in such a way (see below).

Sociologists Oliver and Shapiro (1995) use the term *racialization of the state* to explain how state policies have interfered with the ability of black Americans to accumulate wealth, from the beginning of slavery throughout American history, while simultaneously supporting white wealth accumulation (see Chapter 4). Although their research focuses on blacks and whites, their concept also applies to

BOX 8.2

Racial Justice Activism:
Operation HOPE: From Civil Rights to Silver Rights

Operation HOPE is a nonprofit organization that emerged in Los Angeles in 1992, following the Los Angeles riots, as a way to provide financial education and advice to poor urban minorities and to offer them a "hand-up, not a hand-out," in rebuilding their community (*Economist* 2008). John Bryant, the founder of Operation HOPE, argues that financial literacy is the way to help people help themselves get out of poverty, and he considers it to be the civil rights issue of the twenty-first century, calling it a "silver rights movement" (*Economist* 2008). Operation HOPE believes that "many people in low-wealth communities have big dreams, but no way to put them into action. Those in underserved neighborhoods often have difficulty getting start-up funding for businesses due in part to poor credit, lack of capital, and limited access to bank services. The Operation HOPE Small Business Empowerment Program is designed for aspiring entrepreneurs in low-wealth neighborhoods" (Operation HOPE 2016).

Since the mortgage meltdown of 2008, there has been a push to address widespread financial illiteracy. President George W. Bush established the President's Council on Financial Literacy in response to the mortgage crisis (McGinn and Ehrenfeld 2008). Certainly greed and financial misrepresentation surrounding subprime mortgage loans account for a large part of this crisis; however, if people were financially savvy, they could better avoid being trapped in subprime mortgages. Racial/ethnic minorities are disproportionately victims of subprime lending and thus overrepresented among home foreclosures. While financial illiteracy crosses all racial, class, and educational boundaries, poor people are the most vulnerable during times of crisis because, as this chapter explores, they lack wealth, a financial cushion that can absorb their mistakes (*Economist* 2008).

other racial minorities. For the 240 years of legal slavery, whites in America were legally allowed to appropriate black labor. Government support of slavery qualifies as a particularly blatant example of the racialization of the state, but there are many more subtle instances to consider. In this section, we will explore the evolving relationship between race and social policy, starting with mutual aid societies, which pre-date the emergence of the welfare state; New Deal legislation (such programs as Social Security, the Federal Housing Administration [FHA], and unemployment insurance); and the GI Bill, a program offering government benefits for servicemen and women. Finally, we explore policies that generate intense popular resistance, at least partially due to the perception of them as racial policies: health-care policy, reproductive rights, and affirmative action.

Mutual Aid Societies

One of the dominant themes associated with the American identity is that of "rugged individualism." It portrays Americans as individuals who "pull themselves up by their bootstraps," making it on their own without government handouts. That image is more fiction than reality, however. Historical records reveal that people did in fact join together to create formal organizations, referred to as **mutual aid societies** or benevolent societies, that provided aid to their members and served as safety nets during times when life circumstances overwhelmed members' individual capabilities to provide for themselves or their families. Historians argue that during the late nineteenth and early twentieth centuries, prior to the establishment of the social welfare state, most Americans joined fraternal and mutual aid societies to gain access to basic welfare benefits (Beito 2000).

Marginalized racial/ethnic minority groups and new immigrants to the United States established such organizations for cultural support as well as for economic security, because they could be counted on to provide money when a family was faced with illness or funeral expenses. Examples of such mutual aid societies are the Ancient Order of Hibernians, the Odd Fellows, the Knights of Pythias, and the Zulu Social Aid and Pleasure Club. Most Americans belonged to these kinds of organizations during the late nineteenth century (Beito 2000). However, mutual aid societies were essential for Americans of color and many immigrants, even after the Depression. Minority groups were routinely denied access to many of the government benefits associated with the New Deal that white Americans relied on. Due to discrimination, African American benevolent societies provided the first form of insurance available to members. White hospitals did not have to admit blacks, so as a response to the limited health-care available, many black fraternal organizations built hospitals for blacks throughout the South (Beito 2000). Italian, Polish, Jewish, and Eastern European immigrants formed their own fraternal societies (a type of mutual aid society), as did Chinese and Japanese Americans. Some mutual aid societies, particularly those within Chinese American communities, still exist today, providing economic and social support for immigrants.

The Emergence of the Welfare State

As the Great Depression lingered into the mid to late 1930s, thousands of people dropped their membership to fraternal societies due to an inability to pay even the modest yearly dues (Beito 2000). People began demanding help from the federal government (Piven and Cloward 1979). During President Franklin Delano Roosevelt's four terms in office, he introduced legislation designed to provide relief from the Depression as well as to stimulate recovery. This collection of social programs, known as the New Deal, is the foundation of the American welfare state, providing old-age insurance known as Social Security, unemployment insurance, and Aid to Families with Dependent Children. A **welfare state** refers to "a collection of programs designed to assure economic security to all citizens by guaranteeing the fundamental necessities of life: food, shelter, medical care, protection in childhood, and support in old age" (Katz 2001:9). While common American ideology decries government handouts, social scientists argue that millions of mainstream Americans have happily accepted and supported certain government-provided benefits, such as Social Security (Skocpol 1995). Which social programs generate the support of mainstream American citizens is one of the questions we will look at in this section.

New Deal Policies

Sociologists argue that the welfare state in the United States has been racialized from its inception (Brown 2013; Katznelson 2005; Quadagno 1994; Silverman 2016). For instance, to secure passage of President Roosevelt's New Deal legislation, racial inequality was woven into the policies and programs, thus allowing racial inequality to persist. New Deal policies were designed to protect workers through the establishment of Social Security and unemployment insurance. However, to appease southern Democrats and secure their necessary support of the legislation, agricultural workers and domestic laborers were excluded from these programs. Employers of farmers or domestic workers did not pay into Social Security for their employees; thus, these employees were not able to collect Social Security when they reached the age of eligibility. During this era, the majority of black men were agricultural laborers and the primary form of employment for black women was domestic labor. Sociologists argue that these omissions were intentional, and, as such, excluded three-fifths of black workers from the "universal coverage" of Social Security (Quadagno 1994). Latino workers were also disproportionately affected by these omissions, as they, too, were overrepresented in the agricultural and domestic labor force (Lui 2008).

Another significant piece of legislation that passed during the Roosevelt administration was the National Labor Relations Act, referred to as the Wagner Act of 1935, which granted workers the right to organize unions and the right to collective bargaining. While this provided many unskilled workers with leverage against employer abuses, most labor unions, including the nation's largest union, the American Federation of Labor (AFL), were racially segregated. As the racial exclusion practiced by most labor unions was legal, most African American workers lacked the new protections offered by the Wagner Act. Although African American workers formed their own labor unions, most notably the Brotherhood of Sleeping Car Porters, these unions did not have the same power as white unions because they represented such a small portion of the labor force.

The bulk of social welfare legislation passed under FDR's administration, such as Social Security and union protections, was intended to protect Americans from the ravages of the Great Depression. In practice, most of these measures did not reach Latino or black Americans, despite the fact that blacks experienced significant negative effects and downward social mobility due to the Great Depression (Katznelson 2005).

GI Bill

In the immediate post–World War II era, Americans felt anxious about the hundreds of thousands of veterans returning daily to the workforce. The fear of lapsing into another economic depression without the continued economic boost of the war economy led to the passage of one of the most significant social programs of the twentieth century, the Servicemen's Readjustment Act of 1944, popularly known as the GI Bill. Described by many as "the best investment the US government has ever made" (JBHE Foundation 2003), this legislation provided returning GIs with access to higher education through tuition funding and stipends, low-interest home and business loans, job training and placement, disability payments, and unemployment insurance. This piece of legislation had a profound effect on American society:

> Its educational benefits helped 2.2 million World War II veterans attend college. It helped pay for the training of 450,000 engineers; 180,000 doctors, dentists, and nurses; 360,000 school teachers; 150,000 scientists; 243,000 accountants; 107,000 lawyers; and 36,000 clergy. … Its housing benefits helped 12 million Americans buy a house, farm, or business.
>
> (Winn 2002:179)

During this era, attending college was not the middle-class norm it is today. Researchers estimate that only 7 percent of enlisted men planned to attend college at the close of World War II. This changed dramatically with the availability of the GI Bill (Brown 1946).

The GI Bill is often described as America's first piece of "color-blind social legislation" (Bennett 1996), but it has actually supported racial inequality and contributed to widening the racial wealth gap in postwar American society (Humes 2006; Katznelson 2005). Passage of the GI Bill, like passage of the New Deal policies of the previous decade, required the support of southern Democrats. Mississippi representative John Rankin marshaled his fellow southern Democrats to only allow its passage if the administration of benefits would be at the state level, thus limiting federal oversight of racist state practices. This strategy allowed local administrators to maintain their systems of racial inequality. They discouraged black veterans from attempting to obtain their rightful benefits and sometimes blatantly denied them access. Many black veterans were even denied access to information about their benefits, particularly in the Deep South. Such barriers inhibited black veterans from taking advantage of these new benefits.

WITNESS

"Counselors didn't merely discourage black veterans. They just said no. No to home loans. No to job placement, except for the most menial positions. And no to college, except for historically black colleges" (Humes 2006:95).

Nevertheless, the GI Bill had positive effects on African Americans, as it contributed to an overall increase in education levels in the black community. However, these educational advances lagged behind those of white veterans who took advantage of the GI Bill. The South was still segregated at the close of the war, and thus African American veterans, the bulk of whom were southerners, could only attend historically black colleges and universities (HBCUs), which were not able to absorb the demand. While the enrollments at HBCUs doubled between 1940 and 1950, over

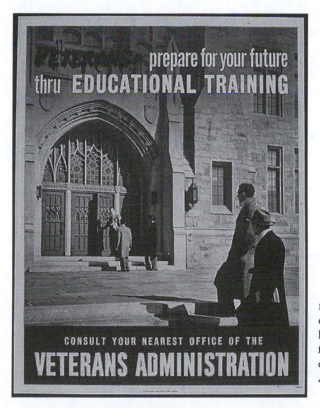

IMAGE 8.1: While the GI Bill is often described as colorblind legislation, the vast majority of the benefits provided by this legislation were denied to otherwise qualified African Americans.

twenty thousand black veterans were turned away in 1946 through 1947 and many more were placed on long waiting lists (Olson 1974). Public universities that exclusively admitted whites also witnessed an explosion in enrollments, but they were supported with increased state funds to meet these demands. While northern universities were not as rigidly segregated as those in the South, many private northern schools did not admit blacks, and at those public universities that did, out-of-state tuition exceeded the benefit levels provided by the GI Bill, thus prohibiting blacks from taking advantage of such opportunities (Humes 2006).

Black veterans who found themselves shut out of a college education often used their funds for vocational training. Even within vocational training programs, blacks were steered toward nonskilled service positions (Pullman porters, for example, as discussed in Chapter 3), while whites were trained for semiskilled jobs. In sum, the GI Bill provided educational opportunities for black and white veterans; they just weren't equivalent opportunities. For whites, the GI Bill opened the door to middle-class, professional occupations. For the majority of blacks, it provided occupational skills that created some economic security, but the opportunities were not nearly as lucrative as those whites enjoyed.

White Ethnics and the GI Bill

For many immigrants and white ethnic veterans, the GI Bill was a fast track to the American Dream. As discussed in Chapter 2, sociologist Karen Brodkin (2008) argues that the GI Bill actually helped Jewish Americans "become white." Prior to the war, anti-Semitism flourished in the United States, particularly in higher education. As Jewish immigrants made up increasing numbers of college enrollments in the early twenty-first century, Protestant elites began to complain about their presence. Leaders of elite American institutions, such as Harvard University, spoke openly of fears of their institutions' being "overrun by Jews." In response, they established widely adopted requirements, such as chapel attendance or the inclusion of a photo with each student's application, or gave preference to children of alumni, now known as legacy enrollments—all ways to limit Jewish enrollment (Brodkin 2008; Karabel 2005). These kinds of restrictions during the early twentieth century resulted in drops in the numbers of Jewish students in law, dental, and medical schools and, thus, restricted Jewish access to many middle-class professions. Such practices were eliminated in the post–World War II era, as American anti-Semitism declined. The restrictions a later generation of African Americans faced due to their limited access to the GI Bill did very much the same thing: it limited their access to middle-class professions.

The GI Bill paved the way for Jews and other white ethnics to enter the white, middle-class mainstream, for many working-class whites to become middle class, and for a small amount of economic security for African Americans who were able to take advantage of the aspects of the GI Bill that were available to them. The significance of the GI Bill was profound. The US government invested more than $95 billion in the GI Bill, which disproportionately went to whites (Desmond and Emirbayer 2010). This led sociologist Ira Katznelson (2005) to describe this period of time as "when affirmative action was white." Whites who previously did not have access to higher education were able to obtain their education and white home ownership increased dramatically, all at least partially due to investments from the federal government (see Chapter 9).

Health-Care

One social program that most citizens of the wealthy, industrialized world can count on is access to health-care. However, the United States is the only wealthy, industrialized nation in the world that does not offer health-care to its citizens as a right. There have been numerous attempts to enact national health insurance over the past century, from FDR through President Barack Obama. In 2010, the latter managed to get through Congress a health-care reform bill, the Affordable Care Act, that provides most citizens access to affordable health insurance. The former, President Franklin D. Roosevelt, intended to include national health insurance in his New Deal policy package but dropped it in fear of opposition from southern Democrats, whose votes he desperately needed to get anything done. For two-thirds of a century, southern Democrats blocked any legislation that would involve the federal

IMAGE 8.2: During the health-care debates of 2010, opposition to healthcare reform proposed by the Obama administration was rampant.

government in local health service delivery. They feared a national health-care system would interfere with local racial practices in the South, such as segregated hospitals and denial of staff privileges to black physicians (Quadagno 2005). Such racialized opposition remained in place during the health-care debates of 2010, yet health-care reform passed primarily because the skyrocketing costs of health-care associated with the private health-care system had become untenable.

The racial politics of the South surely influenced the health-care debate in the first half of the twentieth century, but it is less clear how race has influenced policy debates since the civil rights movement (Quadagno 2005). While the southern strategy of **race-baiting**, using racially derisive language in order to influence the actions or attitudes of a group of people, was blatant prior to the civil rights movement, strategies from the 1970s on have tended to be more subtle. During the health-care reform debates of 2010, race was rarely mentioned. However, it did surface in blatant fashion in an ad widely circulated on the internet and shown in limited television markets. The ad featured what appeared to be ordinary Americans, of all races, claiming they were viewed as racist for merely opposing health-care reform. The ad featured one person after another calmly shrugging their shoulders as they claimed, "I guess that makes me a racist." While the ad is certainly open to interpretation, it might tell us something about some of the resistance to health-care reform.

Many health-care reform opponents expressed their dissatisfaction with the proposed legislation in highly racial ways. For instance, some protesters carried signs protesting health-care reform with the words "Obama's Plan: White Slavery." Another sign generated attention with its portrayal of Obama as an African witch doctor, coupled with the word "Obamacare." Tea Party protesters opposed to health-care reform yelled racial epithets at African American representative John Lewis after the congressional vote on reform (Stein 2010).

Health insurance is a privilege in this country. Prior to the passage of the Affordable Care Act, it was a privilege denied to at least forty-five million Americans because health insurance was tied to employment in the United States, specifically full-time employment at companies that can afford to offer it (Quadagno 2005). Even after health-care reform, an estimated twenty-nine million Americans are without health insurance (Cooper 2016). The number of uninsured Americans continues to decline, with just under twenty-seven million people lacking health insurance coverage in 2016 ("Key Facts …" 2018). As African Americans, Native Americans, and Puerto Ricans face at least double the unemployment rates of whites, they are going to be overrepresented among the uninsured (see Figure 8.4).

As shown in Figure 8.5, when the Affordable Care Act was passed in 2010, health-care reform was supported by the majority of blacks and Latinos but not supported by most whites. As of 2017, support for the Affordable Care Act continues to

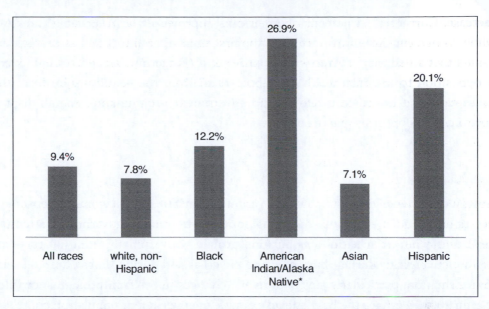

FIGURE 8.4: Percentage of Americans without health insurance coverage, by race and Hispanic origin, 2018.

SOURCES: Rudden 2019; Stats for Native Americans, "Health of American Indian or Alaska Native Population" 2017.

NOTE: * Stats for Native Americans 2017.

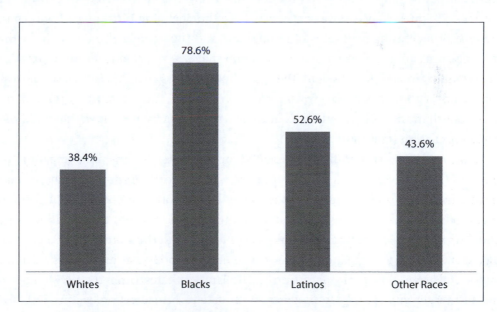

FIGURE 8.5: Support for 2010 health-care reform by race, 2010.

SOURCE: Byrd, Saporta and Martinez 2011.

ently, 54 percent of Americans approve of the Affordable Care Act
nt disapprove, which is the first time since the 2010 health-care law
ajority of Americans approve of it (Fingerhut 2017). To what extent
national health-care about race? Does the hostility stem from the
perception that health-care reform, and government programs in general, disproportionately support people of color?

Reproductive Rights

Governments have long tried, through various means, to control women's reproductive rights through programs known as **population control**, government attempts
to alter the rate of a nation's population growth. Government attention turns to
reproductive policy during times of economic crisis and during times of rapid social
transformation, particularly eras of dramatic changes in the family and gender roles
(Caron 2008). Perhaps the best-known example of government population control is
China's one-child policy, which involved the implementation of strict birth-control
programs in 1979 and heavy financial penalties for noncompliance (Croll 2000).

While such attempts to limit population growth through government policies and
programs are better known, population decline has historically inspired stronger
efforts at controlling women's reproduction. During the late nineteenth century in
the United States, concern was expressed over the declining birthrates of whites in
the face of increasing birthrates of immigrants and the perceived increase in birthrates of racial minority groups, a phenomenon that was referred to rather dramatically by many, including President Theodore Roosevelt, as *race suicide*. Despite great
concern over the danger of a growing black population, the actual black population
in the South in the early twentieth century increased much more slowly than did the
white population (Gordon 1990).

While birth control is a "fundamental prerequisite for the emancipation of
women" (Davis 1983:202), its advocates have also put forth arguments that are blatantly racist. For instance, early proponents of birth control often explicitly claimed
that black and immigrant women had a moral obligation to limit their family size.
Thus, all women are not treated equally when it comes to the state and reproductive
rights. In fact, state regulation of black women's reproduction has always been an
important aspect of racial oppression in the United States (Roberts 1997). Today,
the term *reproductive rights* is generally equated with abortion rights, but, for
women of color, reproductive rights are as much about the right to have their children as they are about the right to terminate a pregnancy. Women of color have
been uniquely sexually exploited throughout American history (see Chapter 4).
Whereas black women were forced to breed and not allowed to mother their children during slavery, since the early twentieth century they have been accused of

reckless fertility (Roberts 1997). White feminists were fighting for the right to safe and legal birth control at the same time that women of color were more likely to be coerced into using it. In other words, "what was demanded as a 'right' for the privileged came to be interpreted as a 'duty' for the poor" (Davis 1983:210). Women of color have embraced the term **reproductive justice** instead of reproductive rights. According to Sister Song—Women of Color Reproductive Justice Collective, reproductive justice is defined as the "human right to maintain personal bodily autonomy, have children, not have children, and parent the children we have in safe and sustainable communities," ("What is …" n.d.).

During the early decades of the twentieth century, a eugenics movement emerged in the United States, composed of scientists, social reformers, and even politicians (see Chapter 2). Eugenics is an extension of scientific racism and refers to programs that promote genetic purity in a society, that work to increase certain desirable characteristics in a society and decrease less-desirable traits. The goals of the eugenics movement coincided with the early birth-control movement, as ideologies surrounding who had a right to procreate took hold. White upper-class women were considered fit to procreate, while socially undesirable women were prevented from procreating.

Forced sterilizations were one of the tactics used to achieve the goals of the eugenics movement. By 1932, at least twenty-six states had passed compulsory sterilization laws that defined thousands of people as "unfit." Initially, the definition of "unfit" was that a person was mentally incapacitated in some way. However, it did not take long

IMAGE 8.3: Poster for a Stop Forced Sterilization rally in 1977. Note that the women shown in the image are all women of color, as they have been the ones disproportionately targeted by sterilization campaigns.

for racial minority women to be classified in this way. By 1970, an estimated 20 percent of all married black women were permanently sterilized, with black women the targets of 43 percent of federally subsidized sterilizations (Davis 1983).

Eugenics ideologies extended beyond the United States and had a global influence. They proliferated throughout Europe, North and South America, the Soviet Union, China, India, South Africa, and Australia (Weindling 1999). Between 1935 and 1976, the Swedish government forcibly sterilized some sixty thousand women. Involuntary sterilization was portrayed as progressive when it began in the 1920s because it was seen as saving people from institutionalization, but it was really part of a program to rid Sweden of "inferior" racial types and promote Aryan features (Cohen 2001; Weindling 1999).

Investigations into surgical sterilizations in the US found that women were often coerced into signing consent forms. They were pressured by hospital staff, sometimes while they were in labor, and often they were not told that the sterilization procedures were irreversible. The consent forms were described as a farce by investigators (Caron 2008). In the South, teaching hospitals performed what were known as "Mississippi appendectomies"—unnecessary hysterectomies on poor black women—merely as practice for their medical residents (Roberts 1997). Even into the 1990s, health officials targeted racial minority women for long-term birth-control options, such as Depo-Provera and Norplant, that were not yet approved by the FDA and in some cases were found to have cancer-causing properties (Caron 2008; Roberts 1997).

Puerto Rican women also found themselves targeted for sterilization. In the 1930s, Puerto Rico was experiencing a population explosion, which contributed to the country's desperate poverty. Population policies in the form of mass sterilizations became the solution to this problem and are an example of whiteness in international development programs (see Box 8.3 Global Perspectives: Whiteness in International Development Programs). This was the beginning of a long period of targeting Puerto Rican women for population control. By the 1960s, one-third of Puerto Rican women of childbearing age had been sterilized. During the development of the birth control pill, the new contraceptive was first tested on Puerto Rican women and resulted in some fatalities (Caron 2008). By the 1960s, women enjoyed the privileges associated with the sexual revolution made available by the birth control pill, a pill that was originally tested on women of color.

Native American women were another target for forced sterilizations, in this case by the Bureau of Indian Affairs' Indian Health Service. By 1976, an estimated 24 to 42 percent of Indian women of childbearing age were sterilized, many without their knowledge (Davis 1983; Jaimes and Halsey 1992). These actions need to be understood within the history of genocidal actions directed at Native Americans by the federal government, such as the Indian Wars, the forced relocation of tribes to

BOX 8.3

Global Perspectives:
Whiteness in International Development Programs

In the late 1940s and early 1950s, Western nations, led by the United States, began promoting international development projects. At the outset, the goal of international development was laudatory: to end global poverty by bringing Western capital, science, and technology to the rest of the world. The introduction of population policies in Puerto Rico is an example of a development project. Development has since been widely criticized for assuming the universality of Western ideas and values and for equating modernization with Westernization (Escobar 1995).

A more recent critique of development pertains to race; specifically, that most of the people delivering aid are white while most of those receiving aid are dark skinned (Loftsdóttir 2009). What effect does this have on the people in both the donor country and in the country receiving aid? Loftsdóttir (2009:6) argues that "whiteness is created and re[-]created through the discourses and actions of development institutions." In her research in Niger from 1996 to 1998, she found that locals saw development projects as belonging to white people, meaning Europeans or Americans. Thus, development is racialized, viewed as belonging to the dominant group rather than to Africans. Africans who worked for development projects in her area always worked in subordinate roles to white, Western supervisors. Africans failed to see themselves as partners in the development process, contrary to goals of development agencies, but "stressed the importance of making friends with 'white' people so as to receive gifts from them" (Loftsdóttir 2009:7). According to Loftsdóttir, Western development workers are not intentionally racializing development; however, it is the result of "the power associated with their whiteness" (2009:7).

reservations, and the Indian boarding school movement, among others. Population policy in the United States has been intimately tied to race as African American, Native American, and Puerto Rican women were disproportionately targeted (Davis 1983). Understanding reproductive rights through a racial lens challenges the dominant white feminist narrative that reproductive rights are all about maintaining the right to terminate a pregnancy.

The fight for reproductive justice for women of color continues today. Infant mortality rates, a statistic that captures the number of babies who die before the first year of life, for black babies is twice the rate for white babies. This disparity is actually wider than in 1850 (Villarosa 2018). Maternal mortality, the death of a woman during childbirth or pregnancy, is also much higher for black and American Indian/Alaska Native women than for white women. As Figure 8.6 shows, maternal

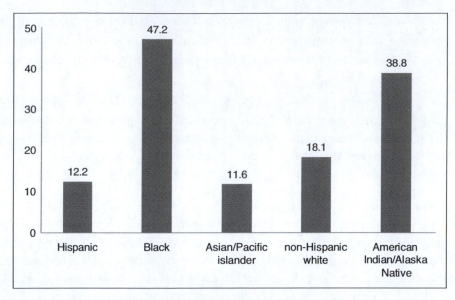

FIGURE 8.6: Maternal Mortality Rates by Race, 2015.

mortality rates by race, with 47.2 black women and 38.8 Native American women dying during pregnancy or childbirth in 2015 compared to 18.1 for whites, 12.2 for Hispanics, and 11.6 for Asian Americans. The infant mortality and maternal mortality rates for black women hold true across class lines as well. Scholars have explored many reasons for this and have recently come to the conclusion that systemic racism is the likely cause. It creates a kind of toxic physiological stress that contributes to hypertension and pre-eclampsia, both of which contribute to infant and maternal mortality (Villarosa 2018).

Affirmative Action

Affirmative action is perhaps the most misunderstood social policy in existence today. On the surface, it challenges the American ideology of meritocracy, the belief that opportunities and rewards are distributed according to effort and ability. Many people, however, have no understanding of what affirmative action is designed to do and tend to believe any number of myths surrounding it. To really understand what affirmative action is, we need to explore when and why it emerged, the controversies surrounding it, and, finally, its effectiveness.

Affirmative action exists primarily because there is real inequality in the labor force—women and people of color have not had the same opportunities that white men have had—and this policy is intended to address such discrepancies. President Lyndon Johnson introduced the rationale for affirmative action in 1965 at a speech at Howard University with the following words:

> You don't take a person who, for years, has been hobbled by chains and liberate him, bring him to the starting line of a race and then say, 'You are free to compete with all the others' and still justly believe you have been completely fair.

Affirmative action is not a single policy but instead a collection of policies that are designed to promote equal employment opportunities for women and racial minorities and to fight institutional racism in the economic sphere. It is designed to keep discrimination from occurring, as opposed to policies that provide avenues to pursue justice after discrimination has taken place (Reskin 1998). In other words, it is intended to be proactive rather than reactive, hence the language "*affirmative* action."

Affirmative action was considered necessary social policy not only because there was ample evidence that women and people of color faced discrimination in the workforce but also because this discrimination was not always intentional. It may be a result of "business as usual" or hiring practices and opportunities for promotion that rely on "custom, habit, self-interest, and people's aversion to risks" (Reskin 1998:6–7). Because white men have been, and still are, most likely to be in management positions and involved in hiring and firing, they inevitably found themselves looking to other white men in their own social networks as potential job prospects. Affirmative action policies required that they go beyond such limited circles.

History of Affirmative Action

President Kennedy was the first to use the term *affirmative action* in 1961, and it was President Lyndon Johnson that issued Executive Order 11246, stating:

> To be eligible for a federal contract, firms had to agree "not to discriminate against any employee or applicant for employment because of race, color, religion, or national origin, and to take affirmative action to ensure that applicants are employed and employees are treated during their employment without regard to race, color, or national origin."
>
> (Reskin 1998:9)

Although Democratic presidents introduced the policies, affirmative action had bipartisan support throughout the 1970s. In fact, Republican president Richard Nixon actually expanded affirmative action to include the establishment of "goals and timetables" for firms with at least $50,000 in federal contracts and at least fifty employees. "Goals and timetables" refers to plans to diversify a company's labor force. For example, in a major law firm, setting up goals and timetables would involve creating written guidelines for the future hiring of partners. This does not mean that an unqualified person has to be hired to fulfill some kind of preexisting quota. Instead, it means the firm could be in violation of affirmative action if it does not hire a qualified minority applicant in favor of a less qualified, or even equally qualified, white male candidate. The law allows for the most qualified person to be hired. It simply no longer allows perfectly qualified minority candidates to be over-looked in favor of a white male candidate.

Myths Surrounding Affirmative Action

Since 1981, affirmative action has been under attack, often due to misconceptions surrounding how it works. Perhaps the most pervasive myth about affirmative action is that it requires employers to establish quotas. In reality, the Office for Federal Con-tract Compliance Programs in the Department of Labor actually prohibits the estab-lishment of quotas. An employer is never required to hire someone less qualified for a position, no matter the job candidate's race or gender. Yet Americans persist in their belief that affirmative action requires employers to hire a certain number of women and people of color, irrespective of their actual qualifications. Only in very rare cases, when a company's hiring and promotion practices are found by federal courts to be discriminatory, can the courts order the company to establish quotas.

A second myth surrounding affirmative action is the belief that white males are now the victims of discrimination due to affirmative action policies, that we are now witnessing "reverse discrimination" against white males (Wise 1991). However, African Americans face double the unemployment rate of whites, and a racial wage gap and a significant racial wealth gap remains. There is no statistical evidence to support the notion of white male workplace discrimination. This myth appears to stem from white privilege. For many whites, affirmative action allows minorities to take "our jobs," although these were not "our" jobs to begin with. It can even be a way to hide white workers' inadequacies. "How sad is it that when white folks suffer some setback [they] are able and willing to turn so quickly to the racist trope of 'some black guy took my job'" (Wise 2005:122).

A third myth that often creates hostility toward affirmative action policies per-tains to the idea that racism is a thing of the past. In that case, why would affirmative action be necessary? Throughout this book, evidence has been introduced that refutes that argument. In fact, racism is very much still part of the fabric of Amer-ican society. Institutional racism in the educational, economic, legal, and political spheres is ongoing, despite the progress that has been made.

REFLECT AND CONNECT

To what extent did you accept some of the myths surrounding affirmative action as true before reading this chapter? Think about where your under-standing of affirmative action comes from: conversation among family members, media coverage, comments from politicians, or employers?

Effects of Affirmative Action

Affirmative action is often portrayed as a race-based policy, and that perception is partly responsible for the general hostility toward it. However, in the language of the original executive order, affirmative action was designed to offset discriminatory practices toward all underrepresented minorities in the labor force. As a package of policies, affirmative action has been more successful at helping some minorities than others. It has succeeded at changing the face of the American labor force by opening doors for women and minorities. White women, for instance, have been its greatest beneficiaries. It has also been more beneficial to middle-class blacks than to impoverished minorities. In the 1970s, African American access to white-collar, professional occupations was due to increases in educational attainment as well as government policies, specifically affirmative action (Brown et al. 2003). Still, some segments of society, such as impoverished blacks and Latinos, have been left in the cold. This is not a policy designed to help the poorest Americans of color.

REFLECT AND CONNECT

What government programs have benefited you or your family? Were these difficult to identify? If so, speculate on the role of the American ideology of individualism in the difficulty you had in identifying these. Ask your parents about the social policies discussed in this chapter (the GI Bill, affirmative action, FHA loans, and so forth) and whether your family has ever benefited from them.

Puerto Rican Debt Crisis

So far in this chapter we have explored government policies and their effects on citizens, particularly in terms of wealth accumulation, employment, and housing opportunities, among others. However, government policies and programs can sometimes have global effects as well, especially in a neocolonial context. *Neocolonialism* refers to the exploitation of impoverished nations by wealthy nations, not through direct political control but instead through economic or cultural influences. Often these relationships are also racialized: the wealthy nations are predominantly white nations while the impoverished nations are populated by people of color. A classic example of neocolonialism is the relationship between the United States and Puerto Rico.

As of 2016, Puerto Rico is facing a $72 billion debt crisis. As a result, schools and hospitals are being forced to close. Puerto Rico's governor, Alejandro Garcia Padilla, and Senator Bernie Sanders called on the US Congress to restructure the debt. In July 2016, Congress passed a bill to help restructure the debt. Part of this deal, though, requires that minimum wage be locked in at \$7.25 per hour for the next five years and allows for the establishment of an outside fiscal board to oversee the Puerto Rican budget. The minimum wage stipulation is likely to keep a significant portion of the population impoverished (Rankin 2016b).

The United States has contributed to Puerto Rico's debt crisis. Like many other poor nations, Puerto Rico was encouraged to take out loans and to direct those funds toward development and modernization projects (for example, in textile manufacturing and pharmaceutical production). Like so many other countries, Puerto Rico then found itself stuck in a cycle of borrowing more money just to stay afloat (Sreenivasan 2015). Puerto Rico wants to declare bankruptcy, but US bankruptcy law does not allow states or territories to declare bankruptcy, as cities and businesses and individuals can (Detroit, for instance, has declared bankruptcy). Thus, Puerto Rico is not in a position to dictate its own economic agenda.

Social Policy Solutions to the Racial Wealth Gap

This kind of racial disparity in wealth accumulation cannot be explained by cultural differences in financial habits, such as savings, investing, or family structure, and increasing educational attainment, and the likelihood of self-employment. The median net worth of a white adult who attended college is 7.2 times more wealth than a black adult who attended college and 3.9 times more wealth than the median Latino adult who attended college. The net worth of a white single parent is 2.2 times that of a black two-parent household and 1.9 times that of a Latino two-parent household (Oliver and Shapiro 2019). Addressing the racial wealth gap is going to take large-scale transformations.

One of the proposed solutions to the racial wealth gap are Baby Bonds, which involves giving every baby born in the US between \$500 and \$50,000 on the day they are born in an attempt to level the playing field for the next generation (Hamilton and Darity 2010; Oliver and Shapiro 2019). This idea has been embraced by New Jersey Senator and Democratic Presidential candidate Corey Booker, who refers to them as "Opportunity accounts." The amount would depend on the family's wealth, but the average middle-class child would receive around \$20,000, which would be available to them when they turn 18 years of age. At this point, they can use the money to pay for college or to buy a home or start a business. This policy holds great potential for closing the racial wealth gap.

A second policy proposal that could address the racial wealth gap is implementing a Universal Basic Income (UBI). This would give every adult American a set amount of monthly income (estimates range from \$600.00 to \$1,200.00 per month). Democratic presidential candidate Andrew Yang (2018) has proposed a UBI to address the impending employment crisis resulting from increasing automation.

CHAPTER SUMMARY

This chapter explores the racial inequities in the economic sphere, how nomic inequalities manifest themselves, and the ways government policies and practices have contributed to economic security for whites and hindered it for racial minorities. The racial wealth gap actually increased just after World War II, when whites, as a group, amassed considerable wealth. Even members of the black middle class, despite the success of the civil rights movement, now have a more precarious economic position than that of the white middle class. They face many of the same problems affecting poor blacks, such as residential segregation, lack of proximity to jobs, poor educational opportunities, and exposure to environmental pollutants.

Such social policies as affirmative action are generally perceived to be racialized policies when, in fact, what this chapter shows is that race has been central to the American welfare state from its inception. We all benefit from government policies and programs through public schools, minimum wage laws, and the old-age protection of Social Security, for instance. However, we all don't benefit equally. The New Deal, the GI Bill, health-care policy, and reproductive policies maintain racial inequality in this country.

Economic transformations, such as deindustrialization, have had a disproportionately negative effect on racial minorities. In the next chapter, we explore racial inequality in housing, including the role of government policies and programs, residential segregation, and environmental racism.

KEY TERMS AND CONCEPTS

Affirmative action	Racial realism
African American mobility trap	Racial signaling
Deindustrialization	Racial wage gap
Discouraged workers	Racial wealth gap
Feminization of poverty	Reproductive justice
Income	Social policies
Joblessness	Spatial mismatch hypothesis
Mutual aid societies	Statistical discrimination
Opportunity hoarding	Underclass
Population control	Underemployed
Poverty line	Unemployment rates
Race-baiting	Urbanization
Racial abilities	Wealth
Racial apathy	Welfare state

PERSONAL REFLECTIONS

1. Interview your parents and your grandparents about their access to key social programs such as the GI Bill, or a government-backed mortgage, or financial aid for higher education. Write a paper, two to three pages, reflecting on your family's current economic status as it relates to race and social policies.
2. To what extent did you enter this class thinking your family had "made it" on their own? Has the material covered in this chapter forced you to rethink that position? If so, why? If not, explain how your family has not been advantaged by government programs (historically or currently).

CRITICAL THINKING QUESTIONS

1. Look for messages in the media that are antiwelfare or antigovernment, or that support the notion of "rugged individualism" (the idea people should "make it" on their own). Critically analyze these in light of what you have learned in this chapter, specifically looking at the role of the government. Why do we cling to these ideologies? To what extent are the messages you find racialized? How do you know they are racialized? Provide evidence to support your answer.
2. How has the economic situation of racial minorities in this country improved since the civil rights movement? What changes since then have resulted in ongoing racial/ethnic economic inequality?
3. Explain the ways racial inequality in the economic and educational spheres are linked. Give evidence that it has become locked in. Does the government have an obligation to address this inequality? Why or why not? Propose two policy solutions that could address racial inequality in the economic sphere.

ESSENTIAL READING

DiTomaso, Nancy. 2013. *The American Non-Dilemma: Racial Inequality Without Racism.* New York: Russell Sage Foundation.

Katznelson, Ira. 2005. *When Affirmative Action Was White: An Untold History of Racial Inequality in Twentieth-Century America.* New York: W. W. Norton and Company.

Quadagno, Jill. 1994. *The Color of Welfare.* New York: Oxford University Press.

Skrentny, John D. 2014. *After Civil Rights: Racial Realism in the New American Workplace.* Princeton, NJ: Princeton University Press.

RECOMMENDED FILMS

Race: The Power of an Illusion, Episode Three: "The House We Live In" (2003). Produced and directed by Llewellyn M. Smith. This documentary goes beyond racism as mere prejudice and instead explores institutionalized racism and how it has created the racial wealth gap. Specifically, it looks at how European ethnic immigrants fared better economically in the post-WWII era due to their access to federal policies and programs that were denied to black Americans.

The Racial Wealth Gap (2018). Part of Netflix's and Vox's *Explained* documentary series, this episode explores the racial wealth gap, from its historical foundations in slavery to today's housing policies.

Unnatural Causes: Is Inequality Making Us Sick? (2008). Created and produced by Larry Adelman and Llewellyn M. Smith. This seven-episode documentary explores how socioeconomic and racial inequality contribute to health inequalities. Unequal health outcomes among racial/ethnic minorities compared to whites, such as the high rates of diabetes among Native Americans, and their possible causes are explored. Culprits range from racism to environmental racism, dangerous employment, poor housing, and the stress of poverty.

Housing

CHAPTER LEARNING OUTCOMES

By the end of this chapter, you should be able to:

- Describe the role of home ownership in the racial wealth gap
- Critically evaluate residential segregation and its origins
- Understand the role of laws, social policies, real estate industry practices, preferences, and the role of social structural sorting processes in creating and maintaining residential segregation
- Describe how the ghetto and the suburbs are intertwined and interconnected in their creation
- Explain environmental racism and the environmental justice movement

I am writing this vignette on August 3, 2019, what would have been my mother's 77th birthday, were she still alive. She was born in 1942, in the middle of World War II. An only child for the first eight and a half years of her life, she and her parents lived in North St. Louis, in a beautiful brick row house. Before she turned 13, the family, including her four-year-old brother, moved to a new suburb in North St. Louis County, taking part in a pattern now known as white flight. She would graduate from Ferguson High School, eventually marry, and have five children and live the rest of her life in Florissant, MO. She and her husband, my father, purchased our modest family home through the help of the GI Bill, since my father was a veteran of the Korean War.

There is nothing exceptional about this story, except that this would be a very different story were my parents not white. My mother's family was able to purchase their suburban home through the relatively new Federal

Housing Administration's government-backed mortgage-loan program at least partially because they were white. The GI Bill was available to my parents not just because my father served his country in Korea, but because he was a *white* GI. He was the child of Irish immigrants and she was the grandchild of a Polish immigrant. Post-WWII social policies helped propel these children and grandchildren of immigrants into the middle class and, of course, contribute to the opportunities I have had in life. Discussions about social policies, the racial wealth gap, housing, and residential segregation may seem abstract, but they are anything but. They are really discussions about opportunities afforded and opportunities lost.

Home ownership in the United States demarcates membership in the middle class and is the embodiment of the American Dream. A sociological analysis of housing involves focusing on more than physical structures. Housing is crucially interconnected with many aspects of people's lives. For instance, where you live often determines your friendship circles, your status, the quality of your schools, your exposure to environmental pollutants, your risk for crime victimization, your access to employment opportunities, among other things. A person's home is often equated to a sanctuary—a "haven from the heartless world." While not all households live up to that motto, the quality of one's housing does contribute to one's health, well-being, and longevity.

When we think of housing, we often think of personal choices—people choose to live where they live based upon their personal preferences—for a rural, urban, or suburban community, for instance. Or, people can opt to buy a home, while others may choose to rent. Some people want a home with a yard while others opt for the low maintenance associated with condominium living. A sociological approach to housing, however, requires that we move beyond a model of personal choice and toward an understanding of the ways structure operates to constrain the options for some people and facilitate those of others. To what extent have people of color in this country been restricted in their housing choices? In what ways have whites benefited from those very restrictions?

In the previous chapter we explored racial inequality in the economic sphere, and its manifestation in the racial wealth gap, the racial income gap, the disproportionate poverty and unemployment rates for people of color, and the role of state policies in facilitating white wealth accumulation and hindering wealth accumulation among racial minorities. This chapter takes up where that chapter left off by exploring the role of home ownership in exacerbating the racial wealth gap, and the government policies and real estate industry practices that contributed to home ownership for generations of whites. New research on social structural sorting processes in perpetuating residential segregation is also introduced. The racialized effects of the 2008 Great Recession, specifically the subprime mortgage crisis, is examined. We then explore racial residential segregation in detail, again focusing on laws, policies, and industry practices that created segregation, the consequences of segregation, and proposed policy solutions to address the problem. We also investigate what sociologist Matthew Desmond (2016) refers to as a new sociology of displacement, which explores racial patterns associated with evictions. We end the chapter with an exploration of environmental inequities, specifically, environmental racism, and the emergence of an environmental justice movement to eliminate these inequities. A sociology of housing focused on race can help us understand many current dynamics, including but not limited to the following examples:

- African American applicants are more likely to be denied a home mortgage in Mississippi than any other state and they face double the rates of denial for home loans than that of white Mississippians (Bologna 2019).
- The foreclosure crisis was racialized, with black, Latino, and integrated neighborhoods facing exceptionally high rates of foreclosure. Additionally, the foreclosure crisis increased racial residential segregation (Hall, Crowder, and Spring 2015).
- Under the Trump administration, HUD (Department of Housing and Urban Development) "is proposing to significantly raise the bar for civil rights groups seeking to prove that a landlord, insurance company or lender is guilty of housing discrimination" (Fadulu 2019).
- President Trump launched unprecedented attacks an African American Congressman and a major American city disproportionately populated by African Americans in July 2019 when he called Rep. Elijah Cummings a "brutal bully" and the city of Baltimore, which he represents, a "disgusting, rat and rodent infested mess" where "no human being would want to live" (Baker 2019).
- In 2014, the government-appointed city manager of Flint, Michigan, decided to save money by getting the city's water from a new source; until the pipeline to the new source was completed, they had to use Flint River water. The water was untreated, which led to the corrosion of pipes, resulting in the lead poisoning of a major American city with, perhaps not coincidentally, a predominantly black population.
- The town of Anniston, AL, was poisoned by Monsanto in their production of chemicals known as polychlorinated biphenyls (PCBs) in the 1960s. By 1969, the plant was discharging 250 pounds of PCBs into a creek that ran through the black section of town. The town is 52 percent African American and the residents are still sick. Much of their community is a biohazard, a dead zone where nothing grows, and perhaps more disturbingly, the effects linger in children's brains. PCBs are known as "brain thieves" because of their ability to erode the structure and functions of the brain and nervous system (Washington 2019).

IMAGE 9.1: The racial wealth gap is at least partially a reflection of racialized rates of home ownership.

HOMEOWNERSHIP BY RACE

As Table 9.1 shows, rates of home ownership vary significantly by race, with almost 70 percent of non-Hispanic whites owning a home versus only 42.3 percent of blacks and 46.2 percent of Hispanics (Duffin 2019). This is a major factor in the racial wealth gap, since, for most Americans, the bulk of their wealth is the equity in their home. *Home equity* is the difference between what you paid for your house and what it is currently worth. Since housing values have risen throughout the twentieth century and into the early twenty-first century, with the exception of the 2008 Great Recession which was spurred by the burst of the "housing bubble," home equity has been a significant source of wealth for those who have been able to purchase homes.

The great majority of Americans rented their homes in the first half of the twentieth century. Home ownership was not financially feasible for most because in order to qualify for a home loan, one had to put down half of the price of the house and pay it off in five to seven years, which was beyond the ability of most Americans. The federal government began taking an interest in American home ownership in the early twentieth century, but as an anti-Communist strategy. The Wilson (1912–1920) administration's reaction to the 1917 Russian revolution was to establish a campaign to encourage home ownership by white Americans: "The idea being that those who owned property would be invested in the capitalist system" (Rothstein 2017:60). The

Race	Percent
Asian American	57.2
White, non-Hispanic	68.5
Black, African American	42.3
Hispanic	46.2
All others	54.5

TABLE 9.1: Home Ownership Rates by Race, 2017
SOURCE: Duffin 2019.

Department of Labor initiated an "own your own home" campaign, complete with the distribution of tens of thousands of buttons, posters, pamphlets, and newspaper advertisements—each with an image of a white couple or family (Rothstein 2017).

This campaign only achieved lukewarm success, though, as most families could simply not afford to buy their own home. When the Great Depression occurred, the economic crisis was exacerbated by a housing crisis, with the escalation of foreclosures and a stagnant construction industry. In 1934, President Franklin D. Roosevelt's administration developed a number of government programs designed to pull the country out of the depression, including one to rescue homeowners who were about to default and one to make first-time home buying possible, which was the beginning of the Federal Housing Administration (FHA). The FHA insured bank mortgages for 80 percent of the purchase price of a home and allowed a twenty-year repayment window, which opened the door to home ownership for countless middle-class families (Rothstein 2017).

In exchange for the government insuring mortgages, the FHA required their own appraisals of properties to ensure a low risk of default; appraisal standards included a whites-only requirement. Essentially, "the FHA judged that properties would probably be too risky for insurance if they were in racially mixed neighborhoods or even in white neighborhoods near black ones that might possibly integrate in the future," (Rothstein 2017:65). In their underwriting manual, the FHA declared that neighborhood stability was contingent upon it remaining occupied by members of the same race and class. Additionally, the FHA discouraged banks from making loans in urban neighborhoods and instead encouraged them to offer loans on new construction in the suburbs (Rothstein 2017). FHA policies privileged single-family, suburban homes as well, rather than multi-family homes, which were more often found in urban areas. The GI Bill offered home loans to returning white GIs, too, following the racially exclusionary policies of the FHA. Suburban developments began expanding in the post–World War II era, spurred by government support in the form of FHA housing policies, the GI Bill, and later the investment in the interstate highway system beginning in 1956. The suburbs were racially segregated, however, so the affordable loans for these new developments sprouting up around every metropolitan area in the country were closed to blacks (more on racial segregation below).

So, the first two to three generations of accessible home ownership for middle-class Americans was reserved for whites; "over 11 million families bought homes backed by the FHA, transforming the American public from a nation of renters to a nation of homeowners. African Americans, and other communities of color, however, could not profit from this government largesse" (Gomer 2018). Even African American families who could afford to buy a home during the mid-twentieth century were denied the opportunity to do so. How much of the racial wealth gap does this explain? Some argue that, "the racial wealth gap is primarily a housing wealth gap" (Jones 2017). As we discussed in the previous chapter, "the median white household has 13 times the wealth of the median black household, and more than 10 times that of the median Latino family" (Gomer 2018).

Research finds that the racial wealth gap cannot be explained by personal choices and behaviors. Instead, factors such as the number of years of homeownership, household income, unemployment, inheritance and family financial support, and whether or not one has a college degree are the best explanatory variables. For instance, the number of years of homeownership explains 27 percent of the black–white wealth gap and is the largest explanatory variable (Shapiro, Meschede, and Osoro 2013). The next variables include household income, which accounts for 20 percent; unemployment, roughly 9 percent; college education, which accounts for 5 percent; and, finally, inheritance and financial support from family combine to 5 percent (see Figure 9.1). When explaining the why years of homeownership was the largest predictor of the racial wealth gap, the authors point out that in addition to historical discrimination, discussed above, one has to acknowledge that whites are more able to assist family members with down payments on homes due to historical privileges associated with homeownership. Today, "white families buy homes and start acquiring equity an average eight years earlier than black families" (Shapiro, Meschede, and Osoro 2013).

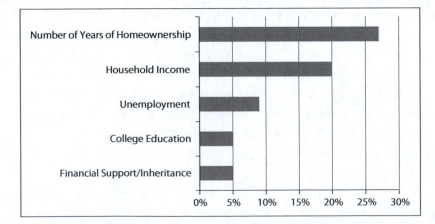

FIGURE 9.1: Factors that explain the racial wealth gap (Shapiro, Meschede, and Osoro 2013).

The Great Recession and the Housing Crisis

A major symptom of the Great Recession (the economic crisis that began in 2008) was the high rate of home foreclosures. There were over 7.1 million foreclosures in the United States from 2007 to 2009. Preyed upon by unscrupulous lenders, people of color were more than three times as likely to have subprime loans as whites, regardless of their credit rating. A subprime loan is a mortgage that is made to borrowers with a lower credit rating; thus, it has a higher interest rate and less-favorable terms than a prime loan. Often subprime loans have fluctuating interest rates; these are referred to as adjustable rate mortgages and result in ballooning payments over time. Thus, a home that is initially affordable for a working-class family can soon consume a larger and larger share of their monthly income and become unsustainable. Because people of color were disproportionately targeted for subprime loans, they were overrepresented in home foreclosures during this period (Dillahunt et al. 2010).

Even black applicants with good credit were steered to subprime lenders, while whites with good credit could get loans through prime lenders. It is estimated that subprime loans have placed more than ninety thousand black borrowers in situations of paying an average of $327 per month more for mortgages than if they had gotten their loans from a prime lender (Wise 2005). As of 2010, approximately 16 percent of Latino homeowners and 10 percent of black homeowners had either lost their homes or were at "imminent risk," compared to 7 percent of white homeowners (Chen 2010). Researchers emphasize the spillover effect on communities with high foreclosure rates: they lose billions in assets, from which it can take generations to recover (Chen 2010). Such organizations as Operation HOPE have emerged to help minority communities avoid being victimized by such mortgages in the future (see Box 8.2 Racial Justice Activism: Operation HOPE: From Civil Rights to Silver Rights). As of 2013, the typical American household had not yet bounced back from the 2008 economic crisis. Yet, the crisis hit black households hardest, as their median net worth fell 42 percent while the median net worth for white households declined by 27 percent (Cortright 2017).

WITNESS

The Illinois attorney general filed a lawsuit against mortgage giant Countrywide for discriminating against blacks and Latinos in home mortgages in Illinois, explaining that "it's disturbingly clear that if you were an African American or Latino borrower who walked into a Countrywide store, you likely paid more for your mortgage than a white borrower. [The lender] effectively imposed a surcharge on mortgage loans based on race and ethnicity" (Tareen 2010).

Low-Income Housing Crisis

The foreclosure crisis of 2008 has increased the number of renters in the United States. Since people of color are less able to own their own homes, they make up a disproportionate share of the rental market. The United States faces a low-income housing shortage for a number of reasons. First, the federal government's investment in the creation of low-income housing through subsidies peaked in the 1970s. Budget cuts under President Reagan resulted in only 25 percent of the number of low-income housing units being subsidized. No president since has reinvested in low-income housing subsidies. The decrease in the supply of affordable housing is also a result of private landlords choosing to remove their properties from subsidized housing programs so that they can charge more for rent. Finally, **gentrification**, the process of renovating deteriorating urban neighborhoods by means of an influx of more affluent residents, has resulted in fewer low-income housing units. Gentrification is a class shift, but it is also characterized by a racial shift as well, from a predominantly black neighborhood to a predominantly white neighborhood. Gentrification is very controversial. It brings with it numerous amenities and improvements that are welcomed in the neighborhood, from parks to bike paths, coffee houses, and grocery stores, yet the process itself results in the displacement of the original low-income residents, as they can no longer afford to live there.

This low-income housing shortage contributes to a number of problems. First, the cost of rent has sky-rocketed, to the point that the majority of low-income families spend over half their income on rent, and one in four spend 70 percent of their income on rent (Desmond 2016). Second, rental housing for the poorest Americans is substandard. We have allowed low-income housing to disappear and it is not being replaced, which results in very low vacancy rates for even the shoddiest housing and no incentive for landlords to improve upon the properties (Desmond 2016). Finally, this has also helped fuel an eviction crisis because landlords are less likely to cooperate with a family facing a temporary crisis, as they know there are plenty of other people willing to rent their over-priced, dilapidated properties.

Sociologist Matthew Desmond (2016) studied evictions in Milwaukee and now leads Princeton University's Eviction Lab, which is the first nationwide database of evictions. He argues that we need to know more about this phenomenon; we need a new **sociology of displacement**, which studies the prevalence, causes, and consequences of evictions (2016:333). In his research, he finds that rather than seeing evictions as a result of poverty, he argues that eviction actually helps create poverty. Some of the earliest research to emerge out of the Eviction Lab finds that the epidemic of evictions has hit African Americans in the South the hardest, with black renters from Louisiana to Virginia disproportionately bearing the burden of the crisis (Image 9.2).

IMAGE 9.2: Sociologist Matthew Desmond and colleagues at Princeton University's Eviction Lab study evictions and find that the epidemic of evictions hit African Americans in the South the hardest.

Specifically, 9 out of 10 of the highest evicting large US cities are located in the South and have populations that are at least 30 percent black. South Carolina has an eviction rate that is four times the national average. This is no mere coincidence; in the South, laws are more protective of landlords than renters. In the rest of the country, renters have some protection. There is also a ripple effect to evictions, affecting individuals through higher rates of depression, stress, and suicide, and affecting communities through the severing of social networks (Blau 2019). Additionally, an eviction stays on one's record, making it difficult to find new housing, resulting in more and more people being forced into homelessness. Desmond (2016:252) points out that evictions affected black women similarly to the way a felony conviction affected so many black men (see Chapter 10):

> Equal treatment in an unequal society could still foster inequality. Because black men were disproportionately incarcerated and black women disproportionately evicted, uniformly denying housing to applicants with recent criminal or eviction records still had an incommensurate impact on African Americans.

WITNESS

As sociologist Matthew Desmond argues, "If incarceration has come to define the lives of men from impoverished black neighborhoods, eviction was shaping the lives of women. Poor black men were locked up. Poor black women were locked out" (2016:98).

Racial Justice Activism:
Fighting Housing Discrimination

As part of the Department of Housing and Urban Development, the Office of Fair Housing and Equal Opportunity's (FHEO) mission is to eliminate housing discrimination and promote equal economic opportunity, through the enforcement of federal fair housing laws and policies. In this text we are primarily focused on race; the FHEO protects against racial discrimination as well as discrimination along the lines of color, religion, sex, national origin, disability, and familial status as well. In their 2017 Annual Report to Congress, cases against disability discrimination represented the largest category of filings (59.4 percent), while 26 percent of complaints were related to race (with 2.3 percent of complaints pertaining to color).

Research by HUD's Office of Policy Development and Research finds that discrimination persists, despite laws and enforcement. They just find it occurs in more subtle forms than in the past. They call it a shift from "door slamming" to more "subtle forms of differential treatment [in which] a landlord or property manager might very apologetically tell a person who is Asian, or Hispanic, or black that there are few apartments available or there are not apartments available; they might not mention that two-month rent special … or they might require a background check—and the white person gets none of that," said Diane Levy, research associate at the Urban Institute, in HUD's quarterly briefing on housing discrimination.

www.huduser.gov/portal/pdredge/pdr_edge_featd_article_081114.html; www.hud.gov/program_offices/fair_housing_equal_opp/housing_discrimination_and_persons_identifying_lgbtq

RESIDENTIAL SEGREGATION

In addition to social programs such as the GI Bill and federal policies administered through the FHA contributing to dramatic differences in home ownership rates between blacks and whites, they also helped create and contribute to the lingering legacy of residential segregation. Residential segregation is a significant feature of American society, something many of us fail to notice. **Residential segregation—** the separation of racial groups into different spaces, specifically, where urban areas are disproportionately composed of people of color while suburban and rural communities are almost all white—seems on the surface to be a natural occurrence, the result of personal preferences. While personal preferences play a role, research evidence shows that residential housing segregation is actually a result of historic and ongoing policies and practices that have restricted housing options for people of color, often with the goal of creating all-white communities. This is referred to as *de jure* **segregation**, segregation that is official policy, enforced by law. As we will see, much racial residential segregation in the United States is an outgrowth of *de jure* segregation. Today, residential racial segregation exists, but it is not enforced by law; it happens by "fact" rather than as a legal requirement. This is referred to as *de facto* **segregation.** Residential racial segregation is neither natural nor harmless. Sociologists Massey and Denton (1993) argue, for instance, that residential segregation is the primary cause of racial inequality, rather than merely an effect of racial inequality. In this section, we explore how racial segregation is measured, the extent of residential segregation, the causes of residential segregation, and its consequences.

Measuring Residential Segregation

One of the most widely used measures of racial segregation is the **dissimilarity index (DI)**, also known as the segregation index, which refers to the evenness with which two groups are distributed across an area. A helpful way to think about this measure is "for any two groups, such as blacks and whites, the segregation index tells us what percentage of a city's black or white population would have to move to another block or census tract in order to have no segregation at all" (Farley 1988:230). The DI ranges from zero to one, zero being the least segregated (or most integrated) and one being the most segregated (or least integrated). For most cities, a DI under 0.3 is considered integrated, those with a DI between 0.3 and 0.6 are understood as moderately segregated, and those above 0.6 very segregated (Massey and Denton 1993).

Extent of Residential Segregation

The DI can show us trends in residential segregation over time. For instance, in the early half of the rural-to-urban migration (1880s–1930s), as blacks were leaving the rural south for the urban north, the average DI for cities increased from 0.49 to 0.68. After World War II through 1970, segregation increased again, to an average DI of 0.73 in 1970, which was peak segregation. Between 1970 and 1990, the average black–white DI was 0.48 within central cities (Boustan 2013; Cutler, Glaeser, and Vigdor 1999). Since 1980, black–white segregation has declined; however, blacks remain severely segregated in the majority of US cities (Charles 2003). The DI also allows us to compare segregation across groups. When we compare the DI of blacks to whites with Hispanics to whites, using the 2000 census, we find that blacks are the most segregated group at 0.67 compared with Hispanics at 0.52 (Boustan

BOX 9.2

Global Perspectives:
Housing Segregation in South Africa

South African apartheid, the system of legal segregation, of white minority rule, and discrimination against people of color, was in place from 1948 to 1994. Twenty-five years after the end of this system, almost 80 percent of white South Africans and 80 percent of black South Africans still live in segregated neighborhoods. Fewer than 40 percent of South Africans socialize with people of another race. Only 11 percent of white children and 15 percent of black children attend racially integrated schools. Despite attempts at reconciliation upon the demise of apartheid, studies still find that it remains a deeply divided nation (Kielburger and Kielburger 2013). One of the explanations for the ongoing racial segregation is that the country also faces extreme economic inequality. So, the racial segregation is also class segregation, as black South Africans face extreme poverty and whites still hold most of the society's wealth. The post-apartheid era "has yet to deliver economic justice for black South Africans. A black-led government presides over an economy that is white-dominated, and which frequently ranks the most unequal in the world. Economic inequality is said to have exploded after the end of apartheid" (Chigumadzi 2017). Until black poverty and extreme economic inequality is addressed, racial segregation will remain.

2013; Iceland and Scopilliti 2008). Asian Americans and Hispanics are moderately segregated from whites, although their segregation from whites has been increasing since 1970 (Charles 2003). Since 1980, we have also seen substantial increases in minority residents in suburban areas; however, they still face high levels of segregation in the suburbs. For instance, in 2000, "nearly 60% of Asians, 50% of Hispanics, and 40% of blacks lived in suburbs, compared to 71% of whites ... [However] Patterns of suburban segregation mirror those of the larger metropolitan area of which they are a part" (Charles 2003:175). In order to understand racial residential segregation, we are going to now explore the origins of these patterns.

Causes of Residential Segregation

We are going to explore the causes of residential segregation, which is really an overview of housing discrimination, because housing segregation simply means that people of color were denied access to housing opportunities. While most of these are illegal today, housing discrimination continues, albeit subtly, resulting in ongoing residential segregation (see Box 9.1)

From Sundown Towns to Whitopias

Residential segregation in America is the result of the exclusion of blacks and other racial minorities from suburban and rural communities, or from white neighborhoods, through violence and racist government policies, some of which linger to this day. Sociologist James Loewen (2005) studied the emergence of all-white communities during the first half of the twentieth century. These communities were known as **sundown towns** because locals used violence to run blacks out and keep them out by placing signs at their city limits declaring "Ni****, Don't Let the Sun Go Down on You in _____" (see Image 9.3).

A key feature of the US historical narrative is the Great Migration, the movement of hundreds of thousands of rural, southern blacks to urban areas, primarily in the North, in the early to mid-twentieth century. This narrative is not so much inaccurate as a shorthand version of history that avoids implicating whites in restricting the residential options of blacks. Many African Americans left the South immediately after the Civil War, initially settling in small towns and rural communities throughout America. They found work as farmers; a way of life familiar to them at

IMAGE 9.3: Sign at the city limits of a sundown town stating, "Warning: Negroes must stay in colored town after dark, unless you are working" (Reprinted with permission from the Tubman African American Museum. Collection of the Tubman African American Museum, Macon, GA).

the time. In the initial decades following the Civil War, goodwill was extended toward former slaves; they were welcomed into many communities.

In the late nineteenth and early twentieth centuries, that goodwill began to fade due to increasing economic tensions, a changing political climate linked to the conclusion of the Indian Wars in 1890, growing anti-immigrant sentiment, and an increasingly imperialist agenda, with the US domination of Puerto Rico, Hawaii, Cuba, the Philippines, Nicaragua, Haiti, and other Caribbean nations. In the face of these trends, the goodwill extended to former slaves faded and whites throughout the country began to engage in practices akin to ethnic cleansing. They used violence, specifically race riots (see Chapter 5), to force African Americans out of rural communities and made it impossible for them to return (Loewen 2005).

Similarly, whites in over two hundred towns in the western United States purged their communities of Chinese Americans, an experience Chinese Americans referred to as being "driven out" (Pfaelzer 2008). These roundups were often led by mayors, governors, judges, and industry leaders and were even discussed in the press. This was an era of high immigration, with unemployment and fear of job competition dominating the public psyche. In addition to pushing out African Americans and Chinese Americans from their homes and communities, whites in other regions of the country used comparable tactics against Mexican Americans, Native Americans, and Jewish Americans. Such actions resulted in extreme racial residential segregation and reinvigorated ideologies of white supremacy.

While sundown towns explain the whiteness of many rural communities throughout the United States, the whiteness of World War II suburban America relies on other explanations. In this era, Levittown, the largest housing development in the country with over seventeen thousand homes, became the model of the suburbanization of America. Levittown, in New York, and suburban developments across the country emerged to take advantage of the availability of government-backed Veterans Affairs (VA) and FHA loans. William Levitt refused to sell his houses to blacks, fearing a negative reaction by whites (Bennett 1996). Housing developments in some regions refused to sell homes to Jews as well. However, even if he had wanted to sell homes to blacks or Jews, the federal government's racially exclusionary policies would have prohibited him from doing so (Rothstein 2017). While the passage of the Fair Housing Act in 1968 made it illegal to refuse to sell a home to someone due to the buyer's religion or skin color, suburban America is still overwhelmingly white. In fact, some of the fastest-growing areas in America today are also the whitest communities in the country, and these areas are defined as **Whitopias**, towns that are much whiter than the nation as a whole (Beale 2009; Benjamin 2009).

New research finds that sundown towns contribute to current black–white inequality (O'Connell 2019). Specifically, the historical presence of a sundown town is linked to lower white poverty in that area, suggesting the prowhite attitudes behind sundown towns result in preferential treatment of and better outcomes for whites. Additionally, whites benefit through opportunity hoarding created through racial segregation established by sundown towns (see Chapter 8).

Federal Policies

Some argue that our current approach to addressing our housing needs amounts to a misplaced "blind faith" in the free market (Gotham 1998). Prior to this "blind faith" era, there was considerable federal investment in housing. However, most of these programs were designed to maintain racial segregation rather than eliminate it. The New Deal buttressed racial segregation through the establishment of the FHA, a government agency that protected lenders from loan defaults, as discussed above. Federal housing policies were implemented during the Great Migration, the rural-to-urban migration of millions of African Americans in the early twentieth century, which dramatically changed the racial composition of US cities. In cities throughout the United States, real estate agents, mortgage brokers, and lenders operated on the assumption that it was best not to allow African Americans to purchase homes in white communities, and they established policies and practices to maintain racial residential segregation (see below). When the federal government sought to establish the FHA through the Housing Act of 1934, prominent leaders in the real estate industry were able to influence what this legislation looked like, while civil rights activists, organized-labor leaders, and interracial-housing activists were excluded from negotiations. Thus, federal housing policy included racially discriminatory policies and practices that had already been instituted in the real estate industry (Gotham 2000; Rothstein 2017).

The 1964 Civil Rights Act did not end racial discrimination in housing, because federal mortgage insurance programs were exempted from antidiscrimination requirements (Lipsitz 2006). Even the passage of the Fair Housing Act in 1968 did not end these discriminatory policies and practices, since the law stipulated that authorities could not punish the perpetrators, which makes this legislation "unique in the annals of legal discourse" (Lipsitz 2006:29).

Real Estate Industry Practices

There have been a number of real estate business practices that contributed to racial residential segregation including redlining, restrictive covenants, racial steering, and blockbusting, each of which was perfectly legal for much of our history. At first glance it seems illogical that real estate agents would artificially limit their sales opportunities through such practices. Why not sell to anyone who can afford a home? Keep in mind two things: first is the power of tradition and, second, the importance of a real estate agent's reputation. Real estate professionals were intimately involved in the creation of the FHA. As powerful white men of the era, they believed in segregation and sought to maintain it; they "were convinced that racial exclusion would enhance their property values" (Rothstein 2017:77). Thus, this became how the industry operated until they were legally required to change. The second factor is that real estate agents work on the power of their reputation—happy clients recommend them to others. In this kind of situation, not "rocking the boat," or not pushing integration, likely seems like the safest bet. Housing discrimination has been illegal since the Fair Housing Act of 1968, yet, racial discrimination continues.

The FHA instituted the practice of **redlining**—labeling areas of the city that are predominantly black as risky to creditors, thus ensuring most black families were ineligible for federally insured loans, which meant banks would not extend loans to them (Quadagno 1994). The FHA literally created color-coded maps of every metropolitan area, with white neighborhoods colored green, emphasizing they were the safest for lending, and neighborhoods that were populated with African Americans or foreigners were colored red and deemed risky (even the presence of ONE black person in the neighborhood could result in it being redlined) (Rothstein 2017). African Americans were confined to ghettos throughout most of the twentieth century due to residential discrimination that emerged directly from actions taken by this federal agency.

The FHA also encouraged residential discrimination through the use of **restrictive covenants**, which refers to language on a deed or sales contract saying that the buyer agrees not to sell the home to a member of a specific group (most often African Americans were stipulated in restrictive covenants, but at different times in US history these were also used to keep Jews and Mexican Americans out of white neighborhoods). Restrictive covenants were enforced by law until 1948. However, even after the Supreme Court ruled that racial clauses could not rely on the government to enforce them, the practice continued for at least another decade (Rothstein 2017).

WITNESS

Wealth is cumulative, so "missed chances at home ownership obviously compound over time … By 1984, when G.I. Bill mortgages had mainly matured, the median white household had a net worth of $39,135; the comparable figure for black households was only $3,397, or just 9 percent of white holdings" (Katznelson 2005:63–4).

Another real estate industry practice involved **racial steering**, which refers to the selective showing of different houses to black home buyers and white home buyers;

blacks are shown houses in black neighborhoods while whites are shown houses in white neighborhoods. Whites attempting to buy homes in integrated or black neighborhoods were discouraged from doing so by real estate agents. This is illegal, yet it is hard to prove, so it still goes on (Farley 1988). Audit studies from the 1970s and 80s found evidence of such practices (Lake 1981; Pearce 1976).

Another real estate industry practice is known as **blockbusting**, which is when unscrupulous realtors play on the fears of whites and the limited housing options of blacks to make more money by encouraging the rapid turnover of a neighborhood from all white to all black (Farley 1988). They spread fear in whites that blacks are moving into the neighborhood. Whites fear their housing values will decrease; thus, they sell for less than the house is worth and the real estate agent profits. That same agent can make higher than normal profit on the other end as well, by selling to a black family who will pay more for a house because their housing choices are limited. Again, these kinds of practices are illegal, but they continue in subtle ways that are hard to prosecute.

Personal Preferences

While the majority of people of all races claim they prefer to live in integrated neighborhoods, they also express a preference for not being outnumbered by other races (Cashin 2009). Some research (Charles 2001; Farley et al. 1978; Farley et al. 1993, 1994; Farley, Bianchi, and Colasanto 1979; Ihlanfeldt and Scafidi 2004; Lake 1981) finds that whites deny moving into communities because they are all white or nearly all white; instead, they claim to move into such communities for their amenities. But in actuality, whiteness is a signal that "implies other qualities that are desirable ... higher property values, friendliness, orderliness, hospitality, cleanliness, safety, and comfort" (Benjamin 2009). Whites are more likely to prefer living in all-white neighborhoods, which explains some housing segregation. According to research from the early 1990s, while some whites are willing to live in integrated neighborhoods, many others expressed an unwillingness to live in a neighborhood that is 30 percent or more black (Farley et al. 1994). Surveys of whites, Latinos, and African Americans in the Houston area find that whites express negative preferences toward black and Latino neighbors. The more Latinos and blacks there are in a neighborhood, the less favorable whites find the neighborhood, while the presence of Asian neighbors had no impact, and the racial composition of the neighborhood had little effect on Latino and black preferences (Lewis, Emerson, and Klineberg 2011). Black preferences, on the other hand, tend toward more racially integrated neighborhoods. Black Americans do not prefer to live in all-white neighborhoods due to fear of white hostility or harassment and also a preference for living near other blacks; many also do not wish to live in all-black neighborhoods, as they are well aware of the lack of amenities associated with all-black neighborhoods (Charles 2001; Farley et al. 1978;

Farley et al. 1993, 1994; Farley, Bianchi, and Colasanto 1979; Ihlanfeldt and Scafidi 2002, 2004; Krysan and Farley 2002; Lake 1981). While research on black preferences finds some blacks do prefer to live in majority-black neighborhoods, black self-segregation explains very little housing segregation (Ihlanfeldt and Scafidi 2002; Krysan and Farley 2002).

Even accounting for personal preferences, recent research finds that African Americans still face housing discrimination. Blacks are given less information from lenders and less encouragement to apply for a loan. They are often told outright that their income and credit are inadequate to qualify for a loan, when whites with similar credit ratings are approved (Wise 2005). Lenders also tend to more aggressively foreclose on black families who are late on loan payments than on similarly late white families. Housing segregation and the racial wealth gap that results from it can be explained by the interaction of white preferences for predominantly white neighborhoods and racism in lending practices.

WITNESS

"Whiteness has a value in our society. Its value originates not in the wisdom of white home buyers or the improvements they have made on their property, but from the ways in which patterns of bad faith and nonenforcement of antidiscrimination laws have enabled the beneficiaries of past and present discrimination to protect their gains and pass them on to succeeding generations" (Lipsitz 2006:33).

Social Structural Sorting Processes

In addition to the intentional efforts at residential segregation, sociologists are now focused on social dynamics that influence people's decision-making surrounding housing decisions, which in turn helps perpetuate racial segregation. For instance, social dynamics such as social networks, life experiences, residential histories, media exposure, and daily activities help inform decision making about where one looks for housing. These social dynamics act as a **social structural sorting processes**, where certain areas of the city are excluded from consideration throughout the decision-making process, in a narrowing down of options. Importantly, people's decision-making process around housing exists within a larger system of racial stratification, which is why residential segregation is perpetuated even through social structural sorting processes (Krysan and Crowder 2017).

When people seek to move, they take their social networks into account. Social networks operate in two ways when it comes to housing choices. First, they are important sources of information about neighborhoods or leads on particular apartments or communities. Second, when making decisions about where to live, people consider the proximity of their friends and family to be significant. In fact, living near friends and family members is one of the most important criteria for people when choosing a neighborhood (Krysan and Crowder 2017). It is easy to see how the use of one's social networks in one's decision about where to move would perpetuate racial segregation: most families are monoracial and many friendship circles are racially homogenous.

People's lived experiences also inform their decision making—perceptions about a neighborhood's desirability based upon driving through it, or areas of a city you might know from your job search or from media coverage, all factor in to one's decision making. Again, it is not hard to envision perpetuating racial residential segregation when taking these kinds of social factors into account when house hunting.

Sociologists Maria Krysan and Kyle Crowder argue that today, "there is ample evidence that, once established, the deep segregation that characterizes many metropolitan areas tends to perpetuate itself with no overt discrimination required … even in the absence of intentionally segregationist policies, residential stratification by race would surely persist well into the future," through residential sorting (2017:11).

Effects of Residential Segregation

In addition to its contribution to the racial wealth gap, the negative effects of racial residential segregation are multiple. Sociologists argue that residential segregation harms minorities through lack of employment opportunities, because job growth tends not to occur in the regions of the country where the most unemployment exists. Policies and practices that encourage and support residential segregation create disparities in education, as most public schools in the United States are neighborhood schools. Communities that are described as "good" neighborhoods are areas that have quality schools, a supportive police presence, public parks, sidewalks, and access to grocery stores, and these neighborhoods are overwhelmingly white (Williams 2008). Residential segregation has had devastating effects on people of color; it concentrates poverty and limits employment and educational opportunities for minorities. The negative effects are particularly problematic for blacks, who may experience **hypersegregation**: extreme segregation in which blacks are so isolated that they only rarely share neighborhoods with whites and are concentrated in very small areas (Massey and Denton 1993). This kind of concentrated poverty amplifies other social problems, such as crime, drugs, dysfunctional schools, joblessness, and isolation; examples include East St. Louis, Illinois; South Central Los Angeles; and Chicago's South Side (Wilson 2010). The disadvantages found in minority communities result in continued racial inequality because economic success is increasingly dependent on people's social networks and access to cultural and social capital

(Patterson 2010). In addition, increasing homogeneity of residents results in less tolerance for differences, damaging the vitality of our democracy.

Sociologists argue that hypersegregation and concentrated poverty are outgrowths of a shift in federal and local housing initiatives in the 1980s and 1990s that emphasized disinvestment of public resources and a "blind faith" in private markets to solve housing needs (Gotham 1998). These housing policies coincided with the economic shift from an industrial, manufacturing economy to a service economy that, as we discussed previously, specifically disadvantaged urban minorities. Gotham argues, "The faith that scholars, policy researchers, and elected officials place in market-centered policies to correct the problems of poverty, homelessness, and segregation is misplaced. ... The problems, instead, are market-induced" (Gotham 1998:22).

WITNESS

"The white power structure has collaborated in the economic serfdom of Negroes [*sic*] by its reluctance to give loans and insurance to Negro [*sic*] business ... There are insufficient economic resources within the ghetto to support its future development ... The suburbs drain the economy of the city—through subsidized transportation, housing development, and the like" (Clark 1989 [1965]:29).

Creating the Ghetto

As the preceding discussion makes clear, government policies created the suburbs. The post-WWII phenomena known as white flight (see Chapter 7) had many contributing factors: housing policies that favored new, suburban construction and privileged white buyers, government investment in the interstate highway system, and white reaction to the Supreme Court decision *Brown v. Board of Education* (1954) that declared segregated schools illegal. It should also be understood that those very same policies created the ghetto. As whites left urban areas and racial minorities moved in, decades of disinvestment followed; under-resourced schools unable to prepare students for the demands of a twenty-first century economy proliferate; lack of decent affordable housing means residents lack the necessary foundation for life; and economic shifts mean employment prospects for urban, minority residents remain grim.

The term *ghetto* originally referred to the Jewish area of sixteenth century Venice, but its use expanded to refer to a crowded, urban section of a city populated by minority groups who are legally, socially, or physically restricted from living outside the designated area. In July 2019, when President Trump described Baltimore as rodent infested and the kind of place where "no human being would want to live," he was tapping into racialized perceptions of the "ghetto" as a dangerous, dirty, crime ridden place: a place that is "not a viable community" (Clark 1989:27). Popular attention to the ghetto tends to focus on the criminal behaviors, alcoholism, drug addiction, and teen pregnancy, which are more heavily concentrated there, as behavioral issues of the inhabitants, painting a picture of people who refuse to comply with middle-class American norms. However, the concentration of these pathologies is more an outgrowth of restricted opportunities: economic marginalization and racial segregation (Wilson 1989).

Chocolate Cities

Importantly, there is more to these regions than pathology and neglect. Many African Americans embrace predominantly black communities and the vibrant, resilient culture that emerges out of them. George Clinton and Parliament Funkadelic released a celebratory album in 1975 entitled *Chocolate City* that captures this vibrancy. Sociologists Marcus Anthony Hunter and Zandria F. Robinson (2018) released the book *Chocolate Cities: The Black Map of American Life* celebrating black agency despite white supremacy; emphasizing the connection between black greatness and place; and recognizing black communities as sites of cultural creation and resistance to oppression. After Hurricane Katrina devastated New Orleans in 2005, then Mayor, Ray Nagin, in a Martin Luther King Jr. day speech on January 16, 2006, declared that New Orleans will remain a "chocolate city." The comment generated significant attention, much of it negative. However, in the face of 80 percent of the city flooding, it remained a question who would return and whether or not New Orleans, a city that owes its entire celebrated culture, from food to music, to its black history and inhabitants, would remain predominantly African American. Disasters do not affect all groups equally (discussed below). Hurricane Katrina was no exception. African Americans were disproportionately displaced and were the least likely to return after the flooding. It remains, however, a chocolate city.

Public Housing

When most Americans envision urban ghettos, they envision public housing complexes: generally high-rise, dilapidated towers in urban areas, cut off from the rest of the city by interstate highways, with a reputation for crime, drugs, and general lawlessness, and populated by impoverished African Americans and Hispanics (Rothstein 2017). **Public housing** refers to housing stock that is owned by the government, specifically HUD. When public housing was initially built in the mid-twentieth century, it was mostly for white working- and lower-middle-class families and was designed to address a need during the Great Depression and post-WWII urban housing shortage. Public housing was racially segregated, mostly built for whites, but some public housing was built for blacks. St. Louis's Pruitt-Igoe project housed whites in one section and blacks in another (Badger 2015).

Two shifts begin happening to public housing in the 1960s: residents were more likely to be poor rather than working class and the population of residents became less white. The reason for this shift was because the federal government established a different program for whites, which involved single-family suburban programs leaving the high-rise urban projects as the program that catered to blacks (Rothstein 2017). While blacks make up 98 to 99 percent of residents in public housing projects in major cities, they are not the majority of residents receiving housing assistance nationwide today; whites are (Badger 2015).

From the beginning, public housing rents were supposed to cover the costs of maintenance and upkeep. This was manageable in the early decades when most residents were working class. However, now that most residents of urban public housing are deeply impoverished, with median family income at only 17 percent of the median family income nationwide in the 1990s, the result is a years-long repair backlog (Badger 2015). Property decline was inevitable. In addition to the repair backlog, public housing projects were built with the cheapest materials, which also meant they were not designed to last.

The failures of public housing projects lead to the establishment of vouchers, a program known as Section 8, which allowed qualifying individuals to use their voucher to supplement their rent almost anywhere. Instead of building new housing projects, old projects were being demolished in cities across the country. Yet, the linkage of public housing with race and crime remained in the public imagination, resulting in Section 8 becoming a racial slur (Badger 2015). Today, the focus has shifted to mixed-income housing developments, reflecting ongoing hostility to poor people.

WITNESS

"Housing is no abstract social and political problem, but an extension of a man's [*sic*] personality. If the Negro [*sic*] has to identify with a rat-infested tenement, his [*sic*] sense of personal inadequacy and inferiority, already aggravated by job discrimination and other forms of humiliation, is reinforced by the physical reality around him [*sic*]. If his [*sic*] home is clean and decent and even in some way beautiful, his [*sic*] sense of self is stronger" (Clark 1989 [1965]:32–33).

ENVIRONMENTAL RACISM

Residential segregation also hurts minorities in terms of their exposure to environmental pollutants and hazards. Sociologist Robert Bullard (1994) describes this phenomenon as **environmental racism**, whereby an industry policy or practice differentially affects a group based upon its race or color, shifting industry costs onto communities of color. Communities of color are targeted by toxic waste facilities, landfills, incinerators, chemical production facilities, and a host of other polluting industries, all of which place their residents in harm's way. This is not an issue of class. Research shows that middle-class black communities are targeted by polluters as often as poor black communities, and more often than poor white communities. Therefore, environmental racism is more of a racial dynamic than a class dynamic (Bullard 1994). Some have argued that instead of polluting industries targeting communities of color, people of color move into polluted neighborhoods. This argument has been soundly refuted: "polluting industries actually single out communities of color more often than not, moving into neighborhoods with high percentages of minority residents" (Pellow 2018).

The recent example of the poisoning of the city of Flint, Michigan, through their water source is an example of environmental racism. In 2014, state and city officials shifted the city of Flint's water source from the Detroit water system to another system to save money. While the pipeline to the new system was being built, the city switched to Flint River water. However, they failed to chemically treat the water, causing corrosion of the pipes and resulting in lead seeping from the pipes into the water supply. Residents drank, bathed in, and cooked with this contaminated water for two years while the government claimed it was perfectly safe to drink. Since then, the ninety-nine thousand residents of Flint, 42 percent of whom are impoverished and 57 percent of whom are black, have discovered they were systematically

IMAGE 9.4: Migrant farmworkers are often expected to pick crops in the fields as pesticides are sprayed.

poisoned. Children are especially vulnerable to lead poisoning, as it affects the development of the brain and nervous system, causing numerous health problems, including decreased intelligence.

Other minority groups also fall victim to environmental racism. For example, Latinos tend to be residentially segregated and lack political clout, so they, too, are targeted by hazardous industries (Ong and Blumenberg 1993). In addition to their disproportionate exposure to environmental toxins in their communities, Latinos experience more work-related hazards and occupational diseases than non-Hispanic whites. Latinos make up the majority of migrant farmworkers, who are exposed to dangerously high levels of pesticides, for example. They are also more likely to be exposed to industrial lead poisoning (Ong and Blumenberg 1993).

Native American communities struggle with environmental racism as well. They are faced with radioactive contamination because so much of the federal government's nuclear weapons production (uranium mining, weapons production, and weapons testing) occurs on tribal lands. The federal government also pays some desperately poor Native American tribes to store radioactive nuclear waste on tribal lands. Over half of all US uranium deposits are in the western United States on Native American reservations. Due to the desperate poverty of Native American tribes and the promise of jobs and royalties, some have signed agreements with the federal government to allow extraction of this dangerous radioactive substance. The Navaho tribe, known as the Dine by tribal members, was one of the tribes to enter into such an agreement in 1952, in exchange for guaranteed mining

IMAGE 9.5: Due to environmental racism, racial minorities are disproportionately exposed to environmental toxins and pollutants. This image shows African American children playing near petrochemical plants in a region of Louisiana known informally as Cancer Alley.

jobs for 150 Dine men. After the mining facility closed in 1980, the toll on the tribe could be actually calculated. By 1980, thirty-eight of the miners had died of radiation-induced lung cancer, ninety-five suffered from respiratory problems, and birth defects had increased dramatically on the reservation (Churchill and LaDuke 1992).

The location of such toxic and polluting industries has *not* been random; instead, minority communities are targeted. They are considered by corporations and the government to be vulnerable precisely because they are poor and politically unorganized (Bullard 1994). The list of targeted communities of color goes on. Corporate hog farms in North Carolina, for instance, present multiple hazards for local black communities, including loss of farm land and environmental degradation associated with industrial swine production (Ladd and Edwards 2000). The Mississippi River corridor between Baton Rouge and New Orleans, home to numerous African American communities, has an extraordinarily high concentration of chemical plants, incinerators, landfills, and petroleum processors in a relatively small area. Louisiana's "petrochemical corridor" is infamously referred to as Cancer Alley by residents and environmentalists because of the disproportionately high cancer rates (Allen 2003). While the United States does have laws and regulations that are meant to protect citizens from polluters, these laws are not applied uniformly (Bullard 1994). The lack of enforcement of existing regulations implicates the government in "exacerbating the already difficult conditions under which many people of color [are] forced to live" (McGurty 2007:117). A new coalition known as the Coalition Against Death Alley has formed to fight polluters in this region. Local residents' fears are real, as a 2015 EPA assessment dear the Denka plant in St. John the Baptist Parish found that they "have a lifetime cancer risk from air pollution 800 times higher than the national average, and the populations in six parish census tracts closest to the Denka facility have the highest risk of air pollution-caused cancer in the country" (Dermansky 2019).

WITNESS

"We are being poisoned …" (Dermansky 2019).

Environmental racism is also evident in lead poisoning in African American communities and increased risk for asthma faced by African American children due to air pollution in inner-city neighborhoods. Communities residing near polluting industries believe their exposure to such pollution manifests in a variety of health problems, including disproportionate cancer rates, reproductive disorders, respiratory illnesses, and skin disorders, and the prevalence of rare childhood cancers, among others (Allen 2003). Environmental racism is a very concrete example of white privilege at work—while we all enjoy the advantages of living in a highly industrialized society, there are environmental costs to that, which are disproportionately borne by people of color.

Targeting racial minority communities with polluting industries is not a new practice. In 1890, San Francisco's board of supervisors passed an ordinance that forced the removal of Chinese Americans from a downtown neighborhood that was targeted for redevelopment and relocated them to a region of the city filled with waste dumps and other environmental pollutants (Lipsitz 2006).

Keep in mind the restricted options people of color face in housing choices; they do not have the same "opportunities to vote with their feet" (Bullard 1994:6) when faced with a toxic polluter as a neighbor. Simply moving away is not always an option, considering the restricted housing market African Americans face. Minorities, however, do not passively accept their victimization. A number of organizations have formed to fight toxic polluters, creating a coalition of similar organizations referred to as the **environmental justice movement**. This movement merges issues and tactics of the 1960s civil rights movement and the environmental movement of the 1970s to challenge polluting industries and their practices, making environmental justice a civil rights issue.

The movement began in 1982 when over four hundred protesters engaged in a six-week protest, physically blocking a road in order to halt the dumping of six thousand truckloads of PCB-contaminated soil. The pollution was destined for a hazardous waste dump recently established in the poor black community of Afton, in Warren County, North Carolina, despite community opposition (Lerner 2005). Despite their actions, the landfill was built and the contaminated soil was delivered. Although the protesters lost this fight, their activism marked the beginning of the national environmental justice movement. Environmental justice activism in North Carolina has also been extended to the fight against corporate hog farming and the myriad negative socioenvironmental impacts of the practice (Ladd and Edwards 2002).

Native peoples have also been successfully mobilizing and engaging in mass demonstrations to resist mining and oil industries that are destroying communities (Gedicks 2001). Native Americans and Chicanos have played integral parts in the environmental justice movement in the Southwest (Bretting and Prindeville 1998). Due to such activism, environmental justice is now part of the mainstream civil rights agenda (Bullard 1994). Environmental justice activism has challenged polluters' assumptions that communities of color lack the political clout and organization necessary to fight. The fight for environmental justice is based on the premise that access to a safe and healthy living environment is a basic human right.

Disasters, like the flooding of New Orleans after the failure of the levees in the face of Hurricane Katrina, are often thought of as random and, thus, equal-opportunity destroyers. On the surface this might seem true. In the case of Hurricane Katrina and

IMAGE 9.6: Damage to a Ninth Ward barber shop after Hurricane Katrina and the flooding of New Orleans after the levee breach in 2005. Poor people and racial minorities are more likely to be underserved during a disaster, and Katrina was no exception.

New Orleans, 80 percent of the city flooded. Who survives, who is able to return, and who is able to rebuild after a disaster are all questions that exemplify the inequality associated with seemingly random events like hurricanes. However:

> Minorities and poor [people] are more likely than all other groups to be underprepared and underserved, and to be living in unsafe, substandard housing. The impact is also cumulative. After a disaster, minorities and the poor suffer a much slower recovery because of the lethargic response of agencies whose participation is critical to their recovery. They often receive less information, are rejected more often for necessary loans, receive less government relief, and endure discrimination and rejection in their search for housing.
>
> (Wright 2009:xx)

Disasters can create **climate refugees**, which is a term used to describe people who are forced to leave their community of origin due to environmental destruction such as soil erosion, drought, or floods, or climate change, which results in the land's inability to support them. The first American climate refugees are a Native American tribe, the Biloxi-Chitimacha-Choctaw, in Isle de Jean Charles, LA. It is not an accident that environmental refugees are often people of color, as the world's most vulnerable people are at the most risk (Davenport and Robertson 2016).

BOX 9.3

Race in the Workplace:
Fighting Environmental Racism

If the description of environmental racism in this chapter has angered you or inspired you, consider making this work your career. Countless organizations are on the front lines, working to end environmental racism. These organizations often need attorneys, for instance, since the battles are often fought in court. A degree from Tulane University's Environmental Law Program, which operates an Environmental Law Clinic, has law students working on real cases of environmental justice, fighting industrial polluters, landfill decisions, destruction of wetlands, or any number of looming environmental threats. (https://law.tulane.edu/clinics/environmental)

You don't have to get a law degree to help. You could work for an organization like the Deep South Center for Environmental Justice, which provides research,

education, community support, and worker training in environmental careers. The center's research is designed to inform local, state, and federal policy makers concerning polices for achieving environmental, climate, and economic justice in Louisiana and the Gulf Coast region. (www.dscej.org/)

Apply for a fellowship focused on environmental justice through Pro-Fellow, such as the Roddenberry Fellowship, the Altshuler Berzon/NRDC Environmental Fellowship, or the Humanity in Action Fellowship. There are a wide range of opportunities here—some require a bachelor's degree, some a master's degree, while others accept current college students. (www.profellow.com/fellowships/11-fellowships-for-activists-fighting-for-environmental-and-social-justice/)

CHAPTER SUMMARY

Home ownership is a significant variable in the racial wealth gap, as whites had a three-generation head start on people of color in terms of home ownership. This was by design, as early social programs designed to encourage home ownership were only available to whites. Residential segregation is by design rather than by default. What started as conflict between whites and minority communities (whether following the Civil War or in times of heavy immigration) became entrenched through government policy and real estate industry practices throughout much of the twentieth century. The negative effects of racial segregation are profound. Racial minorities are more likely to be exposed to toxic pollutants in their communities as well, a phenomenon known as environmental racism. As climate change accelerates, more disasters are occurring and people of color, as some of the most vulnerable people on the planet, will be disproportionately impacted.

KEY TERMS AND CONCEPTS

Blockbusting

Climate refugees

De facto segregation

De jure segregation

Dissimilarity index

Environmental justice movement

Environmental racism

Gentrification

Hypersegregation

Public housing

Racial steering

Redlining

Residential segregation

Restrictive covenants

Social structural sorting processes

Sociology of displacement

Sundown towns

Whitopias

PERSONAL REFLECTIONS

1. Describe the racial composition of the neighborhood you grew up in. If it is close to monoracial (almost all white or almost all Latino, for instance), describe why that might be. To what extent do you think this is intentional? Provide some evidence to support your assumption. Go beyond what you think you know. Conduct web searches for local newspaper reports of Klan activity, for instance; think about community stories you have heard, and so forth.

2. In what way does the community you grew up in or currently live in differ from communities with different racial compositions? In other words, if it is a predominantly white neighborhood, how is it different from predominantly black neighborhoods that you know of? Why do you think your parents chose your particular neighborhood? In what ways do you benefit today, or what disadvantages do you face today, due to the racial composition of your childhood community?

CRITICAL THINKING QUESTIONS

1. Explain the self-perpetuating relationship between residential segregation and environmental racism.

2. Explain the role of social structural variables in housing segregation today. How doe these variables operate in similar ways to real estate industry practices that supported residential segregation in earlier eras? How are they different?

ESSENTIAL READING

Bullard, Robert D. and Beverly Wright. 2012. *The Wrong Complexion for Protection: How the Government Response to Disaster Endangers African American Communities.* New York: New York University Press.

Desmond, Matthew. 2016. *Evicted: Poverty and Profit in the American City.* New York: Crown Publishers.

Hunter, Marcus Anthony and Zandria F. Robinson. 2018. *Chocolate Cities: The Black Map of American Life.* Oakland, CA: University of California Press.

Loewen, James W. 2005. *Sundown Towns: A Hidden Dimension of American Racism.* New York, London: Touchstone/Simon and Schuster.

Krysan, Maria and Kyle Crowder. 2017. *Cycle of Segregation: Social Processes and Residential Stratification.* New York: Russell Sage Foundation.

Martin, Michael E. 2013. *Residential Segregation Patterns of Latinos in the United States, 1990–2000.* New York: Routledge.

Massey, Douglas S. and Nancy A. Denton. 1993. *American Apartheid: Segregation and the Making of the Underclass.* Cambridge, MA: Harvard University Press.

Pattillo-McCoy, Mary. 1999. *Black Picket Fences: Privilege and Peril Among the Black Middle Class.* Chicago, IL: University of Chicago Press.

Rothstein, Richard. 2017. *The Color of Law: A Forgotten History of How Our Government Segregated America.* New York: W.W. Norton & Company.

RECOMMENDED FILMS

Banished: American Ethnic Cleansing (2008). Directed by Marco Williams. This film explores the historical pattern of counties throughout the United States during the early twentieth century that banished their black residents, expelling them from their homes and running them off their land. The film focuses on three specific communities and how they address this aspect of their history. The film also explores the issue of reparations by introducing black descendants of banished community members as they demand justice.

Brick by Brick: A Civil Rights Story (2007). Produced and directed by Bill Kavanaugh. This documentary explores a modern-day civil rights story by following three families from Yonkers, New York, as they fight housing discrimination battles. The film explores the role of government policies in the creation of the ghetto and provides first-person accounts of years of work to achieve racial justice.

Holding Ground: The Rebirth of Dudley Street (2006). Directed by Leah Maham. The inspiring story of a multiracial/multiethnic low-income community that organizes to challenge proposed gentrification of their neighborhood. Witness the twenty-year fight of the Dudley Street Neighborhood Initiative in Roxbury, Massachusetts, as it fights city hall, illegal dumping, open-air drug markets, redlining, and racism to create the change the group wants to see in its community.

Target St. Louis: Environmental Racism and the Cold War (2019). Directed by Sean Slater. The United States Army engaged in open-air studies to test the effects of aerosol radiation in a metropolitan city. These tests were primarily performed in low-income and African American neighborhoods in St. Louis. Generations of St. Louisans were unknowingly exposed to dangerous radiation in these experiments.

RECOMMENDED MULTIMEDIA

Eviction Lab. This website is the first national database of evictions. Explore this site. Write a paper reflecting on the following: Find the eviction rate for your city and state. Explore the cities with the highest eviction rates. Describe any patterns you find. Why do evictions matter? What kinds of policies can curb evictions? https:// evictionlab.org/.

Sundown Towns: A Hidden Dimension of American Racism. Sociologist James Loewen allows you to investigate whether your hometown was a sundown town on his website. Explore the website and write a paper about a sundown town. http:// sundown.afro.illinois.edu/sundowntowns.

Mapping America: Every City, Every Block. The *New York Times* worked with data from the Census Bureau's American Community Survey to offer an interactive map of the racial demographics of every block in the United States. Go to this website and find out how racially segregated your city is: http://projects.nytimes.com/ census/2010/explorer.

CHAPTER 10

Crime and Criminal Justice

CHAPTER LEARNING OUTCOMES

By the end of this chapter, you should be able to:

- Describe the extent of racial/ethnic inequality in the criminal justice system
- Demonstrate the various ways the death penalty is racialized
- Explain the emergence of and the collateral effects of mass incarceration
- Critically analyze the linking of race and crime in the public consciousness

On a cold day in November 2014, 12-year-old Tamir Rice was playing with a toy gun at a public park. A neighbor called 911 to report a boy pointing a gun at passersby and scaring people, adding that the person was likely a juvenile and that the gun was "probably fake." That last bit of information was not relayed to the officers who responded to the call. Two police officers pulled up and ordered the boy to drop his weapon. Within seconds of arriving at the scene, Officer Timothy Loehmann fired his weapon, killing Rice. The shooting sparked outrage and protests nationwide, particularly after a grand jury failed to indict Loehmann. In April of 2016, the city of Cleveland agreed to a $6 million settlement with Tamir Rice's family for the shooting death of their son.

Tamir Rice's story is all too familiar. On July 9, 2010, a Bay Area Rapid Transit police officer was convicted of involuntary manslaughter in the shooting death of an unarmed young black man as he was lying facedown on the concrete, handcuffed and unresisting. The shooting death of Oscar Grant in the Oakland train station on New Year's Day 2009 was caught on video, which contributed to the officer's conviction. Police officers in the United States have rarely been convicted in the shooting deaths of young minority males, as such incidents are overwhelmingly treated as justifiable homicides.

These incidents provide examples of the unconscious racism of jurors, because in the Oscar Grant shooting, the police officer was convicted of involuntary manslaughter rather than the more serious charge of voluntary manslaughter, and in Tamir Rice's case, the grand jury chose not to indict the officer at all. The distinction between voluntary and involuntary manslaughter depends on whether the perpetrator had a reasonable fear of the victim. The jury in the Grant case decided the shooter did reasonably fear the victim. In other words, an unarmed black man, lying on his stomach, handcuffed and unresisting, can still be perceived by a jury as enough of a threat to a white police officer that his killing could be convincingly argued to be reasonable. Similarly, the Tamir Rice case highlights how even typical behavior for a child, such as playing with a toy gun in a park, can be interpreted as threatening to a police officer and warrant the sympathy of a grand jury.

One way to understand the murders of Oscar Grant and Tamir Rice and the fact that these kinds of shootings are not uncommon is to look to the ways unconscious racism operates in the criminal justice system. *Unconscious racism* refers to the ideas, attitudes, and beliefs about race that help create and perpetuate negative feelings and opinions about people of color in our culture. Because we are ensconced in a racist culture where we unconsciously absorb racist beliefs and attitudes, implicit racial prejudices, unless actively addressed, are inevitable (Lawrence 1987; Quillian 2008).

Racism and inequality in the criminal justice field warrant the attention of sociological study. The perpetuation of the myths that link race and crime can have grave repercussions, as the opening vignette shows. These repercussions are evident in the racial discrepancies in death penalty convictions, incidences of police brutality directed against people of color, and the disproportionate number of incarcerated minorities. The racial dynamics between minority communities and the criminal justice system are complex. Examining closely the criminal justice policies and practices that disadvantage racial minorities will lead us to a better understanding of these dynamics and their perpetuation.

SOCIOLOGICAL PERSPECTIVES ON CRIME

When it comes to studying racism and inequality in the criminal justice system, sociologists rely on three primary theoretical perspectives as the basis for their approach. Using theory as a starting point, they seek to better understand the relationship between race and crime as well as its cumulative effects. For example, sociologists have discovered that the disadvantages that racial minorities face in the criminal justice system have amounted to greater advantages for whites. As we saw in the case of Tamir Rice and Oscar Grant in our opening vignette, these effects are both cumulative and complex. Black males, even those as young as twelve years old, are perceived as criminals and dangerous; therefore, their murder is more likely to be understood as justified even when they are unarmed and unresisting. Sociologists approach the study of race and crime from three general perspectives: the conflict perspective, critical race theory, and the white racial frame.

The Conflict Perspective

The conflict perspective argues that the law serves two primary functions: first, it helps to maintain the power of the dominant group in society; second, it is used as a form of social control of subordinate groups. Criminologists use vagrancy laws as classic examples of the conflict theory on crime and the law. Vagrancy is a criminal charge against someone who lives in public spaces, such as sidewalks or parks. Vagrancy, then, is a crime engaged in by poor people. Criminalizing such acts is one way in which the dominant group effectively controls a subordinate group—in this case, poor people. From a conflict perspective, racial inequalities in the criminal justice system are a result of economic, social, and political inequalities. Conflict theorists also emphasize that dominant groups effectively influence what behaviors get defined as criminal and how severely certain crimes are punished, which also serves to advantage them and disadvantage subordinate groups.

Critical Race Theory

CRT, introduced in Chapter 3, sees racism as part of the very foundation of law. A critical race theorist would argue that legal reasoning and constitutional law are not race neutral but instead reflect a white view of the world, and, thus, the law operates to disadvantage racial minorities and advantage whites. The traditional, opposing view is that the US Constitution is presumably color-blind, meaning that it does not afford advantages or disadvantages to individuals based upon their race or ethnic group; under the law, everyone is the same. Similarly, the conservative wing of the US Supreme Court adheres to the position that it is wrong to take note of race, even if taking note of race can provide a remedy to a historical injustice (Delgado and Stefancic 2001).

For instance, as a way to increase minority representation on college and university campuses, many universities used numerical formulas that added points for applicants that were from an underrepresented minority group in their admission decisions. Several white applicants to the University of Michigan challenged this practice in court, resulting in the 2003 Supreme Court case *Gratz v. Bollinger et al.*, in which the court ruled against such affirmative action admission policies. Despite the underrepresentation of minorities in higher education (see Chapter 7), the court found that assigning a certain number of points to the applicant for being a member of an underrepresented minority was unacceptable. Thus, even if such practices were intended to remedy historic and current injustices, such as the marginalization of racial minorities from institutions of higher education, they were no longer deemed constitutional. Simultaneously and somewhat contradictory to this ruling, in *Grutter v. Bollinger et al.* (2003) the Supreme Court upheld affirmative action in admissions at the University of Michigan Law School, claiming the court had a compelling interest in a diverse student body, as long as it was one factor in admission and not a quota system.

CRT also emphasizes the responsibility of institutions rather than individuals in the perpetuation of racism, as the previous example involving college admissions procedures demonstrates. A CRT critique of the criminal justice system, for instance, faults law enforcement for such strategies as imposing curfews on young people to curb gang activity because these are only in place in urban minority communities and, thus, perpetuate the image of minority youth as criminals.

White Racial Frame

The white racial frame is also a useful concept for trying to understand racial inequality in the criminal justice system (see Chapter 3). Sociologist Joe Feagin coined the term to explain the ways in which the beliefs, perspectives, and stereotypes about people of color that are pervasive in our culture help to legitimize forms of systemic racism, which then work to inhibit people from challenging their own racial/ethnic stereotypes and result in discriminatory actions. This frame should be understood as a cultural ideology rather than as an individual attitude, in that it both informs and helps legitimize societal racism. When a white woman locks her car doors at an intersection because a young black male is heading down the street, she is operating out of the white racial frame because her past exposure to stereotypical images of black males as criminals causes her to react as if he is a potential criminal. Within the criminal justice system, the white racial frame exemplifies how beliefs about black criminality inform, and even justify, such police practices as **racial profiling**, which occurs when race is the primary reason for a person to come under police suspicion.

How do these three theoretical perspectives on race and crime compare to popular understandings of race and crime? When you think about crime, what image comes to mind? What types of crimes do you envision? What do the perpetrators of such crimes look like? What do you assume motivates the perpetrators?

RACISM AND INEQUALITY IN THE CRIMINAL JUSTICE SYSTEM

In the United States, African Americans, Latinos, and Native Americans are imprisoned at higher rates than are whites, despite the fact that whites make up the bulk of arrests. Still, racial minorities are disproportionately represented at every stage of the criminal justice system—from arrest to incarceration. What, if anything, does this tell us about minority criminality? Are people of color more likely than whites to commit crimes that will earn them a prison sentence? Or is racial bias in the criminal justice system responsible for high rates of minority imprisonment? Why are so many more whites arrested, while racial minorities disproportionately end up incarcerated? What is the collateral damage associated with the disproportionate rates of incarceration in racial minority communities? These questions do not have simple answers. Consider the following:

- Research finds that the war on drugs has resulted in decreasing numbers of black men attending college, which decreases the odds of them obtaining decent employment opportunities (Borr 2019).
- Twenty-two-year-old African American Symone Marshall died while in police custody in a Texas jail after a car accident on May 10, 2016. Her case is eerily similar to that of Gynnya McMillen, a 16-year-old African American girl detained at a juvenile facility in Kentucky. Both women died due to lack of medical attention while in police custody (Finley 2016; Kates 2016).
- Police violence extends to other communities of color as well, despite the lack of attention from the mainstream media. Rexdale Henry, Mah-hi-vist Goodblanket, Allen Locke, Paul Castaway, and Sarah Lee Circle Bear are all Native Americans who have died at the hands of police since December 2014 (Kilgore 2016).
- A *New York Times* investigation of New York state prisons found extensive racial disparities in disciplinary cases—including who was more likely to face disciplinary action, who was sent to solitary confinement and for how long, parole decisions, and more (Schwirtz, Winerip, and Gebeloff 2016).

- Black males born in 1991 stand a 29 percent chance of imprisonment, a rate that is more than seven times that of whites born in the same year. Latino males are incarcerated at rates four times that of white males (Roediger 2008).
- Black males are linked with crime in the public consciousness, despite the fact that whites are responsible for most of the crime committed in American society (Russell 1998; Walker, Spohn, and DeLone 2007).
- Over 70 percent of arrests are of white people suspected of crimes, a statistic that includes Latinos who do not appear black, while 27 percent of arrests are of African Americans (Walker, Spohn, and DeLone 2007).
- Sixty-six percent of the US prison population is nonwhite.
- Citing concerns over black activism against police brutality, the FBI terrorism unit identified "black identity extremists," such as those involved with Black Lives Matter, to be a violent threat, yet have never declared white supremacist groups a violent threat (Levin 2017).
- Native Americans are disproportionately incarcerated, and for certain crimes, such as assault with a deadly weapon, they receive harsher sentences than do non-Natives charged with the same crime (Dumars 1968; Ross 1998).
- While Native American reservations are officially sovereign nations, federal courts have actually maintained jurisdiction on reservations since the passage of the Major Crimes Act of 1885. Thus, crimes committed by Native people on reservations are treated as federal crimes, which result in harsher sentences (Ross 1998).
- Native American women disappear at double the rate of white women, despite being such a small percentage of the population, and yet there is no database tracking the numbers of Native American women who are missing or murdered every year. Families of victims argue that law enforcement is not taking this epidemic of violence seriously (Hodal 2019).

Racial Disparities in Crime

As discussed in Chapter 1, sociologists look to structural explanations—such as race, gender, and social class, rather than individuals' motivations—for why people behave the way they do. The primary structural explanation for disproportionately high levels of crime, for instance, is poverty. Poverty is an example of what sociologists refer to as a **criminogenic condition**, a condition that contributes to the occurrence and perpetuation of deviance. Communities with more economic and social disadvantages have higher crime rates. In other words, to a certain extent, poverty breeds crime. African Americans, Latinos, and Native Americans, for example, are disproportionately impoverished and disproportionately imprisoned. Most homicide victims are poor and prisons are full of poor people (Prothrow-Stith

1991; Reiman 2009). Whites have more wealth, higher incomes, higher employment rates, and overall more economic stability and opportunities than do people of color, which helps explain why whites make up a smaller proportion of incarcerated persons in the United States.

Conflict theorists also study the kinds of crimes that people are most likely to engage in. In looking at the links between race and crime, they have discovered that African Americans and Latinos are more likely than whites to commit **street crimes**, such as homicide, robbery, auto theft, rape, and aggravated assault. They have also found that **white-collar crime**, which includes embezzlement, tax evasion, forgery, stock manipulation, and identity theft, is generally engaged in by middle- and upper-middle-class individuals. Because racial/ethnic minorities are under-represented in corporate America, these crimes are more often committed by whites. This distinction between types of crime is sometimes referred to as "crime in the streets versus crime in the suites."

Although both street crimes and white-collar crimes result in financial losses and have detrimental effects on human lives, the former lead to a greater number of incarcerations. This is in part because police work is more focused on apprehending street criminals, whose threat to physical safety is more immediate, than white-collar criminals, despite the fact that financial losses associated with white-collar crimes are often far greater than for street crimes and human lives are negatively affected in all types of crime (Drutman 2003; Eitzen, Zinn, and Smith 2009; Reiman 1996). Conflict theorists emphasize the links among the disproportionate represen-tations of racial minorities in the prison system, racial bias, and poverty.

Poverty and crime are linked in other ways as well. When poor people experience criminogenic conditions and react by committing street crimes, law enforcement is well trained to apprehend them. The criminal justice system itself effectively weeds out well-to-do offenders. For the same offense, poor people are more likely to be arrested than are members of the middle or upper class, and they are more likely to be charged, convicted, and sentenced to prison (Reiman 1996). Sociologist Jeffrey Reiman (1996) argues that in the criminal justice system, racism is merely a form of economic bias.

While racial bias is not written into law, there is evidence of its influence at every stage of the criminal justice process—from police practices such as racial profiling, to the prosecutorial decision-making processes used to determine whether someone who has been arrested for a crime is ultimately charged, to criminal sentencing guidelines, to disciplinary treatment while incarcerated. Individual instances of racial bias manifest in a cumulative disadvantage for people of color and provide one explanation for their disproportionate incarceration. Native Americans, for instance, are less than 1 percent of the total population but make up 2.3 percent of federal prison population, according to the Federal Bureau of Prisons (2019). At state levels, the disproportionate incarceration rates between whites and Native Americans are even more glaring. In Montana, Native Americans make up approximately 6 percent of the state's population; however, approximately 22 percent of the prison population is Native American ("Montana Profile" 2010). African Americans make up a much higher percentage of those incarcerated than of those arrested, a fact that implies a substantial bias in the prosecution and sentencing of African Americans. Most of the research on race and the criminal justice system focuses on African Americans and Latinos. The research on Asian American offenders finds that they are punished more like whites than like African Americans or Latinos (Johnson and Betsinger 2009; Kan 2003).

Profiling and Police Brutality

In addition to the everyday police practices that demonstrate racial bias, high-profile cases of police brutality make national headlines every year. While acts of police brutality are far less common than other acts of racism, research finds that the majority of citizens of color experience some form of harassment at the hands of law enforcement officials at some time during their lives. Some racial minorities have reported encounters with police officers whose use of racial slurs qualifies as harassment. An often-cited example of police harassment, unofficially referred to as "driving while black," takes place when a driver is stopped and searched for no reason other than skin color. A more established term for this controversial and well-documented practice is *racial profiling*, which is when race is a significant factor in a police officer's decision to pull someone over. However, any individual who appears to be a member of a racial/ethnic minority group is at risk for racial profiling: black, Latino, and Native American drivers are often the targets of this police practice. The frequency with which these groups are profiled is highly disproportionate to the number of drivers they represent (Cannon 1999).

While the concept of racial profiling is easily grasped, its social repercussions are numerous and complex. If police are looking for minority criminals, they will find more minority criminals. In turn, by focusing their attention on the activities of singled-out racial/ethnic groups, police inevitably neglect to discover many crimes committed by whites (Cannon 1999).

Since the terrorist attacks of September 11, 2001, Arabs and Arab Americans, as well as individuals with racially ambiguous features, have faced increasing instances of racial profiling. Particularly at US borders and airports, people of Middle Eastern origin or descent are more likely to be stopped and detained under the guise of anti-terrorism efforts. In a wry take on the previously cited "driving while black," Middle Eastern communities refer to these instances of profiling and detention as "flying while Arab" (Bonikowski 2005). Since the 9/11 attacks, US leaders and citizens have engaged in what sociologists refer to as a **moral panic**, whereby Arabs are being perceived as a threat to the social order (Cohen 1972). As can be seen in the responses to the 9/11 attacks, moral panics result in irrational responses, such as increasing instances of racial profiling. While there is no evidence that racial profiling actually helps law enforcement to identify criminals, there is ample evidence to demonstrate that a disproportionate number of racial minorities are subject to this unfair practice.

WITNESS

Arab American Omar Jarun describes his experiences with "flying while Arab": "Before 9/11 there were no problems, really. I had always established myself as an American from the Middle East. After 9/11 it was very difficult. My dad would tell me: 'Be careful what you say.' I would get double, tripled-checked at the airport. You know it's for safety for the country, so I don't have many complaints about it" (Montague 2011).

Racial profiling as a police practice has been upheld by the US Supreme Court. In 1996, the Supreme Court decision of *Whren v. United States* declared that any traffic offense committed by a driver could be used as a basis for stopping that driver, regardless of whether the officer's intent is to enforce traffic laws or search for drugs. These are known as **pretextual traffic stops**, in which police use minor traffic violations as reasons to stop someone and then use the stop to search for drugs. The rationale for this practice has been called into question by data that suggest that most individuals stopped and searched are innocent and the entire process is inefficient. One study found that 99 percent of traffic stops made by federally funded narcotics task forces do not result in arrest (Henson 2004).

Incidents of excessive force by police against minorities have increased since the 1990s (Winston 2010). Police encounters with racial minorities occur within a larger context of hostility and distrust, meaning that there is greater likelihood of misunderstanding and overreaction on both sides. Police of all races are socialized in the same way the rest of American society is, into linking race with crime, into the image of racial minorities as inevitable criminals. These images increase the likelihood of an encounter between minority citizens and police and increase the likelihood that the encounter becomes problematic, creating a self-fulfilling prophecy. For instance, police are more likely to approach racial minorities suspiciously, and racial minorities, sharing this distrust, are unlikely to cooperate with police. Lack of cooperation reinforces an officer's suspicions of guilt and can lead to a search and possibly an arrest. In effect, both the officer's and the citizen's assumptions are confirmed.

Police brutality refers to instances in which police use force beyond what is necessary to make an arrest or address a situation. The most egregious form of

IMAGE 10.1: Protesting police brutality in New York City on the anniversary of the police shooting of Tamir Rice.

police brutality, the use of deadly force, while rare, is disproportionately directed at racial minorities, particularly if the police encounter involves an unarmed person (Cullen et al. 1996; Kobler 1975; Takagi 1979; see Figure 10.1). In 1985, in the US Supreme Court case *Tennessee v. Garner*, the court ruled that under certain situations, police officers may use deadly force if the offender poses an imminent threat to the officer or to bystanders (Perkins and Bourgeois 2006). While most of us can agree that police officers must be able to protect themselves or bystanders from imminent threat, deciding what qualifies as an "imminent threat" is not always clear, as the following examples elucidate.

One of the most disturbing examples of police brutality was the 1999 killing of Amadou Diallo by four New York City police officers. All four officers were later acquitted after shooting Diallo forty-one times as he reached for his wallet. In 2010, a Guatemalan immigrant named Manuel Jaminez was shot in the head and killed by Los Angeles police officers who alleged he had a knife. And in Detroit, a seven-year-old girl, Aiyana Stanley-Jones, was killed by a policeman's bullet while sleeping in her family's duplex during an early-morning police raid on the upstairs apartment. Between 2000 and 2005, Phoenix, Arizona, had the highest rate of fatal police shootings. Such statistics have resulted in Maricopa County being identified as one of the most dangerous places to be a Latino in a police encounter. This can be understood as part of the larger anti-immigrant xenophobia of the era (Hoffman 2007) (see Chapter 13).

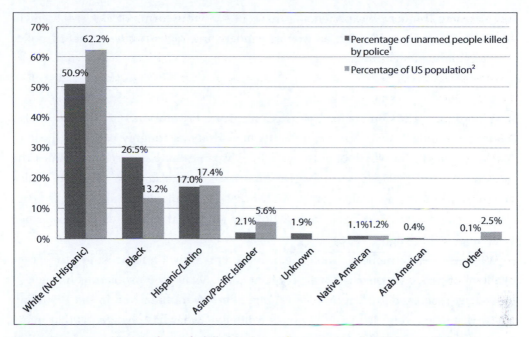

FIGURE 10.1: Unarmed people killed by law enforcement in the US by race/ethnicity, compared to population, 2015.

SOURCE: Beer 2016.

[1]DATA SOURCE: "The Counted" n.d.

[2]DATA SOURCE: Colby and Ortman 2015.

As mentioned in Chapter 1, police killings of unarmed black people have generated considerable media attention in the last five years, to the point that some of the victims have become household names: Stephon Clark, Oscar Grant, Michael Brown, Tamir Rice, Sandra Bland, Freddie Gray, Walter Scott, and Eric Harris, to name a few. In July of 2016, Alton Sterling, an African American father of five was shot four times at point-blank range by Baton Rouge police officers while selling CDs in front of a convenience store. One day later, Philando Castile was shot and killed by a police officer in Minnesota after being stopped for a broken taillight. Stephon Clark was shot and killed by Sacramento police officers in March of 2018 in the backyard of his grandmother's house while he was on the phone.

Others are less well known, including 22-year-old African American Symone Marshall and 16-year-old Gynnya McMillen, both of whom died due to lack of medical attention while in police custody. The violence women of color face at the hands of police is much less visible. The quintessential subject of police brutality is the black or Latino man, yet:

> Women and girls, particularly women of color, are sexually assaulted, raped, brutally strip-searched, beaten, shot, and killed by law enforcement agents with

alarming frequency, experiencing many of the same forms of law enforcement violence as men of color, as well as gender- and race-specific forms of police misconduct and abuse.

(Ritchie 2016:139)

According to the Centers for Disease Control and Prevention, data for 1999–2013 "show per capita Native American deaths in custody as roughly equal to those of Black people and nearly double the rate for Hispanics and almost three times the rates for whites" (Kilgore 2016). Native Americans have also been targets of police violence, including Rexdale Henry, Mah-hi-vist Goodblanket, Allen Locke, Paul Castaway, and Sarah Lee Circle Bear, who have all died at the hands of police since December 2014 (Kilgore 2016).

While this list of names is shocking, it represents only a microcosm of the larger problem of police violence against people of color. While the problem is not new—indeed, we discussed in Chapter 6 that much minority mobilization in the 1960s and 1970s was inspired by the issue of police brutality—what has changed is that many of these shootings have been caught on camera and, therefore, police narratives that they felt their lives were threatened are sometimes being challenged. According to the *Washington Post*, 992 people were killed by police in 2018; most were armed and

IMAGE 10.2: Communities Against Police Brutality is an organization that formed in the Twin Cities to combat police brutality. (Reprinted with permission from Communities United Against Police Brutality).

most were white. But black men, who make up only 6 percent of the population, were 40 percent of unarmed people killed by police (Somashekhar and Rich 2016).

The controversy surrounding these cases helps to bring questions of racial profiling and police brutality to the forefront. In fact, race is the most important determinant in attitudes toward police violence (Thompson and Lee 2004). The definition of "excessive force" depends on whether one is a member of the dominant group in society (Perkins and Bourgeois 2006). **Social dominance orientation**, an idea introduced by psychology professors Jim Sidanius and Felicia Pratto (1999), refers to people's belief that their group is the dominant group in society and their perception of this dominance as legitimate. Its adherence contributes to a wide range of attitudes, including those that perceive abuse against nondominant-group members as legitimate (Perkins and Bourgeois 2006).

For these reasons, throughout the United States there are calls for greater police accountability, from grassroots organizations to formal organizations that have long been involved in the fight for minority rights (see Box 10.1 Race in the Workplace: Diversity Training in Police Departments). The NAACP is working to force more accountability in law enforcement through its Smart and Safe campaign, which encourages more positive interaction between police and minority communities (Winston 2010). The Smart and Safe campaign is also working to encourage communities to recognize that mass incarceration is an issue of "misplaced priorities" and that public dollars can be better spent on education.

The NAACP held a public hearing on police accountability in Houston in response to the videotaped beating of a young African American man, Chad Holley, by a group of Houston police officers in February 2011. Calls for increased accountability often involve the request to form citizen review boards to review police misconduct cases, rather than having such cases handled within the department. Since 1998, Amnesty International has focused its campaign for human rights in the United States on the issue of police brutality and the use of excessive force. Finally, the Fraternal Order of Police, the nation's largest police union, is concerned about increased use of excessive force by police officers, which the union argues is due to the reduced training and standards for officers and the promotion of inexperienced officers, as police departments nationwide have responded to the increased need for law enforcement personnel since 9/11 (Johnson 2007).

War on Cops?

The emergence of the Black Lives Matter movement after the shooting death of African American Michael Brown in Ferguson, Missouri, by white police officer Darren Wilson, led some to speculate that this activism put police officers at risk. In fact, it is one of the reasons the FBI decided that black identity groups like Black Lives Matter were a violent threat. In addition to the "war on cops" narrative, it was argued that such activism has resulted in a "Ferguson effect," in which murder rates rise because the increased scrutiny of police officers results in their being hesitant to do their jobs. No evidence exists to support either claim, and some have argued that it is an insult to the profession to claim that police officers are not doing their jobs out of fears for their safety.

While policing is certainly a dangerous job, it is not the most dangerous job. In fact, out of a list of the top twenty-five most dangerous jobs in 2014, policing came in fifteenth, behind logging, fishing, roofing, and others (Johnson 2016). The year 2015 was the safest year on record for police officers since 1887, with forty-two police shot and killed on the job, down 14 percent from 2014 (Chappell 2015). In 2017, sixty-five police officers were killed on the job: twenty-six in traffic accidents, twenty-three by firearms, and sixteen from other causes, up from fifty in 2016 (Kutner 2017). The idea that police are hesitant to do their jobs has been refuted by former Attorney General Loretta Lynch and former New York City Police Commissioner William Bratton, among others. As journalist Nick Gillespie (2015) states, "It bears repeating: There is no war on cops. There is a long overdue and welcome national conversation about criminal justice reform."

On July 14, 2016, in Dallas, Texas, at a peaceful demonstration protesting the then most-recent incidences of police shootings of black men (Alton Sterling and Philando Castile), a sniper opened fire and shot twelve police officers, killing five of them, seeming to confirm the right-wing narrative of a "war on cops." During police negotiations with the shooter, African American Micah Johnson, he reportedly claimed to be angered by police shootings and said that he wanted to kill white people, especially police officers. Despite this horrific incident, there is no overall pattern of violence directed at police that makes their job any riskier than in the past.

Police Violence in Brazil

Since hosting the 2016 Olympic Games, Rio de Janeiro has increasingly found itself in the global spotlight. One of the issues that has generated international attention is a report by Human Rights Watch that finds a pattern of police killings and cover-ups in Rio de Janeiro slums: there have been over eight thousand extrajudicial killings by law enforcement since 2006 (Licon 2016). In Brazil, social class and skin color are linked (see Chapter 2); thus, Brazilian slums are populated by darker-skinned people with more African features. Thus, police violence targeting slum-dwellers is both a racialized and classed phenomenon. As in the United States, a disturbing number of those killed by police were unarmed, in custody, or trying to flee. Human Rights Watch also identified a lack of investigation and prosecution of the officers responsible. Brazil had a rate of 3.9 police killings per 100,000 people in 2015, which is nearly 10 times the US rate and 5 times the rate of police killings in South Africa (Licon 2016).

BOX 10.1

Race in the Workplace:
Diversity Training in Police Departments

It is estimated that police–citizen conflicts are at the root of 90 percent of major civil disorders in the United States (Coderoni 2002). Grassroots organizations and police departments across the country have responded to calls for increased police accountability. One response to these demands has been the implementation of diversity training, often referred to as cultural sensitivity, cultural diversity, or race-relations training, for cadets as well as experienced officers. Such training is intended to improve police–community relations, particularly the strained relations between police and minority communities.

Support for such training is wide ranging. Police organizations support the training initiatives because they are argued to increase officer safety and effectiveness. They can also potentially protect individual officers and entire departments from charges of police misconduct, brutality, and lawsuits (Barlow and Barlow 1993). Such organizations as the American Civil Liberties Union (ACLU) and NAACP support cultural sensitivity training for police because they believe it will enlighten officers regarding the concerns of minority citizens, thus improving police treatment of these citizens.

Barlow and Barlow (1993) question the efficacy of diversity training programs. They argue that cultural diversity training is unlikely to change the fact that police officers are agents of social control whose job it is to repress certain activities and freedoms. Police often operate in crisis situations where complex understandings of cultural differences are of limited use. Other researchers argue that this kind of training is unlikely to change societal power relations, which are at the core of negative police–community relations. Diversity training demands a level of departmental commitment to cultural sensitivity training. Some police departments are more interested in public relations, conveying the appearance of "doing something" about police–community relations, than they are in actually educating officers in the area of cultural diversity.

Other research has found that the more policing experience police officers have, the more resistant they are to cultural sensitivity training (Gould 1997). Research finds that police cadets responded positively to cultural diversity training, stating that such training would make them better officers. Cadets were open to the idea that they held racial/ethnic biases that needed to be addressed, whereas senior officers felt such programs were a waste of time and that they blamed police for poor police–community relations (Gould 1997).

Despite these limitations, cultural sensitivity training for police officers is still recommended, especially given that the United States is becoming increasingly diverse. Behavior changes

continues

continued

are unlikely to occur after only one training session in cultural sensitivity; training will require reinforcement. A certain amount of "unlearning" culturally insensitive attitudes is necessary. Diversity training should occur early in a police officer's career, when they tend to be more receptive and less cynical (Gould 1997). Ultimately, cultural diversity training can help police officers feel like part of the community rather than "apart from" the community they serve (Coderoni 2002).

Race and the Death Penalty

The use of the death penalty has been controversial since the early days of our nation's history. During the antebellum era, whites could kill a slave for any number of offenses without fear of punishment; postslavery, lynching was used to keep blacks under control. Between 1930 and the 1960s, 90 percent of those executed for rape were African American. During this same time period, African Americans made up 49 percent of the people executed for murder, even though they were just under 10 percent of the population (White 1991).

The death penalty has never been applied objectively; instead, there has been a long history of arbitrary use, particularly against racial minorities (Ogletree and Sarat 2006). In fact, one of the major questions surrounding the validity of its use pertains to race: the race of the victim, race of the defendant, and racial makeup of the jury. A jury that includes 5 or more white men is 40 percent more likely to sentence a defendant to death than is a jury comprising more people of color or more women (Bowers, Steiner, and Sandys 2001). University of Colorado sociologist Michael Radelet and his colleagues studied North Carolina death sentences between 1980 and 2007 and found that when the victim is white, the odds of a death sentence are about three times higher than when the victim is black (Anas 2010). The United States' use of the death penalty continues to be racially discriminatory, though most states still practice it.

The influence of race on the use of the death penalty has been the subject of several US Supreme Court decisions. Congress has attempted to pass legislation that would allow capital defendants to challenge their sentence due to racial bias in capital sentencing. In 2003, former Illinois governor George Ryan placed a moratorium on the use of this form of punishment in that state, at least partially due to evidence of racial bias in sentencing. After almost a ten-year moratorium, the state of Illinois banned the use of the death penalty entirely.

In a significant US Supreme Court case, *Furman v. Georgia* (1972), the defense challenged the constitutionality of capital punishment by bringing evidence of racial bias to the court. The Supreme Court declared the death penalty to be unconstitutional, specifically citing its arbitrary, unpredictable, and capricious use. Three of the judges noted, in particular, its racially discriminatory applications. The court determined that no specific guidelines existed on which to base the sentencing of capital punishment versus a life sentence without parole. Without such guidelines, Justice Thurgood Marshall declared, the option of imposing a sentence of death was an "open invitation to discrimination." Between 1972 and 1976, as a result of this decision, the death penalty was not in use in the United States.

In response, states established guidelines for the imposition of the death penalty, to limit the arbitrariness of its use and to address the concerns of the court. In 1976, the Supreme Court ruled in *Gregg v. Georgia* that as long as juries were provided with specifics as to when the death penalty was acceptable and allowed for mitigating circumstances, the likelihood of arbitrariness and discrimination in sentencing was unlikely. This decision opened the door for states to resume their use of capital punishment. Currently, twenty-nine of our fifty states have the option to use capital punishment and twenty-one, plus the District of Columbia, have abolished it. However, the current trend is away from the use of the death penalty, as the pace of executions hit a twenty-five-year low in 2016 with 31, increasing in 2017 to 39 and

Alaska (1957)	Minnesota (1911)
Connecticut (2012)*	New Hampshire ** (2019)
Delaware (2016)	New Jersey (2007)
Hawaii (1957)	New Mexico (2009)*
Illinois (2011)	New York (2007)#
Iowa (1965)	North Dakota (1973)
Maine (1887)	Rhode Island (1984)^
Maryland (2013)*	Vermont (1964)
Washington (2018)	West Virginia (1965)
Massachusetts (1984)	Wisconsin (1853)
Michigan (1846)	Dist. of Columbia (1981)

TABLE 10.1: States Where Capital Punishment Is Illegal (Year Abolished in Parentheses)

SOURCE: The Death Penalty Information Center 2019b.

NOTES:
* Repeal not retroactive: two people remain on death row in New Mexico; eleven people remain on death row in Connecticut; five people remain on death row in Maryland.
** One prisoner remains on death row.
# In 2004, the New York Court of Appeals held that a portion of the state's death penalty law was unconstitutional. In 2007, it ruled that its prior holding applied to the last remaining person on the state's death row. The legislature has voted down attempts to restore the statute.
^ In 1979, the Supreme Court of Rhode Island held that a statute making a death sentence mandatory for someone who killed a fellow prisoner was unconstitutional. The legislature removed the statute in 1984.

2018 to 42, according to the Death Penalty Information Center. Nebraska countered this trend, however. In 2018, they executed a death row inmate for the first time in twenty years. Years of legal delays, failed attempts to acquire execution drugs, debate over the use of lethal injection, and a vote to repeal capital punishment followed by a vote to reinstate it, all preceded the execution of a man who had been on death row there for thirty-eight years. The federal government announced in July 2019 that they were reinstating the use of the death penalty.

Despite guidelines designed to prevent the arbitrary use of this punishment, research still finds that race—and not the severity of the crime—remains the greatest predictor of who gets the death penalty. And while both the race of the victim and the race of the defendant are influential in whether a death sentence is sought and imposed, the race of the victim is by far the greatest predictor. For instance, evidence finds that blacks who murder whites receive a death sentence at disproportionately high rates (Bright 1995). In 2016, of the almost three thousand people on death row in the United States, 42 percent were black (see Figure 10.2). While only 50 percent of murder victims are white, 75 percent of murder victims in cases resulting in executions were white, according to the Death Penalty Information Center. Are these statistics evidence of discrimination against racial minorities or do such disparities reveal legitimate data about race and criminality?

In 1987, the US Supreme Court considered the issue of racial bias in death penalty sentences in *McCleskey v. Kemp*. In this case, a black man had been convicted by a Georgia court for killing a white police officer. He challenged his death sentence on the grounds that Georgia's death penalty was racially biased. His case was supported by research by David Baldus, professor of law at the University of Iowa, and his colleagues, who found that the race of the victim was statistically

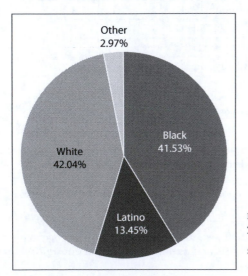

FIGURE 10.2: Race of death row inmates, June 2018.

SOURCE: Death Penalty Information Center 2018.

significant in whether prosecutors sought the death penalty and jurors imposed it (see Figure 10.3). In the Baldus study, researchers analyzed over two thousand murder cases in Georgia between 1973 and 1979 (Baldus, Pulaski, and Woodworth 1990). They controlled for over two hundred variables that could explain disparities in whether defendants were given the death penalty and found that:

> [The] race of the victim continued to exhibit a strong effect on both the prosecutor's decision to seek the death penalty and the jury's decision to impose the death penalty. In fact, those who killed whites were more than four times as likely to be sentenced to death as those who killed African Americans.
>
> (Walker, Spohn, and DeLone 2007:310)

By a one-vote margin, the US Supreme Court rejected McCleskey's claim, stating that he had to prove that the prosecutor in this particular case sought the death penalty for racial reasons or that the jury imposed it for racial reasons; in other words, the court demanded evidence of intentional racial discrimination. The court accepted the statistical evidence as valid but argued that evidence of a conscious racial bias was necessary to prove that the defendant's Fourteenth Amendment rights were violated. Thus, this new standard of proof could only be met by an admission by a prosecutor, judge, or jury to have sought the death penalty because of racial bias. Such evidence is unlikely to ever be available (Alexander 2010).

While the majority of Americans support the death penalty, there is momentum behind abolishing it, largely due to evidence of racial discrimination in its implementation. Since 1988, Congress has attempted to pass the Racial Justice Act, which would provide defendants the opportunity to use statistical evidence of racial

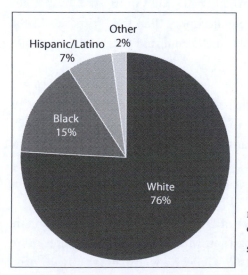

FIGURE 10.3: Race of victims in death penalty cases, April 2018.

SOURCE: Death Penalty Information Center 2019.

discrimination in their states' use of the death penalty to challenge death sentences. This legislation has passed the House twice but has yet to pass the Senate. One senator referred to it as the "so-called Racial Justice Act," meaning that the purpose was not really to seek racial justice and make the use of the death penalty more fair but to take a step toward abolishing the death penalty (Ogletree and Sarat 2006). North Carolina and Kentucky initially passed Racial Justice Acts, while other states, such as California and Georgia, have attempted but failed to do so. However, in 2013, the North Carolina legislature repealed the Racial Justice Act. In 2009, Senator Russ Feingold introduced the Federal Death Penalty Abolition Act, legislation to abolish the death penalty for federal crimes, in part because of the evidence of racial bias in its use.

The cumulative effects of racism in the criminal justice system are manifest in acts as routine as racial profiling and unfair jury selection, but they extend to influence more harmful outcomes, such as police brutality and discriminatory sentencing. One of the most dangerous consequences is the growing disparity with which capital punishment is enforced. But the criminal justice system does not stand apart from the rest of society as somehow more racist. It is instead an institution in which racism is manifest in more profound and damaging ways.

Race and the Juvenile Justice System

Racial discrepancies in arrest and detention rates of juveniles vary along racial/ethnic lines. Blacks make up 16 percent of the population of juveniles in this country, yet they are 28 percent of juvenile arrests, 37 percent of inmates in juvenile jails, and 58 percent of youth sent to adult prisons (Quigley 2010) (see Figure 10.4). The incarceration of juveniles has declined dramatically between 2003 and 2013, however, racial disparities have increased, with black juveniles more than four times as likely to be committed, American Indian juveniles more than three times as likely, and Hispanic juveniles 61 percent more likely to be committed to a facility as white juveniles (Rovner 2016).

While patterns of black and white inequality in the juvenile justice system are more commonly cited, data show similar disparities exist for Latino and Native American youth compared to white youth in certain jurisdictions. Latino youth make up 33 percent of the population of Santa Cruz County, California, yet they account for 64 percent of incarcerated juveniles there. This same pattern is found for Latino youth in Colorado and Native American youth in North Dakota (Walker, Spohn, and DeLone 2007).

The disparate treatment of minority youth offenders and white youth offenders extends to all stages of the juvenile justice system. Minority youth are much more likely to be incarcerated in a juvenile facility than are white youth, especially for drug

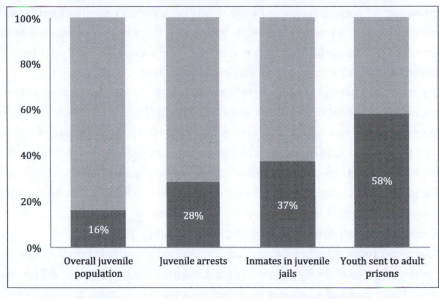

FIGURE 10.4: African American juveniles in the justice system.

SOURCE: Quigley 2010.

crimes. Racial differences in the number of juveniles who are incarcerated in adult prisons are also a concern. When juveniles are charged as adults and sent to adult prisons, they face higher risks of physical and sexual abuse by adult prisoners ("Cruel and Unusual ..." 2008). Even when controlling for severity of crime, race seems to play a role in the harsher treatment of minority juvenile offenders. We are again left with the questions, to what extent do these differences represent racial differentials in offending, and to what extent do they represent differential treatment within the juvenile justice system?

Some research finds that juvenile court authorities perceive minority youth differently than they do white youth. According to this research, the juvenile court system perceives minority youth as more dangerous and as having more negative attitudes, whereas white youth are perceived as less likely to offend and their misbehavior is associated with external factors. Police officers also perceive black boys as older and less innocent than white boys (Goff et al. 2014). Moreover, black youths' families are more likely to be defined as uncooperative than are the families of white juvenile offenders (Brown et al. 2003; Leiber and Stairs 1999; Wordes, Bynum, and Corley 1994). Some research finds that black girls face more-harsh treatment in their encounters with the juvenile justice system than white girls for similar behaviors. One explanation for this is the **adultification** of black girls, where they are viewed as less innocent, needing less support and nurturing, more independent, and knowing more about adult topics, like sex; essentially, they are perceived as more adult-like than white girls of the same age (Epstein, Blake, and González 2017). This kind of perception leads juvenile justice officials to the conclusion that black girls are more responsible for their actions, while white girls have the privilege of being assumed to not know better. Such adultification is a form of dehumanization, because it denies black children a key distinction of childhood: innocence.

Much like the cumulative disadvantages faced by racial minorities in the adult criminal justice system, perceptions informing racial biases influence juvenile sentencing. For example, juvenile authorities are more likely to institutionalize young offenders who come from families that provide what authorities perceive as inadequate supervision. Thus, a young offender from a single-mother household is more likely to be placed in a facility than a youth from a two-parent household. While US rates of children living in single-parent households are high, African Americans have the highest rates of single-parent households (see Figure 10.5).

Justifications for institutionalizing a minority child sometimes include the institution's ability to provide the child with mental health-care or drug rehabilitation, services that their parents may not be able to afford (see Box 10.2 Racial Justice Activism: The Equal Justice Initiative and All of Us or None). Unfortunately, this also means that more minority youth encounter the juvenile justice system, where even minor infractions can result in severe punishment (Brown et al. 2003).

White Privilege in the Criminal Justice System

Although whites are not exempt from police officer suspicion, arrest, and incarceration, their experiences with the criminal justice system differ in several key ways from those of most racial/ethnic minorities. Interestingly, the research on Asian

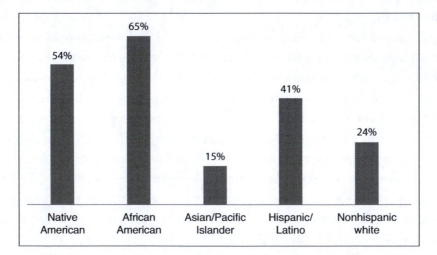

FIGURE 10.5: Percentage of children in single-parent families by race, 2017.

SOURCE: Kids Count Data Center 2016.

BOX 10.2

Racial Justice Activism:
The Equal Justice Initiative and All of Us or None

While many organizations are fighting for the rights of incarcerated individuals and racism in the criminal justice system, we choose to highlight two here: the Equal Justice Initiative (EJI) and All of Us or None. The EJI is a nonprofit organization that provides legal representation to indigent defendants who have experienced some injustice at the hands of the criminal justice system, whether that be a wrongful conviction, prosecutorial misconduct, or some experience with racial bias. They work to end mass incarceration, excessive punishment, racial and economic injustice, and to protect the human rights of the incarcerated.

One of the major issues EJI has been involved in is racial discrimination in jury selection. The organization completed a comprehensive study of racial bias in jury selection in which it interviewed African Americans who had been excluded from juries in eight southern states. EJI also analyzed court documents and records. The resulting report, *Illegal Racial Discrimination in Jury Selection: A Continuing Legacy*, found that people of color are still being excluded from jury service and that such discrimination is more likely in serious criminal trials and death penalty cases. EJI found that some district attorney's offices explicitly train prosecutors to exclude racial minorities from jury service, while teaching them how to mask the racial bias. Additional findings included prosecutors' striking black jurors from jury service for flimsy excuses—for example, they wore glasses, dyed their hair, or walked in a certain way. EJI offered detailed recommendations for ensuring the eradication of racial bias in jury selection. For example, it recommended making prosecutors who repeatedly exclude people of color from juries subject to fines, penalties, and suspension, to deter the practice.

All of Us or None describes itself as a civil and human rights organization whose primary objective is to fight for the rights of formerly and currently incarcerated people and their families. Through political mobilization, they are working to fully restore civil and human rights to formerly incarcerated persons. They have worked on "Ban the Box" campaigns and fought for restoring voting rights for felons, among others. Another key fight for All of Us or None is the Family Unity Project, which helps maintain and strengthen family relationships before and after incarceration by providing legal support, advocacy, training and public education, and developing community partnerships.

Sources: https://eji.org/about-eji and www.prisonerswithchildren.org/our-projects/family-unity-project/

Americans and the criminal justice system finds that they may be benefiting from white privilege in this arena, while still facing racial/ethnic discrimination in others (Johnson and Betsinger 2009; Kan 2003).

The presumption of innocence associated with whiteness is just one example of the many ways in which white privilege plays out within the criminal justice system. Data also show that whites are less likely to be victimized by crime than racial minorities. And although studies have shown that whites fear crime victimization more than do racial minorities, they also place more trust in law enforcement and the criminal justice system. Avoiding detection and arrest is another privilege associated with whiteness, since whites are less likely to be stopped and searched. Some scholars find implicit white favoritism built into criminal law and legal processes to be a major contributor to racial disparities in outcomes in the criminal justice system (Smith, Levinson, and Robinson 2014). In sociologist Nicole Gonzalez van Cleve's (2016) groundbreaking book *Crook County*, she describes a white privilege pipeline in Chicago's Cook County Criminal Courts where white defendants were protected from abuse by courthouse professionals and were more likely to be seen as ill rather than as bad. Mothers of white defendants were viewed as supportive of their child while mothers of black and brown defendants were seen as somehow contributing to the criminality of their children. Regardless of the reasons for a white person's encounter with the criminal justice system—whether an individual is behaving criminally or being victimized—the biases associated with whiteness pose great advantages.

THE ERA OF MASS INCARCERATION

Over the last forty years, one of the most devastating societal changes facing minority communities has been the dramatic increase in America's prison population. The United States incarcerates more people than any other nation and, as of 2008, more than 2.4 million men, women, and children were in custody (Bosworth 2010). The United States incarcerated 612 people per 100,000 in 2014, whereas England and Wales—which most closely resemble the United States culturally and socially—imprisoned only 148 per 100,000 (Bosworth 2010) (see Table 10.2). The dramatic expansion of the penal system has led some to describe the current period as the era of **hyperincarceration**, or **mass incarceration**, in which rates of imprisonment are so high that incarceration is no longer the fate of deviant individuals but a defining feature of entire communities (Garland 2001). Until 2015, incarceration rates had continued to rise. However, as Table 10.2 shows, by 2016, the prison population had begun to slightly decline, decreasing 1 percent between 2015 and 2016. In this section we explore the history of incarceration, the causes of mass incarceration, the consequences of mass incarceration, and current efforts at criminal justice reform.

Year	Total	Rate
1930	129,453	104
1940	173,706	131
1950	166,123	109
1960	212,953	117
1970	196,429	96
1980	315,974	139
1990	739,980	297
2000	1,331,278	478
2009	1,548,721	502
2014	1,561,500	612
2016	*1,506,800*	*582*

TABLE 10.2: Numbers and Rate (Per 100,000) of Sentenced Prisoners in State and Federal Institutions Between 1930 and 2016

SOURCE: "Sourcebook of Criminal Justice Statistics Online" n.d.

A History of Incarceration

The explosion in incarceration rates is a relatively new phenomenon, beginning in the mid-1970s and gaining momentum in the decades that followed. In the early 1970s, there was a serious debate among leading experts in the penology field that called into question the effectiveness of incarceration and pushed for community-based alternatives. At the time, research suggested that incarceration actually created more crime rather than preventing it and that prison conditions inhibited prisoners' successful reentry into society (Pager 2007). Despite this consensus among professionals in the field, incarceration rates increased dramatically and alternatives to prison were underutilized.

Some have argued that the evolution of the prison system has been more strongly influenced by racist attitudes than by crime rates (Perkinson 2010). To better understand the evolution of the prison system, we can look to the racialized origins of prisons in the modern-day United States. At the close of the Civil War, the South grappled with how to maintain its racial hierarchy in a nation undergoing rapid social and political change. The liberal use of prison sentencing, for instance, was one way in which white citizens sought to control former slaves.

WITNESS

"Slavery, prison, capitalism, and race have long been a deadly global cocktail. Prison was a way to subjugate natives or former slaves while serving the white economy's interests" (Dreisinger 2016:72).

Some of the country's most notorious prisons were former plantations—for example, Angola in Louisiana and Parchman Farm in Mississippi. In the post–Civil War era, these prisons emerged as a way of keeping prisoners as slaves, effectively maintaining a small free labor force (Davis 2003). Texas, along with other southern states, began to use an exemption embedded within the Thirteenth Amendment that prohibited slavery "except as a punishment for a crime" to their advantage (Perkinson 2010b). *Vagabond laws* were enacted that made a long list of behaviors illegal, including begging, loitering, panhandling, and looking for work. Someone accused of violating one of these laws could be sent to a hard-labor camp, even without the benefit of a trial. This legalized form of forced labor took the form of *convict-leasing programs*, in which prisoners were hired out to the highest bidder. Black women convicted of crimes were hired out to local families as live-in domestic laborers; black men were sent back to cotton plantations and used to clear swamps and to rebuild the South's infrastructure after the devastation caused by the Civil War. While prisoners were often worked to death under this system, planters, prison wardens, mining companies, and other industrialists grew rich off of free prison labor.

This system was set up to maintain the racial hierarchy at the close of the Civil War. And although it targeted blacks, whites were likewise subject to such laws.

IMAGE 10.3: Chain gang of convicts engaged in road work in Pitt County, North Carolina, 1910. The inmates slept in the wagons in the background. (Courtesy of the Library of Congress, LC-USF344-007541-ZB).

Between 1910 and 1945, the South relied on *chain gangs*, convict labor, to build roads, highways, and bridges. Convicts, black and white, were chained together while working and while sleeping. They were poorly fed and many were worked to death. Convict-leasing programs only ended when labor unions argued the unfairness of competing with free labor, and most chain gangs ended after World War II, when returning soldiers needed jobs (McShane 2008). Chain gangs reemerged in a few states during the 1990s when politicians ran "get tough on crime" campaigns. Alabama was the first state to reintroduce this practice, although the experiment only lasted a year (Cohen 1995). Arizona is the only state that still uses chain gangs (Allen 2011).

For blacks in the post–Civil War South, racism in the criminal justice system was the norm. The guilt of blacks was presumed at every stage of the criminal justice process. Moreover, blacks were more likely to be arrested and sentenced if the victims were white, whereas crimes committed against blacks were treated less seriously by the criminal justice system (Brown et al. 2003). In other words, racism manifested within the criminal justice system in a multitude of forms—from convict-leasing programs and chain gangs to the unfair treatment of black criminals and victims alike—which some have compared to the reenslavement of black citizens (Blackmon 2008).

Political Use of "Law and Order"

In the wake of the civil rights era, several key politicians took up the cause of "law and order." Republican presidents Richard Nixon in the early 1970s and Ronald Reagan in the 1980s made law and order a central theme of their campaigns and used it as a strategy to attract disgruntled white voters who were weary of or unsympathetic to black activism and the civil rights movement. Within this campaign, civil rights for minorities, and specifically the protest tactics of civil disobedience (see Chapter 6), were defined as a threat to law and order. While couched in race-neutral language, the theme of "law and order" had racial implications.

In 1971, Nixon declared a "war on crime," citing drug abuse as "public enemy number one" at a news conference, despite the fact that polls showed that Americans did not view substance abuse as a major problem facing the country. In 1982, Reagan followed with a "war on drugs," despite the fact that substance abuse was declining, and attracted bipartisan support to the cause. Politicians' "get tough on crime" campaign pledges, and their approaches to governance, helped to see through harsh legislation—such as the implementation of the drug war, mandatory minimum sentencing laws, "three strikes" laws, and the virtual elimination of parole.

Mandatory minimum sentences require persons convicted of certain crimes to be punished with at least a minimum number of years in prison, thus eliminating judicial discretion in sentencing that might take into account whether it was a defendant's first offense, for instance. In 1973, New York State was the first state to implement mandatory minimum sentences of fifteen years to life for a drug conviction of possession of more than four ounces of a hard drug. This sentencing trend quickly spread to the rest of the country. A specific type of mandatory minimum sentence, "three strikes" laws, emerged in California in 1994. Three strikes laws require someone facing their third felony conviction to serve a minimum of twenty-five years in prison. All of these have contributed to the rise in US prison population and the fact that the prison population is disproportionately minority. For instance, white offenders are less likely than both black and Latino offenders to receive a mandatory minimum sentence (Vincent and Hofer 1994). Although it is arguable whether racist intent informed the design of these policies, their implementation has had serious racial consequences.

Prison Industrial Complex

Another explanation for the dramatic increase in incarceration rates in the United States is the trend toward **prison privatization**, which takes place when states contract out their correctional services to private businesses. Prison privatization can refer to the contracting of prisons as whole entities, such as when private corporations receive tax dollars to manage prisons, as well as to the contracting of particular services within prisons, such as food preparation, laundry, or medical treatment. In the latter case, services paid for by the state are provided by private businesses (McShane 2008). In either form, prison privatization allows businesses to make a profit off crime—not unlike the profits made from convict leasing and chain gangs.

While chain gangs and convict-leasing programs are mostly obsolete, prison labor has expanded dramatically. Inmates around the country can be forced to work for little to no compensation (sometimes totally uncompensated, sometimes for as little as two cents per hour). If they refuse, they can be severely punished—placed in solitary confinement, have accumulated "good time" revoked, or denied family visits. Prisoners are working in fields, prison kitchens, and in manufacturing. They are being forced to labor in mining, agriculture, garment production, and even as call center personnel. They are not protected by employment law because they are defined not as employees but as prisoners. Countless businesses are making huge profits off of such involuntary labor (Benns 2015).

Prisons are big business. Corrections Corporation of America (CCA), now known as CoreCivic, is the largest private prison operator in the United States and as of 2007 owned and operated sixty-six correctional facilities in the country (Lee 2012). The GEO Group is another private prison corporation, operating not only in the US but throughout the world. Private prison operators such as CoreCivic and GEO Group have a vested interest in the expansion of the incarcerated population. One of Core-Civic and GEO Group's approaches to maintaining financial prosperity has been to lobby Congress to sponsor "get tough on crime" legislation. They write laws that are designed to create more prisoners through criminalizing more behavior and increasing corresponding sentencing. Such legislation has managed to put more people behind bars for longer periods of time than at any point in US history (Harr 1999).

The fact that prisons are businesses has meant that many rural communities experiencing decades of economic decline welcome them. While prisons have historically been viewed as LULUs (locally undesirable land uses), much like polluting industries, for many impoverished, rural, southern communities of color, the situation is more nuanced. People of color are often disproportionately represented among correctional officers, for instance. Research finds that in these rural ghettos, prisons are "neither panacea nor pariah" (Eason 2017:171). While they provide jobs for rural communities with little else to rely on, prison construction is also costly to states already facing budgetary limitations. Eason (2017) further argues that calls for prison abolition (discussed later in this chapter) overlook the negative effects this will have on poor, rural communities of color.

The trend toward increasing prison privatization is part of a larger **prison industrial complex**, a term that refers to the interconnectedness of politicians, government, and private industry and the incentives associated with a commitment to increasing spending on the prison industry, even as crime rates decrease (Schlosser 1998).

While the private prison industry has successfully lobbied Congress to continue funding the war on drugs and the prison industry, it has also sought other ways to maximize profits. A recognized growth area for this industry is the incarceration of undocumented immigrants. When the private prison industry began flooding the prison market in the early years of the twenty-first century, stock prices plummeted and prisons closed (Mencimer 2008). But ultimately the industry's bottom line was saved by a new source of business: the crackdown on illegal immigrants, which took on even greater significance during the George W. Bush administration (Mencimer 2008).

Previously, US immigration policy did not encourage the detaining of undocumented immigrants unless they carried criminal records. Instead, Mexican immigrants were taken back across the border and those from farther away were given court dates to begin their removal proceedings. Because so many failed to show up for their court dates, the Immigration and Customs Enforcement agency changed its policy to one of detaining non-Mexican immigrants pending asylum hearings and maintained the policy of taking undocumented Mexicans back across the border.

As of 2008, these detention facilities hold around thirty thousand people on any given day (Mencimer 2008). Under President Obama, the average daily population of immigrants being detained was between thirty thousand and forty thousand.

As of 2018 under President Trump, over 45,890 immigrants are being held on any given day (Bischoff 2019). Some facilities only house children who have been separated from their parents. There is a lot of money to be made in the warehousing of immigrants, and CoreCivic was awarded millions in contracts. There are now almost two hundred immigration detention centers in the US, housing undocumented immigrants and asylum seekers for indefinite periods of time. Conditions in many of these have been described as "unconscionable," as they are overcrowded, where inmates are held without soap, toothpaste, or beds, and lack adequate food and water. Twenty-two immigrants have died in detention centers during the past two years, including four children by June of 2019.

The idea of prison privatization was initially sold to politicians as a way to cut costs and save the government money. For instance, private prisons save money by cutting personnel and by not filling open positions quickly and instead operating short staffed. They replace guards with video cameras. Programs for prisoners have also been cut. By cutting personnel and programs, and leaving prisoners idle and unattended, private prisons have put their employees and prisoners at greater risk of inmate violence (Bates 1998). Unfortunately, private prisons do not save the state much money, if any at all (Bates 1998). Instead, private prisons have sought tax credits, to be paid by US taxpayers, for prison construction. Despite the lack of savings, politicians have continued to favor the growth in private prisons because so many have become personally and politically invested in the industry.

The War on Drugs

The greatest factor contributing to the growing prison population in the United States, as well as its racial impacts, is the war on drugs. Although it was initiated by the Nixon administration under the banner of a "war on crime," every presidential administration since has used it for political advancement, at the expense of poor and minority communities (Moore and Elkavich 2008).

Between the mid-1980s and the mid-1990s, the number of black men sentenced to prison for drug offenses increased by more than 700 percent (Brown et al. 2003). This figure, however, has not paralleled increasing drug use in the black community. Instead, all research indicates that drug use is equally pervasive, if not more pervasive, in the white community as it is in minority communities. Only approximately 15 percent of illicit drug users are African Americans while 72 percent are white (Moore and Elkavich 2008). The drug war is also responsible for the dramatic increase in the number of Latinos in US prisons, despite the fact that Latinos make up a smaller percentage of illicit drug users than do African Americans or whites. Still, together, blacks and Latinos account for 75 percent of people who go to prison on drug charges (Alexander 2010).

During the 1980s, under the Reagan administration, millions of dollars were funneled toward drug control and prison construction. The administration declared a "war on drugs" in 1982, a curious position to take considering the declining drug use during that period, as well as the fact that public opinion polls of the era found that drugs did not rank high on the list of the most important issues facing the nation. Many have explained the war on drugs as a response to the crack epidemic of the 1980s. However, Reagan's war on drugs actually pre-dates widespread crack use in urban minority communities, a crisis that gained attention around 1984 (Alexander 2010). Since the declaration of the war on drugs, drug-related arrest rates for African Americans have skyrocketed while those for whites have increased only slightly. Between 1965 and the early 1980s, blacks were only twice as likely as whites to be arrested for drug-related offenses. By the end of the 1980s, blacks faced five times the drug-related arrest rates as did whites (Sampson and Lauritsen 1997).

There are many aspects of the war on drugs that have contributed to the disproportionate number of racial minorities who are incarcerated. These range from changes in sentencing laws to changes in policing. In the case of sentencing law, minorities were greatly affected by the Anti-Drug Abuse Act of 1986. This legislation legalized a significant discrepancy between crack sentencing laws and those for powder cocaine. After the passage of this legislation, an individual caught with five grams of crack cocaine received the same prison sentence as did someone convicted of distributing five hundred grams of powder cocaine (Cole 2009). In other words, crack *users* were treated like powder cocaine *dealers* in the eyes of the law. Crack cocaine—which is simply powder cocaine cooked up with baking soda—was associated with urban America and perceived to be primarily an African American drug. In reality, 65 percent of crack users were white, yet only 4.7 percent of white crack users were convicted of crimes involving crack cocaine (Cole 2009).

Many black defendants have challenged the disparity on constitutional grounds, but all have failed in the courts. In July 2010, Congress passed legislation that significantly reduced this crack and powder cocaine sentencing disparity by overturning the previous legislation from 1986 on the understanding that the hundred-to-one ratio (grams of cocaine to grams of crack) was based upon myths and not reality. Scientific evidence, including a major study published in the *Journal of the American Medical Association*, has proven that crack and powder cocaine have identical effects on the body (Hatsukami and Fischman 1996). Still, the new law has only reduced the disparity, from one hundred to one to eighteen to one, rather than eliminating it altogether.

Policing tactics have changed in response to the drug war as well. Police departments around the country are now being trained by the Drug Enforcement Agency to conduct what are known as pretextual traffic stops as a drug interdiction practice. This practice has resulted in an unprecedented roundup of Americans for nonviolent drug crimes. In turn, police departments are rewarded with federal funding. Many people mistakenly conclude that the increase in drug arrests must reflect a surge in drug use. However, what's more significant is the financial incentive the federal government provides to police departments for drug arrests (Alexander 2010).

The drug war, new policing tactics, the emergence of the prison industrial complex, and the political use of campaign promises of "law and order" have all resulted in a growing prison population composed largely and disproportionately of racial minorities. Has mass incarceration made us a safer society by acting as a deterrent to crime?

The Effect on Crime Rates

Changes in policing and legislation regarding drug use and arrests have had profoundly negative consequences on minority communities—socially, economically, and politically. Popular wisdom suggests that the more criminals we incarcerate, the safer our communities will be. But if that were the case, the fact that more than 2.3 million people are incarcerated in the United States would mean crime rates are decreasing and communities are safer. Unfortunately, the relationship between crime rates and incarceration rates is more complicated. During the 1970s and early 1980s, crime rates, specifically for violent crimes, were on the increase, perhaps justifying tougher sentencing laws and increased incarceration rates. However, drug use declined during that period. Shifting our attention from the "war on crime" to the more specific "war on drugs" shifted our attention away from the problem of crime and created additional problems.

To what extent are drugs and crime related? Certainly some criminal acts are drug related. *Drug-related crime* refers to violent behaviors engaged in while under the influence of drugs or to robberies committed so as to get money to buy drugs. However, testing positive for drugs does not mean that drugs caused the person to commit a crime, as the person may have committed the crime without ingesting drugs. Research finds that most violent crimes are not the acts of desperate individuals seeking money to buy drugs. Only 17 percent of people incarcerated claim they committed their offense to obtain money for drugs (Walker 2006). Thus, the link between drugs and crime is complicated.

Since the mid-1990s, crime rates have steadily decreased while our prison population has continued to explode. While there is no single accepted explanation for why crime rates dropped, one argument is that by the 1990s, there was a significant decrease in demand for crack cocaine—a "one generation" drug because its effects were so devastating on users and their loved ones (Egan 1999). Mass incarceration is believed to account for only 10 to 20 percent of this crime drop, according to the National Research Council, which is one of the reasons that crime policies since the

1980s are argued to be expensive and ineffective (Tonry 1995). To have safer communities, taking on violent crime is necessary. However, the mass incarceration of the last thirty years has affected primarily nonviolent offenders. The war on crime has essentially backfired, resulting in overcrowded prisons, depleted state budgets, and an overloaded criminal justice system. In response, corrections officials have recently been forced to release many violent offenders early, since they are not faced with mandatory minimum sentences the way drug offenders are (McCorkel 2013).

Global Effects of Mass Incarceration and the War on Drugs

The war on drugs, mass incarceration, and their negative effects are global. As Baz Dreisinger notes:

> Between 2008 and 2011, the prison population grew in 78 percent of all countries. Some 10.3 million people worldwide are behind bars … Yet the public conversation rarely seemed to turn from America's incarceration crisis to the global prison problem—something the United States built and then foisted on the world.
>
> (2016:19–20)

From the war on drugs, to private prisons, to supermaxes and the increased use of solitary confinement, the US has exported our problematic yet profitable model across the globe. Thailand, for instance, has modeled their tough on drugs stance after the US, resulting in prisons at triple the capacity (Dreisinger 2016).

One of the most significant consequences of the global war on drugs is the dramatic increase in conflict and violence in some of the poorest regions of the world, which are generally populated by people of color. Because there is a high demand for illegal drugs, criminal entrepreneurs enter the market and use violence to control it. Some of this violence is directed at politicians, police, and the military, but much of it is directed at ordinary citizens. In Mexico, for instance, drug cartels and vigilante groups are estimated to have been responsible for over sixty thousand murders between 2006 and 2012 (Bender 2015).

Due to the massive amounts of money involved, the war on drugs has increased corruption and undermined governments throughout the world, including in Mexico, Afghanistan, Nigeria, and Colombia, among others ("Corruption" 2016). Another negative outcome of the global war on drugs is the criminalization of poverty. Faced with limited opportunities, poor people in impoverished nations like Myanmar, Afghanistan, and Colombia turn to drug-crop production to survive. There are negative environmental consequences as well, as increased law enforcement forces drug-crop production deeper and deeper into forested areas, resulting in deforestation and pollution from the spraying of pesticides ("The War on Drugs" n.d.).

Effects on Minority Families and Communities

In the US criminal justice system, the emphasis has been on incarcerating offenders. One result of this emphasis is that we pay much less attention to the consequences of mass incarceration, particularly its effects on families of prisoners and on communities. Only a few crimes warrant life sentences without the possibility of parole or the death penalty. Thus, it is worth examining the collateral damage associated with mass incarceration. The financial burden of incarceration on a family can be crippling. Communities, too, often bear the economic brunt. Ninety-five percent of prisoners are released eventually, once they have served their sentences (Pager 2007). Approximately six hundred thousand prisoners are released from prison every year (Carson 2014). Despite such high numbers, most communities remain untouched by reentry, since "prisoner reentry is highly concentrated in a relatively small number of neighborhoods, generally within metropolitan areas" (Kirk 2016). This means that the most impoverished and vulnerable communities absorb the bulk of returning prisoners.

Minority communities are hit hardest by hyperincarceration. In fact, the costs associated with mass incarceration are so substantial that some have compared it to a hidden tax imposed on poor and minority families (Braman 2004). One out of every six black men and one out of every thirteen Latino men have spent some time in prison, and together they make up 66 percent of the prison population (Perkinson 2010). According to some research, an estimated 28 percent of black men will spend some time in prison during the course of their lives (Brown et al. 2003). Unfortunately, incarceration has become a rite of passage for minority youth with few economic opportunities (Western, Pattillo, and Weiman 2004). A collective cost of mass incarceration that communities of color bear is the increased levels of policing and surveillance of their communities, which increases the odds of residents' contact with the criminal justice system (Pettit and Gutierrez 2018).

REFLECT AND CONNECT

What are some of the consequences of the normalization of incarceration for communities of color? What are some of the consequences of the normalization of incarceration for American society overall?

Economic Effects

When a person is released from prison, finding employment is a major hurdle. While most people in prison arrive there poor, a criminal record can help to ensure they and their families will remain poor following release. A felony conviction, for example, marks a person as unqualified for a wide variety of jobs as well as government assistance programs, such as housing, welfare, and student loans. In a sense, a felony conviction means that employers and government agencies can legally discriminate against released individuals who have served their time (Alexander 2010).

WITNESS

Sociologist Devah Pager finds that the mark of a criminal record severely constrains employment options and "the extremely low callback rate among black ex-offenders (5 per 100 applications) suggests that the combination of minority status and a criminal record results in almost total exclusion from this labor market" (2007:101).

A movement to "ban the box" has emerged that is fighting to have the question "Have you ever been convicted of a felony?" removed from employment applications. The idea is that checking "Yes" essentially ends any consideration of employment, no questions asked. It could be a nonviolent drug conviction that is decades old, but employers who stop considering the application when they hit the answer "yes" are unlikely to find this out. "Banning the box" would force employers to explore the job candidate's qualifications in detail before obtaining details about their potential criminal background. This campaign is working to make prisoner reentry more successful, as statistics on ex-offenders are otherwise quite bleak: one year after release, ex-offenders face 75 percent jobless rates and 45 percent rearrest rates (Pager 2007).

In 2004, there were over thirteen million ex-convicts in the United States, and six hundred thousand more are released from US prisons each year (Gonnerman 2004). Urban minority communities face the most negative consequences, as their young people—overwhelmingly their young men—make up the disproportionate rates of those incarcerated or living with felony convictions. Another impact of incarceration is the financial hardship experienced by the families of prisoners. Two-thirds of people in prison were employed prior to their arrest, albeit mostly in low-wage jobs (Braman 2004). The loss of their income is a significant blow to family members on the outside.

Effects on Families

Incarceration is a major obstacle for families in poor minority communities, especially when those families have children. As Dreisinger explains, "broken homes are acute collateral consequences of incarceration, shattering a family's foundation emotionally and economically" (2016:146). One of the consequences of mass incarceration is the growing number of single-parent families in these communities.

Incarceration is a significant marital stressor, often resulting in divorce. It also limits marriage options once a person is released. Men who have been incarcerated, for instance, are much less likely to be married to or living with the mother of their children than are men who have never been incarcerated (Western, Lopoo, and McLanahan 2004).

Most people in prison are parents; specifically, 75 percent of female prisoners are parents and 2.7 million children have parents who are incarcerated (Dreisinger 2016). Children of incarcerated parents are often cared for by family members, while others end up in foster homes or other forms of state care. In the latter cases, strict timelines limit incarcerated parents' ability to maintain custody of their children and, depending on the terms of the incarceration, can lead to the termination of their parental rights. Many children end up living with the other parent or, in some cases, living on their own, even as minors (Johnson and Waldfogel 2004). Children with incarcerated parents are more likely to be abused, live in poverty, and end up incarcerated (Braman 2004). Many exhibit aggressive behavior, withdrawal, or depression, effects that often hurt their performance in school and limit their relationships with others (Baunach 1985; Kampfner 1995).

Maintaining a relationship with an incarcerated family member is difficult. Because there are so few women's prisons, for example, incarcerated mothers often find themselves imprisoned hours away from their families, limiting visits and weakening family ties. Prisoners have limited access to telephones, and what access they do have can be prohibitively expensive, a privilege few can afford. Collect calls from prisons include a hefty surcharge, making it difficult for families to bear the additional financial burden. All of these factors—increased financial burdens, marital strain, social stigmas, and the effects on children—are symptomatic of the larger problem of mass incarceration and its effects on families and communities.

WITNESS

One mother describes her child's reaction to their separation due to her incarceration: "Her hair was falling out and she wasn't growing. She bit on her nails, she was still in diapers and had bad diaper rash, her nerves were shot—she was in shock" (Poehlmann 2003).

Political Disenfranchisement

In the United States, felons and ex-convicts face restrictions on their political rights. While many countries—including Denmark, Ireland, Finland, and Australia—allow prisoners to vote, only two states in the United States—Maine and Vermont—allow prisoners to retain this right. Thirty-three states bar parolees and probationers from voting. Fourteen states ban all former felons from voting, a practice that is not found in any European country (Manza and Uggen 2006). Factored together, these restrictions disqualify 2.3 percent of potential voters, largely from low-income and African American and Latino communities (Behrens, Uggen, and Manza 2003). In 2002, the US Senate voted against restoring voting rights to ex-felons in federal elections. These data help to demonstrate how the political disenfranchisement of felons and ex-felons affects more than the individuals involved. The needs of entire communities are neglected when such a significant percentage of their members is disenfranchised. In 2018, Florida voted in favor of a state constitutional amendment to restore voting rights to people with felony convictions, allowing the enfranchisement of nearly 1.5 million people. However, in the spring of 2019, Republican lawmakers attempted to again limit many of those very people from being able to vote. They passed a law that requires all people with felony convictions to pay all court fees, fines, and restitution before they are eligible to vote. Florida, like many states, makes defendants pay for their use of a public defender or electronic monitoring devices, things which used to be free. There are over 115 surcharges and fees and the state is known for charging exorbitant fees. This new law will likely deter hundreds of thousands of felons from voting (Racz 2019).

Female Offenders

The United States incarcerates more women than any nation in the world. One of the most significant effects the drug war has had on minority communities is the increasing number of women being incarcerated. The number of women in federal and state prisons has increased by 400 percent since the start of the war on drugs; more than 75 percent are African American or Latina, and the majority have children under the age of eighteen (McCorkel 2013). While men make up the bulk of prisoners, women are the fastest-growing sector of the prison population (Brewer and Heitzeg 2008). The implementation of mandatory minimum sentencing laws and three strikes laws are argued to have a differential impact on women offenders (Meierhoefer 1992). These types of laws were intended to keep repeat, dangerous, violent offenders off the street. However, women are more likely to commit property and drug crimes and are only rarely involved in violent crimes (Casey and Wiatrowski 1996). Some attribute the growing numbers of female prisoners to the feminization of poverty, women's disproportionate likelihood of being impoverished, which is often expressed in petty crimes committed in order to provide for a family. The majority of female offenders are parents. Because women are the primary caretakers in the eyes of the law, incarceration for extended periods of time under mandatory minimum sentencing laws has devastating effects on the children they leave behind (Casey and Wiatrowski 1996).

When it comes to sentencing, however, female defendants of all races appear to be at a relative advantage. Research finds that female defendants receive more lenient sentences than male defendants do, while black and Latino defendants receive less-favorable treatment than do white defendants. However, when exploring the intersection of race/ethnicity and gender, Steffensmeier and Demuth (2006) find that race/ethnicity influences the sentencing of male defendants but not female defendants. Ultimately, gender is a more powerful predictor of sentencing across all racial/ethnic groups.

Religious Discrimination in Prisons: Native Americans and Muslims

Native Americans make up less than 2 percent of the American population. However, like African Americans and Latinos, they are comparatively overrepresented in prisons. They are also more likely to receive harsher prison sentences than are white offenders for similar offenses (McDonald 2007). Native Americans convicted of assault with a deadly weapon on a reservation face federal courts and, thus, receive penalties twice as harsh as someone convicted of the same crime not committed on a reservation and therefore facing a state court (Ross 1998).

Incarcerated Native Americans face discrimination related to religious freedoms. Despite constitutional guarantees and such federal legislation as the American Indians Religious Freedom Act of 1978, Native American prisoners have had to organize and fight to gain access to native religious practices while incarcerated. These practices include pipe ceremonies, sweats, prayer and drum sessions, and the right to wear their hair long (Irwin 2006). In 1984, several Native American prisoners, including political prisoner Leonard Peltier, participated in a fast to raise public awareness of the religious freedom being denied them in prison. Although the courts have ruled in favor of prisoners' right to religious practice, prison staff in many states have consistently refused to accommodate Native prisoner requests (McDonald 2007).

WITNESS

"I am an American Indian (Comanche), imprisoned in the Texas Department of Criminal Justice—Institutional Division. When I first entered prison on April 8, 1987, I knew very little about what legal rights I had. … And I certainly did not know that one of those rights prohibited me from being held down and my hair forcibly cut by prison officials, regardless of my religious beliefs. Nevertheless, that is exactly what took place. That day is so vivid in my mind, the act so offensive, that I even took an oath afterwards that I would not cut my hair ever again as long as I remained incarcerated, let alone allow any prison official to forcibly do so" (Montana 2002).

Native Americans are not the only racial/ethnic minority group to experience religious discrimination while incarcerated; since 9/11, incarcerated Muslims have also witnessed constraints on their right to religious expression. The right to religious expression while institutionalized was passed by Congress in 2000 under the Religious Land Use and Institutionalized Persons Act and later upheld by the Supreme Court in *Cutter v. Wilkenson* (2005). Despite these, incarcerated Muslims complain that their dietary restrictions are not met; they are not allowed to wear religious garb and cannot wear their facial hair more than a quarter of an inch in length; they are denied access to chapel or religious services and to a Koran and other religious materials; their holy days are not observed; and, finally, they complain of being forced to participate in Christian religious services (Marcus 2009). The reason Muslim inmates have faced increasing discrimination since 9/11 is that there is a fear among prison officials that prisons could become breeding grounds for Muslim radicals (Marcus 2009).

Dismantling the Prison Industrial Complex

The United States is beginning to rethink and rein in the prison industrial complex (McCorkel 2013). The initial concerns surrounded costs and state budget shortfalls. Criminal justice reform now includes not only decreasing the US prison population, but reducing overly harsh prison sentences and altering drug sentencing policy. In 2009, the state of California faced a $19.9 billion budget shortfall, due almost entirely to "the state's commitment to 'getting tough' on crime by incarcerating more people, even those convicted of minor drug offenses, for long periods of time" (McCorkel 2013:ix). To address the budget shortfall, Governor Arnold Schwarzenegger cut social programs and capped spending on prisons. He was the first prominent politician to begin backing away from the "law and order" approach that had begun in the 1970s. Every tax dollar spent incarcerating people is, of course, money that could have gone to schools, health-care, or infrastructure. According to the US Department of Education, between 1990 and 2013, state funds allocated per student for education fell by 28 percent while per capita spending on incarceration increased by 44 percent ("State, Local Spending ..." 2016). The Trump administration passed a criminal justice reform bill known as the First Step Act, which reduced some federal prison sentences, allowing some incarcerated federal prisoners to qualify for early release.

Beyond concerns with the costs of mass incarceration, many have begun to question the drug war itself and the logic behind incarcerating so many nonviolent offenders. As of June 2019, eleven states and Washington, DC, have legalized recreational marijuana and twenty-two states and two territories, Puerto Rico and Guam, have made medical marijuana legal. It remains illegal at the federal level. Evidence from Colorado finds that racial discrepancies still exist, despite marijuana legalization. Since it is only legal for adults, juveniles can still be arrested for pot offenses. In Colorado, arrest rates for whites between the ages of 11 and 17 fell by 10 percent between 2012 and 2014, while arrest rates rose 20 percent for Latino youths and 50 percent for black youths during that same time period (Markus 2016). Legal scholar Michelle Alexander has pointed out that marijuana legalization has resulted in white men getting rich in the new industry while in Colorado two hundred thousand men, overwhelmingly racial minorities, remain behind bars for marijuana offenses. She and others argue that we need to go beyond legalization and start talking about reparations for minority communities who were targets of the drug war for forty years and who are still living with the fallout (Flanders 2019; Short 2014).

Mass Incarceration and White Privilege

While white privilege protects many whites from extensive personal experience with the criminal justice system, it is perhaps more effective at keeping mass incarceration invisible; whites are socialized not to see the problem of mass incarceration because its effect on white communities has been minimal. In this way, white people are actually complicit in the system of mass incarceration. White people "have the privilege to imagine [they] will never be in prison, and that prison is only the consequence of proven criminal behavior … to see prisons as functioning solely for punishment, rehabilitation and deterrence to crime" (Mikulich, Cassidy, and Pfeil 2013:6).

Some scholars argue that the black community inadvertently bears some complicity in the creation of the problem of mass incarceration and its unintended disproportionate effect on black communities (Forman 2017). For instance, many African American clergy, activists, police chiefs, journalists, elected officials, prosecutors, and judges supported tough-on-crime policies in the 1970s, in the hope that it would end gun violence and drug crime in their communities. James Forman, Jr., (2017) also emphasizes that during this same period African Americans were fighting for more than harsh punishment for offenders; they also fought for better housing, schools, and job opportunities for those marginalized from the economic mainstream.

LINKING RACE AND CRIME IN THE PUBLIC CONSCIOUSNESS

Americans are exposed to countless media images that incorrectly lead us to believe that most black men are criminals and to automatically link crime with young black men (Russell 1998). "Fear of the black male" that can influence jurors to convict a white police officer of involuntary manslaughter instead of voluntary manslaughter is part of a larger myth perpetrated in American society: namely, that of the black male criminal. George Zimmerman perceived the unarmed Trayvon Martin, a black 17-year-old carrying Skittles and iced tea as a suspect and thus began following him, which led to an altercation and Martin's death. Despite the fact that the only armed person was Zimmerman, the police initially did not even arrest him, instead accepting his story that he killed Martin in self-defense. While explaining his actions at the police station, Zimmerman continually referred to Martin as "the suspect" despite the fact that Martin had committed no crime, and the police officers failed to challenge the inaccurate characterization. A mostly white jury of six women found Zimmerman not guilty of second-degree murder. Zimmerman, the police officers on duty, and the jury seemed to equate "black male" with "criminal."

The perceived link between crime and young black men is pervasive in American culture. Overall racial attitudes have become more progressive over the past few decades; however, the same does not hold true for attitudes about race and crime. Blacks are continually stereotyped by otherwise progressive respondents as prone to violence (Pager 2007). Americans live, for the most part, in racially segregated worlds; thus, stereotypes are often used in place of true understanding of people with different racial and ethnic backgrounds. The problem with stereotypes is that they tend to act as substitutes for actual experience and knowledge.

This image of young men of color as criminal is not class specific. Interviews with middle-class black college students find that they, too, are targeted by police (Barnes 2000). For black men, their encounters with police begin as early as elementary school and become an expected and unpleasant part of their lives. The majority of students interviewed in one study reported being stopped by police whether they were driving or walking in their own neighborhood, and that it was typical for black males driving nice cars to be stopped and searched (Barnes 2000). Sociologist Elijah Anderson (2011) describes the experience of an African American male law student at the University of Pennsylvania who was targeted by police because he fit the description of a perpetrator. As the student waited for a bus and talked on the phone to his girlfriend, holding groceries and a backpack of books, he was approached by police, with guns drawn, and ordered to place his hands on the wall. At least seven other police cars responded to the scene. He was aggressively frisked and handcuffed. He was humiliated as students and professors from the law school began to gather across the street. Ultimately, the police radio announced that the actual suspect they had sought had been apprehended. When the story was later reported on the news, it turned out the suspect had been a white male. Some researchers describe the cumulative effect of dealing with such racial harassment, particularly in predominantly white environments, like that of a college campus, as racial battle fatigue (Smith, Allen, and Danley 2007). **Racial battle fatigue** refers to the physiological and psychological symptoms—such as tension headaches, elevated heartbeat, extreme fatigue, ulcers, hypervigilance, anger, and inability to sleep—associated with the constant exposure to racial slights, indignities and irritations, unfair treatment, and both subtle and overt racial hostilities (Smith, Allen, and Danley 2007). African American males attending predominantly white colleges and universities found that they were under heightened police surveillance on and off campus, repeatedly being defined as "out of place" or "fitting the description" of a suspected criminal there to steal instead of study. They reported a range of psychological reactions to this ongoing surveillance, from frustration and shock to anger, resentment, hopelessness, and fear (Smith, Allen, and Danley 2007). These are young, middle-class black men on their own college campuses who are assumed to be criminal. For poor, urban young black men without opportunities, the assumption of their criminality can become a self-fulfilling prophecy. Black faculty members on college campuses report inspiring similar suspicions while on their own campuses, particularly if it is late at night or a weekend (Rockquemore and Laszloffy 2008).

Racial Minorities and Crime Victimization

An unexpected statistic that defies common perceptions of a race–crime link pertains to victimization: racial minorities are much more likely to be victimized by crime than are whites, with Native Americans having the highest rates of violent crime victimization. Yet the stereotype remains of racial minorities as perpetrators of crimes and not as victims. African Americans are twice as likely as whites to be the victims of robbery, for instance. Latino households are also more likely to be victimized by crime than non-Latino households. African Americans and, to a lesser extent, Latinos suffer much higher rates of robbery than whites. Homicide is the leading cause of death among black and Latino males and females aged 15 to 24 (Sampson and Lauritsen 1997). This information is gathered through the National Crime Victimization Survey (NCVS), data compiled by the Bureau of Justice Statistics. Over the last twenty years, NCVS data has shown that the risk of personally experiencing violent crime is much higher for African Americans than it is for whites (Sampson and Lauritsen 1997).

This is especially true for sexual minority and gender-nonconforming people of color, as homophobic and transphobic violence, from verbal abuse to physical attacks to murder, has escalated dramatically, according to the National Coalition of Anti-Violence Programs. All LGBTQ people are not at equal risk for such violent victimization, however. LGBTQ people of color are disproportionately victimized. For instance, in 2013, 72 percent of LGBTQ murders were of transgender women of color. The year 2017 was the most violent year on record for transgender people: twenty-nine were murdered, most of whom were black or Latina; twenty-six transgender people were murdered in 2018; and as of June 2019, eleven transgender people were murdered, all of whom were trans women of color (Ring 2019).

The predominant image of racial minorities as criminals is exemplified in the media coverage of one of the largest-scale technological disasters in the United States: Hurricane Katrina and the levee breaches which flooded New Orleans. When the levees failed in New Orleans on August 29, 2005, news coverage of the destruction revealed undeniable race and class inequalities. Perhaps the most resounding and disturbing images were those of poor black Americans stranded on the roofs of their homes as the flood waters washed away the city and their lives. The levee breaches resulted in 80 percent of the city of New Orleans being flooded; thus, it was not only black New Orleanians who were negatively affected. However, most poor New Orleanians are black, and, thus, they were the residents who were unable to adhere to the mandatory evacuation, due to lack of transportation or lack of funds to stay in hotels during the evacuation. Seeing these images repeated over the days and weeks to follow, many Americans began to ask: When will the government intervene? How can so many Americans be awaiting rescue?

In the aftermath of the hurricane and levee failure, over fifteen hundred people died and three hundred thousand were displaced. More than thirty thousand New Orleanians, most of whom were black and poor, were trapped for four days in the Superdome and the Convention Center, whose makeshift shelters were unprepared for the disaster and were without food, water, or proper sanitation (Sanyika 2009).

From the moment disaster struck, media coverage of Katrina ran sensationalistic reports of crime, lawlessness, and disorder. Leading politicians, such as the mayor and chief of police of New Orleans, echoed the sensationalistic and undocumented stories, and unfounded accusations were reported to the national media, including stories of babies being raped in the Superdome. Many reports of black lawlessness were accepted by American audiences at face value. The image of a poor black man wreaking havoc on his fellow citizens during a national crisis was believable, if for no other reason than it fit the media-perpetrated image of black lawlessness. While the looting of damaged and unoccupied homes was in fact documented and reported on, the majority of media reports of violence in the immediate aftermath of the hurricane was groundless (Frailing and Harper 2007).

Through the chaos and, to some extent, the breakdown of law and order following the levee failure and the flooding of New Orleans, one can see how unconscious racism influenced the believability of media stories of rampant lawlessness by poor blacks. Media stories of heroism on the part of police also found traction in the cultural narrative of this disaster, much of which was well deserved. Stories of police violence, however, did not fit our cultural narrative and, thus, took more time to surface.

The government response to this catastrophe, at all levels—local, state, and federal—has been criticized as insufficient. Disaster conditions can trigger a breakdown of the social order as well as the ability of institutions to function. But in the case of Katrina, there is some evidence that law and order was valued at the expense of human life.

BOX 10.3

Global Perspectives:
Postapartheid Police Accountability in South Africa

Under South Africa's apartheid regime (1948–1994), a system of legal racial segregation in which blacks were deprived of land, citizenship, and rights, the police force violently enforced the social order. Police abuses and human rights violations, such as the extensive use of excessive force, torture, the deaths of numerous antiapartheid activists while in police custody, and the existence of a South African police hit squad, went unpunished.

In the transition to democracy in 1994, the apartheid police forces were replaced by the South African Police Service, consisting of most of the same personnel from the apartheid police forces. Perhaps not surprisingly, the new police force lacked public confidence.

As part of the country's path to healing, South Africa established a Truth and Reconciliation Commission (TRC) in 1995 under the leadership of Archbishop Desmond Tutu. The commission provided amnesty for political crimes committed between 1960 and 1994 in exchange for full public testimony concerning actions they were responsible for (Worden 2007). National leaders, religious groups, and human rights lawyers had begun discussing how to address the nation's past, acknowledging there could be no new South Africa unless the brutal oppression of the apartheid years was faced honestly (Storey 1997). Under the apartheid regime, whites had been exposed to years of political propaganda that denied the brutality of the apartheid years; thus, the majority of whites refused to acknowledge the torture, abuse, and assassinations that had been carried out by the secret police for decades (Storey 1997).

The TRC held public hearings that were broadcast daily in which both victims and perpetrators told their stories, making white denial of this past difficult. In exchange for full disclosure of abuses committed under apartheid, the TRC process provided amnesty. This process has resulted in many South African police officers recognizing the value of this kind of police accountability and that they were no longer operating within a culture of impunity. Other police officers felt no remorse, claiming instead that, under apartheid, they were engaged in a race war; thus, their actions were justified (Rauch 2005).

In the first days following the disaster, while supplies quickly dwindled in the Superdome and the Convention Center, the state made law enforcement a top priority. A makeshift prison was established, complete with law enforcement personnel, food, water, and working toilets (Eggers 2009). Meanwhile, the 6,500 prisoners already being held in the Orleans Parish Prison were abandoned by the guards and left to fend for themselves (Bosworth 2010). Rather than call the government's actions into question, the media helped perpetuate the myth of the black male criminal with its unbalanced, and often unfounded, coverage of rampant lawlessness and violence, such as looting, carjacking, and rape.

While a focus on law and order prevailed, a number of law enforcement personnel took advantage of their status and contributed to the chaos following the disaster. There have been several ongoing federal investigations of the New Orleans Police Department, one of which resulted in the federal indictment and convictions of five police officers for filing false police reports, covering up crimes committed in the aftermath of Katrina, and murder (Robertson 2010). In another case, six police officers were accused of killing two people and wounding four unarmed civilians who were seeking safety from the storm. These incidents were elaborately covered up by departmental colleagues, many of whom later pleaded guilty to charges of conspiring to obstruct justice (see Box 10.3 Global Perspectives: Postapartheid Police Accountability in South Africa for examples of similar police misconduct in South Africa during apartheid).

The Racial Hoax

More evidence of how unconscious racism and the stereotype of the black male criminal manifests itself can be found in the prevalence of racial hoaxes. A **racial hoax** is when a crime occurs, or someone fabricates a crime, and the perpetrator falsely blames someone else because of that person's race (Russell 1998). A racial hoax that remains in public consciousness took place in 1994 when Susan Smith, a young white woman and mother of two boys, claimed that a black man had carjacked her and kidnapped her children. This story made national headlines with coverage that included a composite drawing of the supposed black male perpetrator. State and federal officials spent nine days looking for a black man before Smith finally confessed to killing her children by driving her car into the lake with the boys in the backseat.

Because we live in a society that unconsciously links race and crime, Smith's story of a black man carjacking her and kidnapping her small children was believed by many law enforcement personnel as well as many members of the public. Sociologists have documented at least sixty-seven racial hoaxes between 1987 and 1996, with 70 percent of the cases involving a white perpetrator charging an African American person with the crime (Russell 1998). Racial hoaxes place individual black men at risk for wrongful imprisonment and help perpetuate the image of black men as deviant criminals in the public mind (Russell 1998).

The Myth of the Immigrant Criminal

While talk of immigration reform is being continually debated in Congress, immigration opponents often cite the link between criminality and immigrants as evidence for why the United States should close its borders. Republican president Donald Trump has made such rhetoric his calling card. We will discuss immigration in detail in Chapter 13, but here we explore the link between criminality and immigrants. Popular perception holds that as the number of undocumented immigrants increases in a community, crime also increases. Such perceptions began as early as the 1920s and ultimately resulted in Congress's passage of restrictive immigration legislation in 1924 (see Chapter 13).

But do immigrants really commit more crime than native-born citizens? The answer appears to be a resounding no. Criminologist Edwin Sutherland (1924) provided the earliest evidence that the link between immigrants and crime did not hold up. In fact, the research is now overwhelming that first-generation immigrants commit less crime than second-generation immigrants or native-born residents (Hagan, Levi, and Dinovitzer 2008). However, undocumented immigrants are increasingly being treated as criminals and placed in detention facilities, part of the ever-expanding prison industrial complex.

CHAPTER SUMMARY

This chapter explores the ways race plays out in the criminal justice system. Race is the most significant variable in whether or not a defendant is sentenced to death, the severity of punishment juvenile offenders face, the odds of experiencing police brutality, or even in one's likelihood of coming under police suspicion.

Such biases have contributed to a prison population that is disproportionately minority. The United States has now entered an era of hyperincarceration in which over 2.3 million Americans are incarcerated and 66 percent of them are people of color. The explanations for the prison boom are the political use of "law and order," a growing prison industrial complex, and the war on drugs. The economic, social, and political costs of mass incarceration on minority communities are profound.

Media-perpetrated stereotypes of race–crime links distort the reality of crime in the United States: while people of color are disproportionately victimized by crime, evidence finds that they are still seen as perpetrators of crimes rather than victims. As an institution, the criminal justice system is not an anomaly. Educational institutions that provide unequal educational opportunities to students of color help feed this culture of imprisonment by limiting the options of children of color.

KEY TERMS AND CONCEPTS

Adultification

Criminogenic condition

Hyperincarceration (or mass incarceration)

Mass incarceration (or hyperincarceration)

Moral panic

Police brutality

Pretextual traffic stops

Prison industrial complex

Prison privatization

Racial battle fatigue

Racial hoax

Racial profiling

Social dominance orientation

Street crime

Unconscious racism

White-collar crime

PERSONAL REFLECTIONS

1. Think about what media coverage of crime you have encountered. After reading this chapter, do you see media coverage of crime as racialized? If so, in what ways is this so? To what extent has this influenced your perception of race and crime?

2. Consider your perception of the drug war prior to reading this chapter. Were you aware the drug war was racialized? Explain. Reconcile this with the current trend toward marijuana legalization (for medical and/or recreational use).

CRITICAL THINKING QUESTIONS

1. Some sociologists have argued that the criminal justice system today is the "new Jim Crow." Based upon what you have learned about race and the criminal justice system in this chapter, explain what they mean by this. Explain how laws are a form of social control.

2. Above and beyond the individuals and communities directly affected, in what way does mass incarceration hurt the United States? What are some negative consequences associated with incarcerating over 2.3 million people?

ESSENTIAL READING

Alexander, Michelle. 2010. *The New Jim Crow: Mass Incarceration in the Age of Colorblindness.* New York: The New Press.

Dreisiner, Baz. 2016. *Incarceration Nations: A Journey to Justice in Prisons Around the World.* New York: Other Press.

Eason, John M. 2017. *Big House on the Prairie: Rise of the Rural Ghetto and Prison Proliferation.* Chicago, IL: University of Chicago Press.

Gonzalez van Cleve, Nicole. 2016. *Crook County: Racism and Injustice in America's Largest Criminal Court.* Stanford, CA: Stanford Law Books.

Guevara, Martin, ed. 2012. *Hispanics in the U.S. Criminal Justice System: The New American Demography.* Springfield, IL: Charles C. Thomas Publishers.

McCorkel, Jill A. 2013. *Breaking Women: Gender, Race, and the New Politics of Imprisonment.* New York: New York University Press.

Pager, Devah. 2007. *Marked: Race, Crime and Finding Work in an Era of Mass Incarceration.* Chicago, IL: University of Chicago Press.

RECOMMENDED FILMS

When They See Us (2019). Directed by Ava DuVernay. A Netflix series on the Central Park Five, which became the most watched series on Netflix. The Central Park Five were a group of African American and Hispanic teenagers wrongfully convicted of raping a white woman jogger in Central Park in 1989. The men were convicted based upon coerced confessions made during police interrogations, without parents or counsel present. The four juvenile defendants served six to seven years while the 16-year-old defendant was tried as an adult and served thirteen years in adult prison. In 2003, the five young men were exonerated.

13th (2016). Directed by Ava DuVernay. This award-winning documentary explores the intersection of race, justice, and mass incarceration in the United States from slavery, to convict leasing, lynching, the war on drugs, and the prison industrial complex.

Black Death in Dixie: Racism and the Death Penalty in the United States (2007). Directed by Peadar King. Explores the history and current use of the death penalty in the South, particularly as an extension of Jim Crow. This film goes beyond the mainstream presentation of capital punishment and instead looks at how it is disproportionately used against African Americans and poor people. Finally, this film explores the issue of wrongful convictions.

The House I Live In (2012). Directed by Eugene Jarecki. This documentary explores the war on drugs, from its negative effects on minority communities to the ways it has changed law enforcement practices.

Slavery by Another Name (2012). Directed by Sam Pollard. Based upon the bestselling book of the same name by Douglas A. Blackmon, this documentary explores how, in the post–Civil War era, new forms of forced labor emerged throughout the South that trapped African Americans almost as completely as slavery had trapped their ancestors.

Tulia, Texas (2007). Directed by Cassandra Herman and Kelly Whalen. This film explores what is considered to be one of the largest drug busts in Texas, in which forty-six people were arrested for selling cocaine to an undercover police officer, in a town of five thousand. Almost all of those arrested were African American and most received extraordinarily long sentences (in some cases, twenty-five, sixty, and ninety years, even when there was no prior criminal record). So many aspects of this case were questionable that residents of Tulia, Texas, began to question the bust itself and, especially, the undercover police officer at the center of it. This film talks to all parties involved, from the initial raids in the summer of 1999 to the perjury trial of the undercover police officer. This incident reveals the ease with which black men are perceived as criminals and the role of unconscious racism in such perceptions.

RECOMMENDED MULTIMEDIA

The NAACP criminal justice department advocates for improved public safety in minority communities, better policing to attain that goal, less reliance on incarceration to solve social problems, and building trust between the criminal justice system and minority communities. It works toward sentencing reform, restoring voting rights for felons, supporting crime victims, and removing employment barriers for formerly incarcerated people. Check this out at www.naacp.org/pages/criminal-justice-about.

Ban the Box Campaign. The Legal Services for Prisoners with Children organized a "ban the box" campaign designed to eliminate the question "Have you ever been convicted of a felony?" from applications for employment, housing, public benefits, and loans. Individuals who have served their time for a crime should not face a lifetime of discrimination for that crime. Check out the campaign at this website: www.prisonerswithchildren.org/our-projects/allofus-or-none/ban-the-box-campaign.

Students Against Mass Incarceration (SAMI). Founded in 2011 at Howard University, SAMI has since spread to other college campuses. Its objective is to dismantle the prison industrial complex by ending mass incarceration. SAMI works to educate the public about the prison industrial complex, help former prisoners overcome barriers to reentry, expose police brutality, and fight for the rights of political prisoners. Check out these websites for more information about this organization and how you can bring a chapter to your campus: https://lionlink.columbia.edu/organization/STUDENTSAGAINSTMASSINCARCERATION; www.facebook.com/events/585302321481443/.

Death Penalty Information Center. This national nonprofit organization provides all the latest information on the death penalty in the United States, including fact sheets, a state-by-state database, information about upcoming executions, and resources for discussing the death penalty in the classroom: www.deathpenaltyinfo. org/.

CHAPTER 11

Race in the Cultural Imagination

CHAPTER LEARNING OUTCOMES

By the end of this chapter, you should be able to:

- Describe the significance of popular culture in reinforcing racial ideologies
- Explore popular culture as an arena for increasing solidarity within groups
- Understand the meaning of and the operation of cultural hegemony
- Identify resistance and counterhegemonic messages in popular culture created by racial/ethnic minorities
- Critically evaluate the images of racial/ethnic minorities in film, television, and video games
- Describe the role of power in the construction of public history and the significance of collective memory

Music is a reflection of culture. One of the best lenses through which to understand the black American experience from the black perspective is through black music such as blues, jazz, and rap/hip-hop. Billie Holiday's famous jazz song "Strange Fruit," recorded in 1939, is a protest of American racism and particularly the practice of lynching. The lyrics vividly describe the bodies of the victims as "strange fruit." (Check out the lyrics in their entirety at www.lyricsfreak.com/b/billie+holiday/strange+fruit_20017859. html.) This song was popular at a time when most whites ignored the practice of lynching and law enforcement refused to prosecute perpetrators for the murders.

Billie Holiday referred to this song as her personal protest song because it reminded her of how her father, and so many black men throughout the Jim Crow era, had died. The song became her biggest-selling record, audiences demanded it, yet it literally made her sick to her stomach when she sang it (Holiday and Dufty 1984).

In 1990, LL Cool J released the song "Illegal Search," protesting racial profiling and police harassment, issues discussed in detail in Chapter 10. (Check out the lyrics in their entirety at www.metrolyrics.com/illegal-search-lyrics-ll-cool-j.html.) Consider the cultural context out of which songs like "Illegal Search" and rap and hip-hop music and culture emerged: urban decay, police brutality, poverty, underfunded schools, and unemployment.

Both songs, sung five decades apart by artists from different musical genres, poignantly expose the racism that black Americans face. Significantly, both Billie Holiday and LL Cool J are black artists who had large white audiences during their careers. While such messages are a way of affirming black reality, they are not just preaching to the choir by telling black Americans about racism they experience. These messages reach white audiences. Some have argued that the crossover success of jazz and blues contributed to the success of the civil rights movement because they helped many white fans rethink racial ideologies of black inferiority (Pomerance 1988). There is no doubt that some of the messages embedded in such black music lyrics as Billie Holiday's "Strange Fruit" contributed to shifting some white perspectives on black reality.

This chapter explores race in the cultural imagination, specifically racialized images in film, television, video games, and new media, as well as the ways history is recorded on the landscape in memorials, monuments, and public history markers, and the potential effects of these on both dominant and subordinate groups. Subordinate groups have long used culture to challenge their oppression. Previous chapter topics exploring race and crime can make coverage of popular culture and public history appear frivolous. However, four ideas need to be kept in mind when thinking about the significance of race, popular culture, and public history.

First, as most Americans still live in racially homogeneous communities, our images of racial/ethnic others emerge disproportionately from popular culture rather than from personal experiences and interracial interactions. Because whites are the most segregated of all racial groups, stereotypical images of racial/ethnic minorities are successful at fueling white misconceptions about race. According to the American Psychological Association, people are more likely to accept media stereotypes as true if they lack real-world information that counters it (Holtzman 2000).

Second, this text pays particular attention to racial ideologies—cultural beliefs about race that help justify exploitation, inequality, and the racial hierarchy—which are perpetuated through the media. The mass media both produce and transmit racial ideologies, "linking symbols, formulas, plots and characters in a pattern that is conventional, appealing, and gratifying" (Dates and Barlow 1990:4).

Third, the history that is told on our landscape, in monuments, historical markers, and memorials, celebrates and validates white culture and Euro-American history while denigrating, marginalizing, or distorting the history of people of color. Not only is race a social construction, but so is history, in the sense that what is defined as American history involves an exercise of power. According to sociologist James Loewen:

> Only one American in six ever takes a course in American history after graduating from high school. Where then do Americans learn about the past? From many sources, of course—historical novels, Oliver Stone movies—but surely most of all from the landscape. History is told on the landscape all across America.
>
> (Loewen 1999:1)

And finally, culture has become an increasingly important aspect of life in the Western world, with the explosion of rock-and-roll music in the 1950s and the countercultural movements of the 1960s and growing scholarly interest in cultural studies since the 1970s (Hall, Neitz, and Battani 2003). Consider some of the following ways culture and race are linked:

- The democratic governor of Virginia, Ralph Northam, and the attorney general, Mark Herring, ignited controversy when yearbook photos emerged of them wearing blackface at parties during the 1980s.
- Part of the education Indian children received at boarding schools was in "civilized" classical music, particularly piano, the cornet, and the violin, as a way to distance them from the musical practices and dances of their parents, which were perceived as "savage" by whites (Troutman 2009).
- Not a single actor of color was nominated for an Oscar for their performance in a film released in 2014 or 2015, inspiring two consecutive years of #OscarsSoWhite protests. By 2019, the following films starring actors of color in the lead (or co-stars) were nominated for Best Picture: *Black Panther, Black KKKlansman* (directed by Spike Lee), *Green Book*, and *Roma*.
- Latinos, Arab Americans, African Americans, Asian Americans, and Native Americans have all been subjected to stereotypical portrayals in television and film.
- Minority groups have long expressed their identity as well as their resistance to their oppression through culture—music, films, literature—producing counter-narratives designed to challenge dominant narratives about race.
- Hate groups use music as a way to recruit young people.

- In most of the United States during the antebellum era, with the exception of Congo Square in New Orleans, whites banned slaves from playing drums, as these were perceived as capable of inciting revolt (Jones 1963).
- In the 1950s in New Orleans, the city where jazz originated, White Citizens' Councils engaged in a campaign to persuade white parents to not buy "Negro records" as a way to help "save the youth of America," declaring that "the savage music of these records are undermining the morals of our white youth" (Feather 1962).
- Partially in response to the massacre of church members in Charleston, South Carolina, in 2015, Governor Nikki Haley signed a bill to remove the Confederate flag from statehouse grounds.
- In December 2015, the city council of New Orleans voted to remove four Confederate monuments in the city. While many residents supported this move, many others were against it, and some engaged in violence against the contractors originally hired to remove the monuments.
- After decades of inaction in the face of student activism demanding the removal of a Confederate monument known as "Silent Sam" on the University of North Carolina's Chapel Hill campus, activists gathered at the beginning of the 2018–2019 academic year and toppled the monument in an act of civil disobedience.
- In 2019, the state of North Carolina agreed to fund an African American memorial on the grounds of the state capital (Vaughan 2019).
- The Southern Poverty Law Center published a report listing every public symbol of the Confederacy, including flags, monuments, statues, school names, and so on, entitled *Whose Heritage? Public Symbols of the Confederacy.*

SOCIOLOGICAL PERSPECTIVES ON RACE AND POPULAR CULTURE

Popular culture refers to a variety of cultural creations, such as television, movies, video games, and comic books, that are created for the masses, particularly for members of the middle and working classes. Sociologists are interested not only in the tangible cultural products created by groups of people, what we refer to as *material culture*, such as films, books, and music, but also in the intangible creations of a group, the values, norms, and beliefs—the *nonmaterial culture*—that are portrayed in the cultural products. While any cultural creation will reflect the nonmaterial culture from which it originated, it can also help perpetuate those values and beliefs; thus, material and nonmaterial culture are self-reinforcing. To put it simply, culture both reflects and creates the world in which we live.

Claiming that media portrayals of racial/ethnic minorities perpetuate racial stereotypes is not the same thing as claiming that these actions are part of a broader conspiracy of racial oppression. Cultural images of racial/ethnic minorities are oppressive, but they are so because they are products of a racist American culture rather than because they are part of some broad conspiracy to keep racial minorities oppressed. Filmmakers, most of whom are white, more than likely share a Eurocentric view of the world, and this is reflected in their films. However, film images do more than reflect societal patterns; they help to perpetuate those patterns, as being repeatedly exposed to certain images results in a sense that these images represent reality. The sheer repetition of racially stereotypical images also helps ensure that we become desensitized to these images, so that we hardly notice them. Repeatedly showing racial stereotypes in media at the exclusion of other images dangerously reinforces existing racial ideologies.

Culture is also always changing; thus, how race is represented in the media changes over time as well. Television programming is dramatically different today in terms of representation of racial/ethnic minorities than it was forty years ago. It represents some of the changes brought on by the minority protest movements of the 1950s through the 1970s, which we discussed in Chapter 6. For instance, minorities are less likely to be invisible in popular culture today, although their increased visibility has too often come at the expense of stereotypical representations, which we will talk about in detail later in this chapter. Another significant change involves the omnipresence of social media and the extent of cyber racism within this new media.

Cultures constantly borrow from one another, something sociologists refer to as *cultural diffusion.* An example of cultural diffusion is the existence of a hip-hop group called the Boo Yaa Tribe, which is made up of Samoans from Carson, California. They enjoy commercial success playing hip-hop music, which is of African American origin, for a largely Chicano audience (Lipsitz 2001). Despite such a multicultural example, keep in mind that cultural diffusion does not occur on a level playing field; some groups have more power than others, and thus, racial representations in popular culture are more likely to reflect the views of the dominant group. This chapter explores key racial imagery in public history and popular culture, specifically within film, television, music, new media, and video games and social media.

Functionalism

The functionalist (introduced in Chapter 3) understanding of popular culture emphasizes how people develop a sense of social solidarity and cohesiveness through the symbols, rituals, and practices reproduced in popular culture. Consider the experience of sixty thousand–plus fans at a U2 concert and the sense of solidarity they have with one another. This solidarity is reinforced through listening to the band on one's iPod or encountering someone wearing a concert shirt from the event. Television can create shared experiences and even *imagined communities* as well (Anderson 1991). An *imagined community* is created when people feel they are members of a collective despite lacking in proximity to one another. The televised images of the historic election of President Barack Obama had this kind of effect on many Americans. Televised sporting events also can create a sense of solidarity and an imagined community.

Conflict Theory

Conflict theorists take a different approach to understand the influence of culture. Their ideas emerge out of the work of Karl Marx and his dominant ideology thesis (introduced in Chapter 3). According to Marx, social institutions such as schools perpetuate the ideologies of the ruling class, beliefs that, in turn, serve to reinforce their power and dominance by justifying the social order. The media can be understood as a cultural institution controlled by dominant groups and perpetuating ideologies that work to their benefit. Marx emphasized that the ideas and values of the ruling class became the dominant cultural values and worked to justify the status quo.

Minstrel shows, the most popular form of entertainment between the 1830s and 1910, provide a good example of Marx's dominant ideology thesis at work. Minstrel shows were designed to appeal to white audiences, who flocked to see white performers blacken their skin with burnt cork and exaggerate their lips with red makeup to portray black characters, or at least black characters in the white imagination. In 1828, T. D. Rice, the father of American minstrelsy, developed a song-and-dance routine that was an exaggerated imitation of the walk of a physically disabled black stablehand named Jim Crow (his name eventually became the name of the system of segregation in the South as well). This was a huge hit with white audiences throughout the country. Soon minstrel troupes were traveling the country, presenting white audiences with lazy, ignorant, and childish black characters, which fit with the image many whites held of blacks at the time.

Minstrel shows presented blacks as happy and content under slavery and as simply too ignorant to be trusted with freedom and the right to vote. Minstrel shows emerged as the abolitionist movement was heating up, sending the message that slavery was really not that bad, a message that contradicted the portrait of slavery as a violent, inhumane institution that was espoused by abolitionists and slaves themselves. After emancipation, minstrel shows were intended to convince northern whites that slaves had been content with their status and to provide southerners with a nostalgic comfort, referencing the "good ole days" when African Americans were perceived by southern whites to be willing participants in their enslavement (Coleman 1998).

Later in the history of minstrel shows, black actors were used to play these stereotypical and degrading characters. Bert Williams, an African American actor and comedian, became a major Vaudeville star during the first decades of the twentieth century. While it might seem counterintuitive for black performers to be perpetuating anti-black stereotypes, African American actors had no other opportunities in theater and few opportunities in other industries at the time.

This history of minstrelsy is why blackface is so controversial today. In 2019, several politicians, including Virginia governor Ralph Northam and the state's attorney general, Mark Herring, were accused of having worn blackface in costume in the 1980s after yearbook photos of them in blackface emerged (Northam first admitted to this, then denied it was him, then admitted to dressing up in blackface to imitate Michael Jackson). Many called for Northam and Herring to resign. They refused. While blackface hasn't been common since the early twentieth century, it hasn't disappeared either. And whites rarely learn about why such caricatures are problematic (Haygood 2019). While blackface has long been a controversial part of American popular culture, it is racist and problematic in its stereotypical portrayals of African Americans. As this chapter is arguing, popular culture helps perpetuate dominant racial ideologies. Ultimately, the popularity of minstrel shows throughout American popular culture "helped cement the nation's perception of black people as hideous and stupid and freakish and dumb and lusty and unworthy of more than torture, exploitation, derision, oppression, neglect, and extermination" (Morris 2019).

Hegemony

Italian theorist Antonio Gramsci expanded on Marx's dominant ideology thesis. He argued that dominant groups were able to control subordinate groups through *hegemony*, which refers to the manufacture of consent, the process through which dominant groups maintain their power by gaining the consensus of subordinate groups rather than by using military power. *Cultural hegemony* is achieved through control of the mass media and the transmission of ideologies that work to the benefit of the dominant group. In this view, the mass media is portrayed as equivalent to cultural and political propaganda. Gramsci introduced this concept to understand class hegemony, how the ruling class maintains the consent of the lower classes, but it can be applied to racial dominance as well. Racial representations in media influence public opinion in seemingly harmless ways and work to the benefit of the dominant group.

Contemporary Cultural Studies

It would be a mistake to assume that only dominant groups use culture and that subordinate groups are regularly duped by dominant groups through cultural manipulation. Hegemony is never "total," meaning it is always being challenged and negotiated, something that neither Marx's dominant ideology thesis nor Gramsci's notion of hegemony acknowledges. A more contemporary body of thought that is used to analyze popular culture is the Birmingham School, or the Centre for Contemporary Cultural Studies, whose theorists build upon both Marx's and Gramsci's work to understand media and its influence; however, they emphasize subordinate-group resistance to dominant-group ideologies transmitted through the mass media. The Marxian/Gramscian perspectives unfairly limit the agency of subordinate groups, portraying them as manipulated by dominant-group ideologies. Instead, subordinate groups challenge these messages and work to win back space with the production of what can be called *counterhegemonic* messages (Gelder 1997). Subordinate groups emphasize their agency through acts of resistance to dominant cultural messages and use culture as a site of resistance to the dominant group. Audiences are always actively decoding media messages, sometimes reinforcing stereotypes, sometimes challenging them in the process (Hall 1980).

An example of counterhegemony can be found in studies of Chicano musicians who emerged out of Los Angeles, such as the bands Tierra and Los Lobos. Through their music, Chicano musicians claim their self-respect in a culture that denigrates them. These musicians assume a bifocal perspective, which implies that they are aware of being watched, while also providing ironic commentary on what is seen. In this way, they are able to acknowledge Anglo stereotypes about them without accepting the stereotypes (Lipsitz 1997). As Latinos from East Los Angeles, Los Lobos claim a public space through their music in a city that has historically denied them. Their music is inherently political in that it is an embrace of Chicano culture, rather than a celebration of assimilation into the white mainstream.

RACIAL IMAGERY IN FILM AND TELEVISION

Hollywood films and the television industry have both contributed to the invisibility of racial/ethnic minorities and helped perpetuate racial/ethnic stereotypes. This is evident from the film industry's beginning in the first two decades of the twentieth century and the origins of the television industry, with the beginnings of regular broadcasting in the early 1930s and its explosion in the 1940s. Stereotypes, introduced in Chapter 4, are oversimplified and formulaic portrayals of a group of people that sometimes contain a kernel of truth, which is why they can be so powerful. Minstrel characters, which are based on an extreme exaggeration of a real person, are a good example of the proliferation of racial stereotypes in popular culture.

Sociologist Bhoomi Thakore (2014, 2016) refers to these as **ethnic characterizations**, where nonwhite characters in TV and film reflect assimilationist stereotypes of media producers and who, in turn, reproduce these stereotypes on screen. An example of such ethnic characterizations involves stereotypical images of South Asian men as non-threatening and effeminate and South Asian women as eroticized,

BOX 11.1

Global Perspectives:
The Effect of Television and the Dismantling of Apartheid

During the years 1949–1994, South Africa had a legal system of racial segregation and discrimination known as apartheid that was designed to ensure white supremacy. Under this system, blacks were severely limited in terms of where they were allowed to live, work, and travel. They were stripped of their citizenship rights and faced extreme police harassment. Antiapartheid resistance emerged, and many activists involved in such opposition found themselves targets of the South African secret police. Any opposition to apartheid was defined as communist inspired, a violation of the Suppression of Communism Act (1950), and a threat to the government. Individuals and organizations that violated the Suppression of Communism Act faced a unique sanction, something that South Africans referred to as "the ban." When under "the ban," it was illegal for images of the banned parties to be published, for their words to be published or broadcast, and for them to be present in any gathering of more than three people (Krabill 2010; Worden 2007). Essentially, any antiapartheid activists placed under the ban were *personae non gratae* because they literally disappeared from public life (Krabill 2010).

As a result of "the ban," most South Africans had no idea what the leaders of the antiapartheid movement looked like. Nelson Mandela, a black political prisoner in South Africa for over

twenty-eight years, spent almost a quarter century under "the ban." This amounted to what social scientist Ron Krabill (2010) refers to as a structured absence of Mandela—invisibility that results from the active exclusion of an individual or group from a particular environment. This concept is different from pure absence, which can be understood as a lack of presence. Structured absence involves power: a person or group must be powerful enough to exclude someone from a particular environment. Mandela and other antiapartheid leaders were intentionally made invisible to their fellow South Africans.

During the apartheid era, television was introduced across the developed world. The South African government, however, resisted television until 1976, despite having the financial and technological capability to make it a reality, because it was viewed as a threat to the apartheid state and the Afrikaner identity (Krabill 2010).

The introduction of television in South Africa in 1976 unintentionally played an indirect role in the dismantling of the apartheid government, according to Krabill (2010). During the 1980s, when antiapartheid activism and government repression of it were at their peak, the most popular television series among all South Africans was *The Cosby Show*. While for many white South Africans, the show did not challenge their views of blacks because it

continues

continued

was "too American," for many other white South Africans, the series significantly influenced how they and their friends viewed black South Africans. While antiapartheid leaders were invisible in the public sphere in South Africa, black American entertainers, such as Bill Cosby, were not only highly visible but also extremely popular among white South Africans.

Although the introduction of television in no way brought about the end of apartheid, it did play a role. Research finds that white South Africans viewed the *Cosby Show* family, the Huxtables, as relatable: like them, rather than foreign to them, the way they had long been socialized to view black South Africans. In the South African context, something this seemingly simple is actually quite revolutionary because it challenges long-held beliefs about race as biological and real. Additionally, one of the unintended consequences of "the ban" was that black South Africans were almost completely invisible to white South Africans, and television filled this void. For the first time, whites learned about black life through television. This example of the influence of television in overturning the South African system of apartheid demonstrates the significance of media in our lives.

as the characters of Raj and his sister, Priya, on the television show *The Big Bang Theory* exemplify (Thakore 2016). Stereotypes and ethnic characterizations are found throughout film and television because they are mental shortcuts; they are used so that audiences can quickly understand the characters introduced and they resonate with white audiences. With a few key stereotypes, audiences understand when they meet the villain or the heroine (Wilson and Gutierrez 1995). Racial/ethnic stereotypes found throughout film and television are damaging. They reinforce white supremacy through the perpetuation of negative racial ideologies about minorities. When racial/ethnic minorities are repeatedly portrayed as lazy, silly, ignorant, or criminal, it reinforces the opposite message as well, which is that whites are hardworking, intelligent, and honest. While it is tempting to believe we all know television and film are not real and, thus, we are not affected by the stereotypical images portrayed in these mediums, it is perhaps more accurate to admit we are all, to some extent, seduced by the images we see on the screen and that these images have a certain power over us (hooks 1996).

Racial stereotypes are not just pandering to a presumed white audience. Research from the Ralph J. Bunche Center for African American Studies at UCLA finds that in 2013 more than half of all frequent moviegoers were racial minorities and that diverse constituencies prefer diverse film and television content. Thus, Hollywood is literally ignoring a big portion of their audience in their decision making; they know their audiences are diverse, yet their decision making reflects presumed white desires.

While this chapter is going to focus on the overwhelming whiteness of lead actors in film and television, research finds that racial inequality and hierarchy in Hollywood is created and maintained through key decision makers in the industry. Gatekeepers, or Hollywood insiders, particularly those with some amount of control or input into the production or distribution of Hollywood movies, employ a racial logic in their decision making. This racial logic links ideas about race and profitability, from expectations that black directors are "unbankable" and should only direct films intended for a black audience, to who should star in a movie and what audiences a movie should be directed toward. The pervasiveness of this kind of racial logic, which goes on long before a film hits the box office, results in the marginalization, ghettoization, and stigmatization of racial and ethnic minorities throughout the industry (Erigha 2019).

Social scientists who study media and popular culture identify a phenomenon they refer to as a *structured absence*, which is when one group has the power to keep others invisible in the media; it is different from a total absence because structured absence is about power, an intentional exercise of power (Krabill 2010) (see Box 11.1 Global Perspectives: The Effect of Television and the Dismantling of Apartheid). The historical omission of people of color from films has long been noted. Today, minority representation has shifted from invisibility to misrepresentation.

As we can see in Figure 11.1, whites are overrepresented among lead actors in Hollywood films, whereas racial minorities are underrepresented: racial minority

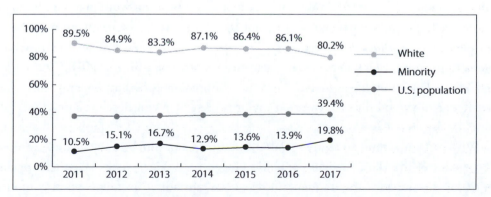

FIGURE 11.1: Percentage of lead actors by race, Top Theatrical Films, 2011–2017.

SOURCE: Hunt, Ramón, and Tran 2019.

representation in leading roles has declined since 2013, but has increased dramatically between 2016 and 2017. However, in 2017 people of color made up only two out
of every ten lead actor roles in film. Exploring racial representation among lead
actors in film is important because story lines revolve around the primary characters
(Hunt, Ramón, and Tran 2019). When racial/ethnic minorities are portrayed, they
are almost always under white control, a practice referred to as *minstrelsy*. While
minstrel shows are a remnant of our past, minstrelsy is still alive. Another pattern
found in film and television involves the assimilation of the main character of color,
emphasizing the "all-American-ness" of the character, who also exists within a
majority white cast (Thakore 2016).

When actors of color do get roles in Hollywood films, they rarely get industry
acclaim for their performances in the form of Oscar nominations and awards. Black
actors and directors have long critiqued the white bias of the Academy Awards.
When we look at the eighty-nine Academy Awards presentations from 1929 to 2015,
white actors won 94.5 percent of the "big five" awards (actor, actress, supporting
actor, supporting actress, and director) (Hughey 2015). In 2015, all the nominees for
these prestigious awards were white—despite exceptional performances by actors of
color in films such as *Selma*, *Concussion*, *Chi-Raq*, *Creed*, and *Straight Outta
Compton*, among others—prompting the #OscarsSoWhite protests, which extended
into 2016 as well. Sociologist Matthew Hughey (2015) argues that on the rare occasions when the Academy does recognize the performance of an actor of color, it is
usually when they star in a white savior film (see below) or when they conform to
racist views of what makes a person of color authentic, such as Hattie McDaniel's
win as the faithful slave in *Gone with the Wind*.

Perhaps due to the #OscarsSoWhite protests, in 2018, the Academy recognized
films with African American lead actors and/or directors with Academy Award
nominations for *Get Out*, *Roman J. Israel, Esq.*, and *Mudbound*. In 2018, *A Wrinkle
in Time*, directed by Ava Duvernay, was released, which was the first film with a production budget of over $100 million dollars directed by a nonwhite woman. In 2019,
the following films starring actors of color in the lead (or co-stars) were nominated
for best picture: *Black Panther*, *Black KKKlansman* (directed by Spike Lee), *Green
Book*, and *Roma*. *Black Panther* was also the top grossing film of 2018. *Crazy Rich
Asians* (2018), directed by Asian American filmmaker Jonathan Murray Chu, was
the first Hollywood film to feature a majority cast of Asian descent since the 1993
film *The Joy Luck Club*.

Why is it important to study racial/ethnic images in film and television? Because
75 percent of the US/Canadian population (aged 2 or older) went to a movie theater
in 2018: 12 percent are frequent moviegoers, attending a movie once a month
or more; more than half the population (53 percent) are occasional moviegoers;
and tens of thousands of people watch movies at home, whether through DVDs,

streaming services, or on various technologies ("Theme Report" 2018). The average American watches 2.9 hours of television every day in 2018, and 99 percent of American households have at least one television ("American Time Use Survey Summary" 2019). Film and television are ubiquitous in our culture; thus, racialized imagery in media likely has some effect.

Another reason it is critical to study racial/ethnic images is that race is the "political unconscious" of American cinema, as Hollywood westerns, war movies, and detective stories are likely to emphasize white males as defenders of women and children against predatory Indians, Asians, blacks, or Mexicans (Lipsitz 2001). The problem is not that racial minorities should never be portrayed as villains or criminals. The problem is that minorities are repeatedly portrayed negatively and rarely portrayed positively, which fuels ideologies of racial inferiority and white superiority. A white criminal on a television show does not have the same effect on viewers because there is no corresponding image of the "dangerous white criminal" in our society; such an image does not reinforce a negative stereotype like that of the black male criminal (discussed in Chapter 10).

African American Images

The stereotypical portrayals of African Americans in Hollywood film have a long history, as they are extensions of stock minstrel characters. Black males fall into one of four primary characters. First, the "musical old darky," who was simple-minded and only good for playing music. Second, the "Uncle Tom," or the good Negro, who was passive, servile, and did not fight his oppression. The Uncle Tom character was actually an argument in support of slavery, even after it had been abolished. It showed that blacks were not unhappy in bondage, a theme carried over from minstrel shows. Third, the "coons," also called the uncles, were black buffoons with eyes that almost always looked as though they were popping out of their head. The coon soon transmuted into one of the most degrading of all racial stereotypes, that of a useless black man, someone who is lazy, crazy, unreliable, and good for nothing. Finally, an image still alive today in television and film is that of the "black buck," a brutally violent, big, bad, oversexed black man, specifically with a desire for white women (Bogle 1994).

The female version of the Uncle Tom is the mammy because she appears to have accepted her subordinate status (Collins 1990). The mammy is passive and asexual, a black domestic servant devoted to her white master. The smiling, singing, overweight mammy image is the most popular cultural image of black women, repeated endlessly in films and advertising images, such as those for Aunt Jemima syrup and Popeye's chicken. The mammy image emerged in popular culture, particularly minstrel shows, before the Civil War. It was repeated in novels and theatrical productions of *Uncle Tom's Cabin*, and was ultimately made famous in the character Hattie McDaniel portrayed in *Gone with the Wind* (Turner 1994). McDaniel's mammy character expresses her loyalty to "her" whites by rejecting the freedom she earns with the signing of the Emancipation Proclamation. These images "perpetuate a mythological Southern past that nearly removed all of the heinous dimensions of slavery" (Turner 1994:47). The mammy image in popular culture is an expression of black women's loyalty to white society; thus, the mammy image in the black community is the image of a race traitor. The mammy image is part of white myth-making about slavery and the Jim Crow era because it is an image of a black woman who is happy and content with her subordinate role as a slave and, later, as a servant (Harris-Perry 2011).

The hit film *The Help* (2011), based upon a book of the same name, is an extension of the mammy image and has been highly criticized by black commentators. It is a film about black domestic workers in the South in the mid-1960s, as told through the lens of Skeeter, a wealthy white woman. *The Help* has been critiqued for avoiding the issue of sexual harassment, which was a very real threat for black domestics of the era, for avoiding discussion of racial violence of the era, for barely broaching the subject of the civil rights movement, despite the time and place in which it was set (Jackson, Mississippi), and for being just another book about black people written by white people, with all the inevitable whitewashing that involves. This particular film and book also expose how white people blithely assumed "their" Negroes were happy.

Beginning in the 1950s, television expanded dramatically and, for the first time, could be found in most American homes. Many of the same racial/ethnic stereotypes from film found a new home in television. For instance, the popular show *Beulah* (1950–1953) portrayed a middle-class suburban white household and their dedicated, loving black housekeeper. In 1981, a new sitcom, *Gimme a Break*, introduced an overweight, dark-skinned, white-identified mammy character into American households, with Nell Carter playing the domestic caretaker of a white household. These images are offensive because they perpetuate the image of black women as devoted to their white families, while their own families remain invisible to viewers. The connotations associated with such images are also problematic. They are always represented by larger, very dark-skinned, asexual black women.

In addition to the mammy image, black women in American film and television have been stereotyped as emasculating matriarchs, welfare recipients, and hypersexual Jezebels. Sociologist Patricia Hill Collins (1990) refers to these stereotypical images as *controlling images*, meaning the images are a major instrument of power as they work to make racism, sexism, and poverty appear normal and natural. The matriarch is the counterpart of the mammy: while mammies are the black mothers in the white homes, matriarchs are black mothers in black homes. Black mothers in

IMAGES 11.1 AND 11.2: The mammy is a black domestic servant devoted to her white master (11.1), while the iconic mammy image is ubiquitous in advertising (11.2). The smiling, singing, overweight mammy image is the most popular cultural image of black women, repeated endlessly in films and in advertising. This commercial image is of Mammy's Cupboard on Highway 61 in Natchez, Mississippi.

black homes are portrayed in popular culture as bad mothers, in that the matriarch has low morals and does not make her family her priority. By not properly supervising their children, their inevitable school failure is her fault. They are overly aggressive and unfeminine; thus, they emasculate black men (Collins 1990).

Another controlling image repeated throughout American popular culture is that of the hypersexual Jezebel. This image, which remains with us today, emerged during slavery as a way to justify white male sexual assaults. These images are interconnected and "transmit clear messages about the proper links among female sexuality, fertility, and Black women's roles in the political economy" (Collins 1990:78). Examples of Jezebel images in our culture are found throughout rap videos and on reality TV shows such as *The Flavor of Love*. In fact, these stereotypical images of black women are some of the most pervasive.

Television shows in the 1970s and 1980s that portrayed black Americans, such as *The Jeffersons* (1975–1985), *What's Happening!!* (1976–1979), and *The Cosby Show* (1984–1992), emphasized black families as economically successful, as "making it." While such images were a welcome relief after decades of stereotypical imagery showing African Americans as inept, these new images were argued to be problematic due to their timing. The portrayal of black success on television during this era reflects the larger cultural backlash against affirmative action and welfare. Such social programs were clearly no longer needed if black families like the Jeffersons and the Huxtables could succeed (Alper and Leistyna 2005).

The Birth of a Nation

Stereotypical black male characters carried over from minstrel shows into Hollywood films from the earliest inception of the medium. In this section, we examine one film in detail because of its considerable influence on creating racial stereotypes: D. W. Griffith's *The Birth of a Nation*. Griffith's 1915 movie, based primarily on Thomas Dixon's novel *The Clansman*, was one of the most popular films ever made. Griffith, a southerner from a relatively poor family, believed that the true story of the Civil War, as seen from the southern white perspective, had not yet been told (Silk and Silk 1990). This film broke from the southern literary tradition of treating blacks as passive, as many of the above stereotypes show, and instead emphasized black male violence and sexual aggression, primarily directed against white women.

The film depicted black political empowerment as a problem, showing blacks as interested in "Negro domination" rather than equality, and as a threat to the white family. Black legislators (played by white actors in blackface, as the intent was to ridicule blacks) were shown sneaking sips of alcohol from flasks, propping their feet up on their desks, eating fried chicken, and leering at white women while discussing legislation allowing interracial marriage (Lipsitz 2001). The film romanticized slavery and portrayed the Reconstruction era as a horrific time of black dominance and corruption (Sullivan 2009). Audiences cheered when the mammy in the film defended the white master's household from Union soldiers (Turner 1994). *The Birth of a Nation* cemented stereotypes of blacks as violent racists, corrupt politicians, faithful servants, and buffoon-like characters for decades. It also is credited with the reemergence of the Ku Klux Klan as a national rather than just a southern organization (Silk and Silk 1990).

The Birth of a Nation was enormously popular with white audiences and there was a special screening of the film at the White House in 1915. Afterward, President Wilson reportedly claimed the film was "like writing history with lightning, and one of my regrets is that it is so horribly true" (Silk and Silk 1990). It was the longest and the most expensive film ever made at the time, and it ran for almost a year in major markets like New York, Chicago, and Boston and was shown throughout the South for fifteen years. It cost $100,000 to make, grossed over $18 million in the first few years after its release, and established the motion picture as the most popular form of entertainment in America (Barry 1965).

The NAACP organized a national campaign against the film, staging protests in numerous cities and working to limit its distribution. They tried to get the film suppressed on the grounds that it would incite violence, since a staged version of *The Clansman* had incited a riot in Philadelphia several years earlier. They were successful in getting a limited release, as some cities, such as Denver, Cleveland, and Albuquerque, refused to grant permits to the film and others demanded that the most objectionable scenes be cut. The NAACP was ultimately unsuccessful in this fight, however (Sullivan 2009).

Griffith's film is considered one of the most important films ever made because of its aesthetic legacy (Wallace 2003). For example, the film used pioneering camera techniques such as panoramic long shots, and it was the first film to include a full musical score. However, its influence on racial imagery in culture lingers. The Civil War is known to most Americans through popular culture rather than through historical literature that may be more accurate (Cullen 1995). Thus:

> *The Birth of a Nation* has stood not only as a dominant fictional account of Reconstruction but as an apologia for the nearly one hundred years of Jim Crow segregation and white supremacist politics that followed in the South and effectively dominated social policies in the West and North.
>
> (Wallace 2003)

Magical Negroes

While traditional stereotypical images of African Americans in films such as that of the mammy, Uncle Tom, and the coon are found less today, there is a new racial stereotype being brought to us by Hollywood, that of the "magical negro" (Hughey

2009). Examples of films that feature "magical negro" characters include *Same Kind of Different as Me* (2017), *The Blind Side* (2009), *Evan Almighty* (2007), *The Green Mile* (1999), *O Brother, Where Art Thou?* (2000), and *The Legend of Bagger Vance* (2000) (see Box 11.2 Race in the Workplace: 40 Acres and a Mule Filmworks). The magical negro is generally an uneducated black person, usually of the lower class, who possesses some supernatural or magical powers that are put to use saving lost whites, almost always men, and turning them into successful, competent people. This stereotype, while positive and certainly an improvement over overt Hollywood racism, is still racist because the white characters remain central while black characters are marginal, and these films ultimately reinforce the status quo while seemingly offering a challenge to racial inequality. This is part of a larger pattern that Hughey (2009) refers to as *cinethetic racism*. Cinethetic racism is characterized by the presence of more people of color, interracial cooperation, and the superficial empowerment of historically marginalized people, which actually misrepresents the extent of racial progress in society. Ultimately, it reinforces the color-blind ideology, the idea that racism is no longer a significant issue in American society.

REFLECT AND CONNECT

Identify two examples of cinethetic racism in films you have seen in the last year. What are some negative manifestations of cinethetic racism?

Native American Images

As American Indians were being physically eradicated from the actual landscape through genocidal strategies and forced relocations, Hollywood was portraying them as stoic, noble savages. Some have argued that John Wayne was the most famous Indian killer, having killed an estimated ten thousand Indians in movies (Chavers 2009). The longest-running television series, *Gunsmoke* (1955–1975), and *Bonanza* (1959–1973) both featured killing Indians as a recurring theme.

Although the violence against Native Americans in film and television is significant, the portrayal of the actual violence directed at Native peoples was sanitized by Hollywood. For instance, *Pocahontas* (1995) turns the violence and brutality associated with colonization and conquest into a voluntary romantic relationship, despite the fact that this film emerged out of criticisms of Disney for its racial stereotypes in previous films (Holtzman 2000; Lipsitz 2001). The notion of Manifest Destiny, that whites had the God-given right to control this country from sea to sea, was reinforced in film with Indians historically portrayed as burning, looting, and scalping whites and, thus, deserving of the violence inflicted upon them during the bloody Indian Wars (Holtzman 2000). White superiority is enforced in films depicting Indians in countless "cowboy and Indian" films, where the good guys are always white and the bad guys, Indians, always lose. Even in the 1990s, the film *Dances with Wolves* reinforced white superiority despite the fact that it portrayed Native–white history such that whites were not completely innocent, because the plot still revolved completely around the white characters, reinforcing Native invisibility in popular culture.

While the Hollywood practice of using white actors in blackface has ceased, white actors playing other racial minority characters, such as Latinos, Asian Americans, or

---

BOX 11.2

Race in the Workplace:
40 Acres and a Mule Filmworks

Due to white dominance in Hollywood, racial/ethnic minorities interested in pursuing film industry careers have often faced significant obstacles, such as being excluded from consideration for roles. Few Hollywood movies feature people of color in leading roles or address subject matters involving minority groups (Tehranian 2009). For example, Will Sampson was the first Native American actor to play a Native American character, in *One Flew Over a Cuckoo's Nest* (1975). In response, many have created their own opportunities and, once successful, have worked to open doors for other talented minority filmmakers, actors, and production staff.

African American actor, director, and filmmaker Spike Lee had tremendous difficulty getting financial backing to make his films, even after his success with *She's Gotta Have It* (1986) and *Do the Right Thing* (1989). In response, he formed his own Brooklyn-based production company, 40 Acres and a Mule Filmworks. The objective of this production company was to provide a venue for African American filmmakers and actors, and other racial minorities interested in pursuing careers in film. Lee and his production company are credited with opening the doors for numerous actors, such as Halle Berry, Rosie Perez, and Samuel L. Jackson. After her film debut in Lee's *Jungle Fever* (1991), Halle Berry went on to become one of the highest-paid actresses in Hollywood and the only African American woman to earn an Academy Award for Best Actress.

40 Acres also focuses on films that explore African American lives, such as *4 Little Girls* (1997), a documentary about the four girls killed in the bombing of an African American Baptist church in Birmingham, Alabama, in 1963, and the films *Malcolm X* (1992) and *Do the Right Thing* (1989). Lee is one of the few black filmmakers who has achieved success in Hollywood. His *Malcolm X* was the first African American film to earn $100 million. 40 Acres and a Mule Filmworks "gave a whole generation of young people … access to the film industry that they did not have before. 40 Acres helped launch the careers of numerous young African American actors and production staff" ("History" n.d.).

Native Americans, continues. As recently as 2013, a major Hollywood film, *The Lone Ranger*, relied on white actor Johnny Depp to play the Native American character Tonto. Similarly, in 2009, Irish American actor Mickey Rourke played a Native American character in *Killshot* (2009) (Chew 2013).

Latino Images

While film and television cemented black stereotypes of mammies, Uncle Toms, and coons, Latinos struggle with gross underrepresentation and misrepresentation in film and television (see Figure 11.2 which shows that racial minority actors are underrepresented in lead roles in broadcast television, but their share of broadcast scripted leads in television has quadrupled since the 2011–2012 season). Latinos are the largest and one of the fastest-growing racial/ethnic groups in the United States, yet the National Association of Hispanic Journalists found that Latinos are virtually absent from national news coverage and that when they are portrayed on the news, they are only portrayed as criminals or illegal immigrants (Picker and Sun 2012). Documentary filmmaker Ken Burns faced criticism from the Latino community for ignoring the contributions of Latinos in two of his documentaries, one on baseball and the other on World War II. The World War II documentary was fifteen hours long and contained no mention of Latino contributions, despite the fact that over half a million Latinos participated in World War II. Burns responded to this criticism by adding two interviews with Latino World War II veterans (Picker and Sun 2012).

Much like the situation of African Americans in film, a handful of Latino stereotypes have proliferated in film. Social scientists identify six basic stereotypes of Latinos in cinema: el bandido/criminal, the harlot, the male buffoon, the female clown, the Latin lover, and the dark lady (Berg 2002). The bandido is always dark

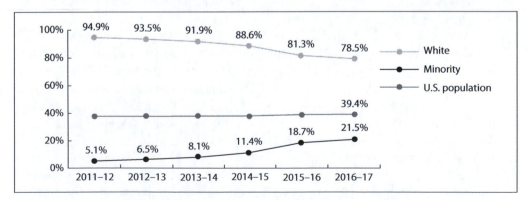

FIGURE 11.2: Leads by race, broadcast scripted, 2011–2012 to 2016–2017 seasons.

SOURCE: Hunt, Ramón, and Tran 2019.

skinned and perceived as a threat to white America. These images began in the silent era. In such films as *Tony the Greaser* (1911), Mexican Americans have been perceived as bandits attacking people and as "greasers," the pejorative term of the era. The Latin lover stereotype emerged very early on, in films such as *The Dove* (1928) and *Bordertown* (1935). Latinas face their own stereotypical representations, with hypersexuality and volatility being the most common.

As African Americans have dealt with blackface in popular culture, Latinos have dealt with *brownface*, where stories about Latinos are told by white directors and writers and, often, played by white actors in brownface. The practice of brownface is faced by Native Americans, Asian Americans, and Arabs in addition to Latinos (Picker and Sun 2012). For example, Ben Affleck played Antonio J. Mendez in *Argo* (2012), a film based upon the work of real-life Hispanic CIA operative, Antonio Mendez. Jack Black played a Mexican character in *Nacho Libre* (2006), Al Pacino played a Latino in *Scarface* (1983), and Will Ferrell played a Latino in *Casa de Mi Padre* (2012).

While Latinos are the largest racial/ethnic group in the United States, they are the most underrepresented on television, remaining ghettoized to Spanish-language stations on cable. Much as in film, Latino representation on television generally is confined to a narrow set of stereotypes: the criminal, the Latin lover, the comic/buffoon, the harlot, and the law enforcer (Mastro and Behm-Morawitz 2005). In the early days of television, ethnic comedies were popular, with shows such as *I Remember Mama* (1949–1957), *The Goldbergs* (1949–1955), and *Life with Luigi* (1952–1953) featuring Norwegian, Jewish, and Italian immigrant families, respectively (Alper and Leistyna 2005). By the 1950s, TV became an all-white world, and it remains predominantly white today (Lichter and Amundson 1994) (see Figure 11.2).

While television sitcoms of the 1970s–1990s began to portray African Americans in a more favorable light, with shows like *The Jeffersons* (1975–1985) and *The Cosby Show* (1984–1992), it wasn't until the 2000s that a sitcom portraying Latino families emerged. The *George Lopez Show* (2002–2010) portrayed an all-American nonwhite family of Hispanic origin, the Lopez family. The critiques of this show were similar to the critiques of *The Cosby Show*. While it was nice to see people of color represented as a "normal" family, their middle-class status meant that the sitcom did not reflect the realities of life for most Latinos. While the Huxtables and the Lopezes succeed financially, nearly a third of black and Latino families are impoverished (see Chapter 8).

Arab Images

Negative portrayals of Arabs, described as *anti-Arab racism*, are found throughout print and visual media, from film to video games (Salaita 2006). One of the dominant patterns found for media images of Arabs is that of "othering," where Arabs and

Muslims are represented as the "other" throughout the media. Negative images of Muslims and Arabs in US media have been documented since World War II (Nurullah 2010).

Researchers have identified five general stereotypes of Arabs in film: villains, sheikhs, Egyptians, Palestinians, and maidens. Since the beginning of the motion picture industry at the turn of the twentieth century, Arabs have been stereotyped as exotic, surrounded by harems and belly dancers. One of the earliest examples of Arab stereotyping in film was *The Sheik* (1921), a popular silent film starring Rudolph Valentino, a white actor, as an Arab sheik. In this film, a white American woman goes to the desert and is captured and possibly raped by the Arab sheik.

Arab women have been stereotyped in humiliating ways, from being demonized to being eroticized. Perhaps the most violent Arab woman image perpetrated by Hollywood is the image of the Arab woman as terrorist, images that are found in films from *Federal Agents vs. Underworld Inc.* (1948) to *Black Sunday* (1977) and *True Lies* (1994) (Shaheen 2007). Another example is the blockbuster film *Rules of Engagement* (2000), in which an angry Arab mob, including women and children, gathers outside a US embassy in Yemen, with US Marines ultimately opening fire on the crowd. The American-Arab Anti-Discrimination Committee has deemed this movie particularly offensive. Even mainstream media outlets such as CNN condemned the bigotry in the film (Tehranian 2009). More recent films that rehash anti-Arab stereotypes include *World War Z* (2013) and *American Sniper* (2014).

Arab stereotypes found in television differ somewhat from those found in film. Sociologist Jack Shaheen (1984) finds that in television Arabs are portrayed as extremely wealthy, as barbaric and uncultured, as sex maniacs with a particular fascination with white slavery, and, finally, as terrorists. Since 9/11, Shaheen (2008) has found more than fifty TV shows that vilify Arab Americans and Muslim Americans. One example is *24*, a television show that portrays a single day in which terrorists threaten to attack the United States. The show's main characters are part of a counterterrorism unit working to stop the terrorists, most of whom are Arab and Muslim. Pressure from the Islamic Council resulted in season five portrayals of some Arab and Muslim characters as patriotic rather than only as terrorists (Nurullah 2010). Despite this adjustment, this television series, which first aired from 2001 to 2010, "depicts the fight against Islamist extremism much as the Bush Administration has defined it: as an all-consuming struggle for America's survival that demands the toughest of tactics by waging war against Muslims" (Nurullah 2010:1042).

The negative images of Arabs in film and television have more potential for harm today than they did forty years ago because today Hollywood images reach an international audience. For any racial/ethnic minority group, stereotypical media portrayals fuel a sense that such people are different and alien, "others," and, thus, increase the likelihood that they will face discrimination and prejudice. For Arab and Muslim Americans, such images are perhaps even more problematic in that they contribute to their being portrayed as threatening to the United States. Sociologist Jack Shaheen (2007) calls this the *new anti-Semitism* because the stereotyping of Arabs continues despite the fact that Hollywood has been working to eliminate negative stereotypical portrayals of blacks and Jews. The image of the harem still exists in Hollywood films. For example, in the Arnold Schwarzenegger film *Around the World in Eighty Days* (2004), Schwarzenegger plays a Middle Eastern prince with a "hundred or so wives" (Shaheen 2007).

Asian Images

Like other racial/ethnic minority groups, Asian Americans also struggle with invisibility and stereotypical portrayals in film and television. In films such as *Lethal Weapon 4* (1998), *Rush Hour* (1998), and *The Year of the Dragon* (1985), Asian and Asian American men are portrayed as violent gangsters involved in a criminal underworld of drug smuggling and human trafficking. Asian Americans are also portrayed as perpetual outsiders, particularly when portrayed using broken English. Asian women are portrayed as sexually exotic and as seductive but untrustworthy, a "dragon lady" who is the female equivalent of the Asian bad guy (Mahdzan and Ziegler 2001).

The TV series *Fresh Off the Boat*, a show about a Chinese immigrant family in the 1990s, based on Eddie Huang's best-selling memoir of the same name, began in 2015 and has been picked up for a third season. This is the first television show to feature a predominantly Asian American cast in twenty years—since Margaret Cho's *All-American Girl* in 1994, which only lasted one season (Hess 2016).

As of 2010, Asian Americans made up almost 6 percent of the population, with South Asians, or Indians, making up 18.4 percent of that population. Research finds that images of South Asians on film and television are limited to those of foreigners, such as convenience store employees who speak heavily accented English, or as model minorities, such as students or scientists (Thakore 2016). In more-current presentations of South Asian characters one finds a shift toward more positive, though limited, characters with an emphasis on their assimilation, to the extent that "these characters know little about their ethnic culture" making them more acceptable to a white audience (Thakore 2016:114). Ultimately, we can look to the concentrated media ownership for such limited representation, as those in positions of authority in film and television "do little to consciously challenge the stereotypes in the media—and they often encourage them for purposes of comedy, staging, or simply othering" (Thakore 2016:115).

Asian American actors have begun protesting their invisibility in television and film. Research by the USC Annenberg Media, Diversity, and Social Change Initiative finds that there was almost no progress in terms of diversity (inclusion of racial/ethnic minorities, women, and transgender characters) between 2007 and 2014 (Gerard 2015). Researchers describe the Asian American presence (or absence) in film as an "epidemic of invisibility," as forty out of the top one hundred films of that period had no Asian characters at all.

Asian American actors are also protesting what they view as **whitewashing**, which refers to the film industry practice of using white actors to play racial/ethnic minority characters, which contributes to the erasure of people of color not only from Hollywood but from history (Hess 2016). There is nothing new about this practice, as whites were cast as Asians in the old Charlie Chan movies. While blackface is no longer still in practice, whitewashing is. Tilda Swinton played a Tibetan monk in *Doctor Strange* (2016). *Ghost in the Shell* (2017), a remake of a Japanese anime film, has been criticized for hiring Scarlett Johansson to play the lead character, a Japanese woman. When criticized for this move, the producers added insult to injury by claiming they were going to alter her appearance to make her look more Asian, "yellowface for the digital age" (Chow 2016).

WITNESS

Actress Lucy Liu starred in Charlie's Angels (2000) and in a television adaptation of the Sherlock Holmes stories. Speaking of the Asian Americans in the media, she states, "I watched a lot of television and, you know, Get Smart and Barney Miller and Brady Bunch and things like that, and at that time there were not many Asian people on television. I think on Barney Miller there was only one person who was on there, and so I didn't grow up thinking that this was a possibility, even though this was something I really wanted to do as a child. I never really thought of myself as the only Asian face out there until somebody pointed that out to me, you know, and said, 'You actually are quite a pioneer, and we hope that this is going to set a new precedent'" ("A Woman as Sherlock's Dr. Watson …" 2012).

White Images

Some racial images in media manage to reinforce white privilege, where whiteness is portrayed as normative, particularly films known as white savior films (WSF). A WSF portrays a white messianic character who saves a lower- or working-class person of color, generally one who is poor, troubled, and oppressed (Hughey 2014). The white character is the hero of the story. Films such as *Green Book* (2018), *Freedom Writers* (2007), *Dangerous Minds* (1995), *The Blind Side* (2009), *Dances with Wolves* (1990), *The Matrix* (1999), *The Help* (2011), and even *The Free State of Jones* (2016) are just a few examples of the WSFs (Hughey 2014, 2016).

While a successful film genre, the WSF is problematic because it frames the person of color as unable to solve their own problems, as incompetent. Often the storyline in a WSF involves a white teacher who touches her impoverished minority students and motivates them to great achievements, or a white coach who leads his poor students of color to victory. While this may hardly seem problematic, it is a storyline that sells only if the teacher is white. For instance, the film *Dangerous Minds* was based upon a true story of a Latina teacher and her students. However, the Hollywood version of this used a white woman, Michelle Pfeiffer, in the leading role. Thousands of teachers of color work in impoverished, underfunded, disproportionately minority schools every day, yet they are not portrayed as capable of saving these children that the rest of society has written off. Indeed, WSFs overlook the reality that communities of color produce their own leaders and heroes and do not have to rely on whites for their salvation. WSFs are problematic because:

> They rely on an implicit message of white paternalism and antiblack stereotypes of contented servitude, obedience, and acquiescence. Whiteness emerges as an iron fist in a velvet glove, the knightly savior of the dysfunctional "others" who are redeemable as long as they consent to assimilation and obedience to their white benefactors.
>
> (Hughey 2014:8)

RACIAL IMAGERY IN NEW MEDIA

Stereotypical images of racial/ethnic minorities also proliferate in video games and other new media, such as YouTube. However, user-generated content sites, also known as Web 2.0, such as YouTube, Wikipedia, and Flickr, hold the potential for underrepresented groups to control some of their representation. Beginning in 2005, blogging, podcasting, social media, and wikis became widespread, dramatically altering the media landscape, as ordinary people now have the technology to publish their thoughts and images.

User-Generated Content

There is some evidence that new media, such as user-generated content (UGC) websites like YouTube, hold potential for racial/ethnic minority groups in terms of their positive and respectful representation. UGC sites are relatively easy to navigate and are free of charge, and draw a larger and larger share of the viewing audience. As of 2013, YouTube had over one billion unique video viewers per month ("YouTube Reaches ..." 2013). Additionally, most users of this new media are young and college educated, and new media have equal numbers of male and female users, all of which leads to the speculation that these users are likely to hold more egalitarian views and, thus, could be expected to produce more positive media representations of racial/ethnic minorities than traditional media sources (Kopacz and Lawton 2010).

Portrayals of Native people on YouTube differ markedly from those in traditional media (Kopacz and Lawton 2010). For instance, Native Americans have appeared as central figures in UGC videos with low incidences of stereotypical depictions. Most Native images were male, however, following a gendered pattern found in traditional media. An additional pattern of representation finds Native Americans portrayed in the post–World War II era, which differs from mainstream media portrayals that only show Native Americans in the past. Issues of tribal sovereignty and racial discrimination faced by indigenous people are also present in YouTube videos, while generally ignored in the mainstream media.

Based upon research findings like these, Native Americans—or any racial minority advocacy group—may find that generating videos for UGC sites is a valuable way to advocate for a group, to boost a group's identity, and to counter mainstream media messages that still subtly or overtly convey racial/ethnic minority inferiority. There were claims that television held the potential for promoting intercultural understanding, yet the medium has not lived up to its potential in this regard (Shaheen 1984). The same potential exists in such new media as UGC. There is some research suggesting that this potential may be being realized as more marginalized groups embrace Web 2.0 sites.

Video Games

Although video games may not appear to warrant the same scholarly attention as other cultural creations such as literature and film, video gaming is a major industry today, rivaling film and book publishing. In fact, video games aren't just for children anymore: research finds that 67 percent of heads of households play computer or video games (Crawford and Gosling 2009). As cultural products, video games are saturated with racialized, sexualized, and gendered meaning (Leonard 2006). While violence in video games has long been debated, the race and gender stereotypes that proliferate in them rarely generate the same kind of attention. Some have argued that racial stereotyping in computer games amounts to "high-tech blackface," a modern-day minstrelsy (Leonard 2004; Marriott 1999).

During the 1980s and 1990s, African American video game characters were rare, as Orpheus Hanley, an African American video game designer describes: "You never saw black characters … If there were black ones, they would get beat up, really whumped so fast, before they had time to get into character" (Marriott 1999). When people of color were depicted in early video games, they were generally portrayed in derogatory and unflattering ways. Today, while racial/ethnic minorities are no longer invisible in video games, racial stereotypes persist and roles for racial minority characters are limited to stereotypes—for instance, criminals or sports stars. Asian characters in such games as *Dynasty Warriors* and *Crouching Tiger*, for instance, are almost always portrayed as foreign, ninjas or martial artists, and speaking poor English (Dickerman, Christensen, and Kerl-McClain 2008; Leonard 2006). Many games, such as *America's Army* and *Desert Storm: Splinter Cell*, portray Arabs as terrorists. Latinos are likely to be portrayed as criminals, as such games as *Grand Theft Auto III* and *Grand Theft Auto: Vice City* show.

Eight out of ten black male video game characters are athletes, reinforcing the idea that African Americans are genetically superior athletes, an idea that reifies race as genetic rather than a social construction (Leonard 2004), an issue we will explore in greater detail in the next chapter. Black male athletes are portrayed as more physical and more verbally aggressive than their white counterparts in video sports games, such as *NFL Street* and *NBA Street*. This fuels dominant ideologies of blacks as innately athletic and aggressive, while white athletic success is portrayed as due to hard work and intelligence, ideas that are found to proliferate among sports commentators as well as fans (see Chapter 12).

Leonard (2004) argues that sports video games are a modern-day form of minstrelsy because they facilitate white control of blackness, an arena where whites can try on blackness. White players are able to sample the "other," to be black, without disrupting dominant beliefs about blackness. It is also a form of minstrelsy in that video games embody "America's simultaneous love and hate of black urbanness, reflecting dominant desires to both police and become the other" (Leonard 2004). While whites play at being black in video sports games, the problem lies in that this play romanticizes urban ghettos from the safety of white suburban players' own homes, which allows them to ignore the social, economic, and political realities of ghetto life and perpetuate the dominant image of urban minority men as only obsessed with street basketball and unconcerned about their communities (Leonard 2004). Although it can be argued that players of color are also able to participate in the ritual of "trying on the other" by playing white characters, the difference is that there are a wide range of roles for white characters as compared to characters of color; thus, this is unlikely to reinforce racial stereotypes about whites (Dunlop 2007).

Video games also provide a good arena for exploring the intersection of race and gender, as white males are central characters in video games and almost 80 percent of female player-controlled characters are white. African American female video game characters are more likely than any other group to be portrayed as victims of violence. Such data show that video games, much like college campuses, as Chapter 7 explored, can be considered racialized as well as gendered spaces: about and for white males.

The presence of white males in the virtual world goes beyond sheer numbers; white males also dominate in terms of the types of characters they portray. White male video game characters are overwhelmingly likely to be the heroes, as Leonard's research finds that out of fifty-three heroes, forty-six were white males.

While video games generally fuel racial stereotypes, only some can be accused of reinforcing explicit white supremacist messages. Some examples of explicit racism in video games are such games as *Ethnic Cleansing* and *White by Law*, which were created by white supremacist groups to fuel messages of white supremacy and racial minority inferiority. However, it is not only white supremacist groups that create blatantly racist games, as a game by the name of *Custer's Revenge* (1982) shows. The objective of the game was for the player, a naked cowboy, to cross the screen to a naked Native American woman who was tied up at a stake. To score points, the player needed to dodge arrows as he made his way toward the woman. Upon reaching her, the character would then have intercourse with her (Dickerman, Christensen, and Kerl-McClain 2008). Another racially offensive video game was *DJ Boy* (1989), in which the villain is Big Mamma, an overweight African American woman with large red lips, an undeniable mammy archetype. One of Big Mamma's weapons was to throw shorter characters that appeared to be her children, fueling negative images of black mothers (Collins 1990). In 2003, a video game called *Border Patrol* was released in which the objective of the game was to kill as many Mexicans as possible.

While racially stereotypical and derogatory images such as these reflect and perpetuate racism, they also tell us something about the audience for video games: it is presumed to be white and male. Many games are designed to allow whites to become the "other," playing on white fantasies while perpetuating white privilege. Thus, video games expose racial power and privilege at work in our society. Who is visible and who is invisible in video games, just as in film and television, sends important messages about power in our society (Dunlop 2007). Video games help reinforce the racial order and can be understood as "vehicles of ideological meaning and cultural products affirming contemporary hegemony" (Leonard 2004:4).

SUBORDINATE GROUP RESISTANCE

Racial/ethnic subordinate groups have long used culture to "talk back" to the dominant group, as an expression of their agency. Even in the face of the most oppressive racism, subordinate racial and ethnic groups have resisted their oppression, and the realm of culture is no exception. Analyzing racial/ethnic images in film and television allows us to understand Marx's dominant ideology thesis and the operation of hegemony. However, just because dominant groups reproduce certain stereotypical images of minority groups throughout popular culture does not mean minority groups passively accept such portrayals. The Centre for Contemporary Cultural Studies provides a theoretical foundation for understanding subordinate-group resistance. In the next sections, we explore subordinate-group resistance in music, film, and television.

Music as the Voice of Resistance

American music has long been an arena where African Americans have "talked back" to the dominant group, countering negative messages and images with affirmations of black life and expressions of black identity and culture. Tricia Rose, professor of history and African American studies at Brown University, explains:

> People learn from experience when and how explicitly they can express their discontent. Under social conditions in which sustained frontal attacks on powerful groups are strategically unwise or successfully contained, oppressed people use language, dance, and music to mock those in power, express rage, and produce fantasies of subversion.
>
> (1994:99)

African American Music: From Slave Songs to Rap

From slave songs to rap, African American music has been one of the most authentic expressions of black life in America. In general, music acts as a reflection of a period—it can capture the mood and attitude of a people during a particular era—and African American musical expressions are no exception.

It has been argued that the only freedom black Americans had during the slave era was linguistic, the freedom to express themselves through song (West 1988). Slave songs were encouraged by slave owners because they were thought to inspire slaves to work harder. What the slave owners did not realize was that revolutionary messages were embedded in slave songs. Slave songs were obsessed with freedom and justice, and some even provided strategies to accomplish this (Fisher 1990). The following lyrics from the song "Steal Away" provide evidence of song lyrics' providing strategies for acquiring freedom for slaves:

> *Steal away, steal away*
> *Steal away to Jesus,*
> *Steal away, steal away home*
> *I ain't got long to stay here.*

These lyrics, while possibly comforting to slave owners due to their Christian message, actually conveyed information about secret meetings of insurrectionary slaves (Fisher 1990). Lyrics of spirituals often use the phrase "down by the river," referring to the River Jordan, and the "promised land." Among slaves, these lyrics were often more literal than the Christian message on which they were based, referring to a nearby river and the promise of freedom for runaway slaves.

Both blues and jazz are African American contributions to American culture that emerged at the turn of the twentieth century. Originally, blues and jazz were labeled as **deviant**, departing from the societal norm, and associated with sin and the devil, at least partially because they were black cultural expressions. For generations, whites and middle-class blacks adhered to this characterization of blues and jazz as sinful.

The *blues* is a term that refers to a particular style of music, originally created by black Americans, that has a twelve-bar, three-line structure and a call-and-response format. It emerged out of the rural black experience during the Jim Crow era. The blues is about more than a style of music; it is a feeling, often described as "nothin' but a good man feelin' bad" (Werner 1998). It is an extension of earlier black musical expression, particularly slave songs and spirituals.

As a reflection of black life in Jim Crow America, the blues mirrored both black emancipation and the constraints on black freedom and translated these ambiguous experiences into song. The blues was the message of an oppressed, yet optimistic, people in a state of flux and the hopes and disappointments of the rural-to-urban migration of black Americans. While the blues originated in the rural South, primarily in the Mississippi Delta, it migrated along with so many black Americans to urban areas in the South, such as Memphis, and those farther north, such as Kansas City, St. Louis, and Chicago.

The blues originated in the late 1800s and early 1900s; the first blues recording was 1920's "Crazy Blues," by Mamie Smith and Her Jazz Hounds. W. C. Handy, a composer and musician known as the "father of the blues," is credited with popularizing both the term and the musical form and with being one of the first to copyright a blues song, with "Memphis Blues" in 1912. With the recording of this musical form, record companies discovered the black consumer and, thus, created a recording category referred to as race records. Race records were commercial recordings of black artists intended only for a black audience. It was assumed by record company executives that whites would not develop a taste for black musical forms.

Jazz originated in the 1890s in New Orleans and almost immediately became popular with white audiences. While blues initially reflected the black rural experience in Jim Crow America, jazz reflected the black urban experience. *Jazz* is a term that refers to music that is more complex in structure than blues and is known for its provocative rhythms and for improvisation, where performers create their parts as they play, making each jazz performance unique (Gridley 1997).

Despite the fact that blues and jazz were designated as "race music," they both became wildly popular with white audiences, particularly once such blues artists as

IMAGE 11.3: Yaaba Funk, an English band with Ghanaian influences, performs at London's Rise Festival in July 2008. The lead singer is wearing a Rock Against Racism T-shirt.

Muddy Waters and Howlin' Wolf migrated north from the Delta and created the renowned Chicago blues scene. Ultimately, blues provided the foundation on which rock and roll was established. Between the 1930s and the 1950s, a type of jazz known as big band was the most popular form of music in the United States. Despite the crossover appeal of jazz, meaning it appealed to both black and white audiences, musical venues were racially segregated. When black musicians played a white club in the South, they were required to enter and exit through the back door, as they were treated like any black person in the Jim Crow South.

White rock musicians, such as Elvis Presley, the Rolling Stones, the Beatles, and Eric Clapton, all took their inspiration from black American musical forms such as the blues. Some would argue that white artists took more than inspiration from black music. In the beginning of this chapter, we argued that cultures inevitably engage in the practice of cultural diffusion, where they borrow ideas from one another. However, sometimes more than simple cultural diffusion is going on and the practice can become **racist appropriation**, where nonwhite groups are denied the profits from their cultural creations (Desmond and Emirbayer 2010). African American rock artist Chuck Berry, for instance, sued the Beach Boys for stealing his song "Sweet Little Sixteen" almost note for note for the title song of their 1963 release *Surfin' USA*, which reached number two on the charts and stayed there for over a year, finding success with predominantly white audiences. Berry won his lawsuit in the mid-1970s and was granted a writing credit and royalties.

WITNESS

Check out Chuck Berry's "Sweet Little Sixteen" at www.youtube.com/
watch?v=ZLV4NGpoy_E and the Beach Boys' "Surfin' USA" at www.
youtube.com/watch?v=sNypbmPPDco and see whether you agree that
the songs are almost identical.

The most recent African American cultural contribution is rap, which emerged out
of urban ghettos in the late 1970s as an "electrified folk poetry of the streets, as a way
for young blacks to speak their minds" (Eyerman and Jamison 1998:105). Rap is
described as a "contemporary stage for the theater of the powerless" (Rose
1994:101). Perhaps surprisingly in the face of the mainstream appeal of rap today,
much like blues and jazz, rap was initially perceived as deviant by mainstream white
culture as well as middle-class black culture. Even such black publications as *Ebony*
and *Essence* ignored the art form, while black radio stations refused to give adequate
airplay to rap (Dyson 1993; Nelson and Gonzales 1991).

Rap functions for today's generation in much the same way blues did for previous
generations, "as a source of racial identity, permitting forms of boasting and asserting machismo for devalued black men suffering from social degradation … fostering
the ability to transform hurt and anguish into art and commerce" (Dyson 1993:9).
While rap music has gone mainstream, the origins of rap can be understood as
reflecting many aspects of 1970s urban black culture: police brutality, poverty, economic stagnation, and educational atrophy. Although the most notorious form of
rap music, gangsta rap, expressed violence, sexism, and homophobia, which inspired
fear and efforts at censorship in white America, there is much more to this musical
form, as it ranges from Christian rap to politically and socially conscious rap. In fact,
early rap artists, such as Public Enemy, sought to disrupt white supremacy with their
radical critiques of institutional racism and urban poverty.

While rap is an art form that emerged out of black America and much of it still
remains a chronicle of black life in America, it is now an international art form—
with both fans and artists from every racial/ethnic group and from all over the
world. Argentine-born Korean American rapper Dumbfoundead is an example of
this. Based in Los Angeles, Dumbfoundead has managed to acquire a sizable black
audience, yet he does not feel he has to be black to be a rapper. He maintains that he
is "bringing his Asian-ness to this art form" (Martin, Michael 2013) (see Recommended Multimedia at the end of the chapter).

Music and the Civil Rights Movement

Both music and African American churches played crucial mobilizing roles in the
civil rights movement; thus, traditional spirituals and gospel songs were the first

BOX 11.3

Racial Justice Activism:
Rock Against Racism

Rock Against Racism (RAR) was an anti-racist organization that was organized by Red Saunders, Roger Huddle, and others in Great Britain in 1976. RAR emerged in response to the rise in white nationalism and anti-immigrant sentiment. A further inspiration were comments made by Eric Clapton at a concert in Birmingham, England. Clapton suggested that England was becoming an overcrowded "black colony," due to immigration. He then shouted, "Keep Britain white!" several times. Clapton later claimed that his comments were a joke and that he was unaware of politics at the time.

RAR sought to use music to promote racial harmony and to help break down barriers between people by organizing RAR festivals with pop, rock, reggae, and punk bands singing songs with antiracist themes. RAR's 1976 concert was the first in England to have black and white bands play together in one show. In 1978, the group organized a Carnival Against the Nazis in London, where one hundred thousand people marched six miles from Trafalgar Square to a RAR concert featuring the Clash, X-Ray Specs, the Ruts, and Generation X, among others.

Rock Against Racism ended in 1981 but was reborn in 2002 as Love Music Hate Racism. www.lovemusichate racism.com/

types of music associated with the movement, primarily because such music was familiar to organizers and activists. Sociologists who study culture from a functionalist perspective point out that music helped ensure solidarity among civil rights movement activists, who varied along class, racial, educational, and geographic lines. Protest songs, such as "We Shall Overcome," inspired protesters and calmed their fears in the face of violent white opposition. The songs of the movement became a significant source of collective identity formation (Eyerman and Jamison 1998).

Music was so central to the civil rights movement that the Student Nonviolent Coordinating Committee (SNCC) formed a band, the Freedom Singers, which traveled throughout the country performing concerts that served the dual purposes of educating northerners about the fight for civil rights, at a time when the mass media failed to devote much time or attention to the topic, and fund-raising. The movement inspired popular white singer-songwriters as well: Bob Dylan's song "Oxford Town" was written in response to the riots that broke out in Oxford, Mississippi, when African Americans tried to integrate the University of Mississippi.

Others have argued that black entertainers of the 1930s through 1950s unintentionally helped facilitate the civil rights movement because the increasing familiarity whites had with black performers in this era, such as Paul Robeson, Bessie Smith,

Billie Holiday, Harry Belafonte, and others, changed the white public's image of blacks (Pomerance 1988). Not only did the talents of these black performers challenge popular stereotypes of black inferiority, but the artists sang and spoke of the black experience in America, a reality white America was oblivious to.

It is worth noting that Britain's struggle with racism was evident through comments made by some musicians. In 1976 Eric Clapton delivered unfortunate statements on stage in England, racist statements that catapulted the movement of Rock Against Racism (see Box 11.3 Racial Justice Activism: Rock Against Racism).

Resistance in Film and Television

African Americans are not the only racial/ethnic minority group that has used popular culture to challenge dominant-group portrayals of them. Latinos, Native Americans, and Asian Americans have resisted cultural stereotypes in numerous ways as well. For some, resistance involves making films from the point of view of minority-group members, as we saw in Box 11.2 on Spike Lee's 40 Acres and a Mule Filmworks. For others, resistance involves protesting the film and television industries, as the NAACP did when *Birth of a Nation* came out in 1915. In 1942, the NAACP's Walter White addressed Hollywood studio heads and threatened a black boycott of Hollywood films unless they increased black employment in Hollywood, both on camera and behind the scenes, and expanded black characters beyond stereotypes.

In 1998, the film *Smoke Signals* was released. It was the first feature film to be written, directed, and cast with American Indians. Telling the story of two young American Indian men of the contemporary era, it used humor to emphasize Indian stereotypes, poverty, and identity issues (Holtzman 2000). In addition to challenging many Indian stereotypes, this film is unique in that it portrays Native Americans as members of the current era, rather than as people from our distant past.

In 1999, the National Council of La Raza encouraged a one-week boycott of television, a "brown out," to protest the paucity of Latino characters. These efforts, however, have not been successful at increasing Latino representation on television. While Latinos are the largest racial/ethnic group in the United States, they comprise only 3 percent of prime-time television characters (Mastro and Behm-Morawitz 2005). That same year, the NAACP encouraged the television industry to consider the fact that from 1999 through 2000, none of the four major networks (ABC, CBS, NBC, and Fox) scheduled programs that had even one racial/ethnic minority actor or character in a leading role (Torres 2003). The National Asian Pacific American Legal Consortium works toward full civil and human rights for Asian Americans, including television diversity, which involves analyzing the underrepresentation of Asian Americans in media and activism to alter stereotypical media representation.

RACE AND PUBLIC HISTORY

Racial imagery is found in more than media. It is also found on the landscape in the form of historical monuments and markers. In fact, some sociologists have argued that white supremacy has literally been erected on the landscape across the United States (Loewen 1999). In August 2011, the first memorial on the National Mall that was not dedicated to a war, a president, or a white man was unveiled. The memorial honors Martin Luther King Jr. and places him in the company of Thomas Jefferson, Abraham Lincoln, and Franklin D. Roosevelt. This is an example of racial progress, considering that in 1922, when the Lincoln Memorial was dedicated, the lone black speaker, Dr. Robert Moton of Tuskegee Institute, was barred from sitting onstage with the white speakers, and blacks in attendance were segregated from whites (Carrier 2004).

The Martin Luther King Jr. Memorial was not the first proposed addition to the National Mall meant to enshrine a black cultural figure. In 1923, Mississippi senator John Williams proposed a bill to establish a national mammy monument to be funded by the Richmond, Virginia, chapter of the United Daughters of the Confederacy. It was to be placed on federal land in the shadow of the Lincoln Memorial, as "a monument in memory of the faithful colored mammies of the South" (Harris-Perry 2011:73). This proposal encountered fierce resistance from ordinary citizens, the black press, and African American women's organizations because it was not intended to honor the lives of actual black women but instead celebrated black women in the white imagination, specifically depicting them as "faithful servants of

IMAGE 11.4: Martin Luther King Jr. memorial on the National Mall in Washington, DC. Dedicated in October 2011, the King memorial is the first memorial on the National Mall that does not commemorate a former president or a war.

white domesticity" (Harris-Perry 2011:74). This memorial never materialized, but the seriousness with which it was proposed tells us something about race, power, and public history. As historian James C. Cobb wrote, "Power over the past, after all, is but a reflection of power over the present" (quoted in Moser 2008:127). Museums, history sites, schools, and universities all have enormous influence over the public perception of the past (Rhea 1997).

Public history sites—markers, monuments, national parks, museums, and battle-fields—are more than symbols of the past. "What a community erects on its historical landscape not only sums up its views of the past but also influences its possible future" (Loewen 1999:14). Public history sites historically have celebrated white culture and Euro-American history while denigrating, marginalizing, or distorting the history of people of color. Celebrating the past through the lens of the dominant group means that subordinate groups must develop strategies to exist within this dominant interpretation of the past (Shackel 2001). Thus, subordinate groups' experiences with public history exacerbate their sense of **double consciousness**, the sense of two-ness that W. E. B. Du Bois (1989) argued that African Americans must feel (Shackel 2001). They must always look at themselves through the eyes of the dominant group. The celebration of dominant groups in public history not only affects our view of the past but has repercussions on the future as well. As long as whites are the subject of our statues, it will always seem right for whites to hold most of the positions of power in our society (Loewen 1999).

We have learned how history has been used to support the dominant group, and public history is no exception. Public history matters if for no other reason than that only one American in six ever takes a course in history after graduating from high school, so we learn much of our history from historical novels, movies, and the landscape (Loewen 1999). There have been intense debates surrounding the *Enola Gay* exhibition, the Holocaust Memorial Museum, the World War II Memorial in Washington, DC, the Vietnam Veterans Memorial, how slavery is represented at Civil War memorial sites, and the Martin Luther King Jr. Memorial, which are all part of the larger **culture wars** over how racial/ethnic groups are represented in culture.

WITNESS

African American Kathe Hambrick-Jackson describes her reaction to visiting Louisiana slave plantations: "One day I decided to take one of these plantation tours. It was all about antiques, furniture, architecture and the wealthy lifestyle. But I wanted to know how many lives of my ancestors did it take to produce one cup of sugar?" (Stodghill 2008). These kinds of experiences inspired her to open the River Road African American Museum in Donaldsonville, Louisiana.

The era of 1890–1920 was a period of massive monument building in the United States. This was also the period when white supremacists reestablished their power and control through the creation of Jim Crow segregation and the oppression of African Americans. It was also the era of imperialist expansion in the Pacific and the Caribbean and the establishment of Native American boarding schools, among other things. White supremacists during this period had the power to determine how the Civil War and Reconstruction would be remembered in the South, which helps explain why so many statues of Confederates were erected during this era (Loewen 1999). They promoted a "Lost Cause" narrative about the Civil War that argued the war was not about slavery but was instead about state's rights and federal intrusion. This narrative was promoted in Confederate monuments. According to the Equal Justice Initiative, over one thousand Confederate monuments had been erected by 1950, with more than three hundred installed on courthouse grounds and every Southern state capital building hosting at least one. Most Confederate monuments were erected forty to fifty years after the Civil War ended (Rushing 2018).

Until recently, Civil War–era historic sites and museums rarely discussed the causes of the Civil War or its consequences, carefully avoiding mention of slavery (Pitcaithley 2006). In Richmond, Virginia, there are so many Confederate museums, monuments, plaques, and statues that it "is almost enough to make a person wonder whether the rebels actually won the war" (Moser 2008:120). Stone Mountain, Georgia, once belonged to the Cherokee and Creek Indians. It is now the site of a Confederate memorial, featuring granite-carved images of Jefferson Davis, Robert E. Lee, and Thomas "Stonewall" Jackson, carved by the same artist who eventually carved Mount Rushmore (Morse 1999). In August 1915, the United Daughters of the Confederacy hired the sculptor to create a monument on Stone Mountain honoring Confederate heroes. The sculpture was not completed and work was delayed due to lack of funds. The project was abandoned until 1958, when the state of Georgia, during the height of desegregation battles, bought the mountain and hired a new sculptor to finish the project, which eventually was completed in 1970 (Morse and Steber 1999). Power over the past reflects power over the present, as this example illustrates.

The post–civil rights era has resulted in a shift in our nation's **collective memory**—the beliefs about the past that a nation's citizens hold in common and publicly recognize as legitimate representations of their history—to better reflect the racial/ethnic diversity of the United States (Rhea 1997). The collective memory and publicly presented past did not shift toward a more inclusive representation of racial/ethnic minorities automatically. Instead, it was due to the minority activists who fought for inclusion in museums, history sites, and schools and universities, dramatically transforming the American identity and landscape (Rhea 1997).

The Custer Battlefield National Monument, for instance, was changed to the Little Bighorn Battlefield National Monument (1991), and the World War II internment of Japanese American citizens is now memorialized at the Manzanar National Historic Site (1992). The massacre of Native Americans is now memorialized at the Sand Creek Massacre Historic Site (2000), and African Americans' struggle for civil rights is memorialized at the Little Rock Central High School National Historic Site (1998), the *Brown v. Board of Education* National Historic Site (1996), and the Selma-to-Montgomery National Historic Trail (1996), among other places. The establishment of these particular monuments has been the result of congressional and National Park Service actions and sends a message that "a useful history must include both painful as well as prideful aspects of the past" (Pitcaithley 2006:172). African American museums have opened across the country, including the National Museum of African American History and Culture, which opened in December of 2016, and a black holocaust museum in Milwaukee, Wisconsin, that was founded in 1988 by James Cameron, a lynching survivor. Many communities, including the states of Louisiana, Alabama, and South Carolina and the cities of Lexington, Kentucky; Cleveland, Ohio; Boston, Massachusetts; and Washington, DC, have established African American heritage trails and sites (Stodghill 2008). The National Civil Rights Museum in Memphis boasted 207,143 visitors between July 2008 and June 2009, and approximately 170,000 people visit the Birmingham Civil Rights Institute every year (Byrd 2010).

Despite this shift, Americans still live in a landscape of white supremacy. For example, Nathan Bedford Forrest, the Confederate general and founder of the Ku Klux Klan, has more state historical markers in Tennessee than does any other historical figure (Loewen 1999). Even though the state claims three presidents of the United States of America as its own—Andrew Jackson, James K. Polk, and Andrew Johnson—Forrest has more markers and monuments in his honor than these three presidents combined.

Public history sites take on a sacred quality, functioning like a **civil religion**, which sociologist Robert Bellah (1967) describes as a set of sacred beliefs so commonly accepted that it becomes part of the national culture (Loewen 1999). The language "In God We Trust" on the dollar bill, for instance, is an example of civil religion. The fact that public history sites take on such sacred qualities explains why there is so much contestation surrounding how history is represented at these sites.

Battles over public history continue. In 2016, Chicago's Field Museum of Natural History stirred controversy when it began showing bronze statues from a 1933 exhibit entitled "Races of Mankind." After being on display for decades, they were banned in 1969 as understandings of race shifted from biological to cultural. The exhibit today is intended to be provocative and to get visitors to see how we understood race historically (Thompson 2016).

After the church shooting in Charleston, South Carolina, in June 2015, Governor Nikki Haley removed the Confederate flag from state grounds. New Orleans mayor

Mitch Landrieu also reacted and declared that the city would remove four Confederate statues, including statues of Jefferson Davis, Robert E. Lee, and P. G. T. Beauregard. His declaration was followed by months of contentious debate, a council vote in support of the mayor's position, legal challenges, and an opposition movement whose motto was "Keep All Monuments." An early contractor hired to remove the monuments resigned after his car was torched, allegedly by someone opposed to the issue. Many supporters of Confederate monuments claim that we should not be using the current climate of political correctness to dictate on this issue, but it is important to know that many people, especially African Americans, actively opposed the monuments at the time they were erected (Palmer and Wessler 2018).

WITNESS

In May of 2017, New Orleans' Mayor Landrieu delivered a speech explaining his decision to remove four Confederate monuments. In response to those who critiqued his actions by stating that the monuments merely reflected history, Landrieu said, "It immediately begs the questions, why there are no slave ship monuments, no prominent markers on public land to remember the lynchings or the slave blocks; nothing to remember this long chapter of our lives; the pain, the sacrifice, the shame … all of it happening on the soil of New Orleans. So for those self-appointed defenders of history and the monuments, they are eerily silent on what amounts to this historical malfeasance, a lie by omission. There is a difference between remembrance of history and reverence of it."

The Southern Poverty Law Center compiles a list of all government-backed Confederate tributes in a publication entitled *Whose Heritage? Public Symbols of the Confederacy.* Some of the tributes identified include 718 monuments and statues, 109 public schools named for Confederates, and 9 official Confederate holidays ("SPLC Study Finds …" 2016). Over the past ten years, over $40 million in tax dollars have gone to Confederate heritage organizations and to maintaining these Confederate monuments (Palmer and Wessler 2018).

The "Woke" Generation? Millennial Attitudes on Race in the US

The "Millennial Attitudes on Race in the US" survey asked respondents two questions about Confederate statues and symbols. The first asked, "Do you personally see the Confederate flag more as a symbol of Southern pride or more as a symbol of racism?" Perhaps unsurprisingly, African Americans (83 percent), Latinos (65

IMAGE 11.5: Soldiers' and Sailors' Monument in Athens, Alabama. The era of 1890–1920 was a period of massive monument building in the United States. Cities throughout the South have monuments to Confederate soldiers similar to the one pictured here, resulting in public history sites overwhelmingly celebrating white history at the expense of the United States' multiracial/multiethnic history.

percent), and Asian Americans (71 percent) view the flag as a symbol of racism (see Figure 11.3). The views among white Millennials were more evenly split, with 55 percent viewing the Confederate flag as a symbol of Southern pride. Respondents were then asked, "Do you support or oppose efforts to remove Confederate statues and symbols from public places such as government buildings and parks?"

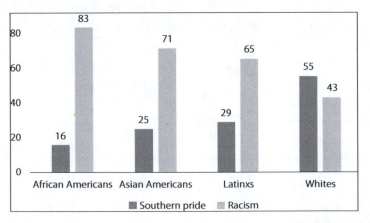

FIGURE 11.3: Millennial attitudes by racial group as to whether Confederate statues and symbols are symbols of southern pride or racism (Cohen et al. 2017).

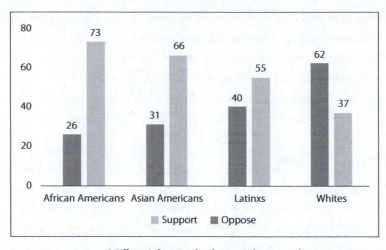

FIGURE 11.4: Millennial attitudes by racial group showing support for removing Confederate statues and symbols from public spaces (Cohen et al. 2017).

Millennials of color were more likely to support removal of Confederate monuments compared to white respondents. Specifically, 73 percent of African Americans, 66 percent of Asian Americans, and 55 percent of Latinos support removal of Confederate statues compared to white Millennials, 62 percent of whom opposed the removal of Confederate symbols (see Figure 11.4).

Slavery and Public History

Visitors who take plantation tours rarely hear the word *slavery* mentioned. This is justified with the claim that people don't want to hear about it because it is unpleasant and conflicts with the perception that American history is about freedom and equality. Until relatively recently, at Monticello, Thomas Jefferson's home and historic site, tour guides did not mention slaves, despite the fact that Jefferson owned over 250 human beings at one point in his life. When the work of slaves was mentioned, they were intentionally misleadingly referred to as "servants." Tours of Monticello included stories of Jefferson's inventions and emphasized the architecture and the grounds (L. Horton 2006). When slaves were mentioned, they were portrayed in as positive a light as possible—for instance, guides said that slaves at this particular plantation were treated well, like family, and so on. Plantation tours help perpetuate the *Gone with the Wind* image of slavery as a benevolent institution.

During the mid-1990s, the director of the National Park Service, Roger Kennedy, began a campaign to modernize the historical interpretations at National Park Service sites, placing particular emphasis on the subject of slavery at Civil War historic sites. As of the mid-1990s, the Gettysburg National Military Park mentioned neither slavery nor slaves in regard to the war. This historic site was attracting nearly two million visitors per year. Over eleven million people visit National Park Service Civil War sites each year (J. Horton 2006). Groups such as the United Sons of Confederate Veterans, the United Daughters of the Confederacy, and the Southern Heritage Coalition were opposed to these moves by the National Park Service and were highly organized and committed to maintaining an interpretation of the Civil War as about states' rights rather than the issue of slavery (J. Horton 2006).

WITNESS

A letter written in protest of the National Park Service's 1998 move to provide more-inclusive historical information about the Civil War at Civil War battlefield historic sites expresses common feelings about the change: "I am completely disgusted with the National Park Service's new policy to post South-bashing propaganda about slavery at National 'Civil War' Battlefield Parks. This mindless South-bashing has to stop if this nation is to continue being united" (Pitcaithley 2006:175).

Opponents of the Park Service's actions feel that national battlefield sites should honor the soldiers who fought at the site and only discuss the specific battle and not the causes of the war or any mention of slavery. This requirement seems to apply only at Civil War battlefield historic sites, as the interpretation at the USS *Arizona* explains the reasons for the Japanese bombing of Pearl Harbor and visitors at Little Bighorn National Historic Site are provided with the battle's larger context (Pitcaithley 2006).

While many plantations still provide tourists a narrative that fails to mention slavery, some plantations have taken it upon themselves to provide a more inclusive history to their visitors. As the owner of the Whitney Plantation in Louisiana, which opened in late 2015, states, "I want to get beyond the moonlight and magnolia myths of the plantation" (Stodghill 2008). The Whitney Plantation is the first in the country dedicated to telling the story of plantation slavery in the United States and was opened by John Cummings, a white man who has spent the last 15 years and $8 million of his own personal fortune to open the museum (Amsden 2015). Cummings's approach has made many uncomfortable, claiming it is too disturbing. Cummings's response is that "it [our slave history] *is* disturbing" (Amsden 2015:52, italics in original).

While there has been some progress in the way we memorialize slavery, there is still too much silence. For instance, New Orleans was the largest slave market in the United States—more people were sold in New Orleans than were brought from Africa to the United States during two centuries of the Middle Passage—and yet the city has only one slavery-related monument, marker, or public history site referencing the domestic slave trade (Ball 2015).

Remember(ing) the Alamo!

The Alamo plays a prominent part in American collective memory, as most school-children learn of the heroic actions of Davy Crockett, Jim Bowie, William Barret Travis, and others bravely fighting to the death against General Santa Anna and the Mexican army. The cry "Remember the Alamo!" is ingrained in our cultural imagination as the rallying cry of Texans seeking independence from Mexican rule. The Alamo historic site is a shrine to Texas freedom (Tate 2004).

However, the 1836 Battle of the Alamo in San Antonio, Texas, has been heavily mythologized, and race is directly tied to this myth (Groneman 2011). The Alamo, in the American memory, was valiantly defended by whites against brown-skinned Mexican foreigners (Hutton 1985). During the late nineteenth century some people began to take an active interest in preserving the battle site, and today the Alamo is the most popular historic site in Texas. The Daughters of the Republic of Texas (DRT) were granted the right to care for the site and arrange for the interpretation of the Alamo to be preserved, and they control its interpretation to this day (Rhea 1997). The DRT is composed of women who can trace their ancestral lineage to white settlers of Texas in the 1820s or to ancestors that were part of Texas's struggle for independence. Under DRT's interpretation, the Alamo is an Anglo history site; they have chosen to glorify only Anglo soldiers by name, ignoring the many Mexicans who died inside the Alamo. Additionally, their interpretation is misleading in that they represent defenders of the Alamo as fighting for Texas's independence, when in reality they were fighting for their rights as Mexican citizens (Rhea 1997).

Mexican Americans in San Antonio have contested DRT's control over this historical site by challenging the organization on legal grounds, particularly its control of the land surrounding the Alamo. The San Antonio city council responded by establishing the Alamo Plaza Study Committee in 1994. In its final report, the committee recommended the inclusion of several interpretive themes of the Alamo, including the area's Spanish and Native American heritage, the battle of 1836, and the modern development of San Antonio (Rhea 1997).

The Alamo's portrayal as a race war between Mexicans and white Texans is inaccurate. On the battlefield were free blacks, slaves, Tejanos (Mexicans who sided with the Americans), Europeans, and Indians from central Mexico. There were also Spanish-speaking defenders of the Alamo, a group completely erased from our collective memory (Tate 2004). In fact, only thirteen native-born Texans were in the group defending the Alamo, and eleven of them were of Mexican descent (Flores 2000).

The DRT's interpretation omits other pieces of history from the Alamo as well. For instance, Anglo-Americans had been flocking into the Mexican territory we now know of as Texas since 1827, quickly outnumbering the Mexican citizens and alarming the Mexican government. The Mexican government outlawed slavery in 1829 as a way to curb immigration from the United States into the Mexican territory. Eventually, this issue, the desire to maintain slavery, became the impetus for the Texas independence movement.

Gilberto Hinojosa, a Tejano historian, began pushing in 1986 for the Alamo historic site to include the role of Mexicans in fighting for the Alamo against Santa Anna's forces. Others have called for a more inclusive historical portrait of the region to be presented at the site, particularly regarding life during the Spanish colonial period. While the DRT resists these suggestions, Latinos still remain uncomfortable with what the Alamo symbolizes, as "they find it a symbol, not of liberty, but of racism" (Flores 2000).

Native Americans, Public History, and the National Parks

Native American activism has resulted in some significant alterations in interpretation at the Little Bighorn Battlefield National Monument, formerly known as the Custer Battlefield National Monument. The fact that the park was initially named the Custer Battlefield National Monument was offensive to Native Americans for several reasons. First, Native Americans had actually won that battle, despite losing the overall war, so naming it after Custer was misleading. Second, there were several battles at the site over several days, and Custer did not participate in all of them. Even Custer's widow remembers the conflicts as the Battle of Little Bighorn (Rhea 1997). To name the entire battlefield after Custer made the site clearly about Custer. Finally, Indian participants were unacknowledged at the historic site, as all the stone markers memorialized army soldiers and none were erected for Indians who died in the battles. Beyond the misnomer, the entire museum portrayed Custer and his men as victims, with Indians described as "hostile" and the Indian side of the story barely presented at all.

During the 1973 occupation of Wounded Knee, discussed in Chapter 6, American Indian Movement (AIM) activists requested permission to place a memorial to the Indians who fought at the Battle of Little Bighorn at the site with a plaque that read, "In memory of our heroic warriors who defended our homes and lands against the hostile aggression of the U.S. Government." The superintendent of the site refused permission to place the plaque at the requested site, but he did agree that they needed to expand their interpretation and include more of the Indian side of the story. The site's staff submitted proposals for including the Indian perspective, with the general idea that all their programs would be presented through the lens of a "clash of cultures" (Rhea 1997).

While the proposals were quite modest, they generated intense hostility from individuals opposed to changing the site. Throughout the 1970s, the National Park

Service remained committed to a strict battlefield history, perceiving this to be objective, neutral history. By the late 1980s, there was more popular support for reinterpretations of the West, and people began pushing the Park Service to include a monument to Indian warriors at the Battle of Little Bighorn site (Rhea 1997). Several significant changes at the site happened in the late 1980s and early 1990s. First was the appointment of Barbara Booher, the first Native American woman superintendent of the park, in 1989. Then in 1991, a bill to change the name of the site from Custer Battlefield to Little Bighorn Battlefield passed Congress with massive support from the public. The conflict over the interpretation of the Battle of Little Bighorn ended in 1991 with Indians victorious. More Indian interpreters were hired to work at the site, with the front desk of the visitor center almost completely staffed by Indians, and Indian interpretations of historical events gained prominence at the site (Rhea 1997). This kind of victory implies that, by the 1990s, Indians had established some power and control over the representation of their past (Rhea 1997).

Another famous national monument, Mount Rushmore, is particularly offensive to Native Americans. The Black Hills are sacred to the Lakota people, the original inhabitants of the region. In 1868, the United States federal government granted the Lakotas the Black Hills in perpetuity. Perpetuity did not last long, as gold was discovered there in the 1870s, which resulted in the Native people being displaced from their land. In addition to the Black Hills being sacred to the Lakota, Mount Rushmore is insulting to them because it celebrates European Americans who killed so many Native Americans and appropriated their land on the very land that the government took from them.

Gerard Baker, the first American Indian superintendent of Mount Rushmore National Monument says that to many Native Americans, Mount Rushmore symbolizes:

> What white people did to this country when they arrived—took the land from the Indians and desecrated it. ... There is a huge need for Anglo-Americans to understand the Black Hills before the arrival of the white men. We need to talk about the first 150 years of America and what that means.
>
> (Perrottet 2006)

Baker has begun expanding educational programs at the monument to include the Indian perspective and to move beyond the image of Mount Rushmore as merely a patriotic symbol. These new programs featuring more-inclusive interpretations of Mount Rushmore have elicited positive responses from visitors, including whites (Perrottet 2006).

WITNESS

Mount Rushmore is "a glittering billboard of imperial supremacy, of might equals right, or white equals right," wrote Tom Saya (2006).

The absence of a memorial can also be telling. Currently, there is no memorial for Wounded Knee, the site of two important historical clashes between Native American tribes and the US federal government. The first was the 1890 massacre in which more than two hundred unarmed Lakota men, women, and children were killed by the US Army, as discussed in Chapter 4. The second was the occupation of Wounded Knee in 1973 by AIM activists, discussed in Chapter 6. In 1986, a group of Lakota people began to commemorate Wounded Knee. They engaged in formal efforts to "renew their stories, remember their ancestors, and to remind themselves of their true history" (Brown 2001:112).

Wounded Knee 1973 survivor groups worked with members of Congress in the 1990s to pass an official apology for what occurred there in 1890 and to establish a Wounded Knee memorial. Congress passed a resolution expressing regret for what occurred. The National Park Service registered the site as a National Historic Landmark in 1965 and offered three proposals for making the site a national park, differing only in terms of who would manage the park. Many Lakota people were hesitant to turn over even more of their land to the federal government, even if it was to be used for a Wounded Knee memorial. In addition to centuries of land loss since the arrival of Europeans, the establishment of the national parks resulted in the removal of Indian tribes from Yosemite, Yellowstone, and Glacier National Park between the 1870s and the 1930s (Burnham 2000; Spence 1999). Another concern among some Lakota was that the Park Service's interpretation of the event would result in the omission of the word *massacre* from the description. Native Americans are unhappy with the interpretation of the events of 1890 as a "battle," as the Lakota victims were unarmed (Brown 2001). Currently, there is no formal memorial to Wounded Knee.

Dispute over a National Historic Site for Japanese Americans

Reparations and conflicts over public history can be intertwined. In 1990, when President George H. W. Bush signed the letters of apology to tens of thousands of Americans of Japanese descent and distributed funds to individuals as reparations for their internment during World War II (see Chapter 13), he also set aside funds for the purpose of educating Americans about the camps (Dubel 2001). Of the ten internment camps established by the federal government during World War II, Manzanar was chosen as the location for the National Historic Site because it was the best preserved, despite the fact that most of the camp had been bulldozed in 1946 by the

Army Corps of Engineers. This site "presents an opportunity for people of all ages and ethnicities to understand the fear, racism, discrimination, and hatred that led to the establishment of ten American concentration camps" (Dubel 2001:94).

More than ten thousand men, women, and children were imprisoned at Manzanar during the war. None of these people were ever charged with a crime. Despite this, there is still considerable controversy surrounding the Manzanar historic site. Some people argue that the federal government engaged in these actions to protect citizens of Japanese descent from others, despite the fact that the historical record shows otherwise. Their internment was due to distrust of Japanese American citizens and was not for their protection. There have been anonymous threats to burn any buildings constructed as replicas of the camp. One of the biggest controversies is over the language on a commemorative plaque that refers to Manzanar as a concentration camp. The plaque has been defaced numerous times by people who believe that equating these camps with concentration camps is inaccurate because that term is often conflated with Hitler's death camps. The Park Service has changed the language on the plaque to read "war relocation center" despite the fact that the historical record shows that the federal government described these as concentration camps (Dubel 2001).

Whitewashing Dutch Slave History

The United States is not the only nation to struggle with its racist past; most European nations are facing similar struggles of how to represent their countries' complicity in slavery, racism, and colonialism. The Netherlands abolished slavery in 1863 after having been involved in the slave trade for over two hundred years and using over an estimated five hundred thousand slaves in their colonies. Their forced labor in the production of cotton, coffee, sugar, tobacco, and cocoa helped make the Netherlands very wealthy (Mitchell, Ricardo, and Sarajilic n.d.).

One example of an ongoing controversy surrounding Dutch slave history is the Dutch royal family's Golden Coach, which was a gift given to the royal family in 1898, long after the eradication of slavery. However, the painted images on the carriage include those of slaves bestowing gifts on colonizers. The continued use of this carriage has generated considerable public debate and controversy, yet most white Amsterdammers agree that the royal family should continue to use it (Mitchell, Ricardo, and Sarajilic n.d.).

For many Europeans, despite their country's intimate involvement in the global slave trade, slavery feels far away, something that is not part of their history. The National Institute for the Study of Dutch Slavery and Its Legacy is working to bring slavery into the public consciousness in the Netherlands. One of its permanent exhibits is entitled "Breaking the Silence."

CHAPTER SUMMARY

Racialized images in popular culture and public history influence how we see our-selves and how we view racial/ethnic others. The power of such controlling images cannot be denied, especially considering how media images saturate our lives. While dominant groups can use media images to reinforce their dominance, subordinate groups also use culture to offer counterhegemonic images. New media, for instance, may be providing a space for such counterhegemonic messages by racial/ethnic minority groups. Public history sites have historically celebrated whiteness, as whites have historically had the power to define history. However, they have become more inclusive since the 1980s, due to cultural activism on the part of racial/ethnic minority groups. It is difficult to predict what kind of an effect this will have on the future of race in the United States, but these kinds of developments lead us in the right direction as a nation.

KEY TERMS AND CONCEPTS

Anti-Arab racism

Brownface

Centre for Contemporary Cultural Studies

Cinethetic racism

Civil religion

Collective memory

Controlling images

Counterhegemonic

Cultural diffusion

Cultural hegemony

Culture wars

Deviant

Double consciousness

Ethnic characterizations

Hegemony

Imagined communities

Material culture

Minstrel shows

Minstrelsy

New anti-Semitism

Nonmaterial culture

Popular culture

Racist appropriation

Structured absence

Whitewashing

PERSONAL REFLECTIONS

1. List your top three favorite television programs from age six to twelve. For each of these, identify the race of the major characters (Latino, African American, white, Asian American, Native American, multiracial). Can you identify any race-related themes in these programs (interracial friendships, racial discrimi-nation, etc.)? Now do the same assignment with your favorite films and/or video games. How have these media images influenced your understandings of race?

2. Think about your most recent encounter with "public history"—a monument, historical marker, or museum. Who or what was being celebrated? After reading this chapter, can you think of any perspective on the person or event that was absent in the interpretation of the person or event? After responding to these questions, listen to the speech New Orleans' Mayor Mitch Landieu gave upon deciding to remove four Confederate monuments from his city (see Recommended Multimedia for a link). To what extent do his comments challenge your perspective on this issue? Why? To what extent are you in agreement with his points? Explain your answer.

CRITICAL THINKING QUESTIONS

1. Explain how minstrel shows are a good example of Marx's dominant ideology thesis. To what extent can rap music be understood through Marx's dominant ideology thesis? Challenge that point by making an argument for understanding rap music as counterhegemonic, the way theorists from the Centre for Contemporary Cultural Studies might understand it.
2. Compare and contrast the racial images of the minority groups discussed in this chapter; speculate on why the images are so similar and why they are sometimes different.

ESSENTIAL READING

Carrier, Jim. 2004. *A Traveler's Guide to the Civil Rights Movement.* Austin, New York: Harcourt, Inc.

Erigha, Maryann. 2019. *The Hollywood Jim Crow: The Racial Politics of the Movie Industry.* New York: New York University Press.

Harris, Leslie. 2019. *Slavery and the University: Histories and Legacies.* Athens, GA: University of Georgia Press.

Holiday, Billie with William Dufty. 1984 [1956]. *Lady Sings the Blues.* London: Penguin Books.

Hughey, Matthew. 2014. *The White Savior Film: Content, Critics, and Consumption.* Philadelphia, PA: Temple University Press.

Loewen, James W. 1999. *Lies Across America: What Our Historic Sites Get Wrong.* New York: Simon and Schuster.

Rose, Tricia. 2008. *The Hip Hop Wars: What We Talk About When We Talk About Hip Hop—And Why It Matters.* New York: Basic Books.

Thakore, Bhoomi K. 2016. *South Asians on the US Screen: Just Like Everyone Else?* Lanham, MA: Lexington Books.

RECOMMENDED FILMS

Ethnic Notions (1987). Produced and directed by Marlon Riggs. Explores the history of racial stereotypes, from faithful and content "mammies," to grinning "coons" and "Sambos," to savage "black brutes" and dehumanized "pickaninnies," all of which have fueled historical and current antiblack prejudice in the United States. These images flourish in our culture, from popular films to cartoons, advertisements, and children's nursery rhymes.

Reel Bad Arabs: How Hollywood Vilifies a People (2006). Directed by Jeremy Earp and Sut Jhally. Explores the long history of offensive images of Arabs and Muslims that proliferate in film, from the silent era to current Hollywood blockbusters, and how the persistence of such images serves to naturalize prejudice against Arabs, Muslims, and Arab culture.

Reel Injuns (2010). Directed by Neil Diamond, Catherine Bainbridge, and Jeremiah Hayes. Looks at the history of images of Native Americans in Hollywood films and the effects such images have on Native people. Stereotypical Indian images in film include the stoic warrior, the noble "Injun," the brutal savage, and the groovy Indian. Indians were some of the earliest subjects of films, and, for the past one hundred years, Hollywood has perpetuated stereotypes of Native Americans in thousands of films that have contributed to a global misunderstanding of millions of indigenous people.

Latinos Beyond Reel: Challenging a Media Stereotype (2012). Directed by Miguel Picker and Chyng Sun. Exposes the media invisibility of this country's largest racial/ethnic minority group and the patterns of gross misrepresentation and underrepresentation that plague Latino media representation and the effects of such.

RECOMMENDED MULTIMEDIA

Mitch Landrieu's Speech on the Removal of Confederate Monuments. Tune in to listen to the speech Mayor Landrieu gave following his contentious decision to remove four Confederate monuments in New Orleans. www.youtube.com/watch?v=csMbjG0-6Ak

Code Switch. This NPR series on race, ethnicity, and culture featured an NPR story about Dumbfoundead, a Korean American rapper. www.npr.org/2013/04/18/177765541/korean-american-rapper-changing-the-face-of-hip-hop.

Life on the Reservation. This YouTube video is one of a half dozen about life on an Indian reservation, from the point of view of the residents. While Native American images are relatively invisible in mainstream media, many Native people have turned to user-generated-content sites like YouTube to present their lives and stories. www. youtube.com/watch?v=mV4QfYWcifM.

Whose Heritage? Public Symbols of the Confederacy. The Southern Poverty Law Center has compiled a list of all symbols of the confederacy, including a map. You can use this information to discover white supremacy on the landscape in your own community. www.splcenter.org/20160421/whose-heritage-public-symbols-confederacy.

PART FOUR

Contemporary Issues in Race/Ethnicity

chapter 12

Arenas of Racial Integration: Interracial Relationships, Multiracial Families, Biracial/Multiracial Identities, Sports, and the Military

CHAPTER LEARNING OUTCOMES

By the end of this chapter, you should be able to:

- Evaluate the extent of racial integration in American society today
- Demonstrate an understanding of the unique dilemmas multiracial families face
- Describe the social control efforts, both formal and informal, directed at limiting interracial relationships
- Critically evaluate the assumption that the increase in people claiming a biracial/multiracial identity can help dismantle the racial hierarchy
- Demonstrate an understanding of the extent of racial integration as well as the ongoing racism within the sports world
- Explain the success racial integration in the US military

African American West Point graduate Captain Benjamin O. Davis Jr. was the commander of the first black squadron of the US Army Air Corps in World War II, known as the Tuskegee Airmen. He eventually became the first African American general in the US Air Force. While a West Point cadet from 1935 through 1936, he was insulted daily and treated as if he were invisible. No one spoke to him for four years, unless it was in the line of duty. His fellow cadets refused to eat with him or sit next to him at football games, and he lived alone in a room designed for two or three cadets. Their goal was to drive him out of West Point, one of the most prestigious military academies in the country. Instead he endured in the face of adversity, graduating 35th in a class of 276. In his first year at West Point, he applied for the Army Air Corps but was rejected because he was black.

When Davis moved to Fort Benning, Georgia, for his first assignment after graduation, the silent treatment continued from his colleagues. He was eventually named captain of the first all-black squadron of airmen, the Ninety-Ninth Pursuit Squadron. This military "experiment" in black airmen proved successful: over nine hundred black airmen flew over fifteen thousand missions during World War II, shooting down over 110 planes. The distinguished performance of the Tuskegee Airmen helped usher in the racial integration of the US military in 1948. After the success of the Tuskegee Airmen, Davis received many letters of apology from his former classmates and colleagues for their ill treatment.

Although only a few African Americans who join the military achieve the kind of success Benjamin O. Davis Jr. did, the military has provided an avenue out of poverty and second-class citizenship for hundreds of thousands of military personnel of color, particularly since the 1970s (Buckley 2002; Swan 2015).

———————————

While much of this text has focused on the extent of racial segregation in America, exploring arenas of racial integration provides an opportunity to see the extent of racial progress as well as ongoing racism. This chapter begins with an exploration of interracial relationships and multiracial families. The extent of these relationships is viewed as the ultimate measure of assimilation. It provides us with an opportunity to understand how multiracial families interact within an over-whelmingly racially segregated world. It also allows us to explore new racial identities—biracial/multiracial identities—and both the liberating aspects of and the particular dilemmas surrounding the embrace of such racial identities.

We then look to the sports world as an arena of racial integration as well as an arena of ongoing racial inequality. Major League Baseball was the first major institution to integrate in 1947, when Jackie Robinson joined the Brooklyn Dodgers. As we know from previous chapters, schools were not ordered to integrate until 1954, with the *Brown v. Board of Education* Supreme Court decision, and the integration of the military occurred one year after that of Major League Baseball, in 1948. Finally, this chapter will explore race in the military. The military can be viewed as an arena of integration not only because it was one of the earliest institutions to integrate but also because it has been so successful in its integration efforts. Despite the progress in each of these arenas, the controversies surrounding multiracial families, interracial relationships, sports, and military affirmative action programs provide us with evidence that we are still a society that is far from color-blind, despite our claims to the contrary. Consider the following points:

- Exploring her self-composed list of biracial people born after the 1967 *Loving v. Virginia* decision overturned prohibitions on interracial marriage, Anna Holmes found that some of the most recognizable and successful black people today were actually biracial. She wonders to what extent their connections to whiteness resulted in this; specifically, their "familiarity with, and therefore accessibility to, the white norms, traditions, and power structures … The common denominator … wasn't necessarily so much white proximity as white acceptance and, in many cases, familial love and close connection to white people. It seemed as if this could indeed have created real opportunities for us" (Holmes 2018).
- In 2018, Britain's royal family made history when Prince Harry married Meghan Markle, a biracial American actress, exciting not only Americans but black Brits, who made up a mere three percent of the population in 2011 and until now had not seen themselves reflected in the royal family (Barry 2018).
- As recently as 1984, a Florida court took child custody away from a white mother because she was married to a person of color, which the court argued would "subject the child to racial hostility" (Dalmage 2000).
- A justice of the peace in Tangipahoa Parish, Louisiana, refused to issue a marriage license to an interracial couple in 2009, out of concern for any future children they may have had, he claimed.
- A group of students at Wilcox County High School in Rochelle, Georgia, organized to put an end to racially segregated proms and had their first integrated prom in 2013. While the school board was willing to hear their case, Georgia governor Nathan Deal said he did not support racially integrated proms (Hanrahan 2013).
- As of 2000, Bob Jones University prohibited interracial dating while simultaneously describing the university as "fully integrated" (Yancey and Lewis 2009).
- There is a long history to black people being harassed at pools, which continues today. In July of 2018, a black woman at a private community pool in North Carolina was asked to provide identification by a white man, who then called the police on her. Because she was the only person he asked to prove her identity, his actions were perceived as racist (Zraick 2018). There is historical precedent to treating black people differently at pools. For instance, in 1931 in Pittsburgh, on opening day of a new pool, blacks were asked to provide

"health certificates" to prove they were disease free, something not asked of whites (Chokshi 2018).

- Research on framing of black and white quarterbacks prior to the NFL draft finds that racial stereotypes predominate: black quarterbacks are primarily described in terms of their physical abilities, while white quarterbacks are described as more mentally prepared (Mercurio and Filak 2010).

- In April 2016, white high school soccer fans in Wisconsin taunted the opposing team, composed of black and Latina players, with chants of "Donald Trump, build that wall" (Gettys 2016).

- Tony Clark, executive director of the Major League Baseball Players Association, proposed a program to bring more African American and Latino fans to the game, claiming that the lack of diversity in professional baseball, especially in management, has undermined its growth (Rhoden 2016).

- The United States Army has the most effective affirmative action program in the nation (Moskos and Butler 1996).

SOCIOLOGICAL PERSPECTIVES ON RACIAL INTEGRATION

Sociologists studying dominant/subordinate group relations are interested in how to lessen intergroup conflict. One view on this, the assimilationist perspective, was introduced in Chapter 1. Assimilation is the theoretical perspective that argues that minority groups gradually become absorbed into the dominant group, which is ultimately desirable, some sociologists argue, because decreasing differences between groups lessens intergroup conflict, resulting in a more harmonious society. Sociologists also argue that decreasing racial prejudice is an important objective and research finds that intergroup contact is a useful tool for achieving that goal.

Stages of Assimilation

Milton Gordon (1964) identified seven stages of assimilation. The first stage is cultural assimilation, which is when the members of a subordinate group adapt to cultural patterns of the dominant group (see Chapter 5). The second phase, structural assimilation, marks the point where subordinate groups are accepted into the dominant group's primary and secondary group structures. In this stage, members of the minority group attend the same schools and participate in the same social organizations as do the members of the dominant group (see Chapter 5). The third stage is **marital assimilation**, which is when there is no difference in societal acceptance levels between interracial and monoracial marriages. The fourth stage, **identificational assimilation**, is when minority-group members no longer see themselves as distinct and thus have no incentive to fight for their own group's

rights. In this stage there is a societal acceptance of the children of interracial marriages. The fifth phase, **attitude-receptional assimilation**, is marked by a significant
decrease in racial/ethnic prejudice (attitudes) in society. This is followed by declining intentional racial/ethnic discrimination (behaviors) against subordinate groups,
behavior-receptional assimilation. The final phase of assimilation, according to
Gordon, is **civic assimilation**, in which power and value conflicts between dominant
and subordinate groups disappear. Eventually, the goal of assimilation is met in that
societal differences between the groups are eliminated.

The assimilation process is marked by **social distance**, the spatial and personal
separation between groups and the degree of sympathetic understanding between
them (Bogardus 1959). The understanding of social distance has expanded to include
the feelings of unwillingness among group members to accept out-group intimacies
(Williams 1964). Social distance between groups declines over time as minority-
group members assimilate into the dominant group.

Prejudice

Integration is correlated with decreasing prejudice, which can ultimately help foster
assimilation. *Prejudice*, as defined in Chapter 1, refers to attitudes rather than behaviors. Prejudice is a preconceived attitude, opinion, or feeling about people due to
their membership in a particular group. While laws can help decrease discrimination, they are less likely to have an effect on an individual's prejudice. Racial integration increases the likelihood of **intergroup contact**, which research finds can be a
prejudice-reducing tool under specific conditions. Sociologist Gordon W. Allport
made the argument over fifty years ago:

> Prejudice ... may be reduced by equal status contact between majority and
> minority groups in the pursuit of common goals. The effect is greatly enhanced
> if this contact is sanctioned by institutional supports ... and provided it is of the
> sort that leads to the perception of common interests and common humanity
> between members of two groups.
>
> (1958:263)

When people are exposed to individuals different from themselves, in certain
situations, they learn that the stereotypes and fears they hold about such people are
unfounded. For intergroup contact to lead to an eradication of racial prejudice, the
people must be of relatively equal status and the contact must be more than superficial. During the antebellum era, southern whites were in daily, intimate contact with
slaves; however, this did not lead them to view black people as fully human. White
contractors who employ Latino workers are unlikely to reduce their prejudice

merely due to the fact that they experience interracial contact. If there is a power and status differential between the two groups, a reduction of prejudice is unlikely. Intergroup contact in the military, particularly in the post-1970s era, for reasons explained later in this chapter, is an example of contact helping reduce racial prejudice. Intergroup contact that requires interdependence and cooperation is also necessary for the contact to help reduce prejudice. This is why interracial contact in organized sports can result in a reduction of racial prejudice (Farley 2005).

Some research finds that being immersed in a more diverse environment with a highly multiracial population can lessen essentialist thinking among white people (Pauker et al. 2018). In order to study this, scholars studied white students from the continental US who moved to Hawaii to attend college. Hawaii was chosen because it is the most racially diverse state, has the largest multiracial population, and is one of the few states with a nonwhite majority. They found that racial essentialist views can change over time and can be reduced at least in part by exposure to racial diversity (Pauker et al. 2018).

INTERRACIAL INTIMACIES: RELATIONSHIPS, FAMILIES, AND IDENTITIES

Gordon's assimilation model identified marital assimilation, also referred to as **amalgamation**, as the most crucial stage of assimilation. The extent to which interracial marriages are accepted in a society is an important determinant of a society's level of assimilation. Dominant groups have historically been slow to accept marital assimilation, preferring to maintain their social distance from subordinate groups in interpersonal, intimate relations (Yancey and Lewis 2009). The extent of interracial relationships in any society is a barometer for how important race remains. The data on interracial intimacies show that we are hardly the color-blind society that we profess ourselves to be. Of course, increasing numbers of interracial relationships have resulted in increasing numbers of multiracial families navigating their way through racially segregated worlds, and have contributed to more fluidity in racial identities for biracial/multiracial individuals.

History of Antimiscegenation Legislation

Interracial marriages were illegal in sixteen states until 1967, when antimiscegenation laws, which made interracial marriage and sexual relations illegal, were finally overturned in the Supreme Court case *Loving v. Virginia.* By the 1930s, thirty-eight states had adopted antimiscegenation laws. Maryland had passed the first antimiscegenation law in 1661, which prohibited whites from marrying African Americans or Native Americans. In the western United States, interracial relationships between whites and Chinese, Japanese, and Filipino Americans were also outlawed, with

Nevada passing the first state law in 1861 to ban marriage between whites and Asians. There was an increased fear of miscegenation after emancipation. Scholar Martha Hodes (1999) explains that "anxiety about sex between white women and black men is not a timeless phenomenon in the United States; rather it is a historical development that evolved out of particular social, political, and economic circumstances" (p. 1). It was with black freedom that such sexual liaisons were viewed as alarming to whites. While these laws made interracial sex illegal, they only applied to consensual sexual relations. Thus, the well-documented practice among white plantation owners of raping slave women was not considered a violation of the law. For over four hundred years, marriage between whites and people of color was either illegal or not constitutionally protected in many states (Frankenberg 1993).

These laws help explain why interracial marriage was incredibly rare prior to 1967. Such laws are examples of **social control**, which are efforts to encourage people to abide by the cultural norms and discourage deviance, or violation of the norm. Laws are an example of **formal social sanctions**, mechanisms designed to prohibit certain deviant behaviors by making them illegal. Social controls that are formalized into laws have the power to punish offenders more seriously than informal sanctions.

Some of the arguments used by whites to support prohibitions on interracial marriage were that God created the races as separate and therefore intended for them to remain so; that interracial marriages dilute white racial purity; that interracial marriages diminish the status of the white partner and his or her family; and finally, that mixed-race children are particularly stigmatized (Romano 2003). Some of these arguments maintained their tenacity well after the 1967 Supreme Court decision, as research finds that, as of 1980, white Americans claimed to be willing to live in integrated neighborhoods, go to integrated schools, and even entertain black people in their homes, but the vast majority of whites disapproved of interracial marriage between blacks and whites (Romano 2003). Whites' approval of interracial marriage has increased since then; this "approval" is conditional. It is often reserved for people other than their own family members (Qian 2005).

Once the Supreme Court declared antimiscegenation laws to be illegal, there were no longer any formal sanctions directed against individuals who chose to engage in interracial relationships. However, while we have seen a dramatic increase in interracial relationships, they still remain remarkably rare. Why is this? Sociologists emphasize the power of **informal social sanctions**: those behaviors directed at people to let them know they are breaking the rules and to encourage them to conform. When strangers glare at an interracial couple in a public space—for instance, at a shopping mall—they are letting their disapproval be known. While a glare from a stranger is hardly as serious as a felony record, such informal social sanctions are actually very effective at maintaining social control: although it's been a little over fifty years since the last antimiscegenation law was struck down by the high court, still, only about 10.2 percent of marriages were interracial in 2016 (Rico, Kreider and Anderson 2018).

REFLECT AND CONNECT

What types of informal social sanctions exist to discourage people from engaging in interracial relationships? Why are such informal sanctions effective?

Limiting interracial relationships, whether through formal or informal sanctions, is a form of **boundary maintenance**; controlling interracial sex and marriage is an integral part of maintaining distinct racial groups (Childs 2009). In the absence of a taboo on interracial relationships, the racial categories of "black" and "white" would not be able to exist in quite the same way. As researchers point out, "the policing of sexual boundaries ... is precisely what keeps a racial group a racial group. ... From the perspective of white supremacism interracial liaisons 'resulted in mixed race progeny who slipped back and forth across the color line and defied social control'" (Jacobson 1998:3). Generally, it has been white Americans who have been the most hostile to interracial families, arguably because the existence of such marriages has been perceived as a threat to the racial order and, thus, their white privilege (Romano 2003; Spickard 1989; Wallenstein 2002).

People in interracial relationships, as well as those in multiracial families, experience what sociologist Heather Dalmage (2000) identifies as a specific kind of informal social sanction known as border patrolling. **Border patrolling** refers to actions by both whites and people of color that send the message that certain behaviors (be they family formation or dating decisions) are against the rules. Ultimately, border patrollers believe that people should stick with their own kind. Dalmage's research finds that "many whites feel both the right and the obligation to act out against interracial couples" (2000:44). White border patrollers let the deviant individuals know that something must be wrong with them to engage in interracial relationships. Border patrolling helps maintain white privilege and the myth of racial purity.

Whites are not the only people who engage in border patrolling; however, when blacks engage in border patrolling, they do it for different reasons. Blacks express concern over race loyalty. Interracially married blacks are sent the message by black border patrollers that they have lost their identity and culture, they are weak, and they are no longer "really black" (Dalmage 2000). Black women may feel a sense of rejection when seeing a black man and a white woman together because, due to the prison industrial complex and economic marginalization, there are fewer marriageable black men than there are black women (Wilson 1987). Another source of their rejection is the fact that women are overwhelmingly judged in terms of their physical beauty, and beauty standards in the United States are Eurocentric, favoring whites. Thus, from a black woman's perspective, a black man in a relationship with a white woman emphasizes just how far removed they are from the dominant beauty standards (Dalmage 2000). Certainly the historical sexual exploitation of black women by white men during slavery lingers as a reason black women are often less accepting of interracial relationships.

Sociological research on the experiences of white partners in interracial relationships finds that they are no longer able to cling to notions of color-blindness as easily as before they entered an interracial relationship. They are forced to see race in ways they could previously ignore. Sociologist Ruth Frankenberg (1993) identified a phenomenon referred to as **rebound racism** to capture the white partner's hurt and pain associated with witnessing racism directed at someone they love. It is a "rebound" in the sense that it does not carry the same sting as it does for the initial target, the partner of color, but watching such hostility and hatred directed at someone you love is painful. This is true for white individuals in interracial relationships as well as for those in multiracial families with biracial children, as discussed later in the chapter.

Sociologist Amy Steinbugler (2012) explores interracial relationships through the lens of **racework**, a term that refers to the everyday actions and strategies that individuals in interracial relationships use to maintain closeness and intimacy across lines of racial stratification. Her research finds that both heterosexual and same-sex interracial couples struggle with visibility issues. Heterosexual interracial couples deal with hypervisibility, where their mere presence generates considerable attention, from curiosity to hostility. They also struggle with invisibility, where, as an interracial couple, they are not seen by strangers as a couple. Same-sex interracial couples face even more profound invisibility, which varies by gender. Gay male interracial couples are more visible than lesbian interracial couples, according to research (Steinbugler 2012). Steinbugler argues that the "joint workings of sexism, racism, and heteronormativity privilege certain bodies and marginalize others" (2012:59).

Attitudes Toward Interracial Relationships

Although formal social control of interracial marriage was altered by the Supreme Court decision in *Loving v. Virginia* in 1967, attitudes toward interracial marriage took much longer to change. Attitudes, particularly toward black–white marriages, have changed enormously since World War II (Romano 2003). In 1958, when Gallup first asked Americans whether they approved of marriage between blacks and whites, only 4 percent approved. By 1983, 50 percent of people surveyed still disapproved of interracial marriage. As of 2007, 77 percent of Americans approved of marriage between blacks and whites and only 17 percent disapproved. As of 2011, approval of black–white marriages was at an all-time high of 86 percent. The most recent Gallup poll found that 96 percent of blacks and 84 percent of whites approved of interracial marriage between blacks and whites (Jones 2011). As of 2015, a record 39 percent of adults viewed the increase in interracial marriage as a good thing for society and only 10 percent say they would oppose a close relative marrying someone of a different race (Bialik 2017). Although this is a dramatic shift in attitudes in the postwar era, it would be a mistake to believe there is no longer resistance to and hostility toward interracial relationships.

Evidence of the resistance and hostility toward interracial relationships is found in a study on adolescent dating. In this research, 71 percent of white adolescents with white boyfriends or girlfriends introduced them to their parents, compared to only 57 percent of those with nonwhite boyfriends or girlfriends. Black adolescents behaved similarly: 63 percent of those with a black boyfriend or girlfriend introduced them to their family, whereas only 52 percent of those with a nonblack boyfriend or girlfriend did so (Qian 2005). It appears that, for both white and black students, there is some hesitation to bring home a partner who is of a different race.

If one looks to images of interracial relationships in popular culture, one can sense some of the ongoing resistance. Mainstream films rarely depict black–white intimate interracial relationships, preferring instead to depict Asian–white relationships (Childs 2009). The film images of interracial couples that do exist follow one of several themes: intimate interracial relationships do not last; the relationship is based upon lust, curiosity, or deception rather than love; negative consequences inevitably arise from such relationships; and/or these relationships exist as part of a larger deviant lifestyle (Childs 2009). When analyzing black–white interracial couples in Hollywood films, sociologist Erica Chito Childs concludes that there is **implicit censorship** going on, where interracial couples fall outside the realm of acceptable subjects. Implicit censorship refers to "operations of power that rule out in unspoken ways what will remain unspeakable" (Butler 1993:130). Hollywood stereotypes of Asian women in relationships with white men have long portrayed the Asian woman as submissive, hyperfeminine, and/or hypersexual, from such films as *Japanese War Brides* (1952) to *Memoirs of a Geisha* (2005) (Nemoto 2009). Asian American men are invisible in Hollywood films, and "when they do appear, they are usually geeky and undesirable men, unable to attract women" (Kao, Balistreri, and Joyner 2018:52). Hollywood is sending the message that interracial couples are deviant, with some, particularly black–white couples, so deviant as to be unacceptable.

Interracial Relationships

In the United States, people tend to adhere to the norm of **endogamy**, meaning they become intimately involved with people racially similar to themselves; thus, rates of interracial marriage in the United States are quite low. As of 2016, only about 10.2 percent of all marriages are interracial, and this statistic includes all possible interracial marriage combinations of Asian Americans, whites, Latinos, blacks, and Native Americans. Interracial marriage rates have more than doubled since 1980 (see Figure 12.1). In 2015, a record 17 percent of all newlyweds were married to someone of a different race (Bialik 2017).

Students often comment on how such statistics make interracial relationships appear rarer than they seem in daily life. There are several ways to consider this. First, where you live partially determines your likelihood of seeing many interracial relationships in your daily life. Interracial marriage is more common on the West Coast of the United States and least common in the Midwest, for instance. Honolulu, HI, has the highest percentage of interracially married couples at 42 percent, followed by Las Vegas at 31 percent, and Santa Barbara, CA, at 30 percent. Cities

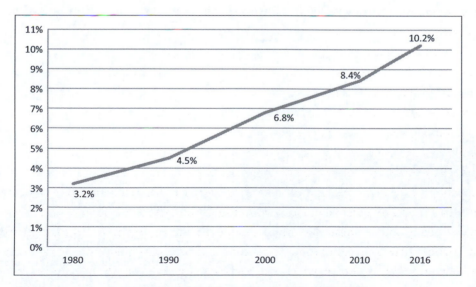

FIGURE 12.1: Increase in interracial marriage trends, 1980–2010.

with the lowest rates of interracial marriage include Asheville, NC, and Jackson, MS, both at just 3 percent of newly married couples (Bialik 2017). Second, interracial dating is more common than interracial marriage; thus, you may see more interracial couples in your life, but many of these people may not end up getting married. Finally, another variable to consider is age, as research finds there is a generation gap on attitudes toward interracial marriage. Traditional-age college students, according to the research, are more open to interracially dating than their parents' generation (Kao and Joyner 2004). Thus, if you are spending time on a college campus, you likely see more interracial dating than what occurs in the nation at large.

Interracial marriage rates vary along gender and group lines. Among recently married couples, Hispanic–white marriages are the most common, while black–white marriages are the least common, making up only 11 percent of interracial marriages in 2015 (see Figure 12.2). While black–white marriages have increased in the last thirty years, they have increased at a slower rate than interracial unions that do not involve a black spouse (Root 2001). White–other marriages, which refers to unions between a white and an Asian American or Native American spouse, have more than doubled since 1980.

The Intersection of Gender and Race in Interracial Dating and Marriage

While there are racial differences in interracial marriage rates, with whites by far the least likely to marry interracially and Native Americans the most likely, there are also gender differences in interracial dating and marriage (Wang 2015). Some research finds that women tend to interracially marry more than their male counterparts, and this is especially true for Asian Americans, as Asian American women are much more likely to marry racial/ethnic others than are Asian American men (Yancey and Lewis 2009). However, this is not true for all groups. Among

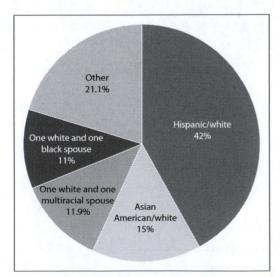

FIGURE 12.2: Intermarriage types, newly married couples, 2015.

SOURCE: "Percent of Newlyweds Who Are Intermarried, 2015." 2015; Bialik 2017.

NOTE: "Other" includes American Indian, mixed race, and "some other" race.

newlyweds, for instance, black men are twice as likely as newlywed black women to be interracially married (Bialik 2017). When we look at gender and race together, the picture gets complicated. Research finds that white women and men are the least open to interracial dating, and it follows that they have the lowest rates of interracial marriage. White women and black women show the greatest preferences toward racially exclusive dating patterns, whereas white men and black men are less racially exclusive in their dating preferences (Robnett and Feliciano 2011). Black men married outside their race 25 percent of the time in 2013, while only 12 percent of black women married outside their race that year (Wang 2015). Among black male newlyweds, 24 percent were intermarried in 2015, while only 12 percent of newly married black women were in interracial relationships (Bialik 2017). Latino males and females show no difference in racial dating preferences, while Asian American women are much less likely to prefer to date only other Asians than their male counterparts (Robnett and Feliciano 2011). Specifically, 36 percent of newly married Asian American women were interracially married in 2015, while only 21 percent of newly married Asian American men were (Bialik 2017).

However, willingness to date outside of one's own racial group does not mean one is open to dating members of all other racial/ethnic groups equally. Research on racial exclusion preferences in internet dating profiles finds that, with the exception of white females, the majority of all race/gender groups are willing to date outside of their own race. Asian Americans, Latinos, and blacks are all more open to dating whites than whites are to dating them. White male racial dating preferences noted that 97 percent of them exclude black women, 48 percent exclude Latinas, and 53 percent exclude Asian American women (see Figure 12.3). White men are excluded

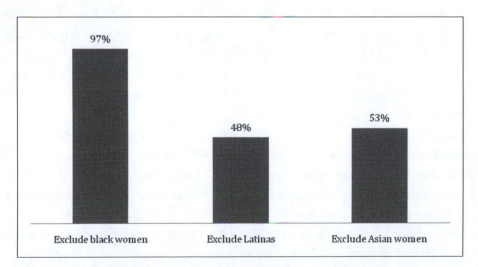

FIGURE 12.3: White male heterosexual racial dating preferences.

SOURCE: Robnett and Feliciano 2011.

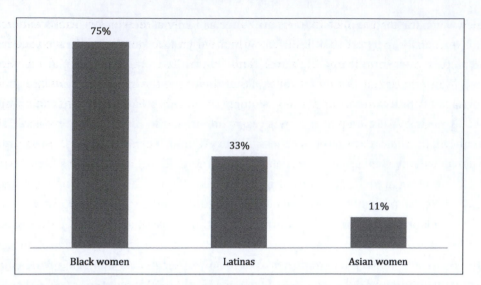

FIGURE 12.4: White male exclusion by racial/ethnic women dating preferences.
SOURCE: Robnett and Feliciano 2011.

by 75 percent of black women, 33 percent of Latinas, and only 11 percent of Asian American women (Robnett and Feliciano 2011) (see Figure 12.4). When stating dating preferences, Latinos, Asian Americans, and blacks are more likely to include whites as possible dates than whites are to include them; thus, social distance between whites and minority groups remains high.

Some research finds that Latinas who describe themselves as open to interracial dating held clear racial preferences and relied on stereotypes to exclude black and Asian American men as romantic partners (Muro and Martinez 2018). Many described themselves as simply "not physically attracted to" Asian men, citing a preference for taller men, for instance. In this research, Latinas expressed fear of disapproval if they dated black men. Racial exclusion patterns in dating begs the question, "When are preferences simply preferences, and when do they hint at subtle and not-so-subtle underlying processes of prejudice and racialization?" (Muro and Martinez 2018:536).

Structural forces such as imperialist policies and wars have influenced the frequency and perceptions of interracial relationships between white men and Asian women. The US involvement in World War II, Korea, and Vietnam all resulted in large increases in war brides as well as sexual liaisons between white soldiers and Asian women overseas. Changes in immigration policy, specifically the passage of the 1965 Immigration Act, have also contributed to an increase in Asian Americans as potential dating partners. This, however, has not resulted in a preponderance of Asian men seeking non-Asian women as partners, as 58 percent of Asian–white relationships involve an Asian American woman and a white man. This pattern holds true despite the fact that Asian American men are typically more educated than white men, a factor that tends to correlate with whether someone is considered marriageable or not (Kao, Balistreri, and Joyner 2018; Qian 2005). Even when looking at adolescent dating patterns, Asian and Asian American males are much more likely to have never dated (60 percent) compared to 40 percent of their white, black and Hispanic classmates having never dated (Kao, Balistreri, and Joyner 2018). No such differences are found for Asian and Asian American women, however, as "the disadvantage is specific to Asian American men" (Kao, Balistreri, and Joyner 2018:52).

Multiracial Families

The increase in interracial dating and marriage has resulted in an increase in multiracial families, with interracial couples joined together as families and often having biracial/multiracial children. Multiracial families occupy a unique place in our racialized society, as they are forced to think about contradictions and complexities surrounding race in ways monoracial families are not. When multiracial families are together in public, others often assume that they are unrelated (Dalmage 2000). Like white partners in interracial relationships, white parents of biracial/multiracial children also experience rebound racism, as defined previously, when they see their child being discriminated against.

WITNESS

A white female student, writing a paper for a university class, describes seeing negative reactions to her biracial child: "For every time I've witnessed that familiar look or attitude of disdain directed not at some generic black person, but at my babies, I understand [racism] more and more."

A specific problem multiracial families encounter is border patrolling in the housing market. As Chapter 9 explores, housing markets in the United States are racially segregated. Multiracial families encounter the same discrimination in the housing market that families of color face, such as redlining, particularly if they try to move into white neighborhoods. Thus, multiracial families have often been forced to find housing in black communities. In the 1960s and 1970s, multiracial families experienced discrimination in black communities as well. There are only a limited number of truly multiracial neighborhoods in the United States, and most of those are upper-middle-class communities; Hyde Park, near the University of Chicago, is a good example (Dalmage 2000).

Biracial/Multiracial Identities

Interracial intimacies may be the most significant barometer of societal assimilation, but looking at the fluid racial identities claimed by biracial/multiracial people allows us to look at how racial integration happens within one's own sense of self, so to speak. Biracial/multiracial people have always recognized the problematic nature of racial segregation as they never fit neatly into our socially constructed racial categories.

Mixed-race individuals have long been portrayed as deviant and mentally unstable, as lacking identity, as longing to be white, and as lonely, being perceived as rejected by both blacks and whites (Fredrickson 1971). This "tragic mulatto" was a popular theme in novels in the late 1800s and a recurrent theme in films, including *The Birth of a Nation* (1915). Since the 1967 Supreme Court decision in *Loving v. Virginia*, there has been an increase in interracial marriages and a resulting biracial baby boom. Even the word *mulatto*, once stigmatized, is having a comeback, and more and more biracial individuals are using this term to describe themselves (Saulny 2011; Spencer 2011).

There is nothing new about biracial people, of course. They have existed since the colonial era. In only two areas of the country were mixed-race people, generally referred to as mulattoes, considered a separate racial status: New Orleans and Charleston, South Carolina, because miscegenation was a more accepted practice in these regions and free mulattoes acted as a buffer between whites and blacks

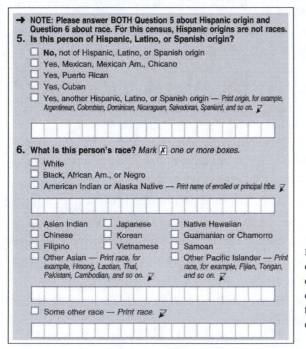

IMAGE 12.1: 2010 US census race question. Census racial categories change over time. In 2000, respondents could check more than one race for the first time. (US Census Bureau, 2010 census questionnaire).

(Rockquemore and Brunsma 2002). Mulattoes became leaders of free black communities and whites relied on them to help control the large numbers of enslaved blacks (Davis 1991). As explored in Chapter 1, several censuses during the 1800s included such racial categories as mulatto, quadroon, and octoroon. Terms for mixed-race people had disappeared by the 1930 census, as the **one-drop rule** was in full effect, which meant that a single drop of "black blood" made a person black. The term **rule of hypodescent** refers to the practice of assigning racially mixed persons the status of the subordinate group (Davis 1991).

The one-drop rule was sometimes enforced through formal sanctions, such as laws, and at other times through informal sanctions. In 1982, Susie Guillory Phipps, a Louisiana woman who looked white and considered herself white, had to sue the state of Louisiana to have herself declared white. She lost her lawsuit because she was found to be one-thirty-second black, which according to Louisiana law (at the time) made her black no matter what she looked like, how she racially identified, or what little she knew of her African ancestry (Dominguez 1986). An example of the lingering influence of the one-drop rule, albeit an informal one, is President Barack Obama. He identifies as black rather than biracial despite his white ancestry. In the United States, as the one-drop rule became ensconced in our culture, the term *mulatto* became a term like *colored*, *Negro*, *black*, and *African American* in that they all referred to people with any known black ancestry.

People who are biracial/multiracial gained a certain amount of legitimacy with the 2000 census when, for the first time, people were allowed to check more than one racial category. In 2000, approximately 2.4 percent of the population marked more than one race (Saulny 2011). According to the 2010 census, nine million people, or about 3 percent of the population, reported more than one race. As of 2015, 14 percent of infants born are multiracial (Bialik 2017). This change was due to the organizing and activism of the **multiracial movement**, which sought to gain public recognition of the multiracial community, to allow people to legally self-identify as biracial/multiracial, and to end the discrimination they faced. The movement initially pushed to have a "multiracial" category on the census; however, this was rejected and instead respondents were allowed to check more than one racial category.

Although there is nothing new about people who are biracial/multiracial, what is new is that so many are claiming a biracial/multiracial identity rather than being constrained in their racial identity choices to black, as the one-drop rule prescribed. People who grew up in the pre–civil rights era are more likely to identify as black while those born in the post–civil rights era show more fluidity in their racial identity, at different points in their lives identifying as black, biracial, and sometimes even white (Harris and Khanna 2010). Blogger Maria Niles, for instance, describes herself as an "undercover black woman" because she looks white while she identifies as black (Niles 2011). Some individuals who are biracial or multiracial argue that through such self-definition they are rejecting the color lines that have long defined our nation (Saulny 2011).

While this represents a dramatic change in our racial categorization system, it also has been controversial. The NAACP, for instance, was against changing the existing census categories. The census does more than provide the nation with a demographic snapshot of our country. The data gathered are also used to address inequalities (Williams 2006). It is through the census, for instance, that we know that African Americans, Native Americans, and Latinos are disproportionately impoverished and uninsured. These census data can then be used to argue that federal funds should be directed toward these communities for the establishment of community health clinics, for instance.

Many argue that the increasing number of people claiming biracial/multiracial identities does not really challenge our existing racial order because it does not challenge whiteness (Dalmage 2004; Ferber 1998; Spencer 2011). Spencer (2011) argues that we are adding new nonwhite categories, which in no way challenges the racial hierarchy that puts whites in a position of privilege. While the fact that more people are claiming biracial/multiracial identities may not disturb the racial hierarchy, the multiracial idea does disrupt notions of race as fixed and biological.

Researchers have also explored another shift in racial/ethnic identity options, that of Native American **reclaimers**, individuals raised as white, with little to no knowledge of their Native American ancestry, who later voluntarily reconnect with their Native heritage (Fitzgerald 2007; Nagel 1996). Their Nativeness becomes a salient aspect of their identity; it informs how they see themselves. Much like the increasing numbers of biracial and multiracial people claiming a nonblack identity, reclaiming a Native American identity does not necessarily upset the racial order, but it does challenge the racial hierarchy because these people are voluntarily rejecting the privileges associated with whiteness.

SPORTS AND RACE

The sports world is an interesting arena for analyzing race primarily because it has undergone significant racial integration. It is also a useful arena for understanding resistance to racial segregation. Studying race and sport provides a unique lens for understanding the social construction of race, primarily because it still fuels overt biological racism through the perpetuation of myths surrounding perceived black dominance in sports. Finally, sports provide a perfect setting for exploring whiteness and lingering racism in the post–civil rights United States and even globally, particularly during apartheid in South Africa (see Box 12.1 Global Perspectives: International Sports Boycotts of South Africa). In other words, the gains made by minority groups are obvious while lingering racism and discrimination tend to be much harder to see.

BOX 12.1

Global Perspectives:
International Sports Boycotts of South Africa

In South African apartheid, sports fell under the same rigid segregation rules and disproportionate investment as other institutions; no racially mixed sports were allowed and international competition was limited to whites only. Even spectators experienced rigid segregation, with people of color banned from some arenas; and in those in which they weren't completely banned, people of color had to use separate entrances, seating, and toilet facilities from whites. Under apartheid, sports were subjected to the Separate Amenities Act, which determined the use of sports facilities for various racial groups. Evidence of the racial disparities found under this provision can be quantified: as of 1987, the province of Natal had six soccer fields, seven tennis courts, and two swimming pools for use by 330,000 nonwhite South Africans. The 212,000 white South Africans of Durban had 146 soccer venues, 15 public swimming pools, and countless tennis courts (Ramsamy 1988).

As activist Sam Ramsamy says, "Apartheid literally punishes all black athletes from birth. Much lower incomes, limited sports facilities, restrictions on travel, vastly inferior schools and equipment, frequent malnutrition, and the fact that whole sections of the black community are almost totally denied access to sports illustrate how apartheid shackles black athletes throughout their lives" (1988).

Sports are very important to white South Africans; thus, Dennis Brutus and other antiapartheid activists concluded that an international sports boycott could help dismantle apartheid. Brutus fought for twenty-five years to have South Africa banned from the Olympic Games. His activism resulted in his being arrested, shot, and jailed, but he ultimately prevailed. There was a campaign to have South Africa banned from the 1964 Olympic Games in Tokyo, but Avery Brundage and the International Olympic Committee rejected the pleas of the campaign. By 1968, antiapartheid activists had garnered the support of other nations in their campaign, so their appeal to have South Africa banned from the 1968 Olympic Games in Mexico City was supported because thirty-eight other countries refused to participate in the games if South Africa were not excluded. Other international sporting bodies followed suit, and by the mid-1970s, the only international sport in which South Africa was still allowed to compete was rugby. The all-white South African rugby team, the Springboks, encountered protesters wherever they played. This kind of international pressure helped to isolate South Africa and contributed to the dismantling of apartheid in 1994.

Racial Integration in Sports

The early years of professional sports generally were not racially segregated. Blacks participated in the first fourteen years of the NFL's existence, from 1920 to 1933. But in 1934, NFL owners began enforcing what was known as a *gentleman's agreement*, an unwritten agreement between owners to keep black players out of the league because of complaints from white players over the lack of jobs (Ashe 1988b). Excluding black players from professional baseball occurred much earlier. In 1889, African American baseball player Moses Fleetwood Walker was the last black player to play in the major leagues until 1947, when Jackie Robinson crossed the "color barrier," as the jargon of the day described racial segregation in baseball. The segregation of professional baseball was also established through a gentleman's agreement, an unwritten agreement between owners to not allow black players into professional baseball. The all-black Harlem Globetrotters basketball club formed during the pre–World War II era, when blacks were not allowed to play in the white professional league. It was a serious basketball team until 1949, when it shifted to an all-entertainment format, as blacks were welcomed into the white professional leagues in 1948 (Ashe 1988b).

The racial integration of Major League Baseball in 1947 pre-dated the integration of the US military, schools, and other public places. Table 12.1 shows the advances racial minorities, particularly African Americans, have made in the major five professional sports. Due to such progress, some have argued that African Americans dominate sports. Such an interpretation deserves careful scrutiny, however. The controversial presence of Tiger Woods in professional golf and Venus and Serena Williams in professional tennis, both of which are still predominantly white sports, during the height of their careers is evidence of the ghettoized nature of black athletic success in professional sports. Despite the amazing career of multiracial golfer Tiger Woods, who won his first major, the Masters, in 1997, and is second in most PGA Tour career wins, including a 2019 Masters win, African Americans still account for only 2.7 percent of golfers nationwide (Leiber 2001). Tennis is an

Racial Group	NFL (2013)	NBA (2013–2014)	WNBA (2014)	MLB (2016)	MLS (2014)
White	31.0	19.5	23.0	59	51.1
African American	67.3	77.0	69.0	8.3	11.3
Latino	0.6	3.1	1.0	28.5	17.0
Asian American	0.7	0.2	0.0	1.7	0.7
Other	0.5	0.2	6.0	2.4	19.8
International	21.5	20.6	14.0	27.5	41.9

TABLE 12.1: Professional Athletes by Sport and Racial Group in Percent, Select Years 2013–2016
SOURCE: Institute for Diversity and Ethics in Sport 2016.

overwhelmingly white middle-class sport that has not always welcomed African Americans. The Williams sisters, for instance, are often booed even by overwhelmingly American crowds and have dealt with the prejudice of the tennis establishment, other players, and the media, as well as fans (Jacques 2003). When Serena Williams lost the 2018 US Open finals match to Naomi Osaka, derogatory caricatures of her as an angry black female appeared in newspapers (Newman 2018).

Professional football, which was much less popular than either professional baseball or college football in the immediate post–World War II era, took a chance on black players in 1946. Six of the eight teams in the All-American Football Conference signed blacks in the first four years of its existence (1946–1950), while only three teams in the NFL signed black players in that same time period. The era between 1946 and 1962 was described as an era of tokenism for black professional football players, as it took seventeen years to fully integrate the NFL, with the Washington Redskins being the last professional football organization to sign black players in 1962 (Ashe 1988). Professional football looked at the success of Jackie Robinson and other African Americans in professional baseball, black Olympic successes, and black success in professional basketball before substantially opening up to black players.

Despite the fact that African Americans are overrepresented in the NFL, NBA, and WNBA, they are underrepresented in the vast majority of collegiate sports. Tennis, golf, swimming, softball, volleyball, and other college sports are overwhelmingly white. It is only in the most visible professional sports of football and basketball that African Americans are disproportionately represented. Major League Soccer is the most diverse sport in the United States, with no one racial group accounting for more than 50 percent of the players (Hoenig 2014).

Resistance to Racism in Sports

In educational, political, legal, and economic systems, minority groups have often resisted discrimination. The sports world is no exception. Resistance to racism in the sports world is global as well (see Box 12.2 Racial Justice Activism: Athletes Against Racism). African American track star Jesse Owens' performance during the 1936 Olympic Games in Berlin was itself a challenge to racism. His unprecedented four gold medals in one Olympiad countered Hitler's master race theory, as Hitler had intended the 1936 Olympics to showcase Aryan superiority.

Jackie Robinson's subtle resistance is well documented. He was chosen to be the person to cross the color barrier in Major League Baseball because not only was he a great baseball player, he was also college educated and had been in the military; thus, Robinson was deemed capable of taking the inevitable abuse that would be directed at him. He was verbally abused by fans wherever he went and was often physically

BOX 12.2

Racial Justice Activism:
Athletes Against Racism

Across the globe, athletes are involved in antiracist activism. Kick It Out began during the 1993–1994 European football (soccer) season as Let's Kick Racism Out of Football and now views itself as English football's equality and inclusion organization. Initially, they sought to educate the public about racism, particularly the racist abuse black footballers experienced. The project was designed to develop antiracist initiatives for maximum public impact. Later, they developed a ten-point plan for professional football organizations to follow to challenge racism and promote equal opportunity within clubs. While some clubs display posters with antiracist messages, the ten-point plan asks clubs to look more closely at racism within their organizations, such as the employment of racial/ethnic minority trainers, coaches, and managers, as a way to ensure their commitment to antiracism is more than superficial (Garland and Rowe 1999).

While Kick It Out originally focused on racism, today the campaign has been extended to challenge homophobia, Islamophobia, anti-Semitism, sexism, and ableism, uniting under the banner "One Game, One Community." The athletes work with communities to increase their participation in football (in Britain, for instance, Asian communities tend to be underrepresented in football), and work with schools and teachers to help them include antiracist lessons in the curricula in ways students will enjoy. They adhere to Nelson Mandela's statement, "Sport has the power to change the world." While researchers argue that football "remains a site of racialized conflict," Kick It Out's sixteen years of antiracist work has helped bring those conflicts into the light—where they can be addressed (Garland and Rowe 1999b).

Despite improvements, racism in football remains. After several high-profile racist incidents on the soccer field, in February 2012, then British prime minister David Cameron requested that England's professional soccer leaders provide a plan for eliminating racism from the sport (Harris 2012). Despite this, racism remains. After an increase in players being targeted for racist abuse at all levels of English soccer, former English prime minister Tony Blair commented, "We thought, not that we had got rid of [racism in soccer], but we thought it had become completely beyond the pale for people to engage in it … and yet now it's back" (Harris 2019).

For more information, visit the Kick It Out website: www.kickitout.org.

abused by white players, even his own teammates, all hoping to provoke a hostile reaction out of Robinson that would signal the end of the integration experiment in professional baseball. He was expected to take this abuse without reacting, which he managed to do, using his baseball prowess as nonverbal resistance to the racism directed at him. The abuse was so severe that, in 2016, the city of Philadelphia issued an official apology for the racist taunts Robinson endured when the Brooklyn Dodgers played the Phillies (Rhoden 2016).

Prior to the 1950s, when African Americans were excluded from professional sports, they responded by forming their own all-black teams and leagues. The most successful of these was the Negro National League. Rube Foster organized the first black professional baseball league in the 1920s, which eventually became the Negro National League. This league became home to some of baseball's greatest players, such as Satchel Paige and Josh Gibson, who were denied the opportunity to play in the white Major League.

The black leagues survived in spite of American racism. Black players traveled the country playing games to sold-out black crowds, negotiating the Jim Crow South and northern racism while traveling overnight in buses from town to town, and often sleeping in the buses because blacks were not allowed to stay in most hotels during this era. The quintessential American freedom, the freedom to travel, was not extended to African Americans in the pre–civil rights era. They had to worry about "sunset laws," laws that said blacks had to be out of a particular town by the end of the day (see Chapter 9). They had to rely on the "Green Book," officially titled *The Negro Motorist Green Book: An International Travel Guide*, to negotiate where a black traveler, or an entire black baseball team, could eat, sleep, and buy gas. In spite of the obstacles, the Negro Leagues became a financial success, for both black baseball organizations and the players, as well as a unifying force for the black community.

Jackie Robinson had played in the Negro Leagues for the Kansas City Monarchs before being brought into Major League Baseball by Branch Rickey of the Brooklyn Dodgers. The integration of Major League Baseball in 1947 brought about the demise of the Negro Leagues by the 1960s because the most successful black players were recruited to play in the Major League, and the fans all went to watch the black players in the white league. The teams also contributed to the demise of the Negro Leagues by refusing to compensate teams for the players they took (Zirin 2013). Satchel Paige, one of the greatest pitchers to ever play the game, played in the Negro Leagues in the 1930s and 1940s and then became the oldest rookie to play Major League Baseball in 1948.

More explicit black athletic resistance to racism occurred in 1967, when African American athletes formed the Olympic Project for Human Rights (OPHR), which organized a boycott of the 1968 Olympic Games in Mexico City as a protest against American racism. The organization's founding statement claimed:

> We must no longer allow the sports world to pat itself on the back as a citadel of racial justice when the racial injustices of the sports world are infamously legendary. … So we ask, why should we run in Mexico only to crawl home?
>
> (Zirin 2005:74)

The athletes involved with the OPHR ultimately decided against a boycott of the Olympics. Instead, during the awarding of the Olympic medals, African American Olympic track stars Tommie Smith and John Carlos bowed their heads during the US national anthem and, wearing black gloves, raised their fists in a Black Power salute; protested black poverty by being barefoot; and protested lynching by wearing a string of black beads around their necks. This silent, symbolic gesture resulted in their being stripped of their medals and expelled from the Olympic Village within hours of the protest (Zirin 2005). They faced harassment and media assaults when they returned to the United States.

This kind of retaliation against athletes' political activism is not rare. Athletes engaged in social and political activism often face negative consequences (Kaufman 2008). NFL player Dave Meggyesy, for instance, found himself benched for his political involvement with the civil rights and anti–Vietnam War movements. Chicago Bulls guard Craig Hodges was cut from the Bulls roster and mysteriously shut out by the rest of the NBA for protesting the Gulf War with a written letter to President Bush when the team was visiting the White House after its 1992 NBA championship (Zirin 2005).

During the fall 1992 semester, four UNC-Chapel Hill football players organized black students and began demanding a black culture center on campus, an expansion of the African Studies curriculum, and improving the pay and working con-

IMAGE 12.2: Iconic image of Olympic track and field champions Tommie Smith and John Carlos at the 1968 Olympics in Mexico City. They are protesting American racism by bowing their heads during the US national anthem, wearing black gloves, and raising their fists in a Black Power salute; protesting black poverty by going barefoot; and protesting lynching by wearing a string of black beads around their necks.

ditions for the university's housekeeping staff. Such athlete-driven activism on the campus continued in 2018, primarily in the form of protests against a Confederate monument in the heart of campus known as Silent Sam (see Chapter 11).

Another example of resistance to racism in sports can be found in the actions of the Black Coaches Association of the National Collegiate Athletic Association (NCAA), which called for a ban on all postseason games in states where "stars and bars" (the official flag of the Confederacy during the Civil War) were part of the state flag or where Confederate battle flags still fly over state capital grounds. Many southern states added the stars and bars to their flags in the late fifties and early sixties as an explicit act of defiance against the civil rights movement and racial integration (Westheider 2008). South Carolina and Mississippi were banned from hosting postseason NCAA sporting events as of 2001. After former South Carolina Governor Nikki Haley signed a bill to remove the Confederate flag from the capital grounds in 2015, Mississippi remains the only state under this NCAA ban.

Resistance to racism in sports remains ongoing and controversial. Professional athletes such as Colin Kaepernick, Eric Reid, Malcolm Jenkins, Megan Rapinoe, and Maya Moore have all become household names not just for their athletic accomplishments but for their anti-racist activism. Colin Kaepernick began protesting police brutality by refusing to stand for the national anthem before games in 2016 when he was quarterback for the San Francisco 49ers. Teammate Eric Reid joined him in the protest, as did others throughout the league. Their protest led to criticism from some fans, other athletes, and then republican presidential candidate Donald Trump. After Donald Trump became president, his criticism increased and he called for the NFL to fire any players who protested in such a way. Despite the criticism, Kaepernick explained, "I love America. I love people. That's why I'm doing this. I want to help make America better" (Mather 2019). His actions involved two and a half years of protest, the loss of his job as a professional football player, and legal action against the NFL. Kaepernick has not played in a professional football game since January of 2017 and many suggest he was being blackballed by the league. He and Eric Reid filed a grievance against the NFL claiming the thirty-two-team league had colluded to keep him out due to his political activism (Reid was eventually signed by the Carolina Panthers). By February of 2019, the NFL reached an undisclosed settlement with Kaepernick and Reid (Mather 2019).

Philadelphia Eagles professional football players Malcolm Jenkins, Chris Long, and others have chosen to use their high-profile positions to fight for criminal justice reform and against racial inequality through an organization known as the Players Coalition. Jenkins' protests began in 2016 with the raising of his fist during the national anthem. Members of the Players Coalition have visited police departments, lawmakers, prisons, and courts to push for criminal justice reform and have pushed the NFL to contribute to the cause. The NFL ultimately agreed to commit up to $89 million over seven years to grassroots groups fighting racial inequality (Belson 2018). Jenkins explains his actions, "when I look at our communities, our country, our justice system, those are things I want to change and I'm committed to changing, and that's going to take sacrifice" (Belson 2018). After the Eagles won the Superbowl in 2017, they were disinvited to the White House for a celebration in reaction to the NFL players' protests and the many Eagles' players who refused to attend the celebration prior to the disinvitation (Sheppard 2018).

In solidarity with Kaepernick and other NFL players protesting racism and police brutality, Megan Rapinoe of the NWSL's Seattle Reign FC and the United States women's national soccer team joined in the protests by kneeling during the national anthem before games, as did members of the WNBA's Indiana Fever, and high school athletes across the country. Rapinoe explained her actions as in part solidarity with Colin Kaepernick and also because:

> Being a gay American, I know what it means to look at the flag and not have it protect all of your liberties. It was something small that I could do and something that I plan to keep doing in the future and hopefully spark some meaningful conversation around it.
>
> (Zirin 2019)

The US Soccer Federation demanded that all players stand for the anthem. During the Women's World Cup in 2019, Rapinoe continued her protest by not singing the anthem, and commented that if the women won the cup, she would not visit the White House, which resulted in Twitter insults from President Trump.

After the police shootings of unarmed African Americans Philandro Castile and Alton Sterling in the summer of 2016 (see Chapter 10), members of the WNBA's Minnesota Lynx, including Maya Moore, protested by wearing black t-shirts over their jerseys with phrases like "Black Lives Matter" and "Change Starts with Us. Justice and Accountability" across the front and back. Moore, one the greatest professional female basketball players, stepped away from her professional playing career in 2018 to fight for Jonathan Irons, an incarcerated man in Missouri, who she believes was wrongly incarcerated (Streeter 2019).

Sports and Racial Essentialism

People easily fall prey to the trap of accepting the notion of black physical superiority, particularly in the world of sports. Black dominance in basketball, football, and track seems to challenge the idea that race is nothing more than a social construction by emphasizing the **essentialist** claim that there is a real, true essence to race. The idea that race is biologically real has been enduring, despite scientific evidence to the contrary, and the sports world, and particularly the sports media, seems to confirm the genetic basis of race. Sports commentators as well as journalists use subtle verbal cues to describe black and white athletes that reinforce racial myths of natural black athletic superiority and white intellectual superiority, what some have referred to as the "black brawn versus white brains" distinction (Davis and Harris 1998; Jackson 1989). Recent research exploring college students' discourse about sports finds this pattern as well (Buffington and Fraley 2011).

There has been a dramatic increase in the number of Asian American athletes in recent years, as they now comprise 2 percent of Major League Baseball and 1 percent of the NFL, with the NBA and NHL lagging behind (Whang 2005). Despite this increase, Asian American athletes face discrimination in the sports world due to stereotypes of Asian Americans. One stereotype is that Asian Americans are smart but not athletic and are too small. In 2005, Timmy Chang entered the NFL draft after a record setting career playing quarterback at the University of Hawaii (he holds the record for most yardage thrown as a quarterback in college football history at 17,072). Despite his notable achievements, he went undrafted after the seventh round, with scouts describing him as "too short." When it was pointed out that he was taller than a number of NFL quarterbacks, including Drew Brees, a member of the New Orleans Saints and a former San Diego Charger, his agent was informed that "he plays short" (Whang 2005).

Research respondents discussed sports in ways that reinforced black physical superiority and white mental superiority as explanations for their athletic success. The respondents avoided using explicit race-based claims and instead relied on coded language and disclaimers to make their point, engaging in **racetalk**, which refers to the ways people use language to construct their social world and to understand race (Bonilla-Silva and Forman 2000). Disclaimers are verbal strategies designed to deter doubt about the claim one is making and to avoid disrupting the social interaction (the line "I'm not prejudiced; some of my best friends are black" is an example of a disclaimer). White respondents described black and white athletic success in the following ways: "Because black men [are] naturally more talented at [the] game" and "*Not many* Caucasian males have great talent" and "African Americans are *usually* fast runners" (Buffington and Fraley 2011:342–3, italics in the original).

The sports media is argued to play a role in disseminating racial stereotypes. For instance, African American athletes are stereotyped as deviant and threatening, out of control, violent, and excessive thugs (Davis and Harris 1998). Television commentators are more likely to focus on the physical characteristics of Latino athletes and to portray them as hot-tempered (Sabo et al. 1996). Asian American female athletes are also portrayed stereotypically by the media in ways that adhere to the model minority stereotype. They are described as hardworking, conforming, self-disciplined, machinelike, and unemotional (Rintala and Kane 1991). Hard work and self-discipline are required of *every* elite athlete—yet this language is not used to describe African American or Latino athletes.

Whiteness in Sports

We can think of the sports world as a racialized space, a concept introduced in Chapters 1 and 7, specifically as a space where whites feel a sense of belonging and racial/ethnic others are defined as outsiders. A historical example of the sports world as a white space are the race riots that exploded across the United States after African American boxer Jack Johnson beat James Jeffries on July 4, 1910. Jack Johnson had won the heavyweight boxing title in 1908, and whites had begun calling for a "great white hope" to reclaim the title that many felt rightfully belonged to whites. White fighter James Jeffries had ceremoniously come out of retirement to win back race pride for whites, to no avail. Immediately after the bout, riots exploded across the country, due to white humiliation at the defeat of Jeffries. Riots in over twenty-five states and fifty cities resulted in dozens of dead African Americans as a result of the sense that the heavyweight boxing championship belonged to whites.

Native American Mascots

There are plenty of more-current examples of the sports world as a racialized space as well. One is the use of Native American mascots, a major source of contention and controversy since the 1960s. Mascots and the ritual performances that surround them—victory dances, school songs, cheers, chants, face painting, shirts and hats with offensive logos—are coming under increasing scrutiny. Examples of offensive mascots involve the Cleveland Indians' mascot, which is problematic because of its cartoonish caricature of an Indian; the Atlanta Braves' "tomahawk chop" fan ritual; and the name of the Washington Redskins. No other racial/ethnic group is demeaned in this way, and the use of these mascots "reveals the latent attitudes whites harbor toward American Indians. These are symbols of dominance and superiority and expose feelings of entitlement not only to our land and resources but also to our religions and identities" (Machamer 2001:220). Native Americans opposed to the use of their names and images as sports mascots argue that these dehumanized, cartooned, and stereotypical images of Indians are damaging to Indian children's self-esteem and even contribute to the high rates of teenage suicides in their community (Harjo 2001).

REFLECT AND CONNECT

Why are Native American mascots considered so offensive? Did you consider them to be offensive prior to reading this chapter? Can you think of other groups who are being denigrated in this way? Why do you think Native American opposition to this practice has not resulted in greater changes? Should professional sporting organizations, such as the Cleveland Indians or the Washington Redskins, have to change their names and mascots if Native Americans find them offensive? Why or why not?

Dozens of high-school, professional, and amateur teams have discontinued the use of their Native American mascots. The Los Angeles Unified School District, the second largest in the nation, was the first to prohibit the use of Native American mascots in 1997 and in 2019, the state of Maine became the first state to ban Native American mascots in all public schools. As of 2019, the Cleveland Indians stopped using the Chief Wahoo logo on their uniforms, an image that first appeared on the club's uniforms in 1948 (Waldstein 2018). The organization did not discuss changing their name.

Despite such progress, more than eighty colleges and universities refuse to retire the offensive mascots, perpetuating these institutions as white spaces. Native American students at the University of North Dakota filed a federal lawsuit in August 2011 to eliminate the school's Fighting Sioux nickname, as its use puts the university at odds with the position of the NCAA, which has declared American Indian nicknames to be "hostile and abusive." The NCAA required that the school retire the nickname unless it got approval from the state's namesake tribes (Kolpack 2011). In the face of NCAA sanctions, the university changed their mascot from the Fighting Sioux to the Fighting Hawks in 2015. Native American organizations have protested the use of Native American mascots, claiming they are as offensive to Native people as Sambos were to African Americans and that they perpetuate inappropriate, inaccurate images of living people and their cultures (King and Springwood 2001).

While it is impossible to claim all Indians are offended by the use of their image as mascots, according to a 2002 *Sports Illustrated* poll, 83 percent of Native Americans believe it is wrong (Price 2002). The term *redskins* is one of the worst racial epithets that can be hurled at a Native American, so the fact that it is the name of Washington DC's professional football team is offensive to many (Harjo 2001). The term is offensive because it comes from the days when bounty hunters were paid for any Indians they brought in, dead or alive. Bounty hunters would bring the bloody scalps of Indians as evidence of their kill. In 1999, Native Americans won their federal lawsuit, *Harjo et al. v. Pro Football, Inc.*, against the organization for its use of the name "Redskins." Despite the decision by the panel of federal judges in this case, the team's owners are still fighting in court to protect their use of the offensive moniker. As of 2013, ten members of Congress urged the organization to change its name due to the term's offensiveness. They sent letters to the team's owner, Dan Snyder, as well as to the NFL Commissioner Roger Goodell, to FedEx, the team's sponsor, as well as to all other thirty-one NFL franchises ("Members of Congress ..." 2013). Despite such efforts, Snyder remains defiant, claiming he will never change the name. While these examples show the whiteness in college and professional sports is being challenged, the resistance to retiring Native American mascots shows ongoing whiteness in sports.

Whiteness at the University of Mississippi

Whiteness is visible at the University of Mississippi sporting events through the omnipresence of the Confederate flag (not at official university-sponsored events, but on cars, in dorm rooms, and at tailgating events) on campus in general and at a specific 2014 event: the hanging of a noose on a campus statue of African American civil rights activist James Meredith. When campus racial incidents like the hanging of a noose around a statue of a civil rights icon happen, university officials respond "with a standard narrative: they condemn the offending individuals and proclaim such actions contradict the ideals of the institution" (Combs et al. 2016:339). Researchers argue that, instead, the 2014 noose incident is hardly an aberration from the norm, as it happened within a context where racial microaggressions occur regularly, where many of the campus buildings were built by slaves, where Confederate soldiers are memorialized while the slaves who built the campus remain invisible, and where campus streets are named "Rebel Drive" and "Confederate Drive" (until 2014, when "Confederate Drive" was changed to "Chapel Drive") (Combs et al. 2016).

While many whites argue that flying the Confederate flag has nothing to do with race and instead is simply a southern tradition, the "tradition" is actually not very old. The flag was rarely seen on the Ole Miss campus before the late 1940s (Newman 2007), when the flag reemerged throughout the South as a symbol of white supremacy and resistance to racial integration.

In the 1980s, black students began organizing and protesting the presence of the Confederate flag at Ole Miss, which they found offensive. White students began a Save the Flag movement, arguing that the flag was not offensive but an endearing symbol of the Old South, and that the demands of the minority should not dictate the desires of the majority (whites were the majority of students on campus). The university chancellor, however, agreed with the black student organizations and banned the flying of the flag at any Ole Miss–sponsored event, including sporting events. But while no rebel flag is carried into the stadium today by cheerleaders, many white fans still insist on flying the rebel flag in the stands. This disregard for the feelings of African American students at a flagship state university in a state that boasts the largest percentage of African Americans in their population is evidence that the campus is a white space.

Perhaps an even more glaring example of whiteness in sports involves the All-American Basketball Alliance (AABA), a new all-white basketball league formed in 2010. Only players who are natural-born United States citizens with both parents of the Caucasian race are eligible to play in the AABA, a move that its organizers describe as not racist but instead an attempt to "get away from the 'street-ball' played by people of color" (Terkel 2010b).

Whiteness and Trash Talking

Fueled by the sports media, trash talking opponents is a central aspect of sports culture, exemplifying competitiveness and transcending "generation, sport, and race. It takes place on and off the field: players, coaches, general managers, and owners do it" (Leonard 2017:65). However, trash talking by white and black athletes is interpreted very differently. African American professional football player Richard Sherman's taunting of opponents is seen as threatening and dangerous, whereas white athletes such as Johnny Manziel's trash talking is perceived as evidence of his competitiveness and feistiness for the game (Leonard 2017).

Lingering Racial Inequality in Sports

Despite the high visibility of African American athletes in the major college and professional sports, ongoing racism in the sports world still exists. It can be found in the practice of **stacking**, which refers to the unequal distribution of whites and blacks in certain sports positions that cannot be explained by a random distribution (Woods 2011). Specifically, whites are disproportionately concentrated in positions that require leadership and intelligence, such as the position of quarterback in football. African Americans tend to be concentrated in more peripheral positions that involve speed, quickness, and strength rather than leadership and intelligence (Eitzen and Sage 2003).

Table 12.2 shows statistical evidence of stacking in the NFL existed well into the 1990s but has declined in the last fifteen years. Most central positions—quarterback, center, and offensive guard—have been held disproportionately by whites. Sports sociologists argue that it is the influence of racial stereotypes concerning blacks' and whites' leadership capabilities that result in stacking. Since schools are still overwhelmingly racially segregated, as Chapter 7 explored, black players must play all positions in order to field a team during high school. It is only as competitiveness increases, as one enters collegiate sports specifically, that we see stacking emerge.

Many black quarterbacks who are recruited to play college football are steered into other positions. African American NFL quarterback Donovan McNabb

Position	1998	2003	2007	2013
Offense				
Quarterback	8	22	19	17
Running Back	87	86	89	83
Wide Receiver	92	86	89	84
Tight End	42	42	42	42
Offensive Tackle	55	55	49	49
Offensive Guard	29	41	35	35
Center	17	12	18	18
Defense				
Cornerback	99	98	97	97
Safety	91	81	97	82
Linebacker	75	81	71	74
Defensive End	79	77	73	83
Defensive Tackle	63	77	76	82

TABLE 12.2: Stacking in the NFL: Percentage of Black Athletes in Each Position, Selected Years 1998–2013

SOURCE: Lapchick et al. 2014.

NOTE: On average, African Americans made up 66 percent of the NFL over these years.

admitted that the advice he received when he turned pro was that he would be treated differently than a white quarterback. He stated:

> When I came into this league [I was advised] to do the extra studying, to work out harder, prepare myself better ... don't give anyone a reason to say that you're uncoachable, that you can't be trusted, that you want to do your own thing. The margin of error [for a black quarterback versus a white quarterback] is different.
>
> (O'Neil 2007)

In 2010, African American University of Miami quarterback Jacory Harris received racially motivated hate messages following the Hurricanes' loss to Ohio State. Harris had an unbeaten 30–0 record during his final two years of high school and led his team to two state championships (Reynolds 2010). The problem of stacking has been decreasing in recent years. It is no longer rare to see an African American NFL quarterback, as there has been a doubling of black NFL quarterbacks since the late 1990s (Woods 2011). As of 2018, there were a record eight black starting quarterbacks in the NFL (Lapchick 2019b).

Evidence of stacking is still found in baseball, where whites are concentrated in the central leadership positions of pitcher, catcher, and infield positions, specifically shortstop and second base (Table 12.3). African American players are overwhelmingly concentrated in the outfield.

Racial Group	Pitcher	Catcher	Infield	Outfield	Overall
White	69	51.6	58.4	51.4	58.8
African American	3.1	0	7.9	25.4	8.3
Latino	25.4	45.3	32.6	19.7	29.3
Asian American	2.2	3.1	2.5	2.1	1.2

TABLE 12.3: Stacking in Major League Baseball: Percentage of Athletes by Race in Each Position, 2015

SOURCE: Lapchick and Salas 2015.

REFLECT AND CONNECT

After reading about the practice of stacking, do you see evidence of it in the sports that you follow? Why does it matter that we have athletes of particular racial groups concentrated in particular positions? Are there any negative consequences to stacking?

The consequences of stacking are significant. First, when whites are concentrated in thinking/leadership positions and African Americans are concentrated in physical positions, it reinforces racial ideologies of white intellectual superiority. Second, individuals who play intercollegiate or professional sports that require speed, quickness, and agility have shorter careers because of the demands of the game on their body, which means lower lifetime income than professional athletes in "thinking" positions. Finally, their shortened careers perpetuate the problem of stacking by reproducing it in coaching and management, since playing at noncentral positions and having a shorter career result in fewer opportunities to become a coach or a manager at the collegiate or professional level (Eitzen and Sage 2003).

The glacial pace of integration at the level of professional coaching is so dire, according to some, it makes "U.S. Congress look like *Soul Train*" because, in 2006, 65 percent of the NFL was African American yet only six coaches, a mere 12 percent, were black (Zirin 2006). In 2002, when there were only two black head coaches in the NFL, a mass antidiscrimination lawsuit was threatened, resulting in the NFL's putting in place rules that require teams to interview at least one minority candidate for every vacancy, a practice known as the Rooney Rule (Zirin 2006).

The Rooney Rule was put in place in 2002 and strengthened in 2018. The new edition of the Rooney Rule requires teams to go outside their own organizations to interview candidates of color. In 2003, 69 percent of NFL players were African American while 29 percent were white. In that same year, 91 percent of head coaches were white and only 9 percent were African American. By 2006, the Rooney Rule was credited with tripling the number of African American head coaches. By 2011, the league had made what many consider to be great progress in terms of head coaching positions, with African Americans making up 22 percent and Latinos constituting 3 percent. However, 67 percent of NFL players in 2011 were African American, a consistent statistic for decades (Lapchick et al. 2012). At the close of the 2012 regular season, eight head coaches lost their jobs. In the interim two weeks, none of those jobs went to a minority candidate, despite the Rooney Rule (Rosenthal 2013). At the start of the 2018 season, there were eight head coaches of color in the NFL—seven African American and one Latino—and four people of color working as general managers. However, by the end of the 2018 season, five of the eight head coaches had lost their jobs and none had been replaced by a person of color (Lapchick et al. 2019).

RACIAL INTEGRATION AND THE MILITARY

While many sports are integrated, racial integration in the sports world is rarely formalized. The military is the only arena where equality of opportunity is formalized, and its racial integration is unmatched (see Figure 12.5). While we can look to the military as a leading organization in racial integration, it is not currently a racial paradise nor has it historically been so. While African Americans and other racial minorities have fought in every war the United States has been involved in, they have experienced considerable discrimination along the way as well. Black cadets were rarely admitted to US military academies, and when they did get accepted, they

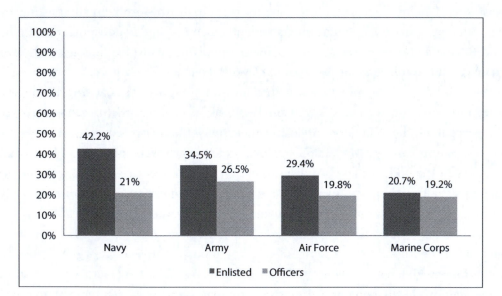

FIGURE 12.5: Percentage of active duty racial minority enlisted members and officers by race and service branch, 2015.

SOURCE: "Percentage of Active duty Racial Minority Enlisted Members and Officers by Race and Service Branch" 2015; Department of Defense 2015

were ostracized by their colleagues and undermined in every way, as the opening vignette exposes. In each military action between the Revolutionary War and the Korean War, the military followed a familiar pattern of discrimination against black soldiers: initially denying them the opportunity to enlist, then enlisting them when there was an obvious manpower shortage but relegating them to menial work rather than combat duty, and denying them positions of authority. Upon conclusion of the conflict, black soldiers were the first to be dismissed (Astor 1998).

The US military provides members the opportunity for interaction with individuals of varying racial/ethnic backgrounds as well as interactions with foreign populations, so interracial interaction is increased simply by living among different people. There is evidence that the extent of interracial interactions has contributed to intercultural understanding in the armed forces (Leal 2003). Research on military race relations has found a number of interesting results: black veterans are less likely to approve of racial separatism, black and white veterans report improved attitudes toward other races due to their military service, Latino veterans had more friendships with Anglos than did Latino nonveterans and experienced increased acculturation, and white veterans had more black friends than did white nonveterans (Leal 2003).

But good race/ethnic relations in the military are the result of formal measures, not merely the increasing potential for interracial contact. Racial integration was imposed by President Harry Truman's Executive Order 9981 in 1948. The Korean War was the first US military operation to have racially integrated fighting units since the Revolutionary War. President John F. Kennedy, a World War II navy veteran, extended Truman's legacy in this arena by issuing an executive order that ordered military commanders to oppose discriminatory practices against military personnel both on and off base (Buckley 2002).

The integration of the armed forces occurred in two phases. The first, **organizational integration**, was when formal discrimination in recruitment, training, retention, and living arrangements on base ended. This phase is referred to as the quiet phase in military race relations because it only involved enlisted men. The second phase, **leadership integration**, refers to full equality in the armed forces, including positions of leadership (Moskos and Butler 1996). Leadership integration took decades to implement after Truman's executive order was signed.

Racial Turbulence in the US Military

Race relations in the military during the Vietnam War were problematic, with racial violence exploding on and around military bases across the world. The Vietnam War was unpopular at home, where there was an active antiwar movement, and many black leaders, including Martin Luther King Jr., condemned the war. Middle-class whites were more successful at avoiding the draft; thus, the image of blacks being disproportionately killed in the war was a major source of racial contention. Research found that blacks were not being disproportionately killed in Vietnam, but there was an absence of blacks in positions of leadership in the military; for example, at the conclusion of the Vietnam War, only three in one hundred army officers were black (Moskos and Butler 1996).

While some blamed racial tensions in the US military on the civilian racial unrest during the era, much of it was caused by the failed racial policies of the US military itself. An example of a failed racial policy was hostility toward expressions of Black Power activism. An African American Vietnam veteran described his anger at the fact that whites were allowed to display Confederate flags on military bases while he was forced to remove a poster from his locker that simply said "Black Is Beautiful" (West-heider 2008). White racists in the armed forces also practiced cross burnings, seemingly with the unspoken approval of those in command. After the assassination of Martin Luther King Jr. in 1968, white racists in the armed forces increased their antagonizing behaviors while anger among African Americans grew, resulting in violence throughout the military, from fistfights to racial gang fights to riots at military prisons in Vietnam and on military training bases in the United States (Westheider 2008).

Addressing Racial Unrest

The military took steps to address these racial problems. One of the solutions to the racial tensions was to increase the number of blacks in command. (Figure 12.6 shows

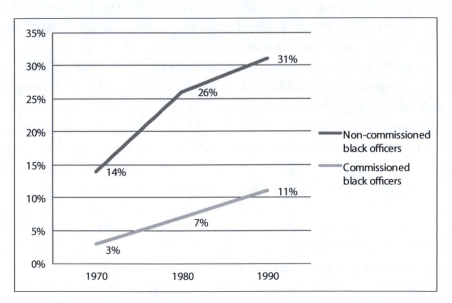

FIGURE 12.6: Increase in Black Leaders in the Army, 1970–1990.

SOURCE: Moskos and Sibley Butler 1996.

specific data on the increase in black officers in the US Army between the years 1970 and 1990.) It is the racial integration of blacks in leadership positions that helped decrease racial tensions and problems in the army. The military also began developing race relations programs for the armed forces. By 1970, officers were required to include information on their handling of race relations in their unit reports. Racial problems in a unit could interfere with an officer's career advancement—an incentive for officers to address racial problems directly.

In 1971, the Department of Defense established the Defense Race Relations Institute (DRRI) to enhance race relations in a military experiencing racial turbulence. The DRRI trained instructors for the race relations classes that were mandatory for all military personnel in 1972 and 1973. Personnel were educated about US racial/ethnic history, minority contributions to American society, and the nature of discrimination. The institute subsequently became the Defense of Equal Opportunity Management Institute (DEOMI) and added emphases on gender issues and sexual harassment (see Box 12.3 Race in the Workplace: Addressing Race the Army Way: Defense Equal Opportunity Management Institute (DEOMI)).

The 1975 revision of the Army Affirmative Action Plan of 1972 was a key development in army race relations (Lawrence and Kane 1995). For the first time, army commanders were made to feel that the quality of race relations in their units was a reflection of their leadership, and, thus, their career progress depended on this. Since the late 1970s, the US military has enjoyed relatively peaceful and harmonious working relations among its racial/ethnic groups. Evidence for this is the lack of openly expressed hostility and violence, promotional and vocational opportunities for all members, and the seriousness with which the military addresses issues of justice and discipline (Lawrence and Kane 1995). The success of the military in dealing with racial issues has to do with their race consciousness rather than color-blindness (Moskos and Butler 1996).

The racial integration of military life spills over into surrounding communities as well, as the most racially integrated communities in the United States are towns with military bases (Moskos and Butler 1996). When the military was segregated, all-black squads often faced intense hostility from their white neighbors. For instance, the famous Tuskegee Airmen, the first black army air force unit, trained at a military base outside of Macon, Georgia, and they experienced considerable antagonism between black airfield personnel and the white town in the early 1940s, with some military personnel experiencing beatings by white locals. In one instance, white police from the town attempted to seize the weapons of black military personnel on base, nearly resulting in a riot (Buckley 2002).

Studying race and the military allows us to see an organization that has been intentionally transformed from one of the most racist public institutions in the United States to the most integrated. While the armed forces are not a racial

BOX 12.3

Race in the Workplace:
Addressing Race the Army Way: Defense Equal Opportunity Management Institute (DEOMI)

DEOMI was founded in 1971 as the Defense Race Relations Institute with the original goal of addressing the racial turbulence affecting the military during this era. Race-relations training was mandated for all military personnel in 1971. The institute has since broadened its agenda to address more than just racial issues and include issues of gender and sexual harassment. In 1979 the organization changed its name to DEOMI to reflect its broadened mission.

The institute offers equal-opportunity training for military personnel. In the US military, equal opportunity is viewed as the responsibility of all commanders, not just a specialized staff. Unit commanders are responsible for the racial climate in their units and for handling charges of discrimination; "a poisoned racial climate is the enemy of any officer who wishes to advance in the Army" (Moskos and Butler 1996:61). Thus, DEOMI offers the training military leaders need to succeed. Military and organizational effectiveness are met through the extension of equal opportunities.

At some level, DEOMI curriculum looks a lot like any multicultural curriculum: topics include African American, Jewish American, Native American, and Arab American history, culture, and so on. However, it differs from traditional multicultural curricula in that it is explicitly tied to the core purpose of the military—readiness to fight. Thus, unit cohesion is the emphasis: the idea that in the army, everyone is "one color—green" is part of the message. Instead of emphasizing diversity itself, the overriding message of DEOMI is that "an overarching, common American identity must override cultural diversity" (Moskos and Butler 1996:58). Essentially, "the Army bombards soldiers with the message that racial divisiveness ruins cohesion, which in turn results in unnecessary deaths in war" (Moskos and Butler 1996:66).

DEOMI approaches diversity training from a position of race consciousness rather than color-blindness. The army, for instance, has a very successful affirmative action program. Instead of lowering its standards to ensure an acceptable racial mix, the army makes every effort to provide people with the necessary education or skill training in order for them to meet the standards. To summarize, "race relations can best be transformed by an absolute commitment to nondiscrimination, coupled with uncompromising standards of performance. To maintain standards, however, paths of opportunity must be created—through education, training, and mentoring—for individuals who otherwise would be at a disadvantage" (Moskos and Butler 1996:13).

For more information, visit the Defense Equal Opportunity Management Institute website: www.DEOMI.org.

utopia, they stand out for their success at racial integration in a nation where racial segregation and discrimination remain rampant in the civilian sector. This transformation has occurred through the implementation of aggressive affirmative action policies:

> During much of the three decades that mainstream America complained about affirmative action, the military quietly developed a system of set-asides and flexible standards that help determine who is assigned, promoted, and retained. ... Without affirmative action, there would be no black officers. The reason is simple: Whites would not even try to recruit blacks and Latinos for officer candidate schools. It's simply too easy to take the next white guy in line.
>
> (Chivers 1995)

The Military, Race, and Naturalization

The American military has also been a path to citizenship for immigrants since 1862, when Congress passed legislation authorizing the naturalization of noncitizens honorably discharged from the armed forces. Since 2001, the US has naturalized 71,638 members of the military ("Citizenship for Military Personnel and Family Members" 2016).

However, race often trumped military service when it came to naturalization, despite the law. Research has found that many noncitizen Asians who served in the

IMAGE 12.3: Retired Native American military veterans, specifically Navaho code talkers, being honored in a Veterans Day parade in New York City.

US military between 1900 and 1952 were denied citizenship on racial grounds despite meeting the military naturalization requirement (Sohoni and Vafa 2007). Despite being willing to fight and possibly die for the United States, many Asians were not deemed worthy of citizenship in the same way Irish or German noncitizens were. The courts were more intent on maintaining a "racialized" concept of citizenship, adhering to the Naturalization Act of 1790, which limited the right to naturalization to "free white persons" (Sohoni and Vafa 2007). Asians were recruited to serve in the US military as US imperialism was directed at Asia with the annexation of the Philippines and Hawaii in 1898. Filipinos began replacing black labor in the navy in this era.

Most of the research on race and the military is framed as black–white, so what we know about Latino, Native American, and Asian American military members' experiences is more limited (Gifford 2005; Leal 2003). Latinos are underrepresented in the US armed forces overall but are more likely to volunteer for combat units, particularly the US Marine Corps, when they do choose to enter the military (Gifford 2005). Native Americans join the military for reasons that overlap with those of others, such as for opportunities they cannot get elsewhere. But Native American military personnel also report unique reasons for their decision to enter the military; for instance, military service is associated with the warrior tradition valued in their family and tribal community (Ledesma 2006).

CHAPTER SUMMARY

While the United States still remains a racially segregated society, there are arenas where racial integration has been achieved: most successfully in the military, but also in the sports world, and to a lesser extent in the sphere of intimate relations. All of the institutions discussed in this chapter face racial struggles, despite their level of racial integration. Interracial intimacies, such as interracial relationships and multiracial families, are increasing as a result of fewer formal obstacles, yet they still face struggles with informal social controls and border patrolling. The increasing numbers of persons claiming a biracial or a multiracial identity expose the fluidity of race, challenging the notion of race as fixed, yet failing to challenge the existence of a racial hierarchy.

This chapter explores institutions, like the sports world, that address racial inequality informally, and the military, which addresses racial integration formally. While both the sports world and the military were two of the earliest institutions to integrate and can be viewed as some of the most progressive on matters of race, racial inequalities remain within both arenas. For instance, in the sports world, racial stereotypes help fuel racial essentialism, and the continued use of Native American mascots remains controversial. The US military is known for having the most effective affirmative action program in place, yet racial/ethnic minorities remain underrepresented in leadership positions.

Ultimately, this chapter outlines some of the most significant examples of racial progress in the United States. While it is too optimistic to argue that shifting racial identities challenge the racial hierarchy, they do create a crack in the racial foundation, just as the increasing presence of people of color in positions of leadership in an integrated military and the decrease in stacking in professional sports challenge notions of color-blindness.

KEY TERMS AND CONCEPTS

Amalgamation	Leadership integration
Attitude-receptional assimilation	Marital assimilation
Behavior-receptional assimilation	Multiracial movement
Border patrolling	One-drop rule
Boundary maintenance	Organizational integration
Civic assimilation	Racetalk
Endogamy	Racework
Essentialist	Rebound racism
Formal social sanctions	Reclaimers
Identificational assimilation	Rule of hypodescent
Implicit censorship	Social control
Informal social sanctions	Social distance
Intergroup contact	Stacking

PERSONAL REFLECTIONS

1. Reflect on your assumptions about racial minorities and sport, or interracial marriage. To what extent do the data presented in this chapter challenge your perceptions of these issues? To what extent do the data support your initial perceptions of these issues? Speculate on the beliefs and influences that created your original assumptions.

2. If you watch sports, do you recognize racetalk occurring among your friends and family when watching sports? If so, had you noticed this before? If you are not a sports fan, can you identify another arena where racetalk occurs?

3. When you see the statistics on interracial marriage, do they ring true to you? Or do they appear too low? If they appear too low or too high, speculate on what factors may be influencing your perception of rates of interracial marriage. Would you consider or have you participated in interracial dating or interracial marriage? Why or why not?

CRITICAL THINKING QUESTIONS

1. To what extent could the success of the integration of the US military be a model for the integration of other institutions (such as the sports world or in the economic sphere?). Based on the information in this chapter, what limitations might exist if we applied the military model to these other institutions? What strengths might exist?

2. Explain why there are such dramatic differences between attitudes toward interracial marriage and interracial marriage rates. Describe three cultural variables that influence interracial marriage.

ESSENTIAL READING

Cashin, Sheryll. 2017. *Loving: Interracial Intimacy in America and the Threat to White Supremacy.* Boston, MA: Beacon Press.

King, C. Richard and Charles Fruehling Springwood. 2001. *Team Spirits: The Native American Mascot Controversy.* Lincoln: University of Nebraska Press.

Korgen, Kathleen Odell. 1998. *From Black to Biracial: Transforming Racial Identity Among Americans.* Westport, CT: Praeger Press.

Leonard, David J. 2017. *Playing While White: Privilege and Power On and Off the Field.* Seattle, WA: University of Washington Press.

Moskos, Charles C. and John Sibley Butler. 1996. *All That We Can Be: Black Leadership and Racial Integration the Army Way.* New York: Basic Books.

Nemoto, Kumiko. 2009. *Racing Romance: Love, Power and Desire Among Asian American/White Couples.* New Brunswick, NJ: Rutgers University Press.

Romano, Renee. 2003. *Race Mixing: Black–White Marriage in Postwar America.* Cambridge, MA: Harvard University Press.

Valenzuela, Freddie, and Jason Lemons. 2008. *No Greater Love: The Lives and Times of Hispanic Soldiers.* Lanham, MD: Ovation Books.

Williams, Kim M. 2006. *Mark One or More: Civil Rights in Multiracial America.* Ann Arbor: University of Michigan Press.

Zirin, Dave. 2005. *What's My Name, Fool? Sports and Resistance in the United States.* Chicago, IL: Haymarket Books.

Zirin, Dave. 2018. *Jim Brown: Last Man Standing.* New York: Blue Rider Press/ Penguin Books.

RECOMMENDED FILMS

The Loving Generation (2018). Directed and produced by Lacey Schwartz and Mehret Mandefro. Four-part documentary series that explores the first generation of Americans to be born legally to one black and one white parent, their experiences with race and identity, and the meaning of their connection to whiteness.

Loving (2016). Directed by Jeff Nichols. This biographical drama explores the couple, Richard and Mildred Loving, behind the Supreme Court case *Loving v. Virginia*, which overturned the sixteen remaining state prohibitions on interracial marriage.

Little White Lie (2014). Directed by Lacey Schwartz and James Adolphus. This documentary explores issues of race and identity through the co-director's experiences growing up in a typical upper-middle-class Jewish household in upstate New York. Despite her belief in her own whiteness, her whole life she was surrounded by questions concerning her dark skin color. She learns at the age of eighteen that her biological father was a black man, not the man who had raised her.

Guess Who's Coming to Dinner? (1967). Directed by Stanley Kramer. In this Academy Award–winning film, released the same year the Supreme Court declared antimiscegenation laws unconstitutional, a white liberal couple, played by Katharine Hepburn and Spencer Tracy, struggle with their own racism when their daughter brings home a black fiancé, played by Sidney Poitier.

Have You Heard from Johannesburg: Fair Play (2010). Directed by Connie Field. Tells the story of athletes and activists who pushed South Africa's apartheid-era teams out of international sports competition, helping to bring global attention to the human rights crisis in South Africa.

In Whose Honor? (1997). Directed by Jay Rosenstein. Explores the controversies surrounding the use of Native American mascots in sports. It looks at the use of these mascots as well as the national movement, begun by Spokane Indian Charlene Teters, to end the use of such mascots and the extremes some communities will go to to maintain this practice.

Multiracial Identity (2010). Directed by Brian Chinhema. Explores the controversies surrounding the embrace of a biracial or a multiracial identity, the social and political impacts of the multiracial movement, and multiraciality as a lived experience. It also explores the ways different races and cultural groups perceive multiraciality. The film weaves biracial/multiracial identities together with larger structural and historical forces surrounding the issue of multiracialism.

Not Just a Game: Power, Politics, and American Sport (2010). Directed by Jeremy Earp. Based on Dave Zirin's critical writings on sport, particularly focusing on how sports have long been at the center of some of the major political debates and struggles of our time. Sports have long glamorized militarism, racism, sexism, and homophobia. This film also examines resistance to the racism in sport by introducing athletes who have stood up to the institution of sport.

Only the Ball Was White (2008). Directed by Ken Solarz. Explores the Negro baseball leagues, with interviews with former players such as Satchel Paige, Roy Campanella, Jimmie Crutchfield, and others.

RECOMMENDED MULTIMEDIA

The National Park Service offers a website with detailed information on "Ethnicity, Race and the Military." Check out the website at www.nps.gov/civilwar/ethnicity-race-and-the-military.htm.

Ending the Era of Harmful "Indian" Mascots. On this website, the National Congress of American Indians outlines their position on Native American mascots, paying specific attention to the controversy over the use of the slur "redskins" by the Washington Redskins football team: www.ncai.org/proudtobe.

CHAPTER 13

The Future of Race

CHAPTER LEARNING OUTCOMES

By the end of this chapter, you should be able to:

- Understand the social construction of race and predictions concerning the future of race in the United States
- Explain how race, racism, and whiteness operate in the political sphere
- Critically evaluate the anti-immigrant climate and the racialization of immigrants
- Define and examine the extent of hate crimes, ethnoviolence, and hate-group activity in the United States
- Explore the history and current status of the reparations movement

While political race-baiting is certainly not new in American politics, the 2016 Republican presidential primary was particularly racist and xenophobic, led by the party's nominee, Donald Trump. Trump's platform included calls for banning Muslims from entering the United States, deporting undocumented immigrants, and building a wall along the US–Mexico border to keep Mexican immigrants out. Islamophobic statements were made in the first GOP presidential primary debate in August 2015, and anti-Muslim political rhetoric surged in September 2015 (Bridge Initiative Team 2016). While Trump's race-baiting inspired concern among many for the fear and hatred it fuels, it also resonated with a majority of Republican primary voters and may be responsible for a dramatic increase in Islamophobic violence.

According to a report by Georgetown University's Prince Alwaleed bin Talal Center for Muslim–Christian Understanding, between March 2015 and March 2016 there were 180 incidents of anti-Muslim violence in the US, including 12 murders, 34 assaults, 56 acts of vandalism, 9 arsons, and 8 shootings and bombings (Hussain 2016). In Grand Rapids, Michigan, a store clerk was called a terrorist while being robbed, and a hijab-wearing sixth-grade girl was attacked in the Bronx. There were twenty-nine attacks on mosques in 2015, which is the highest since records began being kept in 2009. Such violence cannot be understood as separate from the political climate surrounding the 2016 presidential election. According to Ibrahim Hooper of the Council on American–Islamic Relations, "We are seeing an unbelievably toxic, anti-Muslim environment in our society that is being exploited and encouraged by public figures like Donald Trump, Ben Carson, Rick Santorum, and others" (Lazare 2015).

As the opening vignette reveals, race, immigration, incendiary political rhetoric, and hate crimes are intimately and often dangerously interconnected. In this final chapter, we explore the claim made by political pundits immediately after Barack Obama won the 2008 presidential election that we are a postracial society (Wingfield and Feagin 2010). Claiming to be postracial is similar to claiming to be color-blind—it is a claim that race is no longer a major factor in determining one's life chances. This claim should be clearly in question, as evidence of ongoing racial inequality in educational institutions, housing, criminal justice, and even the sports world exists. This chapter will explore the future of race, the operation of racism and whiteness in the political sphere, immigration, hate groups, reparations, and racial reconciliation. Consider the following examples of both the ongoing significance of race in the United States and significant racial progress:

- The Millennial Generation, those individuals born 1981–1996, is the most racially/ethnically diverse generation our country has ever known; we have explored their perspectives on race throughout the book; what this means for future race relations is open to speculation.
- For the first time in over a decade, Congress, specifically the House Judiciary Subcommittee on the Constitution, Civil Rights, and Civil Liberties, held hearings on reparations for slavery in June 2019. Their goal was "to examine, through open and constructive discourse, the legacy of the Trans-Atlantic Slave Trade, its continuing impact on the community and the path to restorative justice" (Scott 2019).
- Although President Obama could not have won the presidency without white votes, he did not win the majority of white votes in either 2008 or 2012.
- Republican presidential nominee Donald Trump successfully based his campaign on racist and xenophobic sound bites, including characterizing Mexicans

as rapists and criminals and proposing to ban Muslims from entering the United States.

- In the first week of August 2019, there were three mass shootings, two within twenty-four hours of one another; two of the three were by gunmen showing at least some allegiance to white supremacist ideologies.
- In June 2016, Rick Tyler, an independent candidate for Congress from Tennessee, put up a billboard with the phrase "Make America White Again" (Bever 2016).
- Anti-immigrant sentiment is racialized. Evidence of this is when President Trump claimed he did not want more immigrants from "shithole countries" and would prefer more from Norway (Watkins and Phillip 2018).
- A campaign to eliminate "the *I* word" ("illegal") from public discourse has enjoyed considerable success in its efforts to stop the description of human beings as "illegal" (as in "illegal immigrants").
- In West Allis, Wisconsin, dozens of black youth began attacking white people at a state fair in August 2011 because the white people were "easy targets" (Cohen 2011).
- On October 27, 2018, a man entered a Pittsburgh synagogue shouting anti-Semitic slurs and opening fire on the congregants, killing eleven and wounding six others, in one of the deadliest attacks against the Jewish community in the United States (Robertson, Mele, and Tavernise 2018).

SOCIOLOGICAL PERSPECTIVES ON THE FUTURE OF RACE

This book began with the argument that race is a social construction, meaning that the concept of race changes across time and place. Groups categorized as racial minorities in 1880 (for example, Chinese Americans) are very different from the groups categorized as racial minorities in 1980 (for example, Mexican Americans). How race is defined in Brazil differs substantially from US racial categorization systems, as they have five official categories: **branco** (white), **pardo** (brown), **preto** (black), **amarelo** (yellow), and indigenous. With the knowledge that racial categories change across time and place, it should come as no surprise that sociologists make the argument that in the future, race will look different than it does today. This means that groups that are currently racialized may not be, and some groups that are not currently racialized may be; essentially, our census will count racial groups differently than it does today. While no one can say for sure what groups will be racialized and what groups will become white, this chapter explores some predictions sociologists offer on what the future may hold. Not all sociologists agree on what the racial future looks like specifically, but there is consensus that we are not now, nor are we likely to be in the near future, a postracial society.

In Chapter 1, we challenged the media interpretation of Pew Research Center data that declared whites would be a "minority" by 2050. One of the reasons this assumption is unlikely to prove true is because sociologists predict that the definition of who is "white" will change (Yancey 2003). Like Irish, Jewish, and Italian Americans in the past, some groups who are currently defined as "nonwhite" today will become white.

Becoming White in the Twenty-First Century

Sociologist George Yancey (2003) argues that the groups most likely to become white in the next forty years are Latinos and Asian Americans. His argument is based on the recognition that African Americans face a greater degree of alienation than other racial groups. Latinos without African features and Asian Americans do not face the same degree of alienation in the United States as African Americans do, although they undeniably face prejudice and racism.

In addition, Yancey argues that Latinos and Asian Americans are more likely to become white for several reasons. The first is that Latinos have some European heritage, which likely results in more social acceptance of them. There has also been a long trend toward **exogamy**, marrying outside one's group, among Latinos (see Chapter 12). An additional argument can be made that Latinos are of value to the dominant group due to their sheer numbers alone. Whites may actually encourage the assimilation of Latinos, as they did the Irish in the mid-1800s, because it is in the political interest of whites to assimilate them rather than having them remain a sizable minority group. Certainly becoming white is alluring to minority groups because of the privileges attached to it, but it can also be beneficial to the dominant group in securing their power. This argument should not be taken to imply that all minority groups desire to distance themselves from their culture and "become white," just that the privileges associated with whiteness can be alluring.

Asian Americans are similar to Southern/Eastern Europeans who were incorporated into an expanded definition of whiteness in the past, according to Yancey (2003). One of the similarities is that the bulk of Asian Americans have entered the United States during roughly the same era, the post-1965 period, making their experiences with racism similar to one another's, rather than having their experiences span multiple generations. Other arguments look to the high interracial marriage rates among Asian Americans, particularly Asian American women, as discussed in Chapter 12, and their model minority status as explanations for their likelihood to become white.

Triracial Stratification System

Sociologist Eduardo Bonilla-Silva (2010) makes a different argument for the future of race in America than the previous one offered by sociologist George Yancey, one he refers to as the **Latin Americanization thesis**. This thesis argues that the United States is shifting from a binary white/nonwhite racial system to a triracial stratification system, similar to that which is found in many Latin American and Caribbean countries. Bonilla-Silva argues that instead of a binary racial status hierarchy with whites at the top and nonwhites at the bottom, in this **triracial stratification system**, whites will be at the top, an intermediary group of "honorary whites" in the middle, and a nonwhite group at the bottom. Unlike Yancey, Bonilla-Silva argues that while some Latinos and Asian Americans are more likely to assimilate into whiteness, not all people and groups that fall under those umbrella categories will be classified as white.

In Bonilla-Silva's triracial stratification system, the white group will be composed of traditional whites, any new white immigrants, and some Latinos, specifically those who have assimilated. Also included in this category are lighter-skinned multiracial individuals. The honorary whites will comprise most light-skinned Latinos, Japanese Americans, Korean Americans, Asian Indians, Chinese Americans, and most Middle Eastern Americans. The bottom rung of the racial hierarchy will be composed of blacks, dark-skinned Latinos with visible African ancestry, Vietnamese, Cambodians, Filipinos, and Laotians (see Table 13.1).

Some of the reasons Bonilla-Silva gives for his Latin Americanization thesis are that Latin America has a long history of race mixing that coexists with rather than supplants white supremacy. In other words, throughout Latin America, white supremacy still exists despite the very different attitudes toward miscegenation. In Brazil, someone who is fair-skinned and has European features generally benefits from white privilege. Thus, while many people argue that the increase in interracial dating and marriages in the United States will result in the dismantling of the racial

"Whites"	"Honorary Whites"	"Collective Black/Non-white"
Whites	Light-skinned Latinos	Vietnamese Americans
New whites (Russians, Albanians, etc.)	Japanese Americans	Filipino Americans
Assimilated white Latinos	Korean Americans	Hmong Americans
Some multiracials	Asian Indians	Laotian Americans
Assimilated (urban) Indians	Chinese Americans	Dark-skinned Latinos
A few Asian-origin people	Middle Eastern	Blacks
	Americans	New West Indians
	Most multiracials	African immigrants
		Reservation-bound Native Americans

TABLE 13.1: Preliminary Map of Triracial Order in the USA
SOURCE: Bonilla-Silva 2010:180.

hierarchy (discussed in Chapter 12), Bonilla-Silva argues that whites will remain privileged and at the top of the triracial hierarchy. One piece of evidence he uses to make his argument that some Asian Americans and some Latinos will become honorary whites is that research finds that whites are significantly more likely to live near people who would fall into the "honorary white" category than those who fall into the "collective black/nonwhite" category (Bonilla-Silva 2010). For instance, dark-skinned Latinos face residential segregation patterns similar to those of African Americans, whereas Latinos who identify as white, such as Cubans and South Americans, are more likely to live in communities with non-Hispanic whites (Logan 2003).

The racial stratification system in Latin America is based on colorism, which implies that racial groups are internally stratified along the lines of skin color (with lighter-skinned people receiving preferential treatment and darker-skinned people experiencing more discrimination). The operation of colorism in the United States was discussed in Chapter 1.

Race and the Millennial Generation

The Millennial Generation, those born between 1981 and 1996, is the most racially and ethnically diverse generation the United States has ever known, and it strongly favored Barack Obama in the 2008 and 2012 presidential elections. In a series of focus groups conducted by the Applied Research Center, Millennials were asked their feelings about race and, specifically, the claim that the United States is a postracial society. While there are differences among Millennials along race and class lines in their beliefs about how much race remains a factor in today's society, as seen throughout this book, one of the overwhelming findings of this report is that a large majority of young people surveyed believe that racism remains a significant force today, particularly within the criminal justice system, educational institutions, economics, and in immigration debates. Research discussed in the previous chapter describes members of this generation as more comfortable with interracial dating, which is often used as evidence of their sense that they are different from previous generations, yet they do not think our society is postracial or that they are beyond race (Apollon 2011).

REFLECT AND CONNECT

Think about your friends and family. What are their feelings about race? Are you more comfortable with interracial dating and relationships than your parents' generation? Explain any differences between your generation and your parents' or grandparents' in terms of the ongoing significance of race in society.

> ## WITNESS
>
> "Ever since Obama came into office, I've noticed that the political climate has become really racist and racial too. First it was kind of towards blacks, and now we are having issues with the borders and 'let's hate Mexicans' … and now it's becoming okay to say some of these things in a political nature in media. And, wow, this is insane." Comment by Theresa, a 24-year-old biracial (Filipina and white) college graduate (Apollon 2011).

RACE, RACIAL INEQUALITY, AND WHITENESS IN THE POLITICAL SPHERE

The election of President Barack Obama is evidence of racial progress in the United States. However, this does not mean that race is insignificant in the political arena. In this section, we explore the ways race manifests itself in the political sphere. How do individuals engage in formal politics? It is useful to think in terms of both rights and responsibilities. As US citizens, we have the right to participate in our government through, at a minimum, voting, and we expect the government to protect our civil rights, those granted to us in the Constitution and the Bill of Rights. In exchange, we have the obligation to pay taxes and obey the law, and we can be called on to defend the country.

Not all Americans have been allowed to fully participate in American political life, however. It is worth remembering that people of color have been marginalized from the political sphere, to varying degrees, throughout the bulk of American history. Native Americans, for instance, were not granted US citizenship until 1924, even though they were required to meet an obligation of citizenship prior to that when they were drafted in World War I. Individual states could grant Native Americans voting rights; however, states with large numbers of Native Americans, such as California and Oklahoma, limited their right to vote by requiring voters to be "civilized," an intentionally vague policy that allowed for various strategies for denying Native peoples suffrage (Markoff 1996). Similarly, African Americans, Chinese Americans, Japanese Americans, and Latinos all paid taxes that supported public schools that their children were often denied entry to (see Chapter 7). Despite the fact that the US Constitution called for "universal suffrage" as a cornerstone of our new democracy, state constitutions often excluded numerous groups from participating in this democracy. Free blacks in the North often lost voting rights they had previously enjoyed under federal statutes upon the establishment of a state constitution. For instance, when New York State issued their constitution in 1821, approximately thirty thousand black men who had previously voted now were denied the right (Markoff 1996).

How race plays out in the political sphere, such as in voting behavior and running for elected office, admittedly is a very narrow look at political activism. In previous chapters we examined political activism in the form of social movements, which essentially is political activism that occurs outside the formal political sphere. This generally happens because those groups engaged in the activism are denied a voice in the formal political sphere.

During the antebellum era, even African Americans who were not enslaved had "no rights a white man was bound to respect," according to the language of the Supreme Court in the 1857 *Dred Scott* decision. Later, racial inequality was built into laws, government policies, and practices. With the exception of the Reconstruction era immediately following the Civil War, throughout most of US history, blacks rarely were allowed to serve as elected officials. African Americans were denied full access to the ballot until the passage of the Voting Rights Act in 1965. However, in 2013, the US Supreme Court significantly limited the effectiveness of the Voting Rights Act by ruling that states would no longer be required to get federal approval before changing their voting laws. In the opinion of the majority, the Voting Rights Act of 1965 was designed to address problems with voter disenfranchisement that no longer exist.

Documentary filmmaker John Wellington Ennis (2016) has explored voter suppression since the 2004 election. His research finds that numerous states engage in a long list of voter suppression techniques, including: voter ID laws that create barriers to voting for poor people and college students, wrongfully purged voter rolls, long lines at the voting booth, provisional balloting, untrained poll workers, confusing polling places, voter intimidation, and faulty voting technology that does not verify your vote, opening the door to fraud.

Fifty years after the Voting Rights Act, an African American was elected to the nation's highest office, president of the United States. This would have been unlikely without the support of white voters. Despite Barack Obama's victory, minorities are still underrepresented in elected office. Currently, there are only three African Americans in the Senate, Kamala Harris of California, Cory Booker of New Jersey, and Tim Scott of South Carolina. The first black woman elected to the Senate was Carol Moseley Braun (D-IL) in 1992. Kamala Harris is only the second black woman to be elected to the Senate. The 116th Congress, which began in January 2019, is the most diverse ever, as almost half of the newly elected representatives are not white men. The 116th Congress is composed of thirteen nonwhite women, and includes the first Muslim women elected to the House, Ilhan Omar of Minnesota and Rashida Tlaib of Michigan. As mentioned in Chapter 1, two Native American women were elected, Deb Haaland of New Mexico and Sharice Davids of Kansas. Ayanna Pressley of Massachusetts is the first black women elected to Congress from that state. Sylvia Garcia is the first Latina to be elected to Congress by the state of Texas.

This increased diversity among elected officials is almost entirely within the Democratic Party. Latinos have made inroads in the political sphere as well; however, they are still underrepresented. There were thirty-six Latinos in the House, including New York's Alexandria Ocasio-Cortez, and four in the Senate when the 116th Congressional sessions began in January of 2019. If Latino Congressional

IMAGE 13.1: The four female Congressional democratic representatives of color, who Trump labeled "The Squad."

representation were proportional to their share of the US population, seventy-seven House members would be Hispanic and eighteen Senators would be Latinos (Gamboa 2018). There is one Latino governor, Michelle Lujan Grisham of New Mexico. The governor of Hawaii, David Ige, is Japanese American.

Of course, there is no guarantee that simply having racial minorities in elected office will ensure that the needs of minority communities will be met. Sometimes there is mere **superficial representation**, where elected officials of color fail to advocate for policies that reflect the interests of their constituency and are generally out of touch with the needs and issues facing minority communities (Swain 1993). When electing a minority to political office, minority constituents hope for **substantive representation**, where politicians work to make the needs of their nonwhite constituents a priority (Swain 1993). History will decide if the nation's first African American president, Barack Obama, offered substantive representation or merely superficial representation for black Americans.

Whiteness in Politics

There has been undeniable political progress for racial minorities in this country, and yet, the political sphere can still be viewed as a white space, one that privileges whiteness. Most black elected officials, for instance, are elected in primarily black districts and few win in majority white districts (Perry and Parent 1995). Even the election of the first nonwhite president doesn't negate this fact, as only a minority of whites (43 percent) voted for Barack Obama in 2008 and even fewer whites supported him in 2012 (Wingfield and Feagin 2013). Another way whiteness is privileged in the political sphere is that black politicians are unlikely to win national campaigns, where winning a significant portion of the white vote is necessary, if they are perceived as affiliated with the civil rights movement. In fact, certain racial issues such as racial disparities in sentencing and racial profiling cannot even be brought up by minority candidates who are seeking to win white votes (Wingfield and Feagin 2010). Another way whiteness is manifest in both major political parties in the United States is through their resistance to the inclusion of Asian Americans. Kim (2007) argues that both parties, in their attempts to appeal to white voters, view Asian Americans as perpetual racialized outsiders.

The overwhelming support Obama received from southern blacks was treated as a given, as if black Americans voted for Obama merely because he was black. Two things are problematic with this assumption. First, it assumes that black Americans supported Obama from the beginning of his candidacy, which simply is not true. Hillary Clinton was the early favorite among most southern black voters while black South Carolinians favored John Edwards (Moser 2008). Second, white voters are not assumed to vote for a candidate merely because they are white, even though there is evidence to support the fact that race matters to white voters, in that "voting became for many white Southerners an expression of cultural unity" (Moser 2008:125). In the South, for instance, blacks and whites vote very differently despite the fact that their positions on issues tend to be similar (Moser 2008).

REFLECT AND CONNECT

When you hear politicians or political pundits refer to voting blocs, do you think they perceive whites to be a voting bloc? Do they explicitly talk about whites as a voting bloc? If not, why do you think that is? Does Republican President Donald Trump treat whites as a voting bloc? Support your answer.

Minority groups have not generated enough **political capital**, the organizational and cultural resources necessary to get political systems to work in their favor (Bourdieu 1991). Policies designed to offer benefits to black Americans (see Chapter 8) generally do not survive the legislative process. Thus, minority groups have relied on the Supreme Court to address the needs of racial minorities. This strategy worked well until the 1980s, when the Reagan administration significantly influenced the direction of the court toward a non–civil rights agenda (Detlefsen 1991).

When political candidates of color run for office, particularly when they are seeking white votes, they are well aware of the need to operate within the white racial

IMAGE 13.2: The election of President Barack Obama, the first African American US president, is evidence of racial progress but not evidence that we are a postracial society. Obama could not have won the presidency without a significant number of white votes. However, most whites did not vote for him, while significant majorities of racial minority voters did. (Courtesy of the Library of Congress, LC-DIG-ppbd-00358).

frame (see Chapter 3). Candidate Barack Obama, for instance, adhered to the white racial frame by rarely speaking publicly of race. As the nation's first black President, his presence could have brought discussions of race, racism, and racial inequality into the open. This did not happen. Obama made one speech addressing race (see Chapter 1), and did not mention the topic again during his candidacy. He has addressed racial issues over the eight years of his presidency, such as when he referenced the killing of African American Trayvon Martin by saying, "If I had a son, he'd look like Trayvon" (Thompson and Wilson 2012), and each time he has faced a white backlash against his invocation of race. The white racial frame requires political candidates of color to downplay issues of race and racism (Wingfield and Feagin 2010).

The 2016 presidential campaign was somewhat unique in terms of the overt race-baiting, particularly by the Republican nominee, Donald Trump. As mentioned in the opening vignette, almost immediately upon declaring his candidacy, he started making anti-immigrant and anti-Muslim statements, and these seem to have resonated with the Republican base. He called Mexican immigrants rapists and criminals, and after these comments gained traction, he declared a federal district court judge from Indiana, Gonzalo Curiel, who was presiding over civil fraud lawsuits against Trump University, to have a conflict of interest because of his Mexican heritage and demanded that he recuse himself from the case. Trump's campaign was accused of being anti-Semitic when they tweeted an image of a pile of money and a Star of David, meant to suggest Clinton's loyalty to Israel and to play on anti-Semitic stereotypes of Jewish people as greedy. The campaign immediately altered the image and Trump claimed it was "just a star." In addition to blatantly disrespecting Mexicans, Muslims, Jews, and immigrants, Trump also refused to distance himself from very vocal white supremacist supporters like David Duke, white nationalist and former Grand Wizard of the Ku Klux Klan.

The Southern Poverty Law Center, through their Teaching Tolerance program, has studied the impact of the 2016 presidential campaign on students. They find alarming levels of fear and anxiety among students of color and immigrant students, who worry about being deported, and that there has been a corresponding increase in bullying and harassment of religious and racial minority students. Teachers reported increased use of the n-word and Muslim students reported being called "ISIS" and "terrorist," rolling back some of the success anti-bullying programs have had ("The Trump Effect …" 2016).

Trump's presidency continued with overt race-baiting. After the 2017 white supremacist rally in Charlottesville, VA, where an anti-racist counter protester was killed, President Trump declared that there were good people on "both sides" of that conflict. In July of 2019, President Trump held a reelection campaign rally in Green-ville, NC. Just days before, he had tweeted that four Congresswomen of color should "go back" to the countries they came from (three of the four were born in the United States and all four are citizens). At the Greenville rally, the crowd began chanting,

"Send her home!" Even some Republicans members of Congress denounced the comments as racist. The message seemed clear, in that the 2020 presidential election "will be a general election focused on race, identity and Mr. Trump's brand of white grievance politics" (Herndon and Medina 2019). The "go back to your country" comment has a long, xenophobic history in the United States and has primarily been used against nonwhite immigrants. For instance, the sentiment had been directed at Chinese workers during the late 1800s, was part of anti-Irish and anti-Catholic sentiment in the 1840s, was an insult hurled at black students bused to white schools during the era of school integration, and was the philosophy behind the American Colonization Society which sought to send freed slaves back to Africa (Rogers 2019). President Trump has also vocally disparaged numerous cities and countries that are disproportionately black, such as referring to Haiti and African countries as "shithole" countries and describing Baltimore, MD, as a "rodent infested mess" where "no human would want to live," among others (Cummings 2019).

WITNESS

"Trump seems to have a vendetta against countries with large percentages of Black and Brown people, as well as those Black and Brown people in the country he leads," (Romero 2018:35).

Sociologists argue that Trump's platform was successful because he appealed to a collection of beliefs known as **ethnonationalism**, which refers to racial resentments that include hostility to immigrants and globalization (Manza and Crowley 2018). White racial resentment in the form of ethnonationalism has always existed. It used to be found in both parties, but today it is more partisan, fueling Republican Party success.

Latino Constituency

In recent decades, Latinos have been actively courted by both major political parties in the United States for several reasons. The first is probably obvious: Latinos are one of the fastest-growing groups in this country and, thus, they are an increasingly significant portion of the electorate. Additionally, Latinos are concentrated in key states with significant electoral votes. This has resulted in southwestern states such as New Mexico and Arizona carrying more weight in national elections than they have in the past (Kershaw 2004). Finally, while Latinos are overwhelmingly Democratic supporters, they tend to be social conservatives on issues like gay marriage and abortion, which put them at odds with the Democratic Party. However, the Republican Party has an image problem in the Latino community because it is viewed as an exclusive and white-dominated party (Coffin 2003). Cubans are the exception as they are overwhelmingly Republican and perceive the Democrats as not hostile enough to Castro and communists (Coffin 2003). With the exception of Cuban Americans, Latino voters behave similarly to African American voters in that race is a more important factor shaping their political party affiliation than class. This has not been the pattern for whites: higher-income whites tend to vote Republican (Coffin 2003), but ascent into the middle class for blacks and Latinos has not shifted their political loyalties in significant ways from Democrat to Republican.

During the 2008 Democratic presidential primary, Latino voters initially supported Hillary Clinton, which at first was interpreted in the media as a sign of interracial tensions between blacks and Latinos. Instead, their support for Clinton over Obama hinged on the fact that she was a more recognizable figure than Obama, who, at the time, was relatively new in the national political landscape. After Obama won the Democratic nomination, Latino voters shifted their support to him, despite ongoing efforts by the Republican Party to attract them (Wingfield and Feagin 2010).

Despite their demographic appeal to both major parties, less than one-quarter of Latinos are registered voters (Perdomo 2004). Latino voting rates are much lower than voting rates for other racial/ethnic groups (Garcia and Sanchez 2008). This is a concern of Latino groups, such as the National Council of La Raza, that engage in voter registration drives in the Latino community. There are several reasons why there is such a low level of political participation among Latinos. First, Latinos tend to be a very mobile population, and this inhibits political participation when they have to reregister in each new location. Second, they may not see the value of voting because they feel that politicians are unlikely to respond to them or address their specific issues. Finally, there is a lack of **political socialization**, how we are taught to be politically conscious, engaged, and active. Many Latinos are not habitual voters, and schools are not teaching this civic responsibility anymore (Garcia and Sanchez 2008; Perdomo 2004).

In 2016, more than three in ten eligible voters were nonwhite for the first time in history. Latinos represent an increasing proportion of eligible voters and are expected to play key roles in states like Colorado, Florida, and Nevada. While Latino voting rates have historically been low, Latino voter registration was described as "skyrocketing" (Bernal 2016) in anticipation of the 2016 presidential election, where they were projected to cast 13.1 million votes. In 2012 Latinos cast 11.2 million votes and in 2008, 9.7 million (Bernal 2016). Polls find that Latinos were reacting to Trump's views on immigration and will overwhelmingly be voting Democratic (Bernal 2016).

Asian American Voting Trends

Sociologists argue that the media portrays Asian Americans and African Americans as in conflict and naturally at odds with one another. They argue that Asian Americans are routinely portrayed in the media as a group that has succeeded and not faced racial discrimination (Wingfield and Feagin 2010). This portrayal in the media ignores historic and current discrimination faced by Asian Americans and instead, conveniently, presents Asian Americans as a model minority, a group that has made it on their own and should act as an example for other racial/ethnic minority groups. Like Latinos, Asian Americans initially supported Hillary Clinton in the Democratic primary in 2008, leading some in the mainstream media to ask, "Does Obama have an Asian problem?" (Cullen 2008). Such racial divisiveness was more of a media creation than a reality as Asian Americans overwhelmingly shifted their support to Barack Obama after he won the 2008 Democratic primary.

In the past twenty years, Asian Americans have shifted from a solidly Republican voting bloc to a solidly Democratic one, with 73 percent of Asian Americans supporting Obama in 2012 (Khalid 2015). While almost half of Asian American voters describe themselves as independents, many voted Republican out of loyalty to Reagan; his anti-communist stance resonated particularly with Vietnamese refugees, for instance. Today, many Asian Americans find the Republican Party has shifted too far to the right. Additionally, many are struggling economically and, thus, find Democratic Party policies more appealing. Finally, the Democratic Party made a concerted effort to woo Asian American voters in the 1990s, which appears to have paid off (Khalid 2015).

Current Trends: The Intersection of Age and Race in Politics

Political sociologists study **voting blocs**: groups of people that tend to vote in ways that support or oppose particular policies, or that vote in a specific way as a reflection of a certain aspect of their identity. Since the 1950s, for instance, African Americans have been a voting bloc that Democrats could count on, while, prior to that, the few American blacks who could vote showed their allegiance to the "party of Lincoln" by voting Republican. To the extent that women can be viewed as a voting bloc, they have been slightly more likely to vote Democratic.

Social scientists who study demographic trends are predicting some serious conflict in the political sphere in the near future. The first trend of interest is the increasing percentage of racial minorities in this country (see Chapter 1). The second trend is one toward an increasingly aged society, a pattern found throughout the industrialized world as baby boomers reach their retirement years. The political consequences of the intersection of these two significant shifts are of interest. Racial minorities have been much more likely to vote Democratic and they are a much younger population; thus, their share of the percentage of the voting age population is predicted to increase markedly in the near future, as "nonwhites make up 44 percent of the under-18 population and are an outright majority of the youth population in seven states" (Brownstein 2010). This racial/generational split was evident in the 2008 and 2012 presidential elections as young people and minorities overwhelmingly supported Democrat Barack

Obama and whites over the age of fifty solidly backed Republicans John McCain and Mitt Romney (Brownstein 2010; Wingfield and Feagin 2010).

Beyond the voting booth, this "generational mismatch" is resulting in significant political struggles over how tax dollars should be spent. The aging white population resists taxes and finds little benefit in public spending on things like schools, while the young minority population tends to see spending on education, health-care, and social welfare programs as essential (Brownstein 2010). Specifically, a Pew Research Center study in the spring of 2010 found:

> Only 23 percent of white seniors said they preferred a larger government that offers more services; 61 percent preferred a smaller government that offers fewer services. Among minorities, the attitude was essentially reversed: 62 percent preferred a larger government and 28 percent a smaller one.
>
> (Brownstein 2010)

Federal spending currently favors the aging white population, spending about seven dollars per senior, primarily due to Medicare and Social Security, while federal investment in children is only one dollar per child (Brownstein 2010). This has set the stage for a generational and racialized battle over resources. What the future holds in terms of the influence of minorities in the political sphere remains to be seen. As the racial demographics of the country change, one can expect political representation of people of color to generate considerable attention.

Some refer to the potential shifts in the electorate as a Rising American Electorate (RAE), an estimated 133 million potential voters, or 59.2 percent of eligible voters, made up of unmarried women, Millennials, and racial minorities, who are concentrated in the South and on the coasts. Between 2012 and 2016, the RAE gained over 8 million votes, while the non-RAE lost 3.5 million votes (Lake, Ulibarri, and Bye 2016).

According to the Pew Research Center predictions, nonwhite voters will account for a third of all eligible voters in 2020, which is their largest share ever, up from one-quarter in 2000. It is projected that Hispanics will be the largest minority group of voters, making them larger than the African American electorate for the first time. Asian American voters will account for 5 percent of 2020 voters, which is more than double the percentage of Asian American voters in 2000. One in ten voters will be members of Generation Z, traditional-aged college students, those between the ages of 18 and 23 in 2020 (Cilluffo and Fry 2019).

IMMIGRANTS AND THE RACIALIZATION OF ANTI-IMMIGRATION SENTIMENT

This section of the chapter explores immigration and hate groups, which are evidence enough that race remains profoundly influential in our culture and that we are not postracial. Anti-immigrant sentiment in the United States today is often racialized and has increased dramatically in the past decade (Buchanan and Holthouse 2006), with politicians proposing building walls along the US–Mexican border (but not the US–Canada border) and with demands for more aggressive border patrols. Efforts to close the border have all failed because, as New Mexico Governor Bill Richardson said, "If you build a 12-foot fence, migrants will use 12-foot ladders" (Johnson 2009). There has been a dramatic increase in nativism, the espousal of ideologies that favor people already in a country, an attitude thus hostile to immigrants. Many states have recently passed extreme anti-immigrant legislation, and similar nativist trends are found throughout Europe (see Box 13.1 Global Perspectives: Immigration Challenges in Europe: A Failure of Multiculturalism?). Historically, US immigration restriction laws have been racialized as well, despite the plea of the Statue of Liberty, to "give me your tired, your poor, your huddled masses yearning to breathe free."

Although America is a nation of immigrants, current levels of immigration are perceived as problematic by many Americans. We are not facing dramatically higher immigration rates than we have in the past (see Table 13.2), but immigration is perceived as problematic during poor economic eras. Even though employment has dramatically improved since the economic crisis of 2008 (see Chapter 8), wages remain stagnant, making the average worker feel like things have not improved. Since January 2000, 13.1 million immigrants, legal and undocumented, have arrived in the United States despite the recessions and the weak economy. However, the numbers of undocumented immigrants declined at the end of the recent decade (Carmarota 2010). Immigrants have been demonized since the 1980s, stereotyped as criminals, terrorists, and drug traffickers (McDowell and Wonders 2009–2010). As discussed previously in this chapter, this narrative has been capitalized on by many politicians, including President Trump.

According to the Southern Poverty Law Center, a group that monitors hate groups and extremist actions, between 2007 and 2009 there was an 80 percent

Year	Size of Immigrant Population (Millions)	Immigrant Share of Total US Population (%)
1970	9.6	4.7
1980	14.1	6.2
1990	19.8	7.9
2000	31.1	11.1
2010	40.0	12.9
2014	42.4	13.3
2017	44.5	13.7

TABLE 13.2: Size and Share of the Foreign-Born Population in the US, 1970–2017

SOURCE: Zong and Batalova 2016; For 2017 data, US Census Bureau n.d.

BOX 13.1

Global Perspectives:
Immigration Challenges in Europe: A Failure of Multiculturalism?

Like the United States, many European nations are faced with growing anti-immigrant sentiment and activism. This was obvious in the Brexit vote in July 2016, in which Great Britain voted to leave the European Union. Most of the arguments made by Brexit supporters were xenophobic and anti-immigrant, and they resonated with many voters. After the vote, there was an increase in racism and anti-immigrant violence. The German chancellor, Angela Merkel, has publicly questioned multiculturalism, calling it a failure because millions of Turks were encouraged to immigrate to Germany yet have been unable to fully integrate into German society (Mortished 2010). Similar comments have been heard in France, the Netherlands, Italy, and Great Britain. Italian political leaders have called for the use of troops to stem the flow of Tunisian immigrants in to their country (Donadio 2011). Politicians have moved to ban head scarves in the Netherlands, a move described as an example of the growing public intolerance of Islamic culture (Mortished 2010).

This kind of anti-immigrant hostility is directed at both documented and undocumented immigrants, and much of it is racialized. Italy's hostility toward Roma immigrants, more popularly known as Gypsies, is expressed by the mayor of Milan with the following statement: "These are dark-skinned people, not Europeans like you and me" (Faiola 2010).

France, a nation that previously boasted of welcoming more immigrants than any other Western country, has expressed intolerance for the increasing numbers of migrants from North Africa by calling for changes in the Schengen Agreement, a hallmark agreement of the European Union that allows immigrants to travel freely between EU nations (Chrisafis 2010; Donadio and Cowell 2011). French president Nicolas Sarkozy ordered that twenty-five thousand undocumented immigrants be expelled from France by the end of 2010, resulting in police roundups outside schools, Métro stations, and businesses and sparking protests from some French people (Chrisafis 2010).

Perhaps the most glaring example of anti-immigrant hostility is the mass murder by Norwegian Anders Behring Breivik, who killed seventy-seven people. After detonating a bomb in Oslo, Norway, Breivik, dressed as a policeman, drove to a summer camp for the youth wing of the Labor Party and opened fire on the young people. The Labor Party has fought for more-liberal policies on immigration, something Breivik considered to be traitorous. His ultimate goal was "to cleanse Europe of Islam" because he believed European Muslims should be forced to convert, be deported, or face death (Seierstad 2011). Although Breivik has been portrayed in the media as a lone wolf, Norway has experienced increasing xenophobia, with one poll finding that one in two Norwegians prefer to halt immigration completely. This kind of support has fueled the Progressive Party, a leader in the anti-immigrant movement in Norway.

increase in nativist extremist groups and groups that are hostile to immigrants (Beirich 2011). Nativist extremists have armed themselves with rifles, night-vision goggles, and body armor and patrolled the Mexico–US border. These groups target day laborers as well.

Economic Contributions of Immigrants

The primary opposition to immigration revolves around economic arguments—that undocumented immigrants take jobs that should go to citizens and are willing to work for so much less money that it hurts all workers. Despite the widespread nature of such beliefs, there is another school of thought that argues that immigrants, both documented and undocumented, contribute more to our economy than they take.

Agriculturalists, many politicians, business owners, and the Chamber of Commerce have long opposed stricter immigration laws because of their embrace of cheap migrant labor, despite the fact that popular sentiment has more often favored restricting immigration (Tichenor 2002). Blanket hostility to immigrants fails to acknowledge the value they bring to a country, as history shows that immigrants bring ideas, vigor, and ambition, as well as their labor (*Economist* 2001). The federal government collects billions of dollars in taxes and Social Security contributions from undocumented immigrants every year, while state governments invest in immigrants in the form of education and social services, such as fire and police protection (Johnson 2009). Foreign labor is needed in both Europe and the United States, specifically to work in the manual and service industries, despite the anti-immigrant sentiment. Importantly, in addition to filling labor needs, immigrants also create jobs because they add to a country's overall economic activity through their consumption of goods and services (*Economist* 2001).

Immigrants fill jobs that many native-born Americans do not wish to do, such as restaurant workers, hotel housekeepers, fruit pickers, gardeners, and garment workers. In the United States, the restaurant industry is the largest employer of foreign labor (Jayaraman 2013). It is not just low-wage work that relies on immigrant laborers. Hog-processing plants offer decent wages and end up filling most of their jobs with immigrant labor because locals do not want to do that work, leading some employers to question the American work ethic (Ludden 2007).

New Immigrant Destinations

Immigrants are now found in small towns throughout the United States instead of being concentrated in major urban areas, prompting dramatic demographic changes in areas such as Garden City, Kansas, and throughout the rural South

(Parker 2001). In 1980, two beef-packing plants opened in Garden City, Kansas, drawing immigrant workers from around the world. Latinos increased from 16 percent of the county population in 1980 to 47 percent in 2010; non-Hispanic whites decreased from 82 percent of the population in 1980 to 30 percent in 2010 (Stull 2011).

Latinos are increasingly populating regions of the country, such as the rural South and Midwest, that have historically had very little racial/ethnic diversity. North Carolina, for instance, has been a premier new destination state for Latinos, experiencing "hypergrowth" with a 394 percent increase in their Latino population since the 1990s (Marrow 2011). According to the census, some North Carolina counties had a 95 percent white population in 1990 and by 2000 one in five people in those counties identified as Latino/Hispanic (Lippard and Gallagher 2011). Tennessee's Latino population increased 278 percent between 1990 and 2000 (Parker 2001). Immigrant workers are moving to such places as North Carolina, Tennessee, and other parts of the South primarily because that is where jobs are. There has been job growth in hog-processing plants, for instance, and they are found throughout the South because their owners are seeking to avoid states with strong unions. These large plants also require a larger workforce than the small rural communities surrounding them can provide, so they inevitably recruit workers far and wide.

Research on southern attitudes toward their new immigrant neighbors finds that despite couching their concerns in color-blind rhetoric, southern whites fear immigrants will take their jobs and use up public resources. Additionally, they also racialize immigrants, conflating "immigrants" and "Mexicans." This is not unusual, as research finds that the anti-immigrant threat is generally focused on "the Latino threat" (Chavez 2008). Finally, they justify the poor treatment of immigrants by comparing their experiences to the experiences of their immigrant ancestors and by suggesting they are all "illegals" (Lippard 2016). Americans have historically simultaneously embraced a racist nativism and a color-blind racism when it comes to immigrants, and the South is no exception (Lippard 2016).

US consumers benefit from immigration directly. We enjoy low-priced goods, from computers to clothing, because immigrant workers are exploited. It is immigrant workers who provide middle- and upper-class consumers with personal services, such as pedicures and domestic labor. By relying on immigrant workers to clean their homes and cook their food, middle- and upper-class consumers are able to focus on their work (Lipsitz 2001). While US consumers benefit from immigration, immigrants themselves are more likely to be exploited by employers who violate wage and labor laws because they recognize that undocumented immigrants are unlikely to turn to the government for recourse (Johnson 2009).

Race, US Immigration Law, and Politics

Although the dominant cultural narrative in the United States portrays the country as welcoming to immigrants, the kind of hostility directed at immigrants actually has a very long history. Examples of racialized hostility toward immigrants are the Chinese Exclusion Act of 1882 and the National Origins Act of 1924. Even Jewish refugees during World War II faced a hostile welcome in the United States. Today, the Trump administration is passing legislation that sends similar messages of hostility to immigrants, particularly those who are racial minorities and from poor nations.

Chinese Exclusion Act

The **Chinese Exclusion Act**, discussed in Chapter 4, was designed to protect the racial purity of American society by banning Chinese immigrants from entry (Tichenor 2002). Hostility toward Chinese immigration was triggered by organized labor, as they resented the use of Chinese workers as strikebreakers. By the late 1860s, the economy was struggling and many mines were closing in the West due to poor productivity. The Transcontinental Railroad had been completed and the population of California continued to climb, exacerbating the economic crisis. The anti-Chinese movement consumed the state of California in the 1870s. Anti-Chinese sentiments gained national prominence when the Democratic Party expressed its support for Chinese exclusion, an extension of its hostility toward racial minorities (Tichenor 2002). By the 1880 presidential election, both parties were seeking votes by promising to restrict Chinese immigration, and by 1882 the Chinese Exclusion Act was signed into law.

National Origins Act

Following the Chinese Exclusion Act was the **National Origins Act** of 1924, part of the Johnson-Reed Act, which was inspired by eugenicist ideas and hostility toward Japanese immigrants. The Japanese government and the US government had reached a gentlemen's agreement in which Japan pledged to discourage Japanese immigration to the United States. Eugenicist beliefs influenced the findings of a congressional commission known as the Dillingham Commission, which in 1909 compiled an extensive body of empirical research that argued that new immigrants to the United States, those primarily from Southern and Eastern Europe, threatened the nation. South and East Europeans were described as the darkest and most primitive of the European "races" in a book entitled *The Races of Europe* (1898), which was influential in the Dillingham Commission's report. This work was later cited frequently in immigration debates of the time (Tichenor 2002).

The National Origins Act limited immigration to 2 percent of each nationality already residing in the United States (based upon 1890 census data) and capped immigration at 186,437 individuals annually. Thus, this legislation established numerical limits on immigration and institutionalized a racial hierarchy, favoring some immigrants over others (Ngai 2004). Such a restriction was projected to result in 84 percent of immigrants coming from Northern and Western Europe while only 16 percent would come from Southern and Eastern Europe. Additional restrictions pushed for gradual Japanese exclusion, an "Asiatic barred zone," and a preference for "near relatives" of current citizens (Tichenor 2002).

Immigration Reform

This legislation remained in place until 1965, when the Immigration and Nationality Act, also known as the Hart-Celler Act, was passed. This act abolished the national origins quota system that had been in place since the 1920s, replacing it with a system that showed preference for an immigrant's skills and their relationships to US citizens. Under this legislation, 170,000 visas were reserved for immigrants from the Eastern Hemisphere (with no country allotted more than 20,000 visas) and 120,000 visas for Western Hemisphere immigrants (Tichenor 2002). Family unification became a priority; thus, spouses, minor children, and parents of American citizens were exempted from these quotas.

President Lyndon Johnson found the national origins quota system to be inconsistent with his civil rights agenda. Immigration reform became a prominent feature of his Great Society programs and was pushed by House liberals, despite the fact that immigration reform was low on the list of priorities among the electorate. It is this legislation that literally changed the face of American society, as it opened the doors for massive immigration from the Caribbean, Asia, and Latin America. These immigrants made up three-quarters of legal admissions in the 1970s and 1980s and currently represent 80 percent of new arrivals (Tichenor 2002).

Was it the intent of legislators to so dramatically change American society with this racially progressive immigration legislation? The answer is "maybe." It appears that while no one foresaw the rapid rise of Asian immigration, some advocates were conscious that this legislation would lead to an increase in Asian immigrants, which they supported. Interestingly, however, there was "no serious discussion of the law's impact" at the time by President Johnson and legislators (Skrentny 2015:14).

The US Government and Jewish Immigration

In addition to anti-Asian hostility, US immigration laws were also influenced by anti-Semitic thought. During the post–World War I era, members of the US Immigration Bureau were explicit in their anti-Semitic beliefs, claiming that Jews were physically and socially deficient and therefore their entry into the United States should be restricted (Tichenor 2002). During the Great Depression, immigration restrictions became even more severe, despite the vast numbers of visas that were requested; restrictions resulted in legal immigration plummeting from 242,000 visas issued in 1931 to 36,000 issued in 1932, of which only 3,000 went to Jews (Tichenor 2002).

When the Nazis came to power in Germany in 1933, they immediately implemented anti-Jewish measures that caused tens of thousands of German Jews to seek refuge in other countries. Many church groups and prominent Americans joined Jewish organizations in pressuring the United States government to provide German Jews with political refugee status. The White House and the consular and visa bureaus of the State Department ignored these pressures. President Franklin Delano Roosevelt was publicly silent on the issue of Jewish refugee relief, unwilling to antagonize southern Democrats. Critics claimed the consular and visa bureaus showed prejudice against Jewish immigrants, because immigrants with Russian passports were perceived as suspicious and anyone with a passport from a country other than the one in which they were a citizen was also considered to be suspicious. Both restrictions worked to limit Jewish entry, since most immigrants from Russian states were Jews and most Jews seeking entry into the United States had fled their original countries due to the rise of Hitler and the Nazis.

Jewish immigration admissions declined in 1934, despite the pressure on the federal government to allow German Jews as political refugees. By the late 1930s, the situation of European Jews was growing more desperate and, thus, pressure on the White House to admit them as political refugees increased. By 1940, Congress passed legislation that extended refugee status to British children facing German bombing during World War II on a nonquota basis, but still maintained the racial/ethnic hierarchy in admissions by denying Jews entry. President Roosevelt finally issued an executive order creating the War Refugee Board to oversee Jewish rescue efforts, after an investigation by Treasury officials accused State Department officials of anti-Semitism and found "the State Department guilty of willful attempts to prevent action from being taken to rescue Jews from Hitler" (Tichenor 2002:167).

Restrictive immigration laws, from the Chinese Exclusion Act to the limits on Jewish immigration, not only reflected a racial hierarchy but also created new categories of racial difference (Ngai 2004). The National Origins Act not only excluded Chinese, Japanese, Indians, and other Asians from immigrating by declaring them ineligible for citizenship, as racial others, it also classified Europeans as white. Thus, Asians were cast as permanently foreign while most Euro-Americans, with the exception of European Jews, were cast as capable of assimilating (Ngai 2004).

Recent Anti-Immigrant Legislation

Strident anti-immigrant legislation that began being passed in several states in 2010 exposed a racial dynamic at work. Arizona was the first to pass what are commonly referred to as racial-profiling laws with SB 1070, formally entitled the Support Our Law Enforcement and Safe Neighborhoods Act. Under this law, if police officers have reasonable suspicion that a person is undocumented, they can request immigration papers as proof of citizenship during the course of any legal traffic stop. Previously police did not have the authority to inquire about an immigrant's legal status. Critics call this racial profiling, as the "reasonable suspicion" a police officer is likely to rely on is being dark skinned. This kind of legislation makes it unlikely that Norwegians who overstay their visas and are thus in the United States illegally will be questioned by police, because their physical features are unlikely to make them appear suspect in ways that Mexican immigrants are, for instance. Although SB 1070 was passed as a law in Arizona, in July 2010 a federal judge blocked key aspects of the law, and in 2012 the Supreme Court rendered a split decision on the law's constitutionality. Much of SB 1070 was struck down, while the "papers please" section, which gave police the right to request immigration papers from anyone they stop, remained (Liptack 2012).

State Immigration Laws

Utah, Indiana, Georgia, South Carolina, and Alabama passed laws similar to Arizona's. The American Civil Liberties Union (ACLU) and other civil rights groups have filed lawsuits against these laws, claiming that they encourage racial profiling and that they preempt federal statutes, such as the Immigration and Nationality Act of 1965, as immigration has always been federally enforced in this country. The Georgia law also includes stipulations that anyone intentionally transporting or housing an undocumented immigrant is in violation of the law, that employers must use a national database to make sure employees are legal citizens, that anyone using false identification to get a job faces fines of up to $250,000 and fifteen years in prison, and finally, that people applying for food stamps and public housing must provide specific forms of identification (Severson 2011). The Alabama law is described as the toughest in the nation because it allows police to jail suspected undocumented immigrants encountered during traffic stops, requires schools to verify the citizenship status of students, and makes it a crime to knowingly assist an undocumented immigrant by providing them with a job, a ride, a place to live, or any form of help. Church leaders have come out strongly against this legislation, arguing that it violates their obligation to minister to the needy.

Key portions of the laws in Georgia, Utah, Alabama, and Indiana have also been blocked from implementation by federal judges. The Obama administration has opposed these laws on the grounds that the state laws conflict with federal immigration laws. States counter that the federal government is not doing enough to curb undocumented immigrants from entering the country (Severson 2011). Attempts to pass similar legislation in Mississippi failed in 2012.

Latino immigrants report negative experiences with police, primarily fears of immigration enforcement (Romero 2006). These laws place a unique strain on police departments, whose relationships with Latino communities are already problematic, and force them to "move between immigrant integration and immigrant exclusion" (Armenta 2016:121).

WITNESS

For Warren Yoder, the executive director of the Public Policy Center of Mississippi, the future for immigrant justice in Mississippi looked bleak: "We could really see ourselves going back to the 1930s and '40s in terms of the new Jim Crow … to have a three-race system with Hispanics at the bottom and using deputy sheriffs to harass people and prevent organizing. It was just scary" (Weishar 2012).

These laws have generated intense opposition in the form of immigrant rights movements and in terms of strategic alliances with other activist groups. In Mississippi, immigrant rights groups have been able to rely on the Legislative Black Caucus and major civil rights and labor organizations in the state to successfully fight anti-immigrant legislation. In 2015, this coalition of activists had helped kill almost three hundred anti-immigrant bills (Brown and Jones 2016).

Xenophobia, the intense fear and dislike of foreigners, and anti-immigrant sentiment are known to increase during difficult economic times, and certainly the recession that began in 2008 is no exception. But while immigrants become easy scapegoats during poor economic periods, the anti-immigrant fervor obscures the necessary role undocumented immigrants play in our economy. After the strict immigration law was passed in Georgia, for instance, their largest industry, agriculture, found itself shorthanded when the 2011 peach-picking season hit. Fruit and vegetable farmers blamed the shortage of farmworkers on the state's new immigration reform law. In the past, migrant farmworkers came to Georgia from Florida when their labor was needed. After the legislation passed, undocumented workers feared entering Georgia, negatively affecting the agricultural industry (Chappell 2011). Because the unemployment rate in Georgia was 9.9 percent in May 2011, local workers should have been able to take the jobs migrant workers formerly did. However, farmers say nonimmigrants won't do the work, claiming it's too hard (Chappell 2011).

In addition to the immigration laws discussed above, the United States has dramatically increased punishment for people who violate immigration laws. The increasing privatization of prisons and increasing immigrant detention are described in Chapter 10. Investigative reports have found links between lobbyists for Corrections Corporation of America (CCA), the largest private prison company in the United States, and the backers of Arizona's immigration law, SB 1070 (Fang 2010). For instance, Arizona governor Jan Brewer's deputy chief of staff was a former lobbyist for CCA and his wife is a CCA lobbyist. CCA was set to receive more than $74 million in tax dollars during 2010 for running immigration detention centers (Fang 2010). Officials at the Immigration and Customs Enforcement Agency (ICE) have covered up abuses and 107 deaths of immigrants in detention (Bernstein 2010).

The Obama administration boasted of their record year of immigrant deportations, at 393,000, under the Department of Homeland Security in 2009. Announcing record deportations is a way for the administration to portray itself as tough on illegal immigration, a stance that tends to be viewed positively by voters. However, the Obama administration's policy preference was for immigration reform that would reward employed undocumented immigrants with citizenship, a position very similar to that of Presidents George W. Bush and Ronald Reagan, but one that is not popular with voters.

The DREAM Act

Another piece of racialized immigrant legislation is the Development, Relief, and Education for Alien Minors (DREAM) Act of 2010. This failed piece of federal legislation would have made the path to citizenship for undocumented immigrants brought to the United States as children easier; their citizenship would have been granted upon their obtaining a college degree or through military service. This legislation would also qualify such students for in-state tuition. Supporters of this act argue that young people brought to the United States illegally, as children, should not be punished for their parents' choices. The DREAM Act is viewed by many as a path to citizenship and productivity for individuals who have already spent the bulk of their lives in this country. Opponents view it as rewarding people for violating immigration laws. While a Gallup poll showed that over half of Americans supported the DREAM Act in 2010, a Senate Republican filibuster defeated the bill. In 2011, President Obama signed an executive order that relaxed deportation laws for DREAMers. While this executive order does not offer citizenship or amnesty to DREAMers, it does give immigration agents flexibility in deciding the fate of immigrants by not requiring their deportation.

Currently, a 1982 Supreme Court decision entitles undocumented immigrants to a free K–12 education. However, once they graduate, they are subject to deportation and do not qualify for federal student aid for higher education; they are also unable to enlist in the military or work legally in the United States. It is estimated that in 2012, there were 1.7 million potential "DREAMers"—undocumented youth between the ages of eighteen and twenty-four—living in the United States, 950,000 of whom are immediately eligible for the benefits of citizenship and 770,000 of whom will be eligible in the future (Passel and Lopez 2012). At least fourteen states have passed legislation allowing undocumented immigrants who have graduated from high schools to attend public colleges and universities in their state at in-state tuition rates.

Minority groups have not simply acquiesced in the face of discrimination. The failure of the DREAM Act's passage has resulted in undocumented youth's engaging in activism to shed light on their plight. In 2011, for instance, five undocumented Latino youth staged a sit-in at the ICE offices in Los Angeles, urging the Obama administration to stop deporting undocumented youth. A national Education Not Deportation (END) campaign was launched and is ongoing (Zimmerman 2011). Other immigrant activists are campaigning to end the use of "the *I* word" ("illegal") (see Box 12.2 Racial Justice Activism: Campaign to Eliminate "The *I* Word").

Anti-Immigrant Legislation and the Trump Administration

As mentioned previously, President Trump embarked on his quest for the highest office in the land by using overtly anti-immigrant rhetoric. His promise to build a border wall between the United States and Mexico resonated with many whites, some of whose incomes had stagnated over the previous decades and who feel

IMAGE 13.3: Immigrant children separated from their families and held in detention by the federal government under President Trump.

BOX 13.2

Racial Justice Activism:
Campaign to Eliminate "The I Word"

A campaign to eliminate the use of the word *illegal* for describing human beings was launched by Colorlines and the Applied Research Center (now known as Race Forward) and embraced by such groups as the General Commission on Religion and Race (GCORR) of the United Methodist Church. It is designed to help people understand how devastating, dehumanizing, and racist the term is. The goals of the campaign are to encourage public awareness of the negative racial impacts of calling people "illegals," to eliminate the racially derogatory term from public discourse and popular usage, and to encourage people to use more respectful and accurate language, such as "undocumented." The use of the term *illegal* to describe undocumented migrants is designed to increase racial and economic anxiety and to make immigrants easy scapegoats for our economic crisis.

Such religious organizations as GCORR emphasize that "no child of God is illegal" and that the use of such hateful rhetoric "patently denies the sacred worth and human dignity of all people as children of God" ("Religion and Race Commission ..." 2010). The goal of GCORR was to engage ten thousand United Methodists in the campaign by December 2011.

A Latin American youth coalition, United 4 the Dream, declared a victory in the "drop the I-word" battle. They gathered outside of radio station WFAE in Charlotte, North Carolina, to protest show host Mike Collins' use of the term *illegal* on air. They peacefully began protesting his show starting in June 2011. After a little over a month, Collins agreed to sign the campaign pledge to "drop the I-word." He also invited Maria Selena and Mary Espinosa, both of United 4 the Dream, on to his radio show to discuss the problem of using the term *illegals* and to think about what that term means. As of 2013, the Associated Press, *USA Today*, *LA Times*, *San Francisco Chronicle*, and many other news outlets have agreed to stop using the word in reference to human beings. The campaign is still working on getting the *New York Times*, the *Washington Post*, and many others on board.

For more information, visit the Colorlines website at http://colorlines.com; the GCORR website at www.GCORR.org; and the Race Forward (formerly the Applied Research Center) website at www.race forward.org.

immigration is to blame. While his campaign rhetoric promised that Mexico would pay for the wall, in July 2019 the Supreme Court approved the Trump administration's plans to use $2.5 billion dollars from the military budget to begin construction of the border wall. The Trump administration has also been separating children from their families at the border as a deterrence strategy to keep people from seeking asylum in the United States, referring to the policy as a "zero tolerance." These immigrant detention centers are criticized for keeping people locked in cages, sleeping on floors, and denied their basic humanity. Even more disturbingly, there are over 1,224 complaints of sexual abuse of women and children in these detention centers (Speri 2018).

In addition to building a border wall along the US–Mexico border and separating immigrant children from their families and detaining them, President Trump also plans to end birthright citizenship by executive order. In accordance with the Fourteenth Amendment, all persons born on US soil are citizens, regardless of the citizenship status of their parents. His administration also attempted to ban foreign Muslims from entering the United States through an executive order, which, after a number of legal challenges, the Supreme Court upheld in a 5:4 vote. Importantly, this list of actions taken by the Trump administration is not comprehensive and it only accounts for his first two years in office.

HATE CRIMES AND HATE GROUPS

Evidence that the election of President Barack Obama was not proof that the United States is a postracial society is the proliferation of hate crimes and hate-group activity since his election; although they decreased between 2011 and 2014, they have increased since 2014. The number of hate groups rose 7 percent between 2017 and 2018, to an all-time high of 1,020 (Beirich 2019). Hate groups are not new; indeed, the first white supremacist organization, the KKK, was organized in 1866 by former Confederate veterans, including former Confederate general Nathan Bedford Forrest, the first Grand Wizard of the Klan, as a way to keep black people in a subordinate place in the post–Civil War era. The Southern Poverty Law Center (SPLC), a nonprofit civil rights organization, has kept track of hate crimes and hate-group activity since its inception in 1971 (see Figure 13.1). According to the SPLC, there has been a marked increase in hate groups and hate crimes as a response to the election of President Barack Obama. President Trump's rhetoric seems to be fueling a resurgence in hate groups and hate crimes as well. In the first two years of Trump's presidency, there has been a 30 percent increase in hate groups (Beirich 2019).

In June 2011, camera footage that was later broadcast nationwide showed a black man in Jackson, Mississippi, being fatally run over by a pickup truck after he was beaten by a group of white teens. The 18-year-old charged with the man's murder is said to have laughed about it afterward and in a phone conversation boasted that he "ran that n— over." In 2009, in Huntington Beach, California, three men and a woman with white supremacist tattoos entered a predominantly Latino neighborhood and attacked and stabbed a Latino man in an alley while yelling racial slurs. In West Allis, Wisconsin, dozens of black youth began attacking white people at a state

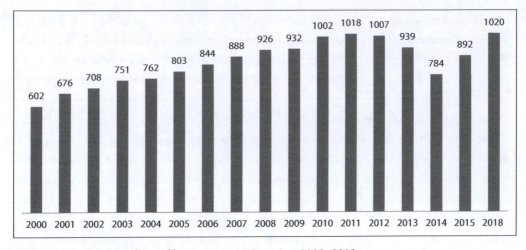

FIGURE 13.1: Numbers of hate groups in America, 2000–2018.

SOURCE: Potok 2016; For 2018 data, Beirich 2019

fair in August 2011 because the white people were "easy targets" (Cohen 2011). These gruesome examples, much like some of the anti-Muslim bias crimes described in the opening vignette, are clear-cut examples of hate crimes.

Ethnoviolence, according to Howard Ehrlich (2009), refers to acts motivated by group prejudice with the intention to cause physical or psychological injury and include intimidation, harassment, property destruction, and physical attacks (see Table 13.3). People targeted due to their race, ethnicity, skin color, national origin, gender, nationality, religion, or sexual orientation are victims of ethnoviolence. The term **hate crime** is more commonly used, but a hate crime specifically refers to legal statutes delineating serious crimes motivated by the same things that motivate ethnoviolence: race, ethnicity, skin color, national origin, and so forth. Ethnoviolence includes illegal hate crimes but also the prejudicial acts that may be outside the realm of legal statutes—for example, bullying in schools that is racially motivated.

These terms are often used interchangeably; however, Ehrlich (2009) argues that the term *hate crime* is less accurate. One reason it is less accurate is that white supremacists are motivated by love of their own kind more than hate of another. Hate is not necessary for an act of ethnoviolence to occur. When African American James Byrd was dragged to his death in Jasper, Texas, in 1998 by three white men, they were all charged under the Texas hate crimes statute. While two of the three men had neo-Nazi tattoos and a history of associating with white supremacist groups, the third man involved did not. His family members resented his actions being attributed to his hatred of African Americans and instead viewed his actions as a result of drinking too much and getting involved with the "wrong crowd." Ultimately, their arguments may have resonated with jurors, as he was sentenced to life in prison without parole while the other two were given the death penalty (Dow and Williams 2003).

Identifying Ethnoviolence	Examples
The use of recognized symbols, slogans, or words of group insult	A University of California, San Diego, student hung a noose off a bookshelf in the main campus library in February of 2010.
	In February 2011, three young men in New Jersey were arrested for a cross-burning hate crime.
Posting or circulating leaflets, including literature of right-wing extremist groups, that contain intimidating statements	Health-care reform protesters in 2010 carried signs declaring "Obama's Plan: White Slavery."
	In the days before the 2008 presidential election, anti-Obama leaflets, distributed throughout a New Jersey town by a white supremacist group, read, "Do you want a black president?"
Defacing or destroying property that is publicly associated with a specific group	In October 2010, the Florence Islamic Center in South Carolina was defaced through the use of bacon slices spelling out the words "pig chump."
	In January 2011, a Northern California man pled guilty to vandalizing two churches and a synagogue in Modesto, CA, by spray painting anti-Semitic and anti-Christian slurs on the buildings.
Acts that occur on or follow holidays or special events associated with a particular group	A white fraternity at the University of California, San Diego, mocked Black History Month with a ghetto-themed party called the "Compton Cookout."
	In 2013, a mosque in the UK was targeted with anti-Muslim graffiti just before Ramadan, the most holy festival of the Muslim calendar.
Acts that fit a pattern of past attacks on the target group	The dragging death of James Byrd in Jasper, TX, in 1998 mirrored lynchings of past eras.
	In the fall semesters of 2012 and 2013, minority students at the University of Texas at Austin were the targets of bleach bombs in a neighborhood near the campus.
The general consensus of the community that this was an act motivated by prejudice	While the crowd went wild as a rodeo clown at the 2013 Missouri State Fair wearing an Obama mask asked whether they would like to see Obama run down by the bull, state fair officials issued an apology and banned the clown from performing at Missouri fairs in the future.
	A 2012 massacre at a Sikh temple in Wisconsin by a white supremacist resulted in six deaths.

TABLE 13.3: Identifying Ethnoviolence
SOURCE: Ehrlich 2009.

Due to the limits of the language of the term *hate crime*, some social scientists have shifted to using the phrase *bias-motivated crime* or *bias-motivated incidents.* Other social scientists prefer the term *ethnoviolence* because it emphasizes that these are violent acts that are committed with the intention to inflict psychological or physical harm on another person and to do so because of prejudice, and because the acts may not necessarily be crimes (Ehrlich 2009).

Latinos have been increasingly targeted for hate crimes and ethnoviolence. Between 2003 and 2007, attacks on Latinos grew 40 percent while the estimated increase in their population during the same period was only 16 percent (Reddy 2008). In the fall of

2008, six white teenagers and one Latino teen, all between the ages of 16 and 17, assaulted two Ecuadoran men in Patchogue, Long Island, beating them and stabbing one to death. The gang told police they were out to hunt Mexicans (Kennedy 2010). Many argue that hate crime data inevitably underestimate the problem because undocumented immigrants are unlikely to report violence directed at them (Potok 2013).

We have already offered some examples of anti-Muslim hate crimes at the beginning of the chapter. In the face of global terrorist acts committed by Muslims, such as the attack on the offices of French magazine *Charlie Hebdo*, the Paris terrorist attacks in November 2015 for which ISIS claimed responsibility, and the Brussels airport attacks in March 2016 by Muslim terrorists, there has been increasing anti-Muslim sentiment. Anti-Muslim groups like Act! for America have been fueling the belief that all Muslims are terrorists and have turned their hostilities toward Syrian refugees (Potok 2016). Their rhetoric influenced several governors to declare they would not allow Syrian refugees into their states, something they do not control because only the federal government can impose immigration restrictions.

WITNESS

"Every hour, someone commits a hate crime. Every day, at least eight blacks, four gays or lesbians, two Jews, two whites, and one Latino become hate crime victims. Every week, a cross is burned, which is an act of intimidation associated with the Ku Klux Klan" (Southern Poverty Law Center 2005).

In the 1990s, Asian Americans were increasingly targeted for hate crimes and ethnoviolence, as violent attacks against Asians increased from 335 in 1993 to 486 in 1999 (Clemetson 2000). In September 2000, a 50-year-old Laotian man was beaten by two teenagers in Baltimore as he stood waiting for a bus. Hate crimes and ethnoviolence against Asian Americans are argued to be vastly underreported. For Asian Americans, there is a cultural reluctance to come forward to police, and those who do come forward are more likely to report it to community groups rather than to authorities (Clemetson 2000). Stereotypes of Asian American success, the model minority image, may fuel anti-Asian bias and ethnoviolence.

Explanations for Increased Nativism and Hate Groups

Latinos and Muslims are being increasingly targeted because of the increasing anti-immigrant and Islamophobic rhetoric in the public sphere, the rise in anti-immigrant legislation, increasingly aggressive immigration control enforcement, and increasing economic inequality. White supremacist activity has been on the rise in Arizona, for instance, since the state passed its recent immigration law. While most people who support the Arizona law are not white supremacists or extremists, the law has created a climate in which white supremacists feel comfortable expressing their extremist views in ways and in places that were unlikely in the past. In Arizona, armed groups have taken it upon themselves to search for undocumented immigrants, using armed weapons and surveillance technology along the Arizona–Mexico border (Groff 2010).

Anti-immigrant rhetoric is increasingly used by politicians and media pundits, helping to create a climate where extremists' views are more likely to be aired. In a campaign ad, former Louisiana senator David Vitter used incendiary images of "illegals"—dirty, brown-skinned young men entering Louisiana through a severed fence—as a way to attract votes during his 2010 reelection campaign for the US Senate. The ad declared that if his opponent were elected, "We may as well put out a welcome sign for illegal aliens." This ad, while containing an obvious misrepresentation of the state of Louisiana by presenting it as sharing a border with Mexico and protected merely by a chain-link fence, was described by one media source as winning the prize for "most vile anti-immigrant ad" (Hing 2010). The ad is a clear example of race-baiting: using racially derisive communication as a way to anger, intimidate, or coerce a group of people, particularly in its dehumanizing use of the term *illegal alien.* It enraged Latino advocacy groups throughout the country, who demanded an apology, claiming the ad had gone too far. The ad was quickly pulled in the face of this opposition (Hing 2010). The demands for meaningful immigration reform have a long history and are clearly valid political issues, but vilifying and dehumanizing immigrants to gain votes is perceived by many as going too far.

Former CNN host Lou Dobbs spent years railing against "illegal aliens" on his nightly news show. He was particularly hostile to employers who hire undocumented immigrants, proposing that employers should face felony charges. Ironically, investigative reporting by *The Nation* magazine found that Dobbs relied on undocumented immigrants for upkeep on his multimillion-dollar estates and horse farm (McCroskey 2010). Dobbs is described as obsessed with immigrants, all of whom are Latino in his portrayals, and he repeatedly propagates myths about immigrants, such as that they are responsible for much of the crime in our communities, and offers the erroneous statistic that they are taking up one-third of our jail cells. His use of incendiary language, describing immigrants as "aliens" and "invading" the country, has also drawn criticism (Lovato 2009). The media watchdog group Media Matters found that in the months between January 1 and June 23, 2009, Dobbs included segments on immigration in 77 out of 140 broadcast hours (Lovato 2009). Dobbs was forced to resign from CNN in November 2009 due to Latino activism and a nationwide advocacy campaign against his anti-immigrant rhetoric.

Many organizations are in the business of fighting hate and bigotry and seeking justice for those victimized by extremists. Two examples of such organizations are the Southern Poverty Law Center and Race Forward (formerly the Applied Research Center) (see Box 13.3 Race in the Workplace: Fighting Hate—The Work of the Southern Poverty Law Center and Race Forward). Organized activism has resulted in successful campaigns, such as the one to force the resignation of CNN's Lou Dobbs for his racist reporting.

Targeting of Arab Americans

If race is a social construction and is always changing, we need to ask whether there are groups that are currently being racialized. The concept of racialization was introduced in Chapter 1 and refers to attaching racial meaning to a previously racially

---

BOX 13.3

Race in the Workplace:
Fighting Hate—The Work of the Southern Poverty Law Center and Race Forward

The Southern Poverty Law Center employs researchers and attorneys who track hate-group activity, bring lawsuits against hate groups in the hopes of crippling them financially, use the courts to win systemic reform on behalf of victims of bigotry, and provide educators with free resources to help teach schoolchildren to reject hate and embrace diversity. The main focus of the Southern Poverty Law Center is to fight hate and extremism, work for justice for immigrants, teach tolerance, and fight for LGBTQ rights.

Race Forward is another organization fighting for racial justice through the use of media, research, and activism. Their research agenda is broad, including focuses on health, immigration, legislative action, poverty, multiracial coalitions, the economy, and green jobs. The center publishes the online news site Colorlines, engages in activist campaigns, such as the Drop the I-Word campaign, provides racial justice training and consulting services, and every two years has a Facing Race conference, which is one of the largest racial justice conferences in the country. Employing researchers, web designers, journalists, video production staff, and communication specialists, this organization might offer internships or employment opportunities to those interested in working to fight hate and bigotry.

There are numerous organizations engaged in such antiracist work, many of which have been introduced in "Racial Justice Activism" boxes throughout this text. Investigate antiracist organizations in your own community or on your college campus and consider getting involved in supporting their mission. Tim Wise, the antiracist activist profiled in Chapter 2, began his career with a local antiracist organization.

For more information, visit the Race Forward website at www.raceforward.org and the Southern Poverty Law Center website at http://splcenter.org.

unclassified group (Omi and Winant 1994). Arab Americans fall into this category. They are increasingly being racialized; particularly since 9/11, Arab Americans have been defined and treated as a racially distinct minority. The racial profiling of Arab Americans, or people who resemble Arab Americans, is evidence of their racialization. The question remains how far this racialization process will go.

While Arab Americans have long experienced discrimination, they have faced particularly intense levels of discrimination since the terrorist attacks of 9/11. These attacks against the United States, during which hijacked passenger jets were crashed into the World Trade Towers in New York City and the Pentagon, were launched by the Islamist terrorist group al-Qaeda. Since this event, men and women of Arab descent, or anyone who resembles someone of Arab descent, have been targeted for hate crimes and other forms of discrimination. In the weeks following the 9/11 attacks, there were over seven hundred documented attacks directed at Arab Americans, according to the American-Arab Anti-Discrimination Committee (Ibish and Stewart 2003). Anti-Muslim organizations depict Islam and Muslims as intolerant, irrational, violent, and a threat to American society. Perhaps most irrationally, these extremists fear that Muslims intend to erode the US legal system by implanting Islamic law, known as Sharia law. These extremists have persuaded some state governments, such as that of Oklahoma, to pass legislation banning Sharia law, something that has never been an actual threat. The federal courts overturned this ban in

IMAGE 13.4: Protest against so-called Ground Zero mosque. (AP Photo/Mel Evans).

2012 (Khan 2012). Sociologist Saher Selod (2018) has argued that since 9/11, South Asian and Arab Muslim Americans have faced increased **racialized surveillance**, which refers to the institutionalized practice of monitoring select bodies by relying on racial cues. Muslim Americans are not the only group who face such racialized surveillance; it is behind the disproportionate incarceration of black and brown men (see Chapter 10), and the targeting of Latinos for deportation. Americans have become increasingly accepting of an increasingly surveilled society, and, yet, surveillance is not race neutral; as Selod (2018) argues, certain bodies face more intense scrutiny than others.

The Globalization of Hate

American white nationalist Richard Bertrand has spent almost a decade designing racist websites, proposing policies for a white nationalist nonprofit he runs from his home in Montana, and holding conferences on topics such as the "future of white people." He has now turned his attention to transnational alliances, specifically, "building bridges to the organized European racist right" (Beirich 2014:37). He is seeking an Aryan homeland in the United States and believes the white race has been dispossessed, resulting in the destruction of European culture.

One of the groups he is reaching out to is a pro-white, anti-Muslim, and antiglobalization movement, the Movement Identitaire, which originated in France. Another is Jobbik, an anti-Semitic organization that is also Hungary's third-largest political party, winning almost 21 percent of the vote in a recent election. Like the anti-Muslim political rhetoric in the US, anti-Semitic rhetoric has been fueled by Hungarian politicians and resulted in an outbreak of anti-Semitic violence (Beirich 2014). These groups are extending their influence into Eastern Europe, and human rights groups have identified both of these organizations as threats to European democracy.

REPARATIONS

The **reparations movement**, the push to right the historical wrong of slavery by offering recompense to descendants of slaves, has a long history. The word *reparations* comes from the Latin word *reparat*, which means "to repair," to make amends for a wrong. The initial idea was suggested in the 1880s by Walter Vaughan, a white southerner concerned about the welfare of former slaves. He lobbied Congress and in 1890 introduced the Ex-Slave Pension and Bounty Bill, which called for maximum payments of $15 per month and maximum bounties of $500 for each ex-slave (Blight 2006). This bill failed, without even garnering the support of the three black congressmen in office at the time. Callie House then took up the cause of a national ex-slave pension bill. She filed a class-action lawsuit in federal court in the names of four African Americans, claiming the Treasury Department owed black people $68,073,388.99, a figure based on the amount of taxes collected on cotton between 1862 and 1868. This suit was dismissed, but it did get attention in the black press (Blight 2006).

African American law professor Randall Robinson argues that slavery is America's great crime and that there must be some restitution for blacks for the damage that was done, since "the psychic and economic injury is enormous, multidimensional and long-running" (2000:9). There are clear precedents for reparations: Germany paid reparations to individual Jews and to the state of Israel following the Holocaust. South Africa has engaged in a reparations campaign, referred to as the Truth and Reconciliation Committee, to try to heal some of the wounds associated with apartheid. The Inuit successfully sued the Canadian government for past wrongs, and Korean women who were forced into prostitution by Japan during World War II have been compensated by the Japanese government. President Lincoln supported a plan during the Civil War to compensate slave owners for their loss of "property," and President Andrew Johnson, Lincoln's successor, vetoed legislation that would have provided compensation to former slaves (Robinson 2000).

In the early 1970s, Yale law professor Boris Bittker wrote a book entitled *The Case for Black Reparations* (1973), arguing that slavery, Jim Crow, and overall racism had resulted in considerable social and economic injury to black Americans (Robinson 2000). In 1989, African American congressman John Conyers introduced a bill into Congress that asked for a commission to study the effects of slavery and to recommend appropriate remedies. The bill has never made it out of committee. Conyers has reintroduced this bill every Congress since (through 2015), and it has never been passed.

WITNESS

"Another reason this bill has garnered so much resistance is because many people want to leave slavery in the past—they contend that slavery happened so long ago that it is hurtful and divisive to bring it up now. It's too painful. But the concept of reparations is not a foreign idea to either the US government or governments throughout the world" (https://ibw21.org/commentary/my-reparations-bill-hr-40/).

Of course, many questions surround the issue of reparations: Why should reparations be paid? Who qualifies for reparations and how much would they get? How much is the promised "forty acres and a mule" worth today? (Cohen 2019). One answer to the first question was suggested by civil rights activist James Forman.

He estimated in 1969 that $500 million would be the price, since unpaid labor of African Americans built this nation's wealth. Economist and reparations scholar William Darity suggests that qualifying for reparations would require that a person have at least one ancestor who was enslaved in the US and that the recipient must have identified as an African American on official documents for at least ten years. By this estimate, some 30 million Americans are eligible today. Coming up with a quantifiable amount is more difficult. Do we calculate the number of hours slaves worked and estimate what they should have earned? Some estimates put the figure at $500 billion dollars. Others, such as William Darity, go back to the unfulfilled promise of forty acres and a mule. What would that be worth at the time, multiply that number by the four million freed slaves, add in compounded interest and inflation, for a grand total of $2.6 trillion dollars. If that amount were divided by 30 million descendants, each would receive roughly $80,000 per descendant, according to Darity (Cohen 2019).

Reparations for Japanese Americans

While the US Congress continues to avoid discussions of reparations for slavery, the United States federal government has shown a commitment to reparations for Japanese Americans who were interned during World War II. Japanese Americans have challenged the dominant national narrative surrounding World War II, perceived as the "good war," by working to preserve the collective memory of the mass internment of Japanese Americans during the war (see Chapter 11). They began by organizing internee reunions in the late 1960s, often accompanied by pilgrimages to the camps where they were formerly interned. A group of Japanese Americans established the Manzanar Committee (named after the internment camp) with the goal of educating people about the camp experience and to campaign for a California state landmark, which was granted in 1972 (Rhea 1997). However, the committee's proposed plaque was rejected by the California state parks system because it included the words *racism* and *greed*; in addition, the parks system insisted on using the term *relocation camp* instead of *concentration camp.*

A national movement to remember the camps of Japanese internment, called the Campaign for Redress, began to grow in the 1970s and early 1980s. They called for an official apology from the US government and reparations, a cash payment to each living internee. President Ford issued a proclamation repealing FDR's order that originally allowed for the internment of the Japanese Americans, and the Senate then established a Commission on the Wartime Relocation and Internment of Civilians, which sought to reconstruct the camp history and make recommendations for possible reparations. The commission eventually recommended a formal apology and a payment of $20,000 for each survivor, which was supported by a strong

IMAGE 13.5: Manzanar War Relocation Camp monument in a cemetery. The inscription reads, "Monument for the Pacification of Spirits." This former Japanese internment camp is now a public history site.

majority in the Senate and the House. President Reagan eventually signed the Civil Liberties Act of 1988, which accepted the commission's recommendations. The $1.65 billion for these reparations was appropriated under President George H. W. Bush (Rhea 1997).

The success of the Campaign for Redress resulted in efforts to memorialize the physical sites associated with the camp experience. National historic sites are approved more readily if they reflect positively on the United States, and, certainly, the Japanese internment camps did not do that, so "they had to work against the understandable desire of many people to forget any injustice which might muddy the image of the good war" (Rhea 1997:65). Due to the ongoing activism of Japanese Americans, Manzanar eventually became a national historic site in 1992.

Rosewood and Reparations in a Black Community

In January 1923, Rosewood, Florida, was the site of the Rosewood massacre, or to use the language of the era, a race riot. Rosewood was a self-sufficient all-black community in rural Florida. An accusation of the rape of a white woman by a black man led to the lynching of an African American man by whites from neighboring communities. After the lynching, black Rosewood residents armed themselves and defended their community from whites, but the white people had gathered hundreds from surrounding communities and they hunted blacks in the surrounding woods, killed six, and burned every building in Rosewood to the ground. The black residents of Rosewood were run out of their community and none ever returned. Survivors hid in nearby swamps for days, and some were lucky enough to catch trains to other communities. No arrests were ever made in this massacre, and few official records of the event exist. In 1993, the Florida legislature commissioned a report on the massacre and, as a result of its findings, became the first US state to compensate survivors and their descendants for damages due to racial violence. In 2004, the state designated Rosewood a Florida Heritage Site, a site designated by the government as important to the cultural heritage of a community.

While there are global examples of reparations for groups who have been wronged, the US government has mostly avoided addressing the wrongs of slavery and the near genocide of Native Americans, although they did respond to demands from Japanese Americans for reparations for their internment during World War II. Ultimately, the avoidance of reparations discussions is evidence of the weakness of the color-blind ideology. Perhaps a more successful approach would be to take a race-conscious approach, or to use the language of Supreme Court justice Harry Blackmun, to "take account of race." In his opinion in the affirmative action case *Regents of the University of California v. Bakke* (1978):

> A race-conscious remedy is necessary to achieve a fully integrated society, one in which the color of a person's skin will not determine the opportunities available to him or her. ... In order to get beyond racism, we must first take account of race. There is no other way. ... In order to treat persons equally, we must treat them differently.

WITNESS

"I changed my name, I was afraid that the whites might track me down and kill me!" said Lonnie Jefferson Carroll (1914–1997), a former Rosewood resident who was in a nursing home by the time Florida began hearings on the Rosewood incident ("Rosewood Survivors" n.d.).

CHAPTER SUMMARY

This chapter begins with speculation on what the racial hierarchy will look like in the future. It is followed by an examination of the role of race in politics; specifically, racialized voting patterns in the 2008 and 2012 elections and the racialized rhetoric surrounding the 2016 presidential election. The ongoing significance of race is evident beyond the political sphere as well. Certainly, the interconnectedness of anti-immigrant hostility, hate groups, hate crimes, and race is evidence of our nation's continuing struggle with race, particularly during the Trump administration. The question of reparations and the hostility to reparations for slavery amounts to a long-standing failure of political will. We end this chapter and this book with a call toward color-consciousness rather than falsely declaring ourselves to be color-blind. Sociologists speculate that the future of race in the United States is bound to be both similar to and distinct from the current racial hierarchy. The future of race is likely to be distinct in that groups currently defined as racial minorities are not likely to be the same groups defined as racial minorities decades from now. It is likely to be similar to race today in that there likely will be some racial hierarchy still in existence, with whites at the top.

KEY TERMS AND CONCEPTS

Campaign for Redress

Ethnonationalism

Ethnoviolence

Exogamy

Hate crime

Latin Americanization thesis

Political capital

Political socialization

Racialized surveillance

Reparations movement

Substantive representation

Superficial representation

Triracial stratification system

Voting blocs

PERSONAL REFLECTIONS

1. To what extent have you experienced political socialization? Explain. To what extent has your political socialization been racialized? Think about family conversations about politics. To what extent do you think your family's race and social class influence how your relatives vote?

2. After reading this book and this chapter's discussion of the reparations movement, do you think reparations for slavery are a good idea? Why or why not? What about reparations for Native American land loss and cultural genocide? Assuming there was broad political support for reparations for slavery and Native American land loss, what form should it take?

CRITICAL THINKING QUESTIONS

1. Explore the "The 'Woke' Generation? Millennial Attitudes on Race in the US" report at https://genforwardsurvey.com/assets/uploads/2017/10/GenForward-Oct-2017-Final-Report.pdf (data from the report has been presented throughout this book). What do you find the most interesting? Why? Are there any

findings that are disturbing to you? Why? Using information from this report and Chapter 13 of this text, speculate on the future of race in America, providing evidence for your argument.

2. Using data from this chapter and major news stories over the past year, explain the links between political rhetoric, immigration, hate groups, and race. To what extent do your findings challenge the standard American narrative—of welcoming immigrants, of a melting pot?

ESSENTIAL READING

Hochschild, Jennifer, Vesla Weaver, and Traci Burch. 2012. *Creating a New Racial Order: How Immigration, Multiracialism, Genomics, and the Young Can Remake Race in America.* Princeton, NJ: Princeton University Press.

Levin, Jack and Jack McDevitt. 2002. *Hate Crimes Revisited: America's War on Those Who Are Different.* New York: Basic Books.

Molina, Natalia. 2014. *How Race Is Made in America: Immigration, Citizenship, and the Historical Power of Racial Scripts.* Berkeley: University of California Press.

Roberts, Dorothy. 2011. *Fatal Invention: How Science, Politics, and Big Business Re-Create Race in the Twenty-First Century.* New York and London: The New Press.

Selod, Saher. 2018. *Forever Suspect: Racialized Surveillance of Muslim Americans in the War on Terror.* New Brunswick, NJ: Rutgers University Press.

RECOMMENDED FILMS

American Blackout (2006). Directed by Ian Inada. Explores recurring patterns of African American voter disenfranchisement during the presidential elections in Florida in 2000 and Ohio in 2004, as well as in a Georgia democratic primary in 2002 in which the state Republican Party led a successful effort to oust African American congresswoman Cynthia McKinney from her congressional seat.

El Norte (1983). Directed by Gregory Nava. The story of indigenous Guatemalan peasants who flee their country after they survive their village massacre at the hands of the Guatemalan army. The siblings make their way to Los Angeles and try to create a new life for themselves, despite being young, poor, uneducated, and undocumented.

Made in L.A. (2007). Directed by Amudena Carracedo. Documents the lives of three Latino immigrants working in Los Angeles sweatshops and their fight for basic labor rights from the trendy clothing retailer Forever 21. This film provides an insider's view of the modern immigrant experience. The women's lives are transformed by their experiences as they find the courage to find their voices.

Rosewood (1997). Directed by John Singleton. A Hollywood portrayal of the 1923 Rosewood massacre that sticks closely to the historical record and the findings of the commission that eventually investigated the massacre seventy years later, which resulted in reparations for survivors and their descendants.

Two Towns of Jasper (2003). Produced and directed by Whitney Dow and Marco Williams. Documents a visit to the town of Jasper, Texas, after the dragging death of African American James Byrd by three white men with white supremacist affiliations. The filmmakers use two crews, one white and one black, to document the aftermath of the crime on the community, resulting in a troubling portrait of race in America.

RECOMMENDED MULTIMEDIA

Watch Live coverage of Danny Glover and Ta-Nehisi Coates testify in a House hearing about slavery reparations. www.bing.com/videos/search?q=reparations+testimony+before+congress&view=detail&mid=8893C0478CACA488EACD8893C0478CACA488EACD&FORM=VIRE.

Southern Poverty Law Center. Want to know if you have organized hate groups in your community? Go to the following website and click on your state: www.splcenter.org/get-informed/hate-map.

Colorlines.org. Go to this website to keep up with the latest on race issues, immigration debates, and the Drop the I-Word campaign: http://colorlines.com/.

"Inside Immigration Reform." PBS *News Hour* on immigration: A Stanford University professor and Rochester Institute of Technology professor debate the economic value of immigrants. www.pbs.org/newshour/extra/daily_videos/could-more-skilled-immigrants-help-the-u-s-tech-industry/.

References

"A Woman as Sherlock's Dr. Watson Is 'Elementary.'" 2012. *Morning Edition*, NPR, September 27. Retrieved June 3, 2013 (www.npr.org/2012/09/27/161859930/sherlocks-dr-watson-as-a-woman-is-elementary).

"AC Milan Players Respond to Racist Chants by Walking off Field, Match Against Pro Patria Ends." 2013. *Huffington Post*, January 3. Retrieved May 2, 2013 (www.huffingtonpost.com/2013/01/03/ac-milan-players-racist-chants-walk-off-pro-patria_n_2403497.html).

Adams, Michael Jacob. 1992. *The Pullman Porter, The Dual Strategy of the Brotherhood of Sleeping Car Porters, and the Civil Rights Movement*. Master's thesis, Department of History, Washington University, St. Louis.

Agger, Ben. 2006. *Critical Social Theories: An Introduction*, 2nd ed. Boulder, London: Paradigm Publishers.

Alba, Richard. 1990. *Ethnic Identity: The Transformation of White Americans*. New Haven, CT, and London: Yale University Press.

Albelda, Randy, Robert W. Drago, and Steven Shulman. 2004. *Unlevel Playing Fields: Understanding Wage Inequality and Discrimination*, 2nd ed. Boston, MA: Economic Affairs Bureau, Inc.

Aldridge, Derrick P. 2002. "Teaching Martin Luther King Jr. and the Civil Rights Movement in High School History Courses: Rethinking Content and Pedagogy." Pp. 3–18 in *Teaching the American Civil Rights Movement: Freedom's Bittersweet Song*, edited by J. B. Armstrong, S. H. Edwards, H. B. Roberson, and R. Y. Williams. New York and London: Routledge.

Alexander, Michelle. 2010. *The New Jim Crow: Mass Incarceration in the Age of Colorblindness*. New York: New Press.

Allen, Barbara. 2003. *Uneasy Alchemy: Citizens and Experts in Louisiana's Chemical Corridor Disputes*. Cambridge, MA: MIT Press.

Allen, Nick. 2011. "Arizona Sheriff Introduces All Female Chain Gangs." *Telegraph*, January 2. Retrieved July 9, 2011 (www.telegraph.co.uk/news/worldnews/northamerica/usa/8236125/Arizona-sheriff-introduces-all-female-chain-gang.html).

Allen, Theodore W. 1994. *The Invention of the White Race*. Vol. 1. London: Verso.

Allport, Gordon W. 1958. *The Nature of Prejudice*. New York: Perseus Books.

Almaguer, Tomas. 1994. *Racial Fault Lines: The Historical Origins of White Supremacy in California*. Berkeley: University of California Press.

Alper, Loretta and Pepi Leistyna. 2005. *Class Dismissed: How TV Frames the Working Class*. Video. Northhampton, MA: Media Education Foundation.

American-Arab Antidiscrimination Committee Research Institute. 2003. *Report on Hate Crimes and Discrimination Against Arab Americans: September 11, 2001 to October 11, 2001*. Boston, MA: American-Arab Antidiscrimination Research Institute.

"American Time Use Survey." 2010. Bureau of Labor Statistics, US Department of Labor. Retrieved June 20, 2013 (www.bls.gov/news.release/archives/atus_06222011.pdf).

"American Time Use Survey Summary." 2019. Bureau of Labor Statistics, US Department of Labor, June 19. Retrieved July 3, 2019. (www.bls.gov/news.release/atus.nr0.htm).

Amsden, David. 2015. "A Peculiar Institution." *New York Times Magazine*, March 1, pp. 48–53, 57.

Anas, Brittany. 2010. "CU Researcher's Study on Death Penalty Shows That Race Matters in Sentencing." *Boulder Daily Camera*, July 22. Retrieved July 22, 2013 (www.coloradodaily.com/ci_155 76796).

Anderson, Benedict. 1991. *Imagined Communities: Reflections on the Origins and Spread of Nationalism.* London: Verso.

Anderson, Elijah. 2011. *Cosmopolitan Canopy: Race and Civility in Everyday Life.* New York: W. W. Norton and Company.

Anderson, Terry H. 1999. *The Sixties.* New York: Longman.

Andrews, Kenneth T., Kraig Beyerlein, and Tuneka Tucker Farnum. 2016. "The Legitimacy of Protest: Explaining White Southerners' Attitudes Toward the Civil Rights Movement." *Social Forces* 94(3):1021–1044.

Andrews, William L. 2019. *Slavery and Class in the American South: A Generation of Slave Narrative Testimony.* New York: Oxford University Press.

Ang, Ien. 2003. "From White Australia to Fortress Australia: The Anxious Nation in the New Century." Pp. 51–69 in *Legacies of White Australia: Race, Culture and Nation*, edited by L. Jayasuriya, D. Walker, and J. Gothard. Crawley. Western Australia: University of Western Australia Press.

Anthony, Arthé A. 2000. "'Lost Boundaries': Racial Passing and Poverty in Segregated New Orleans." Pp. 295–316 in *Creole: The History and Legacy of Louisiana's Free People of Color*, edited by S. Kein. Baton Rouge: Louisiana State University Press.

Apollon, Don. 2011. "Don't Call Them 'Post-Racial': Millennials Say Race Matters to Them." Colorlines, June 7. Retrieved July 21, 2013 (http://colorlines.com/archives/2011/06/youth_and_race_focus_group_main.html).

Aponte, Robert. 1991. "Urban Hispanic Poverty: Disaggregations and Explanations." *Social Problems* 38(4):516–528.

Apple, Michael W. 1999. *Power, Meaning, and Identity: Essays in Critical Educational Studies.* New York, Washington, DC: Peter Lang Publishers.

Applied Research Center. 2013. "ARC Study: Don't Call Millennials Postracial." Retrieved July 20, 2016 (www.raceforward.org/press/toolbox/arc-study-dont-call-millennials-post-racial).

Aptheker, Herbert. 1974 [1943]. *American Negro Slave Revolts.* New York: International Publishers.

Armario, Christine. 2009. "A Darker Side of Columbus Emerges in U.S. Classrooms." *Denver Post*, October 11. Retrieved July 20, 2013 (www.denverpost.com/ci_13539918).

Armbruster-Sandoval, Ralph. 2004. "Looking Backward, Moving *Adelante*: A Critical Analysis of the African American and Chicana/o and Mexicana/o Rights Movements." Pp. 157–195 in *Racial Thinking in the United States*, edited by P. Spickard and G. R. Daniel. Notre Dame, IN: University of Notre Dame Press.

Armenta, Amada. 2016. "Between Public Service and Social Control: Policing Dilemmas in the Era of Immigration Enforcement." *Social Problems* 63(1):111–126.

Armstrong, Julie Buckner, Susan Hult Edwards, Houston Bryan Roberson, and Rhonda Y. Williams. 2002. *Teaching the Civil Rights Movement: Freedom's Bittersweet Song.* New York and London: Routledge.

Asante-Muhammed, Dedrick, Chuck Collins, Josh Hoxie, and Emanuel Nieves. 2016. *The Ever-Growing Gap: Without Change, African-American and Latino Families Won't Match White Wealth for Centuries.* Washington, DC: CFED and Institute for Policy Studies. Retrieved July 13, 2016 (www.ips-dc.org/wp-content/uploads/2016/08/The-Ever-Growing-Gap-CFED_IPS-Final-2.pdf).

Asante-Muhammad, Dedrick, Chuck Collins, Josh Hoxie, and Emanuel Nieves. 2017. "The Road to Zero Wealth: How the Racial Wealth Divide is Hollowing Out America's Middle Class." *Prosperity Now*, September Retrieved May 28, 2019. (https://prosperitynow.org/sites/default/files/PDFs/road_to_zero_wealth.pdf).

Asencio, Marysol and Katie Acosta. 2010. "Introduction: Mapping Latino/a Sexualities Research and Scholarship." Pp. 1–12 in *Latina/o Sexualities: Probing Powers, Passions, Practices, and Policies*, edited by M. Asencio. New Brunswick, NJ: Rutgers University Press.

Ashe, Arthur R. 1988. *A Hard Road to Glory: A History of the African-American Athlete 1919–1945*. New York: Warner Books.

Ashe, Arthur R. 1988b. *A Hard Road to Glory: A History of the African-American Athlete Since 1946*. New York: Warner Books.

Astor, Gerald. 1998. *The Right to Fight: A History of African Americans in the Military*. Navato, CA: Presidio Press.

Back, Les. 2002. "Aryans Reading Adorno: Cyber-Culture and Twenty-First-Century Racism." *Ethnic and Racial Studies* 25(4):628–651.

Badger, Emily. 2015. "How Section 8 Became a 'Racial Slur.'" *Washington Post*, June 15. Retrieved August 3, 2019. (file:///C:/Users/joykat88/AppData/Local/Temp/ProQuestDocuments-2019-08-03-1.pdf).

Bahr, Howard M., Bruce A. Chadwick, and Robert C. Day, eds. 1972. *Native Americans Today: Sociological Perspectives*. New York: Harper and Row Publishers.

Bailey, Stanley R. 2008. "Unmixing for Race Making in Brazil." *American Journal of Sociology* 114(3):577–614.

Baker, Colin. 2006. *Foundations of Education and Bilingualism*, 4th ed. Bristol, UK: Multilingual Matters.

Baker, Peter. 2019. "Trump Assails Elijah Cummings, Calling District a Rat-Infested 'Mess.'" *New York Times* July 27. Retrieved August 2, 2019. www.nytimes.com/2019/07/27/us/politics/trump-elijah-cummings.html.

Baldus, David, Charles Pulaski, and George Woodworth. 1990. *Equal Justice and the Death Penalty*. Boston, MA: Northeastern University Press.

Ball, Edward. 2015. "Slavery's Trail of Tears: Retracing America's Forgotten Migration." *Smithsonian*, November, pp. 58–82.

Bane, Mary Jo and D. T. Ellwood. 1986. "Slipping Into and Out of Poverty: The Dynamics of Spells." *Journal of Human Resources* 21(1):1–23. Retrieved July 21, 2013 (www.vanneman.umd.edu/socy789b/BaneE86.pdf).

Banks, Chloe. 2018. "Disciplining Black Activism: Post-Racial Rhetoric, Public Memory, and Decorum in News Media Framing of the Black Lives Matter Movement." *Continuum* 32(6): 709–720.

Barajas, H. L. and Amy Ronnkvist. 2007. "Racialized Space: Framing Latino and Latina Experience in Public Schools." *Teachers College Record* 109(6):1517–1538.

Barlow, David E. and Melissa Hickman Barlow. 1993. "Cultural Diversity Training in Criminal Justice: A Progressive of Conservative Reform." *Social Justice* 20(3–4):69–84.

Barnes, Annie S. 2000. *Everyday Racism: A Book for All Americans*. Naperville, IL: Sourcebooks, Inc.

Barnes, P. W. and O. R. Lightsey, Jr. 2005. "Perceived Racist Discrimination, Coping, Stress, and Life Satisfaction." *Journal of Multicultural Counseling and Development* 33:48–61.

Baron, Reuben, David Y. H. Tom, and Harris M. Cooper. 1985. "Social Class, Race, and Teacher Expectations." Pp. 251–269 in *Teacher Expectations*, edited by J. B. Dusek. Hillsdale, NJ: Erlbaum.

Barry, Ellen. 2018. "What the Royal Bride-to-Be Means to Black Londoners." *The Seattle Times*, May 12. Retrieved June 29, 2019. (www.seattletimes.com/nation-world/what-the-royal-bride-to-be-means-to-black-londoners/).

Barry, Iris. 1965. *D. W. Griffith: American Film Maker*. Garden City, NY: Doubleday and Company.

Barthelemy, Anthony G. 2000. "Light, Bright, Damn *Near* White: Race, the Politics of Genealogy, and the Strange Case of Susie Guillory." Pp. 252–275 in *Creole: The History and Legacy of Louisiana's Free People of Color*, edited by S. Kein. Baton Rouge: Louisiana State University Press.

Bates, Eric. 1998. "Private Prisons." *Nation*, January 5, p. 13.

Baunach, Phyllis J. 1985. *Mothers in Prison*. New Brunswick, NJ: Transaction Books.

Bayoumi, Moustafa. 2019. "I'm a Brown Arab-American, and the US Census Refuses to Recognize Me." *Guardian*, February 14. Retrieved July 18, 2019. (www.theguardian.com/commentisfree/2019/feb/14/arab-american-census-america-racism/).

Beal, Frances M. 1969. "Double Jeopardy: To Be Black and Female." *New York: Third World Women's Alliance.* Retrieved May 5, 2013 (www.hartford-hwp.com/archives/45a/196.html).

Beale, Lewis. 2009. "Racially Exclusive Suburbs Across U.S. Dubbed the New 'Whiteopia.'" Alternet, October 6. Retrieved July 22, 2013 (www.alternet.org/story/143071/).

Beck, E. M. and Stewart E. Tolnay. 2019. "Torture and Desecration in the American South, an Exclamation Point on White Supremacy, 1877–1950." *Social Currents* 6(4):319–342.

Beer, Todd. 2016. "Police Killing of Blacks: Data for 2015." *Society Pages*, January 20. Retrieved June 22, 2016 (https://thesocietypages.org/toolbox/police-killing-of-blacks/).

Begley, Sharon. 2016. "DNA Testing Wouldn't Settle Spat Over Warren's Ancestry: Genetic Firms Say Native American DNA Lacking." *Boston Globe*, June 30. Retrieved March 16, 2019 (https://search.proquest.com/docview/1800422786?pq-origsite=summon).

Behrens, Angela, Christopher Uggen, and Jeff Manza. 2003. "Ballot Manipulation and the 'Menace of Negro Domination': Racial Threat and Felon Disenfranchisement in the United States, 1950–2002." *American Journal of Sociology* 109(3):559–605.

Beirich, Heidi. 2011. "The Year in Nativism, 2010." *Intelligence Report*, February 23. Retrieved September 7, 2011 (www.splcenter.org/get-informed/intelligence-report/browse-all-issues/2011/spring/the-year-in-nativism).

Beirich, Heidi. 2014. "White Identity Worldwide." *Intelligence Report*, 156:37–41.

Beirich, Heidi. 2019. "White Supremacy Flourishes Amid Feats of Immigration and Nation's Shifting Demographics." *Intelligence Report*, February 20. Retrieved July 28, 2019 (www.splcenter.org/fighting-hate/intelligence-report/2019/year-hate-rage-against-change).

Beito, David T. 2000. *From Mutual Aid to the Welfare State: Fraternal Societies and Social Services, 1890–1967.* Chapel Hill: University of North Carolina Press.

Bell, Joyce M. and Douglas Hartmann. 2007. "Diversity in Everyday Discourse: The Cultural Ambiguities of 'Happy Talk.'" *American Sociological Review* 72(6):895–914.

Bellah, Robert. 1967. "Civil Religion in America." *Daedalus: Journal of the American Academy of Arts and Sciences* 96(1):1–21.

Belson, Ken. 2018. "In a Busy Year, Malcolm Jenkins Raised a Fist and Checked all the Boxes." *New York Times*, January 25. Retrieved August 4, 2019. (www.nytimes.com/2018/01/25/sports/football/malcolm-jenkins-eagles-super-bowl.html).

Bender, Jeremy. 2015. "Mexico's Drug War Is Getting Even Worse." *Business Insider*, May 14. Retrieved July 2, 2016 (www.businessinsider.com/mexicos-drug-war-is-taking-worse-turn-2015-5).

Benjamin, Rich. 2009. "'Clean, Safe and High-Value' Neighborhoods Are a Nice Way of Saying 'White' Without Bringing Race into It." Alternet, October 16. Retrieved July 22, 2013 (www.alternet.org/story/143337/%22clean,_safe_and_high-value%22_neighborhoods_are_nice_ways_of_saying_%22white%22_without_bringing_race_into_it).

Bennett, Lerone. 1961. *Before the Mayflower: A History of the Negro in America, 1619–1964.* New York: Penguin Books.

Bennett, Michael J. 1996. *When Dreams Came True: The GI Bill and the Making of Modern America.* Washington and London: Brassey's.

Benns, Whitney. 2015. "American Slavery, Reinvented." *The Atlantic*, September 21. Retrieved July 1, 2016 (www.theatlantic.com/business/archive/2015/09/prison-labor-in-america/406177/).

Berg, Charles Ramirez. 2002. *Latino Images in Film: Stereotypes, Subversion, Resistance.* Austin: University of Texas Press.

Bergad, Laird W. 2007. *The Comparative Histories of Slavery in Brazil, Cuba, and the United States.* New York, Cambridge: Cambridge University Press.

Berkhofer, Robert E. 1978. *The White Man's Indian.* New York: Vintage.

Bernal, Rafael. 2016. "Hispanic Voter Registration Spikes." The Hill.com, April 27. Retrieved July 9, 2016 (http://thehill.com/latino/277824-hispanics-in-swing-states-create-daunting-electoral-map-for-gop).

Bernstein, Nina. 2010. "Officials Hid Truth of Immigrant Deaths in Jail." *New York Times*, January 9. Retrieved October 12, 2011 (www.nytimes.com/2010/01/10/us/10detain.html).

Berrey, Ellen C. 2011. "Why Diversity Became Orthodox in Higher Education, and How It Changed the Meaning of Race on Campus." *Critical Sociology* 37(5):573–596.

Berrey, Ellen C. 2015. *The Enigma of Diversity: The Language of Race and the Limits of Racial Justice.* Chicago, IL: University of Chicago Press.

Bertrand, Marianne and Sendhil Mullainathan. 2004. "Are Emily and Greg More Employable Than Lakisha and Jamal? A Field Experiment on Labor Market Discrimination." *American Economic Review* 99:991–1011.

Bever, Linsey. 2016. "'Make America White Again': A Politician's Billboard Ignites Uproar." *Washington Post*, June 23. Retrieved July 8, 2016 (www.washingtonpost.com/news/the-fix/wp/2016/06/23/make-america-white-again-a-politicians-billboard-ignites-uproar/).

Bialik, Kristen. 2017. "Key Facts about Race and Marriage, 50 Years after *Loving v. Virginia.*" Pew Research Center, June 12. Retrieved June 29, 2019 (www.pewresearch.org/fact-tank/2017/06/12/key-facts-about-race-and-marriage-50-years-after-loving-v-virginia/).

"Big Racial Divide Over Zimmerman Verdict." 2013. Pew Research Center, July 22. Retrieved July 25, 2013 (www.people-press.org/2013/07/22/big-racial-divide-over-zimmerman-verdict/).

Biggers, Jeff. 2010. "Arizona to Ban Cesar Chavez and Mexican American Studies in Schools?" AlterNet, April 30. Retrieved July 24, 2013 (www.alternet.org/speakeasy/2010/04/30/arizona-to-ban-cesar-chavez-and-mexican-american-studies-in-schools).

Bigler, Rebecca S., Julie M. Hughes, and Sheri R. Levy. 2007. "Consequences of Learning About Historical Racism Among European and African American Children." *Child Development* 78:1689–1705.

Biko, Steven. 1978. *I Write What I Like: Selected Writings by Steven Biko.* Chicago, IL: University of Chicago Press.

Billingham, Chase M. and Matthew O. Hunt. 2016. "School Racial Composition and Parental Choice: New Evidence on the Preferences of White Parents in the United States." *Sociology of Education* 89(2):99–117.

Billingsley, Andrew. 1988 [1968]. *Black Families in White America.* New York and London: Simon and Schuster.

Bischoff, Bea. 2019. "Immigrant Detention Conditions Were Atrocious Under Obama. Here's Why They're So Much Worse Under Trump." *Slate*, June 25. Retrieved June 27, 2019 (https://slate.com/news-and-politics/2019/06/trump-child-immigrant-detention-no-toothpaste-obama.html/).

Bittker, Boris I. 1973. *The Case for Black Reparations.* Boston, MA: Beacon Press.

Black, Donald. 1976. *The Behavior of Law.* New York: Academic Press.

Black, Donald. 1984. "Social Control as a Dependent Variable." In *Toward a General Theory of Social Control*, Vol. 1, *Fundamentals*, edited by D. Black. Orlando, FL: Academic Press.

Blackmon, Douglas A. 2008. *Slavery by Another Name: The Re-Enslavement of Black Americans from the Civil War to World War II.* New York: Anchor Books.

Blalock, Hubert M. 1967. *Toward a Theory of Minority Group Relations.* San Francisco, CA: Wiley and Sons Publishers.

Blau, Max. 2019. "Black Southerners are Bearing the Brunt of America's Eviction Epidemic." *Pew Trusts*, January 18. Retrieved August 1, 2019 (www.pewtrusts.org/en/research-and-analysis/blogs/).

Blauner, Robert. 1969. "Internal Colonialism and Ghetto Revolt." *Social Problems* 16(4):393–406.

Blauner, Robert. 1972. *Racial Oppression in America.* New York, San Francisco: Harper and Row Publishers.

Blay, Y. A. 2011. "Skin Bleaching and Global White Supremacy: By Way of Introduction." *Journal of Pan African Studies* 4(4):4–46.

Bleich, Erik. 2003. *Race Politics in Britain and France: Ideas and Policymaking Since the 1960s.* Cambridge, UK: Cambridge University Press.

Blight, David W. 2006. "If You Don't Tell It Like It Was, It Can Never Be as It Ought to Be." Pp. 19–34 in *Slavery and Public History: The Tough Stuff of American Memory*, edited by J. O. Horton and L. E. Horton. Chapel Hill: University of North Carolina Press.

Blinder, Alan. 2017. "Michael Slaver, Officer in Walter Scott Shooting, Gets 20-Year Sentence." *New York Times*, December 7. Retrieved March 12, 2019 (www.nytimes.com/2017/12/07/us/michael-slager-sentence-walter-scott.html).

Bliss, Catherine. 2012. *Race Decoded: The Genomic Fight for Social Justice.* Stanford, CA: Stanford University Press.

Bloom, Jack M. 1987. *Class, Race, and the Civil Rights Movement.* Bloomington and Indianapolis: Indiana University Press.

Blumberg, Rhoda Louis. 1984. *Civil Rights: The Freedom Struggle.* Woodbridge, CT: Twayne Publishing.

Blumer, Herbert. 1958. "Race Prejudice as a Sense of Group Position." *Pacific Sociological Review* 1(1):3–7.

Bogardus, E. S. 1959. *Social Distance.* Los Angeles, CA: Antioch Press.

Boger, John Charles and Gary Orfield, eds. 2005. *School Resegregation: Must the South Turn Back?* London and Chapel Hill: University of North Carolina Press.

Bogle, Donald. 1994. *Toms, Coons, Mulattoes, Mammies, and Bucks: An Interpretive History of Blacks in American Films,* 3rd ed. New York: Continuum.

Bologna, Giacomo. 2019. "Black Mississippians Twice as Likely to be Denied a Home Loan as Whites, Data Show." *Mississippi Clarion Ledger,* April 22. Retrieved August 3, 2019 (www.clarion ledger.com/story/news/politics/2019/04/22/homes-sale-black-mississippians-denied-loans-more-often/3496801002/).

Bonacich, Edna. 1972. "A Theory of Ethnic Antagonism: The Split Labor Market." *American Sociological Review* 37(5):547–559.

Bonacich, Edna. 1975. "Abolition, the Extension of Slavery, and the Position of Free Blacks: A Study of Split Labor Markets in the United States, 1830–1863." *American Journal of Sociology* 81(3): 601–628.

Bonacich, Edna. 1976. "Advanced Capitalism and Black/White Race Relations in the United States: A Split Labor Market Interpretation." *American Sociological Review* 41(1):34–51.

Bonikowski, Bart. 2005. "Flying While Arab (Or Was It Muslim? Or Middle Eastern?): A Theoretical Analysis of Racial Profiling After September 11th." *Discourse of Sociological Practice* 7(1):315.

Bonilla-Silva, Eduardo. 1997. "Rethinking Racism: Toward a Structural Interpretation." *American Sociological Review* 62(3):465–480.

Bonilla-Silva, Eduardo. 2006. *Racism Without Racists: Color-Blind Racism and the Persistence of Racial Inequality in the United States,* 2nd ed. Lanham, MD: Rowman and Littlefield.

Bonilla-Silva, Eduardo. 2010. *Racism Without Racists: Color-Blind Racism and Racial Inequality in Contemporary America,* 3rd ed. Lanham, MD: Rowman and Littlefield.

Bonilla-Silva, Eduardo and Tyrone Forman. 2000. "'I Am Not a Racist, But …': Mapping White College Students' Racial Ideology in the USA." *Discourse and Society* 11(1):50–85.

Bonvillain, Nancy. 2001. *Native Nations: Cultures and Histories of Native North America.* Upper Saddle River, NJ: Prentice Hall.

Bordt, Rebecca L. 2004. "Only Some Are Dead Men Walking: Teaching About Race Discrimination and the Death Penalty." *Teaching Sociology* 32(4):358–373.

Borr, Tamara Gilkes. 2019. "How the War on Drugs Kept Black Men Out of College." *The Atlantic,* May 15. Retrieved July 27, 2019 (www.theatlantic.com/education/archive/2019/05/war-drugs-made-it-harder-black-men-attend-college/588724/).

Borzi, P. 2012. "Push to Save Fighting Sioux Name Leaves North Dakota in Costly Limbo." *New York Times,* February 18. Retrieved April 20, 2012 (www.nytimes.com/2012/02/19/sports/push-to-save-fightingsioux-name-puts-north-dakota-in-costly-limbo.html).

Bosworth, Mary. 2010. *Explaining U.S. Imprisonment.* Los Angeles, London: Sage.

Bourdieu, Pierre. 1977. "Cultural Reproduction and Social Reproduction." Pp. 487–510 in *Power and Ideology in Education,* edited by J. Karabel and A. H. Halsey. New York: Oxford University Press.

Bourdieu, Pierre. 1991. *Language and Symbolic Power.* Cambridge, MA: Harvard University Press.

Bourdieu, Pierre and Jean-Claude Passeron. 1977. *Reproduction in Education, Society and Culture.* London: Sage Publications.

Boustan, Leah Platt. 2013. "Racial Residential Segregation in American Cities." *National Bureau of Economic Research,* May. Retrieved July 31, 2019 (www.nber.org/papers/w19045/).

Bowers, William, Benjamin Steiner, and Marla Sandys. 2001. "Death Sentencing in Black and White: An Empirical Analysis of the Role of Juror's Race and Jury Racial Composition." *Journal of Constitutional Law* 3(10):171–266.

Bowles, Samuel and Herbert Gintis. 1976. *Schooling in Capitalist America.* New York: Basic Books/Harper.

Bowman, Nicholas A. and Julie J. Park. 2014. "Interracial Contact on College Campuses: Comparing and Contrasting Predictors of Cross-Racial Interaction and Interracial Friendship." *Journal of Higher Education* 85(5):660–690.

Bowser, Benjamin P. 2007. *The Black Middle Class: Social Mobility and Vulnerability.* Boulder, CO: Lynne Rienner Press.

Braman, Donald. 2004. *Doing Time on the Outside: Incarceration and Family Life in Urban America.* Ann Arbor: University of Michigan Press.

Brazeal, Brailsford R. 1946. *The Brotherhood of Sleeping Car Porters: Its Origin and Development.* New York and London: Harper and Brothers.

Bretting, John G. and Diane-Michele Prindeville. 1998. "Environmental Justice and the Role of Indigenous Women Organizing Their Communities." Pp. 141–164 in *Environmental Injustices, Political Struggles: Race, Class, and the Environment*, edited by D. Camacho. Durham and London: Duke University Press.

Brewer, Rose M. 2006. "Thinking Critically About Race and Genetics." *Journal of Law, Medicine and Ethics* 34(3):513–519.

Brewer, Rose M. and Nancy A. Heitzeg. 2008. "The Racialization of Crime and Punishment: Criminal Justice, Color-Blind Racism, and the Political Economy of the Prison Industrial Complex." *American Behavioral Scientist* 51(5):625–644.

Bridge Initiative Team. 2016. "When Islamophobia Turns Violent: The 2016 US Presidential Elections." *Bridge Initiative*, May 2. Retrieved July 8, 2016 (http://bridge.georgetown.edu/when-islamophobia-turns-violent-the-2016-u-s-presidential-elections/).

Bright, Stephen B. 1995. "Discrimination, Death and Denial: The Tolerance of Racial Discrimination in the Infliction of the Death Penalty." *Santa Clara Law Review* 35(2):433–485.

Brodkin, Karen. 2008. "How Jews Became White Folks." Pp. 41–53 in *White Privilege: Essential Readings from the Other Side of Racism*, 3rd ed., edited by P. Rothenberg. New York: Worth Publishers.

Brown, Alleen. 2018. "Five Spills, Six Months in Operation: Dakota Access Track Record Highlights Unavoidable Reality—Pipelines Leak." *The Intercept*, January 8. Retrieved August 1, 2019 (https://theintercept.com/2018/01/09/dakota-access-pipeline-leak-energy-transfer-partners/).

Brown, Cliff and Terry Boswell. 1995. "Strikebreaking or Solidarity in the Great Strike of 1919: A Split Labor Market, Game-Theoretic, and QCA Analysis." *American Journal of Sociology* 100(6): 1479–1519.

Brown, F. 1946. *Educational Opportunities for Veterans.* Washington, DC: American Council on Education.

Brown, Gail. 2001. "Wounded Knee: The Conflict of Interpretation." Pp. 103–118 in *Myth, Memory, and the Making of the American Landscape*, edited by P. Shackel. Gainesville: University Press of Florida.

Brown, Hana E. 2013. "Racial Conflict and Policy Spillover Effects: The Role of Race in the Contemporary U.S. Welfare State." *American Journal of Sociology* 119(2):394–443.

Brown, Hana and Jennifer A. Jones. 2016. "Immigrant Rights Are Civil Rights." *Contexts* 15(2):34–39.

Brown, Mary Jane. 2000. *Eradicating This Evil: Women in the American Anti-Lynching Movement, 1892–1940.* New York, London: Garland Publishing.

Brown, Mary Jane. 2003. "Advocates in the Age of Jazz: Women and the Campaign for the Dyer Anti-lynching Bill." *Peace and Change* 28(3):378–419.

Brown, Michael K., Martin Carnoy, Elliot Currie, Troy Duster, David B. Oppenheimer, Marjorie M. Shultz, and David Wellman. 2003. *Whitewashing Race: The Myth of a Color-Blind Society.* Berkeley, Los Angeles: University of California Press.

Brownmiller, Susan. 1999. *In Our Time: Memoir of a Revolution.* Excerpt, *New York Times on the Web*. Retrieved February 22, 2013 (www.nytimes.com/books/first/b/brownmiller-time.html).

Brownstein, Ronald. 2010. "The Gray and the Brown: The Generational Mismatch." *National Journal Magazine*, July 24. Retrieved July 23, 2013 (www.nationaljournal.com/magazine/the-gray-and-the-brown-the-generational-mismatch-20100724?mrefid=site_search).

Broyard, Bliss. 2007. *One Drop: My Father's Hidden Life—A Story of Race and Family Secrets.* New York: Little, Brown and Company.

Buchanan, Susie and David Holthouse. 2006. "Rising Anti-Immigrant Sentiments Draw Extremist Elements to Issue." *Intelligence Report*, August 11. Retrieved April 15, 2013 (www.splcenter.org/get-informed/intelligence-report/browse-all-issues/2006/summer/white-hot).

Buckley, Gail. 2002. *American Patriots: The Story of Blacks in the Military from the Revolution to Desert Storm*. New York: Random House.

Buenavista, Tracy Lachica, Uma M. Jayakumar, and Kimberly Misa-Escalante. 2009. "Contextualizing Asian American Education Through Critical Race Theory: An Example of U.S. Filipino College Student Experiences." *New Directions of Institutional Research* 142:69–81. Retrieved May 2, 2013 (http://deepblue.lib.umich.edu/bitstream/handle/2027.42/63048/297_ftp.pdf?sequence=1).

Buffington, Daniel and Todd Fraley. 2011. "Racetalk and Sport: The Color Consciousness of Contemporary Discourse on Basketball." *Sociological Inquiry* 81(3):333–352.

Bullard, Robert D. 1994. *Dumping in Dixie: Race, Class, and Environmental Quality*, 2nd ed. New York, London: Garland Publishing.

Bullard, Robert D. and Beverly Wright. 2009. *Race, Place, and Environmental Justice After Katrina: Struggles to Reclaim, Rebuild, and Revitalize New Orleans and the Gulf Coast*. Boulder, CO: Westview Press.

Bullard, Robert D. and Beverly Wright. 2012. *The Wrong Complexion for Protection: How the Government Response to Disaster Endangers African American Communities*. New York: New York University Press.

Bureau of Labor Statistics. 2011. "Unemployment Rates by Race and Ethnicity, 2010." TED: The Economics Daily, October 5. Retrieved July 4, 2016 (www.bls.gov/opub/ted/2011/ted_20111005.htm)

Bureau of Labor Statistics. 2016. "Labor Force Statistics from the Current Population Survey." Retrieved October 10, 2015 (www.bls.gov/web/empsitfcpsee_eK5.htm).

Bureau of Labor Statistics. 2018. "Unemployment Rate Rose to 4.0 Percent in June 2018." TED: The Economics Daily, July 2018. Retrieved July 28, 2019 (www.bls.gov/opub/ted/2018/unemployment-rate-rose-to-4-point-0-percent-in-june-2018.htm).

Burlew, A. K. and L. R. Smith. 1991. "Measures of Racial Identity: An Overview and a Proposed Framework." *Journal of Black Psychology* 17(2):53–71.

Burnham, Phillip. 2000. *Indian Country, God's Country: Native Americans and the National Parks*. Washington, DC: Island Press.

Burton, Orville Vernon, ed. 2008. *Slavery in America*. Vol. 1. San Francisco, New York, Detroit: Gale/Cengage Learning.

Burton, Orville Vernon, ed. 2008. *Slavery in America*. Vol. 2. San Francisco, New York, Detroit: Gale/Engage Learning.

Bush, Melanie. 2011. *Everyday Forms of Whiteness: Understanding Race in a Post-Racial World*, 2nd ed. Lanham, MD: Rowman and Littlefield.

Butler, Anthea. 2015. "Shooters of Color Are Called 'Terrorists' and 'Thugs': Why Are White Shooters Called 'Mentally Ill'?" *Washington Post*, June 18. Retrieved June 4, 2016 (www.washingtonpost.com/posteverything/wp/2015/06/18/call-the-charleston-church-shooting-what-it-is-terrorism/).

Butler, Judith. 1993. *Bodies That Matter: On the Discursive Limits of Sex*. New York: Routledge.

Byrd, Sheila. 2010. "Mississippi Still Lacks a Civil Rights Museum." *Diverse Issues in Higher Education*, December 2. Retrieved July 23, 2013 (http://diverseeducation.com/article/14482/#).

Byrd, Daniel, Carla Saporta, and Rosa Maria Martinez. 2011. "The Role of Race in the Health Care Debate." The Greenlining Institute. Retrieved June 16, 2016 (http://greenlining.org/Zwp-content/uploads/2013/02/HealZhCareReportFINAL28.2.11.pdf).

Byrd, W. Carson. 2017. *Poison in the Ivy: Race Relations and the Reproduction of Inequality on Elite College Campuses*. New Brunswick, NJ: Rutgers University Press.

Cable, Sherry and Tamara L. Mix. 2003. "Economic and Race Relations: The Rise and Fall of the American Apartheid System." *Journal of Black Studies* 34(2):183–203.

Caldas, Stephen J. and Carl L. Bankston III. 2005. *Forced to Fail: The Paradox of School Desegregation*. New York: Praeger.

Calhoun, Craig, ed. 2007. *Sociology in America: A History*. Chicago and London: University of Chicago Press.

Callis, Robert R. and Melissa Kresin. 2016. "Residential Vacancies and Home Ownership in the Second Quarter 2016." US Census Bureau, Current Population Survey, Housing Vacancy Survey, July 3 (www.census.gov/housing/hvs/files/currenthvspress.pdf).

Camp, C. and G. Camp. 1995. *The Corrections Yearbook.* South Salem, NY: Criminal Justice Institute.

Cannon, Angie. 1999. "DWB: Driving While Black." *U.S. News and World Report* 126(10):72.

Carmarota, Steven A. 2010. "Immigration and Economic Stagnation: An Examination of Trends 2000 to 2010." Center for Immigration Studies, November. Retrieved September 10, 2010 (www. cis.org/highest-decade).

Caron, Simone N. 2008. *Who Chooses? American Reproductive History Since 1830.* Gainesville: University Press of Florida.

Carrier, Jim. 2004. *A Traveler's Guide to the Civil Rights Movement.* Austin, New York: Harcourt, Inc.

Carson, E. Ann. 2014. *Prisoners in 2013.* Bureau of Justice Statistics Bulletin. Washington, DC: US Department of Justice.

Carter, Andrew. 2018. "24 Years Before the Protests Over Silent Sam, UNC Athletes United Over Another Cause." *Raleigh News and Observer,* December 21. Retrieved July 1, 2019 (www. newsobserver.com/sports/article223319670.html).

Carter, Dorinda J., Stella M. Flores, and Richard J. Reddick. 2004. *Legacies of Brown: Multiracial Equity in American Education.* Cambridge, MA: Harvard Educational Review.

Carter, Robert. 2007. "Genes, Genomes and Genealogies: The Return of Scientific Racism." *Ethnic and Racial Studies* 30(4):546–556.

Casey, Karen A. and Michael D. Wiatrowski. 1996. "Women Offenders and 'Three Strikes and You're Out.'" Pp. 222–243 in *Three Strikes and You're Out: Vengeance as Public Policy,* edited by D. Shichor and D. K. Sechrest. Thousand Oaks, CA: Sage Publications.

Cashin, Sheryll. 2009. "Race, Class, and Real Estate." Pp. 59–66 in *Breakthrough Communities: Sustainability and Justice in the Next American Metropolis,* edited by M. P. Pavel. Cambridge, MA: MIT Press.

Cashin, Sheryll. 2017. *Loving: Interracial Intimacy in America and the Threat to White Supremacy.* Boston, MA: Beacon Press.

Cassel, Susie Lan, ed. 2002. *The Chinese in America: A History from Gold Mountain to the New Millennium.* Walnut Creek, CA: Alta Mira Press.

Cassidy, Laurie M. and Alex Mikulich, eds. 2007. *Interrupting White Privilege: Catholic Theologians Break the Silence.* Maryknoll, NY: Orbis Books.

Chan, Sucheng. 1991. *Asian Americans: An Interpretive History.* New York: Twayne Publishers.

Chandrasekhar, S., ed. 1992. *From India to Australia: A Brief History of Immigration; The Dismantling of the 'White Australia' Policy; Problems and Prospects of Assimilation.* La Jolla, CA: Population Review Books.

Chandrasekhar, S. 1992. "A Short History of Australian Immigration Policy with Special Reference to Indian's Nationals." Pp. 11–35 in *From India to Australia,* edited by S. Chandrasekhar. La Jolla, CA: Population Review Books.

Chang, Mitchell J., Alexander Astin, and Dongbin Kim. 2004. "Cross-Racial Interaction among Undergraduates: Some Consequences, Causes, and Patterns." *Research in Higher Education* 45(5):529–553.

Chappell, Bill. 2011. "Georgia Farmers Say Immigration Law Keeps Workers Away." NPR, May 27. Retrieved October 20, 2012 (www.npr.org/blogs/thetwo-way/2011/05/27/136718112/georgia-farmers-say-immigration-law-keeps-workers-away).

Chappell, Bill. 2015. "Number of Police Officers Killed by Gunfire Fell 14 Percent, Study Says." NPR, December 29. Retrieved July 8, 2016 (www.npr.org/sections/thetwo-way/2015/12/29/461402091/number-of-police-officers-killed-by-gunfire-fell-14-percent-in-2015-study-says).

Charles, Camille Zubrinsky. 2001. "Processes of Racial Residential Segregation." Pp. 217–271 in *Urban Inequality: Evidence from Four Cities,* edited by A. O'Conner, C. Tilly, and L. D. Bobo. New York: Russell Sage Foundation.

Charles, Camille Zubrinsky. 2003. "The Dynamics of Racial Residential Segregation." *Annual Review of Sociology* 29:167–207.

Chigumadzi, Panashe. 2017. "Why is South African Still So Anti-Black, So Many Years After Apartheid?" *Guardian*, March 10. Retrieved August 5, 2019 (www.theguardian.com/commentisfree/2017/mar/10/south-africa-anti-black-violence-afrophobic).

Chavers, Dean. 2009. *Racism in Indian Country*. New York: Peter Lang Publishing.

Chavez, Leo R. 2008. *The Latino Threat: Constructing Immigrants, Citizens, and the Nation*. Stanford, CA: Stanford University Press.

Chemerinsky, Erwin. 2005. "The Segregation and Resegregation of American Public Education: The Court's Role." Pp. 29–50 in *School Resegregation: Must the South Turn Back?*, edited by J. C. Boger and G. Orfield. Chapel Hill: University of North Carolina Press.

Chen, Michelle. 2010. "No End in Sight for Foreclosures in Communities of Color." *RaceWire*, June 24. Retrieved July 23, 2013 (www.commondreams.org/view/2010/06/24-0).

Chen, Michelle. 2011. "Muslim 'Terrorists,' White 'Lone Wolves,' and the Lessons of Oslo." Colorlines, July 27. Retrieved July 11, 2013 (www.colorlines.com/articles/muslim-terrorists-white-lone-wolves-and-lessons-oslo).

Chen, Sammi. 2018. "Racial Wealth Snapshot: Asian Americans." *Prosperity Now*, May 10. Retrieved July 27, 2019 (https://prosperitynow.org/blog/racial-wealth-snapshot-asian-americans).

Chew, Kristina. 2013. "Hey, Hollywood! Race Does Matter." *Truthout*, July 7. Retrieved June 21, 2016 (www.truth-out.org/opinion/item/17422-hey-hollywood-race-does-matter?tmpl=component).

Childs, Erica Chito. 2009. *Fade to Black and White: Interracial Images in Popular Culture*. Boulder, CO: Rowman and Littlefield.

Chivers, C. J. 1995. "Race and the Military: Looking for a Few Good (Black) Men." *Nation*, October 16, pp. 428–430.

Chokshi, Niraj. 2018. "Racism at American Pools Isn't New: A Look at a Long History." *New York Times*, August 1. Retrieved June 29, 2019 (www.nytimes.com/2018/08/01/sports/black-people-pools-racism.html).

Chou, Rosalind. 2012. *Asian American Sexual Politics*. Lanham, MA: Rowman and Littlefield Publishers.

Chow, Keith. 2016. "Why Won't Hollywood Cast Asian Actors?" *New York Times*, April 22. Retrieved July 6, 2016 (www.nytimes.com/2016/04/23/opinion/why-wont-hollywood-cast-asian-actors.html).

Chrisafis, Angelique. 2010. "Europe Immigrant Communities Under Pressure: Police Roundups: Crackdown on 'Sans Papiers.'" *Guardian*, November 17, p. 23. Retrieved September 8, 2011 (www.theguardian.com/world/2010/nov/16/france-immigration-police-roundups).

Churchill, Ward and Winona LaDuke. 1992. "Native North America: The Political Economy of Radioactive Colonialism." Pp. 241–266 in *The State of Native America: Genocide, Colonization, and Resistance*, edited by M. A. Jaimes. Boston, MA: South End Press.

Cilluffo, Anthony and Richard Fry. 2019. "An Early Look at the 2020 Electorate." *Pew Research Center Social and Demographic Trends*, January 30. Retrieved July 21, 2019 (www.pewsocialtrends.org/essay/an-early-look-at-the-2020-electorate/).

"Citizenship for Military Personnel and Family Members." 2016. US Citizenship and Immigration Services, May 23. Retrieved October 9, 2016 (www.uscis.gov/military/citizenship-military-personnel-family-members).

Clark, Kenneth B. 1989. *Dark Ghetto: Dilemmas of Social Power*, 2nd ed. Middletown, CT: Wesleyan University Press.

Clemetson, Lynette. 2000. "The New Victims of Hate: Bias Crimes Hit America's Fastest Growing Ethnic Group." *Newsweek*, November 6, p. 61.

Clotfelter, Charles T. 2002. "Private Schools, Segregation, and the Southern States." Paper presented at the Conference on the Resegregation of Southern Schools, Chapel Hill, NC, August.

Coates, Ta-Nehisi. 2017. *We Were Eight Years in Power: An American Tragedy*. New York: One World Books.

Coderoni, Gary R. 2002. "The Relationship Between Multicultural Training for Police and Effective Law Enforcement." *FBI Law Enforcement Bulletin* 71(11):16–18.

Coffin, Malcolm. 2003. "The Latino Vote: Shaping America's Electoral Future." *Political Quarterly* 74(2):214–222.

Cohen, Adam. 1995. "Back on the Chain Gang." *Time*, May 15. Retrieved July 9, 2011 (www.Time.com/time/magazine/article/0,9171,982949,00.html).

Cohen, Cathy J., Matthew Fowler, Vladimir E. Medenica, and Jon C. Rogowski. 2017. "The 'Woke' Generation? Millennial Attitudes on Race in the US." GenForward, October. Retrieved March 14, 2019 (https://genforwardsurvey.com/assets/uploads/2017/10/GenForward-Oct-2017-Final-Report.pdf).

Cohen, J. Richard. 2011. "Hate Crimes Are a National Problem." CNN.com, August 18. Retrieved September 11, 2011 (www.cnn.com/2011/08/17/opinion/cohen-racial-violence).

Cohen, Patricia. 2019. "What Reparations for Slavery Might Look Like in 2019." *New York Times*, May 26. Retrieved July 30, 2019 (www.nytimes.com/2019/05/23/business/economy/reparations-slavery.html).

Cohen, Stanley. 1972. *Folk Devils and Moral Panics: The Creation of Mods and Rockers.* Oxford, UK: Basil.

Cohen, Stanley. 2001. *States of Denial: Knowing About Atrocities and Suffering.* Cambridge, UK: Polity Press.

Cohn, D'Vera and Andrea Caumont. 2016. "10 Demographic Trends Shaping the U.S. and the World in 2016." Pew Research Center, March 31. Retrieved April 3, 2020. (www.pewresearch.org/fact-tank/2016/03/31/10-demographic-trends-that-are-shaping-the-u-s-and-the-world/).

Colby, Sandra L. and Jennifer M. Ortman. 2015. "Projections of the Size and Composition of the U.S. Population: 2014 to 2060." US Census Bureau. Retrieved June 22, 2016 (www.census.gov/content/dam/Census/library/publications/2015/demo/p25-1143.pdf).

Cole, David. 2009. "No Equal Justice: The Color of Punishment." Pp. 219–224 in *Rethinking the Color Line: Readings in Race and Ethnicity*, 4th ed., edited by C. Gallagher. New York, St. Louis: McGraw-Hill.

Cole, Nicki Lisa. 2019. "Understanding the School-to-Prison Pipeline." *ThoughtCo.* January 25. Retrieved May 27, 2019 (www.thoughtco.com/school-to-prison-pipeline-4136170).

Cole, Wade M. 2006. "Accrediting Culture: An Analysis of Tribal and Historically Black College Curricula." *Sociology of Education* 79(4):355–388.

Coleman, James S. 1966. *Equality of Educational Opportunity.* US Department of Health, Education, and Welfare. Washington, DC: US Government Printing Office.

Coleman, Robin R. 1998. *African American Viewers and the Black Situation Comedy.* New York: Garland Publishing.

Collier, Peter. 1972. "The Red Man's Burden." Pp. 51–68 in *Native Americans Today: Sociological Perspectives*, edited by H. M. Bahr, B. A. Chadwick, and R. C. Day. New York: Harper and Row Publishers.

Collins, Patricia Hill. 1990. *Black Feminist Thought: Knowledge, Consciousness, and the Politics of Empowerment.* New York: Routledge.

Collins, Patricia Hill. 1994. "Shifting the Center: Race, Class, and Feminist Theorizing About Motherhood." Pp. 45–65 in *Mothering: Ideology, Experience and Agency*, edited by E. N. Glenn, G. Chang, and L. Forcey. New York: Routledge.

Collins, Randall and Michael Makowsky. 1993. *The Discovery of Society*, 5th ed. St. Louis, New York: McGraw Hill.

Combs, Barbara Harris, Kirsten Dellinger, Jeffrey T. Jackson, Kirk A. Johnson, Willa M. Johnson, Jodi Skipper, John Sonnett, James M. Thomas, and Critical Race Studies Group, University of Mississippi. 2016. "The Symbolic Lynching of James Meredith: A Visual Analysis and Collective Counter Narrative to Racial Domination." *Sociology of Race and Ethnicity* 2(3):338–353.

"Confederate Iconography in the 20th Century." 2018. *Equal Justice Initiative.* Retrieved July 17, 2017 (https://segregationinamerica.eji.org/report/confederate-icongraphy.html).

Contenbader, Virginia and Samia Markson. 1998. "School Suspension: A Study with Secondary School Students." *Journal of School Psychology* 36:59–82.

Cook, Kevin. 2012. "Viva Moulin Rouge!" *Smithsonian* 43(9):62–70.

Cooper, Lara. 2016. "Even with Obamacare, 29 Million People Are Uninsured: Here's Why." *Fiscal Times*, May 10. Retrieved October 9, 2016 (www.thefiscaltimes.com/2016/05/10/Even-Obamacare-29-Million-People-Are-Uninsured-Here-s-Why).

Cornell, Stephen. 1988. *Return of the Native: American Indian Political Resurgence.* New York, Oxford: Oxford University Press.

Cornell, Stephen and Douglas Hartmann. 1998. *Ethnicity and Race: Making Identities in a Changing World.* Thousand Oaks, CA: Pine Forge Press.

"Corruption." 2016. *Drug War Facts.* Retrieved August 25, 2016 (www.drugwarfacts.org/cms/Corruption#sthash.80V5rGuF.dpbs).

Cortright, Joe. 2017. "How Housing Intensifies the Racial Wealth Gap." *City Lab*, September 22. Retrieved August 1, 2019 (www.citylab.com/equity/2017/09/how-housing-intensifies-the-racial-wealth-gap/540879/).

Corzine, Jay, James Creech, and Lin Corzine. 1983. "Black Concentration and Lynchings in the South: Testing Blalock's Power-Threat Hypothesis." *Social Forces* 61(3):774–796.

Cox, Oliver Cromwell. 1945. "Lynching and the Status Quo." *Journal of Negro Education* 14(4): 576–588.

Cox, Oliver Cromwell. 1948. *Caste, Class, and Race: A Study in Social Dynamics.* Garden City, NY: Doubleday.

Crawford, Garry and Victoria K. Gosling. 2009. "More Than a Game: Sports-Themed Video Games and Player Narratives." *Sociology of Sport Journal* 26(1):50–66.

Crenshaw, Kimberle. 1989. "Demarginalizing the Intersection of Race and Sex: A Black Feminist Critique of Antidiscrimination Doctrine, Feminist Theory, and Antiracist Politics." *University of Chicago Legal Forum* 1989(1):139–167.

Croll, Elisabeth. 2000. *Endangered Daughters: Discrimination and Developments in Asia.* London, New York: Routledge.

Cross, W. E., Jr., T. A. Parham, and J. E. Helms. 1991. "The Stages of Black Identity Development: Nigrescence Models." Pp. 319–338 in *Black Psychology*, 3rd ed., edited by R. Jones. San Francisco, CA: Cobb and Henry.

Crow Dog, Mary and Richard Erdoes. 1990. *Lakota Woman.* New York: Harper Perennial.

"Cruel and Unusual: Sentencing 13- and 14-Year-Old Children to Die in Prison." 2008. Equal Justice Initiative. Montgomery, AL: Equal Justice Initiative.

Cullen, Frances T., Liquin Cao, James Frank, Robert H. Langworthy, Sandra Lee Browning, Renee Kopache, and Thomas J. Stevenson. 1996. "Stop or I'll Shoot: Racial Differences in Support for Police Use of Deadly Force." *American Behavioral Scientist* 39(4):449–460.

Cullen, Jim. 1995. *The Civil War in Popular Culture: A Reusable Past.* Washington, DC: Smithsonian Institute.

Cullen, Lisa Takeuchi. 2008. "Does Obama Have an Asian Problem?" Time.com, February 18. Retrieved August 21, 2010 (www.time.com/time/politics/article/0,8599,1714292,00.html).

Cullinan, Bernice, ed. 1974. *Black Dialects and Reading.* Urbana, IL: ERIC Clearinghouse on Reading and Communication Skills, National Council of Teachers of English.

Cummins, Jim. 2000. *Language, Power, and Pedagogy: Bilingual Children in the Crossfire.* Buffalo, Toronto, Sydney: Multilingual Matters LTD.

Cummings, William. 2019. "Trump Called Al Sharpton a 'Con Man.' Sharpton Said He Makes 'Trouble for Bigots.' A Look at their Twitter Feud." *USA Today*, July 29. Retrieved July 29, 2019 (www.usatoday.com/story/news/politics/2019/07/29/trump-al-sharpton-twitter-feud-baltimore-tweets/1856787001/).

Curtis, Lewis Perry. 1997. *Apes and Angels: The Irishman in Victorian Caricature*, Rev. ed. Washington, DC: Smithsonian Institution Press.

Cutler, David M, Edward L. Glaeser, and Jacob L. Vigdor. 1999. "The Rise and Decline of the American Ghetto." *Journal of Political Economy* 107:455–506.

Dailey, Jane. "The Theology of Massive Resistance: Sex, Segregation, and the Sacred After *Brown*." Pp. 151–180 in *Massive Resistance: Southern Opposition to the Second Reconstruction*, edited by C. Webb. Oxford, New York: Oxford University Press.

Dalmage, Heather M. 2000. *Tripping on the Color-Line: Black–White Multiracial Families in a Racially Divided World.* New Brunswick, NJ: Rutgers University Press.

Dalmage, Heather M. 2004. *The Politics of Multiracialism: Challenging Racial Thinking.* Albany: State University of New York Press.

Dalton, Harlon. 2008. "Failing to See." Pp. 15–18 in *White Privilege: Essential Readings on the Other Side of Racism*, 3rd ed., edited by P. Rothenberg. New York: Worth Publishers.

Daniels, Jesse. 2009. *Cyber Racism: White Supremacy Online and the New Attack on Civil Rights*. Lanham, MD: Rowman and Littlefield.

Daniels, Roger. 1998. *Not Like Us: Immigrants and Minorities in America, 1890–1924*. Chicago, IL: Ivan R. Dee Publishers.

Darity, William, Jr., Darrick Hamilton, Mark Paul, Alan Aja, Anne Price, Antonio Moore, and Caterina Chiopis. 2018. "What We Get Wrong About Closing the Racial Wealth Gap." Samuel DuBois Cook Center on Social Equity, April. Retrieved May 28, 2019 (https://socialequity.duke.edu/sites/socialequity.duke.edu/files/site-images/FINAL%20COMPLETE%20REPORT_.pdf).

Darling-Hammond, Linda. 2007. "Race, Inequality and Educational Accountability: The Irony of 'No Child Left Behind.'" *Race, Ethnicity and Education* 10(3):245–260.

Dates, Jannette L. and William Barlow, eds. 1990. *Split Image: African Americans in the Mass Media*. Washington, DC: Howard University Press.

Davenport, Coral and Campbell Robertson. 2016. "Resettling the First American 'Climate Refugees.'" *New York Times*, May 2. Retrieved August 4, 2019 (www.nytimes.com/2016/05/03/us/resettling-the-first-american-climate-refugees.html).

David, Gary C. 2007. "The Creation of 'Arab American': Political Activism and Ethnic (Dis)Unity." *Critical Sociology* 33(5/6):833–862.

Davis, Angela Y. 1983. *Women, Race, and Class*. New York: Vintage Books.

Davis, Angela Y. 2003. *Are Prisons Obsolete?* New York: Seven Stories Press.

Davis, Bonne M. 2005. *How to Teach Students Who Don't Look Like You: Culturally Relevant Teaching Strategies*. New York: Corwin Press/Sage Publications.

Davis, F. James. 1991. *Who Is Black? One Nation's Definition*. University Park: Pennsylvania State University Press.

Davis, Laurel R. and Othello Harris. 1998. "Race and Ethnicity in US Sports Media." Pp. 154–169 in *Media Sport*, edited by L. A. Wenner. London, New York: Cengage.

De La Rosa, Mario. 2000. "An Analysis of Latino Poverty and a Plan of Action." *Journal of Poverty* 4(1/2):27–62.

Death Penalty Information Center. 2018. "Current U.S. Death Row Population by Race," October 1. Retrieved June 26, 2019 (https://deathpenaltyinfo.org/policy-issues/race/race-and-the-death-penalty-by-the-numbers).

Death Penalty Information Center. 2019. "Race of Victims." June 21.

The Death Penalty Information Center. 2019b. "Facts About the Death Penalty." June 21. Retrieved June 26, 2019. (https://files.deathpenaltyinfo.org/documents/pdf/FactSheet.f1561126387.pdf).

DeBerry, Jarvis. 2016. "B.R. Police Have History of Brutality Complaints." *The Times-Picayune*, July 8, p. B6.

Deering, T. E. and A. Stanutz. 1995. "Pre-Service Field Experience as a Multicultural Component of a Teacher Education Program." *Journal of Teacher Education* 46(5):390–394.

Dees, Morris with James Corcoran. 1996. *Gathering Storm: America's Militia Threat*. New York: HarperCollins.

Degler, Carl N. 1971. *Neither Black Nor White: Slavery and Race Relations in Brazil and the United States*. New York, Toronto: Macmillan Publishing Co.

Delgado, Richard and Jean Stefancic. 2001. *Critical Race Theory: An Introduction*. New York: New York University Press.

Deloria, Vine, Jr. 1988 [1969]. *Custer Died for Your Sins: An Indian Manifesto*. Norman: University of Oklahoma Press.

Deloria, Vine, Jr. 1992. *God Is Red: A Native View of Religion*, 2nd ed. Golden, CO: North American Press.

D'Emilio, John D. and Estelle B. Freedman. 2012. *Intimate Matters: A History of Sexuality in America*, 3rd ed. Chicago, IL: University of Chicago Press.

DeNavas-Walt, Carmen, and Bernadette D. Proctor. 2015. "Income and Poverty in the United States: 2014." Current Population Reports, US Census Bureau, September (www.census.gov/content/dam/Census/library/publications/2015/demo/p60-252.pdf).

DeNavas-Walt, Carmen, Bernadette D. Proctor, and Jessica C. Smith. 2010. "Income, Poverty, and Health Insurance Coverage in the United States: 2009." US Census Bureau, September. Retrieved June 28, 2016 (www.census.gov/prod/2010pubs/p60-238.pdf).

Department of Defense. 2015. "Demographics: Profile of the Military Community." Retrieved July 2, 2019 (http://download.militaryonesource.mil/12038/MOS/Reports/2015-Demographics-Report.pdf).

Dermansky, Julie. 2019. "Outraged, New Coalition Emerges Against Louisiana's Expanding—and Polluting—Petrochemical Industry." *Resilience*, April 30. Retrieved August 3, 2019 (www.resilience.org/stories/2019-04-30/outraged-new-coalition-emerges-against-louisianas-expanding-and-polluting-petrochemical-industry/).

Desmond, Matthew. 2016. *Evicted: Poverty and Profit in the American City.* New York: Crown Publishers.

Desmond, Matthew. 2019. "In Order to Understand the Brutality of American Capitalism, You Have to Start on the Plantation." The 1619 Project of *New York Times Magazine*, August 18. Retrieved August 31, 2019 (www.nytimes.com/interactive/2019/08/14/magazine/slavery-capitalism.html).

Desmond, Matthew and Mustafa E. Emirbayer. 2010. *Racial Domination, Racial Progress: The Sociology of Race in America.* St. Louis, New York: McGraw-Hill.

Desmond, Matthew and Carl Gershenson. 2016. "Housing and Employment Insecurity Among the Working Poor." *Social Problems* 63(1):46–67.

Detlefsen, Robert R. 1991. *Civil Rights Under Reagan.* San Francisco, CA: ICS Press.

Dettling, Lisa J., Joanne W. Hsu, Lindsay Jacobs, Kevin B. Moore, and Jeffrey P. Thompson, with Elizabeth Llanes. 2017. "Recent Trends in Wealth-Holding by Race and Ethnicity: Evidence from the Survey of Consumer Finances." FEDS Notes. Washington: Board of Governors of the Federal Reserve System, September 27. Retrieved May 28, 2019 (www.federalreserve.gov/econres/notes/feds-notes/recent-trends-in-wealth-holding-by-race-and-ethnicity-evidence-from-the-survey-of-consumer-finances-20170927.htm).

Dewey, John. 1916 [1926]. *Democracy and Education.* New York: Macmillan.

Diamond, John B., Amanda E. Lewis, and Lamont Gordon. 2007. "Race and School Achievement in a Desegregated Suburb: Reconsidering the Oppositional Culture Explanation." *International Journal of Qualitative Studies in Education* 20(6):655–679.

DiAngelo, Robin. 2018. *White Fragility: Why It's So Hard for White People to Talk about Racism.* Boston, MA: Beacon Press.

Dickerman, Charles, Jeff Christensen, and Stella Beatriz Kerl-McClain. 2008. "Big Breasts and Bad Guys: Depictions of Gender and Race in Video Games." *Journal of Creativity in Mental Health* 3(1):20–29.

Dierenfield, Bruce J. 2008. *The Civil Rights Movement*, revised ed. London, New York: Pearson Longman.

Dill, Bonnie Thornton, Sandra Murray Nettles, and Lynn Weber. 2001. "Defining the Work of the Consortium: What Do We Mean by Intersections?" *Connections: Newsletter for the Consortium on Race, Gender, and Ethnicity*, Spring, p. 4. Retrieved June 15, 2013 (www.crge.umd.edu/pdf/RC2001_spring.pdf).

Dillahunt, Ajamu, Brian Miller, Mike Prokosch, Jeannette Huezo, and Dedrick Muhammad. 2010. *State of the Dream 2010: Drained, Jobless and Foreclosed in Communities of Color.* Boston, MA: United for a Fair Economy.

Dillard, J. L. 1973. *Black English: Its History and Usage in the United States.* New York: Vintage Books, Random House.

Dinnerstein, Leonard and David M. Reimers. 1982. *Ethnic Americans: A History of Immigration and Assimilation.* New York: Harper and Rowe.

DiTomaso, Nancy. 2013. *The American Non-Dilemma: Racial Inequality Without Racism.* New York: Russell Sage Foundation.

Dobbs, Michael. 2003. "Education 'Miracle' Has a Math Problem." *Washington Post*, November 9. Retrieved April 12, 2005 (www.washingtonpost.com/archive/politics/2003/11/08/education-miracle-has-a-math-problem/20a51c3b-0100-4b1b-be23-edeb78b7debc/).

Doering, January 2016. "Visibly White: How Community Policing Activists Negotiate Their Whiteness." *Sociology of Race and Ethnicity* 2(1):106–119.

Dolan, Jay P. 2008. *The Irish Americans: A History.* New York: Bloomsbury Press.

Dominguez, Virginia. 1986. *White by Definition: Social Classification in Creole Louisiana.* New Brunswick, NJ: Rutgers University Press.

Donadio, Rachel. 2011. "Italy Seeks to Use Forces to Halt Illegal Immigrants from Tunisia." *New York Times*, February 14, p. A4. Retrieved September 8, 2011 (www.lexisnexis.com/lnacui2api/delivery/PrintDoc.do?jobHandle=1826%3A3052815).

Donadio, Rachel and Alan Cowell. 2011. "French and Italian Leaders Seek Tighter Controls on Migration." *New York Times*, April 27, p. A4. Retrieved September 8, 2011 (www.lexisnexis.com/lnacui2api/delivery/PrintDoc.do?jobHandle=2828%3A3052815).

Donato, Ruben. 1997. *The Other Struggle for Equal Schools: Mexican Americans During the Civil Rights Era.* Albany: State University of New York Press.

Dong, Harvey. 2014. "Transforming Student Elites into Community Activists: A Legacy of Asian American Activism." Pp. 186–205 in *Asian Americans: The Movement and the Moment*, edited by S. Louie and G. Omatsu. Los Angeles, CA: UCLA Asian American Studies Center Press.

Dow, Whitney and Marco Williams. 2003. *Two Towns of Jasper.* Arlington, VA: PBS Video.

Dowling, Julie A. 2014. *Mexican Americans and the Question of Race.* Austin: University of Texas Press.

Downs, Jim. 2015. *Sick from Freedom: African American Illness and Suffering during the Civil War and Reconstruction*, reprint ed. Oxford, New York: Oxford University Press.

Dreisinger, Baz. 2008. *Near Black: White-to-Black Passing in American Culture.* Amherst, MA: University of Massachusetts Press.

Dreisinger, Baz. 2016. *Incarceration Nations.* New York: Other Press.

Drutman, Lee. 2003. "Corporate Crime Acts Like a Thief in the Night." *Los Angeles Times*, November 4. Retrieved July 24, 2013 (http://articles.latimes.com/2003/nov/04/opinion/oe-drutman4).

Dubel, Janice L. 2001. "Remembering a Japanese American Concentration Camp at Manzanar National Historic Site." Pp. 85–102 in *Myth, Memory, and the Making of the American Landscape*, edited by P. Shackel. Gainesville: University Press of Florida.

Du Bois, W. E. B. 1899. *The Philadelphia Negro: A Social Study.* Philadelphia: University of Pennsylvania Press.

Du Bois, W. E. B. 1935. *Black Reconstruction, 1860–1880.* Oxford: Oxford University Publishers.

Du Bois, W. E. B. 1989 [1903]. *The Souls of Black Folk.* New York: Penguin Books.

Du Bois, W. E. B. 2003 [1920]. *Darkwater: Voices from within the Veil.* New York: Humanity Books.

Duffin, Erin. 2019. "Rate of Home Ownership in the United States in 2017, by Race." Statista, US Census Bureau, April 29. Retrieved July 28, 2019 (www.statista.com/statistics/639685/us-home-ownership-rate-by-race/).

Duffin, Erin. 2019b. "Poverty Rate in the US in 2017, by Ethnic Group." Statista, US Census Bureau, April 29. Retrieved July 27, 2019 (www.statista.com/statistics/200476/us-poverty-rate-by-ethnic-group).

Dumars, T. 1968. "Indictment Under the 'Major Crimes Act': An Exercise in Unfairness and Unconstitutionality." *Arizona Law Review* 10:691–705.

Dunaway, Wilma A. 2003. *Slavery in the American Mountain South.* Cambridge, New York: Cambridge University Press.

Dunbar-Ortiz, Roxanne. 2014. *An Indigenous Peoples' History of the United States.* Boston, MA: Beacon Press.

Dunker, Chris. 2019. "UNL Project Illustrates History of Slaves Suing for their Freedom." *The Lincoln Journal Star*, May 17. Retrieved May 21, 2019 (https://journalstar.com/news/local/education/unl-project-illustrates-history-of-slaves-suing-for-their-freedom/article_bc748d1b-b536-5dc7-a292-e0534358ef51.html?fbclid=IwAR2zKkMuZeMn_2WGtgKghLkF_NvK6UG-cvd0KmNsDBfsq-fZSdbjwPvI4oE).

Dunlop, Janet C. 2007. "The U.S. Video Game Industry: Analyzing Representation of Gender and Race." *International Journal of Technology and Human Interaction* 3(2):96–109.

Durkheim, Émile. 1964. *The Rules of the Sociological Method.* New York: Free Press.

Durkheim, Émile. 1967. *The Division of Labor in Society.* New York: Free Press.

Duster, Troy. 1995. "Review Symposium: The Bell Curve." *Contemporary Sociology* 24(2):158–161.

Duster, Troy. 2003. *Backdoor to Eugenics*, 2nd ed. New York: Routledge.

Duster, Troy. 2005. "Race and Reification in Science." *Science* 307(5712):1050–1051.

Duster, Troy. 2011. "Ancestry Testing and DNA: Uses, Limits and *Caveat Emptor*." Pp. 99–115 in *Race and the Genetic Revolution: Science, Myth, and Culture*, edited by S. Krimsky and K. Sloan. New York: Columbia University Press.

Dworkin, Anthony Gary. 1968. "No Siesta Manana: The Mexican-American in Los Angeles." Pp. 389–439 in *Our Children's Burden: Studies of School Desegregation in Nine American Communities*, edited by R. W. Mack. New York: Vintage Books.

Dyson, Michael Eric. 1993. *Reflecting Black African American Cultural Criticism*. Minneapolis: University of Minnesota Press.

Eason, John M. 2017. *Big House on the Prairie: Rise of the Rural Ghetto and Prison Proliferation*. Chicago, IL: University of Chicago Press.

Easter, Luke. 2011. "Akron Mom Incarcerated? Kids to a Better School?" *Salem-News*, February 16. Retrieved July 24, 2013 (www.salem-news.com/articles/february162011/akron-mom-jailed-le.php).

Economist. 2001. "Let the Huddled Masses In." *Economist*, March 29. Retrieved September 31, 2001 (www.economist.com/node/554349).

Economist. 2008. "Getting It Right on the Money." *Economist*, April 3. Retrieved October 9, 2016 (www.economist.com/node/10958702).

Edin, Kathryn and Laura Lein. 1997. *Making Ends Meet: How Single Mothers Survive Welfare and Low-Wage Work*. New York: Russell Sage Foundation.

Egan, Timothy. 1999. "Crack's Legacy: A Special Report." *New York Times*, September 19. Retrieved July 1, 2016 (www.nytimes.com/1999/09/19/us/crack-s-legacy-a-special-report-a-drug-ran-its-course-then-hid-with-its-users.html?pagewanted=all).

Eggers, Dave. 2009. *Zeithoun*. New York: Vintage Books.

Ehrlich, Howard J. 2009. *Hate Crimes and Ethnoviolence: The History, Current Affairs, and Future of Discrimination in America*. Boulder, CO: Westview Press.

Eitzen, D. Stanley, Maxine Baca Zinn, and Kelly Eitzen Smith. 2009. *Social Problems*, 11th ed. Boston, New York, San Francisco: Pearson.

Eitzen, D. Stanley and George H. Sage. 2003. *Sociology of North American Sport*, 7th ed. Boston, St. Louis, New York: McGraw-Hill.

Eligon, John. 2019. "Busing Worked, So Why are Its Schools Becoming More Segregated?" *New York Times*, July 28. Retrieved August 3, 2019 (www.nytimes.com/2019/07/28/us/busing-louisville-student-segregation.html).

Elmelech, Yuval. 2008. *Transmitting Inequality: Wealth and the American Family*. Lanham, Boulder, New York: Rowman and Littlefield Publishers.

Embrick, David G. 2011. "The Diversity Ideology in the Business World: A New Oppression for a New Age." *Critical Sociology* 37(5):541–556.

Embrick, David G. 2015. "Two Nations, Revisited: The Lynching of Black and Brown Bodies, Police Brutality, and Racial Control in 'Post-Racial' Amerikka." *Critical Sociology* 41(6):835–843.

Emery, Kathy, Linda Reid Gold, and Sylvia Braselmann. 2008. *Lessons from Freedom Summer: Ordinary People Building Extraordinary Movements*. Monroe, MN: Common Courage Press.

Eng, Aimee and Daniel McFarland. 2006. *The Japanese Question: San Francisco Education in 1906*. Stanford, CA: Stanford University School of Education.

Ennals, Richard. 2007. *From Slavery to Citizenship*. Oxford, UK: John Wiley and Sons.

Ennis, John Wellington. 2016. "Confronting Voter Suppression in 2016." *Huffington Post*, April 29. Retrieved July 9, 2016 (www.huffingtonpost.com/john-wellington-ennis/confronting-voter-suppres_b_9812612.html).

Epstein, Rebecca, Jamilia J. Blake, and Thalia González. 2017. "Girlhood Interrupted: The Erasure of Black Girls' Childhood." Center on Poverty and Inequality Georgetown Law. Retrieved June 26, 2019 (www.blendedandblack.com/wp-content/uploads/2017/08/girlhood-interrupted.pdf).

Erdmans, Mary. 1995. "Immigrants and Ethnics: Conflict and Identity in Chicago Polonia." *The Sociological Quarterly* 36(1):175–195.

Erigha, Maryann. 2019. *The Hollywood Jim Crow: The Racial Politics of the Movie Industry*. New York: New York University Press.

Escobar, Arturo. 1995. *Encountering Development: The Making and Unmaking of the Third World.* Princeton, NJ: Princeton University Press.

Espenshade, Thomas J., and Alexandria Walton Radford. 2009. *No Longer Separate, Not Yet Equal: Race and Class in Elite College Admissions and Campus Life.* Princeton, NJ: Princeton University Press.

Espiritu, Yen Le. 1992. *Asian American Panethnicity: Bridging Institutions and Identities.* Philadelphia, PA: Temple University Press.

Espiritu, Yen Le. 2009. "Asian American Panethnicity: Contemporary National and Transnational Possibilities." Pp. 87–93 in *Rethinking the Color Line: Readings in Race and Ethnicity,* 4th ed., edited by C. A. Gallagher. St. Louis and New York: McGraw-Hill.

Essed, Philomena. 1991. *Understanding Everyday Racism: An Interdisciplinary Theory.* Newbury Park, CA: Sage.

Estes, Nick. 2019. *Our History is Our Future: Standing Rock Versus the Dakota Access Pipeline and the Long Tradition of Indigenous Resistance.* New York: Verso.

Eubanks, W. Ralph. 2003. *Ever Is a Long Time: A Journey into Mississippi's Dark Past.* New York: Basic Books.

Eyerman, Ron and Andrew Jamison. 1998. *Music and Social Movements: Mobilizing Traditions in the Twentieth Century.* Cambridge, UK: Cambridge University Press.

Fadulu, Lola. 2019. "HUD Proposes to Raise Bar for Housing Discrimination Cases." *Raleigh News and Observer*, August 4, p. 4A.

Faiola, Anthony. 2010. "Italy Closes the Door on Gypsies." *Washington Post*, suburban ed., October 12, p. A1. Retrieved on September 8, 2011 (www.lexisnexis.com/lnacui2api/delivery/PrintDoc.do?jobHandle=2827%3A3052817).

Fairlie, Robert W. 2002. "Private Schools and 'Latino Flight' from Black Schoolchildren." *Demography* 39(4):655–674.

Fang, Lee. 2010. "Prison Industry Funnels Donations to State Lawmakers Introducing SB1070-Like Bills Around the Country." *Think Progress*, September 16. Retrieved September 5, 2011 (http://thinkprogress.org/politics/2010/09/16/117661/sb1070-prison-lobby/).

Farber, Henry. 2005. "What Do We Know about Job Loss in the United States? Evidence from the Displaced Workers Survey, 1984–2004." *Economic Perspectives* 2:13–28.

Farley, John E. 1988. *Majority-Minority Relations,* 2nd ed. Englewood Cliffs, NJ: Prentice Hall.

Farley, John E. 2005. *Majority-Minority Relations,* 5th ed. Upper Saddle River, NJ: Prentice Hall.

Farley, Reynolds, Suzanne Bianchi, and Diane Colasanto. 1979. "Barriers to the Racial Integration of Neighborhoods: The Detroit Case." *Annals of the American Academy of Political and Social Science* 441:97–113.

Farley, Reynolds, Howard Schuman, Suzanne Bianchi, Diane Colasanto, and Shirley Hatchett. 1978. "Chocolate City, Vanilla Suburbs: Will the Trend Toward Racially Separate Communities Continue?" *Social Science Research* 7(4):319–344.

Farley, Reynolds, Charlotte Steeh, Tara Jackson, Maria Krysan, and Keith Reeves. 1993. "Continued Racial Residential Segregation in Detroit: 'Chocolate City, Vanilla Suburbs.'" *Journal of Housing Research* 4(1):1–38.

Farley, Reynolds, Charlotte Steeh, Tara Jackson, Maria Krysan, and Keith Reeves. 1994. "Stereotypes and Segregation: Neighborhoods in the Detroit Area." *American Journal of Sociology* 100(3):750–80.

Feagin, Joe. 2006. *Systemic Racism: A Theory of Oppression.* New York: Routledge.

Feagin, Joe. 2010. *The White Racial Frame: Centuries of Racial Framing and Counter-Framing.* New York and London: Routledge.

Feagin, Joe. 2012. *White Party, White Government: Race, Class and U.S. Politics.* New York and London: Routledge.

Feagin, Joe. 2013. *The White Racial Frame: Centuries of Racial Framing and Counter-Framing,* 2nd ed. New York: Routledge.

Feagin, Joe R. and Hernan Vera. 2008. *Liberation Sociology,* 2nd ed. Boulder, CO: Paradigm Publishers.

Feagin, Joe R., Hernan Vera, and Pinar Batur. 1995. *White Racism: The Basics.* New York and London: Routledge.

Feagin, Joe R., Hernan Vera, and Nikitah Imani. 1996. *The Agony of Education: Black Students at White Colleges and Universities.* New York and London: Routledge.

Feather, Leonard. 1962. *Encyclopedia of Jazz.* New York: Bonanza Books.

Federal Bureau of Prisons. 2019. "Inmate Race." June 22. Retrieved June 26, 2019 (www.bop.gov/about/statistics/statistics_inmate_race.jsp).

Feimster, Crystal N. 2011. *Southern Horrors: Women and the Politics of Rape and Lynching.* Boston, MA: Harvard University Press.

Feimster, Crystal. 2018. "Ida B. Wells and the Lynching of Black Women." *New York Times*, April 28. Retrieved February 28, 2020. (www.nytimes.com/2018/04/28/opinion/sunday/ida-b-wells-lynching-black-women.html).

Ferber, Abby. 1998. *White Man Falling: Race, Gender, and White Supremacy.* Lanham, MD: Rowman and Littlefield.

Ferguson, Ronald E. 1998. "Teachers' Perceptions and Expectations and the Black–White Test Score Gap." Pp. 273–317 in *The Black–White Test Score Gap*, edited by C. Jencks and M. Phillips. Washington, DC: Brookings Institution.

Fiel, Jeremy E. 2013. "Decomposing School Resegregation: School Closure, Racial Imbalance, and Racial Isolation." *American Sociological Review* 78(5):828–848.

Fingerhut, Hannah. 2017. "Support for 2010 Health Care Law Reaches New High." Pew Research Center, February 23. Retrieved August 4, 2019 (www.pewresearch.org/fact-tank/2017/02/23/support-for-2010-health-care-law-reaches-new-high/).

Finley, Taryn. 2016. "Texas Woman Dies in Police Custody After Two Weeks of 'Gross Negligence.'" *The Huffington Post*, May 19. Retrieved February 28, 2020 (www.huffpost.com/entry/texas-woman-dies-in-police-custody-after-two-weeks-of-gross-negligence_n_573dc687e4b0aee7b8e91a11).

Fins, Deborah. 2013. "Death Row USA." *NAACP Legal Defense and Education Fund*, Winter, pp. 1–64.

Fischer, Claude S., Michael Hout, Martin Sánchez Jankowski, Samuel R. Lucas, Ann Swidler, and Kim Voss. 1996. *Inequality by Design: Cracking the Bell Curve Myth.* Princeton, NJ: Princeton University Press.

Fisher, Miles Mark. 1990. *Negro Slave Songs in the United States.* New York: A Citadel Press Book.

Fitzgerald, Kathleen J. 2001. "White Like Me: Reproducing the Racial Hierarchy in a Teacher Education Program." Paper presented at the Midwest Sociological Society Annual Meeting, St. Louis, MO, April.

Fitzgerald, Kathleen J. 2007. *Beyond White Ethnicity: Developing a Sociological Understanding of Native American Identity Reclamation.* Lanham, MD: Lexington Books.

Fitzgerald, Kathleen J. 2014. "Interrogating the Invisibility of White Privilege." Paper presented at the Association for Humanist Sociology Annual Meeting, Cleveland, OH, October.

Fitzgerald, Kathleen J. 2014b. "Reifying Race: Genetic Genealogy and the Maintenance of the Racial Hierarchy." American Sociological Association Annual Meetings, San Francisco, CA, August.

Fitzgerald, Kathleen J. 2017. "Understanding Racialized Homophobic and Transphobic Violence." In *Violence Against Black Bodies*, edited by S. Weissinger, E. Watson, and D. Mack. New York: Routledge.

Fitzgerald, Kathleen and Diane M. Rodgers. 2000. "Radical Social Movement Organizations: A Theoretical Model." *Sociological Quarterly* 41(4):573–592.

Flanders, Laura. 2019. "Pot Industry Owes Reparations to Those Criminalized for Drug Use." *Truthout*, May 25. Retrieved June 27, 2019 (https://truthout.org/articles/pot-industry-owes-reparations-to-those-criminalized-for-drug-use/).

Fletcher, J. J. 1989. *Clean, Clad, and Courteous: A History of Aboriginal Education in New South Wales.* New South Wales: Southwood Press.

Flores-Gonzalez, Nilda. 2002. *School Kids/Street Kids: Identity Development in Latino Students.* New York: Teachers College Press.

Flores, Richard R. 2000. "The Alamo: Myth, Public History, and the Politics of Inclusion." *Radical History Review* 77:91–103.

Foley, Neil. 2008. "Becoming Hispanic: Mexican Americans and Whiteness." Pp. 49–60 in *White Privilege: Essential Readings on the Other Side of Racism*, 3rd ed., edited by P. Rothenberg. New York: Worth Publishers.

Fordham, Signithia and John Ogbu. 1986. "Black Students' School Success: Coping with the 'Burden of "Acting White." ' " *Urban Review* 18(3):181.

Forman, James, Jr. 2017. *Locking Up Our Own: Crime and Punishment in Black America*. New York: Farrar, Straus and Giroux.

Forman, Tyrone A. 2004. "Color-Blind Racism and Racial Indifference: The Role of Racial Apathy in Facilitating Enduring Inequalities." Pp. 43–66 in *The Changing Terrain of Race and Ethnicity*, edited by M. Krysan and A. Lewis. New York: Russell Sage Foundation.

Forman, Tyrone A. and Amanda Lewis. 2006. "Racial Apathy and Hurricane Katrina: The Social Anatomy of Prejudice in the Post–Civil Rights Era." *Du Bois Review* 3(1):175–202.

"Forum: What Does a Genuine Commitment to Diversity Look Like?" 2016. *Chronicle of Higher Education*, May 15. Retrieved June 15, 2016 (http://chronicle.com/article/Forum-What-Does-a-Genuine/236449).

Fountain, Ben. 2018. "Slavery and the Origins of the American Police State." *Medium* Sept. 17. Retrieved Feb. 28, 2020. (https://medium.com/s/story/slavery-and-the-origins-of-the-american-police-state-ec318f5ff05b).

Fox, Helen. 2001. *When Race Breaks Out: Conversations About Race and Racism in College Classrooms*. New York, Washington, DC: Peter Lang Publishers.

Fox, Helen. 2009. *When Race Breaks Out: Conversations About Race and Racism in College Classrooms*, revised ed. New York, Washington, DC: Peter Lang Publishers.

Frailing, Kelly and Dee Wood Harper. 2007. "Crime and Hurricanes in New Orleans." Pp. 51–70 in *The Sociology of Katrina: Perspectives on a Modern Catastrophe*, edited by D. L. Brunsma, D. Overfelt, and J. S. Picou. Lanham, MD: Rowman and Littlefield Publishers.

Frankenberg, Ruth. 1993. *White Women, Race Matters: The Social Construction of Whiteness*. Minneapolis: University of Minnesota Press.

Franklin, John Hope. 2009. "Foreword." Pp. xi–xii in *One America in the 21st Century: The Report of President Bill Clinton's Initiative on Race*, edited by S. F. Lawson. London and New Haven, CT: Yale University Press.

Franklin, John Hope and Alfred A. Moss, Jr. 2000. *From Slavery to Freedom: A History of African Americans*, 8th ed. Boston, St. Louis: McGraw-Hill.

Frazier, E. Franklin. 1939. *The Negro Family in the United States*. South Bend, IN: University of Notre Dame Press.

Frazier, E. Franklin. 1947. "Sociological Theory and Race Relations." *American Sociological Review* 12(3):265–271.

Frazier, E. Franklin. 1957. *Black Bourgeoisie*. Glencoe, IL: Free Press.

Frazier, E. Franklin. 1966 [1939]. *The Negro Family in the United States*. Chicago, IL: University of Chicago Press.

Fredrickson, G. M. 1971. *The Black Image in the White Mind: The Debate on Afro-American Character and Destiny, 1817–1914*. New York: Harper and Row.

Freire, Paulo. 1993 [1970]. *Pedagogy of the Oppressed*. New York: The Continuum Publishing Company.

Fry, P. G. and L. J. McKinney. 1997. "A Qualitative Study of Pre-Service Teachers' Early Field Experiences in an Urban, Culturally Different School." *Urban Education* 32(2):184–201.

Fujimura, Joan H. and Ramya Rajagopalan. 2011. "Different Differences: The Use of 'Genetic Ancestry' Versus Race in Biomedical Human Genetic Research." *Social Studies of Science* 41(1):5–30.

Fuller, M. L. 1992. "Teacher Education Programs and Increasing Minority School Populations: An Educational Mismatch?" Pp. 182–199 in *Research and Multicultural Education: From the Margins to the Mainstream*, edited by C. Grant. London: Falmer.

Gallaher, Carolyn. 2003. *On the Fault Line: Race, Class, and the American Patriot Movement*. Lanham, MD: Rowman and Littlefield.

Gamboa, Suzanne. 2018. "Latinos Show Record Gains in Congress, though Numbers Are Still Low." NBC News November 15. Retrieved July 20, 2019 (www.nbcnews.com/news/latino/latinos-show-record-gains-congress-though-numbers-are-still-low-n936781).

Gamson, William A. 1992. "The Social Psychology of Collective Action." Pp. 53–76 in *Frontiers in Social Movement Theory*, edited by A. D. Morris and C. M. Mueller. New Haven, CT: Yale University Press.

Gans, Herbert J., ed. 1979. *On the Making of Americans: Essays in Honor of David Riesman*. Philadelphia: University of Pennsylvania Press.

Garafoli, Joe. 2012. "Asian American Immigrants Outpace Latinos." *San Francisco Chronicle*, June 19. Retrieved June 20, 2013 (www.sfgate.com/politics/joegarafoli/article/Asian-American-immigrants-outpace-Latinos-3643191.php).

Garcia, F. Chris and Gabriel R. Sanchez. 2008. *Hispanics and the U.S. Political System: Moving into the Mainstream*. Upper Saddle River, NJ: Pearson/Prentice Hall.

Garland, David, ed. 2001. *Mass Imprisonment: Social Causes and Consequences*. Thousand Oaks, CA: Sage Publications.

Garland, Jon and Michael Rowe. 1999. "Field of Dreams? An Assessment of Anti-Racism in British Football." *Journal of Ethnic and Migration Studies* 25(2):335–344.

Garland, Jon and Michael Rowe. 1999b. "Selling the Game Short: An Examination of the Role of Antiracism in British Football." *Sociology of Sport Journal* 16(1):35–53.

Gedicks, Al. 2001. *Resource Rebels: Native Challenges to Mining and Oil Corporations*. Cambridge, MA: South End Press.

Geggus, David P. 2001. *The Impact of the Haitian Revolution in the Atlantic World*. Columbia: University of South Carolina Press.

Geiger, A. W. 2017. "Many Minority Students Go To Schools Where at Least Half of Their Peers Are Their Race or Ethnicity." Pew Research Center Fact Tank, October 25. Retrieved May 25, 2019 (www.pewresearch.org/fact-tank/2017/10/25/many-minority-students-go-to-schools-where-at-least-half-of-their-peers-are-their-race-or-ethnicity/).

Gelder, Ken. 1997. "Introduction to Part 2: The Birmingham Tradition and Cultural Studies." Pp. 83–89 in *The Subcultures Reader*, 2nd ed., edited by K. Gelder and S. Thornton. London: Routledge.

Genovese, Eugene D. and Elizabeth Fox-Genovese. 2008. *Slavery in White and Black: Class and Race in the Southern Slaveholders' New World Order*. London, UK: Cambridge University Press.

Gerard, Jeremy. 2015. "Hollywood's Diversity Gap Has Spawned an 'Epidemic of Invisibility'—Study." Deadline.com, August 5. Retrieved July 6, 2016 (http://deadline.com/2015/08/study-reveals-epidemic-of-invisibilty-in-movie-casting-usc-annenberg-center-1201492361/).

Gettys, Travis. 2016. "Black and Latino Girls Walk Off Soccer Field After Whites Chant 'Donald Trump, Build That Wall.'" Rawstory.com, April 11. Retrieved July 6, 2016 (www.rawstory.com/2016/04/black-and-latina-girls-walk-off-soccer-field-after-whites-chant-donald-trump-build-that-wall/).

Gibbons, Robert and Lawrence Katz. 1991. "Layoffs and Lemons." *Journal of Labor Economics* 9:351–80.

Gibson, Donald P. 1989. "Introduction." Pp. vii–xxxviii in *The Souls of Black Folk*, by W. E. B. Du Bois. New York: Penguin Books.

Gifford, Brian. 2005. "Combat Casualties and Race: What Can We Learn from the 2003–2004 Iraq Conflict?" *Armed Forces and Society* 31(2):201–225.

Gillborn, David. 2005. "Education Policy as an Act of White Supremacy: Whiteness, Critical Race Theory and Education Reform." *Journal of Education Policy* 20(4):485–505.

Gillespie, Nick. 2015. "There Is No 'War on Cops'; There Is a Long Overdue Conversation About Police Brutality." Reason.com, September 3. Retrieved July 7, 2016 (https://reason.com/blog/2015/09/03/there-is-no-war-on-cops-there-is-a-long).

Glazer, Nathan and Daniel Patrick Moynihan. 1970 [1963]. *Beyond the Melting Pot*. Cambridge, MA: MIT Press.

Glymph, Thavolia. 2008. *Out of the House of Bondage: The Transformation of the Plantation Household*. New York: Cambridge University Press.

Goff, Phillip Atiba, Matthew Christian Jackson, Brooke Allison Lewis Di Leone, Carmen Marie Culotta, and Natalie Ann DiTomasso. 2014. "The Essence of Innocence: Consequences of Dehumanizing Black Children." *Journal of Personality and Social Psychology* 106(4):526–545.

Goffman, Erving. 1961. *Asylums: Essays on the Social Situation of Mental Patients and Other Inmates.* Garden City, NY: Anchor Books.

Goffman, Erving. 1963. *Stigma: Notes on the Management of Spoiled Identity.* New York: Touchstone Books.

Golash-Boza, Tanya Marie. 2012. *Yo Soy Negro: Blackness in Peru.* Gainesville: University Press of Florida.

Goldberg, Carey. 1997. "Hispanic Households Struggle Amid Broad Decline in Income." *New York Times,* January 30, p. A1.

Goldberg, David Theo. 1997. *Racial Subjects: Writings on Race in America.* Thousand Oaks, CA: Routledge.

Goldberg, Robert A. 1996 [1991]. *Grassroots Resistance: Social Movements in Twentieth-Century America.* Prospect Heights, IL: Waveland Press.

Golden, Marita. 2003. *Don't Play in the Sun: One Woman's Journey Through the Color Complex.* New York: Doubleday.

Goldsby, Jacqueline. 2006. *A Spectacular Secret: Lynching in American Life and Literature.* Chicago, IL: University of Chicago Press.

Gomer, Justin. 2018. "Housing and the Racial Wealth Gap: A Historical Overview." KCET.org, September 4. Retrieved July 31, 2019 (www.kcet.org/shows/city-rising/housing-and-the-racial-wealth-gap-a-historical-overview).

Gonnerman, Jennifer. 2004. *Life on the Outside: The Prison Odyssey of Elaine Bartlett.* New York: Picador.

Gonzales-Day, Ken. 2006. *Lynching in the West, 1850–1935.* Durham, NC: Duke University Press.

Gonzalez van Cleve, Nicole. 2016. *Crook County: Racism and Injustice in America's Largest Criminal Court.* Stanford, CA: Stanford Law Books.

Good, Thomas L. and Jere E. Brophy. 2000. *Looking in Classrooms,* 8th ed. New York, Sydney: Longman.

Gordon, Linda. 1990. *Woman's Body, Woman's Right: Birth Control in America,* revised ed. New York: Penguin Books.

Gordon, Milton. 1964. *Assimilation in American Life.* New York: Oxford University Press.

Gotham, Kevin Fox. 1998. "Blind Faith in the Free Market: Urban Poverty, Residential Segregation, and Federal Housing Retrenchment, 1979–1995." *Sociological Inquiry* 68(1):1–31.

Gotham, Kevin Fox. 2000. "Racialization and the State: The Housing Act of 1934 and the Creation of the Federal Housing Administration." *Sociological Perspectives* 43(2):291–317.

Gotham, Kevin Fox. 2014. "Racialization and Rescaling: Post-Katrina Rebuilding and the Louisiana Road Home Program." *International Journal of Urban and Regional Research* 38(3):773–790.

Gould, Larry A. 1997. "Can an Old Dog Be Taught New Tricks? Teaching Cultural Diversity to Police Officers." *Policing* 20(2):339–349.

Graham, David A. 2016. "What's the Goal of Voter ID Laws?" *The Atlantic,* May 2. Retrieved July 6, 2016 (www.theatlantic.com/politics/archive/2016/05/jim-demint-voter-id-laws/480876/).

Grann, David. 2017. *Killers of the Flower Moon: The Osage Murders and the Birth of the FBI.* New York: Doubleday.

Grant, Carl A. 2004. "'Brown' for All." *Rethinking Schools* 18(3):12–14.

Grant, Donald. L. 1975. *The Anti-Lynching Movement: 1883–1932.* San Francisco, CA: R and E Research Associates.

Greely, Henry T. 2008. "Genetic Genealogy: Genetics Meets the Marketplace." Pp. 215–234 in *Revisiting Race in a Genomic Age,* edited by B. A. Koenig, S. S. Lee, and S. S. Richardson. New Brunswick, NJ: Rutgers University Press.

Greenberg, Jack. 1994. *Crusaders in the Courts: How a Dedicated Band of Lawyers Fought for the Civil Rights Revolution.* New York: Basic Books.

Gregory, Anne, Russell J. Skiba, and Pedro Noguera. 2010. "The Achievement Gap and the Discipline Gap: Two Sides of the Same Coin?" *Educational Researcher* 39:59–68.

Gridley, Marc C. 1997. *Jazz Styles: History and Analysis,* 6th ed. Upper Saddle River, NJ: Prentice Hall.

Griffith, Janelle. 2019. "Stanford University Investigating Noose Found on Campus." *NBC News*, July 17. Retrieved July 17, 2019 (www.nbcnews.com/news/nbcblk/stanford-university-investigating-noose-found-campus-n1030931).

Groff, Garin. 2010. "Activists: White Supremacist Activity on the Rise in Arizona." *East Valley Tribune*, August 1. Retrieved September 10, 2011 (www.lexisnexis.com/lnacui2api/delivery/PrintDoc.do?jobHandle=1828%3A305535).

Groneman, William, III. 2011. "Misremembering the Alamo: Ten Things About the 1936 Battle Every American Knows—Whether They Happened or Not." *Wild West* 23(5):36–43.

Grzanka, Patrick A. 2014. *Intersectionalities: A Foundations and Frontiers Reader.* Boulder, CO: Westview Press.

Guevara, Martin, ed. 2012. *Hispanics in the U.S. Criminal Justice System: The New American Demography.* Springfield, IL: Charles C. Thomas Publishers.

Guggenheim, Charles. 1995. *The Shadow of Hate: A History of Intolerance in America.* Montgomery, AL: Southern Poverty Law Center.

Guimaraes, Antonio Sergio Alfredo. 1995. "Racism and Anti-Racism in Brazil: A Postmodern Perspective." Pp. 208–226 in *Racism and Anti-Racism in World Perspective*, edited by B. P. Bowser. Thousand Oaks, CA: Sage Publications.

Gungwu, Wang. 2003. "Introduction." Pp. vii–ix in *Legacies of White Australia: Race, Culture, and Nation*, edited by L. Jayasuriya, D. Walker, and J. Gothard. Crawley, Western Australia: University of Western Australia Press.

Gunn-Allen, Paula. 1998. *Off the Reservation: Reflections on Boundary-Busting, Border-Crossing, and Loose Cannons.* Boston, MA: Beacon Press.

Gurr, Ted R. 1970. *Why Men Rebel.* Princeton, NJ: Princeton University Press.

Gutierrez-Jones, Carl Scott. 2001. *Critical Race Narratives: A Study of Race, Rhetoric and Injury.* New York: New York University Press.

Gutierrez, Kris D. and Peter McLaren. 1995. "Pedagogies of Dissent and Transformation: A Dialogue About Postmodernity, Social Context, and the Politics of Literacy." Pp. 125–148 in *Critical Multiculturalism: Uncommon Voices in a Common Struggle*, edited by B. Kanpol and P. McLaren. Westport, CT: Bergin and Garvey Publishers.

Hacker, Andrew. 1995. *Two Nations: Black and White, Separate, Hostile, Unequal.* New York: Ballantine Books.

Hacsi, Timothy A. 2002. *Children as Pawns: The Politics of Educational Reform.* Cambridge, MA: Harvard University Press.

Hagan, John, Ron Levi, and Ronit Dinovitzer. 2008. "The Symbolic Violence of the Crime–Immigration Nexus: Migrant Mythologies in the Americas." *Criminology and Public Policy* 7(1):95–112.

Hagerman, Margaret A. 2014. "White Families and Race: Colour-Blind and Colour-Conscious Approaches to White Racial Socialization." *Ethnic and Racial Studies* 37(14):2598–2614.

Hagerman, Margaret A. 2018. *White Kids: Growing Up with Privilege in a Racially Divided America.* New York: New York University Press.

Hahn, Steven. 2003. *A Nation Under Our Feet: Black Political Struggles in the Rural South from Slavery to the Great Migration.* Cambridge, MA: Belknap Press of Harvard University Press.

Hale, Janice E. 2004. "How Schools Shortchange African American Children." *Educational Leadership* 62(3):34–38.

Hall, John R., Mary Jo Neitz, and Marshall Battani. 2003. *Sociology on Culture.* London, New York: Routledge.

Hall, Matthew, Kyle Crowder, and Amy Spring. 2015. "Neighborhood Foreclosures, Racial/Ethnic Transitions, and Residential Segregation." *American Sociological Review* 80(3):526–549.

Hall, Stuart. 1980. "Encoding/Decoding." Pp. 128–138 in *Culture, Media, Language: Working Papers in Cultural Studies, 1972–1979*, edited by Stuart Hall, Dorothy Hobson, Andrew Lowe, and Paul Willis. London: Hutchinson.

Hamilton, Darrick and William Darity, Jr. 2010. "Can 'Baby Bonds' Eliminate the Racial Wealth Gap in Putative Post-Racial America?" *The Review of Black Political Economy* 37(3–4):207–216.

Handlin, Oscar. 1972. *A Pictorial History of Immigration.* New York: Crown Publishing Group.

Haney Lopez, Ian F. 1996. *White by Law: The Legal Construction of Race*. New York: New York University Press.

Haney Lopez, Ian F. 2006. "Colorblind to the Reality of Race in America." *Chronicle of Higher Education*, November 3. Retrieved July 24, 2013 (http://chronicle.com/article/Colorblind-to-the-Reality-of/12577).

Hannah-Jones, Nikole. 2017. "The Resegregation of Jefferson County." *New York Times Magazine*, September 6. Retrieved May 25, 2019 (www.nytimes.com/2017/09/06/magazine/the-resegregation-of-jefferson-county.html).

Hannah-Jones, Nikole. 2019. "Our Democracy's Founding Ideals Were False When They Were Written. Black Americans Have Fought To Make Them True." 1619 Project of *New York Times Magazine*, August 18. Retrieved August 31, 2019 (www.nytimes.com/interactive/2019/08/14/magazine/black-history-american-democracy.html).

Hannon, Lance. 2015. "White Colorism." *Social Currents* 2(1):13–21.

Hanrahan, Mark. 2013. "Segregated Prom: Wilcox County, GA, High School Students Set Up First Integrated Prom." *Huffington Post*, April 4. Retrieved April 14, 2013 (www.huffingtonpost.com/2013/04/04/segregated-prom-wilcox-county-ga-high-school_n_3013733.html).

Hansen, Claire. 2018. "Do Chief Diversity Officers Help Diversify a University's Faculty? This Study Found No Evidence." *The Chronicle of Higher Education*, September 6. Retrieved March 30, 2019 (www.chronicle.com/article/Do-Chief-Diversity-Officers/244460).

Hansen, Marcus Lee. 1996 [1938]. "The Problem of the Third Generation Immigrant." Pp. 202–215 in *Theories of Ethnicity: A Classical Reader*, edited by Werner Collors. London: MacMillan Press.

Harjo, Suzan Shown. 2001. "Fighting Name-Calling: Challenging 'Redskins' in Court." Pp. 189–207 in *Team Spirits: The Native American Mascot Controversy*, edited by C. R. King and C. F. Springwood. Lincoln: University of Nebraska Press.

Harper, Philip Brian. 1998. "Passing for What? Racial Masquerade and the Demands of Upward Mobility." *Callaloo* 21(2):382.

Harr, Daniel. 1999. "The New Slavery Movement." *Social Policy* 29(4):28–32.

Harris, Cherise A. and Nikki Khanna. 2010. "Black Is, Black Ain't: Biracials, Middle-Class Blacks, and the Social Construction of Blackness." *Sociological Spectrum* 30(6):639–670.

Harris, Leslie. 2019. *Slavery and the University: Histories and Legacies*. Athens, GA: University of Georgia Press.

Harris, Norene, Nathaniel Jackson, and Carl E. Rydingsword. 1975. *The Integration of American Schools: Problems, Experiences, Solutions*. Boston, London: Allyn and Bacon.

Harris, Paul. 2012. "How the End of Slavery Led to Starvation and Death for Millions of Black Americans." *Guardian*, June 16. Retrieved May 21, 2019 (www.theguardian.com/world/2012/jun/16/slavery-starvation-civil-war).

Harris-Perry, Melissa V. 2011. *Sister Citizen: Shame, Stereotypes, and Black Women in America*. New Haven, CT: Yale University Press.

Harris, Rob. 2012. "British PM Cameron Wants Soccer Anti-Racism Plan." CNSNews.com, February 22. Retrieved October 13, 2016 (www.cnsnews.com/news/article/british-pm-cameron-wants-soccer-anti-racism-plan).

Harris, Rob. 2019. "AP Interview: Blair on Racism, Human Rights at Sports Events." *Fox News*, April 26. Retrieved July 1, 2019 (www.foxnews.com/world/ap-interview-blair-on-racism-human-rights-at-sports-events).

Harris, William H. 1977. *Keeping the Faith: A. Philip Randolph, Milton P. Webster, and the Brotherhood of Sleeping Car Porters, 1925–37*. Chicago and Urbana: University of Illinois Press.

Hartmann, Douglas. 2015. "Reflections on Race, Diversity, and the Crossroads of Multiculturalism." *Sociological Quarterly* 56(4):623–639.

Hartocollis, Anemona. 2018. "What's at Stake in the Harvard Lawsuit? Decades of Debate over Race in Admissions." *New York Times*, October 13. Retrieved August 4, 2019 (www.nytimes.com/2018/10/13/us/harvard-affirmative-action-asian-students.html).

Harstock, Nancy C. 1987. "The Feminist Standpoint: Developing the Ground for a Specifically Feminist Historical Materialism." Pp. 157–180 in *Feminism and Methodology*, edited by S. Harding. Bloomington, Indianapolis: Indiana University Press.

Hatsukami, Dorothy K. and Marian W. Fischman. 1996. "Crack Cocaine and Cocaine Hydrochloride: Are the Differences Myth or Reality?" *JAMA* 276(19):1580–1588.

Haygood, Wil. 2019. "Why Won't Blackface Go Away? It's Part of America's Troubled Cultural Legacy." *New York Times*, February 7. Retrieved July 2, 2019 (www.nytimes.com/2019/02/07/arts/blackface-american-pop-culture.html).

"Health of American Indian or Alaska Native Population." 2017. National Center for Health Statistics. Retrieved July 28, 2019 (https://ftp.cdc.gov/pub/Health_Statistics/NCHS/NHIS/SHS/2017_SHS_Table_P-11.pdf).

Hedges, Chris. 2011. "The Obama Deception: Why Cornel West Went Ballistic." Truthdig, May 16. Retrieved July 5, 2011 (www.truthdig.com/report/item/the_obama_deception_why_cornel_west_went_ballistic_20110516).

Helms, Janet. 1990. "Toward a Model of White Racial Identity Development." Pp. 49–66 in *Black and White Racial Identity: Theory, Research and Practice*, edited by J. Helms. Westport, CT: Praeger.

Henricks, Kasey. 2015. "Bursting Whose Bubble? The Racial Nexus Between Social Disaster, Housing Wealth, and Public Policy." *Social Justice Research* 28(3):318–338.

Henson, Scott. 2004. *Flawed Enforcement: Why Drug Task Force Highway Interdiction Violates Rights, Wastes Tax Dollars, and Fails to Limit the Availability of Drugs in Texas*. Austin: American Civil Liberties Union of Texas. Retrieved July 24, 2013 (www.aclu.org/racialjustice/racialprofiling/15897pub20040519.html).

Herman, Arthur. 2008. *Gandhi and Churchill*. New York: Bantam Books.

Herndon, Astead W. and Jennifer Medina. 2019. "Trump Sets the Terms of Racial Division. Do Democrats Know What to Do?" *New York Times*, July 21. Retrieved July 21, 2019 (www.nytimes.com/2019/07/21/us/politics/trump-race-democrats.html?action=click&module=Top%20Stories&pgtype=Homepage).

Herrnstein, Richard J. and Charles Murray. 1994. *The Bell Curve: Intelligence and Class Structure in American Society*. New York: Free Press.

Hess, Amanda. 2016. "Asian American Actors Are Fighting for Visibility: They Will Not Be Ignored." *New York Times*, May 25. Retrieved July 8, 2016 (www.nytimes.com/2016/05/29/movies/asian-american-actors-are-fighting-for-visibility-they-will-not-be-ignored.html).

Hewlett, Sylvia Ann, Nancy Rankin, and Cornel West. 2002. *Taking Parenting Public: The Case for a New Social Movement*. Lanham, MD: Rowman and Littlefield Press.

Higham, John. 1963. *Strangers in the Land*. New York: Atheneum.

Hing, Julianne. 2010. "David Vitter Wins the Prize: Most Vile Anti-Immigrant Ad." Colorlines, October 15. Retrieved September 11, 2011 (http://colorlines.com/archives/2010/10/latino_groups_livid_over_david_vitters_vile_anti-immigrant_ad.html).

"History." n.d. 40 Acres and a Mule Filmworks. Retrieved May 5, 2013 (www.40acres.com/history/).

Hobbs, Allyson. 2014. *A Chosen Exile: A History of Racial Passing in American Life*. Cambridge, MA: Harvard University Press.

Hobgood, Mary Elizabeth. 2007. "White Economic and Erotic Disempowerment: A Theological Exploration in the Struggle Against Racism." Pp. 40–55 in *Interrupting White Privilege: Catholic Theologians Break the Silence*, edited by L. M. Cassidy and A. Mikulich. Maryknoll, NY: Orbis Books.

Hobson, Mellody. 2014. "Color Blind or Color Brave?" TED Talk, March. Retrieved July 15, 2019 (www.ted.com/talks/mellody_hobson_color_blind_or_color_brave/).

Hochschild, Jennifer L. and Nathan Scovronick. 2003. *The American Dream and the Public Schools*. Oxford, New York: Oxford University Press.

Hochschild, Jennifer, Vesla Weaver, and Traci Burch. 2012. *Creating a New Racial Order: How Immigration, Multiracialism, Genomics, and the Young Can Remake Race in America*. Princeton, NJ: Princeton University Press.

Hodal, Kate. 2019. "A Young Woman Vanishes: The Police Can't Help Her; Her Desperate Family Won't Give Up." *Guardian*, February 25. Retrieved June 26, 2019 (www.theguardian.com/us-news/2019/feb/25/a-young-woman-vanishes-the-police-cant-help-her-desperate-family-wont-give-up?CMP=fb_gu&fbclid=IwAR3JNtvNN38XlI9lImVB4mDUHi4jToK4kCBdpYZpNHHxTO61HLfeHP4ZlXA).

Hodes, Martha. 1999. *White Women, Black Men: Illicit Sex in the Nineteenth Century South.* New Haven, CT: Yale University Press.

Hoenig, Chris. 2014. "The Measure of Diversity That Only One US Pro Sport Meets." Diversity Inc., July 16. Retrieved July 6, 2016 (www.diversityinc.com/news/measure-diversity-one-u-s-pro-sport-meets/).

Hoffman, Frederick. 1896. "Race Traits of the American Negro." *Publication of the American Economic Association* 11(1/3):1–329.

Hoffman, Jessica. 2007. "Why So High?" Colorlines, November/December, pp. 24–27.

Holden, Robert H. and Eric Zolov. 2000. *Latin America and the United States: A Documentary History.* Oxford, New York: Oxford University Press.

Holiday, Billie with William Dufty. 1984 [1956]. *Lady Sings the Blues.* London: Penguin Books.

Holmes, Anna. 2018. "Black with (Some) White Privilege." *New York Times*, February 10. Retrieved June 29, 2019 (www.nytimes.com/2018/02/10/opinion/sunday/black-with-some-white-privilege.html).

Holtzman, Linda. 2000. *Media Messages: What Film, Television, and Popular Music Teach Us About Race, Class, Gender, and Sexual Orientation.* Armonk, NY: M. E. Sharpe Publishers.

Honey, Michael K. 2007. *Going Down Jericho Road: The Memphis Strike, Martin Luther King's Last Campaign.* London, New York: W. W. Norton and Company.

hooks, bell. 1996. *Reel to Real: Race, Class and Sex at the Movies.* New York and London: Routledge.

Horowitz, Julianna Menasce, Anna Brown, and Kianna Cox. 2019. "Race in American 2019." Pew Research Center, April 9. Retrieved August 4, 2019 (www.pewsocialtrends.org/2019/04/09/race-in-america-2019/).

Horsman, Reginald. 1975. "Scientific Racism and the American Indian in the Mid-Nineteenth Century." *American Quarterly* 27(2):152–168.

Horton, James Oliver. 2006. "Slavery in American History: An Uncomfortable National Dialogue." Pp. 35–56 in *Slavery and Public History: The Tough Stuff of American Memory*, edited by J. O. Horton and L. E. Horton. Chapel Hill: University of North Carolina Press.

Horton, Lois E. 2006. "Avoiding History: Thomas Jefferson, Sally Hemings, and the Uncomfortable Public Conversation on Slavery." Pp. 135–150 in *Slavery and Public History: The Tough Stuff of American Memory*, edited by J. O. Horton and L. E. Horton. Chapel Hill: University of North Carolina Press.

Horwitz, Tony. 1998. *Confederates in the Attic: Dispatches from the Unfinished Civil War.* New York: Pantheon Books.

Howard, Gary. 2006. *We Can't Teach What We Don't Know: White Teachers, Multiracial Schools*, 2nd ed. New York: Teachers College Press.

Howard, Jeff. 1995. "You Can't Get There from Here: The Need for a New Logic in Education Reform." *Daedalus* 124(4):85–93.

Hughes, Everett C. 1963. "Race Relations and the Sociological Imagination." *American Sociological Review* 28(6):879–890.

Hughey, Matthew. 2009. "Cinethetic Racism: White Redemption and Black Stereotypes and in 'Magical Negro' Films." *Social Problems* 56(3):543–577.

Hughey, Matthew. 2010. "The (Dis)Similarities of White Racial Identities: The Conceptual Framework of 'Hegemonic Whiteness.'" *Ethnic and Racial Studies* 33(8):1289–1309.

Hughey, Matthew. 2012. *White Bound: Nationalists, Anti-Racists, and the Shared Meanings of Race.* Stanford, CA: Stanford University Press.

Hughey, Matthew. 2014. *The White Savior Film: Content, Critics, and Consumption.* Philadelphia, PA: Temple University Press.

Hughey, Matthew. 2015. "The Whiteness of Oscar Night." *Contexts*, January 19. Retrieved July 5, 2016 (https://contexts.org/blog/the-whiteness-of-oscar-night/).

Hughey, Matthew. 2016. "Of Tarzan and Knight: Our Cinematic Addiction to White Saviors." *Huffington Post*, July 1. Retrieved July 1, 2016 (www.huffingtonpost.com/entry/of-tarzan-and-knight-our-cinematic-addiction-to-white_us_577693aae4b00a3ae4cdbc48).

Humes, Edward. 2006. "How the GI Bill Shunted Blacks into Vocational Training." *Journal of Blacks in Higher Education* 53:92–104.

Hunt, Darnell, Ana-Christina Ramón, and Michael Tran. 2019. *Hollywood Diversity Report 2019: Old Story, New Beginning.* UCLA College Social Sciences. Retrieved July 3, 2019 (https://social sciences.ucla.edu/wp-content/uploads/2019/02/UCLA-Hollywood-Diversity-Report-2019-2-21-2019.pdf).

Hunt, Scott A. and Robert D. Benford. 1994. "Identity Talk in Peace and Justice Movements." *Journal of Contemporary Ethnography* 22(4):488–518.

Hunter, Marcus Anthony and Zandria F. Robinson. 2018. *Chocolate Cities: The Black Map of American Life.* Oakland, CA: University of California Press.

Hunter, Margaret. 2007. "The Persistent Problem of Colorism: Skin Tone, Status, and Inequality." *Sociological Compass* 1(1):237–254.

Hussain, Murtaza. 2016. "Hate Crimes Rise Along with Donald Trump's Anti-Muslim Rhetoric." The Intercept.com, May 5. Retrieved July 8, 2016 (https://theintercept.com/2016/05/05/hate-crimes-rise-along-with-donald-trumps-anti-muslim-rhetoric/).

Huston, Caitlin. 2015. "Airbnb Hosts Discriminate Against Black People, Study Finds." Marketwatch, December 11. Retrieved June 6, 2016 (www.marketwatch.com/story/airbnb-hosts-discriminate-against-black-people-study-finds-2015-12-10).

Hutson, Brittany. 2011. "Race and Heath Care." *Atlanta Post*, March 22. Retrieved July 31, 2011 (http://atlantapost.com/2011/03/22/how-much-is-race-a-factor-behind-health-care-reform/).

Hutton, Paul Andrew. 1985. "Introduction." Pp. 1–15 in *Alamo Images: Changing Perceptions of a Texas Experience*, edited by S. P. Schoelwer and T. W. Glaser. Dallas, TX: Southern Methodist University Press.

Ibish, Hussein and Anne Stewart. 2003. "Report on Hate Crimes and Discrimination Against Arab Americans: The Post-September 11 Backlash." American-Arab Anti-Discrimination Committee. Retrieved April 15, 2013 (www.adc.org/PDF/hcr02.pdf).

Iceland, John, and Melissa Scopilliti. 2008. "Immigrant Residential Segregation in US Metropolitan Areas, 1990–2000." *Demography* 45:79–94.

Ignatiev, Noel. 1995. *How the Irish Became White.* New York, London: Routledge.

Ihlanfeldt, Keith R. and Benjamin Scafidi. 2002. "Black Self-Segregation as a Cause of Housing Segregation: Evidence from a Multi-city Study of Urban Inequality." *Journal of Urban Economics* 51:366–390.

Ihlanfeldt, Keith R. and Benjamin Scafidi. 2004. "Whites' Neighbourhood Preferences and Neighbourhood Racial Composition in the United States: Evidence from the Multi-City Study of Urban Inequality." *Housing Studies* 19(3):325–359.

Ingram, Catherine. 1990. *In the Footsteps of Gandhi: Conversations with Spiritual Social Activists.* Berkeley, CA: Parallax Press.

Institute for Natural Progress. 1992. "In Usual and Accustomed Places: Contemporary American Indian Fishing Rights Struggles." Pp. 217–240 in *The State of Native America: Genocide, Colonization, and Resistance*, edited by M. A. Jaimes. Boston, MA: South End Press.

Intagliata, Christine. 2007. *Race to Execution.* Documentary. Washington, DC: Lioness Media Arts, Inc.

Irving, Debby. 2014. *Waking Up White and Finding Myself in the Story of Race.* Cambridge, MA: Elephant Room Press.

Irwin, Lee. 2006. "Walking the Line: Pipe and Sweat Ceremonies in Prison." *Nova Religio: Journal of Alternative and Emergent Religions* 9(3):39–60.

Jackson, Derrick. 1989. "Calling the Plays in Black and White: Will Today's Super Bowl Be Black Brawn vs. White Brains?" *Boston Globe*, January 22, p. A25.

Jacobs, Margaret D. 2009. *White Mother to a Dark Race: Settler Colonialism, Maternalism, and the Removal of Indigenous Children in the American West and Australia, 1880–1940.* Lincoln: University of Nebraska Press.

Jacobson, Matthew Frye. 1998. *Whiteness of a Different Color: European Immigrants and the Alchemy of Race.* Cambridge, MA: Harvard University Press.

Jacques, Martin. 2003. "Tennis Is Racist—It's Time We Did Something About It." *Guardian*, June 25. Retrieved April 14, 2013 (www.guardian.co.uk/sport/2003/jun/25/wimbledon2003.tennis11).

Jaimes, M. Annette, ed. 1992. *The State of Native America: Genocide, Colonization, and Resistance.* Boston, MA: South End Press.

Jaimes, M. Annette with Theresa Halsey. 1992. "American Indian Women: At the Center of Indigenous Resistance in North America." Pp. 311–344 in *The State of Native America: Genocide, Colonization, and Resistance*, edited by M. A. Jaimes. Boston, MA: South End Press.

Jawort, Adrian. 2012. "Montana Schools Try to Keep Indian Students Engaged by Teaching Indian Culture to All." Indian Country Today Media Network, April 12. Retrieved June 21, 2016 (http://indiancountrytodaymedianetwork.com/2012/04/12/montana-schools-try-keep-indian-students-engaged-teaching-indian-culture-all-107543).

Jayaraman, Saru. 2013. *Behind the Kitchen Door.* Ithaca, NY: ILR Press.

Jayasuriya, Laksiri, David Walker and Jan Gothard, eds. 2003. *Legacies of White Australia: Race, Culture, and Nation.* Crawley, Western Australia: University of Western Australia Press.

JBHE Foundation. 2003. "How the GI Bill Widened the Racial Higher Education Gap." *Journal of Blacks in Higher Education* 41:36–37.

Jencks, Christopher, Marshall Smith, Henry Acland, Mary Jo Bane, David Cohen, Herbert Gintis, Barbara Heyns, and Stephen Michelson. 1972. *Inequality: A Reassessment of the Effect of Family and Schooling in America.* New York: Basic Books.

Jenkins, Sally. 2007. "The Team That Invented Football." *Sports Illustrated*, April 23, pp. 60–73.

Jensen, Arthur. 1969. "How Much Can We Boost IQ and Scholastic Achievement?" *Harvard Educational Review* 39:1–123.

Johansen, Bruce E. 2005. *The Native Peoples of North America: A History.* Vol. II. London, Westport, CT: Praeger.

Johnson, Brian D. and Sara Betsinger. 2009. "Punishing the 'Model Minority': Asian American Criminal Sentencing Outcomes in Federal District Courts." *Criminology* 47(4):1045–1090.

Johnson, David. 2016. "The Most Dangerous Jobs in America." *Time*, May 13. Retrieved July 9, 2016 (http://time.com/4326676/dangerous-jobs-america/).

Johnson, Elizabeth I. and Jane Waldfogel. 2004. "Children of Incarcerated Parents: Multiple Risks and Children's Living Arrangements." Pp. 97–134 in *Imprisoning America: The Social Effects of Mass Incarceration*, edited by M. Pattillo, D. Weiman, and B. Western. New York: Russell Sage Foundation.

Johnson, Kevin. 2007. "Police Brutality Cases on Rise Since 9/11." *USA Today*, December 17. Retrieved July 2, 2011 (http://usatoday30.usatoday.com/news/nation/2007-12-17-Copmisconduct_N.htm).

Johnson, Kevin. 2009. "Immigration and America: How the Undocumented Add Up for California: Why We Need Reform from Washington; Yes, They're 'Illegal,' but They Contribute." *Sacramento Bee*, June 21, p. E1.

Johnson, Luke. 2012. "Mike Turzai, Pennsylvania GOP House Majority Leader: Voter ID Will Allow Mitt Romney to Win State." *Huffington Post*, June 25. Retrieved May 21, 2013 (www.huffingtonpost.com/2012/06/25/mike-turzai-voter-id_n_1625646.html).

Johnson, Robert. 2003. *British Imperialism.* New York: Palgrave Macmillan.

Johnston, Hank, Enrique Larana, and Joseph R. Gusfield. 1994. "Identities, Grievances, and New Social Movements." Pp. 3–35 in *New Social Movements: From Ideology to Identity*, edited by E. Larana, H. Johnston, and J. R. Gusfield. Philadelphia, PA: Temple University Press.

Jones, Antwan. 2006. "The Effects of Wealth on Homeownership Propensity and Ethnic Spatial Distribution for Latinos in the United States." Paper presented at the American Sociological Association Annual Meeting, Montreal, Canada, August.

Jones, Gavin W. 2003. "White Australia, National Identity, and Population Change." Pp. 110–128 in *Legacies of White Australia: Race, Culture and Nation*, edited by L. Jayasuriya, D. Walker, and J. Gothard. Crawley, Western Australia: University of Western Australia Press.

Jones, Janelle. 2017. "The Racial Wealth Gap: How African Americans Have Been Shortchanged Out of the Materials to Build Wealth." Economic Policy Institute, February 13. Retrieved July 31, 2019 (www.epi.org/blog/the-racial-wealth-gap-how-african-americans-have-been-shortchanged-out-of-the-materials-to-build-wealth/).

Jones, Jeffrey N. 2011. "Record High 86% Approve of Black–White Marriages." Gallup, September 12. Retrieved April 14, 2012 (www.gallup.com/poll/149390/Record-High-Approve-Black-White-Marriages.aspx).

Jones, Leroi. 1963. *Blues People: The Negro Experience in White America and the Music That Developed from It*. New York: Morrow Quill Paperbacks.

Jones-Rogers, Stephanie E. 2019. *They Were Her Property: White Women as Slave Owners in the American South*. New Haven, CT: Yale University Press.

Jones, Susan and Debra Myhill. 2004. "Seeing Things Differently: Teachers' Construction of Underachievement." *Gender and Education* 16(4):531–546.

Jordan, M. L. R. 1995. "Reflections on the Challenges, Possibilities, and Perplexities of Preparing Pre-Service Teachers for Culturally Diverse Classrooms." *Journal of Teacher Education* 46(5): 369–374.

Jordan, Winthrop. 1968. *White Over Black: American Attitudes Toward the Negro, 1550–1812*. Chapel Hill: University of North Carolina Press.

Joseph, Peniel E. 2006. *Waiting 'Til the Midnight Hour: A Narrative History of Black Power in America*. New York: Henry Holt and Company.

Kahn, Jonathan. 2011. "BiDil and Racialized Medicine." Pp. 129–141 in *Race and the Genetic Revolution: Science, Myth, and Culture*, edited by S. Krimsky and K. Sloan. New York: Columbia University Press.

Kahn, Jonathan. 2013. *Race in a Bottle: The Story of BiDil and Racialized Medicine in a Post-Genomic Age*. New York: Columbia University Press.

Kalmbacher, Colin. 2019. "White Supremacist Designated as Terrorist in Major First for New York Learns his Fate." *Law & Crime*, Fen/13. Retrieved March 12, 2019 (https://lawandcrime.com/high-profile/white-supremacist-designated-as-terrorist-in-major-first-for-new-york-learns-his-fate/).

Kampfner, Christina J. 1995. "Post-Traumatic Stress Reactions in Children of Imprisoned Mothers." Pp. 89–102 in *Children of Incarcerated Parents*, edited by K. Gabel and D. Johnston. New York: Lexington Books.

Kan, Yee W. 2003. "Race and the Death Penalty: Including Asian Americans and Exploring the Desocialization of Law." *Journal of Ethnicity and Criminal Justice* 1(1):63–92.

Kantor, Jodi. 2012. "For President, a Complex Calculus of Race and Politics." *New York Times*, October 21, p. A1.

Kao, Grace and Kara Joyner. 2004. "Do Race and Ethnicity Matter Among Friends? Activities Among Interracial, Interethnic, and Intraethnic Adolescent Friends." *Sociological Quarterly* 45(3):557–573.

Kao, Grace, Kelly Stamper Balistreri, and Kara Joyner. 2018. "Asian American Men in Romantic Dating Markets." *Contexts* 17(4)48–53.

Kaplan, Karen. 2005. "Ancestry in a Drop of Blood." *The Los Angeles Times*, August 30. Retrieved June 16, 2019 (www.latimes.com/archives/la-xpm-2005-aug-30-sci-indiandna30-story.html/).

Karabel, Jerome. 2005. *The Chosen: The Hidden History of Admission and Exclusion at Harvard, Yale, and Princeton*. Boston, New York: Houghton Mifflin Company.

Karoub, Jeff. 2013. "Some Patients Won't See Health Care Workers of a Different Race." *Times-Picayune*, February 24, p. A17.

Kates, Graham. 2016. "Lawsuit: Juvenile Detention Staffer Watched as KY Girl Took 'Last Gasps.'" CBSNews.com, September 6. Retrieved February 28, 2020. (www.cbsnews.com/news/gynnya-mcmillen-lawsuit-juvenile-detention-staffer-watched-as-kentucky-girl-died/).

Katz, Michael B. 2001. *The Price of Citizenship: Redefining the American Welfare State*. Philadelphia: University of Pennsylvania Press.

Katznelson, Ira. 2005. *When Affirmative Action Was White: An Untold History of Racial Inequality in Twentieth-Century America*. New York, London: W. W. Norton and Company.

Kaufman-Osborn, Timothy V. 2006. "Capital Punishment as Legal Lynching?" Pp. 21–54 in *From Lynch Mobs to the Killing State: Race and the Death Penalty in America*, edited by C. J. Ogletree, Jr. and A. Sarat. New York and London: New York University Press.

Kaufman, Peter. 2008. "Boos, Bans, and Other Backlash: The Consequences of Being an Activist Athlete." *Humanity and Society* 32:215–237.

Keen, Mike Forrest. 1999. *Stalking the Sociological Imagination: J. Edgar Hoover's FBI Surveillance of American Sociology*. Westport, CT: Greenwood Press.

Kendall, Francis. 2006. *Understanding White Privilege: Creating Pathways to Authentic Relationships Across Race*. New York: Routledge.

Kennedy, Helen. 2010. "Long Island Teen Thugs Accused of Killing Ecuadoran Immigrant Preyed on Random Latinos, Says DA." *NY Daily News*, March 19. Retrieved October 9, 2016 (www.nydaily news.com/news/crime/long-island-teen-thugs-accused-killing-ecuadoran-immigrantpreyed-random-latinos-da-article-1.165376).

Kershaw, Sarah. 2004. "The 2004 Campaign: The Hispanic Vote." *New York Times*, February 2. Retrieved July 24, 2013 (www.nytimes.com/2004/02/02/us/2004-campaign-hispanic-vote-vital-bloc-realizing-its-power-measures-its-suitors.html).

"Key Facts about the Uninsured Population." 2018. Fact Sheet. Henry J. Kaiser Family Foundation. Retrieved May 28, 2019 (http://files.kff.org/attachment//fact-sheet-key-facts-about-the-uninsured-population).

Khalid, Asma. 2015. "How Asian American Voters Went from Republican to Democrat." It's All Politics, NPR, September 16. Retrieved July 9, 2016 (www.npr.org/sections/itsallpolitics/2015/09/16/439574726/how-asian-american-voters-went-from-republican-to-democratic).

Khan, Huma. 2012. "Oklahoma's Ban on Sharia Law Struck Down by Federal Appeals Court." ABC News, January 11. Retrieved April 15, 2013 (http://abcnews.go.com/blogs/politics/2012/01/oklahomas-ban-on-sharia-law-struck-down-by-federal-appeals-court/).

Kharem, Haroon. 2006. *The Curriculum of Repression: A Pedagogy of Racial History in the United States*. New York: Peter Lang Publishers.

Kibria, Nazli. 1997. "The Construction of 'Asian American': Reflections on Intermarriage and Ethnic Identity Among Second-Generation Chinese and Korean Americans." *Ethnic and Racial Studies* 20(3):523–544.

Kids Count Data Center. 2016. "Children in Single-Parent Families by Race." Retrieved June 28, 2015 (http://datacenter.kidscount.Org/data/tables/107-children-in-single-parent-families-by#detailed/1/any/false/869,36,868,867,133/10,11,9,12,1,185,13/432,431).

Kielburger, Craig and Marc Kielburger. 2013. "Why South Africa is Still Dealing with Segregation and Poverty." *Huffington Post*, December 18. Retrieved August 5, 2019 (www.huffingtonpost.ca/craig-and-marc-kielburger/post-apartheid-south-africa_b_4460819.html).

Kilgore, James. 2016. "Mass Incarceration Since 1492: Native American Encounters with Criminal Justice." *Truthout*, February 7. Retrieved June 20, 2016 (www.truth-out.org/news/item/34725-mass-incarceration-since-1492-native-american-encounters-with-criminal-injustice).

Kim, Thomas P. 2007. *The Racial Logic of Politics: Asian Americans and Party Competition*. Philadelphia, PA: Temple University Press.

Kimmel, Michael S. and Abby L. Ferber, eds. 2014. *Privilege: A Reader*. Boulder, CO: Westview Press.

Kinder, D. R. and Sanders, L. M. 1996. *Divided by Color*. Chicago: University of Chicago Press.

King, C. Richard and Charles Fruehling Springwood. 2001. *Team Spirits: The Native American Mascot Controversy*. Lincoln: University of Nebraska Press.

Kirk, David S. 2016. "Prisoner Reentry and the Reproduction of Legal Cynicism." *Social Problems* 63(2):222–243.

Kivel, Paul. 2008. "How White People Can Serve as Allies to People of Color in the Struggle to End Racism." Pp. 127–136 in *White Privilege: Essential Readings on the Other Side of Racism*, 3rd ed., edited by P. Rothenberg. New York: Worth Publishers.

Kivel, Paul. 2011. *Uprooting Racism: How White People Can Work for Racial Justice*, 3rd ed. Gabriola Island, BC, Canada: New Society Publishers.

Klarman, Michael J. 2005. "Why Massive Resistance?" Pp. 21–28 in *Massive Resistance: Southern Opposition to the Second Reconstruction*, edited by C. Webb. Oxford, New York: Oxford University Press.

Klein, Alyson. 2016. "No Child Left Behind: An Overview." *Education Week*, June 21. Retrieved June 21, 2016 (www.edweek.org/ew/section/multimedia/no-child-left-behind-overview-definition-summary.html).

Knutsen, Elise. 2013. "Israel Forcibly Injected African Immigrants with Birth Control, Report Claims." *Forbes*, January 28. Retrieved August 5, 2019 (www.forbes.com/sites/eliseknutsen/2013/01/28/israel-foribly-injected-african-immigrant-women-with-birth-control/#3190269e67b8).

Knutson, April A. 2004. "Haitian Women in the New World Order." Pp. 154–180 in *Women and Globalization*, edited by D. D. Aguilar and A E. Lacsamana. New York: Humanity Books.

Kobler, Arthur. 1975. "Police Homicide in a Democracy." *Journal of Social Issues* 31(1):163–184.

Kochhar, R., R. Fry, and P. Taylor. 2011. *Twenty-to-One: Wealth Gaps Rise to Record Highs Between Whites, Blacks and Hispanics.* Washington, DC: Pew Research Center.

Kochhar, Rakesh and Anthony Cilluffo. 2017. "How Wealth Inequality Has Changed in the US Since the Great Recession, by Race, Ethnicity, and Income." Pew Research Center, November 1. Retrieved July 27, 2019 (www.pewresearch.org/fact-tank/2017/11/01/how-wealth-inequality-has-changed-in-the-u-s-since-the-great-recession-by-race-ethnicity-and-income/).

Kolpack, Dave. 2011. "Students File Lawsuit Over ND School's Nickname." *Crookston Times*, August 12. Retrieved October 14, 2016 (www.crookstontimes.com/article/20110812/NEWS/308129976).

Kopacz, Maria and Bessie Lee Lawton. 2010. "The YouTube Indian: Portrayals of Native Americans on a Viral Video Site." *New Media and Society* 13(2):330–349. Retrieved September 21, 2011 (http://nms.sagepub.com/content/13/2/330).

Korgen, Kathleen Odell. 1998. *From Black to Biracial: Transforming Racial Identity Among Americans.* Westport, CT: Praeger.

Kozol, Jonathan. 1991. *Savage Inequalities: Children in America's Schools.* New York: Harper Perennial.

Kozol, Jonathan. 2005. *The Shame of the Nation: The Restoration of Apartheid Schooling in America.* New York: Crown Publishers.

Krabill, Ron. 2010. *Starring Mandela and Cosby: Media and the End(s) of Apartheid.* Chicago, IL: University of Chicago Press.

Krysan, Maria and Kyle Crowder. 2017. *Cycle of Segregation: Social Processes and Residential Segregation.* New York: Russell Sage Foundation.

Krysan, Maria and Reynolds Farley. 2002. "The Residential Preferences of Blacks: Do They Explain Persistent Segregation?" *Social Forces* 80:937–979.

Kurtz, Lester R. 1984. *Evaluating Chicago Sociology: A Guide to the Literature, with an Annotated Bibliography.* Chicago, IL: University of Chicago Press.

Kutner, Max. 2017. "Police Killed on the Job: Number Spikes in 2017, as New York Mourns Murdered Officer." *Newsweek*, July 13. Retrieved June 26, 2019 (www.newsweek.com/police-line-duty-deaths-increase-2017-636064).

LaCelle-Peterson, M. W. and C. Rivera. 1994. "Is It Real for All Kids? A Framework for Equitable Assessment Policies for English Language Learners." *Harvard Educational Review* 64(1):55–75.

Ladd, Anthony E. and Bob Edwards. 2002. "Corporate Swine and Capitalist Pigs: A Decade of Environmental Injustice and Protest in North Carolina." *Social Justice* 29(3):26–46.

Ladson-Billings, Gloria. 1999. "Preparing Teachers for Diverse Student Populations: A Critical Race Theory Perspective." *Review of Research in Education* 24:211–247. Retrieved July 24, 2013 (www.brianscollier.com/wp-content/uploads/2015/05/Preparing_Teachers_for_Diverse_Student_Populations_A_Critical_Race_Theory_Perspective1.pdf).

Ladson-Billings, Gloria. 2006. "From the Achievement Gap to the Education Debt: Understanding Achievement in U.S. Schools." *Educational Researcher* 35(7):3–12.

Ladson-Billings, Gloria and William F. Tate. 1995. "Toward a Critical Race Theory of Education." *Teachers College Record* 97(1):47–69.

Lake, Celinda, Joshua E. Ulibarri, and Caroline Bye. 2016. "A Demographic Profile of the Rising American Electorate in 2016." The Voter Participation Center. Retrieved July 21, 2019 (https://data.voterparticipation.org/wp-content/uploads/2017/09/Report.VPC_.RAE-Demo-Report.2017.12.04-firev.pdf).

Lake, Marilyn and Henry Reynolds. 2008. *Drawing the Global Colour Line: White Men's Countries and the International Challenge of Racial Equality.* Cambridge, New York: Cambridge University Press.

Lake, Robert. 1981. *The New Suburbanites: Race and Housing in the Suburbs.* New Brunswick, NJ: Center for Urban Policy Research, Rutgers University.

Landrieu, Mitch. 2017. "Mitch Landrieu's Speech on the Removal of Confederate Monuments in New Orleans." *New York Times*, May 23. Retrieved July 17, 2019 (www.nytimes.com/2017/05/23/opinion/mitch-landrieus-speech-transcript.html?auth=login-facebook&login=facebook).

Lang, Sabine. 1997. "Various Kinds of Two-Spirit People: Gender Variance and Homosexuality in Native American Communities." Pp. 100–118 in *Two-Spirit People: Native American Gender*

Identity, Sexuality and Spirituality, edited by S. Jacobs, W. Thomas, and S. Lang. Urbana: University of Illinois Press.

Langston, Donna Hightower. 2003. "American Indian Women's Activism in the 1960s and 1970s." *Hypatia* 18(2):114–132.

Lapchick, Richard. 2019a. "The 2018 Racial and Gender Report Card: National Football League." TIDES: The Institute for Diversity and Ethics in Sport. Retrieved July 21, 2019 (https://docs.wix static.com/ugd/7d86e5_0fea53798fdf472289d0966a8b009d6c.pdf).

Lapchick, Richard. 2019b. "The 2019 Racial and Gender Report Card: National Football League." TIDES: The Institute for Diversity and Ethics in Sport, October 30. Retrieved March 1, 2020 (https://43530132-36e9-4f52-811a-182c7a91933b.filesusr.com/ugd/7d86e5_19da9197093641d1b7 cc8aade3929b46.pdf).

Lapchick, Richard and Diego Salas. 2015. "The 2015 Racial and Gender Report Card: Major League Baseball." Institute for Diversity and Ethics in Sports, April 15.

Lapchick, Richard, Philip Costa, Tamara Sherrod, and Rahman Anjorin. 2012. "The 2012 Racial and Gender Report Card: National Football League." Institute for Diversity and Ethics in Sport, September 13. Retrieved July 24, 2013 (www.tidesport.org/RGRC/2012/2012_NFL_RGRC.pdf).

Lapchick, Richard, Drew Donovan, Stephens Rogers, and April Johnson. 2014. "The 2014 Racial and Gender Report Card: National Football League." Institute for Diversity and Ethics in Sport, September 10. Retrieved July 11, 2016 (http://nebula.wsimg.com/1e912077d1fd5c5c7ee7c4633806 cfb5?AccessKeyId=DAC3A56D8FB782449D2A).

Lareau, Annette and Erin McNamara Horvat. 1999. "Moments of Social Inclusion and Exclusion: Race, Class and Cultural Capital in Family-School Relationships." *Sociology of Education* 72(1):37–53.

Laville-Wilson, Debra and Judi Anne Caron Sheppard. 2001. "Explaining Concern About Police Brutality: How Important Is Race?" Paper presented at annual meeting of the Society for the Study of Social Problems, Anaheim, CA, August.

Lawrence, Charles R. III. 1987. "The Id, the Ego, and Equal Protection: Reckoning with Unconscious Racism." *Stanford Law Review* 39(2):317–388.

Lawrence, George H. and Thomas D. Kane. 1995. "Military Service and Racial Attitudes of White Veterans." *Armed Forces and Society* 22(2):235–255.

Lawrence, S. M. 1997. "Beyond Race Awareness: White Racial and Multicultural Teaching." *Journal of Teacher Education* 48(2):108–117.

Lazare, Sarah. 2015. "'Off the Charts' Violence Against Muslims Ravaging US Communities." Common Dreams.org, December 18. Retrieved July 8, 2016 (www.commondreams.org/news/ 2015/12/18/charts-violence-against-muslims-ravaging-us-communities).

Leacock, E. B. 1969. *Teaching and Learning in City Schools.* New York: Basic Books.

Leal, David L. 2003. "The Multicultural Military: Military Service and the Acculturation of Latinos and Anglos." *Armed Forces and Society* 29(2):205–226.

Lebron, Christopher J. 2017. *The Making of Black Lives Matter: A Brief History of an Idea.* New York: Oxford University Press.

Ledesma, Rita. 2006. "Entrance and Exit from the Military: Reflections from American Indian and Alaska Native Veterans." *Journal of Ethnic and Cultural Diversity in Social Work* 15(1/2):27–53.

Lee, Sharon M. 1994. "Poverty and the U.S. Asian Population." *Social Science Quarterly* 75(3): 541–559.

Lee, Stacey J. 2009. *Unraveling the Model Minority Stereotype: Listening to Asian American Youth*, 2nd ed. New York: Teachers College Press.

Lee, Suevon. 2012. "By the Numbers: The U.S.'s Growing For-Profit Detention Industry." *ProPublica*, June 20. Retrieved July 25, 2013 (www.propublica.org/article/by-the-numbers-the-u.s.s-growing-for-profit-detention-industry).

Leiber, Jill. 2001. "Golf on New Course." *USA Today*, August 15. Retrieved April 14, 2013 (http://usa-today30.usatoday.com/sports/golf/_stories/2001-08-14-cover.htm).

Leiber, Michael J. and Jayne M. Stairs. 1999. "Race, Contexts, and the Use of Intake Diversion." *Journal of Research in Crime and Delinquency* 36(1):56–87.

Leonard, David J. 2004. "High Tech Blackface—Race, Sports Video Games and Becoming the Other." *Intelligent Agent* 4(4):1–5.

Leonard, David J. 2006. "Not a Hater, Just Keepin' It Real: The Importance of Race—and Gender-Based Game Studies." *Games and Culture* 1(1):83–88.

Leonard, David J. 2017. *Playing While White: Privilege and Power On and Off the Field.* Seattle, WA: University of Washington Press.

Leonardo, Zeus. 2004. "The Color of Supremacy: Beyond the Discourse of 'White Privilege.'" *Educational Philosophy and Theory* 36(2):137–52.

Leonardo, Zeus. 2007. "The War on Schools: NCLB, Nation Creation and the Educational Construction of Whiteness." *Race Ethnicity and Education* 10(3): 261–278.

Leondar-Wright, Betsy. 2008. "Black Job Loss Déjà Vu." Pp. 153–162 in *The Wealth Inequality Reader*, edited by Dollars & Sense and United for a Fair Economy. Boston, MA: Dollars & Sense—Economic Affairs Bureau.

Leonhardt, David. 2013. "Hispanics, the New Italians." *New York Times*, April 20. Retrieved May 20, 2013 (www.nytimes.com/2013/04/21/sunday-review/hispanics-the-new-italians.html).

Lerner, Steve. 2005. *Diamond: A Struggle for Environmental Justice in Louisiana's Chemical Corridor.* Cambridge, MA: The MIT Press.

Levin, Jack and Jack McDevitt. 2002. *Hate Crimes Revisited: America's War on Those Who Are Different.* New York: Basic Books.

Levin, Sam. 2017. "FBI Terrorism Unit Says 'Black Identity Extremists' Pose a Violent Threat." *Guardian*, October 7. Retrieved June 26, 2019 (www.theguardian.com/us-news/2017/oct/06/fbi-black-identity-extremists-racial-profiling).

Lewis, Amanda E. 2003. *Race in the Schoolyard: Negotiating the Color Line in Classrooms and Communities.* New Brunswick, NJ: Rutgers University Press.

Lewis-McCoy, R. L'Heureux. 2014. *Inequality in the Promised Land: Race, Resources and Suburban Schooling.* Stanford, CA: Stanford University Press.

Lewis, Valerie A., Michael O. Emerson, and Stephen L. Klineberg. 2011. "Who We'll Live With: Neighborhood Racial Composition Preferences of Whites, Blacks and Latinos." *Social Forces* 89(4):1385–1407.

Lewontin, Richard C. 2012. "Is There a Jewish Gene?" *New York Review of Books*, December 6. Retrieved March 18, 2013 (www.nybooks.com/articles/2012/12/06/is-there-a-jewish-gene/).

Lichtenberg, Illya. 2006. "Driving While Black (DWB): Examining Race as a Tool in the War on Drugs." *Police Practice and Research* 7(1):49–60.

Lichter, S. R., and D. Amundson. 1994. *Distorted Reality: Hispanic Characters in TV Entertainment.* Washington, DC: Center of Media and Public Affairs.

Licon, Adriana Gomez. 2016. "Rights Group: Police Executions Undermine Brazil Security." *Times-Picayune*, July 8, p. A11.

Lieb, Emily. 2017. "How Segregated Schools Built Segregated Cities." City Lab, February 2. Retrieved May 25, 2019 (www.citylab.com/equity/2017/02/how-segregated-schools-built-segregated-cities/515373/).

Lieberson, Stanley. 1980. *A Piece of the Pie: Blacks and White Immigrants Since 1880.* Berkeley, CA: University of California Press.

Linzer, Dafna and Jennifer Lafleur. 2001. "Presidents More Likely to Pardon White Felons." *Times-Picayune*, December 5, p. A3.

Lippard, Cameron D. 2016. "Playing the 'Immigrant Card': Reflections of Color-Blind Rhetoric Within Southern Attitudes on Immigration." *Social Currents* 3(1):24–42.

Lippard, Cameron D. and Charles Gallagher, eds. 2011. *Being Brown in Dixie: Race, Ethnicity, and Latino Immigration in the New South.* Boulder, CO: First Forum Press.

Lipsitz, George. 1992. "The Politics and Pedagogy of Popular Culture in Contemporary Textbooks." *Journal of American History* 78(4):1395–1400.

Lipsitz, George. 1997. "Cruising Around the Historical Block: Postmodernism and Popular Music in East Los Angeles." Pp. 350–359 in *The Subcultures Reader*, 2nd ed., edited by K. Gelder and S. Thornton. London: Routledge.

Lipsitz, George. 2001. *American Studies in a Moment of Danger.* Minneapolis: University of Minnesota Press.

Lipsitz, George. 2006. *The Possessive Investment in Whiteness: How White People Profit from Identity Politics*, revised and expanded ed. Philadelphia, PA: Temple University Press.

Liptack, Adam. 2012. "Blocking Parts of Arizona Law, Justices Allow Its Centerpiece." *New York Times*, June 25. Retrieved May 1, 2013 (www.nytimes.com/2012/06/26/us/supreme-court-rejects-part-of-arizona-immigration-law.html).

Littlefield, Holly. 2001. *Children of the Indian Boarding Schools*. Minneapolis, MN: Carolrhoda Books.

Litwack, Leon F. 1998. *Trouble in Mind: Black Southerners in the Age of Jim Crow*. New York: Alfred A. Knopf.

Lockette, Tim. 2010. "The New Racial Segregation at Public Schools." Alternet, February 4. Retrieved July 24, 2013 (www.alternet.org/story/145553/).

Loewen, James. 1999. *Lies Across America: What Our Historic Sites Get Wrong*. New York: Simon and Schuster.

Loewen, James. 2005. *Sundown Towns: A Hidden Dimension of American Racism*. New York: Touchstone.

Loewen, James. 2007. *Lies My Teacher Told Me: Everything Your American History Textbook Got Wrong*, revised ed. New York: Simon and Schuster.

Loftsdóttir, Kristín. 2009. "Invisible Colour: Landscapes of Whiteness and Racial Identity in International Development." *Anthropology Today* 25(5):4–7.

Logan, John R. 2003. "How Race Counts for Hispanic Americans." University of Albany, Lewis Mumford Center for Comparative Urban and Regional Research, July 14. Retrieved April 14, 2013 (http://mumford.albany.edu/census/BlackLatinoReport/BlackLatino01.htm).

Logan, John R., Jacob Stowell, and Deirdre Oakley. 2002. "Choosing Segregation: Racial Imbalances in American Schools, 1990–2000." University of Albany, Lewis Mumford Center for Comparative Urban and Regional Research. Retrieved July 24, 2013 (https://s4.ad.brown.edu/Projects/USSchools/reports/report4.pdf).

Lopez, Linda and Adrian D. Pantoja. 2004. "Beyond Black and White: General Support for Race Conscious Policies Among African Americans, Latinos, Asian Americans, and Whites." *Political Research Quarterly* 57(4):633–642.

Louie, Steven G. and Glenn Omatsu, eds. 2006. *Asian Americans: The Movement and the Moment*. Los Angeles, CA: UCLA Asian American Studies Center Press.

Loury, Glenn C. 2003. *The Anatomy of Racial Inequality*. Cambridge, MA: Harvard University Press.

Lovato, Roberto. 2009. "Latinos to CNN: Dump Lou Dobbs Now!" Alternet, September 16. Retrieved September 11, 2011 (www.alternet.org/module/printversion/142680).

Loveman, Mara. 2014. *National Colors: Racial Classification and the State in Latin America*. New York: Oxford University Press.

Lowery, Wesley. 2016. "Study Finds Police Fatally Shoot Unarmed Black Men at Disproportionate Rates." *Washington Post*, April 7. Retrieved June 14, 2016 (www.washingtonpost.com/national/study-finds-police-fatally-shoot-unarmed-black-men-at-disproportionate-rates/2016/04/06/e494563e-fa7).

Ludden, Jennifer. 2007. "No Americans Need Apply? Work Ethic Questioned." All Things Considered, NPR, January 2. Retrieved September 10, 2011 (www.npr.org/templates/story/story.php?storyId=6712257).

Luhman, Reid. 2002. *Race and Ethnicity in the United States: Our Differences and Our Roots*. Belmont, CA: Thompson/Wadsworth.

Lui, Meizhu. 2008. "Doubly Divided: The Racial Wealth Gap." Pp. 44–51 in *The Wealth Inequality Reader*, 2nd ed., edited by Dollars & Sense and United for a Fair Economy. Boston, MA: Dollars & Sense—Economic Affairs Bureau.

Lui, Meizhu, Barbara Robles, Betsy Leondar-Wright, Rose Brewer, and Rebecca Adamson, with United for a Fair Economy. 2006. *The Color of Wealth: The Story Behind the U.S. Racial Wealth Divide*. New York: The New Press.

Luker, Kristin. 1997. *Dubious Conceptions: The Politics of Teenage Pregnancy*. Cambridge, MA: Harvard University Press.

Luttmer, Erzo F. P. 2001. "Group Loyalty and the Taste for Redistribution." *Journal of Political Economy* 109(3):500–528.

Macartney, Suzanne, Alemayehu Bishaw, and Kayla Fontenot. 2013. "Poverty Rates for Selected Detailed Race and Hispanic Groups by State and Place: 2007–2011." American Community Survey Briefs, US Census Bureau. Retrieved March 11, 2013 (www.census.gov/prod/2013pubs/acsbr11-17.pdf).

Machamer, Ann Marie (Amber). 2001. "Last of the Mohicans, Braves, and Warriors: The End of American Indian Mascots in Los Angeles Public Schools." Pp. 208–220 in *Team Spirits: The Native American Mascots Controversy*, edited by C. R. King and C. F. Springwood. Lincoln: University of Nebraska Press.

Macionis. John J. 2010. *Sociology*, 13th ed. Upper Saddle River, NJ: Prentice Hall.

MacLeod, Celeste Lipow. 2006. *Multiethnic Australia: Its History and Future*. London: McFarland and Company, Inc.

Maddox, Keith B. and Stephanie A. Gray. 2002. "Cognitive Representations of Black Americans: Re-exploring the Role of Skin Tone." *Personality and Social Psychology Bulletin* 28(2):250–259.

Mahdzan, Farah and Norlinda Ziegler. 2001. "Negative Stereotyping of Asian Americans." Model Minority, July 4. Retrieved April 12, 2013 (http://modelminority.com/joomla/index.php?option=com_content&view=article&id=58:negative-stereotyping-of-asian-americans&catid=44:media&Itemid=56).

Maltz, Earl M. 2007. *Dred Scott and the Politics of Slavery*. Lawrence: University Press of Kansas.

Manza, Jeff and Christopher Uggen. 2006. *Locked Out: Felon Disenfranchisement and American Democracy*. Oxford, New York: Oxford University Press.

Manza, Jeff and Ned Crowley. 2018. "Ethnonationalism and the Rise of Donald Trump." *Contexts* 17(1):28–33.

Maran, Meredith. 2000. *Class Dismissed: A Year in the Life of an American High School, A Glimpse into the Heart of a Nation*. New York: St. Martin's Press.

Marcus, Kenneth. 2009. "Jailhouse Islamophobia: Discrimination in American Prisons." *Race and Social Problems* 1(1):36–44.

Markoff, John. 1996. *Waves of Democracy: Social Movements and Political Change*. Thousand Oaks, CA: Pine Forge Press.

Markus, Ben. 2016. "As Adults Legally Smoke Pot in Colorado, More Minority Kids Arrested for It." *Morning Edition*, NPR, June 29. Retrieved July 1, 2016 (www.npr.org/2016/06/29/483954157/as-adults-legally-smoke-pot-in-colorado-more-minority-kids-arrested-for-it).

Marriott, Michel. 1999. "Blood, Gore, Sex and Now: Race." *New York Times*, October 21. Retrieved July 24, 2013 (www.nytimes.com/1999/10/21/technology/blood-gore-sex-and-now-race.html).

Marrow, Helen B. 2011. *New Destination Dreaming: Immigration, Race, and Legal Status in the Rural American South*. Stanford, CA: Stanford University Press.

Marshall, Barbara. 2001. "Working While Black: Contours of an Unequal Playing Field." *Phylon* 49(3/4):137–150.

Martin, Areva and Arshya Vahabzadeh. 2014. "Children of Color and Autism: Too Little, Too Late." *Huffington Post*, November 10. Retrieved July 3, 2016 (www.huffingtonpost.com/areva-martin/children-of-color-and-aut_b_6133354.html).

Martin, Ben L. 1991. "From Negro to Black to African American: The Power of Names and Naming." *Political Science Quarterly* 106(10):83–107.

Martin, Jonathan and Alan Blinder. 2019. "Second Virginia Democrat Says He Wore Blackface, Throwing Party into Turmoil." *New York Times*, February 6. Retrieved March 12, 2019 (www.nytimes.com/2019/02/06/us/politics/virginia-blackface-mark-herring.html).

Martin, Michael. 2013. "Korean-American Rapper Changing the Face of Hip-Hop." Radio WVTF, April 18. Retrieved February 28, 2020 (www.wvtf.org/post/korean-american-rapper-changing-face-hip-hop#stream/0).

Martin, Michael E. 2013. *Residential Segregation Patterns of Latinos in the United States, 1990–2000*. New York: Routledge.

Martinez, E. 1997. "Unite and Overcome!" *Teaching Tolerance* 11. Retrieved March 3, 2014 (www.tolerance.org/magazine/number-11-spring-1997/feature/unite-and-overcome).

Martinez, Miranda. 2005. "The Nuyorican Movement: Community Struggle Against Blocked Mobility in New York City." Pp. 289–305 in *Minority Voices: Linking Personal Ethnic History and the Sociological Imagination*, edited by J. P. Myers. New York: Pearson.

Massey, Douglas, ed. 2008. *New Faces in New Places: The Changing Geography of American Immigration.* New York: Russell Sage Foundation.

Massey, Douglas and Nancy Denton. 1993. *American Apartheid: Segregation and the Making of the Underclass.* Cambridge, MA: Harvard University Press.

Mastro, Dana E. and Elizabeth Behm-Morawitz. 2005. "Latino Representation on Primetime Television." *Journalism and Mass Communication Quarterly* 82(1):110–130.

Mather, Victor. 2019. "A Timeline of Colin Kaepernick vs. the NFL." *New York Times*, February 15. Retrieved July 1, 2019 (www.nytimes.com/2019/02/15/sports/nfl-colin-kaepernick-protests-timeline.html).

McAdam, Doug. 1988. *Freedom Summer.* New York, Oxford: Oxford University Press.

McAuley, Christopher A. 2004. *The Mind of Oliver C. Cox.* Notre Dame, IN: University of Notre Dame Press.

McCarthy, John D. and Mayer N. Zald. 1977. "Resource Mobilization and Social Movements: A Partial Theory." *American Journal of Sociology* 82(6):1212–1241.

McCorkel, Jill A. 2013. *Breaking Women: Gender, Race, and the New Politics of Imprisonment.* New York: New York University Press.

McCroskey, S. 2010. "Lou Dobbs, American Hypocrite." *The Nation*, October 7. Retrieved September 11, 2011 (www.thenation.com/print/article/155209/lou-dobbs-american-hypocrite).

McCrum, Robert, William Cran, and Robert MacNeil. 1986. *The Story of English.* New York: Viking Publishers.

McDermott, Monica and Frank L. Samson. 2005. "White Racial and Ethnic Identity in the United States." *Annual Review of Sociology* 31:245–261.

McDonald, Steve, Lindsey Hamm, James R. Elliott, and Pete Knepper. 2016. "Race, Place and Unsolicited Job Leads: How the Ethnoracial Structure of Local Labor Markets Shapes Employment Opportunities." *Social Currents* 3(2):1–20.

McDonald, Suzanne. 2007. "Help for Incarcerated Native Americans." *Guild Notes*, Spring, pp. 16–17.

McDowell, Meghan G. and Nancy A. Wonders. 2009–10. "Keeping Migrants in Their Place: Technologies of Control and Racialized Public Space in Arizona." *Social Justice* 36(2):54–72.

McGinn, Daniel and Temma Ehrenfeld. 2008. "Clues for the Clueless." *Newsweek*, April 14, p. 38.

McGuinn, Patrick J. 2006. *No Child Left Behind and the Transformation of Federal Education Policy, 1965–2005.* Lawrence: University Press of Kansas.

McGuire, Danielle L. 2010. *At the Dark End of the Street: Black Women, Rape, and Resistance—A New History of the Civil Rights Movement from Rosa Parks to the Rise of Black Power.* New York: Vintage Books.

McGurty, Eileen. 2007. *Transforming Environmentalism: Warren County, PCBs, and the Origins of Environmental Justice.* New Brunswick, NJ: Rutgers University Press.

McIntosh, Peggy. 1988. "White Privilege and Male Privilege: A Personal Account of Coming to See Correspondences Through Work in Women's Studies." Working Paper 189. Center for Research on Women, Wellesley College, Wellesley, MA.

McIntosh, Peggy. 2008. "White Privilege: Unpacking the Invisible Knapsack." Pp. 97–102 in *White Privilege: Essential Readings on the Other Side of Racism*, 3rd ed., edited by P. Rothenberg. New York: Worth Publishers.

McIntyre, Alice. 1997. *Making Meaning of Whiteness: Exploring Racial Identity with White Teachers.* Albany: State University of New York Press.

McIntyre, Alice. 1997b. "Constructing an Image of a White Teacher." *Teachers College Record* 98(4):653–682.

McKee, James B. 1993. *Sociology and the Race Problem: A Failure of Perspective.* Urbana and Chicago: University of Illinois Press.

McRae, Elizabeth Gillespie. 2005. "White Womanhood, White Supremacy, and the Rise of Massive Resistance." Pp. 181–202 in *Massive Resistance: Southern Opposition to the Second Reconstruction*, edited by C. Webb. Oxford, New York: Oxford University Press.

McRae, Elizabeth Gillespie. 2018. *Mothers of Massive Resistance: White Women and the Politics of White Supremacy.* New York: Oxford University Press.

McShane, Marilyn D. 2008. *Prisons in America.* New York: LFB Scholarly Publishing, LLC.

Meier, Deborah and George Wood. 2004. *Many Children Left Behind: How the No Child Left Behind Act Is Damaging Our Children and Our Schools.* Boston, MA: Beacon Press.

Meier, Matt and Feliciano Rivera. 1972. *The Chicanos: A History of Mexican Americans.* New York: Hill and Wang Publishers.

Meierhoefer, Barbara S. 1992. *The General Effect of Mandatory Minimum Prison Terms: A Longitudinal Study of Federal Sentences Imposed.* Washington, DC: Federal Judicial Center.

Melcher, Joan. 2009. "A History in the Making." *Miller-McCune,* May–June, pp. 24–29.

Melucci, Alberto. 1980. "The New Social Movements: A Theoretical Approach." *Social Science Information* 19(2):199–226.

"Members of Congress Urge Redskins to Change Name." 2013. *Times-Picayune,* May 29, p. A-3.

Menchaca, Martha. 2001. *Rediscovering History, Constructing Race: The Indian, Black, and White Roots of Mexican Americans.* Austin: University of Texas Press.

Mencimer, Stephanie. 2008. "Texas Hold 'Em." *Mother Jones* 33(4):56–57.

Mercurio, Eugenio and Vincent F. Filak. 2010. "Roughing the Passer: The Framing of Black and White Quarterbacks Prior to the NFL Draft." *Howard Journal of Communications* 21(1):56–71.

Merton, Robert. 1938. "Social Structure and Anomie." *American Sociological Review* 3(5):672–682.

Metcalf, George R. 1983. *From Little Rock to Boston: The History of School Desegregation.* Westport, CT: Greenwood Press.

Metzl, Jonathan M. 2019. *Dying of Whiteness: How the Politics of Racial Resentment is Killing America's Heartland.* New York: Basic Books.

Meyer, Doug. 2015. *Violence Against Queer People: Race, Class, Gender, and the Persistence of Anti-LGBT Discrimination.* New Brunswick, NJ: Rutgers University Press.

Mickelson, Roslyn Arlin. "Why Does Jane Read and Write So Well? The Anomaly of Women's Achievement." Pp. 149–172 in *Education and Gender Equality,* edited by J. Wrigley. London, Washington, DC: The Falmer Press.

Mikulich, Alex, Laurie Cassidy, and Margaret Pfeil. 2013. *The Scandal of White Complicity in U.S. Hyper-Incarceration: A Nonviolent Spirituality of White Resistance.* New York: Palgrave Macmillan.

Miller, Kerby A. 1985. *Emigrants and Exiles: Ireland and the Irish Exodus to North America.* New York, Oxford: Oxford University Press.

Millman, Jennifer. 2008. "Slavery Ties: Bush's Long-Held 'Family Secret.'" DiversityInc.com, February 20. Retrieved July 11, 2013 (www.juneteenth.us/news7.html).

Mills, Charles W. 1997. *The Racial Contract.* Ithaca, NY: Cornell University Press.

Mills, C. Wright. 2000 [1959]. *The Sociological Imagination.* Oxford, UK: Oxford University Press.

Mingus, William and Bradley Zopf. 2010. "White Means Never Having to Say You're Sorry: The Racial Project in Explaining Mass Shootings." *Social Thought and Research* 31:57–77.

Minow, Martha. 2004. "Surprising Legacies of *Brown v. Board.*" P. 9 in *Legacies of Brown: Multiracial Equity in American Education,* edited by D. J. Carter, S. M. Flores, and R. J. Reddick. Cambridge, MA: Harvard Educational Review.

Mitchell, Amelia, Marie-Anne Ricardo, and Belma Sarajilic. n.d. "Whitewashed Slavery Past? The (Lost) Struggle Against Ignorance About the Dutch Slavery History." Humanity in Action.org. Retrieved July 11, 2016 (www.humanityinaction.org/knowledgebase/434-whitewashed-slavery-past-the-lost-struggle-against-ignorance-about-the-dutch-slavery-history).

Mitchell, Thomas G. 2007. *Antislavery Politics in Antebellum and Civil War America.* Westport, CT: Praeger.

Mogul, Joey L., Andrea J. Ritchie, and Kay Whitlock. 2011. *Queer (In)Justice: The Criminalization of LGBT People in the United States.* Boston, MA: Beacon Press.

Molina, Natalia. 2014. *How Race Is Made in America: Immigration, Citizenship, and the Historical Power of Racial Scripts.* Berkeley: University of California Press.

Montague, James. 2011. "An American Soccer Star Playing for Palestine." CNN.com, July 4. Retrieved July 3, 2013 (http://edition.cnn.com/2011/SPORT/football/07/01/palestine.american.omar.jarun/index.html).

Montana, Alex. 2002. "Alex Montana's Story." Albert Eissing's Native Home Page, April 30. Retrieved May 21, 2013 (http://members.home.nl/aeissing/montanae.html).

"Montana Profile." 2010. *Prison Policy Initiative.* Retrieved June 26, 2019. www.prisonpolicy.org/profiles/MT.html.

Moody, Aaron. 2018. "Silent Sam's History Has Been Marked by Protests." *The Raleigh News & Observer.* August 22: 6A.

Moore, Jan and Raquel Pinderhughes, eds. 1993. *In the Barrios: Latinos and the Underclass Debate.* New York: Russell Sage Foundation.

Moore, Joan and Harry Pachon. 1976. *Mexican Americans.* Englewood Cliffs, NJ: Prentice Hall.

Moore, Lisa D. and Amy Elkavich. 2008. "Who's Using and Who's Doing Time: Incarceration, the War on Drugs, and Public Health." *American Journal of Public Health* 98(5):782–786.

Moore, Wendy Leo. 2008. *Reproducing Racism: White Space, Elite Law Schools, and Racial Inequality.* Lanham, MD: Rowman and Littlefield.

Moore, Wendy Leo and Joyce M. Bell. 2011. "Maneuvers of Whiteness: 'Diversity' as a Mechanism of Retrenchment in the Affirmative Action Discourse." *Critical Sociology* 37(5):597–613.

Moore, Wendy Leo and Joyce M. Bell. 2017. "The Right to Be Racist on Campus." *Law & Policy* 39(2):99–120.

Morales, Rebecca and Frank Bonilla, eds. 1993. *Latinos in a Changing U.S. Economy: Comparative Perspectives on Growing Inequality.* Newbury Park, CA: Sage Publications.

Morris, Aldon D. 2007. "Sociology of Race and W. E. B. Du Bois: The Path Not Taken." Pp. 503–534 in *Sociology in America: A History,* edited by C. Calhoun. Chicago, IL: University of Chicago Press.

Morris, Aldon D. 2015. *The Scholar Denied: W. E. B. Du Bois and the Birth of Modern Sociology.* Oakland: University of California Press.

Morris, Edward W. and Brea L. Perry. 2016. "The Punishment Gap: School Suspension and Racial Disparities in Achievement." *Social Problems* 63(1):68–86.

Morris, Wesley. 2019. "The Governor Who Partied Like it's 1884." *New York Times,* February 3. Retrieved July 3, 2019 (www.nytimes.com/2019/02/03/arts/-blackface-governor-northam.html?module=inline/).

Morse, Minna. 1999. "The Changing Face of Stone Mountain." *Smithsonian* 29(10):56–66.

Morse, Minna and Maggie Steber. "The Changing Face of Stone Mountain." *Smithsonian* 29(10) (January 1999):56.

Mortished, Carl. 2010. "The Confusing, and Perilous, State of European Immigration." *Globe and Mail (Canada),* October 19, p. B15. Retrieved September 8, 2011 (www.lexisnexis.com/lnacui2api/delivery/PrintDoc.do?jobHandle=1826%3A3052817).

Moser, Bob. 2008. *Blue Dixie: Awakening the South's Democratic Majority.* New York: Holt Paperback.

Moskos, Charles C. and John Sibley Butler. 1996. *All That We Can Be: Black Leadership and Racial Integration the Army Way.* New York: Basic Books.

Mueller, Jennifer C. 2017. "Producing Colorblindness: Everyday Mechanisms of White Ignorance." *Social Problems* 64:219–238.

Muñoz, Carlos, Jr. 2007. *Youth, Identity, Power: The Chicano Movement,* revised and expanded ed. New York: Verso Books.

Muro, Jazmin A. and Lisa M. Martinez. 2018. "Is Love Color-Blind? Racial Blind Spots and Latinas' Romantic Relationships." *Sociology of Race and Ethnicity* 4(4):527–540.

Murphy, Heather. 2019. "How White Nationalists See What They Want to See in DNA Tests." *New York Times,* July 12. Retrieved July 20, 2019 (www.nytimes.com/2019/07/12/us/white-nationalists-dna-tests.html).

Murray, Gail S. 2004. *Throwing Off the Cloak of Privilege: White Southern Women Activists in the Civil Rights Era.* Gainesville: University Press of Florida.

Myrdal, Gunnar. 1944. *An American Dilemma: The Negro Problem and Modern Democracy.* New York: Harper and Brothers.

Nagel, Joane. 1996. *American Indian Ethnic Renewal: Red Power and the Resurgence of Identity and Culture.* New York and Oxford: Oxford University Press.

Nagel, Joane. 2003. *Race, Ethnicity, and Sexuality: Intimate Intersections, Forbidden Frontiers.* New York and Oxford: Oxford University Press.

Nakanishi, Don T. 1989. "A Quota on Excellence? The Asian American Admissions Debate." *Change*, November/December, pp. 39–47.

Nanda, Serena. 2020. "Multiple Genders Among Native Americans." Pp. 64–71 in *The Kaleidoscope of Gender: Prisms, Patterns, and Possibilities*, 6th ed., edited by Catherine G. Valentine, Mary Nell Trautner, and Joan Z. Spade. Los Angeles, CA: Sage Publishing.

Naples, Nancy. 1998. *Grassroots Warriors: Activist Mothering, Community Work, and the War on Poverty*. New York and London: Routledge.

National Center for Education Statistics. 2014. "Digest of Education Statistics." Table 322.20. Retrieved July 2, 2016 (https://nces.ed.gov/programs/digest/d14/tables/dt14_322.20.asp).

National Center for Education Statistics. 2014b. "Certificates and Degrees Conferred by Race/Ethnicity." Retrieved July 2, 2016 (https://nces.ed.gov/programs/coe/pdf/coe_svc.pdf).

Nash, Gary B. 1974. *Red, White and Black: The Peoples of Early North America*. Upper Saddle River, NJ: Prentice Hall.

Nelson, Alondra. 2008. "The Factness of Diaspora: The Social Sources of Genetic Genealogy." Pp. 253–270 in *Revisiting Race in a Genomic Age*, edited by B. A. Koenig, S. S. Lee, and S. S. Richardson. New Brunswick, NJ: Rutgers University Press.

Nelson, Alondra. 2016. *The Social Life of DNA: Race, Reparations, and Reconciliation after the Genome*. Boston, MA: Beacon Press.

Nelson, Havelock and Michael A. Gonzales. 1991. *Bring the Noise: A Guide to Rap Music and Hip-Hop Culture*. New York: Harmony Books.

Nemoto, Kumiko. 2009. *Racing Romance: Love, Power and Desire Among Asian American/White Couples*. New Brunswick, NJ: Rutgers University Press.

Newman, Brooke. 2018. "The Long History Behind the Racist Attacks on Serena Williams." *Washington Post*, September 11. Retrieved July 1, 2019 (www.washingtonpost.com/outlook/2018/09/11/long-history-behind-racist-attacks-serena-williams/?utm_term=.a1bc73e56482).

Newman, Joshua I. 2007. "Old Times There Are Not Forgotten: Sport, Identity, and the Confederate Flag in the Dixie South." *Sociology of Sport Journal* 24(3):261–282.

Newman, Louise Michele. 1999. *White Women's Rights: The Racial Origins of Feminism in the United States*. Oxford and New York: Oxford University Press.

Newton, Nell Jessup. 1999. "Indian Claims for Reparations, Compensation, and Restitution in the United States Legal System." P. 41 in *When Sorry Isn't Enough: The Controversy over Apologies and Reparations for Human Injustice*, edited by R. L. Brooks. New York: New York University Press.

Ngai, Mae. 2004. *Impossible Subjects: Illegal Aliens and the Making of Modern America*. Princeton, NJ: Princeton University Press.

Nies, Judith. 1996. *Native American History*. New York: Ballantine Books.

Nieto, Sonia, ed. 2000. *Puerto Rican Students in U.S. Schools*. Mahwah, NJ: Lawrence Erlbaum.

Niles, Maria. 2011. "Black History Month: Why I Identify as Black." Blogher.com, February 28. Retrieved April 14, 2013 (www.blogher.com/black-history-month-why-i-identify-black).

Nisbett, Richard. 1995. "Race, IQ, and Scientism." Pp. 36–57 in *The Bell Curve Wars: Race, Intelligence and the Future of America*, edited by S. Fraser. New York: Basic Books.

Nix, Emily and Nancy Qian. 2015. "The Fluidity of Race: 'Passing' in the United States, 1880–1940." NBER Working Paper 20828. National Bureau of Economic Research. Retrieved July 9, 2016 (http://aida.wss.yale.edu/~nq3/NANCYS_Yale_Website/resources/papers/NixQian_20150101.pdf).

Noble, Safiya Umoja. 2018. *Algorithms of Oppression: How Search Engines Reinforce Racism*. New York: New York University Press.

Noel, Donald L. 1968. "A Theory of the Origin of Ethnic Stratification." *Social Problems* 16(2):157–172.

Noel, Donald L. 1972. *The Origins of American Slavery and Racism*. Columbus, OH: Charles E. Merrill Publishing Co.

Noguera, Pedro A. 2004. "Social Capital and the Education of Immigrant Students: Categories and Generalizations." *Sociology of Education* 77(2):180–183.

Noguera, Pedro A. 2008. *The Trouble with Black Boys: And Other Reflections on Race, Equity, and the Future of Public Education*. San Francisco, CA: Jossey-Bass.

Nojeim, Michael. 2004. *Gandhi and King: The Power of Nonviolent Resistance.* London, Westport, CT: Praeger.

Noriega, Jorge. 1992. "American Indian Education in the United States: Indoctrination for Subordination to Colonialism." Pp. 371–402 in *The State of Native America: Genocide, Colonization, Resistance*, edited by M. A. Jaimes. Boston, MA: South End Press.

Nurullah, Abu Sadat. 2010. "Portrayal of Muslims in the Media: '24' and the 'Othering' Process." *International Journal of Human Sciences* 7(1):1020–1046.

Oakes, J. 1985. *Keeping Track: How Schools Structure Inequality.* New Haven, CT: Yale University Press.

Oakley, Giles. 1997. *The Devil's Music: A History of the Blues*, 2nd ed. New York: Da Capo Press.

O'Connell, Heather A. 2019. "Historical Shadows: The Links between Sundown Towns and Contemporary Black–White Inequality." *Sociology of Race and Ethnicity* 5(3):311–325.

O'Connor, Lydia and Daniel Marans. 2016. "Here are 13 Examples of Donald Trump Being Racist." *Huffington Post*, February 29. Retrieved March 13, 2019 (www.huffingtonpost.com/entry/donald-trump-racist-examples_us_56d47177e4b03260bf777e83).

Ogbar, Jeffrey O. G. 2001. "Yellow Fever: The Formation of Asian American Nationalism in the Age of Black Power, 1966–1975." *Souls* 3:29–38.

Ogbu, John. 1978. *Minority Education and Caste.* New York: Academic Press.

Ogbu, John. 1990. "Minority Education in Comparative Perspective." *Journal of Negro Education* 59(1):45–57.

Ogbu, John. 2003. *Black American Students in an Affluent Suburb: A Study of Academic Disengagement.* Mahwah, NJ: Lawrence Erlbaum Associates Publishers.

Ogletree, Charles. 2012. *The Presumption of Guilt: The Arrest of Henry Louis Gates, Jr. and Race, Class and Crime in America.* New York: Palgrave Macmillan.

Ogletree, Charles J., Jr. and Austin Sarat. 2006. "Introduction." Pp. 1–17 in *From Lynch Mobs to the Killing State: Race and the Death Penalty in America*, edited by C. J. Ogletree, Jr. and A. Sarat. New York and London: New York University Press.

Ohlheiser, Abby. 2012. "Report Shows 'Stunning' Increase in Anti-Government Groups." Slatest at Slate.com, March 8. Retrieved May 20, 2012 (http://slatest.slate.com/posts/2012/03/08/southern_poverty_law_center_hate_group_report_obama_election_triggers_patriot_organization.html).

Okamoto, Dina G. 2014. *Redefining Race: Asian American Panethnicity and Shifting Ethnic Boundaries.* New York: Russell Sage Foundation.

Oliver, Melvin L. and Thomas M. Shapiro. 1995. *Black Wealth/White Wealth: A New Perspective on Racial Inequality.* New York, London: Routledge.

Oliver, Melvin L. and Thomas M. Shapiro. 2019. "Disrupting the Racial Wealth Gap." *Contexts* 18(1):16–21.

Olivo, Antonio. 2008. "By 2050, Nearly 1 in 5 U.S. Residents to Be Immigrants." *Chicago Tribune*, February 12. Retrieved February 24, 2008 (www.chicagotribune.com/20080212-TB-Study-By-2050-nearly-1-in-5-residents-to-be-immigrants-0212).

Olson, Keith W. 1974. *The G.I. Bill, the Veterans, and the Colleges.* Lexington: University Press of Kentucky.

Olzak, Susan. 1990. "The Political Context of Competition: Lynching and Urban Racial Violence, 1882–1914." *Social Forces* 69(2):395–421.

Olzak, Susan. 1992. *The Dynamics of Ethnic Competition and Conflict.* Stanford, CA: Stanford University Press.

Olzak, Susan and Joane Nagel, eds. 1986. *Competitive Ethnic Relations.* Orlando, FL: Academic Press.

Omi, Michael and Howard Winant. 1994. *Racial Formation in the United States: From the 1960s to the 1990s*, 2nd ed. New York, London: Routledge.

O'Neil, Dana Pennett. 2007. "McNabb and the Grating Expectations." *Philadelphia Daily News*, September 19. Retrieved November 15, 2007 (www.philly.com/philly/sports/eagles/200070919_GRATING_EXPECTATIONS.html).

Ong, Paul and Evelyn Blumenberg. 1993. "An Unnatural Trade-Off: Latinos and Environmental Justice." Pp. 207–225 in *Latinos in a Changing U.S. Economy*, edited by R. Morales and F. Bonilla. Newbury Park, CA: Sage.

Operation HOPE. 2016. "HOPE Small Business Empowerment Program." Retrieved October 9, 2016 (www.operationhope.org/small-business).

Orfield, G. and M. Kornhaber, eds. 2001. *Raising Standards or Raising Barriers? Inequality and High-Stakes Testing in Public Education.* New York: Century Foundation.

Oshinsky, David M. 1996. *"Worse Than Slavery": Parchman Farm and the Ordeal of Jim Crow Justice.* New York: The Free Press.

Pager, Devah. 2007. *Marked: Race, Crime, and Finding Work in an Era of Mass Incarceration.* Chicago, IL: University of Chicago Press.

Paley, Vivian Gussin. 2000. *White Teacher*, 2nd ed. Cambridge, MA: Harvard University Press.

Palmer, Brian and Seth Freed Wessler. 2018. "The Costs of the Confederacy." *Smithsonian*, December. Retrieved July 30, 2019 (www.smithsonianmag.com/history/costs-confederacy-special-report-180970731/).

Parenti, Michael. 1994. *Land of Idols: Political Mythology in America.* New York: St. Martin's Press.

Parisi, Nicolette, Michael R. Gottfredson, Michael J. Hindelang, and Timothy J. Flanigan, eds. 1979. *Sourcebook of Criminal Justice Statistics, 1978.* Washington, DC: US Government Printing Office.

Park, Robert E. 1950. *Race and Culture.* Glencoe, IL: The Free Press.

Park, Robert Ezra and Herbert Miller. 1921. *Old World Traits Transplanted.* Chicago, IL: University of Chicago Press.

Parker, Karen F. 2008. *Unequal Crime Decline: Theorizing Race, Urban Inequality, and Criminal Violence.* New York and London: New York University Press.

Parker, Laura. 2001. "USA Just Wouldn't Work Without Immigrant Labor." *USA Today*, July 22. Retrieved September 10, 2011 (www.usatoday.com/news/washington/july01/2001-07-23-immigrant.htm).

Parker, Robin and Pamela Smith Chambers. 2007. *The Great White Elephant: A Workbook on Racial Privilege for White Anti-Racists.* Mount Laurel, NJ: Beyond Diversity Resource Center.

Passel, Jeffrey and D'Vera Cohn. 2008. "U.S. Population Projections 2005–2050." Pew Research Hispanic Center, February 11. Retrieved April 22, 2013 (www.pewhispanic.org/2008/02/11/us-population-projections-2005-2050/).

Passel, Jeffrey and Mark Hugo Lopez. 2012. "Up to 1.7 Million Undocumented Youth May Benefit from New Deportation Rules." Pew Research Center, August 14. Retrieved April 15, 2013 (www.pewhispanic.org/2012/08/14/up-to-1-7-million-unauthorized-immigrant-youth-may-benefit-from-new-deportation-rules/).

Patten, Eileen. 2016. "Racial, Gender Wage Gaps Persist in U.S. Despite Some Progress." Pew Research Center Fact Tank, July 1. Retrieved May 28, 2019 (www.pewresearch.org/fact-tank/2016/07/01/racial-gender-wage-gaps-persist-in-u-s-despite-some-progress/).

Patterson, Orlando. 2010. "Can't Call It Progress: African-Americans Are Earning Less Than Their Parents Did." *Nation*, July 7. Retrieved July 25, 2013 (www.alternet.org/story/147452/can%27t_call_it_progress%3A_african-americans_are_earning_less_than_their_parents_did).

Pattillo, Mary. 2015. "Everyday Politics of School Choice in the Black Community." *Du Bois Review* 12(1):41–71.

Pattillo, Mary, David Weiman, and Bruce Western, eds. 2004. *Imprisoning America: The Social Effects of Mass Incarceration.* New York: Russell Sage Foundation.

Pattillo-McCoy, Mary. 1999. *Black Picket Fences: Privilege and Peril Among the Black Middle Class.* Chicago, IL: University of Chicago Press.

Pauker, Kristin, Colleen Carpinella, Chanel Meyers, Danielle M. Young, and Diana T. Sanchez. 2018. "The Role of Diversity Exposure in Whites' Reduction in Race Essentialism Over Time." *Social Psychological and Personality Science* 9(8):944–952.

Paying for Senior Care. 2019. "Health and Human Services Poverty Guidelines/Federal Poverty Levels." Retrieved July 28, 2019 (www.payingforseniorcare.com/longtermcare/federal-poverty-level.html).

Payne, Charles M. 2008. *So Much Reform, So Little Change: The Persistence of Failure in Urban Schools.* Cambridge, MA: Harvard Education Press.

Pearce, Diana. 1976. *Black, White, and Many Shades of Gray: Real Estate Brokers and their Racial Practices.* Unpublished PhD dissertation, The University of Michigan, Ann Arbor. Retrieved

August 2, 2019 (https://leerebookes.com/ebookfile/read.php?book=BLACK%20%20WHITE%20
%20AND%20MANY%20SHADES%20OF%20GRAY%20%20REAL%20ESTATE%20BROKERS%20
AND%20THEIR%20RACIAL%20PRACTICES).

Pearce, Sarah. 2005. *You Wouldn't Understand: White Teachers in Multiethnic Classrooms.* Stafford-shire, UK: Trentham Books.

Pellegrini, Anthony D. and Peter Blatchford. 2000. *The Child at School: Interactions with Peers and Teachers.* London and Oxford, UK: Arnold/Oxford University Press.

Pellow, David Naguib. 2018. *What is Critical Environmental Justice?* Cambridge, UK: Polity Press.

Pember, Mary Annette. 2010. "The Bitter Legacy of American Indian Boarding Schools." *USA-RiseUp*, March 10. Retrieved July 24, 2013 (www.usaonrace.com/feature-stories/bitter-legacy-american-indian-boarding-schools).

Perdomo, Yolanda. 2004. "Political Growing Pains." *Hispanic* 17(6):15.

Perdue, Theda. 1997. "Writing the Ethnohistory of Native Women." Pp. 73–86 in *Rethinking American Indian History*, edited by D. L. Fixico. Albuquerque: University of New Mexico Press.

Perkins, James E. and Martin J. Bourgeois. 2006. "Perceptions of Police Use of Deadly Force." *Journal of Applied Social Psychology* 36(1):161–177.

Perkinson, Robert. 2010. *Texas Tough: The Rise of America's Prison Empire.* New York: Henry Holt and Company.

Perkinson, Robert. 2010b. "Texas Justice, American Injustice." *Truthout*, April 10. Retrieved July 23, 2010 (www.truth-out.org/texas-justice-american-injustice58409).

Perrottet, Tony. 2006. "Mt. Rushmore." *Smithsonian* 37(2):78–83.

Perry, Huey L. and Wayne Parent. 1995. "Black Politics in the United States." Pp. 3–10 in *Blacks and the American Political System*, edited by H. L. Perry and W. Parent. Gainesville: University Press of Florida.

Persons, Stow. 1987. *Ethnic Studies in Chicago: 1905–1945.* Champaign: University of Illinois Press.

Peterson, Ruth D. and Lauren J. Krivo. 2009. "Race, Residence, and Violent Crime: A Structure of Inequality." *Kansas Law Review* 57(4):303–333.

Pettit, Becky and Carmen Gutierrez. 2018. "Mass Incarceration and Racial Inequality." *The American Journal of Economics and Sociology* 77(3–4):1153–1182.

Pfaelzer, Jean. 2008. *Driven Out: The Forgotten War Against Chinese Americans.* Berkeley: University of California Press.

Phillips, Kristine. 2018. "A Black Child's Backpack Brushed up against a Woman. She Called 911 to Report a Sexual Assault." *The Washington Post*, October 16. Retrieved March 12, 2019 (www.washingtonpost.com/nation/2018/10/13/black-childs-backpack-brushed-up-against-woman-she-called-report-sexual-assault/?utm_term=.cba62c646a58).

Phillips, Ulrich. 1918. *American Negro Slavery.* Baton Rouge, LA: Louisiana State University Press.

Picker, Miguel and Chyng Sun. 2012. *Latinos Beyond Reel: Challenging a Media Stereotype.* North-hampton, MA: Media Education Foundation.

Pinar, William F. 2001. *The Gender of Racial Politics and Violence in America: Lynching, Prison Rape, and the Crisis of Masculinity.* New York, Washington, DC: Peter Lang Publishers.

Pinho, Patricia de Santana. 2009. "White but Not Quite: Tones and Overtones of Whiteness in Brazil." *Small Axe: A Caribbean Journal of Criticism* 29:39–56.

Pitcaithley, Dwight T. 2006. "'A Cosmic Threat': The National Park Service Addresses the Causes of the American Civil War." Pp. 169–186 in *Slavery and Public History: The Tough Stuff of American Memory*, edited by J. O. Horton and L. E. Horton. Chapel Hill: University of North Carolina Press.

Piven, Frances Fox and Richard A. Cloward. 1979. *Poor People's Movements: Why They Succeed, How They Fail.* New York: Vintage Books/Random House.

Poehlmann, J. 2003. "Family Matters: Update on Health Insurance." *A Family Impact Seminar Newsletter for Wisconsin Policymakers* 3(2):1–2. Retrieved July 25, 2013 (www.purdue.edu/hhs/hdfs/fii/wp-content/uploads/2015/06/pnl_v03i01_0603.pdf).

Pomerance, Alan. 1988. *Repeal of the Blues.* New York: Citadel Press.

Popp, Evan. 2016. "White Youths Yelling Racial Slurs Chase Black Teenager to His Death." *Think Progress*, June 3. Retrieved June 14, 2015 (http://thinkprogress.org/justice/2016/06/03/3784578/new-york-teen-dies-after-racist-teenagers-hunted-him/).

Portales, Marco. 2004. "A History of Latino Segregation Lawsuits." Pp. 124–136 in *The Unfinished Agenda of Brown v. Board of Education*, edited by The Editors of Black Issues in Higher Education. Hoboken, NJ: Wiley and Sons, Inc.

Potok, Mark. 2013. "DOJ Study: More Than 250,000 Hate Crimes a Year, Most Unreported." Southern Poverty Law Center, March 26. Retrieved April 15, 2013 (www.splcenter.org/blog/2013/03/26/doj-study-more-than-250000-hate-crimes-a-year-a-third-never-reported/).

Potok, Mark. 2016. "The Year in Hate and Extremism." *Intelligence Report*, February 17. Retrieved July 8, 2016 (www.splcenter.org/fighting-hate/intelligence-report/2016/year-hate-and-extremism).

"Poverty Rate by Race/Ethnicity." 2017. Henry J. Kaiser Family Foundation. Retrieved August 4, 2019 (www.kff.org/other/state-indicator/poverty-rate-by-raceethnicity/?currentTimeframe=0&sortModel=%7B%22colId%22:%22Location%22,%22sort%22:%22asc%22%7D).

Price, S. L. 2002. "The Indian Wars." *Sports Illustrated*, March 4. Retrieved April 11, 2012 (www.si.com/vault/2002/03/04/8100154/the-indian-wars-the-campaign-against-indian-nicknames-and-mascots-presumes-that-they-offend-native-americansbut-do-they-we-took-a-poll-and-you-wont-believe-the-results).

Prince, Zenitha. 2009. "Black Intellectuals Decry White House 'Beer Summit.'" *Los Angeles Sentinel*, August 6. Retrieved July 7, 2011 (www.lasentinel.net/Black-Intellectuals-Decry-White-House-Beer-Summit.html).

Prothrow-Stith, Deborah. 1991. *Deadly Consequences*. New York: HarperCollins Publishers.

Qian, Zhenchao. 2005. "Breaking the Last Taboo: Interracial Marriage in America." *Contexts* 4(4):33–37.

Quadagno, Jill. 1994. *The Color of Welfare*. Oxford, New York: Oxford University Press.

Quadagno, Jill. 2005. *One Nation Uninsured: Why the U.S. Has No National Health Insurance*. Oxford, New York: Oxford University Press.

Quigley, Bill. 2010. "Fourteen Examples of Systemic Racism in the U.S. Criminal Justice System." CommonDreams.org, July 26. Retrieved July 26, 2010 (www.commondreams.org/view/2010/07/26-2).

Quillian, Lincoln. 2008. "Does Unconscious Racism Exist?" *Social Psychology Quarterly* 71(1):6–11.

Quillian, L. and D. Pager. 2001. "Black Neighbors, Higher Crime? The Role of Racial Stereotypes in Evaluations of Neighborhood Crime." *American Journal of Sociology* 107(3):717–767.

Race: The Power of an Illusion. Vol. I. 2003. Documentary. San Francisco, CA: California Newsreel.

Racz, Erica. 2019. "Florida Gave Felons Like Me the Vote Again. Then the State Took It Away." *Washington Post.com*, June 26. Retrieved June 27, 2019 (www.washingtonpost.com/outlook/florida-gave-felons-like-me-the-vote-again-then-the-state-took-it-away/2019/06/26/9d2efef4-978b-11e9-916d-9c61607d8190_story.html?utm_term=.98318eac0f3f).

Ramsamy, Sam. 1988. "Keep South African Sports in Isolation." *New York Times*, December 11, sec. 8 p. 8. Retrieved August 14, 2011 (www.lexisnexis.com/lnacui2api/delivery/PrintDoc.do?jobHandle=1826%A301068).

Randolph, Antonia. 2013. *The Wrong Kind of Different: Challenging the Meaning of Diversity in American Classrooms*. New York: Teachers College Press.

Rankin, Kenrya. 2015. "Unemployment Rate Ticks Up for Blacks, Declines Overall." Colorlines, September 4. Retrieved July 6, 2016 (www.colorlines.com/articles/unemployment-rate-ticks-blacks-drops-overall).

Rankin, Kenrya. 2016. "Report: Black Women's Wages Now Even Further Behind Those of White Men." Colorlines, March 9. Retrieved June 14, 2016 (www.colorlines.com/articles/report-black-womens-wages-now-even-further-behind-those-white-men).

Rankin, Kenrya. 2016b. "House Introduces New Bill to Address Puerto Rican Debt Crisis." Colorlines, May 19. Retrieved July 11, 2016 (www.colorlines.com/articles/house-introduces-new-bill-address-puerto-rican-debt-crisis).

Rauch, Janine. 2005. "The South African Police and the Truth Commission." *South African Review of Sociology* 36(2):208–237.

Ray, Victor. 2019. "A Theory of Racialized Organizations." *American Sociological Review*, 84(1):1–28.

Reddy, Sumathi. 2008. "Attacks Against Hispanics Rising." *Desert Morning News*, November 24. Retrieved September 10, 2011 (www.lexisnexis.com/lnacui2api/delivery/PrintDoc.do?jobHandle=2828%A305535).

Rediker, Marcus. 2007. *The Slave Ship: A Human History.* New York: Penguin.

Reed, Adolph, Jr. 2001. "Race and Class in the Work of Oliver Cromwell Cox." *Monthly Review* 52(9):23–33.

Reese, William J. 2005. *America's Public Schools: From the Common School to "No Child Left Behind."* Baltimore, MD: Johns Hopkins University Press.

Reiman, Jeffrey. 1996. *… And the Poor Get Prison: Economic Bias in American Criminal Justice.* Boston, MA: Allyn and Bacon.

Reiman, Jeffrey. 2009. "… And the Poor Get Prison." Pp. 234–245 in *Rethinking the Color Line: Readings in Race and Ethnicity*, 4th ed., edited by C. Gallagher. St. Louis and New York: McGraw-Hill.

"Religion and Race Commission Urges United Methodists to 'Drop the I-Word.'" 2010. United Methodists of the California-Nevada Annual Conference, December 6. Retrieved October 6, 2016 (www.cnumc.org/news/7566).

Renzulli, Linda A. and Lorraine Evans. 2005. "School Choice, Charter Schools, and White Flight." *Social Problems* 52:398–418.

Reskin, Barbara F. 1998. *The Realities of Affirmative Action in Employment.* Washington, DC: American Sociological Association.

Resnicow, K. and D. Ross-Gaddy. 1997. "Development of a Racial Identity Scale for Low-Income African Americans." *Journal of Black Studies* 28(2):239–254.

Reyhner, Jon and Jeanne Eder. 2004. *American Indian Education: A History.* Norman: University of Oklahoma Press.

Reynolds, Tim. 2010. "Jacory Harris Received Racist Message." *Huffington Post*, September 19. Retrieved September 20, 2010 (www.huffingtonpost.com/college/the-news/2010/09/19/).

Rhea, Joseph Tilda. 1997. *Race Pride and the American Identity.* Cambridge, MA: Harvard University Press.

Rhoden, William C. 2016. "Baseball Has Yet to Deliver the Greatest Tribute to Robinson." *New York Times*, April 17, Sports, p. 4.

Rico, Brittany, Rose M. Kreider, and Lydia Anderson. 2018. "Growth in Interracial and Interethnic Married-Couple Households." *United States Census Bureau*, July 9. Retrieved June 29, 2019 (www.census.gov/library/stories/2018/07/interracial-marriages.html).

Riley, Glenda. 1997. "The Historiography of American Indian and Other Western Women." Pp. 43–70 in *Rethinking American Indian History*, edited by D. Fixoco. Albuquerque: University of New Mexico Press.

Ring, Trudy. 2019. "These are the Trans People Killed in 2019." *The Advocate*, June 22. Retrieved June 27, 2019 (www.advocate.com/transgender/2019/5/22/these-are-trans-people-killed-2019#media-gallery-media-10).

Rintala, K. and Mary Jo Kane. 1991. "Culturally Constructed Factors That Mediate the Media's Portrayal of Female Athleticism: The Case of Age, Race, and Disability." Paper presented at North American Society for the Sociology of Sport Conference, Milwaukee, WI, November.

Ritchie, Andrea J. 2016. "Law Enforcement Violence Against Women of Color." Pp. 138–156 in *Color of Violence: The INCITE! Anthology*, edited by INCITE! Women of Color Against Violence.

Rivera, Zayda. 2008. "The Housing Crisis: Blacks and Latinos Targeted." DiversityInc. Retrieved October 10, 2008 (www.freerepublic.com/focus/f-news/2082183/posts).

Rivett, Kenneth. 1992. "From White Australia to the Present." Pp. 58–75 in *From India to Australia*, edited by S. Chandrasekhar. La Jolla, CA: Population Review Books.

Rizvi, Fazal. 2005. "Representations of Islam and Education for Justice." Pp. 167–178 in *Race, Identity, and Representation in Education*, 2nd ed., edited by C. McCarthy, W. Crichlow, G. Dimitriadis, and N. Dolby. New York: Routledge.

Robbins, Rebecca L. 1992. "Self-Determination and Subordination: The Past, Present, and Future of American Indian Governance." Pp. 87–122 in *The State of Native America: Genocide, Colonization, Resistance*, edited by M. A. Jaimes. Boston, MA: South End Press.

Roberts, Donald F., Lisa Henriksen, and Peter G. Christenson. 1999. "Substance Use in Popular Movies and Music." Washington, DC: Office of National Drug Control Policy and Department of Health and Human Services. Retrieved July 24, 2013 (www.ncjrs.gov/pdffiles1/Digitization/176359NCJRS.pdf).

Roberts, Dorothy. 1997. *Killing the Black Body: Race, Reproduction, and the Meaning of Liberty*. New York: Vintage/Random House Books.

Roberts, Dorothy. 2011. *Fatal Invention: How Science, Politics, and Big Business Re-Create Race in the Twenty-First Century*. New York and London: The New Press.

Robertson, Campbell. 2010. "5 Officers Indicted in Killing After Storm." *New York Times*, June 12, p. A-10.

Robertson, Campbell, Christopher Mele, and Sabrina Tavernise. 2018. "11 Killed in Synagogue Massacre; Suspect Charged with 29 Counts." *New York Times*, October 27. Retrieved July 29, 2019 (www.nytimes.com/2018/10/27/us/active-shooter-pittsburgh-synagogue-shooting.html).

Robinson, Randall. 2000. *The Debt: What America Owes to Blacks*. New York: Dutton.

Robnett, Belinda. 1997. *How Long? How Long? African-American Women in the Struggle for Civil Rights*. New York and Oxford: Oxford University Press.

Robnett, Belinda. 2004. "Women in the Student Non-Violent Coordinating Committee: Ideology, Organizational Structure, and Leadership." Pp. 131–168 in *Gender and the Civil Rights Movement*, edited by P. J. Ling and S. Monteith. New Brunswick, NJ: Rutgers University Press.

Robnett, Belinda and Cynthia Feliciano. 2011. "Patterns of Racial-Ethnic Exclusion by Internet Daters." *Social Forces* 89(3):807–828.

Rockquemore, Kerry Ann and David Brunsma. 2002. *Beyond Black: Biracial Identity in America*. Thousand Oaks, CA: Sage Publications.

Rockquemore, Kerry Ann and Tracey Laszloffy. 2008. *The Black Academic's Guide for Winning Tenure—Without Losing Your Soul*. Boulder, CO: Lynne Rienner Publishers.

Rodriguez, Clara E. 1989. *Puerto Ricans: Born in the U.S.A.* Boulder, CO: Westview Press.

Rodriguez, Victor M. 2005. "The Racialization of Mexican Americans and Puerto Ricans: 1890s–1930s." *CENTRO Journal* 17(1):71–105.

Roediger, David R. 1991. *The Wages of Whiteness: Race and the Making of the American Working Class*. London, New York: Verso.

Roediger, David R. 2008. *How Race Survived U.S. History: From Settlement and Slavery to the Obama Phenomenon*. London, New York: Verso.

Rogers, Katie. 2019. "The Painful Roots of Trump's 'Go Back' Comment." *New York Times*, July 16. Retrieved July 21 (www.nytimes.com/2019/07/16/us/politics/aoc-trump-tlaib-omar-pressley.html?action=click&module=RelatedCoverage&pgtype=Article&region=Footer).

Roithmayr, Daria. 2014. *Reproducing Racism: How Everyday Choices Lock In White Advantage*. New York: New York University Press.

Rollins, Judith. 1986. "Parts of a Whole: The Interdependence of the Civil Rights Movement and Other Social Movements." *Phylon* 47(1):61–70.

Romano, Renee C. 2003. *Race Mixing: Black–White Marriage in Postwar America*. Cambridge, MA: Harvard University Press.

Romero, Mary. 2006. "Racial Profiling and Immigration Law Enforcement: Rounding Up of Usual Suspects in the Latino Community." *Social Problems* 63(1):111–126.

Romero, Mary. 2018. "Trump's Immigration Attacks, In Brief." *Contexts* 17(1):34–40.

Romero, Simon. 2019. "Lynch Mobs Killed Latinos across the West. The First to Remember These Atrocities is Just Starting." *New York Times*, March 2. Retrieved March 13, 2019 (www.nytimes.com/2019/03/02/us/porvenir-massacre-texas-mexicans.html).

Rondilla, Joanne L. 2009. "Filipinos and the Color Complex: Ideal Asian Beauty." Pp. 63–80 in *Shades of Difference: Why Skin Color Matters*, edited by E. N. Glenn. Stanford, CA: Stanford University Press.

Rondilla, Joanne L. and Paul Spickard. 2007. *Is Lighter Better? Skin-Tone Discrimination Among Asian Americans*. Lanham, MD: Rowman and Littlefield Publishers.

Root, Maria. 2001. *Love's Revolution: Interracial Marriage*. Philadelphia, PA: Temple University Press.

Rose, Margaret. 1995. "'Women Power Will Stop Those Grapes': Chicana Organizers and Middle-Class Female Supporters in the Farm Workers' Grape Boycott in Philadelphia, 1969–1970." *Journal of Women's History* 7(4):6–37.

Rose, Tricia. 1994. *Black Noise: Rap Music and Black Culture in Contemporary America*. Hanover and London: Wesleyan University Press.

Rose, Tricia. 2008. *The Hip Hop Wars: What We Talk About When We Talk About Hip Hop—And Why It Matters.* New York: Basic Books.

Rosenberg, Pearl M. 2004. "Color Blindness in Teacher Education: An Optical Illusion." Pp. 257–272 in *Off White: Readings on Power, Privilege, and Resistance*, 2nd ed., edited by M. Fine, L. Weis, L. P. Pruitt, and A. Burns. New York: Routledge.

Rosenthal, Gregg. 2013. "No African American NFL Head Coaches Hired in 2013." NFL.com, January 17. Retrieved July 25, 2013 (www.nfl.com/news/story/0ap1000000127869/article/no-africanamerican-nfl-head-coaches-hired-in-2013).

"Rosewood Survivors." n.d. *Remembering Rosewood*, Displays for Schools. Retrieved May 21, 2013 (www.displaysforschools.com/survivor.html).

Ross, Luana. 1998. *Inventing the Savage: The Social Construction of Native American Criminality.* Austin: University of Texas Press.

Ross, Sonya and Jennifer Agiesta. 2012. "Poll Shows Racial Attitudes Deteriorate." *Times-Picayune*, October 28, p. A-12.

Roth, Wendy. 2016. "The Multiple Dimensions of Race." *Ethnic & Racial Studies* 39(8):1316–1338.

Roth, Wendy D. and Biorn Ivemark. 2018. "Genetic Options: The Impact of Genetic Ancestry Testing on Consumers' Racial and Ethnic Identities." *American Journal of Sociology* 124(1):1 50–184.

Rothenberg, Paula S., ed. 2008. *White Privilege: Essential Readings on the Other Side of Racism*, 3rd ed. New York: Worth Publishers.

Rothstein, Richard. 2017. *The Color of Law: A Forgotten History of How Our Government Segregated America.* New York: Liveright Publishing Corporation/W.W. Norton.

Rovner, Joshua. 2016. "Policy Brief: Racial Disparities in Youth Commitments and Arrests." *The Sentencing Project*, April. Retrieved June 26, 2019 (www.sentencingproject.org/wp-content/uploads/2016/04/Racial-Disparities-in-Youth-Commitments-and-Arrests.pdf).

Royster, Deirdre A. 2003. *Race and the Invisible Hand: How White Networks Exclude Black Men from Blue-Collar Jobs.* Berkeley: University of California Press.

Rubin, Lillian. 1994. *Families on the Fault Line.* New York: Harper Perennial.

Rudden, Jennifer. 2019. "Percentage of People Without Health Insurance in the United States from 2019 to 2018, by Ethnicity." Statista, United States Centers for Disease Control, May 28. Retrieved July 28, 2019 (www.statista.com/statistics/200970/percentage-of-americans-without-health-insurance-by-race-ethnicity).

Ruhm, Christopher. 1991. "Are Workers Permanently Scarred by Job Displacement?" *American Economic Review* 81:319–324.

Rush, Sharon E. 2006. *Huck Finn's "Hidden" Lessons: Teaching and Learning Across the Color Line.* Lanham, MD: Rowman and Littlefield.

Rushing, Wanda. 2018. "Setting the Record Straight on Confederate Statues." *Contexts* 17(1):18–20.

Russell, Katheryn K. 1998. *The Color of Crime: Racial Hoaxes, White Fear, Black Protectionism, Police Harassment, and Other Macroaggressions.* New York and London: New York University Press.

Russell, Kathy, Midge Wilson, and Ronald Hall. 1992. *The Color Complex: The Politics of Skin Color Among African Americans.* New York: Harcourt Brace Jovanovich Publishers.

Sabo, Don, Sue Curry Jansen, Danny Tote, Margaret Carlisle Duncan, and Susan Leggett. 1996. "Televising International Sport: Race, Ethnicity, and Nationalistic Bias." *Journal of Sport and Social Issues* 20(1):7–21.

Saenz, Victor B. 2010. "Breaking the Segregation Cycle: Examining Students' Precollege Racial Environments and College Diversity Experiences." *Review of Higher Education* 34(1):1–37.

Salaita, Steven George. 2006. "Beyond Orientalism and Islamophobia: 9/11, Anti-Arab Racism, and the Mythos of National Pride." *New Centennial Review* 6(2):245–266.

Samora, Julian and Patricia Vandel Simon. 1993. *A History of Mexican American People.* London, Notre Dame, IN: University of Notre Dame Press.

Sampson, Robert J. and Janet L. Lauritsen. 1997. "Racial and Ethnic Disparities in Crime and Criminal Justice in the United States." *Crime and Justice* 21:311–374.

San Miguel, Guadalupe, Jr. 2004. *Contested Policy: The Rise and Fall of Federal Bilingual Education in the United States 1960–2001.* Denton: University of North Texas Press.

Sanyika, M. 2009. "Katrina and the Condition of Black New Orleans: The Struggle for Justice, Equity, and Democracy." Pp. 87–114 in *Race, Place and Environmental Justice After Hurricane Katrina*, edited by R. D. Bullard and B. Wright. Boulder, CO: Westview Press.

Sater, Terry. 2016. "Student Announces White Privilege Day in Class, School Officials Say." *ABC Wisconsin*, June 2. Retrieved June 4, 2016 (www.wisn.com/news/student-announces-white-privilege-day-at-nicolet-hs-school-officials-say/39854496).

Saulny, Susan. 2011. "Race Remixed: Black? White? Asian? More Young Americans Choose All of the Above." *New York Times*, January 29. Retrieved April 5, 2013 (www.nytimes.com/2011/01/30/us/30mixed.html).

Saya, Tom. 2006. "The Whiteness of Mount Rushmore." *Midwest Quarterly* 47(2):144–154.

Schlosser, Eric. 1998. "The Prison-Industrial Complex." *Atlantic Monthly*, December 1. Retrieved July 25, 2013 (www.theatlantic.com/magazine/archive/1998/12/the-prison-industrial-complex/304669/).

Schwirtz, Michael, Michael Winerip, and Robert Gebeloff. 2016. "The Scourge of Racial Bias in New York State Prisons." *New York Times*, December 3. Retrieved June 26, 2019 (www.nytimes.com/2016/12/03/nyregion/new-york-state-prisons-inmates-racial-bias.html).

Schwirtz, Michael, Michael Winerip, and Robert Gebeloff. 2007. "Domination and the Arts of Resistance." Pp. 199–214 in *On Violence: A Reader*, edited by B. B. Lawrence and A. Karim. Durham, NC: Duke University Press.

Scott, Eugene. 2019. "Congressional Hearing Could Help Move the Needle on Support for Reparations." *The Washington Post*, June 13. Retrieved July 18, 2019 (www.washingtonpost.com/politics/2019/06/13/congressional-hearing-could-help-move-needle-support-reparations/?utm_term=.98c26d3b3091).

Scott, James C. 1992. *Domination and the Arts of Resistance: Hidden Transcripts.* New Haven, CT: Yale University Press.

Seguin, Charles. 2018. "How Northern Newspapers Covered Lynchings." *New York Times*, June 11. Retrieved May 21, 2019 (www.nytimes.com/2018/06/11/opinion/northern-newspapers-lynchings.html).

Seierstad, A. 2011. "What Now, Little Country? In the Wake of a Devastating Massacre, Norway Reexamines Its Values—and Its Fears." *Newsweek*, September 12. Retrieved September 9, 2011 (www.lexisnexis.com/lnacui2api/delivery/PrintDoc.do?jobHandle=1828%3A3054403).

Selod, Saher. 2018. *Forever Suspect: Racialized Surveillance of Muslim Americans in the War on Terror.* New Brunswick, NJ: Rutgers University Press.

Sen, Rinku. 2003. *Stir It Up: Lessons in Community Organizing and Advocacy.* San Francisco, CA: Jossey-Bass.

Senechal de la Roche, Roberta. 2001. "Why Is Collective Violence Collective?" *Sociological Theory* 19(2):126–144.

The Sentencing Project. 2003. *New Inmate Population Figures Demonstrate Need for Policy Reform.* Washington, DC: The Sentencing Project.

Severson, Kim. 2011. "Parts of Georgia Immigration Law Blocked." *New York Times*, June 27. Retrieved April 20, 2012 (www.nytimes.com/2011/06/28/us/28georgia.html).

Shackel, Paul A. 2001. "An Exclusionary Past." Pp. 17–19 in *Myth, Memory, and the Making of the American Landscape*, edited by P. A. Shackel. Gainesville: University Press of Florida.

Shaheen, Jack G. 1984. *The TV Arab.* Bowling Green, OH: Bowling Green State University Popular Press.

Shaheen, Jack G. 2001. *Reel Bad Arabs: How Hollywood Vilifies a People.* New York: Olive Branch Press.

Shaheen, Jack G. 2007. "Hollywood's Reel Arab Women." *Media Development* 54(2):27–29.

Shaheen, Jack G. 2008. *Guilty: Hollywood's Verdict on Arabs After 9/11.* North Hampton, MA: Olive Branch Press.

Shapiro, Thomas, Tatjana Meschede, and Sam Osoro. 2013. "The Roots of the Widening Racial Wealth Gap: Explaining the Black–White Economic Divide." *Institute on Assets and Social Policy.* Retrieved July 31, 2019 (https://heller.brandeis.edu/iasp/pdfs/racial-wealth-equity/racial-wealth-gap/roots-widening-racial-wealth-gap.pdf).

Sheppard, Samantha N. 2018. "Close-Up: Sports, Race, and the Power of Narrative. Introduction." *Black Camera: An International Film Journal* 10(1):156–161.

Short, April M. 2014. "Michelle Alexander: White Men Get Rich from Legal Pot, Black Men Stay in Prison." Alternet, March 16. Retrieved July 1, 2016 (www.alternet.org/drugs/michelle-alexander-white-men-get-rich-legal-pot-black-men-stay-prison).

Shreve, Bradley G. 2011. *Red Power Rising: The National Indian Youth Council and the Origins of Native Activism.* Norman: University of Oklahoma Press.

Shriver, Mark D. and Rick A. Kittles. 2008. "Genetic Ancestry and the Search for Personalized Genetic Histories." Pp. 201–214 in *Revisiting Race in a Genomic Age*, edited by B. A. Koenig, S. S. Lee, and S. S. Richardson. New Brunswick, NJ: Rutgers University Press.

Sidanius, Jim and Felicia Pratto. 1999. *Social Dominance: An Intergroup Theory of Social Hierarchy and Oppression.* Cambridge, UK: Cambridge University Press.

Sidran, Ben. 1971. *Black Talk.* New York: Da Capo Press.

Silk, Catherine and John Silk. 1990. *Racism and Anti-Racism in American Popular Culture: Portrayals of African Americans in Fiction and Film.* Manchester, NY: Manchester University Press.

Silva, Christianna. 2018. "Trump's Full List of 'Racist' Comments about Immigrants, Muslims, and Others." *Newsweek*, January 1. Retrieved March 13, 2019 (www.newsweek.com/trumps-full-list-racist-comments-about-immigrants-muslims-and-others-779061).

Silverman, Robert Mark. 2016. "Urban Policy Without Broaching the Topic of Race, Really? Response to David Imbroscio's 'Urban Policy as Meritocracy: A Critique.'" *Journal of Urban Affairs* 38(1):105–109.

Simon, Mallory and Sara Sidner. 2019. "Inside the GM Plant where Nooses and 'Whites-Only' Signs Hung." CNN, January 17. Retrieved March 12, 2019 (www.cnn.com/2019/01/16/us/gm-toledo-racism-lawsuit/index.htm).

Simon, Mallory and Sara Sidner. 2019b. "Black Workers in Ohio Accuse UPS of Allowing Hate at Work." CNN, March 13. Retrieved March 15, 2019 (www.cnn.com/2019/03/13/us/black-workers-in-ohio-sue-ups-racism/index.html?fbclid=IwAR1LJ91b0bbqbzyro96y9Gyr9lxBFvQ6CQhsw34o18Vld1Lorp1-JECK0NY).

Skocpol, Theda. 1995. *Social Policy in the United States: Future Possibilities in Historical Perspective.* Princeton, NJ: Princeton University Press.

Skrentny, John D. 2014. *After Civil Rights: Racial Realism in the New American Workplace.* Princeton, NJ: Princeton University Press.

Skrentny, John D. 2015. "Did Congress Vote for Whites to Become a Minority?" *Contexts* 14(2):14–15.

Skutnabb-Kangas, Tove. 2000. *Linguistic Genocide in Education: Or Worldwide Diversity and Human Rights.* Mahwah, NJ: Lawrence Erlbaum Associates Publishers.

Sleeter, Christine. 1994. "A Multicultural Educator Views White Racism." *Education Digest* 59(9):33–37.

Sleeter, Christine. 2005. "How White Teachers Construct Race." Pp. 243–256 in *Race, Identity and Representation in Education*, edited by C. McCarthy, W. Crichlow, G. Dimitriadis, and N. Dolby. New York and London: Routledge.

Smedley, Audrey. 2007. *Race in North America: Origin and Evolution of a Worldview*, 3rd ed. Boulder, CO: Westview Press.

Smedley, Audrey and Brian D. Smedley. 2012. *Race in North America: Origin and Evolution of a Worldview*, 4th ed. Boulder, CO: Westview Press.

Smith, Andrea. 2005. *Conquest: Sexual Violence and American Indian Genocide.* Cambridge, MA: South End Press.

Smith, Andrea. 2009. "Rape and the War Against Native Women." In *The Matrix Reader: Examining the Dynamics of Oppression and Privilege*, edited by A. Ferber, C. M. Jimenez, A. O. Herrara, and D. R. Samuels. New York, St. Louis: McGraw-Hill.

Smith, Dorothy. 1987. *The Everyday World as Problematic: A Feminist Sociology.* Boston, MA: Northeastern University Press.

Smith, Gary. 2007. "Blindsided by History." *Sports Illustrated*, April 9, pp. 66–75.

Smith, Heather and Owen V. Furuseth, eds. 2006. *Latinos in the New South: Transformations of Place*. Burlington, VT: Ashgate Publishing.

Smith, Paul Chaat and Robert Allan Warrior. 1996. *Like a Hurricane: The American Indian Movement from Alcatraz to Wounded Knee*. New York: The New Press.

Smith, Robert J., Justin D. Levinson, and Zoë Robinson. 2014. "Implicit White Favoritism in the Criminal Justice System." *Alabama Law Review* 66(4):871–923.

Smith, William A., Walter R. Allen, and Lynette L. Danley. 2007. "'Assume the Position … You Fit the Description': Psychosocial Experiences and Racial Battle Fatigue Among African American Male College Students." *American Behavioral Scientists* 51(4):551–578.

Snipp, C. Matthew. 1989. *American Indians: The First of This Land*. New York: Russell Sage Foundation.

Sohoni, Deenesh and Amin Vafa. 2007. "The Fight to Be American: Patriotism, Military Naturalization and Asian Citizenship." Paper presented at the Annual Meeting of American Sociological Association, New York, August.

Sokol, Jason. 2006. *There Goes My Everything: White Southerners in the Age of Civil Rights, 1945–1975*. New York: Vintage Books.

Sollors, Werner. 1996. *Theories of Ethnicity: A Reader*. New York: New York University Press.

Solnit, Rebecca. 2016. "Standing Rock Protests: This is Only the Beginning." *Guardian*, September 12. Retrieved July 22, 2019 (www.theguardian.com/us-news/2016/sep/12/north-dakota-standing-rock-protests-civil-rights).

Somashekhar, Sandhya and Steven Rich. 2016. "Final Tally: Police Shot and Killed 986 People in 2015." *Washington Post*, January 6. Retrieved July 6, 2016 (www.washingtonpost.com/national/final-tally-police-shot-and-killed-984-people-in-2015/2016/01/05/3ec7a404-b3c5-11e5-a76a-0b5145e8679a_story.html).

Soule, Sarah. 1992. "Populism and Black Lynching in Georgia, 1890–1900." *Social Forces* 71(2): 431–449.

"Sourcebook of Criminal Justice Statistics Online." n.d. University at Albany, School of Criminal Justice (www.albany.edu/sourcebook/pdf/t31122008.pdf).

Southern Poverty Law Center. 2005. *Ten Ways to Fight Hate: A Community Response Guide*, 3rd ed. Montgomery, AL: Southern Poverty Law Center.

Spear, Jennifer M. 2007. "Race Matters in the Colonial South." *Journal of Southern History* 73(3):579–588.

Spence, Mark David. 1999. *Dispossessing the Wilderness: Indian Removal and the Making of the National Parks*. New York, Oxford: Oxford University Press.

Spencer, Rainier. 2011. *Reproducing Race: The Paradox of Generation Mix*. Boulder, CO: Lynne Rienner Publishers.

Speri, Alice. 2018. "Detained, Then Violated." The Intercept, April 11. Retrieved July 29, 2019 (https://theintercept.com/2018/04/11/immigration-detention-sexual-abuse-ice-dhs/).

Spickard, Paul. 1989. *Mixed Blood: Intermarriage and Ethnic Identity in Twentieth-Century America*. Madison: University of Wisconsin Press.

Spickard, Paul and G. Reginald Daniel. 2004. *Racial Thinking in the United States: Uncompleted Independence*. Notre Dame, IN: University of Notre Dame Press.

"SPLC Study Finds 1,500 Government-Backed Confederate Tributes." 2016. *SPLC Report* 46(2):3.

Sreenivasan, Hari. 2015. "Everything You Should Know About Puerto Rico's Debt Crisis." PBS *News Hour*, July 11. Retrieved July 11, 2016 (www.pbs.org/newshour/bb/everything-know-puerto-ricos-debt-crisis/).

Stampp, Kenneth. 1956. *The Peculiar Institution*. New York: Knopf.

Staples, Brent. 2008. "As Racism Wanes, Colorism Persists." *New York Times*, August 22. Retrieved August 28, 2011 (http://theboard.blogs.nytimes.com/2008/08/22/as-racism-wanes-colorism-persists/).

Staples, Robert. 2006. *Exploring Black Sexuality*. Lanham, MA: Rowman and Littlefield Publishers.

"State, Local Spending on Prisons Outpaces Education Funding." 2016. *Inside Higher Ed*, July 8. Retrieved July 8, 2016 (www.insidehighered.com/quicktakes/2016/07/08/state-local-spending-prisons-outpaces-education-funding).

Stavans, Ilan. 2000. "The Gravitas of Spanglish." *Chronicle of Higher Education* 47(7):B7.

Stearn, E. Wagner and Allen E. Stearn. 1945. *The Effects of Smallpox on the Destiny of the Amerindian.* Boston, MA: Bruce Humphries, Inc.

Stearns, Elizabeth, Claudia Buchmann, and Kara Bonneau. 2009. "Interracial Friendships in the Transition to College: Do Birds of a Feather Flock Together Once They Leave the Nest?" *Sociology of Education* 82(2):173–195.

Steffensmeier, Darrell and Stephen Demuth. 2006. "Does Gender Modify the Effects of Race-Ethnicity on Criminal Sanctioning? Sentences for Male and Female White, Black and Hispanic Defendants." *Journal of Quantitative Criminology* 22(3):241–261.

Stein, Howard and Robert F. Hill. 1977. *The Ethnic Imperative: Examining the New White Ethnic Movement.* University Park: Pennsylvania State University Press.

Stein, Sam. 2010. "Tea Party Protests: 'Ni**er,' 'Fa**ot' Shouted at Members of Congress." *Huffington Post*, May 20. Retrieved August 4, 2016 (www.huffingtonpost.com/2010/03/20/tea-party-protests-nier-f_n_507116.html).

Steinberg, Stephen. 1981. *The Ethnic Myth: Race, Ethnicity and Class in America.* New York: Atheneum.

Steinberg, Stephen. 2007. *Race Relations: A Critique.* Stanford, CA: Stanford University Press.

Steinbugler, Amy C. 2012. *Beyond Loving: Intimate Racework in Lesbian, Gay, and Straight Interracial Relationships.* New York: Oxford University Press.

Stevens, Matt and Sarah Mervosh. 2019. "White Police Officer Placed on Leave after Detaining Black Man Picking Up Trash in Front of his Building." *New York Times*, March 7. Retrieved June 10, 2019 (www.nytimes.com/2019/03/07/us/boulder-police-detain-black-man.html/).

Stewart, Jeffrey C. 1992. "Introduction." Pp. xix–xx in *Race Contacts and Interracial Relations*, by Alain LeRoy Locke. Washington, DC: Howard University Press.

Stewart, Nikita. 2019. "'We are Committing Educational Malpractice': Why Slavery is Mistaught—and Worse—in America's Schools." The 1619 Project of *New York Times*, August 18. Retrieved August 31, 2019 (www.nytimes.com/interactive/2019/08/19/magazine/slavery-american-schools.html).

Stiffarm, Lenore A. and Phil Lane, Jr. 1992. "The Demography of Native North America: A Question of American Indian Survival." Pp. 23–54 in *The State of Native America: Genocide, Colonization, and Resistance*, edited by M. A. Jaimes. Boston, MA: South End Press.

Stodghill, Ron. 2008. "Driving Back into History: Stretching from New Orleans to Shreveport, the Louisiana African-American Heritage Trail Is a Road Paved with Memories Both Painful and Proud." *New York Times*, May 25. Retrieved July 25, 2013 (www.nytimes.com/2008/05/25/travel/25trail.html).

Storey, Peter. 1997. "A Different Kind of Justice: Truth and Reconciliation in South Africa." *Christian Century* 114(25):788–793.

Streeter, Kurt. 2019. "Maya Moore Left Basketball. A Prisoner Needed Her Help." *New York Times*, June 30. Retrieved July 1, 2019 (www.nytimes.com/2019/06/30/sports/maya-moore-wnba-quit.html).

Strmic-Pawl, Hephzibah V. 2015. "More Than a Knapsack: The White Supremacy Flower as a New Model for Teaching Racism." *Sociology of Race and Ethnicity* 1(1):192–197.

Stull, Donald D. 2011. "Harvest of Change: Meatpacking, Immigration, and Garden City, Kansas." Paper presented at the Kansas Economic Policy Conference, Kansas City, KS, October 13. Retrieved April 15, 2013 (www.ipsr.ku.edu/conferen/kepc11/HarvestofChange.pdf).

Sturgis, Ingrid. 2006. "Spike Lee: Two Decades on the Big Screen." *The Crisis* 113(5):39.

Sue, S. and S. Okazaki. 1990. "Asian American Educational Achievements: A Phenomenon in Search of an Explanation." *American Psychologist* 45(8):913–920.

Sullivan, Patricia. 2009. *Lift Every Voice: The NAACP and the Making of the Civil Rights Movement.* New York: The New Press.

Sunderman, Gail L. and Jimmy Kim. 2004. *Expansion of Federal Power in American Education: Federa–State Relationships Under the No Child Left Behind Act, Year One.* Cambridge, MA: The Civil Rights Project at Harvard University.

Sutherland, Edwin. 1924. *Criminology.* Philadelphia, PA: Lippincott.

Swain, Carol M. 1993. *Black Faces, Black Interests: The Representation of African Americans in Congress.* Cambridge, MA: Harvard University Press.

Swalwell, Katy. 2012. "Confronting White Privilege." *Teaching Tolerance* 42. Retrieved July 25, 2013 (www.tolerance.org/magazine/number-42-fall-2012/feature/confronting-white-privilege).

Swan, Sarah. 2015. "Learn About African American History at National Museum of the US Air Force." National Museum of US Air Force, January 28. Retrieved October 8, 2016 (www.national-museum.af.mil/Upcoming/ArticleDisplay/tabid/466/Article/579843/learn-about-african-american-history-at-national-museum-of-the-us-air-force.aspx).

Takagi, Paul. 1979. "Death by 'Police Intervention.'" Pp. 31–38 in *A Community Concern: Police Use of Deadly Force,* edited by R. N. Brenner and M. Kravitz. Washington, DC: US Government Printing Office.

Takaki, Ronald. 1979. *Iron Cages: Race and Culture in 19th Century America.* Oxford, New York, Toronto: Oxford University Press.

Takaki, Ronald. 1989. *Strangers from a Different Shore: A History of Asian Americans.* Boston, MA: Little, Brown and Company.

Takaki, Ronald. 1993. *A Different Mirror: A History of Multicultural America.* London, Boston, MA: Little, Brown and Company.

Takei, Isao. 2008. "Poverty Among Asian Americans: Evidence from the 2000 Census." Paper presented at the American Sociological Association Annual Meeting, Boston, MA, August.

Tallbear, Kimberly. 2008. "Native-American-DNA.com: In Search of Native American Race and Tribe." Pp. 235–252 in *Revisiting Race in a Genomic Age,* edited by B. A. Koenig, S. S. Lee, and S. S. Richardson. New Brunswick, NJ: Rutgers University Press.

Tan, Clement. 2010. "Study: Wealth Gap Widens." *Times-Picayune,* May 20, p. A-13.

Tannehill, Brynn. 2015. "Ohio and the Epidemic of Anti-Transgender Violence." *Huffington Post,* February 20. Retrieved January 12, 2016 (www.huffingtonpost.com/brynn-tannehill/ohio-and-the-epidemic-of-_b_6720892.html).

Tareen, Sophia. 2010. "Countrywide Lawsuit: Racial Discrimination in Subprime Loans Alleged by Illinois Attorney General." *Huffington Post,* June 30. Retrieved July 25, 2013 (www.huffingtonpost.com/the-news/2010/06/30/).

Tate, Bronson. 2004. "Remembering the Alamo." *Smithsonian* 35(1):64–72.

Tate, Emily. 2017. "Digging Deeper into Campus Diversity." *Inside Higher Ed,* February 6. Retrieved August 4, 2019 (www.insidehighered.com/news/2017/02/06/study-finds-negative-diversity-experiences-affect-student-learning).

Tate, Katherine and Sarah Harsh. 2005. "'A Portrait of the People': Descriptive Representation and Its Impact on U.S. House Members' Ratings." Pp. 216–231 in *Diversity in Democracy: Minority Representation in the United States,* edited by G. M. Segura and S. Bowler. London and Charlottesville: University of Virginia Press.

Tatum, Beverly Daniel. 1992. "Talking About Race, Learning About Racism: The Application of Racial Identity Development Theory in the Classroom." *Harvard Educational Review* 62(1):1–24.

Tatum, Beverly Daniel. 1994. "Teaching White Students About Racism: The Search for White Allies and the Restoration of Hope." *Teachers College Record* 95(4):462–476.

Teaching Tolerance. 2016. "About Us." Southern Poverty Law Center (www.tolerance.org/about).

Tehranian, John. 2009. *Whitewashed: America's Invisible Middle Eastern Minority.* New York: New York University Press.

Telles, Edward. 2004. *Race in Another America: The Significance of Skin Color in Brazil.* Princeton, NJ: Princeton University Press.

Telles, Edward. 2009. "The Social Consequences of Skin Color in Brazil." Pp. 9–24 in *Shades of Difference: Why Skin Color Matters,* edited by E. N. Glenn. Stanford, CA: Stanford University Press.

Terkel, Amanda. 2010. "Arizona Expands Its Discriminations: Teachers with Heavy Accents Can't Teach English, Ethnic Studies Are Banned." *Think Progress,* April 30. Retrieved July 25, 2013 (http://thinkprogress.org/politics/2010/04/30/94567/arizona-teachers/).

Terkel, Amanda. 2010b. "New All-White Basketball League: Not Racist At All!" *Think Progress,* January 21. Retrieved July 25, 2013 (www.alternet.org/story/145312/new_all-white_basketball_league %3A_not_racist_at_all!).

Terry, Robert W. 1970. *For Whites Only.* Grand Rapids, MI: William B. Eerdmans Publishing.

Thakore, Bhoomi. 2014. "Must-See TV: South Asian Characterizations in American Popular Media." *Sociology Compass* 8(2):149–156.

Thakore, Bhoomi. 2016. *South Asians on the US Screen: Just Like Everyone Else?* Lanham, MD: Lexington Books.

"Theatrical Market Statistics." 2014. Motion Picture Association of America. Retrieved October 9, 2016 (www.mpaa.org/wp-content/uploads/2015/03/MPAA-Theatrical-Market-Statistics-2014.pdf).

"The Counted." n.d. *Guardian.* Retrieved June 22, 2016 (www.theguardian.com/us-news/ng-interactive/2015/jun/01/the-counted-police-killings-us-database).

"THEME Report: A Comprehensive Analysis and Survey of the Theatrical and Home Entertainment Market Environment." 2018. *Motion Picture Association of America.* Retrieved July 3, 2019 (www.mpaa.org/wp-content/uploads/2019/03/MPAA-THEME-Report-2018.pdf).

Thomas, Lynn M. 2009. "Skin Lighteners in South Africa: Transnational Entanglements and Technologies of the Self." Pp. 188–210 in *Shades of Difference: Why Skin Color Matters,* edited by E. N. Glenn. Stanford, CA: Stanford University Press.

Thomas, William and Florian Znaniecki. 1918–20. *The Polish Peasant in Europe and America: Monograph of an Immigrant Group.* Boston, MA: Richard G. Badger.

Thompson, Brian L. and James Daniel Lee. 2004. "Who Cares If Police Become Violent? Explaining Approval of Police Use of Force Using a National Sample." *Sociological Inquiry* 74(3): 381–410.

Thompson, Derek. 2016. "The Liberal Millennial Revolution." *The Atlantic,* February 29. Retrieved March 14, 2019 (www.theatlantic.com/politics/archive/2016/02/the-liberal-millennial-revolution/470826/).

Thompson, Ginger. 2009. "Where Education and Assimilation Collide." *New York Times,* March 14. Retrieved July 24, 2013 (www.nytimes.com/2009/03/15/us/15immig.html).

Thompson, John. 1984. *Studies in the Theory of Ideology.* Cambridge, UK: Polity.

Thompson, Krissah and Scott Wilson. 2012. "Obama on Trayvon Martin: 'If I Had a Son, He'd Look Like Trayvon.'" *Washington Post,* March 23 (www.washingtonpost.com/politics/obama-if-i-had-a-son-hed-look-like-trayvon/2012/03/23/gIQApKPpVS_story.html).

Thompson, Megan. 2016. "Once Banished, Controversial Race Exhibit Resurfaces at Chicago Museum." *PBS Newshour,* March 4. Retrieved July 5, 2016 (www.pbs.org/newshour/bb/once-banished-controversial-race-exhibit-resurfaces-at-chicago-museum/).

Thornhill, Ted. 2018. "We Want Black Students, Just Not You: How White Admissions Counselors Screen Black Prospective Students." *Sociology of Race and Ethnicity* Sept:1–15.

Thornton, Russell. 1987. *American Indian Holocaust and Survival: A Population History Since 1492.* Norman: University of Oklahoma Press.

Tichenor, Daniel J. 2002. *Dividing Lines: The Politics of Immigration Control in America.* Princeton, NJ: Princeton University Press.

Tilly, Charles. 1998. *Durable Inequality.* Berkeley, CA: University of California Press.

Tolnay, Stewart E. and E. M. Beck. 1995. *A Festival of Violence: An Analysis of Southern Lynchings, 1882–1930.* Urbana and Champaign: University of Illinois Press.

Tolnay, Stewart E., E. M. Beck, and James L. Massey. 1989. "Black Lynchings: The Power Threat Hypothesis Revisited." *Social Forces* 67(3):605–623.

Tonry, Michael. 1995. *Malign Neglect: Race, Crime, and Punishment in America.* New York: Oxford University Press.

Torres, Sasha. 2003. *Black, White and in Color: Television and Black Civil Rights.* Princeton, NJ: Princeton University Press.

Trafzer, Clifford, Jean A. Keller, and Lorene Sisquoc. 2006. "Introduction: Origin and Development of the American Indian Boarding School System." Pp. 1–34 in *Boarding School Blues: Revisiting American Indian Educational Experiences,* edited by C. E. Trafzer, J. A. Keller, and L. Sisquoc. Lincoln: University of Nebraska Press.

Troutman, John W. 2009. *Indian Blues: American Indians and the Politics of Music, 1879–1934.* Norman: University of Oklahoma Press.

"The Trump Effect: The Impact of the Presidential Campaign on Our Nation's Schools." 2016. Southern Poverty Law Center. Retrieved July 4, 2016 (www.splcenter.org/20160413/trump-effect-impact-presidential-campaign-our-nations-schools).

Tucker, Belinda M. and Claudia Mitchell-Kernan. 1995. "Social Structural and Psychological Correlates of Interethnic Dating." *Journal of Social and Personal Relationships* 12(3):341–361.

Tucker, Norma. 1969. "Nancy Ward: Gighau of the Cherokees." *Georgia Historical Quarterly* 53:192–200.

Turner, Corey. 2016. "Why Preschool Suspensions Still Happen (and How to Stop Them)." *All Things Considered*, NPR, June 20. Retrieved June 20, 2016 (www.npr.org/sections/ed/2016/06/20/482472535/why-preschool-suspensions-still-happen-and-how-to-stop-them).

Turner, Patricia A. 1994. *Ceramic Uncles and Celluloid Mammies: Black Images and Their Influence on Culture*. New York: Anchor Books.

Turner, Ralph H. and Lewis W. Killian. 1987. *Collective Behavior*. Englewood Cliffs, NJ: Prentice Hall.

Tyler, Jasmine. 2010. "Congress Passes Historic Legislation to Reduce Crack/Powder Cocaine Sentencing Disparity." *Huffington Post*, July 28. Retrieved July 25, 2013 (www.huffingtonpost.com/jasmine-tyler/congress-passes-historic_b_662625.html).

Tyson, Karolyn. 2002. "Weighing In: Elementary-Age Students and the Debate on Attitudes Toward School Among Black Students." *Social Forces* 80(4):1157–1189.

Tyson, Karolyn. 2011. *Integration Interrupted: Tracking, Black Students, and Acting White After Brown*. New York: Oxford University Press.

Tyson, Karolyn, William Darity, and Domini R. Castellino. 2005. "It's Not a 'Black Thing': Understanding the Burden of Acting White and Other Dilemmas of High Achievement." *American Sociological Review* 70(4):582–605.

Tyson, Timothy B. 2004. *Blood Done Sign My Name*. New York: Three Rivers Press.

Udoh, Roberta. 2018. "Can Schools Nurture the Souls of Black and Brown Children? Combating the School-to-Prison Pipeline." Pp. 101–109 in *Lift Us Up, Don't Push Us Out: Voices from the Front Lines of the Educational Justice Movement*, edited by Mark R. Warren. Boston, MA: Beacon Press.

US Census Bureau. 2017. "Quick Facts: United States." Retrieved March 15, 2019 (www.census.gov/quickfacts/fact/table/US/PST045217).

US Census Bureau. 2019. "CPS Historical Time Series Tables." Retrieved May 25, 2019 (www.census.gov/data/tables/time-series/demo/educational-attainment/cps-historical-time-series.html).

US Census Bureau. n.d. "American Fact Finder." Retrieved July 28, 2019 (https://www.census.gov/programs-surveys/sis/resources/data-tools/aff.html).

Valenzuela, Freddie, and Jason Lemons. 2008. *No Greater Love: The Lives and Times of Hispanic Soldiers*. Lanham, MD: Ovation Books.

Vaughan, Dawn Baumgartner. 2019. "Monument to African Americans Would Join Others at the Capital." *Raleigh News and Observer* July 20:1A, 6A.

Vaughan, Ed. 2001. *Sociology: The Study of Society*. Upper Saddle River, NJ: Prentice Hall.

Vera, Hernan and Andrew M. Gordon. 2003. *Screen Saviors: Hollywood Fictions of Whiteness*. Lanham, MD: Rowman and Littlefield Publishers.

Vertuno, Jim. 2010. "Simkins Hall Name Change? Texas Dorm Named for KKK Leader May Be Renamed." *Huffington Post*, July 14. Retrieved July 24, 2013 (www.huffingtonpost.com/college/the-news/2010/07/14/).

Vieira, Rosangela Maria. 1995. "Black Resistance in Brazil: A Matter of Necessity." Pp. 227–240 in *Racism and Anti-Racism in World Perspective*, edited by B. P. Bowser. Thousand Oaks, CA: Sage Publications.

Vigil, Ernesto B. 1999. *The Crusade for Justice: Chicano Militancy and the Government's War on Dissent*. Madison: University of Wisconsin Press.

Villarosa, Linda. 2018. "Why America's Black Mothers and Babies are in a Life-or-Death Crisis." *New York Times Magazine*, April 11. Retrieved May 28, 2019 (www.nytimes.com/2018/04/11/magazine/black-mothers-babies-death-maternal-mortality.html).

Vincent, B. S. and P. J. Hofer. 1994. *The Consequences of Mandatory Minimum Prison Terms: A Summary of Recent Findings*. Washington, DC: Federal Judicial Center.

Waldstein, David. 2018. "Cleveland Indians Will Abandon Chief Wahoo Logo Next Year." *New York Times*, January 29. Retrieved July 1, 2019 (www.nytimes.com/2018/01/29/sports/baseball/cleveland-indians-chief-wahoo-logo.html).

Walker, David. 2003. "Race Building and the Disciplining of White Australia." Pp. 33–50 in *Legacies of White Australia: Race, Culture and Nation*, edited by L. Jayasuriya, D. Walker, and J. Gothard. Crawley, Western Australia: University of Western Australia Press.

Walker, Samuel. 2006. *Sense and Nonsense About Crime and Drugs: A Policy Guide*, 6th ed. Belmont, CA: Thompson Wadsworth.

Walker, Samuel, Cassia Spohn, and Miriam DeLone. 2000. *The Color of Justice: Race, Ethnicity, and Crime in America*, 2nd ed. Belmont, CA: Thompson Wadsworth.

Walker, Samuel, Cassia Spohn, and Miriam DeLone. 2007. *The Color of Justice: Race, Ethnicity, and Crime in America*, 4th ed. Belmont, CA: Thompson Wadsworth.

Wallace, John M., Sara Goodkind, Cynthia M. Wallace, and Jerald G. Bachman. 2008. "Race, Ethnic, and Gender Differences in School Discipline Among U.S. High School Students: 1991–2005." *Negro Educational Review* 59:47–62.

Wallace, Michele Faith. 2003. "The Good Lynching and 'The Birth of a Nation': Discourses and Aesthetics of Jim Crow." *Cinema Journal* 43(1):85–104.

Wallenstein, P. 2002. *Tell the Court I Love My Wife: Race, Marriage and the Law—An American History.* New York: Palgrave Macmillan.

Walters, Pamela Barnhouse. 2001. "Educational Access and the State: Historical Continuities and Discontinuities in Racial Inequality in American Education." *Sociology of Education* 74, extra issue:35–49.

Wang, Wendy. 2015. "Interracial Marriage: Who Is Marrying Out?" Pew Research Center, June 12. Retrieved July 7, 2016 (www.pewresearch.org/fact-tank/2015/06/12/interracial-marriage-who-is-marrying-out/).

"The War on Drugs: Undermining International Development and Security, Increasing Conflict." n.d. Count the Costs. Retrieved July 1, 2016 (www.countthecosts.org/sites/default/files/Development_and_security_briefing.pdf).

Warren, Mark R. 2010. *Fire in the Heart: How White Activists Embrace Racial Justice.* Oxford, New York: Oxford University Press.

Warren, Mark R. 2018. *Lift Us Up, Don't Push Us Out: Voices from the Front Lines of the Educational Justice Movement.* Boston, MA: Beacon Press.

Washington, Harriet. 2019. "Monsanto Poisoned this Alabama Town—And People Are Still Sick." Buzzfeed News, July 25. Retrieved August 4, 2019 (www.buzzfeednews.com/article/harriet washington/monsanto-anniston-harriet-washington-environmental-racism?fbclid=IwAR3n120p C4j33U6ew5MI7ArSeKKGys1paKHSpR_XettkFd4rppDj85JTtjo).

Waters, Mary. 1990. *Ethnic Options: Choosing Identities in America.* Berkeley: University of California Press.

Watkins, Eli and Abby Phillip. 2018. "Trump Decries Immigrants from 'Shithole Countries' Coming to US." CNN Politics, January 12. Retrieved July 29, 2019 (www.cnn.com/2018/01/11/politics/immigrants-shithole-countries-trump/index.html).

Weatherford, Jack. 1991. *Native Roots: How the Indians Enriched America.* New York: Fawcett Columbine.

Webb, Clive, ed. 2005. *Massive Resistance: Southern Opposition to the Second Reconstruction.* Oxford, New York: Oxford University Press.

Wei, William. 2004. "The Asian American Movement: A Quest for Racial Equality, Social Justice, and Political Empowerment." Pp. 196–220 in *Racial Thinking in the United States: Uncompleted Independence*, edited by P. Spickard and G. R. Daniel. Notre Dame, IN: University of Notre Dame Press.

Weissinger, Sandra E., Dwayne A. Mack, and Elwood Watson. 2017. *Violence against Black Bodies: An Intersectional Analysis of How Black Lives Continue to Matter.* New York: Routledge.

Wells, Amy Stuart and Robert L. Crain. 1992. "Do Parents Choose School Quality or Social Status? A Sociological Theory of Free Market Education." Pp. 65–82 in *The Choice Controversy*, edited by P. W. Cookson, Jr. Newbury Park, CA: Corwin Press.

Wells-Barnett, Ida B. 2002. *On Lynchings.* New York: Humanity Books.

Weinberg, Meyer. 1977. *A Chance to Learn: A History of Race and Education in the United States.* Cambridge and London, UK: Cambridge University Press.

Weinberg, Meyer. 1983. *The Search for Quality Education: Policy and Research on Minority Students in School and College.* Westport, CT: Greenwood Press.

Weinberg, Meyer. 1997. *Asian American Education: Historical Background and Current Realities.* Mahwah, NJ: Erlbaum Associates Publishers.

Weindling, Paul. 1999. "International Eugenics: Swedish Sterilizations in Context." *Scandinavian Journal of History* 24(2):179–197.

Weishar, Sue. 2012. "Mississippi Rejects Immigration Enforcement Bill." *Just South Quarterly,* Summer. Retrieved April 15, 2013 (http://loyno.edu/jsri/mississippi-rejects-immigration-enforcement-bill).

Weist, Lynda. 1998. "Using Immersion Experiences to Shake Up Pre-Service Teachers' Views About Cultural Differences." *Journal of Teacher Education* 49(5):358–366.

Werner, Craig. 1998. *A Change Is Gonna Come: Music, Race, and the Soul of America.* New York: Penguin.

West, Cornell. 1988. "On Afro-American Popular Music: From Bebop to Rap." Pp. 177–187 in *Prophetic Fragments.* Grand Rapids, MI: Wm. B. Eerdmans Publishing Company.

Western, Bruce, Leonard M. Lopoo, and Sara McLanahan. 2004. "Incarceration and the Bonds Between Parents in Fragile Families." Pp. 21–45 in *Imprisoning America: The Social Effects of Mass Incarceration,* edited by M. Pattillo, D. Weiman, and B. Western. New York: Russell Sage Foundation.

Western, Bruce, Mary Pattillo, and David Weiman. 2004. "Introduction." Pp. 1–20 in *Imprisoning America: The Social Effects of Mass Incarceration,* edited by M. Pattillo, D. Weiman, and B. Western. New York: Russell Sage Foundation.

Westheider, James E. 2008. *The African American Experience in Vietnam: Brothers in Arms.* Lanham, MD: Rowman and Littlefield Publishers.

Whang, Yun-Oh. 2005. "More Than Just a Game: Asian and Asian American Athletes in Major Professional Sports." *Harvard Asia Pacific Review* 8(1):45–48.

"What is Reproductive Justice?" n.d. Sister Song Women of Color Reproductive Justice Collective. Retrieved February 28, 2020. (www.sistersong.net/reproductive-justice).

White, Welsh. 1991. *The Death Penalty in the Nineties.* Ann Arbor: University of Michigan Press.

" 'White Privilege' Lesson in Delavan-Darien High School Class in Wisconsin Draws Ire." 2013. *Huffington Post,* January 16. Retrieved May 2, 2013 (www.huffingtonpost.com/2013/01/16/white-privilege-class-at-_n_2489997.html).

Whitfield, Stephen J. 1997. "Introduction." Pp. ix–xxxi in *Culture and Democracy in the United States,* by Horace Kallen. Piscataway, NJ: Transaction Publishers.

Wilkerson, Isabel. 2010. *The Warmth of Other Suns: The Epic Story of America's Great Migration.* New York: Random House.

Wilkinson, J. Harvie, III. 1979. *From Brown to Bakke: The Supreme Court and School Integration, 1954–1978.* Oxford and New York: Oxford University Press.

Williams, Juan. 1987. *Eyes on the Prize: America's Civil Rights Years, 1954–1965.* New York: Viking Penguin Press.

Williams, Kim M. 2006. *Mark One or More: Civil Rights in Multiracial America.* Ann Arbor: University of Michigan Press.

Williams, Linda Faye. 2003. *The Constraint of Race: The Legacies of White Skin Privilege in America.* University Park: Pennsylvania State University Press.

Williams, Patricia J. 2005. "Genetically Speaking." *The Nation,* June 2. Retrieved July 24, 2013 (www.thenation.com/article/genetically-speaking#).

Williams, Patricia J. 2008. "Uncooperative Housing." *The Nation,* November 13. Retrieved July 24, 2013 (www.thenation.com/article/uncooperative-housing#axzz2a2q7pjCi).

Williams, R. M., Jr. 1964. *Strangers Next Door: Ethnic Relations in American Communities.* Englewood Cliffs, NJ: Prentice Hall.

Wilson, Clint C. and Felix Gutierrez. 1995. *Race, Multiculturalism, and the Media*, 2nd ed. Thousand Oaks, CA: Sage Publications.

Wilson, William Julius. 1978. *The Declining Significance of Race: Blacks and Changing American Institutions.* Chicago, IL: University of Chicago Press.

Wilson, William Julius. 1989. "Introduction to the Wesleyan edition." Pp. ix–xxii. In *Dark Ghetto: Dilemmas of Social Power*, 2nd Edition. Kenneth B. Clark. Middletown, CTL Wesleyan University Press.

Wilson, William Julius. 1987. *The Truly Disadvantaged: The Inner City, the Underclass, and Public Policy.* Chicago, IL: University of Chicago Press.

Wilson, William Julius. 1996. *When Work Disappears: The World of the New Urban Poor.* New York: Alfred A. Knopf.

Wilson, William Julius. 2010. *More Than Just Race: Being Black and Poor in the Inner City.* New York and London: W. W. Norton and Company.

Winders, Jamie. 2005. "Changing Politics of Race and Region: Latino Migration to the US South." *Progress in Human Geography* 29(6):683–699.

Wing, Adrien Katherine. 2000. *Global Critical Race Feminism: An International Reader.* New York and London: New York University Press.

Wingfield, Adia Harvey and Joe R. Feagin. 2010. *Yes We Can? White Racial Framing and the 2008 Presidential Campaign.* New York and London: Routledge.

Wingfield, Adia Harvey and Joe R. Feagin. 2013. *Yes We Can? White Racial Framing and the Obama Presidency*, 2nd ed. New York and London: Routledge.

Winn, Peter. 2002. "Back to the Future: A GI Bill for the Twenty-First Century." Pp. 175–206 in *Taking Parenting Public: The Case for a New Social Movement*, edited by S. A. Hewlett, N. Rankin, and C. West. Boulder, CO: Rowman and Littlefield.

Winston, Bonnie V. 2010. "The NAACP's New Smart and Safe Campaign Calls for Law Enforcement Accountability." *The Crisis* 117(1):41.

Wise, Tim. 1991. "Affirmative Action and the Politics of White Resentment." *Blueprint for Social Justice* 45(3):1–6.

Wise, Tim. 2001. "School Shootings and White Denial." Alternet, March 5. Retrieved August 20, 2009 (www.alternet.org/story/10560/school_shootings_and_white_denial).

Wise, Tim. 2005. *White Like Me: Reflections on Race from a Privileged Son.* Brooklyn, NY: Soft Skull Press.

Wise, Tim. 2005b. "Oh, Give Me A Home." Alternet, March 10. Retrieved July 25, 2013 (www.alter net.org/story/21469/oh,_give_me_a_home).

Wise, Tim. 2008. "Membership Has Its Privileges: Thoughts on Acknowledging and Challenging Whiteness." Pp. 107–110 in *White Privilege: Essential Readings on the Other Side of Racism*, 3rd ed. New York: Worth Publishers.

Wise, Tim. 2013. "Terrorism and Privilege: Understanding the Power of Whiteness." TimWise.org, April 16. Retrieved May 21, 2013 (www.timwise.org/2013/04/terrorism-and-privilege-understanding-the-power-of-whiteness/).

Wodtke, Geoffrey T. 2016. "Are Smart People Less Racist? Verbal Ability, Anti-Black Prejudice, and the Principle-Policy Paradox." *Social Problems* 63(1):21–45.

Wolters, Raymond. 1984. *The Burden of Brown: Thirty Years of School Desegregation.* Knoxville: University of Tennessee Press.

Wong, K. Scott. 1998. "Cultural Defenders and Brokers: Chinese Responses to the Anti-Chinese Movement." Pp. 3–40 in *Claiming America: Constructing Chinese American Identities During the Exclusion Era*, edited by K. S. Wong and S. Chan. Philadelphia, PA; Temple University Press.

Wood, James L. and Maurice Jackson. 1982. *Social Movements: Development, Participation and Dynamics.* Belmont, CA: Wadsworth Publishing Company.

Woods, Ronald. 2011. *Social Issues in Sport*, 2nd ed. Champaign, IL: Human Kinetics.

Worden, Nigel. 2007. *The Making of Modern South Africa: Conquest, Apartheid, and Democracy*, 4th ed. Malden, MA: Wiley-Blackwell.

Wordes, Madeline, Timothy S. Bynum, and Charles J. Corley. 1994. "Locking Up Youth: The Impact of Race on Detention Decisions." *Journal of Research in Crime and Delinquency* 31(2):554–570.

Wray, Matt. 2006. *Not Quite White: White Trash and the Boundaries of Whiteness*. London and Durham, NC: Duke University Press.

Wright, Beverly. 2009. "Preface." Pp. xix–xxii. In *Race, Place, and Environmental Justice After Hurricane Katrina: Struggles to Reclaim, Rebuild, and Revitalize New Orleans and the Gulf Coast*, edited by Robert D. Bullard and Beverly Wright. Boulder, CO: Westview Press.

Yancey, George. 2003. *Who Is White? Latinos, Asians, and the New Black/Nonblack Divide*. Boulder, CO: Lynne Rienner Publishers.

Yancey, George. 2008. *Black Bodies, White Gazes: The Continuing Significance of Race*. Lanham, MD: Rowman and Littlefield.

Yancey, George and Richard Lewis, Jr. 2009. *Interracial Families: Current Concepts and Controversies*. New York: Routledge.

Yang, Andrew. 2018. *The War on Normal People*. New York: Hachette Books.

Yen, Hope. 2011. "Wealth Gap Between Whites, Minorities Widens to Greatest Level in a Quarter Century." *Huffington Post*, July 26. Retrieved July 27, 2011 (www.huffingtonpost.com/politics/the-news/2011/07/26/).

Yosso, Tara J. 2005. "Whose Cultural Capital? A Critical Race Theory Discussion of Community Cultural Wealth." *Race, Ethnicity and Education* 8(1):69–91.

Young, Richard and Jeffrey Meiser. 2008. "Race and the Dual State in the Early American Republic." Pp. 31–58 in *Race and American Political Development*, edited by J. Lowndes, J. Novkov, and D. T. Warren. New York: Routledge.

"YouTube Reaches 1 Billion Users Milestone." 2013. CNBC, March 21. Retrieved July 10, 2013 (www.cnbc.com/id/100575883).

Zellner, Bob and Constance Curry. 2008. *The Wrong Side of Murder Creek: A White Southerner in the Freedom Movement*. Montgomery, AL: New South Books.

Zimmerman, Arely M. 2011. "A Dream Detained: Undocumented Latino Youth and the DREAM Movement." *NACLA Report on the Americas*, November/December, pp. 14–17. Retrieved March 20, 2013 (http://immigrationintheheartland.files.wordpress.com/2012/04/the-dream-movement.pdf).

Zinn, Howard. 2003. *A People's History of the United States: 1492–Present*. New York: Harper Perennial Modern Classics.

Zinn, Howard. 2009. "Drawing the Color Line." Pp. 9–16 in *Rethinking the Color Line*, 4th ed., edited by C. A. Gallagher. New York, St. Louis: McGraw-Hill.

Zirin, Dave. 2005. *What's My Name, Fool? Sports and Resistance in the United States*. Chicago, IL: Haymarket Books.

Zirin, Dave. 2006. "Racism and Coaching in the NFL." Alternet, January 6. Retrieved January 6, 2006 (www.alternet.org/story/30460/).

Zirin, Dave. 2013. "Five Fears About '42.'" *The Nation*, April 1. Retrieved June 20, 2013 (www.thenation.com/blog/173606/five-fears-about-42#axzz2Y1aiz9Ry).

Zirin, Dave, 2019. "Megan Rapinoe is Right to Not Sing the Anthem." *The Nation*, June 14. Retrieved February 29, 2020. (www.thenation.com/article/archive/megan-rapinoe-sports-soccer/).

Zong, Jie and Jeanne Batalova. 2016. "Frequently Requested Statistics on Immigrants and Immigration in the United States." Migration Policy Institute, April 14. Retrieved July 6, 2016 (www.migrationpolicy.org/article/frequently-requested-statistics-immigrants-and-immigration-united-states).

Zopf, Bradley J. 2018. "A Different Kind of Brown: Arabs and Middle Easterners as Anti-American Muslims." *Sociology of Race and Ethnicity* 4(2):178–191.

Zraick, Karen. 2018. "Man Labeled 'ID Adam' Fired After Calling the Police on a Black Woman at Pool." *New York Times*, July 6. Retrieved February 28, 2020. (www.nytimes.com/2018/07/06/us/pool-racial-profiling-white-man.html).

Zuckerman, Phil, ed. 2004. *The Social Theory of W. E. B. Du Bois*. Thousand Oaks, London: Pine Forge Press.

Index

Page numbers in **bold** denote tables, those in *italics* denote figures.

343; influence of 386; intersection of 447; invocation of 530; issues of 530; and juvenile justice system 390–2; Millennials on 30–2, 37–8, *38*, **38**, 459–61; and no child left behind 288–9; note on terminology 32–4; pride movement 223; privilege 23, 61; problem 4, 47; resisting 19–20; significance of 7–9; social construction 23–9, 492; in society 524; sociology of 10–12; speaking "race" honestly 21–3; theoretical perspectives on 86; in US 237; validity of 23; in workplace 439, 512, 552

race and social policy 315–17; affirmative action 330–3; emergence of welfare state 318–19; GI Bill 320–3; health-care 323–6; mutual aid societies 318; new deal policies 319–20; Puerto Rican debt crisis 333–4; reproductive rights 326–30; social policy solutions to racial wealth gap 334

race-baiting 324, 551

race/ethnicity: and gender 408; scientific understandings of 86; sociology of 11

Race Forward 552

race, future of 519–21; age and race in politics 533–4; Asian American voting trends 532–3; becoming white in twenty-first century 522; economic contributions of immigrants 537; globalization of hate 554; hate crimes and groups 547–50; immigrants and racialization of anti-immigration sentiment 534–7; Latino Constituency 531–2; and Millennial Generation 524; nativism and hate groups 550–2; new immigrant destinations 537–8; racial inequality, and whiteness in the political sphere 524–31; reparations 554–8; sociological perspectives on 521–2; targeting of Arab Americans 552–4; triracial stratification system 522–4; US immigration law, and politics: anti-immigrant legislation 542–7; Chinese Exclusion Act 539; government and Jewish immigration 541–2; immigration reform 540; National Origins Act 539–40

race relations 97, 106, 157–9, 199–201; Arab American Activism 234; Asian American activism 231–3; *Brown* power strategies and tactics 228; organizing farmworkers 229; urban organizing 229–30; civil rights movement *see* civil rights movement; cultural activism 226; cycle 159–60; ideologies, institutions, and identities 204–5; Indian women's activism 226–7; late twentieth and early twenty-first centuries 233; Long Civil Rights Movement 235–7; Mexican American and Chicano activism 228; Native American activism 222–4, 239; nativism *see* nativism; from reconstruction to Jim Crow 162–78; Red Power movement 228; Red Power strategies *see* Red Power strategies; social and cultural context 202–4; sociological perspectives on intergroup relations 159–62; sociological perspectives on social movements 201–2; training 512; White Backlash 234–5; "woke" generation 237–8; women and Chicano activism 230–1

race riots 170–1, **171**

racetalk 501

racework 483

racial abilities 307

racial achievement gap 284

racial apathy 316

racial battle fatigue 411

racial beliefs 291

racial bias in sentencing 386

racial categorization 25, 28–9, 52, 492; nature of 178; and power 48–51

racial challenges 60

racial classification 34

racial dating preferences 487, *487*

racial democracy 131

racial demographics 32f

racial dictatorship 131

racial differences 391; categories of 541

racial discrimination 186, 258, 389, 532; in schools 276–9

racial disparities: in crime 376–8; interpretation of 286; in sentencing and racial profiling 528

racial essentialism, sports and 500–2

racial/ethnic groups 12, 125, 130; demographic breakdown of 30f; in United States 441, 454

racial/ethnic identity, symbolic interactionism on 106–7

racial/ethnic inequality 125, 127–8, 130–1; Marxist analyses of 128; sociological theories on 136

racial/ethnic minorities 9, 145, 250, 313, 430, 432, 446–7; children 283; cultural images of 425; groups 13, 58, 227, 454, 532–3; images of 422; media portrayals of 424–5; sexualizing 12–13

racial/ethnic relations, history of 125–6

racial/ethnic stereotypes 428, 434

racial/ethnic stratification 127

racial/ethnic subordinate groups 448

racial/ethnic women dating preferences 487–8, *488*

racial exclusion patterns 488

racial formations 86, 107

racial-group membership 131–2, 298–9
racial groups 246, 524
racial harmony 176
racial hierarchies 59, 158
racial hierarchy 128
racial hoax 415
racial identities 35–6, 476
racial ideologies 37, 70; attention to 422–3; of color-blindness 68–70; institutional privilege 73–4; Native American land loss 74–5; wealth accumulation 75–6; white racial identity 70–3
racial imagery in film and television 428–33, 455; African American images 433–8; Arabs 441–3; Asian 443–4; Latinos 440–1; Native Americans 438–40; user-generated content 445–6; video games 446–8; white 444–5
racial inequality 61, 105, 135, 308, 340, 476, 499, 26, 530; achievement gap 283–7; bilingual education 279–81; current funding inequities 281–3; demise of 315; race and no child left behind 288–9; racial issues in higher education 289–91; school-to-prison pipeline 287–8; scientific research on 35; tracking 283; US system of 203
racial integration 475–8, 492; arenas of 476; interracial intimacies *see* interracial intimacies; lingering racial inequality in sports 505–8; of Major League Baseball 494; and military *see* military; sociological perspectives on: prejudice 479–80; stages of assimilation 478–9; sports and race 492–500; sports and racial essentialism 500–2; whiteness in sports 502; Native American mascots 502–4; and trash talking 505; University of Mississippi 504–5
racialization 234; process 143; of state 131, 316
racialized medicine 86
racialized organizations 115
racialized social systems theory 107–8
racialized space 8
racialized surveillance 553
racialized tracking 256
Racial Justice Act 389, 390
racial justice activism 22, 65, 496, 546
racial microaggressions 504
racial minorities 74, 161, 311, 372, 379, 431–2, 508, *508*, 533; communities 364, 375–6; and crime victimization 412–15; groups 298; marginalization of 374; needs of 529; political progress for 528; predominant image of 413; urbanization of 203
racial oppression 97, 186, 424–5
racial order 4

racial orthodoxy 112
racial 'othering' 54
racial preferences 488
racial profiling 28, 374, 378, 379, 528
racial purity 481
racial realism 307–8
racial resentment 79
racial segregation 176, 221, 490, 494; and discrimination 513
racial self-awareness 60
racial separatism 509
racial signaling 307
racial socialization 61; of white children 62
racial status hierarchy 523
racial steering 354–5
racial stereotypes 436, 501; influence of 505
racial stratification, lines of 483
racial subordination 168–71, 179
racial terminology 32
racial unrest 510–13
racial violence 434
racial wage gap 301, 302
racial wealth gap 302–3, 342, 344, *344*, 356; proposed solutions to 334; social policy solutions to 334
racism 8, 14, 61, 63, 126, 128, 202, 220, 234, 497, 530, 556, 558; African American resistance to *214*; cumulative effects of 390; and discrimination 492; in Europe 203; issues of 530; nonverbal resistance to 496–7; operation of 520; past and present 13–15; resistance to 495, 499; scientific 87–8; societal 374; unacknowledged side of 60–1
racist appropriation 451
RAE *see* Rising American Electorate (RAE)
Randolph, A. Philip 176
rape 170, 557–8
rap functions 452
Raphael Weill School in San Francisco 263
Rapinoe, Megan 500
Ray, Victor 115
Reagan, Ronald 233, 254, 313, 346, 397, 401, 529, 544, 557
Rebel Drive 504
rebound racism 483
reclaimers 492
Reconstruction era 163–6
redlining 354
Red Power activism 223
Red Power activists 223–4
Red Power movements 200, 202–4, 222, 223–4, 226, 227, 276
Red Power strategies 224; Indian Occupations 224–5; Wounded Knee 1973 225